LINDLEY J. STILES

Professor of Education for Interdisciplinary Studies,
Northwestern University

ADVISORY EDITOR TO DODD, MEAD & COMPANY

CHALLENGES TO EDUCATION:

Readings for Analysis of Major Issues

CHALLENGES TO EDUCATION

Readings for Analysis of Major Issues

Emanuel Hurwitz, Jr.
Charles A. Tesconi, Jr.

University of Illinois at Chicago Circle

Dodd, Mead & Company

NEW YORK   1972   TORONTO

LC
191
.H78

ISBN 0-396-06540-6
Library of Congress Catalog Card Number: 74-180933

Printed in the United States of America

TO THE SPECIAL PEOPLE IN OUR LIVES

Judi Lynn Hurwitz

AND

Marie Sadler Tesconi

Editor's Introduction

TO SELECT from the mass of contemporary literature pertinent and significant views and information is a challenge for one interested in education today. This book presents a digest of significant writings about the relationships between school and society, along with penetrating analyses and suggestions for further study. The contrasting positions taken by the various authors in relationship to critical problem areas, together with a unique issue-analysis approach developed by Drs. Hurwitz and Tesconi, make this book a genuine stimulus to creative thought. Such an issue-oriented approach breaks with tradition for books in the field of education and brings to the reader chances to interact with the dynamic ideas of authors who are "telling it like it is."

While the focus is on fresh ideas about educational issues, the scholarship is sound and comprehensive. By studying this book one can gain insights into the contemporary crises in education; the turmoil that surrounds students, teachers, and citizens who are struggling to improve their schools; and the reasons why controversy has become a constant companion with education at all levels. The editors have developed a book, furthermore, that helps the student of education to consider the problems of learning and teaching in positive rather than negative terms. Throughout, help is given the reader to think constructively about what might be, in place of the frustrating failures that schools currently confront.

The editors of this book are representative of a new brand of creative educators who are leading educational reforms today. They are both associated with the University of Illinois at Chicago Circle, an institution that lives daily with the educational challenges of urban society. From first-hand experience, they know how schools are failing to serve various economic, ethnic, and racial groups, and have observed the forces that today are changing schools. Out of such personal experiences, as well as an in-depth acquaintance with contemporary literature, this new type of educational resource book has evolved. Readers will find it both a challenge to their thinking and a valuable reference to understanding the great controversial educational issues of the times.

LINDLEY J. STILES

Preface

THE FORMAL educational system of any society is shaped by the major social forces present in that society. Indeed, the history of education in the United States is a record of this kind of school-society relationship. Our theocratic Colonial ancestors saw to it that their children were schooled in the Bible, the basal reader of the time, in order to encourage children and youth to reach accommodation with their God. Their eighteenth-century successors added the concerns of this world to the curriculum, making certain that their children learned to read, write, and cipher in order to prosper in the here and now. In the nineteenth century, a people in the process of industrialization asked their schools to educate the young in the secular subjects of history, mathematics, living languages, and science, and to train them specifically for occupational skills such as agriculture and the mechanical arts. Now, in the twentieth century, our schools are expected to provide curricular offerings addressed to the scientific and technological demands of advanced industrialized society.

Right from their beginnings, schools in this country have not only responded to the polity in devising curricular offerings, administrative structure, and the like, they have also reflected the mien, the temper, the cultural flavor, as it were, of society. This is made the more obvious when we reflect upon the fact that what we call the "public or common school" movement is a generalized way of referring to the political and social forces which made such a movement a reality. American schools are thus, in the main, dependent variables in the school-society relationship. It is true, of course, that there is always a lag between emerging social developments and school response. But few thinking persons would deny that American schools, like most schools every-where—for good or bad—are not only the creatures, but microcosmic facsimiles of the larger society.

This kind of school-society relationship has not gone unchallenged. And its critics, as some of the selections in this book make clear, are increasing in number. But whatever one's position on such matters, the problems and social developments in contemporary society make the study of schools in relation to that society a study of great importance. Urban blight, poverty amidst plenty, cancerous racism, the war in Indo-China, the doomsday forecasts in the light of continued prostitution of our natural environment, the counter-culture movement, technological complexity—all these and many more are shaking the foundations of our society. The consequence of such staggering and persistent forces is a society which, at the very least, is in a state of transition. We know that we are going through a terribly rough time, we are frightened by it, do not know how to get out of it, and the future is difficult to contemplate.

The school is in turmoil. Pushed and pulled from all quarters, it is feeling the pressure of the times more than most institutions. This is a logical consequence of its relationship to the larger society. As the chief socializing agent of the young, it becomes the major object of attention in times of social stress. But a paradox of such times is that even as many people see the school as a major vehicle for getting us out of troubled waters, many others lose confidence in it. This compounds the school's difficult position and places it, like the society it serves, in a transitional state.

Given the centrality of the school in contemporary America, we believe it important for the student of American education to gain an understanding of the major social forces that affect or involve the operation of the school. Furthermore, we think it is imperative for the student to achieve a basic comprehension of the sociopolitical questions which underlie educational decision-making processes. This kind of rationale is the backbone-support for foundations of education course offerings. Claims that such courses are basic and necessary ingredients in vital teacher education programs are legion. We make no apology for adding to such claims. The existence of this book manifests our support of them. As the approach of this book suggests, however, we are not committed to the traditional means typically used to express the rationale behind those claims.

It is our belief that a valuable approach to the study of schools and society is through an issue-analysis approach: more specifically, that is, through a method or procedure wherein teacher and student systematically examine issues which are of major importance to schools and the society in which they operate. Accordingly, readings in this book are centered around crucial social-educational issues of our times.

Furthermore, these readings are offered within the framework of an analytical scheme described in Chapter 1.

The issues examined in this book arise out of the social forces contributing to the transitional state of society and schools (discussed earlier in this preface). In many ways they are formative issues in the sense that the discord which surrounds them sets in motion activities out of which emerge new ideas, systems, and processes. There is of course a danger involved in building a book around contemporary issues and conflict: the live issue of today may be dead tomorrow. While we accept the risk involved in an issue-analysis approach, we are convinced that the nature of the issues we have selected minimizes the gamble. For it is unlikely that the questions and problems surrounding school finance, student protest, racial and ethnic conflict, the role of the courts in education, the control of schools, teacher militancy, and the question of the school-society relationship itself will disappear in the foreseeable future.

Most of the issues examined in this book grow out of and are intensified by urban problems and social developments. That a book on American education should have such a focus in the 1970's should not be surprising because nearly 80 percent of the population in this country is urban. Nevertheless, the issues in this book have no geographical-political boundaries. The problems of school finance, student unrest, teacher militancy, and all the others with which this book is concerned are far from unknown in small town, rural America.

On a personal note, we would like to thank our friend and colleague, Professor Van Cleve Morris, for the painstaking effort he invested in reading and commenting upon our manuscript. His suggestions for improvement were invaluable to us.

Finally, our names appear in alphabetical order on the cover. There is no "first" or "second" author-editor. We have both contributed equally to the development and production of the book.

EMANUEL HURWITZ, JR.
CHARLES A. TESCONI, JR.

Contents

Chapter 3. THE POLITICS OF SCHOOL CONTROL 142

Chapter 4. TEACHER POWER 193

INTRODUCTION

AMERICAN public schools are not immune to the major social conflicts, trends, and cultural values which are dominant in our society. It is true that curricular offerings, organizational patterns, and classroom activities may, and often do, treat such phenomena as if they did not exist—as the saying goes, education can indeed be "irrelevant"—but the public school is a social institution and as such is inextricably bound up in social and cultural proceedings. By way of example, the school may choose to ignore the problems of race or student rights, but as very recent events indicate, it is certainly affected by them. It follows, therefore, that the study of American public education must include, and perhaps begin with, examination of the social and cultural forces which have an impact upon the school.

The identification and differentiation of these forces for purposes of critical study is no easy task. There is a wealth of such phenomena to choose from and the relative impact of each upon the schools is not easily determined. The serious student of education does not treat these matters lightly, although he must admit that the choice of studying one as opposed to another is, ultimately, a value choice. Furthermore, most if not all of these matters are intimately related to one another. The financial crises of the urban schools, for example, cannot be divorced from racial dissonance: one social force is tied into, and its boundaries blurred, by others. Social forces do not come packaged in neat, mutually exclusive categories. Finally—and this can be a major problem in the foundations of education field—there is the quandary of selecting an appropriate disciplinary or cognitive framework for analyzing those social forces and attendant issues which have been staked out for study. Such matters and their analysis are not the exclusive domain of any one academic discipline. These are just a few problems associated with the study of education as it is affected by its social and cultural milieu. We cite them so that the reader may better understand the rationale behind the procedures and organization employed in this text.

1

Concerning the problem of identification and differentiation, we have chosen readings centered around social-educational issues which are functions of major social forces of the times. These are issues in the sense that they are the focus of major debate, dissension, and even violence. The parties to these issues take very strong, often stubborn stands. The issues are social in that they have consequences for society at large —its people and structures. The issue of alternative schools, for example, has implications for schooling which could effect vital social changes in such areas as control and financing of the public schools, manpower training, race and ethnic relations, to cite just a few. The issues are educational in the sense that schooling, both as process and institution, is more intimately affected by them than perhaps any other public institution. Student protest, for example, is obviously a social issue which involves the school to a greater extent than other social institutions. On the other hand, the pollution of our environment, while certainly a pressing formal educational concern, is not as central to the formal schooling process as it is—or should be—to other institutions. Finally, we should add that these issues are critical in that their very existence and solution (or nonsolution) could lead to conditions which would dramatically reshape or even do away with public education as we now know it.

As noted earlier, we recognize that social issues do not come neatly wrapped in mutually exclusive categories. We have therefore made repeated reference in our editorial contributions and in the questions and exercises at the end of each chapter to some of the ways in which a particular issue relates to other issues included in this book. Thus, when we discuss the politics of the school-control issue, we note some of the ways in which it is related to the school-society relationship issue, the ethnicity question, and so on.

These few comments suggest the major purpose of this book: to introduce the reader to selected, critical social-educational issues of the day. Furthermore, it has been designed to involve the reader in a systematic, critical analysis of these issues, the understanding of which is crucial to a basic comprehension of the social and intellectual foundations of American public education.

These objectives could be approached in a number of ways. The conventional procedure is to draw heavily upon selected content from history, philosophy, and sociology (i.e., those disciplines believed to be basic to foundations of education study). Such content has been considered appropriate for orienting students to the study of education and, hence, to their prospective roles as teachers. It is well known, however, that such an approach leaves much to be desired.

The method employed in this book differs greatly from the conventional procedure referred to above. Growing out of an attempt to deal with the difficulty of selecting an appropriate disciplinary or cognitive framework for examining important social issues, our procedure is centered around a conceptual framework designed for systematic analysis of social-educational issues, the boundaries of which are not limited or defined by a particular discipline.

The Conceptual Framework

Each chapter is devoted to a particular issue. Each issue is examined, through editorial comments and selected readings, within the bounds of a four-sided conceptual framework. Each "side" or dimension of this framework serves a particular function. We call these dimensions (1) Description, (2) Illustration, (3) Analysis, and (4) Projection. It is the reader's encounter with the issues through all of these dimensions which will lead, we believe, to a better understanding and deeper involvement in crucial educational concerns than is usually realized in conventional approaches to the study of educational issues. Here are some brief descriptions of the functions served by these dimensions.

1. *Description.* The function of description is to identify a particular issue, and the major actors and variables involved in the issue—all the while avoiding, as much as possible, evaluation and justification. These are rather stringent limitations to place upon accounts which purport to describe "hot" issues. But the major thrust of such accounts, however, will be

Identification of the issue. What is the issue? What subissues are involved? What does it imply for education? What are its origins?

Identification of the major actors and variables involved in the issue. Who is involved? Why? How are they involved? What is at stake for the parties to the issue? What ideas, philosophies, or ideologies are involved? How are prevailing ideas affected by the issue?

2. *Illustration.* Once an issue has been described, an illustration of the ways in which it functions (affects people, institutions, processes) helps the examiner to lift it out of the realm of the academic or abstract into the world of experience. To study a description of the financial plight of the urban school is one thing; to read an account of the closing of a large city school system for lack of funds is quite another. The selections

in the illustrative sections, therefore, attempt to provide the reader with material which gives life to the descriptive accounts.

The reader is invited to examine the appropriateness of the illustrative accounts, to seek out other illustrative accounts, to compare them with those which appear here, and to make some judgments about the relative worth of the different accounts. In short, he has an opportunity to get involved in the examination process and, hence, with the issue itself.

3. *Analysis.* The function of this dimension is to separate an issue into its constituent parts and to reveal their relation to the whole and to one another. Analysis deals with cause-and-effect relationships and explains "why." It refers principally, therefore, to dissection aimed at "getting to know." But it means more than this. Analysis also means moving from knowledge toward a more critical perspective on the known.

In the analytical dimension the reader will encounter directly the approaches and perspectives of those disciplines—history, philosophy, sociology, and political science, principally—which comprise foundations of education study. Each issue will be analyzed from perspectives employing the intellectual tools and patterns of inquiry which inhere in these disciplines. This is not to suggest that the articles which appear in other dimensions lack attachment to a specific academic discipline (or disciplines). On the contrary, some sociological, philosophical and other articles do indeed appear in the other three dimensions. But these articles have been placed in contexts outside the analytical dimension because their nature and function are not, essentially, analytical. They may rely upon philosophical tools for description, or historical tools for projection, not upon analysis as such.

We would like to note, furthermore, that not all the analyses herein offer purely one disciplinary approach as opposed to another. Some reflect one approach; others are combinations—that is, they rely upon an assortment of disciplinary tools and perspectives in analyzing a particular article. In any case, an intended by-product of all the selections serving the analytical function is to provide the reader with impressions, insights, and knowledge into the ways particular academic disciplines relate to the study of education. The reader is invited to seek out analyses which differ from those which appear here. In other words, he has another opportunity for involvement in the issues to be examined.

4. *Projection.* By definition, issues are not closed. They speak to and follow from problems, disagreements, and conflicts which will continue to be open to question and doubt. Accordingly, scholars and others who

examine particular issues often engage in making predictions and offering prescriptions on these matters. They speculate about what the future may hold in light of the parameters surrounding an issue at a given moment in time. Or they often prescribe what should happen, what should be done, what kind of resolution should be reached regardless of (or in spite of) present conditions.

Selections in this section, then, will serve to focus attention on what some writer believes will or should happen regarding a particular issue. On the issue of teacher power, for example, selections serving the projection function deal with what the future is likely to hold for this movement (given related developments), as well as with what some people wish to happen to it. The projection selections, perhaps more than others, provide the reader an opportunity to become intimately involved in the issues at hand. Here he confronts conditions as they may be in education when he will very likely be a professional in that field. Moreover, in these selections he encounters beliefs and values openly—and often polemically—expressed. In brief, we hope many of the selections here will touch the sensibilities of the reader.

This, then, is the conceptual framework in which the selections in this book have been cast. Designed for a systematic analysis of crucial issues which affect or involve schooling in America, it is a unique approach and one which we believe will stimulate and aid the prospective teacher to come to grips with important aspects of the field which he will shortly be entering. It is also designed to involve the student intellectually and emotionally in educational issues. To insure this kind of involvement, each chapter closes with several questions and some suggested topics for further study which provide the reader with additional opportunity for expressing his thoughts, beliefs, and feelings.

Chapter 1. THE RELATIONSHIP
BETWEEN SCHOOL AND SOCIETY

SINCE public schools are social institutions ordained to carry out certain functions deemed appropriate by the dominant groups in the society in which they operate, it is not surprising that schools reflect the professed beliefs, values, and ideals of the dominant groups. Schools also mirror the unprofessed values—that is, the values revealed in the actual behavior of the controlling groups. If the dominant group claims to cherish brotherhood, the school seeks to transmit the value as an ideal for its students. However, if the life styles and behavior of the controlling groups favor competition and chauvinistic nationalism, then the schools come to mirror these values. Schools tend to mirror the professed, the ideal, and the "good." But they also reflect the real and the "bad."

This is not to deny that the school has often been out of touch with both the "good" and "bad" in society. As indicated in the Introduction, the school can indeed be out of touch with emerging trends and social needs. Nevertheless, it is the dependent variable in the school-society relationship. Many people are unhappy with this fact. Some claim that it has contributed to the impotency of the school, keeping it from making *direct* contributions to necessary social change. In any case, the school-society relationship, always a topic of debate, has become in recent times the center of raging controversy.

In a relatively stable, homogeneous society, there is little controversy surrounding the tasks and functions of the school. Under such circumstances, formal schooling consists of teaching and learning the basic skills, as well as the knowledge and values traditionally regarded as necessary and "good." In other words, although there may be disagreement about how well the school is functioning relative to these basic tasks, there is virtually no controversy over what the tasks and functions ought to be.

On the other hand, a society pervaded by rapid social and cultural change—encountering vast and unanticipated social complexities of population growth, urbanization, and large-scale technology; wrenched by racial and age-gap strife—will produce conflicting ideas and beliefs about the tasks and functions of the school. This is not difficult to understand. The conflicting ideas are symptoms of the uncertainties and fears which unanticipated social change always induces in members of society. And these conflicting ideas almost always lead to conflicting demands upon the school.

Rapid social change and its concomitant social complexities create new social environments which in turn, and quite naturally, give rise to new ways of thinking, feeling, and acting. The turned-on youth culture, the drug culture, the politics of confrontation, the "group-think" syndrome of Madison Avenue, the Black Power movement, the "de-sublimated" participant (vicarious or otherwise) in Hugh Hefner's *Playboy* world of slick erotica, the anti-establishment man on the street, the switched-on world of the jet set, the middle-aged, middle-class pot smoker, the world of sensitivity training—all these and many more are functions of a new social environment. But the new ways do not register simultaneously and equally with all people. Some bitterly resent them; others violently resist them. Many are confused, fearful, and uncertain. No wonder, then, that we debate the quarrel over the new ways and the role of the school. Some people would have the school ignore contemporary realities and stick to the transmission of time-tested ideas and values. Others feel that it should embrace what they perceive as a newly emerging culture. Some urge the school to become the agent for cultural renewal, the architect of a blueprint for a new society. Still others urge the school to behave as neutral observer, to serve as the referee or intellectual arbiter between the old and new ways. Some would have us give up on the public school and turn attention to the creation of alternatives to public schooling. There are even those who would have us burn down the system. Thus we come to the issue which is the object of our attention in this chapter: *What should be the relationship between the school and the society in which it operates?*

The prospective teacher may wonder why he should be concerned about this issue. His job will be to teach some academic specialty. Are not these specialties basically the same regardless of the social system in which the school operates? Isn't knowledge in an academic field and the methods and skills necessary to the teaching of it all one needs to know?

What direct bearing does the relationship between school and society have upon classroom activity?

It is essentially true that knowledge of and involvement in the issue of the school-society relationship is not necessary to effective teaching as such. Yet, most of the disputes over the schools center around basic functions and roles of schooling. And the classroom teacher is centrally, crucially, and inextricably involved in these matters. For example, all of these disputes have implications for the overall objectives of the school and, hence, the instructional program. The teacher is *the* catalyst in the instructional program. While the student, the administration, the curriculum, and the community are all limiting or liberating factors in the instructional program, it is the teacher who gives life to it. Furthermore, these disputes have something to say about the types of individuals (and the relationships among them) that our schools ought to produce. Again, it is the teacher, through his beliefs, his values, and the ways in which they are acted out in the classroom, who, ultimately, has the most to say and contribute for good or bad to such disputes.

The teacher, then, is necessarily caught in the ebb and flow of school controversies. To be uninvolved in them is impossible. To ignore them is possible, but to do so is to remove oneself from a crucial arena of the school's activity.

Ralph L. Pounds and James R. Bryner

CONTRASTING VIEWPOINTS AS TO THE SCHOOL'S ROLE

The following article is taken from the second edition of a pioneering textbook on American society and education. In it the authors describe major, conflicting views on the nature of schooling and the school-society relationship, and present the underlying assumptions and philosophical perspectives of these points of view. Each point of view described by Pounds and Bryner is addressed to the large issue of the nature of education and the general question of the school-society relationship. But each position is also examined in terms of its outlook on the school's role in a

From Ralph L. Pounds and James R. Bryner, *The School in American Society* (Second Edition) (New York: The Macmillan Company, 1967), pp. 491–510. Footnotes omitted. Copyright © 1967 The Macmillan Company. Reprinted by permission of the publisher.

time of rapid change. Moreover, each position has clear implications concerning most of the issues which make up this book.

The Pounds and Bryner article does not exhaust the existing and possible positions on the school-society relationship. Furthermore, it does not include what might be considered "radical" notions. We have purposely selected an article which excludes such ideas because the radical positions that appear, explicitly or implicitly, in later articles are then set in bold relief from those which appear here. And this ought to be the case. Radical ideas are radical because they dramatically depart from traditional and generally accepted ideas. The points of view described by Pounds and Bryner are, by and large, those turned to by most educators (and those concerned about education) when problems and conflicts lead to debates on the school-society relationship.

Ralph L. Pounds is Professor of Education at the University of Cincinnati and the author or coauthor of several books and articles. James R. Bryner, a former public school superintendent, is Associate Professor of Education at the University of Saskatchewan.

[I] Schools for the Development of the Intellect—Humanism, Religious and Classical

Of the several points of view that are to be discussed in detail in this and the following sections, humanism is the one whose history goes back the farthest in an unbroken line. The continuity between classical humanism, which developed during the Renaissance period at the end of the Middle Ages, and modern "neo"-humanism is almost unbroken.

Central Ideas Related to the Nature of Education. Most of the persons we are here classifying as humanists hold that the universe is organized on a relatively few changeless principles. It is assumed that these principles can be ascertained by an intellectual-rational process by those persons who have minds capable of grasping such principles. The central purpose of education is thought to be the development of the intellect —that capacity of mind that is necessary for the grasping of these unchanging principles.

According to this position, the great classics that have come down to us from the past are examples in print of the efforts of great minds. One of the best ways to develop intellect is to come into contact with a great mind. The great minds are so few that the contact with the written result of a great mind (a great book) becomes the best way of touching the mind itself. Some of the humanists are not so much interested in teaching by means of the great classics as are others. These latter are usually interested in the organization of subject matter of the great subject disciplines, which have been produced by the great minds just as the classics have been.

The way in which the school can best serve present society, according to the humanist position, is in concentrating its efforts on the mental development of outstanding individuals who can become the leaders of our present society. It is the job of the schools carefully to select the best thoughts of the past, representative of the best minds, and transmit them to the present—at least to those persons who are capable of understanding and utilizing these thoughts in the solution of our pressing problems. . . .

Basic Philosophical Assumptions. Certain main metaphysical assumptions are for the most part held in common by persons having this point of view, whether they are classical or religious humanists.

By and large this group adheres to the concept of a dualistic world composed of two substances or essences, the one of matter and the other of ideas (or spirit or form). The student of philosophy will recognize this concept as going back historically as far as the ancient Greek controversies on the nature of matter. It includes both the Platonic and the Aristotelian concepts. The student of philosophy will also recognize that there is a wide variety of viewpoints that may be taken with respect to the nature of these two types of essences and also with respect to the relationships between them. Also, it will be recognized that some individuals holding the other points of view may be dualists to a greater or less extent.

In general, the theory of knowledge that is adhered to by those in the humanist tradition places less emphasis upon the scientific development of knowledge in the modern connotation of the word "science" as necessarily involving careful experimentation, and more upon the securing of knowledge through the use of reason or the rational process. In some cases, of course, faith, intuition, or revelation is added to other methods for arriving at ideas of values. The scientific method in general *is* accepted by this group only as a method of securing knowledge concerning the material world. For more basic knowledge, including that of the metaphysical principles and certainly for the realm of values, we must go to other processes. These are held to lie in the realm of ideas where the scientific method is not applicable.

Man himself is considered to differ from animals because he possesses mind. Mind is the "quality of rationality" that makes man different from animals. In general, the chief values for this group are those that are in harmony with the unchanging values that have been accredited by the great figures and writers of the past.

While the American adherents to the humanist view are for the most part enthusiastic supporters of our democratic society, there certainly is a difference between their point of view toward democracy and some of the points of view to be described later. In general, those in the humanist position accept only the political definition of democracy: namely that it is a form of government in which the main officers or representatives are chosen by the people. Political equality is not held to mean social or intellectual equality. This group emphasizes quite strongly that everyone should recognize that there is a difference in the kind of contribution different individuals can make to our society. The humanists advocate improvement of the ability of the masses to select as their leaders members of the intellectual elite who can make the proper decisions for the rest of us. The humanists, for the most part, believe very strongly in the individual's civil liberties and think that we should protect them because individuals must be free to make decisions they wish to make.

Ideas on the School in Relationship to Social Change; Other Suggestions as to Curriculum and Methods. In general, . . . matters [related to] social change . . . are held by those in the humanist position not to be changes in the basic ideas underlying the universe. Consequently, although these changes pose problems, it becomes all the more important that we should not lose sight of the unchanging principles. The main job of the school, therefore, in times of slow change as well as in times of rapid change, is to see to it that methods of rational thinking are used in facing our problems. Thinking through to the basic principles that underlie solution of the problems we face is held central and paramount in the educational process.

One of the implications of this, of course, is that the school should not be basically concerned with current events. By being too much taken up with current problems, we lose perspective and sometimes do not get at the basic principles in the crosscurrents of our political and other problems. Once our minds have been trained to think rationally by coming in contact with the great minds through study of the great books or of the subject disciplines, we shall then be able to use our trained intellects in the solution of the present problems with which we are faced.

This apparent lack of interest by formal education in our present social problems does not mean that none of the persons adhering to this philosophy is concerned about them. Many of them are. Robert Hutchins, for example, tends to be a social liberal, even though, in his educational philosophy, he harks back to an earlier form of education, which he thinks will enable us to develop leaders to help us solve the social problems we face.

In the humanist point of view, the best form of education, at least the education of the intellectual elite, is that which was used in our schools in an earlier period: namely contact with the great classics and the lecture method, perhaps supplemented by discussion in seminars with professors familiar with the classics. The student will thereby be stimulated to think, through contact with the ideas that are being promulgated in the great books curriculum or in the subject disciplines. Contact with a great mind that uses rational thinking is more important than practice in the utilization of proper procedures in the actual solving of concrete problems. After it has been ascertained in elementary school or early in high school that certain individuals cannot attain any very great intellectual accomplishment, they should be given vocational training and training for citizenship so that they will be able to make wise decisions in choosing their political leaders. Such training should not be called "education," because real education is the development of the intellect.

Some of the statements contained in above paragraphs are too extreme for some of the persons who would adhere at least partially to the ideas expressed. There are many differences, for example as to the number of persons who can be trained intellectually, among those people who basically adhere to this point of view. There is also a difference of opinion as to the kind of education for other persons. We have already seen that only a few humanists would strictly follow the great books curriculum. There are also some individuals, particularly those adhering to a traditional religion, who would accept the basic *philosophical assumptions* set forth in this view but would accept in part *educational ideas* similar to those to be described later.

[II] Schools to Pass on the Tested Heritage from Man's Historical Development—Social Evolutionism

Again, as in the case of the humanists, what we have called *social evolutionism* represents a number of related points of view. In this case the points of view probably are more similar in their basic philosophical assumptions. This general point of view differs markedly from that of the humanists with respect to its naturalistic approach to the universe and to man. This point of view, and the others of the series to follow, date (in their more mature forms) from the period after man had discovered the scientific method. What is here called social evolutionism probably can be traced at least as far back as Spencer, the scientist who first applied the Darwinian point of view to the field of social evolution. It is most definitely found within the scientific-evolutionary view as to the nature of man and of the universe.

In contrast to this emphasis on change, the conclusions for education tend to be of a conservative nature. Whereas the humanists tend to go back to an earlier period both for the subject matter of the schools and for the methods, the social evolutionists for the most part are satisfied with the present curriculum of the school, although some of them may have suggestions for the improvement of methods of teaching. In this group there are wide differences of opinion with respect to certain matters. For example, there is a difference of opinion as to the validity of intelligence tests. William C. Bagley was very critical of the use that was being made of their results in his time. There are also differences as to emphases. Bagley emphasized adaptability of methods to the individual, Morrison carefully worked out detailed units of study for the various subjects, and Judd emphasized the cultivation of the higher mental processes. . . .

In the discussion of social evolutionism to follow, under the same four subheadings under which we discussed neo-humanism, we shall limit ourselves to those positions that for the most part are held in common by the persons to be indicated later as the proponents of this general point of view.

Central Ideas Related to the Nature of Education. The social evolutionists look to man's evolutionary development in order to get a basis for their ideas about the specific purposes of the school. They note that a study of man's social development indicates that man has been enabled to make progress because of specific adaptations or inventions he has made. Man learned to associate with his fellows for improved ability to secure food and to protect himself from danger. Later, speech developed and still later, the art of writing. Various forms of organization that enabled man more effectively to carry on his group organization were developed. Many kinds of adaptation of technology and food-getting were discovered and then passed on culturally.

The net result of all this is that man owes his very quality of "humanness" to the social environment in which he is found. Society is preeminent. Man gets his individuality from his contact with the society in which he is found.

Education, according to the social evolutionist view, develops as a separate institution when its functions become so important or so complex that they must be performed by specialists. The main function of education is to see to it that those great inventions of the past that have enabled man to make such progress are passed on to the young. The school acts as a preserver of the cultural heritage. The school as an institution must carefully study the past, determine those aspects of the past that are worthy of being passed on, and see to it that the new generation is then given the necessary skills, attitudes, and character traits that have been validated by societies of the past. By and large, the traditional curriculum, consisting of the subjects that incorporated the past successful discoveries of mankind, did contain those elements that needed to be passed on to the new generation. The school must do the most effective job possible in seeing to it that these essentials of our time-tested cultural heritage are passed on. . . .

Basic Philosophical Assumptions. . . . For the most of the persons in this school of thought, the approach to the problem of knowledge, of course, comes largely through the scientific method. (The historical method is one aspect of the scientific.) Certainly the scientific method should be used to verify facts concerning the nature of the world and of man. The scientific method can also be used in establishing the facts of history. It is from history that, according to this point of view, the values for the use of the school are obtained. The values lie in the preservation of those things that have been validated through their success in man's previous history. The purpose of life therefore seems to be to build a society that would operate in terms of those values that have been fully established in man's previous social history.

Ideas on the School in Relationship to Social Change; Suggestions as to Curriculum and Methods. Since the school is to validate its curriculum and its values by a study of the history of the race, educators need not be concerned about the events that are happening contemporaneously in the society. Indeed at this very point, when society is in a state of crisis, the school is needed most to act as a conservator or "balance wheel" to support basic social values. This does not mean that there is no change (over a long period of time) in certain basic values as man goes onward in his societal evolution and has new insights. For example, the development of democracy was a new insight that arose out of man's experience and was gradually proved to be helpful for his onward and upward evolution. The school plays no part, however, in these advances of society. It is enough that the school's program assures that the time-tested values and essentials of our culture are passed on, once they are established. By so doing, it will prevent the various societies from moving rather hastily in unknown directions. Any lack of attention to essential values and to man's past heritage may cause a society to deteriorate. As a matter of fact, they note, a study of history indicates this. In many cases a more gradual, and therefore a better, evolution of society would have occurred had the school done a more effective job of passing on the time-tested values of a culture.

For the social evolutionist, the curriculum of the school should consist of those essentials of subject matter, skills, attitudes, and character traits that have been time-tested and therefore have proved to be good in terms of man's past history. These essentials, for the most part, have traditionally (at least in the recent past) been held to be of most importance in the curriculum of the school. The present school subjects are satisfactory as far as they contain the essentials (knowledge and skills).

On the question of school methods, several social evolutionists have had suggestions to make. [Henry] Morrison, for example, proposed the Morrison unit. For this type of unit (which is still widely used, sometimes with modifications) he listed in detail plans for teaching adapted to the different kinds of subject matter. William C. Bagley was also a specialist on methods. In each case, they believed that the *real essentials* could be taught to practically all persons regardless of their reputed slowness in learning ability. Bagley particularly decried the undue emphasis on the intelligence test and the implied notion that some people could not learn. He also opposed the separation of students by homogeneous grouping. He and Morrison both believed that methods could be adapted to the learning level of the various students involved. Morrison in particular stressed the mastery of the essentials. If certain items had been proved essential in the onward development of civilization, it was mandatory that the schools teach for *mastery* and *continue to teach* until there was mastery. He was very much opposed to the idea of developing a quite extensive curriculum that could not be fully taught. Some of the items that had at times been included in the curriculum were considered to be definitely unnecessary.

The central idea of this point of view can be summarized in the statement, "It is the school's job to pass on the essentials as effectively as possible to the greatest number of persons in our culture in order to insure the optimum conditions necessary for the further onward development of our society." To this group the main function of the school is to facilitate the onward development of our civilization by seeing to it that the essentials of our cultural heritage are passed on as unimpaired as possible to the next generation. Emphasis was upon mastery of essentials by all; no provision was made for leadership training for the gifted few.

[III] Schools to Adjust Individuals to Present Society—Social Realism

The point of view here called *social realism* tends to represent more of a social philosophy than a general metaphysical point of view. For the most part, however, its proponents do adhere to a general philosophical point of view—that of realism. There are many kinds of realism, so we have attempted to differentiate them by calling this one *social realism*. The precise nature of the metaphysical assumptions will be set forth in a later section. . . . This point of view is a currently prevailing one among school administrators.

Central Ideas Related to the Nature of Education. In general, this point of view arose (as did social evolutionism) in response to the scientific movement, which came about in the Western world in the latter part of the seventeenth century. The scientific movement did not affect seriously the study of psychology until late in the nineteenth century with the work of Wundt and others in Europe and the group in America under the stimulation of William James. The point of view underlying almost all of science of that time was a strongly realistic one, philosophically speaking. It was felt that by a careful use of the scientific method we could amass a whole set of facts, each one established in an isolated investigation. These individual facts could then be added together until man could establish all knowledge, and on the basis of this knowledge he could develop the kind of world he wanted. In the field of science and in the scientific study of man, there was little place for values. As a matter of fact, in the early part of this period it was felt that, in order to be scientific, it was necessary to lay aside for the moment all questions of values. Consequently this group was very little interested in the problem of values as such. Indeed some of this group were, and are, quite antagonistic toward philosophy. In the period of the 1920's, when certain extreme aspects of this point of view were quite evident, in the movement of education called *scientism,* there was very little interest in a philosophical approach to the problems of education.

The social realists felt that the job of education is to insure that individuals are prepared to adjust to the present society. The emphasis was upon the preparing of individuals to *live in our present society.* Consequently one of the main procedures to be used in the selection of a curriculum was to conduct a careful study of the present society, in order to determine just what would be demanded of the students when they get out of school.

Another aspect of the problem was the desirability of helping the individual to fit into his proper place in society. This necessitated a careful study of the individual. It was found that individuals varied greatly with respect to their abilities. Each person probably had a definite place in society, which could be ascertained by a careful study of his abilities. It was then necessary to assist in fitting him into his niche. . . .

Basic Philosophical Assumptions. The basic philosophical assumptions of the social realists are similar in some respects to those of the social evolutionists. The social realists believe very definitely in a real, knowable world that can be known apart from the particular knower. In other words, this is not a subjective world. It can be known objectively. The means of knowing the world is through the scientific method, whereby knowledge can be validated. Most of the realists formerly thought that knowledge could be obtained by careful isolation of a phenomenon and by examining it in piecemeal fashion in accordance with the Newtonian scientific tradition. The newer point of view of Eisteinian science indicates that phenomena must always be studied in the total field of interrelationships. The realists hold that, when mankind has determined the facts concerning the world in which he lives, the problem remaining is to use them in accordance with the prevailing purposes and values of his culture. For the most part the implication is that as teachers and educators we may arrive at these values by a careful study of our culture. For example, as school administrators, we must objectively study our culture to determine its prevailing values and then we must proceed to develop the practices of the institution called the school so that it operates in such a way as to achieve those prevailing values.

The realists recognize that we live in a changing world. Consequently the school as an institution must change, both to keep up with the world and to be in touch with whatever values may become predominant at different times in our culture. The realists would agree with those points of view that hold that the values predominant in a democratic culture are different from those in, let us say, a feudalistic culture, and that the school at present must reflect in its practices the democratic nature of our culture.

Ideas on the School in Relationship to Social Change; Other Suggestions as to Curriculum and Methods. We have seen that the proponents of the social-realist point of view by and large desire that the school keep up with the changes in our society. A special problem arises when we recall that, if in an era of social change we are preparing people for the now-present society, the society to which they will have to adjust will be a different one within the next few years. Some of the social realists have recognized this problem and have arrived at answers similar to those of the experimentalists. They have become more concerned about the development of adaptable individuals because of the changing nature of our society. Another point that many of this group apparently have neglected is the existence of many conflicts in our society. It is difficult to find out what values are predominant. At any given time a whole series of values is in conflict. Sometimes sudden changes are made, perhaps reversions to previous ideas or values. Do we get our values merely by "counting noses" at a particular time? Does the school follow every change in the political and social weather vane? This issue appears to be faced in two different ways by different groups of realists. One approach is to ignore for the most part these values that are in serious conflict. Instead we may look at the fundamental activities in which man engages and attempt to duplicate them in the school, so that a man can learn as a child or youth to make proper adjustments in his social activities. Another approach among the realists is to handle this problem in a fashion similar to that of the experimentalists. The school would teach the student to handle problems of a controversial nature in a scientific manner and attempt to help him to arrive at satisfactory answers to the problems with which individuals and groups in our society are faced. In this latter process, an attempt is made to help the student to clarify his own values among the varieties of multiconflicting values found in our society. This latter approach would differ very little in operation from the methods usually used by the experimentalists. Only the underlying philosophical assumptions would be somewhat different.

To return now to the discussion of social realism in general, the curriculum of the school should be made up of those activities and selected subject matter that would be of direct, functional, practical value to the persons who are going to live and operate in our culture. The learning situation should be such as to secure maximum learning of facts and skills.

The emphasis on the part of some realists on the wide differences among individuals in regard to capabilities and the activities they will pursue later in life leads them to set up a number of differentiated curricula, particularly in the secondary school, according to the kind of life the individual plans to pursue later. Of course there will be a core of common studies, but there will also be curricula of many kinds, differentiated for persons of differing abilities and with respect to the quite different vocations into which they will enter. Some of the realists advocate plans that use homogeneous grouping of the students with respect to their abilities, so that both curriculum and methods can be more readily adapted to students of similar ability. This point of view has been manifest, of course, in some contemporary secondary schools. While there is still emphasis on special classes for those people requiring special help, such as the slow learner and the gifted, the general trend today is away from such a heavy emphasis on homogeneous grouping, even among some of the realists.

The realists in general advocate that the methods of teaching should be discovered through scientific research to determine the most effective way of accomplishing whatever purposes or values can be arrived at by the methods described above.

[IV] Schools to Develop Individuals with Ability to Refine Critically the Social Heritage and to Improve Society—Experimentalism

Experimentalism is the point of view that has been ascribed to John Dewey and others of his school of philosophy. In the field of general philosophy, it is based on what is called the pragmatic viewpoint. It is more commonly known as experimentalism as far as the implications for education are concerned. The word *instrumentalism* has sometimes been applied to it because of the stress upon the instrumental nature of the hypothesis or idea in assisting the human organism in solving its problems. This point of view has developed primarily within the American democratic culture, and it stems from democratic values coupled with the scientific method of getting at knowledge and with the general "practical" realistic point of view found in American society. John Dewey assimilated these elements into an integrated point of view to form his pragmatic philosophy.

Central Ideas Related to the Nature of Education. Most of the persons adhering to the experimentalist position place emphasis on the process of getting at knowledge through the method of tested human experience. Education as the construction and progressive "reconstruction of experience" is John Dewey's way of stating the relation of the educational process to ongoing activity.

The main purpose of education, then, is to develop critically minded individuals who are capable of seeking and finding (at least tentatively) creative answers to the problems they face in their society. Not only should they develop capabilities of finding answers to their own personal problems, but also abilities of being able to work well with others in a group solution to common problems. There is emphasis among the experimentalists on the clarification of the values of the students as a part of the educational process.

The above concepts mean that the curriculum is primarily to be thought of in terms of carefully selected experiences under the guidance of the teacher, in order to develop the kind of individuals who will be capable of the solution of their own problems and of common problems in conjunction with fellow students and later with fellow men.

Basic Philosophical Assumptions. John Dewey held that there are some metaphysical problems the solution of which we can never hope to find. Consequently we should begin to work on our practical problems without trying to settle in advance the answers to all those that are metaphysical. There is, however, a necessary set of assumptions under which the experimentalist operates. The earlier idealistic philosophy held that there were two basic essences of the universe, matter and spirit. The experimentalist tries to resolve this dualism, and along with it many other types of dualisms, by holding that reality is one, the reality of human experience. It is within this reality of human experience that mankind must seek the answers to its problems. This world of human experience in which we find ourselves and in which we attempt to solve our problems is a dynamic, changing world, the parts of which are in constant interaction with each other. All knowledge in that universe is tentative and is based upon tested human experience. Each new hypothesis for human action must be tested in terms of consequences for further human action. Hypotheses as to values arise out of human experiences in the same way that hypotheses as to facts do, and they are tested in that human experience. Both knowledge and values are tentative and must be continually retested.

Almost all experimentalists find three values emerging out of their experience that seem to be fairly universal. These values, also central to our democracy, can be summarized as follows: (1) respect for individual personality; (2) use of the reflective-scientific method as a basis for the solution of human problems; and (3) widening of the area of common concern through the increasing participation of all in the solution of problems.

These basic principles, which are much simpler than those of most of the other philosophies, are held by the experimentalists to be sufficient to define a point of view, but they are broad enough to be susceptible to a variety of meanings related to human experience as such experiences change through enrichment and through contact with a changing world. These assumptions are not held to be absolute but are subject to scrutiny and possible change from time to time.

Ideas on the School in Relationship to Social Change; Other Suggestions as to Curriculum and Methods. In general, the experimentalists hold it to be the school's job to help individuals to develop so as to become creative in problem-solving in line with the scientific method. The curriculum is to be selected experiences under the guidance of the teacher. The following principles of procedure in teaching, generally characteristic of experimentalists, can be listed: (1) experiential learning; (2) student participation in the selection and development of learning experiences; (3) integrated learnings; (4) individualization of the study of the child; (5) emphasis on intrinsic motivation; (6) continuous evaluation by group and self; (7) emphasis on social adjustment; (8) teaching as guidance; (9) emphasis on cultivation of problem-solving abilities; and (10) emphasis on refinement of the cultural heritage.

Some of these principles are accepted also by persons holding other points of view, and, of course, individual experimentalists may well interpret them quite differently in light of their own individual experiential background. In general, these points of view do serve to define a pragmatic approach to the problems of the curriculum and methods of the school.

[V] *Schools to Develop Individuals for a New Society Based on Best Solutions to Present Conditions and Trends—Reconstructionism*

The point of view called *reconstructionism* has become clearly defined only in quite recent years. Theodore Brameld, now at Boston University, has played a prominent part in its inception. Reconstructionism has stemmed from the experimentalist point of view and agrees with it in many of the basic philosophical assumptions. The reconstructionists however, have become quite impatient with the experimentalist teacher, who, they say, hesitates to take a position as a teacher with respect to a definite answer to the problems that the student faces, holding that the student must be "free" to make his own decisions.

Central Ideas Related to the Nature of Education. To the reconstructionists, the main purpose of education is to develop individuals with the ability and the desire to create the new social order now possible. The method to be used in discovering and developing the new social order is the scientific method. The school, however, must have examined available knowledge and must have arrived in advance at a possible solution as to the kind of society that we need in light of our present knowledge and of problems with which we are faced. The teacher then presents this solution to the student, with the evidence pro and con. The student, of course, is permitted to make his own decision with respect to whether or not he accepts or rejects the kind of society that the reconstructionist, in light of his interpretation of the evidence, has found that we need in order to deal effectively with the very crucial problems that we face. . . .

Basic Philosophical Assumptions. The assumptions of the reconstructionist as to the nature of the world and their answers to other metaphysical problems are similar to those of the experimentalists. At times, some of them do stress the greater emphasis upon the hypothesis as a necessary determinant of the way in which we approach the solution of a problem. There is also on the part of those named, such as Harold Rugg, a greater emphasis on the esthetic and on other aspects related to the validating of knowledge or values than that of the tested experience emphasized by the experimentalists. For example, Rugg holds that an esthetic experience is intrinsically good in and of itself, rather than because it has been validated by testing its consequences for further human action.

Ideas on the School in Relationship to Social Change; Other Suggestions as to Curriculum and Method. In determining the curriculum of the school, the reconstructionists feel that teachers and others concerned with education must first examine the facts and principles of knowledge that have been discovered by the social sciences and from them determine the kind of society we need. Then they should set up the school's curriculum in such a way as to present these facts and principles, including the "blueprint of the new society," so that the student may know what is needed to solve the social problems we face. Although the individual would be given arguments on other sides and would be permitted to choose whether or not he wanted to accept the new society, it is felt that in general he would accept the new society because it would be based upon scientific knowledge and principles. The nature of the new society is held to be readily apparent, given the facts of the situation and the facts and principles developed by the social sciences. It will be acceptable to the student if it is presented fairly to him along with the evidence. The main job of the school, then, is to prepare individuals to have the various skills needed and to know how to use the various procedures needed to bring about the new society.

[VI] *Schools with Emphasis on Self-creativity and Individual Growth—Educational Laissez-Faire*

The point of view with emphasis on "self-creativity and individual growth" is [what we label] *educational laissez-faire. . . .* On the contemporary scene, this point of view does not exist in any sharply defined form. Sometimes we find it approximated among some persons who lay extreme emphasis on the child-study approach, or sometimes among those who have an extremist approach stemming originally from psychiatry (or at least from a smattering of psychology). In this point of view, there is very little emphasis upon society itself as a basis for determining the nature of the curriculum of the school. The emphasis is upon the individual child and his developmental trends. The main purpose of education is to encourage the fullest development of the individual. The stress of educational method is on individuality in the handling of pupils. There is great emphasis upon the individual's physical environment (to be sure that we have an environment that is conducive to his good development), and there is an emphasis upon trying to bring out the individual's creative expression. Particularly, there is an emphasis in opposition to positive efforts that might serve to thwart the individual's creative expression and his direction of wholesome development.

Some of the persons holding this point of view realize that the pupil does live in and grow with a dynamic, pervasive society, and do help him to understand his society and to learn to live within it. In this case, the point of view does not differ too greatly from that of experimentalists. The extreme point of view that some popular writers erroneously associate with the term "progressive education," that of "permitting a child to do as he pleases," stems philosophically from the laissez-faire point of view. This extreme point of view has been erroneously ascribed to John Dewey, even though Dewey in *Experience and Education,* and Boyd Bode in *Progressive Education at the Crossroads,* have clearly set forth the differences between their point of view, experimentalism, and an extreme point of view among some "progressive" educators of that time, similar to educational laissez-faire.

Experimentalism does have a very definite social philosophy in order to give it a definite direction, which Bode described as "democracy." The Progressive Education Association was organized originally by persons whose only common philosophy was a desire to move away from traditional practices. Some of them perhaps did go to extremes. In 1941, however, the society did officially adopt a philosophic point of view within the experimentalist position.

[VII] *Existentialism*

Existentialism as a point of view and as a well-defined system of thinking goes back to at least the nineteenth century. Some persons have held that it goes back to some aspects of Thomas Aquinas' thinking or even to Socrates and the ancient Greeks. In its more modern version, it has a great deal of acceptance among French intellectuals. It arose largely in the nineteenth century as a theological point of view in order to explain the nature of religion in a world in which scientific explanation seemed to do away with any logical basis. However, in the modern form it has two branches—a theistic and a nontheistic, or atheistic branch. Jean-Paul Sartre is the most prominent proponent of the nontheistic branch. There are many prominent representatives of the theistic point of view. Examples are Martin Buber, Jacques Maritain, Paul Tillich, representing as they do respectively three different theological traditions, Jewish, Catholic, and Protestant.

Basically the existentialists hold that man lives in a world of despair that is bound to end up in an absurd, tragic finish. In this world in which there is no meaning to be found outside a man's own efforts to find or determine a meaning for himself, the most important thing is for man to recognize the necessity for choosing, and to accept his responsibility to live in accord with his particular choice. One cannot get the answer to one's existence from science or any other study discipline. Certainly the extent to which man has attempted to probe the meaning of existence in literature and the arts may help other persons to some extent, but basically the question comes back to one's own self, and each must finally make his own choice. What is the nature of my existence and what do I wish to become? "Existence precedes essence." We first recognize we exist; we then choose; and then we develop into the "essence" (or nature) of our choice. This point of view has implications for education in terms of getting youngsters ready to recognize the necessity for choice and to prevent them from being pushed into conformity and standardization without facing up to the necessity for their own choice. This whole point of view is an anti-system. Consequently, there is *no* well-defined program of action for education. It is more of an attitude or temper than a programmatic point of view.

[VIII] *Eclectic Point of View*

There are many persons who work in the field of education, including indeed some who are definitely students of philosophy of education, who have points of view that do not fit into the classification structure used in this chapter. The word *eclectic* has been frequently applied to those whose point of view does not fit into a standard philosophical position. In the first place, it should be noted that many eclectics are so classified only because they do not happen to fit into a particular structure as it has been set up by someone else. Were the structure different, they might well fit. Second, there is a sense in which all persons who have thought clearly and creatively develop ideas somewhat different from others whose general points of view are similar. This, of course, means they quite often have ideas that are also found in some other point of view. This would automatically make them "eclectics" by definition. Their particular combination of ideas may be very consistent (according to their assumptions) and may fit together into a well-coordinated point of view even though it does not fit into a "standard" classification.

In a sense, each of the philosophical positions discussed in preceding sections may be "eclectic" according to one of the other points of view. If, for example, we were to ask an experimentalist how he would handle the problems of passing on the cultural heritage (in which we might be somewhat critical of his apparent lack of emphasis upon past tradition), the experimentalist would probably indicate that he had taken care of the matter because of his emphasis upon the "clarification or refinement of the cultural heritage." In other words, he would not ignore some of the things that are emphasized in other points of view; he would merely stress them in other ways. Similar questions directed at other groups, such as the place of scientific thinking for the humanist or of the importance of cultural change for the essentialist, would be answered in ways to indicate that they had taken into account that particular point but had answered it in a different way. All of them would deny that they were overlooking the emphasis of the other points of view.

Literally hundreds of ongoing controversies about schooling are direct functions of, or have implications for, the school-society relationship issue. No wonder, then, that much of the present fury over education can be traced to different views about the role of schools in relation to the society they serve. Accordingly, there exists a wealth of material which can be used to illustrate this issue. Take the question of black studies. According to Charles Hamilton in the article which follows, this movement is intimately wedded to student, faculty, and community dissatisfaction with prevailing curricular offerings, with the traditional authorities and sanctions turned to in justifying and legitimizing courses of study, and with substantive gaps and shortcomings in our typical and traditional school curriculums.

Whatever one's position on the black studies question, it can be traced to or related to the school-society relationship issue. Are social changes reflected in the black studies movement to be ignored by the schools? Is the movement a passing fancy? Is the present curriculum, largely devoid of black studies as such, satisfactory to the extent that it offers means necessary for black students to adapt successfully to the natural and social environment? Questions such as these, raised at a more general level in the Pounds and Bryner article, are logically and naturally raised in any analysis of the black studies question. So too with sex education, drug education, and so on. Indeed, most if not all questions which deal with curriculum innovation, particularly those which are related to meeting relevant or current needs, give rise to further questions concerning the relationship between school and society. The reader should not be surprised, therefore, to discover that he recurrently turns to the Pounds and Bryner article as he proceeds through this book.

Charles V. Hamilton

THE QUESTION OF BLACK STUDIES

In the following article, Charles Hamilton contends that demands for black studies are essentially political demands for academic innovation and relevance. He argues that the black studies movement is a consequence of much dissatisfaction with prevailing curricular offerings relative to the place and prospects of black people in our society, traditional authorities and values turned to in legitimizing educational programs, and the lag between pressing needs of the black student and educational offerings. Although the black studies movement has been most evident on college campuses, it is not limited to institutions of higher learning. Indeed, with increasing regularity the demands for black studies is being made at lower levels of formal schooling.

From *Phi Delta Kappan*, 7 (March, 1970), pp. 362–364. Some footnotes omitted. Reprinted by permission of the publisher.

Charles V. Hamilton is Professor of Political Science and Urban Studies at Columbia University. Author of several articles on race and education, he coauthored, with Stokely Carmichael, *Black Power: The Politics of Liberation in America.*

Several years from now, when historians studying race and politics in the United States look back on the 1960's, they will see a decade of innumerable phrases and labels. They will see such terms as *integration, busing, nonviolence, violence, freedom now, law and order, black power, community control, white racism, institutional racism, separatism, black nationalism, revolution, black studies.* Hopefully, those historians will realize the intense political environment out of which these terms came. These terms were abbreviated ways—and therefore dangerous because of the great possibility of oversimplification—of explaining or projecting complicated phenomena. Arising out of an emotional, intense political struggle, these terms became less the subject for penetrating, in-depth analyses and more the basis on which a polemical, momentarily dramatic debate was engaged.

The black studies issue is one example of this sort of treatment. The term rose out of the protest demands of black students on college campuses in the late 1960's. The demands generally were summed up in another phrase: "a relevant education." The black students wanted their exposure to higher education to be "relevant" to them as black people. They were dissatisfied with the nature of the college curriculum as it existed in most places around the country—and they were specific in their criticisms, with particular emphasis on the humanities, history, and the social sciences. They pointed out major substantive gaps in American academia, and many of them concluded that these gaps were as much a function of a value system that deliberately chose the kinds of subjects to include in the curriculum as they were simply the result of scholarship yet to be done. In other words, the failure to depict the true role of black people in American history, or the exclusion of black writers from the reading lists of courses in American literature, for example, was a clear reflection of the values of American academia. Law schools and other professional schools were vehemently criticized for offering a course of study which did not "relate" to the developmental needs of a depressed black community.

Thus the students began to demand black studies as an academic mechanism to overcome these normative and substantive problems. One has to understand that these demands were *political* precisely because they reflected—explicitly and implicitly—a feeling among the students that the colleges and universities were not "legitimate." That is, the students were demanding that the institutions change in many ways: in how they recruited black students, in what they did with the black students once they were on campus, in how the schools related to black communities, in the recruitment of black professors, in the kinds of courses offered. Therefore, as *political* demands for *academic* innovation, the demands were subject to negotiation and compromise. At all times, the demands were focal points of a political struggle. The struggle was political in the sense that the right of the college and university to rule unchallenged in the traditional ways was being questioned. *This was the central question: the question of legitimacy.*

Most schools readily admitted that changes (in curriculum, recruitment, community relations) had to be made. But then ensued an unfortunate period when many of the specific alternatives—which had to be understood as products of a political struggle—were taken as absolute academic ends. And before there was time to examine perceptively the kinds of *academic* changes that could be made, many people began to join the polemical debate. Black studies were called "soul courses"; they were seen as places where a cadre of revolutionaries would be trained; respected scholars admonished that black students needed "higher education" in order to compete, not something called black studies.

If one examined closely some of the black studies proposals, there is no question that he would find many of them being concerned with issues of ideology and what might be called subjective matters. This is so precisely because the proposals were trying to—and in many instances did—articulate a new system of legitimacy. The proposals were rejecting, for example, traditional and widely accepted political science literature that argued in favor of the virtual inviolability of a two-party system. The proposals in that field called for courses that attempted to explore new ways to approach socio-political change in modern America —at least from the vantage point of black Americans. Perhaps those courses were aimed at "getting ourselves together" and at developing political power among black people. Why are these "soul courses"—in the catharsis-serving and demeaning sense of that phrase? Have not some political science courses traditionally been dealing with how groups operated "effectively" in the society? Have not many of the economics courses not only dealt with mere descriptions of the existing economic order but also with ways to strengthen and make that order more viable? Are we unaware of the mass of research carried on on the college campuses by scholars under contract with the government in the natural, physical, and policy sciences? Indeed, virtually all of American education (and surely this would apply to any educational system) has served as a socializing process.

The black students—perceiving blatant weaknesses in that process vis-à-vis their own lives and experiences—were calling for a substantive alternative. They no longer believed in the myth that higher education was value-free, objective, above the social turmoil. Traditional American scholarship has been geared to maintenance of the status quo. The black studies proposals were out to alter that orientation. Professors Seymour Martin Lipset and Philip G. Altbach—who cannot be accused of being generally and unequivocally sympathetic to the black student demands —made an interesting observation on the nature of the university:

> In the developing countries, there is an intrinsic conflict between the university and the society, thereby creating a fertile ground for student political awareness and participation. The university, as one of the primary modernizing elements in largely traditional societies, necessarily finds itself opposed to other elements in its society, and must often fight to protect its values and orientation. Students are often involved in these conflicts and are key protectors of the modern orientation of the university. . . . In the developed nations, on the other hand, no such conflict exists. The university is a carrier of the traditions of the society, as well as a training agency for necessary technical skills. It is a participant in a continuing modernizing development, rather than in the vanguard of such development. University students are not called upon to protect the values of their institutions against societal encroachments. In most cases, they are merely asked to gain the qualifications necessary for a useful role in a technological society.[1]

This is an interesting observation because the black students *are* asking their universities to be in the vanguard of development.

The black students and the black studies demands have a valid *political* point. If this is generally accepted, as very many thoughtful people have conceded, it would appear that the next step would be to begin to work out the kinds of *academic* changes those demands call for. Clearly, the students who have served as the catalyst for this should not be expected to come up with the final answers. Those people who style themselves scholars have the burden of proceeding to try to develop new knowledge consistent with a new orientation.

Much of the empirical work has yet to be done, because the questions

---

[1] Seymour Martin Lipset and Philip G. Altbach, "Student Politics and Higher Education in the United States," in *Student Politics*, Seymour Martin Lipset (ed.). New York: Basic Books, Inc., 1967, p. 242.

have never been asked. What is the feasibility of massive economic co-operative ventures in rural and urban black communities? What is the nature of and significance of the black culture vis-à-vis new forms and styles of political action in the black community? Is it possible to talk about a peculiar "black experience" that has relevance to the way black Americans organize themselves and conduct their lives? What is the impact of the oral tradition on social, economic, and political phenomena? Black Americans have a heritage, a black experience of abrupt cultural transformation to traumatized conditions of slavery in a distant, alien land with a different language and different life styles; to legal freedom from legal slavery in the same place and economic position; to an urban, atomized, technological environment from a rural, intimate, agrarian environment. What is the meaning of this heritage and experience in terms of new adaptive cultural characteristics, characteristics that can sustain black Americans as a viable people? What are the implications of all this for enlightened public policy? What does it mean for the kinds of effort made to bridge tradition and modernity in the black community? What is meant by the "crisis-oriented" nature of the black political experience? What is meant by "political traumatization" (as opposed to "political apathy") that makes this distinction relevant to one trying to understand and deal with the problems of black community development?

These are some of the kinds of questions that their proponents want black studies to deal with. Are these "soul courses"? Are they "separatist," "violent advocacy of revolution," "catharsis-serving" courses? Do they take one *out* of "higher education"?

I believe that, *if these courses are carefully thought out, they will be the epitome of higher education.* They will prepare the student to engage the total society, not to withdraw from it. One is not going to know much about how to proceed with black economic development or with black educational development or with black political development without knowing a great deal about the total economic, educational, and political systems. And if one listens carefully to the major thrust of the student arguments—rather than focusing on particular polemical sentences here and there—this point will come through clearly.

One must understand that the demands made in a particular environment—political, suspicious, hostile—have many functions: They serve to wrench an entrenched, closed system into a new awareness; they serve to state specifically a rejection of old values and to state generally a framework for new values. The new directions *cannot* be very specific; they are new programs for experimental times. All answers are not known. There is a tendency on the part of some people to require certainty of results and consequences before they are willing to innovate. In social dynamics, this is hardly reasonable. Of course, there is the possibility of unanticipated consequences. But if those who led the fight in the American colonies to break with England in the 1770's had waited until they knew the precise consequences, they probably would not have moved. Or, to take a less "ruptured" case, those who began to implement New Deal measures in the crises of the 1930's could not wait until they had definitive answers about results. They were faced with crises, and, hopefully bringing the best judgment to bear, they had to act.

American higher education faces a serious series of crises. The demands for black studies simply point up one area of intense concern. It is unfortunate, but understandable (if one agrees with Lipset and Altbach) that some *so-called* culturally disadvantaged black students had to take the lead in pointing out serious educational weaknesses. And precisely because *they* had to assume the role of innovator in an area traditionally felt to be in the province of "experts," it is quite possible that many people in power positions have forfeited their claim to authenticity. Many of them have been lax and unimaginative and listless for so long that many black students now view them as anachronisms.

If all the colleges and universities now rushing to set up some sort of black studies department are sincere in agreeing to the validity of their moves, then why—the black students ask—did they not recognize the need before now? Why did they have to be prodded and poked and seized? (If they are acting now simply to avoid another sit-in or disruption, then they should be exposed as spineless hypocrites!) The point is that the credibility of many of the schools in the eyes of many black students is so low—the students, indeed, in some instances, question their integrity—that the students do not trust the traditional administrators and faculty to set up and implement a viable program. And this is the crux of the control problem. *The students do not want control because they want to insure easy grades, but because they want to insure a quality program.* They ask: How can the people who have been so negligent and value-oriented in harmful ways now be *trusted* to administer this exciting, vibrant new educational innovation? These are important questions.

In a sense, it is the *pride* of established academia that is hurt. And frequently their vanity requires its representatives to call for assurances that "high standards" be maintained—in evaluation of class work, recruitment of professors, etc. It is rather strange to hear such calls issue from a group that has admitted its own failure and ineptness. How could a scholar in American intellectual history, for example, not recognize the genius of W.E.B. DuBois? What sort of standards must have prevailed that permitted such a scholar to assume a position of authority?

Let us consider proposals for black studies submitted by black students. Do the black students have the answers? Obviously not; they are still in the early stages of their formal education. But they have enough insights gleaned from their black experience (a term which some people have come to see as delightfully mystic or just quaint) to know that much of what has been taught is inconsistent with—indeed, irrelevant to—the lives they lead as black Americans. *And it is this recognition that accounts for a great part of the thrust for black studies.* Many of the proposals may sound, and in fact are, extreme and farcical. But one should not be too quick to dismiss the entire "movement."

A Harvard University faculty committee on African and Afro-American studies made the following statement:

We are dealing with 25 million of our own people with a special history, culture, and range of problems. It can hardly be doubted that the study of black men in America is a legitimate and urgent academic endeavor.[2]

Is American academia seriously prepared to embark on such an important intellectual pursuit? Or will there continue to be nit-picking and polemics and energy-wasting efforts over momentarily glamorous and dramatic issues (kicking white students out of black studies classes, separatism, etc.)? The black students have performed an invaluable educational service by raising in a political context the hard academic questions—a political context, incidentally, which many students perceived to be absolutely necessary, given the arrogance, smugness, and entrenched nature of many sources of power. The question now becomes whether higher education can be perceptive and intelligent enough to deliver the empirical goods.

American professors and deans are not unfamiliar with political struggles on their campuses. Campus politics has a long history in this country: interdepartmental rivalries; personality clashes; competition for promotion and tenure; faculty-wife gossip and clashes; at times, in some places, vindictive vetoing of each others' Ph.D. candidates; bitter ma-

[2] Report of the Faculty Committee on African and Afro-American Studies, Harvard University, January 20, 1969, p. 14.

neuvering for fewer and smaller classes (and larger office space) at choice (i.e., not 8 A.M.) hours of the day and week.

But the demands and the criticisms leveled by many black students today will make those perennial squabbles seem like tea parties—or perhaps one should say panty raids. The demands of the black students are not nearly so frivolous. The black students are raising serious politico-academic questions that cut to the core, to the very nature of the university and college systems. The black students are political modernizers vis-à-vis higher education in a way never before experienced on American campuses. And traditional American academia may well flunk the test (a metaphor not entirely unintended) if it does not do its homework (hard, empirical, relevant research and teaching).

As we have suggested, any analysis of the school-society relationship issue must at some point consider the expectations which members of society have for the school. These expectations will provide some insight into the reasons for the prevailing school-society relationship, the difficulties faced by the school within that relationship, and will indicate as well what other kinds of relationships are possible. What is possible is always difficult to identify because perhaps more than any other public institution the American school is expected to transmit and preserve our cultural heritage and at the same time prepare its clients for a future which is not known. The school is expected both to impress upon young people the value of intellectual activity as an end in itself, yet prepare them for college and/or vocations. Schools are expected to treat each student as a unique being, to instill in each a respect for self and his own "kind." Yet schools also deal with "masses" of boys and girls and are expected to instill respect for other selves and other "kinds." The school is expected to be apolitical, yet it depends upon political processes for its funding and, in some cases, its governance. All these sometime contradictory expectations, and more, limn the character of the school-society relationship.

David A. Goslin

THE FUNCTIONS OF THE
SCHOOL IN MODERN SOCIETY

David A. Goslin, a sociologist with the Russell Sage Foundation, addresses himself to those functions which most members of society expect their schools to perform and, indeed, which most schools do in fact set

From David A. Goslin, *The School in Contemporary Society* (Glenview, Ill.: Scott, Foresman and Company, 1965), pp. 1–11. With deletions and some footnotes omitted. Reprinted by permission of the author and publisher.

out to serve. The author is particularly concerned with how common expectations influence the processes and the institution of education.

Goslin identifies and analyzes three general functions of the school: (1)
transmission of culture; (2) supporting the discovery of new knowledge;
and (3) allocating individuals to positions in society. In studying Goslin's
analysis, keep in mind the different points of view described by Pounds
and Bryner, especially reflecting upon those which might logically suggest
that any or all of the above functions are inappropriate. In which ways
might these functions best be served by the public school?

. . . The purpose of this chapter is to examine the relationship of that
part of the modern society concerned with the maintenance and transmission of culture—the institution of education—to the other parts of
the society as a whole. In particular we shall be concerned with what
members of the society expect from their schools and how these expectations influence the educational process in the United States.

Each of the different institutions within the society, including the educational system, have important functions in relation to the system as a
whole and to its other parts. Thus many of the decisions made by government will have important consequences not only for the society as a
whole but also for the functioning of other parts of the system, such as
the family or the school. And, conversely, child rearing practices in the
family are likely to affect what goes on in the school and, at least in the
long run, governmental processes.

The conception of society as a system of interrelated parts is neither
novel nor particularly sophisticated, yet it is frequently overlooked in efforts to understand the workings of a particular part of the system. For
example, if one wishes to make any real headway in the analysis of the
teaching process in American elementary schools, the particular student-teacher relationship must be set in a context that includes some
consideration of the various functions performed by education as well as
the ways in which other aspects of the social system influence the
school. To consider only one of many possible consequences of this interdependence, if certain groups within the society view the elementary
school primarily as a place to send children to get them out of the
house, then this view of the school's function will almost certainly have
an effect on what goes on in the school.

The Transmission of Culture

From the standpoint of the society as a whole, and often of groups
within the society, the primary function of education is the maintenance

of culture. "Man's capacity to learn, to organize learning in symbolic forms, to communicate this learning as knowledge to other members of the species, and to act on the basis of learning or knowledge is the source of all cultural phenomena. . . . Any culture and the civilization based upon that culture must depend upon the ability of the civilization to articulate and transmit its learning as semiautonomous, cognitive systems. These represent the accumulated knowledge in every field of inquiry and comprise the subject matter in all education. This is what we mean when we speak of the school's responsibility in transmitting a cultural heritage." [1]

Culture, of course, includes more than just the "accumulated knowledge in every field of inquiry." It includes the values, beliefs, and norms which have been passed down from generation to generation, albeit with frequent modifications, throughout the history of the society. "Education transmits a common cultural fund to the next generation and in the process helps to bring hordes of young barbarians to adult ways that are continuous with the past." [2]

The transmission and accumulation of culture from generation to generation has been the distinguishing characteristic of man since the earliest beginnings of human society. The role of formal education in this process has thus been significant throughout only a fraction of man's history. As Burton Clark points out, "the earliest 'educational systems' were no more than a woman instructing a daughter or a man and a boy walking, talking, and working together. In the Stone Age, we may bet, there were no elementary classes in flint chipping; a boy learned to chip flints by watching adults." [3] As the store of man's knowledge has grown and the groups in which he lives have become more complex, the development of specialized facilities to take over where the family leaves off in this process of cultural transmission has become necessary. During most of recent history and extending as far back as the days of the Greek and Roman civilizations, formal education was restricted to a tiny minority of the society's members, usually the ruling elite or members of religious orders. The Industrial Revolution, however, in addition to producing a flood of innovations that caused the reservoir of man's knowledge and technical skills to burst its heretofore relatively narrow confines, radi-

---

[1] Vincent Ostrom, "Education and Politics," in *Social Forces Influencing American Education,* ed. Nelson B. Henry (Chicago: The National Society for the Study of Education, 1961), pp. 10–12. Distributed by the University of Chicago Press.

[2] Burton R. Clark, *Educating the Expert Society* (San Francisco: Chandler Publishing Company, 1962), p. 11.

[3] *Ibid.,* p. 12.

cally altered the social structure of the society. No longer was the family the primary unit of production, as was the case in a predominantly agrarian economy. Instead a large number of men (not to mention women and children) found themselves leaving the home every day to work in manufacturing plants or offices. This shift in the basic social structure of the society (which tended to split up the family unit), together with a growing variety of available occupational positions (each requiring somewhat different skills and knowledge), made it impossible for new members of the society to continue to learn by observation of their parents alone. Not only did the young have more choices as to what skills they might acquire, than their parents, but no longer did the breadwinner of the family work where his children could watch him and learn from him.

"In brief, formal schooling became a necessity as the home and the community became ineffectual, even incompetent, in training the young for adulthood through informal contact. A new class of cultural agents —the teachers of the commoners—grew up. The changing nature of knowledge and work brought the children of the common man into the schoolhouse and gave to the schools a greatly broadened and deepened role in cultural transmission and continuity." [4]

To the extent that current trends in our society continue to accentuate this separation of occupational and family roles, we may predict that the function of the school as a primary agent of cultural transmission will be enhanced. We may not conclude, however, that the family is no longer important as a socializing agent, or that the school has taken over all of what used to be the family's functions in regard to the socialization of the young and the transmission of culture. Although there appears to be a trend toward admission of children to schools in this country at earlier ages, the family still serves as virtually the sole agent of socialization during the critical first four or five years of the child's life. It is during this period that the child learns to talk and forms the initial significant social relationships that will greatly influence his adaptation and accommodation in subsequent interpersonal situations. The child also begins to internalize the social values and normative prescriptions and proscriptions that will make it possible for him to function as a member of an orderly society during the remainder of his life.

Nor does the family lose its interest in the child when he reaches school age. In most cases parents, brothers and sisters, and members of

[4] *Ibid.*, p. 15.

the extended family (aunts, uncles, cousins, et cetera) will continue to exert strong socializing influences throughout the period of the child's formal education and, to a lesser extent, thereafter. As we shall see in subsequent discussions, it is likely that many of the special problems with which the school must contend stem from this division of responsibility for socialization of the young. Not only must the school begin with children who have already acquired a set of values (some of which may conflict with values that the school is committed to inculcating), but it must continue to deal with parallel and sometimes competing influences from the family (not to mention the child's peer group) during the time that the child is in its care.

These problems are further complicated by the fact that in this country the school traditionally has been viewed in a service relationship to the family, rather than as a legitimate independent socializing influence. This relationship between the family and the school is perhaps understandable in light of the fact that it is the family that is usually held responsible for faulty socialization and not the school. But this does not make the school's task any easier. Our society has come to expect the school to transmit to the child an enormously complex culture which includes not only a great deal of accumulated knowledge and many complex skills, both intellectual and physical, but an even more sophisticated and complicated set of values and norms which comprise the ideological basis of our cultural heritage.

It is a frequently acknowledged fact that the stability and continuity of our society as presently constituted depends not only on the ability of its citizens to read, write, and complete their income tax forms, but on their belief in and adherence to the political, religious, and social principles on which the institutions of the society are based. Thus the school is expected to teach the child something about such diverse ideals as democracy, the rule of law, free enterprise, and even the desirability of monogamous marriage. And it is also expected to persuade future citizens of the society of the necessity of behaving in accordance with these principles and practices.

Socialization, even within the context of a formal educational system such as the school, involves much more than the learning of skills and the acquisition of information about how the society works or how it should work. Learning that results from more or less formal pedagogical procedures constitutes only a part of the preparation of the child for behaving in accordance with the roles of a participating adult member of the society. Perhaps the most important part of the socialization process involves the unconscious assimilation and internalization of beliefs, values, and patterns of behavior of significant others with whom the individual comes in contact. The preschool child soon begins to emulate aspects of the behavior of his parents, his brothers and sisters, and certain of his peers. As new figures are added to the circle of significant others surrounding the child—his teacher, his classmates, perhaps certain television personalities—the resulting influences on his behavior become increasingly diverse and complex. The possibility of conflict in the emulated behaviors is also increased, and the child must face the task of ranking the people with whom he deals, consciously or unconsciously, in terms of the influence he will permit them to have on his behavior.

Since most children spend a considerable part of their waking hours in school or in school-related activities, it is not surprising that those whom the child encounters in school can have an important influence on his behavior, including the formation of his value system, his attitudes about various social norms, and his behavior in general. It is only through widening his circle of significant others that the individual has an opportunity to prepare himself adequately for the diverse roles which the adult in our society must assume. To function adequately as an adult, the child must learn not only the roles of father or mother but also those of student, teacher, group leader, and, eventually, wife or husband. Boys must learn something about the role of family provider, be he businessman or factory worker; while girls frequently must be able to assume the role of secretary or career woman along with their roles as wife and mother. Although it is obvious that children do not for the most part learn a great deal about some of these roles until they have reached the status of an adult, many of the decisions that a child must make (and in which, although he may receive assistance from his family, his teacher or guidance counselor, or other adults, he is often left on his own) require him to know something about what is expected of individuals occupying various positions in the adult society. In addition, a child begins to acquire more generalized capacities for assuming adult roles at an early age. The school plays a major role, for example, in helping children learn to control their emotions, to deal with as well as assume positions of authority, and to recognize the existence of status hierarchies in social groups.

It is also clear that even if it were deemed desirable to keep children from learning about adult roles, such a course would be impossible without isolating young people from all contact with the adult world. With the rapid development of the mass media, especially television, children are exposed to this world earlier, with greater frequency, and in greater detail than ever before. The influence of the mass media is clearly a fact of modern life that must be considered in any discussion of the processes of socialization and cultural transmission.

A frequently overlooked aspect of the socialization process that has great relevance to any discussion of the functions of the school in modern society concerns the nature of the intellectual process itself. Among other things, socialization involves learning how to solve problems of all sorts. The acquisition of problem-solving techniques is an integral part of the educational process, although this is not always made explicit, perhaps in part because of the current state of our understanding of intellectual processes. It is not completely clear, for example, which of the various ways of going about solving different kinds of problems is of greatest overall usefulness and whether certain techniques are more useful in some situations than in others. Many scholars have advocated an essentially inductive approach to certain kinds of problems, whereas others have maintained that a deductive approach is of greatest usefulness. Learning theorists have not yet fully explored the relative roles of reward and punishment in the learning process, and although during recent years most educators have clung steadfastly to the assumption that optimum learning takes place under conditions of reward, it is not entirely clear that this is the case in all learning situations. Even assuming that some kind of positive reinforcement is most felicitous to learning, it might turn out that rewards intrinsic to the learning situation itself—for example, enjoyment in the activities involved—are all that are needed in certain kinds of learning. The intrusion into the situation of potentially conflicting external rewards from a teacher or parent may serve only to impede the process.

Although new insights into learning and thinking processes are forthcoming all the time, relatively little attention has been given to the problem of how these discoveries relate to what is going on in the school and, more importantly, to what should go on in the school. If one of the most important functions of the school is to teach children how to learn and to solve problems, then it would appear to be reasonable to inquire about what young people are being taught along these lines and whether the techniques they are learning will be of greatest usefulness to them as they assume responsibilities as adult members of the society. Obviously it is important for those individuals who are in positions where they must make decisions affecting the society to be able to adapt effectively to the continually changing demands upon them and to learn how to handle their responsibilities in the most efficacious way. The responsibility of the school in preparing society's members for such positions involves more than the inculcation of technical knowledge along with a smattering of tradition. Of even greater importance is the school's responsibility for teaching the child how to use whatever skills and knowledge he may possess. The educator's responsibility does not permit him to ignore the question of how children are being taught to solve problems and absorb new knowledge. The technique for approaching new information that is acquired by the child in the course of his experiences in school may turn out to be the most important part of the educational process.

Supporting the Discovery of New Knowledge

Although the primary function of the school may be the transmission of existing knowledge and tradition, educational institutions have paradoxically also been expected to play an important role in the encouragement and implementation of change. The university has always been a focal point of the search for new knowledge, and a great part of the flood of new ideas and innovations that have produced such rapid change in our society has originated in institutions of higher learning. During the past half century, as the rate of discovery has accelerated, the emphasis on research as a major function of colleges and universities has become of even greater significance. The result has been that the highest academic standing and prestige are increasingly being awarded to those members of the faculty who contribute the most to knowledge and the discovery of new ways of dealing with the physical, psychological, and social world. Much to the distress of many educators and despite frequent claims to the contrary, the teacher in higher education is not accorded prestige and financial rewards commensurate with those received by the researcher. That this trend is having and will continue to have an effect on the quality of the educational process, at all levels, is hard to deny (perhaps, for example, it will improve secondary school teaching by driving dedicated teachers out of the college ranks).

The role of educational institutions in fostering change and innovation is particularly notable at the college and university level, but elementary and secondary schools are expected to play their part in this process as well. Both through the encouragement of creative activities on the part of students and through the inculcation of social values having to do with the desirability of progress based on achievements in the sciences and in other fields of knowledge, the school plays a major role in influencing the rate of change in the society.

Not only does it have a responsibility to prepare children for dealing with the rapidly changing society they will encounter as adults, but if the society is to continue to progress at its current pace, the educational system must continue to produce individuals who will take over the task of developing new knowledge and techniques. As the cultural heritage on which our technology is based expands, the amount of preparation necessary before an individual can make a contribution to our basic store of knowledge grows along with it. The increasing technological complexity of the society has therefore had a profound effect on elementary and secondary education. Even in the primary grades, for example, efforts are being made to revise traditional curriculum content, particularly in mathematics and the sciences, at least in part in order to meet the demands of a society that has accepted change as an ideal to be strived for with all of the resources at its disposal.

Allocating Individuals to Positions in Society

Every society must make some provision for deciding which of its members shall occupy the various positions in the society and perform the roles necessary for its continuation and development. Although the number and variety of positions to be filled varies from society to society, it has thus far been true in every society that the available positions have carried with them unequal responsibilities for and demands upon their occupants. Some jobs are more difficult than others, some are more dangerous, and some are more distasteful; some require special training or skills. For this reason and because it is fairly clear that the skills required for some positions are rarer than for others (e.g., the doctor, the judge), the world has not yet seen a society in which the occupants of all positions were accorded equal rewards or status. As a result there is competition among the members of the society (at least within those groups in which competition is permitted) for those positions receiving the greatest rewards and carrying with them the greatest responsibility and prestige. In his utopian *Walden Two*, B. F. Skinner solved this problem by mandating that the occupants of the most distasteful or boring positions would work significantly *fewer* hours but would receive equal rewards from the community—thus making garbage collection a particularly attractive occupation, especially for the artist or musician who values free time more than having an interesting job.[5] Thus far, however, although we have perhaps been moving in these directions, the desirability as well as the possibility of attaining such an ideal is open to question.

Traditionally, most societies have made use of a variety of ascribed or inherited characteristics in allocating individuals to positions or at least in deciding which groups of individuals will have an opportunity to compete for certain classes of positions. Family background, race, religion, order of birth, and sex are examples of ascribed characteristics which have been and frequently still are used as major determiners of the positions an individual may hold in society. However, the rapidly expanding technology of modern society has created a situation in which it has become increasingly important that individuals occupy positions for which they are well suited. As Ralph Linton pointed out in his analysis of status and role in human societies, the better adjusted the members of any society are to their statuses and roles, the more smoothly the society is likely to function. As the requirements for fulfilling various positions become more complex and require not only longer training but greater ability, ascribed characteristics of individuals turn out to be less useful as criteria for allocating positions efficiently than measures of the individual's achievement and ability.

As the school has taken over from the family a greater share of the responsibility for socializing the young, it has also become the focus of many of the child's activities. The performance of the child in school serves therefore as one of the most important early measures of his abilities and energy. With the rise of mass education the school functions as an integral part of the process of status allocation in four ways: (1) by providing a context in which the individual can demonstrate his abilities, (2) by channeling individuals into paths that lead in the direction of different occupations or classes of occupations, (3) by providing the particular skills needed to fulfill the requirements of various positions, and finally (4) by transferring to the individual the differential prestige of the school itself.

In theory, development of public educational facilities in the United States has made it possible for any child to acquire the skills necessary to fulfill virtually any position in the society within the limitations of the individual's own abilities. Although the theory does not always work in practice (we shall examine some of the reasons for this in a subsequent

[5] B. F. Skinner, *Walden Two* (New York: Macmillan Company, 1962).

chapter), it is nevertheless true that the school offers most children a unique opportunity to show what they can do. Although we have not as yet reached the point where access to all the different positions in the society is determined by an individual's abilities or even his educational background—ascribed characteristics still play an important part in influencing selection for many positions—the evidence is overwhelming that educational achievement makes a great deal of difference in the kinds of opportunities open to a given individual, regardless of what other attributes he may have.

From the beginning the school operates as the arbiter of the individual's achievement. As the child progresses through the educational system, the decisions that must be made about the kinds of training he may select and the opportunities for advancement open to him are, for the most part, left to the school. The child and his parents may influence these decisions, but in the majority of cases the school plays the major role. It is in this process that the school probably exerts its greatest influence on the allocation of status. The decision as to whether the student will be allowed to take the courses required for college admission, for example, looms as one of the critical choice points in determining the individual's subsequent occupational status.

The skills and knowledge the individual acquires during the course of his education are, of course, important factors in the process of job allocation. But schools are not all equal in the quality of the education they provide or even in the kinds of specific training they offer. Consequently, the individual's long-range occupational opportunities may be determined by the kinds and quality of the educational experiences open to him. We have not yet reached the point where all members of the society have equal access, limited only by their abilities, to the various kinds of training possible. Regional and local differences in resources available for educational facilities, and discrimination in the allocation of what resources there are, severely restrict the opportunities of many members of the society. The situation has been improved in recent years, and the prospect of increased Federal government involvement in education has brightened the picture considerably, both with respect to increasing the total supply of resources available and to ensuring their equitable distribution. As our society becomes technologically more complex, continued progress in providing access to educational facilities will be an important factor in the maintenance of our present rate of growth.

Finally, because some schools are better than others, the reputation and prestige of the school is likely to become a factor in subsequent evaluations of the individual, regardless of his actual training or capabilities. Thus the young man who graduates from an Ivy League college may find that there are more job opportunities available to him than to the graduate of a less prestigious college, even though the latter student might be equally qualified. Similarly, the private preparatory school graduate has less trouble getting into many colleges than his public school counterpart (excluding students who attend a few highly prestigious public schools), not only because he may have received better training but in part because of the reputation and prestige of his school. Although there is little data available on this point, the prestige of one's secondary school or college probably makes less difference at present due to the growing demand for well-trained personnel and to the increasing use of objective measures of ability and achievement (e.g., standardized tests) in both college admissions and job allocation. Indeed, one series of studies has indicated [6] that where social class background is taken into account in evaluating the influence of the reputation of one's school or college on subsequent opportunities, the hypothesized relationship disappears. . . .

George D. Spindler

EDUCATION IN A TRANSFORMING AMERICAN CULTURE

In the second selection of this analytical section George D. Spindler, an educational anthropologist, seeks to explain the origins of conflicts over education. He describes and analyzes a continuum of values ranging from those he calls "traditional" to those "emerging." Spindler sees much of the conflict over education as a result of different value orientations. He does not predict any easy transition period nor does he advocate one end of the value continuum in preference to the other. He does argue, however, that the value changes which he analyzes are conditions of our social existence to which education and educators, whatever their philosophical persuasion, must adjust. Again, therefore, Spindler's article returns us to the introductory one by Pounds and Bryner: Which of the positions described by Pounds and Bryner is most appropriate for anticipating and dealing

From *Harvard Educational Review* (Summer, 1955), pp. 145–156. Copyright © 1955 by President and Fellows of Harvard College. Reprinted by permission of the publisher.

[6] Alexander W. Astin, " 'Productivity' of Undergraduate Institutions," *Science*, CXXXVI (April 13, 1962).

with the problems suggested in Spindler's analysis? What role, if any, should the schools play regarding value changes? Should they critically examine value conflicts? Are recent analyses of value changes merely analyses of superficial or surface phenomena? Should the schools attempt to arbitrate differences which appear to follow from "traditional" and "emergent" value attachments?

A difficulty encountered in using an analysis such as Spindler's is that social mores and values change. Such aspects of human existence are not static. Since Spindler's article was published in 1955, we should not, therefore, accept at face value the mores and values described in it. This is not to deny the quality or worth of Spindler's analytical scheme, however. On the contrary, it is a valuable tool for examining the nature of conflicts over education and the school-society relationship. As you study this article, however, ask yourself if the values identified in it are accurate reflections of today's value conflicts. If not, which values would be? Do they impinge upon the school in ways which Spindler suggests they might? Are they the basis of current conflicts over education?

George D. Spindler is Professor of Education and Anthropology at Stanford University. His many books and articles have served to make educators and anthropologists aware of the contributions that anthropology can make to the study of education.

The American public school system, and the professional educators who operate it, have been subjected to increasingly strident attacks from both the lay (non-educationist) public, and from within the ranks. My premise is that these attacks can best be understood as symptoms of an American culture that is undergoing transformation—a transformation that produces serious conflict. I shall discuss this transformation as a problem in culture change that directly affects all of education, and everyone identified with it.

The notion of social and cultural change is used persuasively, if carelessly, by too many writers to explain too much. Generalized allusions to technological change, cultural lag, the atomic age, and mass society, are more suggestive than clarifying. We must strike to the core of the change. And my argument is that this core can best be conceived as a radical shift in values.

The anthropologist, and I speak as one but not for all, sees culture as a goal-oriented system. These goals are expressed, patterned, lived out by people in their behaviors and aspirations in the form of values— objects or possessions, conditions of existence, personality or characterological features, and states of mind, that are conceived as desirable, and act as motivating determinants of behaviors. It is the shifts in what

I believe are the core values in American culture, and the effect of these shifts on education today, that I wish to discuss. I will present these shifts in values as the conditions of life to which education and educators, whether progressives, experimentalists, conservatives, or in-betweens, must adapt—and to which they are adapting, albeit confusedly. My emphasis within the value frame-work will be upon shifts in the conception of the desirable character type, since education can never be freed from the obligation to support, if not produce, the kind of personality, or social character deemed desirable in society.

But first I must specify what sources are to be used as the factual baseline for generalization, even though there is no avoiding the necessity of going beyond these facts in the discussion to follow. There is a body of literature on American culture, as a culture, and the changes within it. I have drawn most heavily from the anthropologists, like Margaret Mead, Clyde and Florence Kluckhohn, Gregory Bateson, Lloyd Warner, and Geoffrey Gorer, and a few sociologists, like David Reisman. Their writings range from the highly intuitive to the relatively observation-based. Though there is consensus, and a surprising degree of it, on the part of these students of American culture, little they say can be or is intended by them to be taken as proven.

These writings are useful, but most emphasize static patterning in values more than change in values. To extend my factual baseline I have been collecting relevant data from college students for the past four years. The sample consists of several hundred students, ranging in age from 19 to 57 years, mainly graduates in professional education courses, and representing socio-economic strata describable as lower-middle to upper-middle class. The sample is as representative of this professional group and these economic strata as any regionally biased sample can be. I have used two simple value-projective techniques. The aim has been to find out what features of social character (the term I will use to designate those personality elements that are most relevant to social action) the students in the sample hold as being valuable and that presumably determine much of their behavior in classrooms. . . .

These are the characteristics of the ideal American boy seen as most important by the students in the sample. Leadership, independence, high intelligence, high academic ability, individuality, are mentioned relatively infrequently (in about 20% of the descriptive paragraphs). But individuals do vary in the pattern of characteristics that are combined in the paragraph. Some emphasized the high achievement and individualized characteristics just mentioned. Some include elements from the modal list and combine them with these latter items. But the majority emphasize the sociable, well-rounded, average characteristics ranked above.

The implications seem clear. The keynote to the character type regarded as most desirable, and therefore constituting a complex of values, is *balance, outward-orientedness, sociability,* and *conformity* for the sake of harmony. Individuality and creativity, or even mere originality, are not stressed in this conception of values. Introspective behavior is devaluated (even intellectuals are suspicioned by many). Deviancy, it seems, is to be tolerated only within the narrow limits of sociability, of general outwardness, of conformity for harmony ("Artists are perverts"). The All-American Boy is altogether average. . . .

From this point on, I shall use the implications of this data, along with the content of anthropological and sociological writings on American culture, without further reference to the factual baseline itself. The purpose is to sketch in bold strokes the major dimensions of culture changes in our American society and relate them in explanatory style to the contretemps of modern public education and educators.

In doing this, I cannot indicate all of the logical and analytic steps between data and generalization, since this is not a research report. The statements I will make now about American values, their shift, and the effect on education, are based upon the varying responses of different age groups in the sample, upon person-to-person variation in responses, and upon variations in response and particularly contradictions of response within single individual protocols (the total set of responses for a single individual).

On the basis of these kinds of data, and in the light of the perceptive works of the fore-mentioned writers on American Culture, I believe it is clear that a major shift in American values has, and is taking place. I find it convenient to label this shift as being from *traditional* to *emergent*. The values thus dichotomized are listed under their respective headings with explanatory statements in parentheses.

I believe American Culture is undergoing a transformation, and a rapid one producing many disjunctions and conflicts, from the traditional to the emergent value systems outlined above. It is probable that both value systems have been present and operating in American Culture for some time, perhaps since the birth of the nation. But recently, and under the impetus of World Wars, atomic insecurities, and a past history of "boom and bust," the heretofore latent tendencies in the emer-

TRADITIONAL VALUES	EMERGENT VALUES
Puritan morality (Respectability, thrift, self-denial, sexual constraint; a puritan is someone who can have anything he wants, as long as he doesn't enjoy it!)	*Sociability* (As described above. One should like people and get along well with them. Suspicion of solitary activities is characteristic.)
Work-Success ethic (Successful people worked hard to become so. Anyone can get to the top if he tries hard enough. So people who are not successful are lazy, or stupid, or both. People must work desperately and continuously to convince themselves of their worth.)	*Relativistic moral attitude* (Absolutes in right and wrong are questionable. Morality is what the group thinks is right. Shame, rather than guilt-oriented personality, is appropriate.)
Individualism (The individual is sacred, and always more important than the group. In one extreme form, the value sanctions egocentricity, expediency, and disregard for other people's rights. In its healthier form the value sanctions independence and originality.)	*Consideration for others.* (Everything one does should be done with regard for others and their feelings. The individual has a built-in radar that alerts him to other's feelings. Tolerance for the other person's point of view and behaviors is regarded as desirable, so long as the harmony of the group is not disrupted.)
Achievement orientation (Success is a constant goal. There is no resting on past glories. If one makes $9,000 this year he must make $10,000 next year. Coupled with the work-success ethic, this value keeps people moving, and tense.)	
Future-time orientation (The future, not the past, or even the present, is more important. There is a "pot of gold at the end of the rainbow." Time is valuable, and cannot be wasted. Present needs must be denied for satisfactions to be gained in the future.)	*Hedonistic, present-time orientation* (No one can tell what the future will hold, therefore one should enjoy the present—but within the limits of the well-rounded, balanced personality and group.)
	Conformity to the group (Implied in the other emergent values. Everything is relative to the group. Leadership consists of group-machinery lubrication.)

gent direction have gathered strength and appear to be on the way towards becoming the dominant value system of American Culture.

Like all major shifts in culture, this one has consequences for people. Culturally transitional populations, as anthropologists know from their studies of acculturating Indian tribes, Hindu villages, and Samoan communities (among others), are characterized by conflict, and in most severe form—demoralization and disorganization. Institutions and people are in a state of flux. Contradictory views of life are held by different groups and persons within the society. Hostilities are displaced, attacks are made on one group by another. And this applies as well to the condition of American culture—the context of American education.

The traditionalist views the emergentist as "socialistic," "communistic," "spineless and weak-headed," or downright "immoral." The emergentist regards the traditionalist as "hidebound," "reactionary," "selfish," or "neurotically compulsive." Most of what representatives of either viewpoint do may be regarded as insidious and destructive from the point of view of the other. The conflict goes beyond groups or institutions, because individuals in our transitional society are likely to hold elements of both value systems concomitantly. This is characteristic, as a matter of fact, of most students included in the sample described previously. There are few "pure" types. The social character of most is split, calling for different responses in different situations, and with respect to different symbols. So an ingredient of personal confusion is added that intensifies social and institutional conflict.

I hypothesize that the attacks upon education, which were our starting point, and the confusion and failure of nerve characterizing educators today, can be seen in clear and helpful perspective in the light of the conflict of traditional and emergent values that has been described. It is the heart of the matter. The task then becomes one of placing groups, institutions and persons on a continuum of transformation from the one value system to the other. Without prior explanation, I should like to provide a simple diagram that will aid at least the visual-minded to comprehension of what is meant. With this accomplished I will provide the rationale for such placement and discuss the implications of it in greater detail.

The diagram is meant to convey the information that different groups operating in the context of relations between school and community, educator and public, occupy different positions on the value continuum, with varying degrees and mixtures of traditional and emergent orientations. It should be understood that the placements indicate hypothecated tendencies, that no one group representing any particular institution ever consists of "pure" value types, but that there is probably a modal tendency for the groups indicated to place on the transformation, or continuum line, in the way expressed in the diagram.

The rationale for the placement of the various groups on the value continuum is fairly complex, but let me try to explain some salient points. School boards are placed nearest the *traditional* end of the continuum because such boards are usually composed of persons representing the power, *status-quo*, elements of the community, and of persons in the higher age ranges. They are therefore people who have a stake in keeping things as they are, who gained their successes within the framework of the traditional value system and consequently believe it to be good, and who, by virtue of their age, grew up and acquired their value sets during a period of time when American culture was presumably more tradition-oriented than it is today.

TRADITIONAL VALUES				EMERGENT VALUES
	General public and Parents		School administrators	
School boards		Students		Students
			Older teachers	
				Younger teachers

The general public and parent group, of course, contains many elements of varying value predilection. It is therefore unrealistic to place this public at any particular point in the value continuum. But I hypothesize that the public *tends* to be more conservative in its social philosophy than the professional education set. The placement to the left of center of the continuum ("left" being "right" in the usual sense) takes on further validity if it is seen as a placement of that part of the public that is most vocal in its criticism of educators and education—since most of the criticisms made appear to spring out of value conflicts between traditionalist and emergentist positions. Parents complain that their children are not being taught the "three R's" (even when they are), that educators want to "socialize" the competitive system by eliminating report cards, that children are not taught the meaning of hard work. These all sound, irrespective of the question of their justification or lack of it, like traditionalist responses to change in an "emergent" direction.

Students are placed at two points on the transformation line because it is clear that those coming from traditionalist family environments will tend to hold traditionalistic values, but hold them less securely than will their parents (if our hypothesis for over-all change is valid), while other students who come from emergent-oriented families will tend to place even further, as a function of their age and peer groups, towards the emergent end of the line than their parents would. This is only partially true, indeed, for such a rationale does not account for the fact that offspring in revolt (and many American children from 6 to 16 are in a state of revolt against parental dictums) may go to extremes in either direction.

School administrators, older, and younger teachers, place at varying points on the emergent half of the transformation line. I have placed them there because I believe that the professional education culture acquired in the schools and colleges of education has a clear bias toward an emergent-oriented ethos. Many of my educationist colleagues will reject this interpretation, and indeed, such interpretations are always guilty of over-generalization. Others of my colleagues will welcome such a characterization, but still question its validity. My case must rest on the basis of contemporary educational philosophy, theory, and practice. The emphasis is on the "social adjustment" of the individual, upon his role as a member of the group and community. Most of the values listed under the *emergent* heading are explicitly stated in educational literature as goals. Some of them, such as conformity to the group, are implicit. This value, in particular, grows out of the others, is more or less unintended, and constitutes a *covert* or *latent* value, by definition. This is, admittedly, a little like accusing a man of hating his mother, but not knowing it, and such accusations are usually rejected, or rationalized out of existence. But I believe that it is literally impossible to hold the other values in this system and avoid placing a strong emphasis on group harmony, and group control of the individual. My data, at least, gathered largely from graduate students in professional education courses, indicate that this is the case.

But educators and schools do not all come off the same shelf in the supermarket. Older teachers will tend, I hypothesize, to hold relatively traditionalist views by virtue of their age, and time of their childhood training (when they acquired their basic values)—a period in American culture when the traditionalist values were relatively more certain and supported than they are at present. Younger teachers were not only children and acquired their personal culture during a relatively more emergent-oriented period of American history, but they have been (I hypothesize) exposed to a professional education culture that has become rapidly more emergent-oriented in its value position. They are therefore placed near the extreme of the transformation line of the emergent direction.

School administrators come from a different shelf in the same section of the supermarket. They, to be sure, range in age from young to old, come from different family backgrounds, and have been exposed in varying degrees to the professional education culture. But sociological and anthropological studies of the influence of status and role on behavior and perception indicate that these factors tend to over-ride others, and produce certain uniformities of outlook. The school administrator's role is a precarious one—as any school principal or superintendent knows. He faces toward several different audiences, each with different sets of demands—school boards, parents, power groups, teachers, and students—as well as other administrators. He has to play his role appropriately in the light of all these demands. The fact that many cannot, accounts for the increasingly short tenure of personages like school superintendents. But to the extent that he plays *across the board* he will place somewhere toward the center of the line of transformation. Furthermore, his dependence upon the school board, and the power groups in the community, in many cases will tend to make his outlook relatively more conservative, and probably more traditionalistic, than that of his teachers—at least the younger ones. There are many exceptions, of course. I am only claiming *tendencies.*

My thesis, I hope, is clear by now. I am attempting to explain, or help explain, the increasingly bitter and strident attacks on schools and educators, and the conflict and confusion within the ranks. I have claimed that this situation can better be understood as a series of complex but very real conflicts in core values. And I have tried to show the direction of the values shift in American culture and place the various actors in the drama upon a transformation line within this shift.

In this perspective, many conflicts between parents and teachers, school boards and educators, parents and children, and between the various personages and groups within the school system (teachers against teachers, administrators against teachers, and so on) can be understood as conflicts that grow out of sharp differences in values that mirror social and cultural transformation of tremendous scope—and for which none of the actors in the situation can be held personally accountable. This is the real, and perhaps only, contribution of this analysis. If these conflicts can be seen as emerging out of great sociocultural shifts—out of a veritable transformation of a way of life—they will lose some of their sting. To understand, the psychiatrist says, is to forgive.

But now, though it seems indeed improper at this point, permit me to add another complication to an already complicated picture. I have tried to make it clear that not only are there variations in values held by groups and different parts of the social body and school institutions, but that there are also various values, some of them contradictory, held by single individuals as diverse streams of influence in their own systems. This is always true in rapid culture-change situations, as the anthropologist and philosopher knows.

This means that the situation is not only confused by groups battling each other, but that individuals are fighting themselves. This has certain predictable results, if the anthropological studies of personal adaptation to culture change have any validity. And I believe that those results can be detected in the behaviors of most, if not all, of the actors in the scene. Let me try to clarify this.

I will deal only with teachers, as one of the most important sets of actors on this particular stage. I hypothesize that the child training of most of the people who become teachers has been more tradition than emergent-value-oriented. They are drawn largely from middle to lower-middle social class groups in American society, and this segment of the class structure is the stronghold of the work-success ethic and moral respectability values in our culture (even in a culture that is shifting away from these values). Furthermore, it seems probable that a selective process is operating to draw a relatively puritanistic element into the public school teaching as an occupation. Self-denial, altruism, a moralistic self-concept, seem to be functional prerequisites for the historically-derived role of school teacher in American society (I might have said "schoolmarm").

If this can be granted, then only one other ingredient needs to be added to explain several persistent types of personal adaptation to value conflicts observable among school teachers. That ingredient is one already spelled out—the relatively heavy emphasis, within the professional education culture, on this emergent-oriented value system. Teachers-to-be acquire their personal culture in a more tradition-oriented familiar environment, but they encounter a new kind of culture when in training to become school teachers—in the teacher-training institutions. There is, in this experience, what the anthropologist would call a discontinuity in the *enculturation* of the individual. This is a particular kind of culture-conflict situation that anthropologists have recently begun to study, but mostly in non-western societies undergoing rapid change towards a western way of life.

On the basis of observation of a fair sample of teachers in coastal communities and in the Middle West, I hypothesize that three types of adaptation to this personal culture-conflict situation and experience are characteristic.

Ambivalent: This type is characterized by contradictory and vacillating behavior, particularly with respect to the exercise of discipline and authority. The type tends to be *laissez-faire* in some classroom situations, and authoritarian in others, depending upon which behavior is called into being as a defense against threat of loss of control.

Compensatory: This type is characterized by one of two modes of behavior. The teacher overcompensates consistently either in the direction of the emergent or the tradition-centered values. In the first mode he (or she) tends to become a member of a *group-thinkism* cult—a perversion of progressive educational philosophy in action. The total stress is placed on social adjustment. Individuality is not sanctioned to any significant degree. Conformity to the group becomes the key to success. The type, in its extreme form, is a caricature of the better features of the emergent-centered value set. The second type compensates for internal culture-conflict in the opposite direction, and becomes an outright authoritarian. Tight dominance is maintained over children. All relationships with them are formalized and rigid. No deviation is allowed, so curiously enough, there is a convergence in the end-results of both types. This type is a caricature of the better features of the tradition-centered values set.

Adapted: This type can be either traditional or emergent value-oriented. But the compensatory and ambivalent mechanisms operating in the first two types are much less intense, or absent. The teacher of this type has come to terms with the value conflict situation and experience, and has chosen (consciously or unconsciously) to act within the framework of one or the other value set. There is consequently a consistency of behavior, and the mode of classroom management and teacher-student relationship is not a caricature of either value system.

No one is in a position to say which of these types is represented in greatest numbers among American public school teachers today, and there are few "pure" types. Certainly there are many traditional and emergent-oriented teachers who have adapted successfully to the personal culture-conflict situation and discontinuity of enculturative experience described. But equally certainly there are many school teachers who fall more clearly into one or the other typologies. It would be asking too much to suppose that a cultural values-conflict situation as intense as the one transforming American culture could be handled without strain by the key agent of the culture-transmission process—the school teacher. But again, to understand is to forgive.

In any event, it seems clear that if conditions are even partially of the nature described, the group culture-conflict situation resulting in attacks by representatives of those groups upon each other is intensified and at the same time confused by the personal culture-conflict problem. Both processes must be seen, and understood, as resultants of a larger culture-transformation process.

In conclusion to this by-far unfinished analysis (the next 20 years may tell the more complete story), let me make it clear that I am not castigating either the emergentists, or the traditionalists. Value systems must always be functional in terms of the demands of the social and economic structure of a people. The traditional mode has much that is good about it. There is a staunchness, and a virility in it that many of us may view with considerable nostalgia in some future time. But rugged individualism (in its expedient, ego-centered form), and rigid moralism (with its capacity for displaced hate) become non-functional in a society where people are rubbing shoulders in polyglot masses, and playing with a technology that may destroy, or save, with a pushing of buttons. The emergentist position seems to be growing in strength. Social adaptability, relativistic outlooks, sensitivity to the needs and opinions of others, and of the group, seem functional in this new age. But perhaps we need, as people, educators, anthropologists, and parents, to examine our premises more closely. The emergentist can become a group conformist—an average man proud of his well-rounded averageness—without really meaning to at all.

And lastly I would like to reiterate the basic theme of this article. Conflicts between groups centering on issues of educational relevance, and confusions within the rank and file of educators can be understood best, I believe, in the perspective of the transformation of American culture that proceeds without regard for personal fortune or institutional survival. This transformation, it is true, can be guided and shaped to a considerable degree by the human actors on the scene. But they cannot guide and shape their destiny within this transformation if their energies are expended in knifing attacks on each other in such a central arena as education, or if their energies are dissipated in personal confusions. I am arguing, therefore, for the functional utility of understanding, and of insight into the all-encompassing transformation of American culture and its educational-social resultants.

Americans have never been shy about criticizing their schools. In the past two decades, however, criticism has reached such stinging proportions that cries of "burn down the schools" are not uncommon. And no one group has a monopoly on criticism. Persons from all walks of life and political persuasions seem to have no problems in finding something wrong with the schools. Even some professional educators when addressing parent groups as to how parents can best serve the educational needs of their children are given to such prescriptions as "boycott the schools," "take your children out of the public schools and establish your own neighborhood schools!"

People who administer and staff public schools often respond to the wide-ranging criticism with claims that they have been unfairly blamed for ills for which their responsibility is minimal at best. After all, it does seem a bit absurd to attribute perceived moral decay to a failure of the schools, or to blame them for juvenile delinquency, widespread drug abuse, or even the low quality of television programming. However absurd or brutish the charges associated with it, this far-flung criticism constitutes an unintended and indirect tribute to the schools. It attests to the centrality and significance of education in contemporary society. Moreover, the criticism has moved a host of observers to reflect upon and speculate about where education is going and where it should go.

As you study the readings in this projective section—readings which suggest both where the school *is* headed and where it *should* be going—review the Spindler essay and consider if the articles which follow take into account (explicitly or implicitly) the kinds of questions he raises.

William H. Boyer

EDUCATION FOR SURVIVAL

Cries for relevance in education are not necessarily new, but given the temper of our times they are certainly more strident than ever before and are perhaps receiving more attention. Demands for relevance, of course, strike at the heart of the school-society relationship issue. What does "relevance" mean? What are the social and natural pressures which lead to demands for it? Do such demands follow from what are merely superficial social changes and, hence, should they be ignored by the schools? Can

From *Phi Delta Kappan*, (January, 1971), pp. 258–261. Reprinted by permission of the author and publisher.

we afford to wait to see if such demands are functions of more enduring social changes before responding to them through education? These are just a few of the questions to which Boyer's article is addressed. The author is convinced that the schools must reconstruct themselves in order to meet demands for relevance which he perceives as following from urgent and legitimate needs.

William H. Boyer is Professor of Educational Foundations at the University of Hawaii. He has written a book titled *Education for Annihilation*.

Fear of the future increasingly corrodes modern life. We are beginning to sense the ways in which we have become locked into old institutional habits and their supporting mythologies, permitting technology and organizational technique to become the central determiners of social change. The tail usually wags the dog, and we do what is technologically possible, whether or not it is humanly desirable. Established systems become self-perpetuating and create their own goals, defining their own meaning of reality and progress. People are finally beginning to ask whether change is synonymous with progress or whether some change is destructive and even suicidal. Through our lack of qualitative standards we have often accepted all change as synonymous with social progress—the more the better. The gross national product is still the primary official indicator of national achievement. It lumps together the total dollar units of cigarette commercials and cancer therapy, automobile sales and mortuary fees, napalm and sulfa drugs.

The arrogant use of modern power has implications which are not only political and economic but ecological as well. Particularly in the West, where the Judeo-Christian traditions have flourished, man has encouraged himself to believe that he is above nature and that he can dictate to nature without showing respect for it. This arrogance is producing a dangerous ecological crisis to which the United States is the foremost contributor. The early rape and exploitation of seemingly boundless land and natural beauty still continues. The ugly consequences become more and more apparent. The beauty of irreplaceable giant redwood trees is increasingly denied to all future generations, as corporation profits and the chain saw continue to triumph over nature's ancient monuments. Lakes, streams, underground water, and even the oceans are headed rapidly toward pollution levels so high that they will be irreversible. In some areas of the United States, the air has become so polluted that it kills increasingly larger numbers of people as well as forests and vegetation. Increasingly, the birds that we don't see because of the smog are not there anyway, for our insecticides often hit wide of their mark. "Overkill" has become the symbol of our age.

Technology itself is not inherently evil, but when it develops without corresponding political, economic, and educational advances, a society becomes glutted with physical change unguided by integrated social planning. A society without control over change is a society with its future out of control. We are now at the dawn of a growing awareness that we must choose our destiny. The race is now on between more fundamental planning than we have ever engaged in and catastrophe.

Modern institutions, sustained by an immense amount of knowledge, paradoxically also require an abundance of ignorance to perpetuate them. Ignorance is the cement that continues to stabilize most contemporary institutions. Blindness to the ways in which old habits support intolerable levels of population, pollution, social inequality, and international violence is a prerequisite to the continuation of the world as it is.

Schools, also paradoxically, are usually one of the instruments for the perpetuation of ignorance. This is achieved primarily by isolating knowledge within separate compartments and by focusing on knowledge which is the least relevant, therefore meeting the traditional requirements of transmitting knowledge without disturbing the existing order. This is neither an intentional nor a stated goal of most schools, yet by isolating students from the major problems of the world the results are usually no less effective than if the goals were intended. Schools are usually so intertwined with the larger culture (educators often proclaim that enculturation is their main objective) that they often fail to see the dangers, even the suicidal consequences, of adjusting students to obsolete aspects of the culture.

Schools that fail to develop the capacity of students to participate intelligently in the control of their society not only emasculate them but alienate them from the dominant culture. Furthermore, this approach guarantees that social decision making is kept where it is—in the hands of a few who use such power to preserve the personal advantages enjoyed only by the decision-making elite. This process, which in the past has produced social injustice, now has brought us to the point where life on this planet cannot long continue without a new relationship of both man to man and man to nature. Therefore, students are engaged in a new quest for relevance.

A Definition of Relevance

There are a variety of current uses of the word "relevance," so I would like to suggest how relevance might be defined. This will lead to a proposal for planning a relevant future through education. Then I will focus particularly on planning for survival and suggest how all this applies to social studies.

I will define an education as being relevant when it has a vital connection to human life—either to the conditions which sustain life or to the conditions which give life meaning. An education that contributes to the knowledge of health, food production, nutrition, population control, and war prevention is the kind of education which can help sustain life. Education that provides knowledge of esthetic, social, and religious quality is the kind that helps give meaning to life.

Relevance Through Planning

An education that is relevant must connect knowledge and social change so that the student becomes a causal agent in historical change. Such education should help him participate in the development of the future by directing him into the mainstream of human events, by giving him experience in making effective social decisions, and by illuminating the alternative choices and their consequences. The student should be taught to join others in cooperatively planning the future.

The essential data in all planning involves information about the direction of trends which permits likely forecasts of the future. This requires information about present conditions, historical data to plot the rate and direction of change, and projections based on locating present trends at some point in the distant future. Short-term prediction is more reliable than long-term prediction, and unexpected events may alter even short-term predictions. The purpose of planning is to minimize accidental change and to maximize intentional change. The motive for the entire enterprise is based on the unwillingness to continue what Michael Harrington has called our Accidental Century, a century which has been based on a faith in history and the marketplace and the belief that when you get into trouble you will inevitably come out smelling like roses.

Planning can occur through an elitist top-down system, or it can be based on bottom-up participation, the relative emphasis being reflective of an autocratic or democratic social philosophy. Specialists are needed in either system to provide accurate information about the consequences of alternative plans, but value judgments are necessary to define the kind of future to be planned. This role cannot be performed by a specialist. The failure of schools to help students become participants in planning processes virtually predetermines that social planning will be elitist, representing the values of those who have the power to affect social policy.

Some types of planning are already well developed, particularly in large industries. This type is well described in John Galbraith's book, *The New Industrial State*. But such planning is aimed either at anticipating trends and then adapting to them or else at manipulating the larger public into the acceptance of a goal that may serve the corporation at the expense of the larger public.

Government planning is similar, usually with even less anticipation of trends and more reliance on ad hoc crisis treatment. The manipulation of public consent is also well established, but government even includes a self-predatory addition where branches of government withhold information from other branches, each in an attempt to achieve its own special interest.

Virtually all current social planning is *expansive* planning, based on the anticipation of trends. We are told that certain kinds of jobs will be increasingly available in the next decade, with the assumption that the enterprising citizen will prepare himself to become more marketable; but another kind of planning, which might be called *reconstructive* planning, assumes that what is needed is not mainly planning *for* the future, but planning *of* the future. The reconstructive planner does not assume that people need necessarily adjust to trends but rather that trends should be adjusted to people. Reconstructive planning requires integrative social planning—with the larger social unit being given priority. If it is a question of what is good for General Motors or what is good for the American people, the latter should have the overriding claim. If it is a matter of what is good for the United States or what is good for the human race, the human race should be given priority.

The difference between expansive national defense planning and reconstructive defense planning can be illustrated as follows: The effort to build ABM's and fallout shelters to protect against the radioactivity of World War III is an example of expansive planning. The Clark-Sohn plan for World Peace Through World Law, which is designed to *avert* cataclysmic war, is an example of reconstructive planning.

Areas of Planning

In order to teach planning, it is advisable to set up areas of study. Such classifying involves the danger of once again separating problems and neglecting their interrelatedness, but some problems are more urgent than others, at least from the standpoint of survival, so distinctions in the kinds of problems permit the appropriate allocation of energy and time. Planning areas might be usefully classified under problems of 1) social justice, 2) environmental quality, and 3) survival.

Social justice involves the study of human exploitation and plans to remedy such exploitation. *Environmental quality* involves planning which increases the desirability of living in a particular society. *Survival* planning minimizes the chances of unnecessary death.

If existence does precede essence, survival planning should be given central emphasis. This is the kind of ordering understood by Martin Luther King. In spite of his deep concern for increasing social justice, he saw that it would be no victory to achieve integration of radioactive corpses. He recognized the priority of the problems of international violence in the atomic age. It is this comparative perspective that must be cultivated if planning is to order energies toward the most important problems.

Statistics are necessary but are not sufficient for describing the consequences of trends. The *meaning* of a future can be illuminated by having some sense of what it would be like to live in a world suggested by particular trends. Futurist novels, plays, any dramatic and artistic form that provides vicarious experience of alternative futures is useful to the assessment of the desirability of living in such a world. That is why novels like *1984*, films like *On the Beach* and *Seven Days in May* make future possibilities real in a way that usually cannot be achieved by statistics. It is one thing to know what the statistical probabilities are for cigarette lung cancer. But many people require a more vivid and personal event (such as the death of Edward R. Murrow) to illustrate what the statistics mean.

Planning to Survive

Four major survival problems are cataclysmic war, uncontrolled population, resource depletion, and pollution of the biosphere on which human life depends. Projections in each of these three areas give little hope that mankind can long survive. If nothing is done to change trends in any of these areas, even short-range future survival chances are very low—most of the human race is not likely to survive this century. It is increasingly possible to predict the approximate time and place where autogenocide from overpopulation, pollution, and resource depletion will take place, but the war system is somewhat different. It combines the comparatively fixed probabilities of a mutual deterrence—mutual annihilation system. Estimates of the odds for the system failing range from 1% to 10% per year. Assuming that a 2% per year probability of mutual annihilation is an optimistic figure, the current war system itself is not likely to get most of the human race through the twentieth century.

The war system, however, may be one of the easier systems to reconstruct if enough people come to see that the atomic age has fundamentally transformed the meaning of national defense. Nations no longer have effective defense against nuclear arms, therefore the national "defense" they have is largely in name only. Current defense systems are examples of institutions locked into the constraints and habits of expansive planning. To move to the level of reconstructive planning requires a careful examination of alternative forms of world order. By patterning our changes according to old habits, we merely add new technology to old pre-atomic systems, giving virtually no attention to reconstructive possibilities such as an international system of national defense.

Survival and the Social Studies Teacher

The social studies programs in most schools would be transformed if they included a commitment to futurist goals directed toward the development of a world with greater social justice, improved quality of the physical environment, and increased chances for human survival. Such a commitment would provide new criteria for the selection of subject matter. History would no longer be largely an antiquarian excursion into the particular events that have come to be a dreary part of the perennial puberty rites of American youth. History should not be ignored in futurist studies, but it should be selectively studied to understand current problems. History is *always* written and studied selectively, but instead of merely chronicling battles, they could be examined not only to find out what seemed to be the primary causes but to question whether better ways might have been used to resolve the conflict. Causes of historical events include not only the precipitating factors, but also the structures that were *not* present. It is not only what people do that causes wars; it is also what they failed to do in the way of developing procedures, habits, norms, and political machinery for averting war. This use of *negative causality*, or what was omitted in the system, can be an exceedingly useful concept for analyzing historical events for the purpose of planning a future that avoids some of the pitfalls of the past.

Clearly it will be necessary to reorient our study of history to focus on those events that are the most productive. In most current history texts, very little consideration is given to the bombing of Hiroshima and the political-military implications of this nuclear era. The Nuremberg trials, the Cuban missile crisis, and the Vietnam War can be used as case studies to raise questions about the need for new principles of international law and new peace-keeping systems. The assumptions on which American policy has been based, which include atomic threat systems and a mutual deterrence theory, are crucially in need of more critical examination.

Earlier, I suggested that the four main crisis areas are war, population, resource depletion, and pollution. In all these problems, a basic strategy is to explore alternative futures and then to make comparisons of alternative goals and strategies of change as a basis for commitment to social action. New information becomes necessary. In the case of teaching about population problems, demographic and birth control information is basic. In the case of pollution, the information describing trends, danger levels, and causes becomes basic. Understanding causes should include knowledge of the resistance to pollution control offered by organizations that have a vested interest in pollution, such as the automobile industry.

But knowledge of how to bring about change must go beyond the usual mere assimilation of facts and theory. It must include direct experience. For example, if high school students were to identify a problem of air or water pollution in their own community, they could inquire into the reasons for the problem. They may find there is a lack of appropriate legislation, or lack of monitoring and enforcement. Their findings could be used to illuminate the local needs. They would at the minimum obtain more understanding of the politics of pollution control and at the maximum they would help effect actual changes. Futurist education must link theory and practice if the goal of teaching planning is to be really effective. It involves a change in the meaning of social education—away from competitive individual success, toward cooperative social action.

The basic model of reconstructive planning is not difficult to understand, but the task of reorienting a curriculum toward planning, even toward survival planning, is likely to be difficult because of the entrenched commitments to obsolete practices. The self-righteous autonomy of schools is a major obstacle. Psychologists have often defined intelligence as that which I.Q. tests measure, and the same quaint logic is often used by schools to define education as that which schools do. Without some outside theory of man, history, and the good life, schools have no outside standard of measurement and they easily commit a kind of Cartesian fallacy in which they say, "Schools are, therefore relevance exists." The most common traps include some of the following assumptions: 1) that state-adopted materials are necessarily relevant, 2) that the traditional content of social studies is necessarily relevant, 3) that the mass media concentrates on problems that are necessarily relevant, 4) that regents examinations and college entrance requirements are necessarily relevant, 5) that materials prepared by university academicians are necessarily relevant. A reexamination of these assumptions may threaten the self-interest of existing bureaucracies, but may provide a breath of fresh air in the midst of the present educational stagnation.

Danger—University Ahead

The increased influence of universities on social studies curricula is a mixed blessing. To the unwary and the innocent, the university can be one more snare to trap the social studies teacher. When the university is treated as the citadel of the philosopher-king, a kind of tragic comedy can result—a case of the blind leading the blind. Theodore Roszak is even more critical:

Until the recent rash of campus protest related to the Vietnam war, nothing has so characterized the American academic as a condition of entrenched social irrelevance, so highly developed that it would be comic if it were not sufficiently serious in its implications to stand condemned as an act of criminal delinquency. (*The Dissenting Academy*, p. 12)

"Criminal delinquency" is strong language, but a teacher who deprives his students of knowledge that might literally save his life could be said to be committing a type of criminal act. Universities often are Parkinsonian bureaucracies where words expand to fill the time available. They are often places to learn many reasons why nothing can be done—a kind of staging area for intellectual paralysis. A teacher who wants knowledge to be an instrument of action for helping people participate in social change will need to be aware that this is not the dominant meaning of knowledge in American universities. The academician carries an implicit theory of knowledge with him, and most academicians are not concerned with the kind of knowledge that makes futurist education possible.

The disciplinary compartmentalization of knowledge is one of the major traps, but even when knowledge becomes interdisciplinary, it is not necessarily relevant to the problems of our age. The new Fenton High School Social Studies Series is a case in point. The texts are more interdisciplinary and integrative than most texts, but the particular type of inquiry method that is used is aimed at inducting students into the language and problems of behavioral *science*. The mode of inquiry is analytic and scientific. If it were also philosophical and critical, it would move beyond description into normative questions—judgments about values and questions of what ought to be, not merely what has been and what is. This would make it more suitable for futurist study. As it stands, it encourages the kind of neutrality that characterizes most behavioral science. Education for planning requires the use of scientific inquiry skills, but it also requires movement toward commitment rather than toward neutrality—an instrumental use of knowledge rather than interest in scientific inquiry as an end in itself. But Fenton himself does have social goals in mind. He points out that the students who are successful with his curriculum are not learning merely as an end in itself; the material does serve other needs—it helps them "pass the college board examinations." Middleclass "success" values once again take precedence over the more existential values of survival. What appears to be a new approach to social studies turns out not really to be an instrument of reform, but only one more way of aiming at adaptive individual middleclass success in a society that desperately needs reconstruction. The Fenton series is typical of the academic traps that reinforce old social systems under the guise of reform.

So even what is called the "new social studies" can be a way of actually preserving old ideologies. This is achieved by ignoring the more fundamental problems of our age. If by contrast we give precedence to life rather than death, beauty rather than ugliness, human equality rather than exploitation, we can then use science to see if present practices are likely to lead in such a direction. Previous illustrations have focused on social studies, but futurism is applicable to all areas of the schools. Selective use of social science, natural science, and philosophy can then become integrated educational tools that help people learn the ecological limits of human action and learn to plan the best of possible worlds.

Conclusion

This is the first period in human history where man has the means to reflect not only on his social policies, but also on the values that underlie them. His new capacity to engage in fundamental replanning, including intentional reconstruction of the culture itself, is the most important achievement of the twentieth century. This capacity is not yet being realized, yet no institution can be more useful than the schools in helping to bring this new knowledge to the general citizenry. But to do so schools must extricate themselves from many of their old habits and avoid merely trying to adapt the young to a world gone by. Schools are inextricably involved in social change, either because of what they do or what they fail to do. In an age when relevant education is desperately urgent, the ritualistic trivia and bureaucratic games that occupy most schools are not merely a waste of time but a form of pathology.

There are some old values, such as maximum freedom of choice, that are still important, but schools must *illuminate the new context* in which choices must be made. They should help students identify trends that are suicidal and also those which perpetuate social injustice and exploitation. Then the job is to collectively design optimum futures, first focusing on classes, next on schools expanding local communities, the nation, and a new world order. Such planning should include implementing and testing effective strategies for change.

If people were less alienated from the forces of social change, more aware of the problems of common survival, and more accustomed to cooperating to create the future, we could then be optimistic about the future. Schools have a crucial survival role: They can either continue to reinforce pathological trends or else by reconstructing themselves they can help divert history from the suicidal path on which it is now embarked.

Joe R. Burnett

CHANGING THE SOCIAL ORDER: THE ROLE OF SCHOOLING

One of the positions described by Pounds and Bryner calls for the school to act as the chief agent for social and cultural reconstruction. In the following selection Joe R. Burnett examines some recent developments which he perceives as carrying implications for the role of schooling in the reconstruction of the social order.

Burnett, a philosopher, addresses himself to three main themes: (1) the way in which the increase in teacher power may relate to the role of the school as an agent of cultural renewal and social reconstruction; (2) some reasons why past advocates of social reconstructionism failed to attract the kind of following necessary for their goals; and (3) where those who do dare to change the social order through the schools are likely to find ideological and philosophical support. Burnett concludes with six speculative or projective observations. His article has some major implications for the teacher-power movement examined in Chapter 4.

Joe R. Burnett is Professor of Philosophy of Education at the University of Illinois, Urbana. He is the author of many articles and books in the general area of philosophy of education and a past president of the Philosophy of Education Society.

. . . By way of a synopsis, let me indicate [what] I will do in this address.

First, I will argue that the evidence favors an increase in "teacher power" in this country—that is, an increase in the power of the key people in the elementary and secondary schools. They are "key" in the sense that their numbers and their contemporary orientation give them, as we say in Illinois, "political clout." They obviously *do* dare change the social order and *are* doing so.

Second, I will hazard a guess as to why the admonition to change the social order—made most provocatively by George S. Counts thirty-seven years ago (1932), but by others much earlier—was not heeded.

Third, I will suggest that now, when teachers do dare change the so-

From *Philosophy of Education 1969: Proceedings of the Twenty-Fifth Annual Meeting of the Philosophy of Education Society, Denver, 1969*, Donald Arnstine, editor (Edwardsville, Ill.: Southern Illinois University, 1969), pp. 233–242. Some footnotes deleted. Reprinted by permission of the publisher and Joe R. Burnett.

cial order, some of the systematic philosophies which would help them do this democratically and wisely are out of vogue. Paradoxically, when some of the philosophies *were* in vogue, there was not the organizational "clout," the large numbers of interested people and the militancy necessary to carry through a philosophically-grounded program of change. . . .

I begin by speculating—critically and suggestively, I trust—about some important consequences which could result if the national teachers' organizations (the National Education Association and the American Federation of Teachers) continue to increase their political power or, as it is sometimes called, their "Teacher Power." By teacher power I refer to the demonstrated ability of organized classroom teachers at the elementary and secondary levels of American public education to cause other societal groups to accept demands which they (the other groups) consider troublesome, not fair, repugnant in the extreme, or even illegal and immoral.

I see virtually no reason to think that organized teachers will be significantly blocked in gaining greater power. Granted, racial conflict ("community power" vs. "teacher power" as it emerged in Ocean Hill-Brownsville) may call into question the democratic ethos of teacher organizations, and perhaps the conflict could seriously weaken teacher organizations; but, equally well, it could cause teachers in increasing numbers to seek membership in the organizations as a mode of protection, thereby strengthening the organizations. Granted, severe economic depression (which, like racial conflict, *could* have the opposite effect), severe political repression, or expanded military confrontations could create a cultural base uncongenial for growth in power of the teacher organizations.

In any event, there obviously are factors which might curtail growth of power vested in teacher organizations. Let me just say that, if things continue very much as they are, we seem a long way from seeing teacher power "peak out" or "hit a plateau."

Let me cite a few reasons why this seems true.

First, successes such as the teachers organizations have had over the past decade breed further success—not indefinitely, but for a long period and often at something like an exponential rate. As Toynbee puts it in talking about cultures, the successful meeting of challenges produces in the group an enthusiasm which makes them desirous of finding new challenges. It also gives them a "mind set" which—to a point—provides an edge in meeting the new challenges.

Second, the times seem propitious for a merger of the two national organizations. As Myron Lieberman has remarked, it seems likely that the ". . . emerging organization will put great pressure on teachers to join, and we can expect a dramatic increase in teacher organizational membership at all levels." No longer will funds and energies be needed by the two national organizations to fight one another, and thus they can concentrate on what has apparently come to be *the* task: creation of one powerful, comprehensive organization without internal control by administrators.[1]

Third, it would seem that the stances of a number of groups are going to threaten teachers into realizing that they have no security except in a "united-we-stand-divided-we-fall" policy. The threats of minority groups seeking to gain more community control of the schools furnishes us one instance. But I also call attention to the vilification of teachers during some of the recent strikes, boycotts, and leveling of professional sanctions. Teachers, we hear from some financial and political interests, are motivated by greed rather than a concern for children, they are being non-professional, they are the tools (in the case of the A. F. of T.) of organized labor, they are dupes of a left-wing conspiracy.

There are too many teachers, too many people who are relatives of teachers, and too many people who otherwise know teachers well, for such charges to "stick." Classroom teachers, as little as any group in America, can be so stigmatized. We are talking about 1.8 million teachers alone, and probably one can quadruple this figure in voting power and additional support if he talks about those who know the conditions of teaching and the plight of teachers with respect to such things as historic status, low financial rewards, civil liberties, and even academic freedom. Such blanket charges seem sure to bring a defensive and unifying reaction within teachers' ranks.

Fourth, and perhaps the most important and the most impressionist reason I offer for expecting more teacher militancy: we seem to be getting a new breed of teacher trainee, and he is going to be a force to be reckoned with when he becomes a teacher. Our teacher trainees increasingly "know the context." They are a wing—ill-defined at this point—of the youth revolt. Let me elaborate on this point briefly.

More and more of our teacher trainees are the children of professional and union parents. If what is attacked is the very source of their parents' upward socio-economic mobility, *via* their parents' use of professional

[1] Myron Lieberman, "Implications of the Coming NEA-AFT Merger," *Phi Delta Kappan*, I (Nov., 1968), 142.

organizations and unions, then what is being attacked is near sacred. One cannot attack political organization techniques so absolutely as we have recently seen in the case of teachers, and expect those attacked to simply "lie down." Today one is probably stupid to attack such things respected by youth who often heard discussions of "scabs," "company unions," "company co-opting of dissenters," etc. in the context of family welfare. One does not wisely send the present broadsides against teacher and teacher trainees whose parents are of the professional class and know full well the significance of such things as group insurance, retirement policies, standard cost-of-living arrangements, bonuses for extra competence or performance.

Like most youth today, teacher trainees may be unhappy with, and revolting against, their parents; but not many will settle for less than their parents had in the way of *live* options for socio-economic aesthetic mobility routes. They know well how their parents "made it."

There are some other things which seem to be significant in discussing —however impressionistically—the new breed of teacher trainee and teacher. Ever increasingly, they are *not* a cloistered, normal-school lot. Compared to students of other departments, schools, and colleges on a university campus they still are a fairly quiet and tame breed. But they are not non-political in the old, normal-school pattern, and they are not non- or anti-intellectual. In the old days—say two decades ago!—they often *were* cloistered, even on university campuses, and the only major concern one could elicit from them was some kind of nebulous love of children when he asked them why they wanted to be teachers of children.

If I am not mistaken, they are jaded today by comparison with their counterparts of only a few decades ago. Contemporary studies of teachers' political attitudes do not show this—perhaps because the studies are of teachers of the older breed.

Teacher trainees are still talking about some sort of nebulous love of children; but, oddly, so are the students in physics, math, chemistry, philosophy, and the social sciences. This is odd when one considers the concerns of the latter group; no less odd is the concern of teacher trainees with some of the concerns of the latter group: pot, the pill, pornography, and political power.

But let me turn back to the theme of contemporary teacher power and what it may portend.

I earlier indicated that, by use of the expression "teacher power," I refer to the demonstrated ability of organized, classroom teachers at the elementary and secondary levels of American public education to cause other societal groups to accept demands which they (the other groups) consider troublesome, not fair, repugnant in the extreme, or even illegal and immoral.

There is no question that teachers' organizations are beginning to have power in this regard, at least in certain cities and states. While not constituting a power factor of major proportions in American society, it is evident that the teachers' organizations represent a new element in the power calculus of the President of the United States, several governors, several state boards of education, many mayors, and many leaders in the labor and industrial complexes.

If we project the growth of teacher power, then it would seem destined to end with the same kind of power held by other, large, special interest groups in America. And, although attaining success has sometimes taken many, many decades in this country, even for movements strongly begun and widely joined, it is a commonplace that they can succeed. The hallmark of success is, of course, control over entry of others into full, practitioner status.

A crucial point, albeit a speculation for the teachers' organizations, is that control of entry to practitioner status *includes control over training prerequisite to entry.* It may be the type of control exercised by the American Medical Association, which "farms out" prerequisite training but exercises strong control over both pre-medical and regular medical education; or it may be the type of control which some of the unions exercise through their own apprenticeship programs; but in the context of teacher power, put concretely, this augurs for *control of courses for certification, control by representatives of teaching practitioners who are organized into a powerful collectivity.*

There is another especially noteworthy phenomenon associated with control of entry to practitioner status in the strong labor and professional organizations. It is that what constitutes a "practitioner" becomes very rigorously defined. This has been a necessity in the past for organizations in America, whether they have been labor unions, scientific organizations, medical associations, or even organized criminal elements such as the Mafia. It is necessary to protect the organization and also to protect the organization's clientele. One always knows just who is responsible for what. Full status is highly-guarded status, given only when the candidate follows a stipulated training pattern and is, as a result of the training, not only basically competent but sure to be without conflict of interest. Whom one excludes is quite as important as whom one includes: assured allegiance demands rigorous standards of inclusion-exclusion. Sometimes they are standards which on occasion turn out to be silly, stupid, or even criminal. But, as Mosca argues, they tend to be necessary for maintaining a position of strength in the societal balance of power.

This is a *highly* speculative projection of a trend, but I think that you will admit that the trend is there. Projecting it, as one might have done for certain labor and professional groups at the turn of the century, gives one an idea of what enormous power could come to lie in the hands of teachers: a large measure of control over certification and accreditation; almost full control over curriculum; almost full control over teacher-learning techniques; the ability to make school boards and communities bargain—as perhaps we already see in a few cases—in better than just token good faith.

In the recently developed trend we may be seeing something new; something not widely recognized; and something *not* widely recognized because in recent decades we have come to believe that it could never exist in viable form.

Let me "back up" a bit. It well may be that the social foundations, the progressive, and the social reconstructionist movements were, until recently, idea systems without the ability to specify the *political* agents and vehicles necessary to carry the idea systems to fruition. If one traces back these movements he will find, ordinarily at least, that there was a very vague notion of just who were to be the political agents of social change *via* education or schooling.

Lester Frank Ward, generally credited with being the spiritual forerunner of the social foundations movement, was almost completely vague. Ward found a cosmic *telos* which was emerging in such a way as to make of education the natural *via royale* to the future, and educators were seen as emergent architects of the coming, democratic and sociocratic society which Ward envisioned. But he did not specify just who was an educator, and just how the cosmic end was to find political means.

Albion W. Small (Ward's student, a colleague of Dewey's at Chicago, and one of George S. Count's mentors) found the promise of social change and betterment in the revelations of sociology. Here too there may have been a *telos,* but obviously a more modest one than Ward's. While a critic of Comte, he on at least one occasion makes Sociology seem the emergent Prime Mover for social reform that Comte made it. Let me quote the passage, since it is such a beautiful example of what we all recognize today as "sociological sanctimoniousness":

Sociology demands with . . . confidence: first that for everybody the study of *society* shall begin with the nursing bottle, and continue so long as social relations continue; second, that for most people the study of sociology shall never begin at all. . . .

Sociology demands of educators . . . that they shall not rate themselves as leaders of children, but as makers of society. Sociology knows no means for the amelioration or reform of society more radical than those of which teachers hold the leverage.[2]

Certainly in the case of Ward, and seemingly in the case of Small, changing the social order meant wielding concerted political power—either in spiritual concert or in *that* plus special interest group organization. Again, the idea was there, but there was no obvious stipulation of viable agents and/or vehicles. "Educators" and "teachers," when Ward and Small wrote, simply were not terms which connoted or denoted viable political actors. Both gentlemen knew where they wanted to go, but they could not specify the routes.

For one individual, in truth a member of all three movements, the agents and vehicles were obvious—or, at least, they were obvious to him at one point in his career. The agents were the select group of educators in the Progressive Education Association and in the New Educational Fellowship of the World. In a 1937 statement, which today may seem ludicrous, Harold Rugg commented:

There are in the Western world two important liberal educational forums—The Progressive Education Association of America and The New Educational Fellowship of the World. It is through these two agencies that we shall most effectively coordinate the power of individual teachers to remake the world.

These two groups have both potential world vision and educational initiative. We who belong to these organizations are not bound by the traditional fears and stereotypes of the mass education associations. We owe no allegiance to the fears created by local and nationalistic climates of opinion. We pay allegiance only to the integrity of our own judgments of problems and issues in the modern world, to our own concept of the kinds of national personalities that we wish to develop in the world.[3]

___

[2] "Demands of Sociology Upon Pedagogy," in Merle L. Borrowman's (ed.) *Teacher Education in America* (New York: Teachers College Press, 1965), pp. 138–39. Small made these remarks in an address published in 1896—and republished in (circa) 1897 with John Dewey's *My Pedagogic Creed*.

[3] "Education and International Understanding," *Progressive Education* (VIII: Apr., 1931), p. 300. I am indebted to Helen A. Archibald for bringing this specific passage to my attention.

Of course, the Progressive Education Association *is* no longer. The New Educational Fellowship of the World survives, but I doubt that many of our younger members have heard of it. The John Dewey Society and the Philosophy of Education Society—both, I take it, born in America mainly by the same intellectual spirits who gave birth to the Progressive Education Association—do not exactly "flourish."

Like Ward, Small, and many, many others, Rugg thought that the schools and educators could and should change the social order. Perhaps we are seeing today that indeed they *can* change the social order: deliberately, quickly, and hopefully with an eye to the profound betterment of society. Ward and Small were lacking in specificity with respect to attaining the end; Rugg probably erred in the opposite direction. But, in terms of strategy, who could have said that it was an error in 1937? He picked two special interest groups composed of educators who *were* giving signs of militantly working for rapid social change. Rugg, at least, tried to specify who the educators were that could and should change the social order. It just may have been, as I think it was, that there was no group of educators which then was organized for the type of political action which was necessary. For want of the agents and the institutional vehicles, the battle was lost and probably was not even joined in any significant sense.

There is a presently obscure, side issue involved in reflections about the feasibility of educators' changing the social order. Perhaps you recall Mark Twain's statement after being informed by someone to the effect that there was a report of his death. Twain remarked that "the reports of my death are greatly exaggerated." If we let the movements under discussion be equated with Twain, there was "news" to the effect that they could not even be born—or, if they were born, they would be ineffective. Issac Kandel, writing in 1938, seems to have had spokesmen of the movements in mind when he penned the following:

There has . . . been injected into discussions of education and social change the suggestion that schools should, in a period of change, educate for a new social order, and that teachers should ally themselves with some political group and use their classrooms to propagate certain doctrines. Schools and teachers should, in other words, participate more directly and vitally in projecting particular ideas, or patterns, of social change and in their execution. The whole history of education emphasizes the impossibility of this idea, for society establishes schools to provide a firm basis for itself and to sustain the common interest. . . . Society changes first and schools follow.[4]

---

[4] I. L. Kandel, *Conflicting Theories of Education* (New York: Macmillan, 1938), pp. 85–86.

One probably could have said the very same thing of medicine, law, engineering, and many other professional endeavors in the pre-1900 centuries. Society changed, and most of the professional endeavors followed; but today many of those endeavors both "lead" and follow. The perspective which I have used Kandel to represent has been and is widely held. Durkheim is without a doubt one of the best intellectual sources of European scepticism with regard to the ineffectualness of the schools as agents of social change; William Graham Sumner is probably the best American counterpart of Durkheim. But if one can accuse Ward, Small, Rugg and others of the "sin" of Utopianism, then one can as well accuse Kandel (and such kindred souls as Durkheim and Sumner) of the "sin" of traditionalism—the sin, that is, of claiming that what has been and is must always be.

Historians of education may be perpetrating the traditionalist error. Some recent historical analysis of the social foundations, progressive, and social reconstructionist endeavors seems to suggest that the idea systems represented by these movements were doomed to failure because they did not and could not find their agents and vehicles in their own time. Agents and vehicles may never mature in an historical epoch, and they may cease to be if they do give evidence of maturing, but this does not mean that new agents and vehicles will not come to the fore. For instance, there is no reason to think that progressivism died because the Progressive Education Association ceased to exist in 1955 and the journal, *Progressive Education*, "folded" two years later—which is, I take it, what Professor Cremin would have us infer.[5]

Let me conclude with six observations which I hope you will find have speculative merit.

First, it appears that for many decades an idea system associated with educators' changing the social order was developing, but that there were no viable agents or vehicles to serve as the political force essential to objectifying the idea system.

Second, the lack of agents and vehicles seems to have served to convince some educators that the particular type of idea system was not feasible—which is the "traditionalist fallacy" as exemplified in the quotation from Kandel.

Third, the conviction that it was not feasible seems gradually to have led to the notion that it is not desirable that educators function as one of society's dominant power groups in directing social change.

[5] Lawrence A. Cremin, *The Transformation of the School: Progressivism in American Education, 1876–1957* (New York: Alfred A. Knopf, 1961).

Fourth, at the very time the idea system is being neglected and/or is in bad repute, the agents and vehicles have come to the fore in the form of the two national teachers' organizations.

Fifth, because many of the problems of today are so much like those of three or four decades ago, one can suspect that we will see a resurgence of interest in social foundations, progressivism, and social reconstructionism. We likely will rediscover them, as we must do with so many things in educational history and philosophy. Our students and our society want education to be socially relevant today, and what could be more relevant than such things as the concept of community; that of social consensus; that of social conflict and crisis; that of social —as contrasted with political—democracy?

Sixth, it well may be that it is going to be professionally important for us to stress social philosophy of education much more, and this just at a time when the emphasis seems to be on high specialization and fewer general, philosophically-oriented courses for teacher trainees. For if we get a massive, powerful organization of classroom teachers, it could degenerate into a "racket" (as George Axtelle has characterized certain other, professional organizations) without a set of rich, humane, philosophical perspectives.

Questions for Discussion

1. Which one or which combination of positions discussed by Pounds and Bryner do you think underlies the relationship which now seems to prevail between our schools and society?
2. Can you think of any way(s) in which public schools have taken the lead in solving major social problems?
3. Do any of the selections in this chapter cause you to question the motives behind your choice to become a teacher? Why?
4. Do you think you have been steamrollered into attending college? If so, did your school experiences contribute to this situation?
5. In your opinion, are the schools producing youngsters who will promote or at least be tolerant of social and cultural change?

Topics for Further Study

1. Examine curriculum guides in such fields as social studies, English, and natural science that have been prepared by an urban school system and a rural school system. Do you find any evidence of the influence of the six points of view described by Pounds and Bryner? What evidence do you think you ought to find through such an examination? What differences between the guides prepared by the two different types of systems reflect underlying philosophies about the school-society relationship?

2. In the description of the school-society relationship issue, attention was drawn to the fact that radical positions on this issue would be avoided in the descriptive selection. Now, using the framework presented by Pounds and Bryner, develop what you would consider to be a radical position on education. Then look for elements of your position which may have appeared in some of the selections in this chapter.

3. What criteria would you develop to indicate whether the schools are meeting the generally agreed-upon goals for education?

Chapter 2. THE COURTS: AN INCREASING INFLUENCE ON LOCAL SCHOOL POLICY-MAKING

EVEN though there is a continuing debate over the role of the school in relation to society, there is agreement by most citizens that the school is to perform certain specific functions. David A. Goslin, in "The Functions of the School in Modern Society," has summarized some of these for us (see Chapter 1). As the reader will recall, Goslin cites the school's responsibility in perpetuating a cultural heritage as its primary function. Included in this cultural heritage are the values, beliefs, and norms accumulated through the years as well as the sum total of knowledge in every field of inquiry. In addition, Goslin notes that education is expected to play a major role in influencing the rate of change in our society. Schools are also expected to sort out and select those whose abilities are commensurate with certain vocational and occupational roles in society. Certainly this does not work out equitably in practice. As Goslin indicates, there are several reasons why this happens. One basic cause which even the most inexperienced observer can detect is the difference in resource allocations to various school districts.

The general acceptance of the goals of education described above and their sacrosanct nature have led to a situation in which the entire educational establishment has been basically immune from the checks and balances applied to other institutions in our society. Since the governance of education has been left to the states, one might assume initially that the state legislatures would hold the power to ensure that the agreed-upon educational functions were, in fact, being performed. But such is not the case. The state legislatures have in fact chosen to relinquish most of their powers in education to local school boards, whose members are theoretically state officials but who, in actuality, are local representatives serving local constituencies. This allegiance to the concept of local school control has prevented the executive, legislative, and judicial branches of our government from having any significant influence in educational decision-making.

There has been some indication in recent years, however, that this era of educational immunity from legitimate checks on its progress in carrying out agreed-upon goals has come to an end. The federal government has, for example, provided the states with at least one means of checking upon certain aspects of the school's attempts to meet societal obligations—that is, through passage of the Elementary and Secondary Education Act of 1965. Admittedly, the powers acquired through this means have been extremely limited. More significant has been the influence of both federal and local courts in educational decision-making.

Foremost among the reasons why the schools are no longer immune from intervention by those wishing to review their progress is that the schools have recently become the focal point of many societal problems. Boards of education are now, more than ever before, expected to rectify, through the schools, long-neglected social injustices. Evidence of this observation is the insistence by student protesters that school boards confront the issues at the roots of these injustices. A brief examination of Chapter 5, "Students in Rebellion: Unrest in the Public Schools," will reveal the pressure placed upon boards of education to deal directly and effectively with such issues as racial imbalance in the schools, as well as with the issues of poverty and bureaucratic control of social institutions. The reason for the student protest examined in this chapter is a perceived gap between the role of the schools and the needs of society. The schools, in the view of a growing number of critics, have simply failed to recognize most of the current trends in our society. This has been interpreted by many as negligence in accomplishing the expected and agreed-upon goals for education.

It has been the courts that have most dramatically drawn attention to the problems of the schools in achieving their goals. Since 1954, the courts have increasingly challenged educational decisions that have not coincided with society's expectations of the schools. Until the historic *Brown v. Board of Education of Topeka, Kansas* case of 1954, the schools had rarely been subjected to judicial review. It had been a matter of precedent that American public education generally functioned outside the sphere of courts of law. For this reason, local boards of education had been granted extensive discretionary authority in making their decisions. Even to this day, courts tend not to intervene in school board affairs unless there has been an invasion of the constitutional rights of an individual or unless the board has failed to act when it had the responsibility to do so. This latter point is highly controversial today because the courts seem to be interpreting it more and more broadly and, as they do so, resistance to judicial review of school decisions is becoming a major issue. The courts are, in effect, forcing the schools to attack overall social injustices by withdrawing much of their self-restraint toward educational policy-making bodies.

In an effort to examine the role of the courts regarding their checking function on the progress of school boards toward achieving society's goals for education, this chapter will probe the extent to which the judicial review of recent years has affected public education institutions. Despite their traditional tendency to avoid intervention in public education, the courts have made considerable impact upon certain educational decisions. Noteworthy among these are decisions concerning church-state matters, teacher rights, student discipline, and school board rules. In the church-state area alone, the Supreme Court has in the past few years upheld a New York statute that provides textbooks for parochial school students (*Allen v. Board of Education*) and overturned a half-century old precedent to allow taxpayers to challenge federal appropriations. This latter decision (*Flast v. Cohen*) was brought to a head by the passage of the Elementary and Secondary Education Act of 1965, which relied heavily upon state and local administration of its various titles. Such practice raised serious legal problems because of wide variation in implementation policies.

Recently considerable controversy has arisen regarding the role of both federal and lower courts in local educational decision-making. Much of the controversy has centered on the decisions handed down by federal district courts relating to the status of racial segregation in the public schools. The issue of the role of the courts in local school policy-making came to national prominence with the landmark *Hobson v. Hansen* decision (1967), in which Judge J. Skelly Wright ordered the desegregation of the 90 percent black, *de facto* segregated Washington D.C. school system.* Although the courts have entered the education field in the various other areas mentioned previously, this chapter will focus for illustrative purposes on an exploration of court influence in the area of

---

* In *Hobson v. Hansen* Judge J. Skelly Wright declared that the constitution required elimination of school segregation if Negro children are to receive equal educational guarantees. His remedies to provide integrated education for the Washington Public School system drew national attention because they were seemingly impractical. The reader may at this time wish to familiarize himself with the *Hobson v. Hansen* case by studying the summary which appears in this chapter.

urban racial imbalance or *de facto* school segregation, as exemplified in the Hobson case. Examples were selected from this particular area (1) because of the impact of racial matters on almost all educational issues and (2) because of its continuing importance to the civil rights movement. However, while the illustrations in this chapter will be drawn from *de facto* segregation litigation, there is a general issue to be examined in depth in the following pages: *What, if any, should be the role of the courts in local educational decision-making?*

It is not surprising to discover that the courts have been hesitant to intervene in local educational decision-making related to big-city, *de facto* school segregation. Prior to the *Hobson v. Hansen* case the courts had already undertaken a major task in correcting racially motivated educational policies in the South. The *Hobson* litigation was clearly designed to test whether the courts would set precedent by ordering a school board in the North to correct policies which were not responsive to the needs of the blacks and the poor. As noted above, the courts did take this step, but the resulting remedy for the Washington, D.C. problem was idealistic, complex, and impossible to administer. Judge Wright was not concerned with the impracticability of his decision because he was mainly trying to show the nation that the courts must intervene in this type of local educational policy-making. Controversy, which had been building up for several years, came to a head immediately after the *Hobson* decision was announced. As the historical review in this section indicates, *Hobson* was not the first *de facto* segregation case. It has been, however, the most dramatic to date.

The controversy arose for many reasons. First, as far as the legal profession was concerned, the *Hobson* doctrine had no clear precedent; its scope was too great; and it clearly threatened the prestige of the judiciary.

Second, many people felt that the issue in the *Hobson* case should have been dealt with by other social institutions. In other words, they felt it was not a problem for the courts to decide because *de facto* segregation does not mean a deliberate attempt to deprive certain children of equal opportunity. It was obvious, of course, that the political system— of which the schools are a subsystem—could not solve the housing pattern problem nor could any other governmental institution. The controversy was given added impetus when the question was asked who would attempt to solve the problems of providing equal educational opportunity to minority groups if the courts refused to do so. There is no doubt that when asked this question any court would have to intervene in local school policy-making, even at the expense of entering an area in which the court has no real expertise. The judge in the *Hobson* case was willing to sacrifice all conventional conceptions of the judicial process because he felt strongly motivated by the obvious injustice being perpetrated against black children in Washington and other big cities.

A third reason why the court intervention was and still is such a sensitive matter is that it obligates local government to strive to improve the education of those in the minority. This implies an additional expense for any system and, more importantly, it suggests that the system will have to take clear-cut actions to alleviate some of the aspects of poverty that it has been avoiding for years.

Fourth, further controversy arose when the education profession was criticized for not providing the expertise to create more reasonable solutions than those offered by the courts. In *Hobson v. Hansen,* the court abolished ability grouping and challenged the use of standardized tests as a criterion for such grouping anywhere, when used on disadvantaged children. In a sense, the decision in *Hobson* was a judicial reprimand directed against all school administrators under whose jurisdiction problems similar to those in Washington had been allowed to grow. Some critics of the nation's educators feel that professional people should be able to create remedies such as busing and school-pairing plans, even in large districts. Such plans would then render decisions like Judge Wright's unnecessary.

Finally, court intervention in local school decision-making regarding *de facto* segregation has far-reaching ramifications for the civil rights movement. There has for years been a split among civil rights leaders in their attitudes toward attempts to improve the educational opportunity for ghetto children. Some leaders oppose a major commitment of ghetto schools, while others have campaigned for better schools in the ghetto. The former attitude assumes that the best approach to equal educational opportunity is through integrated classrooms. Such a view was implicit in the *Hobson* case. If the court assumes that an integrated education is prerequisite to a quality education (as it does in *Hobson*), then another controversial question is raised. Should the court demand integrated education when it has neither the power nor the resources necessary to follow up on this demand? Such demands may lead to false hopes and to the conclusion that integrated education is the only path to equal education for all.

These, then, are but a few of the reasons why the question of the role of the courts in local educational decision-making is so intriguing. They are also some of the reasons why the court-school relationship is a significant contemporary issue in education and society at large.

It is interesting to note that Judge Wright anticipated the adverse reaction and the controversy that would be focused on the *Hobson* case. He wrote, in a section of his decision called "Parting Words," what might be considered to be an apology for his lack of expertise in education:

It is regrettable, of course, that in deciding this case this court must act in an area so alien to its expertise. It would be far better indeed for these great social and political problems to be resolved in the political arena by other branches of government. But these are social and political problems which seem at times to defy such resolution. In such situations, under our system, the judiciary must bear a hand and accept its responsibility to assist in the solution where constitutional rights hang in the balance.

J. Skelly Wright

PUBLIC SCHOOL DESEGREGATION: LEGAL REMEDIES FOR *DE FACTO* SEGREGATION

This excerpt from an article by Judge J. Skelly Wright prior to his historic decision provides an excellent description of the issue under consideration in this chapter. Judge Wright, who clearly thought long and hard about the role of the court in local school decision-making, comes to grips with the issue directly in this selection.

V. Remedial Action of the Courts to Correct Racial Imbalance

. . . What can a state do—what can a court require a state to do— to relieve racial imbalance? In short, what, if any, remedies are available?

A. *Current Approaches and Their Limitations.* Initially, public school authorities must be cured of the neighborhood school syndrome. The neighborhood school, like the little red school house, has many emotional ties and practical advantages. The neighborhood school serves as the neighborhood center, easily accessible, where children can gather to play on holidays and parents' clubs can meet at any time. But Twentieth Century education is not necessarily geared to the neighborhood school.

From *Western Reserve Law Review,* May, 1965, pp. 489–501. Footnotes omitted. Reprinted by permission of the publisher.

In fact, the trend is definitely in the opposite direction. Educational parks, each consisting of a complex of schools, science buildings, libraries, gymnasiums, auditoriums, and playing fields are beginning to replace the neighborhood school. Although the development of the educational park idea in education is unrelated to the question of racial segregation, its use in relieving racial imbalance in public schools is obvious. Instead of having neighborhood schools scattered through racially homogeneous residential areas, children of all races may be brought together in the educational parks.

In many areas where the educational park is not feasible, simple changes in the existing school district lines may relieve racial imbalance. For example, the homogeneous character of a school in a segregated neighborhood may be changed by redrawing its district lines along with the district lines of the nearest white school so as to include Negro and white pupils in both schools. Also, under the well known Princeton Plan, where the district lines of two racially diverse schools are contiguous, the racial imbalance can be relieved by limiting the grades in one school from kindergarten to third and in the other from fourth to sixth. And where new schools are to be built to accommodate the expanding school population, the sites for those schools should not be in Negro or white residential areas, but near the dividing line so that the children living in both areas may be included in each school district. These plans, alone or in combination, when properly used, may well suffice to eliminate the inequality arising from the segregated school in most areas. But in some sections of our large cities, because of the density of the residential segregation, Negro schools are back to back. Princeton Plans and the like are not geared to this problem, but educational parks do provide the answer to Harlem-type residential situations. And pending the construction of the educational parks, open enrollment may be used as a temporary expedient.

B. *Relieving Inequality Between Suburban and City Schools.* An even more difficult problem is presented by the flight of the white population to the suburbs. The pattern is the same all over the country. The Negro child remains within the political boundaries of the city and attends the segregated slum school in his neighborhood, while the white child attends the vastly superior white public schools in the suburbs. The situation is accurately described in the 1964 Advisory Panel Report to the Board of Education of the City of Chicago:

Finally, it cannot be too strongly stressed that programs to effect school integration must reckon with the fact that the white elementary school child is already in the minority in the public schools of Chicago and the time is not far off when the same will be true of the white high school student. Unless the exodus of white population from the public schools and from the City is brought to a halt or reversed, the question of school integration may become simply a theoretical matter, as it is already in the nation's capital. For integration, in fact, cannot be achieved without white students.

While a court, in proposing or approving a plan of desegregation, may find no great difficulty in ordering the local school authorities to use the Princeton Plan, or one of its variants, or, under the authority of *Griffin v. County School Bd.*, in ordering the local taxing authority or the state to levy taxes to raise funds to build an educational park, relieving the inequality between the suburban public school and the segregated city slum public school presents a greater challenge. Obviously, court orders running to local officials will not reach the suburbs. Nevertheless, when political lines rather than school district lines shield the inequality, as shown in the reapportionment cases, courts are not helpless to act. The political thicket, having been pierced to protect the vote, can likewise be pierced to protect the education of children.

Education, as stated in *Brown,* is "the most important function of the state." And, as shown in *Hall v. St. Helena Parish School Bd.,* and *Griffin v. County School Bd.,* that important function must be administered in all parts of the state with an even hand. The State operates local public schools through its agents, the local school boards. It directly supplies part of the money for that operation, it certifies the teachers, it accredits the schools, and, through its department of education, it maintains constant supervision over the entire operation. The involvement of the state in the operation of its public schools is complete. Indeed, the state is the conduit through which federal money in increasing amounts is being funnelled into the public schools. Certainly federal money may not be used to indurate an inequality. Thus, no state-created political lines can protect the state against the constitutional command of equal protection for its citizens, or relieve the state from the obligation of providing educational opportunities for its Negro slum children equal to those provided for its white children in the affluent suburbs.

When the Supreme Court decided the first reapportionment case, *Baker v. Carr,* just as when it decided *Brown,* it left to the district courts the task of fashioning the remedy. Undoubtedly, if and when the Supreme Court tackles the suburban problem vis-à-vis the city slum school problem, it will again remit the remedy to the district courts with instructions to ignore the state-created political lines separating the school boards; and it will make its orders run directly against state as well as local officials.

VI. The Question of Judicial Intervention

I am aware, of course, that what is said here will not find favor with the advocates of judicial restraint—many of whom have already expressed the view that *de facto* segregation is a political and social matter which requires a political, not a judicial, solution; that the Congress and the states are equipped to remedy any inequality which may exist in the public schools, and that any attempted judicial resolution of the problem would adversely affect the balance of our federalism by trenching on states' rights.

These objections to judicial intervention into *de facto* segregation all have a slightly familiar ring. The Supreme Court's opinion in *Brown* was subjected to just such criticism. Yet because of that decision definite progress has been made toward the recognition of Negro rights. The Court's action unquestionably moved other branches of government to act. Is there anyone who seriously thinks that the Civil Rights Act of 1964 would be a reality today without *Brown* and other Supreme Court decisions exposing racial injustice? Is it conceivable that the Southern states would have abolished segregation compelled by law without prodding from the federal courts?

The reapportionment cases are also in point. Does anyone really believe that the state legislatures would have reformed themselves? Legislators elected via the rotten borough system ordinarily would not be expected to vote for its abolition. Perhaps the reapportionment cases do trench on states' rights, but the people who now have a full vote are not complaining.

The advocates of judicial restraint have also been critical of the Supreme Court's work in the field of criminal justice. It is true that the Court has insisted on civilized procedures in state as well as federal criminal courts. An accused in a serious criminal case must now have a lawyer available to represent him, coerced confessions must be excluded from state and federal criminal trials, and state as well as federal police must now respect the fourth amendment. How long should the Supreme Court have waited for the states to civilize their own criminal procedures before it undertook to protect the constitutional rights of persons accused of crime?

The Supreme Court's intervention into these fields of primary state responsibility was not precipitous. The states were given ample opportunity to correct the evils themselves. Before *Brown*, the Supreme Court handed down a series of decisions in the field of education indicating quite clearly that if the states did not act to eliminate racial segregation compelled by law it would. The persistence with which reapportionment cases continued to reach the Supreme Court after it had refused to exercise jurisdiction in *Colegrove v. Green*, should have been warning enough to the states that one way or the other vote dilution was on the way out. And civilizing of state criminal procedures under gentle urging from the Supreme Court has been going on since *Brown v. Mississippi*, where the Court set aside a death sentence based solely on a confession obtained by hanging the accused from a tree.

There is no indication that the Supreme Court will rush into the *de facto* segregation arena. Two circuit courts of appeals have already denied relief from *de facto* segregation and the Supreme Court has stayed its hand. But this is no guarantee that the Court will not act if the problem persists and the states fail to correct the evil. Proper judicial restraint does not include a failure to act where a state has abdicated its responsibility to protect the constitutional rights of its citizens.

John Kaplan

PLESSY AND ITS PROGENY

The noted legal scholar John Kaplan has devoted much of his legal research to the study of *de facto* school segregation litigation in the North. His in-depth study of the general Northern problem and, specifically, *Bell v. School City of Gary, Indiana*, have brought him considerable respect from both legal scholars and educators. In "Plessy and Its Progeny," Kaplan describes several of the noneducation-oriented cases which preceded *Brown v. Board of Education of Topeka, Kansas*.

In any examination of the Supreme Court's treatment of segregation in education, the fountainhead case must be *Plessy v. Ferguson*, decided in 1896. Plessy brought an action to forestall his criminal prosecution for violation of a Louisiana statute requiring Negro and white passengers to ride in equal but separate railway cars. Plessy, who had attempted to

From John Kaplan, "Segregation Litigation and the Schools, Part II: The General Northern Problem," *Northwestern University Law Review*, May–June, 1963, pp. 157–167. Reprinted by permission of the author and publisher.

ride in the car reserved for whites, alleged that he was not a Negro, being of seven-eighths Caucasian blood and, further, charged that in any event the statute requiring this racial segregation was unconstitutional. The Supreme Court found it necessary only to consider the latter question and upheld the segregation statute against constitutional challenge. The impact of the *Plessy* case would not have been so great had the Court confined its decision to segregation on railway cars which, after all, affects only a relatively small percentage of the population for relatively short periods of time. The opinion of the Court, however, was much broader than required by the facts of the case before it, and relied in great part upon the authority of previous state court decisions allowing segregation of white and colored races in the schools. For this reason the Court's reasoning was taken as a blanket declaration that in all areas, so long as facilities were equal, state-imposed segregation was inoffensive to the Constitution.

In approving the separate but equal doctrine, the Court had to meet two basic arguments. First, Plessy's attorney contended that if segregation on the basis of race were permitted, other types of segregation would have to be allowed, such as of those "whose hair is of a certain color, or who are aliens, or who belong to certain nationalities," and that it would be permissible to enact "laws requiring colored people to walk on one side of the street and white people upon the other, upon the theory that one side of the street is as good as the other." The Court, however, stated:

The reply to this is that every exercise of the police power must be reasonable and extends only to such laws as are indicated in good faith for the promotion of the public good, and not for the annoyance or oppression of a particular class.

This facet of the Court's reasoning would seem much more appropriate to overturning the statute than to upholding it. While an examination of the Louisiana statute alone might not show any "oppression of a particular class," the historical context of the statute makes its basic motivation and effect crystal clear. The segregation statutes enacted by the various Southern states were part of a concerted plan to remove the newly freed slaves from the political, social, and economic life of the South. For instance, in 1896, the year *Plessy* was decided, 130,334 Negro voters were registered in Louisiana. Eight years later, this number had been cut almost a hundredfold to 1,342. Similar effects were accomplished in other Southern states. Moreover, political rights were not the only ones affected by this movement. Statutes such as that of South Carolina which prohibited employers from allowing white and Negro workers to work together in the same room or to use the same entrances or toilets made it uneconomical for employers to hire Negro workers, other than as floor scrubbers who, by an exception to this segregation edict, were allowed to associate with white men in the factory. So long as the Court, as it did in *Plessy*, viewed the segregation issue as a simple, enforced separation between two equal groups, it could find no oppression. The fact was, however, that the white race in the South was dominant in terms of economic and political power. It would seem that the attempt by the state government to use its authority to accomplish the isolation of the Negro from this power would be oppressive enough.

Plessy's next argument, that both the motive of those exacting segregation statutes and the effect of such acts was to disadvantage the Negro psychologically, was answered by the Court:

We consider the underlying fallacy of the plaintiff's argument to consist in the assumption that enforced separation of the two races stamps the colored race with a badge of inferiority. If this be so, it is not by reason of anything found in the Act, but solely because the colored race choose to put that construction upon it.

Again, although it may be difficult to imply any assertion of inferiority in the bland requirement that separate railway cars be provided for the two races, the contention assumes a different light when the context of segregation is considered. Many Southern states have held that a white person can recover damages for the humiliation of being forced to sit next to a Negro in a common carrier. Moreover, the Court's assertion that segregation did not in any way imply inferiority of the Negro is somewhat inaccurate as applied to jurisdictions which regard the imputation of Negro blood to a white man as so serious a charge that recovery may be allowed without any proof of damages.

Lastly, the Court buttressed its reasoning by asserting that segregation was not an evil since legislative and constitutional provisions, in any event, could not achieve equality for the Negro. "If the two races are to meet upon terms of social equality, it must be the result of natural affinities, a mutual appreciation of each other's merits and a voluntary consent of individuals."

This argument might be perfectly appropriate to a situation where the state by statute had attempted forcibly to mix the races, but here exactly the opposite situation was at issue. Here the state was attempting to prevent just the individual contact which the Supreme Court asserted was essential to equality.

The *Plessy v. Ferguson* decision may be explained, if not defended, by noting that it was decided relatively near the beginning of the drive to exclude the Negro from participation in the life of the Southern states. Since this drive reached full momentum only after the turn of the century, the Supreme Court may very well have not appreciated how completely state law would disadvantage the Negro. Viewed in this manner, the decision was wrong when it was handed down, although perhaps only a Court especially sensitive to the political mood of the South might have realized this at that time.

With the benefit of hindsight, the doctrine of *Plessy v. Ferguson* might be counted wrong on another, more pragmatic, ground. It is fair to say that, at least as applied to public education, the separate but equal doctrine in practice had turned out to be a failure. The Negro schools, which were undeniably separate, were generally by no means equal in their most obvious physical characteristics, let alone in more subtle matters such as their quality of education. For instance, in 1950, some 54 years after *Plessy v. Ferguson,* Mississippi, which had almost equal numbers of white and Negro students, had half again as many teachers in the white schools. Moreover, the widespread belief that from the 1940's on, the Southern states had moved with great energy and rapidity to ease the obvious inequalities in its schools, seems to be refuted by statistics. For instance, in 1952, 56 years after *Plessy*, rather than spending more on the Negro student to close the gap previously created between him and the white student, Mississippi's current educational expenditure per Negro pupil was 30 per cent of that per white pupil; South Carolina's was 60 per cent; Arkansas', 66 per cent; and Georgia's, 68 per cent. Roughly similar figures could be given for the capital expenditures on Negro and white schools. With only two exceptions, Southern states, rather than attempting to make up the deficiency in quality of buildings between white and Negro schools, were still spending more per pupil on the white schools. Georgia was spending 53 per cent as much per pupil on Negro school construction as on white school construction; Alabama, 60 per cent; South Carolina, 46 per cent. Generally, the same type of disparity was noticeable in the salaries paid teachers, the number of books purchased for school libraries, and almost every other characteristic investigated.

The reported lower court cases highlighted the flouting of *Plessy v. Ferguson* more graphically than could mere statistics. In a not atypical case in 1949, over 50 years after *Plessy*, the district court found that the city of DeWitt, Arkansas, provided a Negro elementary school which differed from the white one in that it had no indoor drinking fountain, an outdoor open pit instead of indoor toilet facilities, and furniture which the court characterized as "outmoded and in bad repair." In addition, the term in the Negro school was one month shorter than that in the white school. As if this inequality were not great enough, the community had embarked upon the construction of a new white elementary school which the court characterized as "luxurious." This additional white elementary school was being built at a cost of $140,000, as contrasted with the Negro school's value of $6,000. Nor was the discrepancy in the elementary schools the only one faced by the Negro students; while the DeWitt High School had an A rating, the Negro high school, some distance away, had a rating of only C. In this situation, however, the court decided that the admission of Negro children to the white schools was "not necessary for the protection of the constitutional rights of the plaintiffs."

The separate but equal doctrine was a failure not only because it was so openly and widely flouted, but because it was impossible to administer rationally. While equality of one railway car with another was susceptible of reasonably accurate measurement, equality of schools was not. For instance, how was a court to balance the fact that a Negro high school was in a newer building against the fact that it was a forty minute bus ride away for Negro students who lived within easy walking distance of a white high school? How could a court balance the availability of fine courses in woodworking in the Negro schools with the absence of a course in trigonometry there? As one district court judge stated,

[The separate but equal doctrine] present[s] problems which are more than judicial and which involve elements of public finance, school administration, politics, and sociology. . . . The federal courts are not school boards; they are not prepared to take over the administration of the public schools of the several states.

The treatment of *Plessy* over the years in the Supreme Court shows a gradually growing awareness of its inadequacy. The first case applying the *Plessy* doctrine to education, and the high-water mark of the doctrine itself, was *Cummings v. Board of Education*, decided just three years after *Plessy*. There the Supreme Court was faced with a situation in which a Georgia county maintained a high school for white children but none for Negroes on the ground that it could not afford to maintain both.

The Court, in an opinion by Justice Harlan, who had dissented vigorously in *Plessy*, admitted that the benefits and burdens of public taxation must be shared by all citizens without discrimination against any class on account of their race. It went on to hold, however, that since the county had discontinued its operation of the Negro high school only temporarily and because of economic pressures, it had not violated the constitutional rights of the Negro students who were without any school. The Court therefore refused to enjoin expenditures on the white high school until Negroes could have equal rights.

The next case involving segregation in education came before the Court nine years later. There, in the case of *Berea College v. Kentucky*, the Court upheld the validity of a statute which provided that no educational institution could teach both white and Negro students at the same time. The Court's opinion did not even cite *Plessy v. Ferguson*, but rather proceeded on an entirely different ground—that the state had an absolute authority to control the corporations which it had chartered and hence could require them to segregate. The Court, however, did recognize that if the state attempted to prevent an individual, as distinguished from a corporation, from teaching white and Negro students together, "Such a [segregation] statute may conflict with the Federal Constitution in denying to individuals powers which they may rightfully exercise." . . . No reported case appears to have raised this question, however.

The first real indication of any weakening in the *Plessy* philosophy came 21 years after *Plessy* in *Buchanan v. Warley*, where the Court was confronted with a zoning ordinance which in effect segregated an entire city by race. Although the Court stated that *Plessy* was controlling insofar as segregation in education and transportation were concerned, it refused to carry the doctrine into the field of housing. It is difficult to determine the precise reasoning of the Court since the notions of civil rights for Negroes and property rights to dispose of land seem inextricably interwined in the opinion. *Buchanan*, however, did reject a rationale which, although unexpressed in the *Plessy* opinion, had been one of the primary justifications for all types of segregation. The Court stated:

It is urged that this proposed segregation will promote the public peace by preventing race conflicts. Desirable as this is, and important as is the preservation of the public peace, this aim cannot be accomplished by laws or ordinances which deny rights created or protected by the federal Constitution.

Buchanan v. Warley is significant for yet another reason. It has been suggested that the case rests on the historical idea that each piece of land is unique and therefore it makes no sense to talk about equality of land within the separate but equal doctrine. If this is so, one might argue that no great insight into the educational process is required to see that a school and its student body are at least as unique as a piece of land.

Ten years later, in *Gong Lum v. Rice,* the Supreme Court was faced with its first case involving actual segregation in public education. There, however, the validity of the *Plessy* doctrine was conceded by the plaintiff, who was Chinese. He merely insisted that children of Chinese descent were properly placed in the white, as distinct from the colored, schools. The Court held that the state had the power, under the *Plessy* decision and cases cited therein, to classify Chinese in the same category as Negroes. In its opinion, however, the Court not only pointed up the fact that the validity of the *Plessy* doctrine had been conceded, but seemed gratuitously to cast a certain doubt upon it. The opinion by Chief Justice Taft stated that had it not been so often previously approved, the *Plessy* doctrine would call for "very full argument and consideration," and ruled against the plaintiff, "assuming the cases [such as *Plessy*] to be rightly decided. . . ."

It was not until 1938, in *Missouri ex rel. Gaines v. Canada,* that the Supreme Court struck down a state statute providing for segregation in education. Missouri maintained a law school for whites only and no equal, or even unequal, one for Negroes. Rather it offered to pay the tuition of any Missouri Negro at a law school in an adjacent state. In an opinion by Chief Justice Hughes, the Court rejected the state's contention that by paying tuition at equal law schools it had complied with the *Plessy* doctrine. Although Chief Justice Hughes seemed to base his decision entirely on the principle that a state was not providing equal education by requiring resort to another state's facilities, he did advert to the possibility that "equality" under the separate but equal doctrine might mean more than simple parity in physical facilities.

Twelve years after the *Gaines* case, in 1950, the Supreme Court was given an opportunity actually to analyze the ingredients of equality under the *Plessy* doctrine. The Court in two companion opinions, both written by Chief Justice Vinson, examined not only the intangible values associated with a particular school, but also considered the educational process itself. In *Sweatt v. Painter* the Court went beyond the mere physical facilities to find Texas' Negro law school inferior to Texas Law School in "those qualities which are incapable of objective measurement." These included the position and influence of the alumni, standing in the community, traditions and prestige. Moreover, for the first time in this context, the Court overtly recognized that in the United States the two races were not on an equal footing. It stated that the segregation deprived the Negro of educational contact with the dominant racial groups, which comprised 85 per cent of the population of the state and included most of the lawyers, jurors, judges, and other officials with whom a lawyer inevitably deals. On the same day that *Sweatt v. Painter* was decided, the Supreme Court handed down *McLaurin v. Oklahoma State Regents,* involving a closely related issue. There, Oklahoma, while admitting the Negro petitioner to its graduate school, had insisted that he conform to certain regulations:

Thus he was required to sit apart at a designated desk in an anteroom adjoining the classroom; to sit at a designated desk on the mezzanine floor of the library, but not to use the desks in the regular reading room; and to sit at a designated table and to eat at a different time from the other students in the school cafeteria.

The Court held that these restrictions "impair and inhibit his ability to study, to engage in discussions, and exchange views with other students and, in general, to learn his profession." Chief Justice Vinson's opinion then struck another blow at the separate but equal doctrine and the rationale of *Plessy* by stating:

There is a vast difference—a Constitutional difference—between restrictions imposed by the state which prohibit the intellectual commingling of students, and the refusal of individuals to commingle where the state presents no such bar.

Accordingly, when the Brown case and four other cases challenging state-imposed segregation in public grade and high schools finally reached the Supreme Court in 1952, the question was not so much whether the *Plessy* doctrine would be overruled as how it would be overruled. . . .

Stephen F. Roach

THE FEDERAL COURTS AND RACIAL IMBALANCE IN PUBLIC SCHOOLS

In this article, Stephen F. Roach of Boston College, School of Education, noted school law authority and long-time editor of the prestigious *School Law Review,* discusses several significant federal court decisions

From *Phi Delta Kappan,* January, 1966, pp. 254–257. Some footnotes omitted. Reprinted by permission of the author and publisher.

between 1954 and 1965 in an effort to summarize what the courts have said concerning *de facto* segregation and racial imbalance in Northern public school systems. The inconsistencies in lower federal court decisions become apparent as one reads this descriptive article, but it must be remembered that these conflicting decisions accumulated because the Supreme Court had not as yet acted in *de facto* segregation cases. There have of course been several important decisions since 1965 which have been designed to test the role of the courts in influencing local educational decision-making. The most significant of these, as already noted, has been the *Hobson v. Hansen* case. Another important decision, however, was that of Judge Alfred Getelson, in which he accused the Los Angeles Board of Education in 1970 of deliberately perpetuating segregation among students and then instructed the board to develop a plan that would lead to immediate integration of all schools in the city.

One of the more significant questions raised by the increasingly controversial struggle for Negro equality in the field of civil rights is whether the racial imbalance [1] which now exists in some Northern and Western urban public school systems is to be corrected.

An analysis of recent decisions in the higher federal courts, for the purpose of determining the legal principles which these courts considered to be controlling in this regard, should be of value. A compilation of such principles should be of particular interest to public school authorities, local or state, who may themselves be faced with the issue at some future date.

A starting point in any discussion of racial imbalance in the schools is the basic principle, established by the U.S. Supreme Court in its decision in the 1954 case of *Brown vs. Board of Education of Topeka* (347 U.S. 483), that racial discrimination in public education is contrary to the "equal protection" clause of the Fourteenth Amendment. State or local school authorities are therefore prohibited from maintaining racially segregated public schools.

The *Brown* decision is of course a landmark in the field of school segregation litigation. A brief further examination of it will be worthwhile.

In this case, Brown and other Negro children living in Topeka, Kansas, had been denied admission to certain elementary schools attended by white children on the basis of a Kansas statute which permitted cities to maintain separate school facilities for Negro and white students. On the strength of this statute, the Topeka Board of Education had chosen to segregate its elementary schools.

---

[1] In this paper, "racial imbalance" will be the term used to describe the situation where, in a community's public schools, Negro pupils are largely concentrated in one set of schools and white pupils in another.

In bringing their suit, the Brown children contended, essentially, that segregated public schools were not, and could not be, "equal" to nonsegregated schools; therefore the children were being deprived of equal protection of the laws guaranteed to them by the Fourteenth Amendment. By a unanimous vote, the Supreme Court agreed with this contention.

It is perhaps important to note that the highest federal court specifically described the issue in this case in these words: "Does segregation of children in public schools solely on the basis of race deprive the children . . . [so segregated] of equal educational opportunities?" To this query the court answered: "We believe that it does."

The Brown case, as brought, clearly dealt with de jure segregation in public schools, i.e., segregation overtly forced or imposed by the action of governmental authority, in this instance by the resolution of the local school board. Brown, per se, did not involve de facto segregation.[2] However, in its decision and throughout its opinion, the court uses the term "segregation" unmodified by either de jure or de facto.

For example, the opinion says:

Our decision . . . must look . . . to the effect of segregation itself on public education. . . . We must consider . . . if segregation in public schools deprives these [children] of the equal protection of the laws. (pp. 492–93)

Segregation of white and colored children in public schools has a detrimental effect upon the colored children. The impact is greater when it has the sanction of law; for the policy of separating the races is usually interpreted as denoting the inferiority of the Negro group. (p. 494)

We conclude that in the field of public education the doctrine of "separate but equal" has no place. Separate educational facilities are inherently unequal. (p. 495)

Segregation [in public education] is a denial of the equal protection of the laws. (p. 495)

A Controlling Principle

In any event, Brown furnishes the fundamental controlling principle:
1. *Racial discrimination in the public schools violates the U.S. Constitution.*

Brown makes clear also that all provisions of federal, state, or local

[2] De facto segregation, as used herein, refers to the adventitious racial concentration of Negro students caused by such circumstances as housing patterns, job availability, a preponderantly white enrollment in the nonpublic schools, plus the utilization of a "neighborhood school" policy in the public schools and its concomitant "attendance zone" districting. Racial imbalance may thus be a result of de facto segregation.

law requiring or permitting such racial discrimination must yield to this principle.

The rationale behind this basic principle would appear to be that segregation based on race is an unlawful denial of equal educational opportunity. It will help if this rationale is kept in mind as we turn our attention to what the next-highest federal courts, i.e., the several U.S. Courts of Appeals, have recently said concerning racial imbalance in Northern and Western public school systems. In 1964 and 1965 these courts were asked to rule with regard to school racial imbalance litigation arising in Indiana, Kansas, Massachusetts, and New York.

U.S. Courts of Appeals

Gary, Indiana: In chronological order, the first case arose in Gary, where under the public school system's "neighborhood school" policy pupils residing within a particular school's "attendance zone," as that zone had been determined by the school authorities, were expected to attend that school. Requests for the transfer of students between schools were handled, generally, on an individual basis. A request was allowed, or denied, depending "upon the apparent reasonableness and desirability of the transfer."

Negro children, who made up some 53 per cent of the public school enrollment at the time of the suit, protested: 1) their assignment, under the system's neighborhood school plan, to certain predominantly Negro schools; and 2) the proposal of the Gary school authorities to locate schools—and draw school attendance zone lines—entirely within the predominantly Negro areas of the city. The Negro children contended, essentially, that: 1) regardless of school attendance zone boundaries or the place of residence of its Negro students, the Gary school authorities had a constitutional duty to provide a racially integrated school system; and 2) the Gary school authorities, by establishing school attendance zones entirely within the predominantly Negro areas, were purposely maintaining a racially segregated school system in violation of the Fourteenth Amendment.

This suit resulted, eventually, in the U.S. Court of Appeals for the Seventh Circuit affirming a lower federal (district) court judgment that the Gary Board of Education was not *required,* under the federal Constitution, to take steps to eliminate or reduce the racial imbalance which admittedly existed in the Gary public school system. In its opinion, the Court of Appeals made the following significant comments: 1) The U.S.

Constitution does not compel integration or racial balance in the schools, it merely forbids discrimination; 2) The mere fact that certain schools in a public school system are completely or predominantly Negro does not necessarily mean that the school authorities are maintaining a segregated school system; and 3) a "neighborhood school" plan, honestly and conscientiously constructed with no intention to segregate the races, need not be abandoned because a resulting effect is to have a racial imbalance in certain schools.

In May, 1964, the U.S. Supreme Court refused to review the Court of Appeals decision.[3]

Kansas City, Kansas: The next case originated in a public school system which also operated under a neighborhood school plan. In addition, a "feeder-school" policy was also in effect, under which students from a particular elementary school, upon graduation, were required to attend a designated junior high school.

In 1960, "in order to equalize the student load," the local board had divided the attendance zone then in effect for one of its predominantly Negro elementary schools, with the result that those graduates who resided in the area of heaviest Negro concentration in the attendance zone were assigned to a predominantly Negro junior high school. Previously, all the elementary school's graduates were fed into a predominantly white junior high school. Along with the 1960 order, the board adopted a policy of granting transfer permits to students who wished to transfer from a school "where a majority of the students are of a different race."

Negro children living in the areas which, under the new board order, would feed into the predominantly Negro junior high school (rather than into a predominantly white one, as heretofore) sued to enjoin the board from carrying out the change. The case was decided in the U.S. Court of Appeals, Tenth Circuit, in September, 1964.

Basically, the Tenth Circuit ruling reiterated the October, 1963, Seventh Circuit decision in the Gary case and held that the Kansas City Board of Education was under no obligation, under the federal Constitution, to correct racial imbalance. This court made the following noteworthy comment: "A 'neighborhood school' plan is not objectionable in

[3] While the practical effect of such refusal may be to allow the decision of the lower court to stand, it must not be concluded—as is done all too frequently—that such refusal also means that the Supreme Court *approved* the lower court decision. A refusal to review means no more than that the Supreme Court, for reasons of its own, which it may or may not choose to reveal, does not wish to hear and decide a case on its merits, *at the time.*

the absence of a showing that it is being operated so as to discriminate against students because of their race or color."

It is of interest to note that this court also enunciated three significant *restrictions* on local board procedures relating to racial imbalance in its schools: 1) The local board could not justify continuing the unlawful segregation of Negro students on the ground that the classrooms in a predominantly white school, to which the Negro students could conceivably be transferred, were "already overcrowded." 2) The local board could not operate a "feeder" policy under which Negro elementary pupils were routinely promoted to predominantly Negro junior high schools and which required such pupils, when they applied for transfers to predominantly white schools, to meet criteria to which white transferees were not subject; and 3) The local board could not classify students by race, for transfer purposes, by adopting a rule under which a student might transfer out of a desegregated school if a majority of the students in that school were of a different race.

The court made two other significant comments: 1) The school authorities, rather than the courts, must assume the burden of initiating desegregation in the public schools, since it is the former who "have the primary responsibility for assessing and solving" the local school problems thus arising; and 2) "The constitutional right of a student not to be discriminated against in the public schools on grounds of race or color . . . can neither be nullified openly and directly by state legislators or state executive or judicial officers, nor nullified indirectly by them through evasive schemes for segregation whether attempted ingeniously or ingenuously."

In March, 1965, the U.S. Supreme Court refused to review this decision.

Springfield, Massachusetts: The third case originated in Springfield, Massachusetts, in which city the elementary and junior high schools were operated under a "neighborhood school" policy, with the children generally required to attend the school within the attendance zone in which they lived.

Negro children residing in areas with a heavy racial concentration brought suit to bar the school authorities from assigning them to schools with predominantly Negro enrollments. The children contended that the Springfield School Committee's continued rigid adherence to its neighborhood school policy, in combination with the existing racial imbalance in certain schools, was tantamount to governmentally imposed segregation.

The testimony showed that in September, 1963, prior to the institution of this suit, the Springfield School Committee had recognized that integrated education was desirable and had resolved to "take whatever action is necessary to eliminate, to the fullest extent possible, racial concentration in these schools within the framework of effective educational procedures." These voluntary activities ceased, assertedly on advice of counsel, upon the institution of this suit in January, 1964.

This case resulted in a First Circuit U.S. Court of Appeals ruling in July, 1965, to the effect that the federal Constitution does not require, as an absolute right, the removal of racial imbalance in the public schools as being tantamount to segregation.

It is perhaps significant to note also, in connection with this case, that the U.S. Court of Appeals, though it did not agree with the earlier U.S. District Court decision that the Springfield school authorities should be ordered to prepare and present "a plan to eliminate to the fullest extent possible racial concentration," did make the following comment: "If defendants [Springfield School Committee] permanently disregard their previously announced purpose to reduce imbalance so far as educationally feasible, a new action may be brought to determine whether the plaintiffs are, in that event, entitled to relief." It was the view of the U.S. Court of Appeals here that no such local school committee plan was necessary *at this time,* since the committee had, prior to the suit, recognized the necessity for such a plan.

Additional Controlling Principles

Thus, if we summarize the controlling legal principles which were advanced in 1964–65 by the three U.S. Courts of Appeals cited, we might add the following to the one already mentioned:

2. Because a particular public school is completely or predominantly Negro does not necessarily mean that the school authorities are unlawfully maintaining a segregated school system.

3. The U.S. Constitution does not compel racial balance in the public schools; hence a local school board is under no constitutional obligation to correct existing racial imbalance in the schools.

4. A "neighborhood school" plan, constructed originally with no intention to segregate the races, need not later be abandoned because it

results in racial imbalance in certain schools, unless it can be shown to be operating so as to discriminate against students because of their race or color.

5. School authorities, rather than the courts, must initiate actions to correct the racial imbalance in the schools.

U.S. Supreme Court

As we have already seen, the U.S. Supreme Court has held that governmentally imposed racial segregation is unconstitutional. It has not yet spoken directly concerning racial imbalance in the schools, *per se,* though we have seen that it refused to review the U.S. Courts of Appeals decisions in two of the three cases we have discussed.

Though we must not read more into the U.S. Supreme Court's refusal to review than is justified, it cannot be denied that the practical effect of these refusals—one in May, 1964, the other in March, 1965—was to leave standing the pertinent U.S. Court of Appeals decisions. The thrust of these earlier decisions—as is evident from the controlling principles enumerated above—is that local school authorities are under no federal constitutional duty to correct racial imbalance in the public schools.

On the other hand, it should be noted that on three other occasions— in October, 1964, in October, 1965, and in November, 1965—the Supreme Court also refused to review still other lower court decisions relating to racial imbalance in the schools. In each of these cases the lower court rulings had held that there was no federal constitutional bar to local (or state) school authorities *taking steps, if they wished, to correct* racial imbalance.

In the first case, the New York City Board of Education had determined to take the factor of racial balance into account in establishing the attendance zone boundaries for a new school; in the second, the state school authorities had ordered the Malverne, N.Y., local school board to reorganize its attendance zone boundaries so as to eliminate racial imbalance; and in the third, the New York City local board determined to pair a predominantly Negro elementary school with a nearby predominantly white school in order to correct racial imbalance.

A Final Controlling Principle

As has been pointed out earlier, it is misleading and often erroneous to attempt to read any positive significance into the refusal of the U.S.

Supreme Court to review a case. And that caveat most assuredly applies here.

But I wonder if some significance might not be found in the fact that on the five occasions—two in 1964 and three in 1965—when the Supreme Court did refuse to review school racial imbalance cases, the effect of those refusals has been to uphold the contentions that: 1) the school authorities *have no constitutional obligation* to correct racial imbalance in the public schools; or 2) school authorities *are not constitutionally prohibited from taking steps* to correct such imbalance, *if they wish to do so.*

Thus, I submit that to the five controlling judicial principles developed earlier, one other might be added:

6. *While local school authorities may have no affirmative constitutional duty to correct racial imbalance in the schools, there is no constitutional bar to prevent them from taking reasonable steps to do so should they so desire.*

This last principle is obviously not as firmly grounded as the five others, being based only on what are considered to be the logical implications of the U.S. Supreme Court's refusal to review certain cases during 1964 and 1965.

Obviously, this last principle, along with the four based on the decisions of the U.S. Courts of Appeals, can be modified or even overturned by the Supreme Court at such time as it chooses to rule on the issue of racial imbalance in the schools.

But until that time the judicial principles herein developed might well serve as helpful guidelines for action by public school authorities faced with school racial imbalance controversies.

The preceding descriptive selections show the rapidly increasing influence of the courts on local educational decision-making. One is immediately struck by the many ramifications of court intervention in school policy-making, particularly for social institutions other than the school. But equally important to the prospective teacher is the threat to the education profession created by the apparent trespassing of the courts on formerly inviolable areas of educational expertise. The problem of racial imbalance in large Northern cities has brought into clear focus many of the conflicting goals of the courts and the public schools that will eventually have to be resolved by the Supreme Court.

HOBSON V. HANSEN (SUMMARY)

These excerpts from *Hobson v. Hansen* illustrate the role of the courts as an influence in educational decision-making. The *Hobson* case suggests the immensity of the societal problems confronted by big-city school systems which have large minority populations, and it exemplifies the recent so-called dictatorial trend on the part of judges to use the schools for curing social ills.

[1] In *Bolling v. Sharpe,* 347 U.S. 497, 74 S.Ct. 693, 98 L.Ed. 884 (1954), the Supreme Court held that the District of Columbia's racially segregated public school system violated the due process clause of the Fifth Amendment. The present litigation, brought in behalf of Negro as well as poor children generally in the District's public schools, tests the current compliance of those schools with the principles announced in *Bolling,* its companion case *Brown v. Board of Education of Topeka,* 347 U.S. 483, 74 S.Ct. 686, 98 L.Ed. 873 (1954), and their progeny. The basic question presented is whether the defendants, the Superintendent of Schools and the members of the Board of Education, in the operation of the public school system here, unconstitutionally deprive the District's Negro and poor public school children of their right to equal educational opportunity with the District's white and more affluent public school children. This court concludes that they do.

In support of this conclusion the court makes the following principal findings of fact:

1. Racially and socially homogeneous schools damage the minds and spirit of all children who attend them—the Negro, the white, the poor and the affluent—and block the attainment of the broader goals of democratic education, whether the segregation occurs by law or by fact.

2. The scholastic achievement of the disadvantaged child, Negro and white, is strongly related to the racial and socio-economic composition of the student body of his school. A racially and socially integrated school environment increases the scholastic achievement of the disadvantaged child of whatever race.

3. The Board of Education, which is the statutory head of the public schools in the District, is appointed pursuant to a quota system which, until 1962, for over half a century had limited the Negro membership of

U.S. Federal Court 269, Federal Supplement 401, 1967.

the nine-man Board to three. Since 1962 the Negro quota on the Board has been four, one less than a majority. The city of Washington, which is the District of Columbia, presently has a population over 60% Negro and a public school population over 90% Negro.

4. Adherence to the neighborhood school policy by the School Board effectively segregates the Negro and the poor children from the white and the more affluent children in most of the District's public schools. This neighborhood school policy is relaxed by the Board through the use of optional zones for the purpose of allowing white children, usually affluent white children, "trapped" in a Negro school district, to "escape" to a "white" or more nearly white school, thus making the economic and racial segregation of the public school children more complete than it would otherwise be under a strict neighborhood school assignment plan.

5. The teachers and principals in the public schools are assigned so that generally the race of the faculty is the same as the race of the children. Thus most of the schools can be identified as "Negro" or "white," not only by reference to the predominant race of the children attending, but by the predominant race of the faculty as well. The heaviest concentration of Negro faculty, usually 100%, is in the Negro ghetto schools.

6. The median annual per pupil expenditure ($292) in the predominantly (85–100%) Negro elementary schools in the District of Columbia has been a flat $100 below the median annual per pupil expenditure for its predominantly (85–100%) white schools ($392).

7. Generally the "white" schools are underpopulated while the "Negro" schools generally are overcrowded. Moreover, all of the white elementary schools have kindergartens. Some Negro schools are without kindergartens entirely while other Negro schools operate kindergartens in shifts or consecutive sessions. In addition to being overcrowded and short on kindergarten space, the school buildings in the Negro slums are ancient and run down. Only recently, through the use of impact aid and other federal funds, have the Negro slum schools had sufficient textbooks for the children's use.

8. As they proceed through the Washington school system, the reading scores primarily of the Negro and poor children, but not the white and middle class, fall increasingly behind the national norm. By senior high school the discrepancy reaches several grades.

9. The track system as used in the District's public schools is a form of ability grouping in which students are divided in separate, self-contained curricula or tracks ranging from "Basic" for the slow student to "Honors" for the gifted.

10. The aptitude tests used to assign children to the various tracks are standardized primarily on white middle class children. Since these tests do not relate to the Negro and disadvantaged child, track assignment based on such tests relegates Negro and disadvantaged children to the lower tracks from which, because of the reduced curricula and the absence of adequate remedial and compensatory education, as well as continued inappropriate testing, the chance of escape is remote.

11. Education in the lower tracks is geared to what Dr. Hansen, the creator of the track system, calls the "blue collar" student. Thus such children, so stigmatized by inappropriate aptitude testing procedures, are denied equal opportunity to obtain the white collar education available to the white and more affluent children. . . .

In sum, all of the evidence in this case tends to show that the Washington school system is a monument to the cynicism of the power structure which governs the voteless capital of the greatest country on earth.

Remedy

To correct the racial and economic discrimination found in the operation of the District of Columbia public school system, the court has issued a decree attached to its opinion ordering: 1. An injunction against racial and economic discrimination in the public school system here. 2. Abolition of the track system. 3. Abolition of the optional zones. 4. Transportation for volunteering children in overcrowded school districts east of Rock Creek Park to underpopulated schools west of the Park. 5. The defendants, by October 2, 1967, to file for approval by the court a plan for pupil assignment eliminating the racial and economic discrimination found to exist in the operation of the Washington public school system. 6. Substantial integration of the faculty of each school beginning with the school year 1967–68. 7. The defendants, by October 2, 1967, to file for approval by the court a teacher assignment plan fully integrating the faculty of each school. . . .

The increasing controversy surrounding the court-school relationship centers theoretically on the wisdom of using the schools as initiating agents for social change. In practice, as we have seen, the conflict reduces to one of defining the limits of the judiciary in school policy-making. The overriding issue which emerges for subsequent analysis is whether the courts will, in fact, be able to provide their historical checks and balances in the formerly inviolable area of school decision-making, or whether the job of ensuring equal educational opportunity for all children will be left to the educators. It is important to note, furthermore, that the controversy has arisen because housing patterns and other factors in the Northern cities, to date, have not allowed local educational leaders to create workable measures for guaranteeing equal educational opportunity.

David Cohen

JURISTS AND EDUCATORS ON URBAN SCHOOLS: THE WRIGHT DECISION AND THE PASSOW REPORT

In the following article by David Cohen, the *Hobson v. Hansen* case is discussed together with the Passow Report, a survey of the Washington, D.C., school system conducted by Columbia University. As Cohen points out, the two investigations were not related but some of their findings are surprisingly similar. His article analyzes the different responsibilities of the educator as compared to the jurist in seeking solutions to serious societal problems. David Cohen is a faculty member of the Harvard Center for Law and Education. His scholarly work has been in the area of educational politics, and his articles have appeared in numerous national journals.

In sum, all of the evidence in this case tends to show that the Washington school system is a monument to the cynicism of the power structure which governs the voteless capital of the greatest country on earth.

Judge J. Skelly Wright's
decision in *Hobson v. Hansen*

Education in the District is in deep, and probably worsening trouble. . . . With its poverty, slums, and obsolete schools and schooling, presently the District is exemplary only of the worst of the urbanized setting.

Passow Report

To no one's great surprise, Judge Wright's decision and Professor Passow's Columbia University Survey of the Washington schools found abysmally poor education in the schools serving the District's mostly poor and Negro students. As Passow observed, this finding "might be applied to other large city school systems." [1] Well it might, for in most

From *The Record*, December, 1968, pp. 233–245. Some footnotes omitted. Reprinted by permission of the author and publisher.

[1] A. Harry Passow, *A Study of the Washington, D.C. Public Schools* (Mimeo). New York, 1967, p. 42.

essentials—racial and socio-economic segregation, poor fiscal and teaching resources, paralyzing bureaucracy, and a generally worsening situation vis-à-vis suburban education—the District schools present only a somewhat more intense version of the problems that afflict the nation's other great cities.

Therein lies the great interest of these two investigations of education in the District. There are very substantial differences in their tone and treatment of the problem, yet they share—almost in spite of themselves—important basic similarities. Since they reflect very different positions, drawn up and hardened over the past ten or twelve years, this is the more surprising. In finding for the plaintiffs, as a recent essay by the General Counsel of the NAACP reveals,[2] Judge Wright championed the claims and validated the grievances of Northern civil rights and community groups. On the other side, the Passow report reflects the more serious recent efforts by school systems and universities to improve segregated education in the cities.

These important differences seem to have given way, however, to similarities imposed by the District's considerable educational problems. Significantly, the similarities are negative and derive chiefly from the great existing barriers to remedial action. First, although they agree that the aim of reform in urban education is to provide equality of educational opportunity, Wright and Passow are unclear on what the standard for such equality should be. Second, the immediate effect of their proposals for remedy is to reveal the fiscal and political impotence of the District to implement them.

The Meaning of Equality. The common perplexity over the meaning of equality of educational opportunity arises in large part from the problem of massive segregation. Judge Wright found that the defendant Board and Superintendent did ". . . unconstitutionally deprive the District's Negro and poor public school children of their rights to equal educational opportunity . . ." But his decision contains at least three separate essays at defining this equality: desegregation; equality of resources invested in segregated schools; positive inequality of resources to segregated schools to produce equality of results. The last two seem mutually exclusive; and, taken together they conflict with the views on which the court's first standard rests: that "racially and socially homogeneous schools damage the minds and spirit of the children who attend

[2] Robert L. Carter, "School Integration is Still on the Agenda," *The Saturday Review*, October 21, 1967.

them . . . and block the attainment of the broader goals of democratic education, whether the segregation occurs by law or by fact."

The Passow report also speaks with many tongues on this question. In some places it seems to side with the court's first alternative, but in others it clearly favors a positive inequality of resources. Passow vigorously argues that segregation is given, and writes that "in the meantime, for the hundreds of thousands of youngsters who come through the schools an appropriate and adequate education must be designed." Not surprisingly, his report does not meet the question of whether this would provide equality of opportunity.

These problems of definition arise from the obstacles to remedial action. It has become tiresome to repeat that segregation will be difficult to overcome. Less fashionable to mention are the fiscal, educational, and political barriers to effective education in ghettoes, but they probably are at least as formidable. Although the political status of the District creates additional problems, it shares with the other great cities a growing inability to control the critical educational resources—students, teachers, and sufficient money. This is basic to an understanding of these two examinations of the D.C. schools, and is increasingly central to most problems of urban education.

Desegregation and Achievement. In the early 1950's, as now, the relevant policy question was whether equality could be attained in racially segregated schools. But clarity on the standard by which "attainment" is to be judged has progressively diminished. Under the *Plessy* doctrine the standard was thought to be equality of objective "inputs" to the educational process. Then the series of cases which culminated in *Brown* attacked this doctrine on its own terms, by arguing that were all objective inputs equal, racial segregation itself was an input which caused there to be an inequality in the schools.

Although this apparently destroyed the principles of *Plessy* and seemed to erect a clear standard of equal opportunity on its ruins, in fact *Brown* still rested on the old foundation. The *Brown* standard was new—no state-operated segregation—but its foundation was the *Plessy* notion of *input equality*. Under *Brown* the attainment of equal opportunity could only be measured by the degree of desegregation, on the assumption that segregation was like books and teachers, an operative if less tangible input to education.

Yet this entire intellectual structure gives way to the simple question: "why equal inputs—tangible or intangible?" Apparently, it was presumed that equal inputs would have racially equal results. Inherent in the *Brown* standard of equality was an implicit performance or "output" standard. *Brown* seems to have embodied the assumption that desegregation, by equalizing *all* the relevant inputs, would racially equalize the outcomes.

If all school segregation in America had been clearly *de jure* this intellectual frailty might not have reached the level of policy significance for at least another generation. Only then would there have been long and wide enough experience with school desegregation to show that (in terms of school achievement) it alone does not fully satisfy the implicit *Plessy-Brown* performance standard. But most segregation is not plainly *de jure*. As the pressure for desegregation mounted in Northern and Western cities, lacking judicial resolution or any widely accepted standard of equality, increasing attention was given to performance standards, mostly reading achievement. This tendency was firmly set—and the policy problem posed clearly for the first time—when Northern school authorities responded to demands for desegregation by promising to improve schools so as to raise performance, but rejected the idea of desegregation. If academic competence could be equalized given segregation, why eliminate the segregation?

That question, and recognition of massive *de facto* segregation, collide again and again in the Passow report and the Wright decision, as they have in local and federal policy debates for the last decade. In the abstract the answer seems clear: if performance is the sole standard of equality, and the sole standard of performance is academic competence, then desegregation would not be required to provide equality.

Agonizing Uncertainties. Neither Passow nor Wright are that clear on the matter, however. The Passow report consistently favors better-than-equal treatment for predominantly Negro and/or predominantly lower-class schools. In spite of this it is never apparent what the standard is against which the sufficiency of such efforts will be judged. Reference repeatedly is made to depressed reading achievement, which suggests a presumption that it should be raised to equality. But there also is a heavy emphasis on tailoring education to the needs of "urban" children.

The chapter on the track system recommends, for example, that ability grouping be retained in the junior high years, but that:

The criteria for placement should be developed on the basis of the population *in the school* rather than on the basis of external District or national norms.

The impression left by such passages is reinforced by the lack of many references to equality of educational opportunity, but rather a proliferation of such terms as "quality education," "adequate education," and education "appropriate" to Negro and poor children.

This uncertainty is most apparent in the chapter on integration, which seems agonizingly divided. Early note is taken of the fact that:

. . . it would be absurd to deny or ignore the special problems that a racially isolated school faces in preparing its pupils for life in an open society.

Because of these special problems it is asserted that each child:

. . . should have the help he needs to reach maturity prepared to compete on fair terms in an open society. . . . The schools must furnish unequal education . . . to provide equal opportunity. . . .

If we assume this means something that the report never clearly says —that the criterion of equal opportunity is the *average white achievement*—a major difficulty still remains. The court in *Brown* spoke of emotional and psychological, as well as more "objective," forms of damage. On this point the Passow report is quite at odds with itself. To begin with it defers, in a curious way, to the *Brown* tradition:

If children are to obtain reliable knowledge about people whose backgrounds differ from their own, if they are to learn to respect rather than to distrust differences, if they are to appreciate the commonalities which unite as well as the distinctions which divide humanity, those who attend segregated schools must obviously receive special help.

Although this group of children includes virtually all of those schooled in the Washington metropolitan area—to say nothing of the entire United States—*nothing* (save one quick reference to integrated textbooks) *ever* is said again about what such "special help" might be. There is not a hint of how Passow proposed to "compensate" for the psychological and attitudinal effects of segregation in segregated schools.

A bit further on, the author weighs the prospects of school desegregation, and essays the view that:

So far as the children now in the Washington schools are concerned, it is in one sense too late and in another too early . . .

Then, after a review of the policies which would provide integration in the future, he concludes:

But none of this is likely to happen—*indeed, all of it is certain not to happen* —until enough Marylanders, Virginians, Washingtonians, and Americans are convinced that their interests will be better served by making the national capital area a well-integrated metropolitan community . . . (emphasis added).

That sequence of three passages boggles the mind, because as the first one suggests, "enough Marylanders . . ." will never be convinced, as long as they and their children live and learn in all white and all black neighborhoods and schools. If, as these passages suggest, psychological and emotional factors might be counted as elements of equal opportunity by the Columbia Survey, it seems that their report cannot promise equality for the District's children.

On this matter one would expect a jurist, by definition closely tied to the *Brown* tradition, to be more clear; Judge Wright is. His first finding of fact cites the damage to the "mind *and spirit*" of "Negro and white" children, in support of his opinion that there was an unconstitutional deprivation of the right to equal opportunity in education. Here the court was unequivocal, and did not suppose that any such "special measures" to remedy attitude damage as alluded to in the Passow report would be possible:

School segregation, whatever its genesis, *always* imposes a twofold disadvantage (emphasis added).
[Second] segregation in the schools precludes the kind of social interaction between Negroes and whites which is an indispensable attribute of education for citizenship in a democratic society.

Judicial Unclarities. On these grounds the racial composition of schools would be an indispensable standard for determining denials of equal opportunity. But like Passow, the court could provide no remedy in a 90 percent Negro school system. Apparently as a result, desegregation is not the only standard contemplated in the decision; indeed, an apparently contrary one also is smartly applied to the defendant school system. Finding rather severe racial inequalities in the allocation of resources to schools, the court held that these inequalities were both a deprivation of equal opportunity and unconstitutional, and ordered that there should be racial equality in all "objective" resources allocated to schools.

The rationale, however, is substantively unclear.

The constitutional principle from which this modern separate-but-equal rule draws its sustenance is, of course, equal protection. Orthodox equal protection doctrine can be encapsulated in a single rule: *government action which without justification imposes unequal burdens or accords unequal benefits is unconstitutional.*

This only returns us to the submerged difficulties in the *Brown* tradition: by what standard to determine "unequal burdens or . . . benefits"?

The court's language in this section of the opinion leaves little

question as to its view. Rehearsing the inequities with respect to kindergartens, for example, it comments that:

The children of the slums absolutely must be brought into the culturally rich
atmosphere of the school at the earliest age . . .

The rationale for preschool education, of course, is to increase academic
competence. Therefore there is a meta-rule behind the one enunciated
by Judge Wright, a rule which in the *Brown* tradition embodies the
notion of equal results.

But by any such rule, *if equality of opportunity in education is denied
by inequality of inputs it cannot be provided by their simple equality.*
The court was not insensible of this, as evidenced in its closing discussion of plans for remedy:

Where because of the density of residential segregation or for other reasons
children in certain areas, particularly in the slums, are denied the benefits of
an integrated education, *the court will require that the plan include compensatory education sufficient at least to overcome the detriment of segregation and
thus provide, as nearly as possible, equal educational opportunity to all school
children* (emphasis added).

But no rationale for this requirement was enunciated; if it were, it could
only be the latent performance principle of *Brown*.[3] Here the same difficulties which plague the Passow report come to light. If Judge Wright
had enunciated an equal-result standard upon which to base his compensatory remedy ideas he would have shattered a major element of the
Brown tradition, for to so hold would assume that one of the major performance criteria implicit in Brown—achievement—could be equalized
given segregation. Although the Judge seems to have believed this possible, his reluctance to say so openly is understandable in view of the
very persuasive evidence on the attitudinal and psychological damage of
segregation—the other criterion in the *Brown* tradition. He could not,
however, fail to actively employ an equal result standard, for given segregation, mere equality of inputs would not basically change the relative
educational standing of rich and poor, Negro and white.

[3] Any doubt that Judge Wright contemplated a result criterion is dispelled by his
ruling on the legality of the track system. The ground for this ruling is the finding
that ". . . the track system is fatally defective, because for many students placement
is based on traits [poverty and race] other than those on which the classification
purports to be based." (174) The basis for this, in turn, is the court's view that ". . .
the limits on his [any student's] academic progress, and ultimately the kind of life
work he can hope to attain, are set by the orientation of the . . . curricula. Those in
the lower tracks are, for the most part, molded for various vocational assignments;
those in the upper tracks, on the other hand, are given the opportunity to prepare
for the higher ranking jobs and, most significantly, for college." (172)

The Problem of Standards. Thus Wright and Passow share the same perplexity, although with very different external emphases. The Columbia study team was not obviously pro-integration, as was the court, but all the same it did give reluctant recognition to psychological and attitudinal damage, it did suggest some desegregation of students, and then it proposed massive compensatory treatment. And like the court, the Columbia survey could not say which one or combination of these, if any, would provide equal opportunity.

That two such different approaches to the same problem should arrive at a common difficulty on an important point is evidence of its fundamental character. The difficulty may persist for some time, because it is rooted not only in a basic constitutional tradition but also in the economic and demographic realities underlying our current dilemmas about education and race. The *Brown* tradition rests upon the notion of dual (academic and psychological-attitudinal) damage. Although it is sometimes conceded that in theory at least academic results could be equalized between races given segregation, no one seriously pretends that the psychological-attitudinal damage could thus be repaired. Yet situations such as those in the District seem to cry out for a simple achievement standard. As long as we lack remedies for the cities' educational problems, it will seem that we should either abandon one element of the *Brown* tradition and adopt such an achievement standard of equality, or cease the effort to apply constitutional guarantees to city schools. Since the first would probably be an incorrect measure of equality of opportunity, and the second a disaster, it seems likely the confusion will continue.

Remedy: Prescriptions and Problems. Defining equality of educational opportunity, then, is not a mere philosophical charade; quite the contrary, it is the setting of standards for school systems' behavior. As the preceding discussion showed, the lack of a clear definition of equality arises in large part from the fact that the fruitful application of any standard seems impossible.

The same circumstances which obscured the meaning of equal opportunity also impeded clear discussion of remedial action. Again, the two documents differ not so much in their essential conclusions about remedy as in the emphasis and tone with which they approach the dilemmas. Both Passow and Wright urged the virtual or actual abolition of the track system, and both proposed limited desegregation through busing and/or education parks. Both urged the use of education parks as a tentative, limited foundation for metropolitan cooperation, but both were skeptical of suburban interest. Their approaches, of course, were very different; the court was almost passionate in emphasizing the need for the little desegregation possible, while the Passow report's tone in urging similar steps often was grudging. But more important, neither seemed to hold out much hope that in the foreseeable future any one or combination of these measures would make a serious dent in the District's educational problem. Thus both turned to compensatory education, the Court in one sentence and the Columbia survey team in hundreds of turgid pages.

In the tradition of recent education school theory and public school practice the Passow report concentrates upon its definition of the District's task:

. . . providing massive remediation of existing learning difficulties for those now in school and designing developmental and compensatory programs for thousands of children who will be entering school in the years ahead.

Although many changes to this end were proposed, the central recommendations can be readily summarized.

Extend preschool education to all four-year-olds, and the needy three's.
Upgrade teacher competence by devoting 20 percent of teachers' time to retraining, employ teachers on a twelve month basis, and hire teacher aides.
Upgrade teaching and totally redevelop curriculum, using as the main vehicle curriculum supervisors—one for every twenty teachers.
Recruit a new breed of teachers through the creation of joint school-university staff development centers.

More important than any single recommendation is the hope running throughout the report that if the recommendations were put in motion the District would begin to create a "model urban school system," by virtue of which competent and dedicated teachers could be attracted and held.

As an educational matter it would be difficult to fault these proposals on any intrinsic grounds. They are responsive to the deep problems found in the District schools.

There were, however, some basic things left unsaid. It is not surprising that a teacher-training institution should place a heavy emphasis upon the improvement of curricula and teaching. Yet there is a substantial body of research, culminating in the Coleman Report, which shows that independent of teacher quality the racial and social class composition of student bodies have a powerful impact upon student achievement. James Coleman has summarized the policy significance of these research findings well, in pointing to the need for a radical reconstruction of children's social and intellectual environments in schools:

It is such reconstruction that is important—whether it be provided through other children, through tutorial programs, through artificial environments created by computer consoles, or by some other means.[4]

This line of thought is wholly absent from the Passow report's discussion of and recommendations for compensatory education. Instead it proceeds on the unfortunate and by-now classical model of improved education for "disadvantaged" children in ghetto schools; enrich instruction to compensate for individual deficiencies, but leave unchanged the achievement-depressing social and intellectual structure of the student environment. This course has proven just as fruitless as other efforts to change only school organization without improving the quality of instruction.[5] In its wholesale disregard of the need—especially given the acceptance of segregation—to deal with the academically devastating effects of weak student environments, the Passow report reflects the deficiencies of both education school theory and public school practice. It seems likely that the implementation of Passow's recommendations— although they would substantially improve the District schools—would not fundamentally alter the relative status of Negro and white students' school achievement in the Washington metropolitan area.[6]

Teachers and Environments. These comments on the matter of student environment also bear on the strictly teacher-oriented proposals made in the Passow report. They are based upon the underlying hope that beginning to create a "model urban school system" would bring positive change in teacher recruitment patterns. It is an attractive idea, and to the extent that teachers value challenge above status it might be true. But that appears to be quite a limited extent; teachers' preferences are very closely tied to the color, class, and achievement composition of student bodies. This is not surprising, since the chief mark of teachers' success is their students' achievement—which of course is very closely related to schools' color, class, and achievement composition.[7] Lacking change in schools' social class and racial composition, satisfactory aca-

---

[4] James Coleman, "Toward Open Schools," *The Public Interest*, No. 9, Fall 1967, p. 23.

[5] Daniel Fox, *Expansion of the More Effective School Program.* New York: Center for Urban Education, 1967, p. 112.

[6] This may seem paradoxical, but it is not. The MES program in New York City has much improved some ghetto schools, but has not improved achievement; Fox, pp. 44–68; 101–114.

[7] Coleman, pp. 347–366.

demic performance and/or radical restructuring of schools' organization would seem to be the only factors which might broadly affect teachers' preferences. It is precisely the absence of such performance which produces negative preferences, but there is not a word in the Passow report directly addressed to how the structure and status of schools and student environments might be changed so as to make them more attractive to teachers.

In a sense, however, it is almost beside the point to raise even such critical educational objections. Far more important difficulties inhere in the fiscal and political implications of the compensatory education urged in the Passow report and ordered in the Wright decision.

The Columbia survey team did not attach line-by-line cost estimates to its recommendations. In the section on finance, however, it observed that meeting the educational needs of "disadvantaged" children in the District schools may entail ". . . as much as three or four times the cost of meeting the educational needs of the child whose home environment has already done a good portion of the job . . ." This estimate—which translates into per-pupil expenditure of about $2,000—is more or less consistent with other discussions of the subject.[8] Indeed, it may well turn out to be conservative, for there is some evidence that simply to extend existing compensatory programs *at present levels of intensity* to the entire educational experience of the affected children would cost roughly four times (about $2,000) present per-pupil expenditures.[9]

If funds at this level were allocated to District pupils presently eligible for aid under Title I ESEA they would amount to about $50,000,000 annually. That is fifteen or twenty times the current annual federal education aid for District children in poverty under ESEA, and about two thirds of the total annual District school operating budget. Were the criterion also to include underachievement, as the Passow report suggests it should,[10] this figure could be nearly doubled.

[8] Edmund Gordon, "Compensatory Programs in the Equalization of Educational Opportunity" (mimeo), Yeshiva University, 1967; the estimate given here is $2,500; p. 47. See also Cohen, "Policy for the Public Schools: Compensation and Integration," *Harvard Educational Review*, Winter, 1968.

[9] In Cincinnati, for example, the existing compensatory program provides concentrated remedial reading in "deprived" schools for roughly 15–20 percent of the student's average day, at a per-pupil cost of about $250.00 over the average per-pupil expenditure for instruction of about $500. To extend this remedial approach to the entire school day would entail a total expenditure of about $2,000. Cohen, *Race and Equality of Educational Opportunity in Cinicinnati, Ohio* (mimeo), The Joint Center for Urban Studies of Harvard and MIT, 1968.

[10] Passow, p. 259. Wright, p. 139, note 144, suggests that slightly over half of the upper elementary children read below grade level, and that a good deal more than half do in the secondary schools.

The political implications of such expenditures are potent. First, it is unlikely that in Washington—or for that matter in any city, or nationally—the parents of advantaged children or their representatives would consent to expenditure of three or four times as much on disadvantaged children as on their own. By roughly the same token, secondly, it would be a bit unreal to expect that the Congress would give such special attention to the District alone. The Passow report calls for just that, asking that Congress create "a model urban school system." But apart from all other considerations, racial inequality of educational opportunity is a national problem, and it would probably be politically impossible to legislate for it on a locality-by-locality basis. Legislation on such a scale (a 15- or 20-fold increase annually in ESEA), only for the national constituency represented by children of the urban poor, seems unlikely. For one thing, this would require a very substantial revision in federal budgetary and political priorities, for a relatively small group of people. For another, one of the chief group of agencies which could provoke, promote, and assist such a revision are the states, and for the most part they are not vociferous supporters of categorical aid to schools, let alone education aid to the urban children of poverty.

The comparative magnitudes of the cost and the constituency suggests that although it might be somewhat more expensive to provide integrated schools of high quality, that could well be the best way to broaden potential support for improved education for poor urban children.

State Responsibilities. The problems of urban schools, however, do not lie neatly along an uncluttered federal-municipal axis, and they probably cannot be dealt with by those two units of government alone. The disparities in resource allocation from which Washington and the other great cities suffer organically involve the suburbs—whether the resource in question is students, teachers, or tax base. If the great cities do not control the student resources required to fully desegregate, no more do they control those required to improve their relative status in respect to teacher quality or financing education.

The states alone possess the authority—by law and tradition—to affect the flow of educational resources within their limits, and thus within most metropolitan areas. The local school districts are their creatures. Whether it is a matter of changing the allocation of funds, quality teachers, or students, historically the authority to regulate and apportion lies not with the local district or the federal government, but with the state.

This authority has been exercised to promote equality of opportunity only in a few states, and even there only in a limited fashion. The question of whether the states have such an obligation in their cities has not been tried in court, let alone established. Yet were the will to act everywhere present, the states themselves command the authority, but not all the necessary resources.

The conclusion in the District is yet to occur. But let us suppose that racial inequities in the District schools were eliminated. It is a foregone conclusion that if the plaintiffs returned to court they could claim continued denial of equal opportunity on the grounds that most Negro and poor children still were performing far below normal. This claim could be based on the implicit equal-result standard of equality. What, then, could the court do?

It has been fashionable to point out that its jurisdiction does not extend to those school districts whose students would be needed if the District schools were to be desegregated. But does it extend any more to the sources of the funds, or the mechanisms of teacher production and recruitment whose control would be required to mount programs which might result in equality of achievement? In the rush to point out the obvious, the equally great obstacles to ghetto school improvement have been quite consistently overlooked.

This is perhaps the chief conclusion which emerges from analysis of these two documents. Washington, like the nation's other great cities, no more controls the resources to mount effective education programs in ghetto schools than it controls those required to desegregate the schools. Both approaches require a much greater commitment to solving educational problems in the great cities than presently exists, vastly increased allocation of resources to the development and implementation of solutions, and reallocations in the production of educational resources for metropolitan areas.

This is not to say, as Wright and Passow properly point out, that more effective use should not be made of existing opportunities, for clearly they should. Judge Wright's decision in *Hobson v. Hansen* has revealed that existing educational resources are terribly misused and misallocated: to correct only these abuses is a major task, and of the first importance. Nor is it to say that alternative solutions to those discussed here should not be undertaken. But there is a great gulf between such limited efforts and the elimination of inequality of opportunity in education. Whether we judge the latter by a simple achievement standard or by the more complex *Brown* standard, its attainment will require the three types of basic change just enumerated. Lacking such changes neither effective compensation in segregated city schools, nor quality education in integrated metropolitan schools is likely to become a reality. Absent either or both there probably will not be fundamental change in the relative educational status of Negro and white children, and little progress toward any standard of equality of educational opportunity.

The future role of the courts in local school decision-making is a topic of considerable interest to educators. Legal scholars and educators look particularly to the treatment of *de facto* segregation cases for indications of the future school-court relationship. To date, as mentioned earlier, the Supreme Court has refused to hear a *de facto* segregation case. Despite this fact, there are those who believe that—in light of Judge Wright's decision and others, including the Los Angeles ruling by Judge Gitelson in 1970—it will not be long before the courts order total integration of the Northern schools. They believe that the next step of the courts will be to order *de jure* integration of all public schools. Furthermore, they expect to see the courts intervening to ensure not only that a black-white balance is achieved, but also that the proportion of the poor in each school equals the percentage of poor in the entire city. This group speculates that the courts will expect this goal to be achieved even if it requires involuntary exchanges of pupils from across school district and state lines. The effect of such court action would be to make homogeneous schools of any kind illegal. Those predicting that a doctrine of *de jure* integration will soon be adopted have a good reason for doing so. Recent decisions in the lower courts appear to be moving away from the theory that *de facto* segregation should be left to the local school board for solution.

Even though there are those who predict that the courts will adopt a more visible role in local educational decision-making, especially in the area of racial imbalance and desegregation, there is reason to speculate that the opposite might also occur. Those inclined to believe that the courts will cease to intervene in local school decision-making base their predictions on the changing composition of the United States Supreme Court. By appointing Chief Justice Warren Burger, President Nixon indicated that he intended to lead the nation away from the liberalism and "judicial activism" that marked the Earl Warren Court from 1953 to 1969. For the entire Warren era, the Court used its power to bring about sweeping changes in the political, social, and economic life of the country. The 1954 *Brown v. Board of Education of Topeka, Kansas* case was the beginning of a series of decisions that ultimately banned racial discrimination in all forms by the federal government, the states, and even in private housing and employment.

Since the Burger Court is likely to adopt judicial restraint and to hesitate to solve societal problems through court decree, there is good reason to presume that the High Court will not continue the trend toward intervention in local school matters. Burger will probably not lead the court toward social reform because his philosophy admits that the court will encounter some problems for which it can offer no solution. Unlike Warren, Burger does not view the court as an instrument of national conscience to correct the social and political inequities which have been neglected by other governmental institutions. With this understanding of the Burger (and Nixon) philosophy of the role of the court, it is safe to predict that when the Supreme Court is called to rule upon the constitutionality of *de facto* segregation in Northern schools, the decision will be made with judicial restraint in mind. For this reason, many speculate that boards of education will not be forced to take affirmative action to desegregate *de facto* segregated school systems and, furthermore, the courts will not tend to intervene in local school policy-making. At least, it can be anticipated that the Supreme Court can be expected to slow the trend begun by the Wright and Gitelson decisions on *de facto* segregation.

Carl F. Hansen

HANSEN V. HOBSON: JUDICIAL INTERVENTION IS BEING TESTED

This chapter, using the example of racial imbalance in the public schools, indicates the current uncertainty surrounding the role of the court in local educational decision-making. The next selection is the text of a speech delivered by Carl F. Hansen, former Superintendent of the Washington, D.C., Public Schools (the Hansen in *Hobson v. Hansen*). In this projective selection, Hansen discusses, with considerable emotion, the school-court relationship that he would like to see prevail. His outright attack on the court and his anger two years after leaving Washington are clear indications that one of the nation's leading school administrators has serious questions about the role of the court as it intervenes in school decision-making.

An accelerating effort is developing to hold public boards of education responsible for enforcing integration by race and, in accord with the Wright opinion in *Hobson vs. Hansen*, by social class as well.

The new doctrine emerging from court decisions, Federal civil rights legislation, and actions of a number of state legislatures and boards of education may properly be called *de jure* integration. The purpose is to require a recalcitrant society to do by law what it is unwilling to do by free choice.

From *Integrated Education: Race and Schools Magazine,* September–October, 1969, pp. 23–29. Reprinted by permission of the publisher.

Conceived as desirable by social theorists, the commingling of the black and poor with the white and affluent must be brought about by the force of law in this same manner as separation by race was once required by law in a number of jurisdictions.

When the state, whether through its legislative or judicial branches, thus orders children to attend any school on race or income lines, whether or not this order maintains the appearance of voluntarism, the effect is integration by law, and the term for this concept is *de jure* integration.

At this juncture the effect of *de jure* integration is applied only to the public schools in about the same way that *de jure* segregation was mainly concerned with education.

It is a mistake that *de jure* integration as public policy applies to children only. Now that the demand is being clearly enunciated in such cases as the Wright opinion, adults in that class called teachers are also subject to enforced mixing, at this point, on race alone. School systems that fail to carry adult integration into the staffing of all branches of the service—building maintenance, busing, clerical—are subject to close scrutiny by the courts as well as by pressure groups of various kinds.

The effect is to say of teachers, "You are black, and therefore you must accept assignment to a predominantly white staff, or your whiteness of skin, variable as it may be from pallid to profound brown, entitles you to select, if you want a job in this school district, placement in a black school."

Up to date, not even in the notable Wright opinion, has a requirement been stipulated that affluent white or black teachers be integrated with poor white or black teachers. Mainly, no doubt, because the rather uniform low income class from which most of this nation's teachers spring, offers little comfort to those who espouse with utmost self-righteousness the importance of the rich sharing their cultivation, not their dollars, their cultivation, with the denizens of the lower middle class deeps.

But along simple racist lines alone, based on the unjustified view that the shade of skin affects the quality of teaching, *de jure* integrationists from the Supreme Court on down now seek to require faculty mixing as an essential step toward ultimate integration.

Origins of Doctrine

At this point, it is necessary to deal with two specific questions. The first is, what are the origins of the *de jure* integration doctrine? The second, what is the predictable effect of the doctrine, assuming that it is constitutional and can then prevail even against the public will?

One of the earliest examples of a legislative action occurred in 1954 when the New York City Board of Education was seduced into stating that "racially homogeneous public schools are educationally undesirable" and as a consequence it must prevent the "further development of such schools" and at the same time take the responsibility of achieving racial balance in all of its schools.

The New York policy proved worse than useless. It produced almost endless protests, boycotts, and sit-ins resulting from the frustrations of civil rightists who complained that the city board of education was failing to pay up on its promissory note.

In 1964, an official study group commented, "No act of the Board of Education from 1958 through 1962 has had a measurable effect on the degree of school segregation. . . . Not a single elementary or junior high school that was changing toward segregation after 1958 by virtue of residential changes and transfers of whites into parochial and private schools was prevented from becoming segregated by Board action." [1]

Unimpressed by the failure of the New York City effort to reverse the segregation trend, proponents of *de jure* integration gained strong footholds in a number of state departments of education and in state legislatures.

On the premise that homogeneous schools "impair the ability to learn," the New York Board of Regents ordered the State Department of Education to seek solutions to the problem of residential segregation. In 1960, it declared that:

"Modern psychological knowledge indicates that schools enrolling students largely of homogeneous ethnic origin may damage the personality of the minority group children. Such schools decrease their motivation and thus impair the ability to learn. Public education in such a setting is socially unrealistic, blocks the attainment of the goals of democratic education, and is wasteful of manpower and talent, whether this situation occurs by law or fact."

California, Massachusetts, New Jersey, Wisconsin, and Connecticut have also taken the position "in executive or judicial statements that racial isolation in the schools has a damaging effect on the educational op-

[1] "Desegregating the Public Schools of New York City. A Report Prepared for the Board of Education of the City of New York" by the State Education Commissioner's Advisory Committee on Human Relations and Community Tensions. May 12, 1964, p. 5.

portunities of the Negro pupils." In 1965 the Massachusetts Legislature enacted a Racial Imbalance Act. Schools with racial imbalance were required to file with the Massachusetts State Board a plan to correct the condition. (A school with more than 50 percent non-whites is here considered racially imbalanced.)

Equally important as the concept of the need for enforcing racial balance is the now clearly defined theory that school quality reflects social class, and that therefore adjustments to effect balance in social class are as mandatory as those needed to achieve racial balance.

While the Wright decision is the first court action that asserts the evils of *de facto* segregation by social class, the literature on this subject is growing at a rate which suggests that there is impending a strong likelihood that public schools will soon be required to bring about social class balance as a constitutional duty.

In its 1967 report, the United States Civil Rights Commission devoted a full chapter to the racial-social class isolation factor and its connection with school outcomes. Evidence is mounting that income level is a more effective predictor of reading achievement than race. With some justification, conclusions are being drawn that black children do better in predominantly white schools than in predominantly black schools. The error here is the over-simplification of the causes of the benefits as stemming solely from the mixing of races.

If these conditions lead to the conclusion that the only way to improve achievement among lower social class pupils is to integrate them with higher income pupils, then a vast manipulation of school populations is in prospect.

The prospect of introducing a benign despotism capable of arranging children by income-race levels on the school chess board is clearly contained in the following declaration in Wright's *de facto* segregation decision:

"Racially and socially homogeneous schools damage the minds and spirit of all children who attend them—the Negro, the white, the poor and the affluent—and block the attainment of the broader goals of democratic education, whether the segregation occurs by law or by fact."

Because the Wright decision is closest to my experience, although certainly the Brown Doctrines set forth in 1954 by the Supreme Court were also very close, I want to present my analysis of the meaning of this far-reaching opinion.

On what to me were really secondary issues, the Appellate Court of the Second Circuit construed a number of Wright conclusions in such a manner as to make them ineffectual. On ability grouping, specifically the track system, the appeals bench seemed to say that after all the abolishment of the track system meant nothing more than its modification.

The Appellate Court believes the lower court ruling abolishing the track system "provides adequate scope for ability grouping in the administration of the school system." Thus, it is argued that the track system only as it existed at the time of the Wright decree was abolished. In effect, a modification for correction of its ills is all that is required.

While I would still insist that the lower court improperly intervened in the management of the Board's educational program when it ordered it to abolish the track system, to find now that this action does not trammel its discretion in organizing for instruction is reassuring.

Homogeneity Harmful

The real heart of the Wright decision is not any of these things—tracking, busing, faculty integration, optional zones. It is the determination that homogeneous schools, either by race or social class or both, are harmful, thus acting to deprive children of the equal protection of the law under the 14th amendment.

In its confirmatory ruling, the Appellate Court for the District of Columbia admonished the Board to discontinue discrimination against the Negro and the poor. The sleeper in the decision at both levels is that the Board is required to "submit to the court a long-range plan of pupil assignment to alleviate racial imbalance among the District schools."

The Board is required to submit plans for correcting segregation, a court order based on the views of the damaging effect of schools that are homogeneous by race and class; the Board is further required to include in its building plans the application of desegregation principles, as well as to anticipate the possibility that integration may be accomplished through cooperation with suburban schools. Clearly remaining without the slightest change in meaning in the Appellate Court's opinion is the mandatory rule requiring the local board to seek ways to integrate its schools, and to submit plans for doing so for the approval of the lower court.

In Wright is clearly established a *de jure* integration rule affecting both race and social class. While the application of the rule is tempered by the realities of the situation, the order to proceed is clear and unmistakable. Thus, after more than eight earlier court rulings, including the notable Gary and Kansas City actions, holding it not to be the duty of a board of education to eliminate *de facto* segregation, there came into being an affirmative ruling applicable to all school systems burdened with *de facto* segregation by race and class.

Integration by class is not the figment of someone's overheated imagination. Proposed by Wright for the Washington schools, the ruling led to a massive program of boundary changes in the schools that required the moving of more than ten thousand pupils in the fall of 1968. This was done mainly for class integration because very little racial mixing is possible where the enrollment in a public school is 94 percent black.

Class integration is a going business in the schools of the Nation's capital and follows, clearly, income rather than race lines. When you apply the doctrine of *de jure* integration by class to the public schools in this nation, you can visualize, if the operation takes place, a gigantic ordering of pupils from one school to another, into massive educational parks, or possibly away from them, into travel patterns where the buses conveying the affluent to the poor and the poor to the affluent pass each other in the mists of the early morning and the gloom of the early evening, for the hopeful objective of getting a beneficial racial and social mix. As I contemplate the scene, I cannot put off the opinion that freedom seems to have diminishing meaning in a society in search of social equality.

In three opinions [2] issued May 27, 1968, the Supreme Court enunciated the doctrine of affirmative responsibility for the disestablishment of state-imposed school segregation where such a condition existed prior to 1954.

While the freedom of choice plan was not declared unacceptable in every case, the effect of the three decisions was to require pairing, as in the case of Gould, Arkansas, or zoning without freedom of choice, as is likely to be imposed upon Jackson City, Tennessee.

The freedom of choice plan allowing both Negroes and whites to elect any school in the district in which capacity is available does not provide the kind of rapid, affirmative action leading to the disestablishment of all-Negro schools required by the Supreme Court. In reality, of course, the disestablishment doctrine requires state-imposed integration in those states where state-imposed segregation existed prior to 1954. This ruling is only a short step removed from one requiring the disestablishment of

---

[2] *Green vs. Kent County, Virginia School Board*, No. 695; *Raney vs. Gould, Arkansas Board of Education*, No. 825 and *Mear vs. Commissioners, Jackson City, Tennessee*, No. 740. Opinions issued May 27, 1968.

de facto segregation, a finding which is the main burden of Wright in *Hobson* vs. *Hansen.*

To support the conclusion that racially imbalanced schools deny pupils the equal protection of the law guaranteed by the 14th amendment, the courts must take the position that predominantly black schools are inferior not only because of neglect and lack of support but also by virtue of cultural isolation.

In the Wright opinion, therefore, the conclusion was inevitably negative on the quality of education in Washington's predominantly Negro schools. The charge of discrimination against the black and the poor was hurled with vindictive vigor at the school administration. The premise formed the basis for the ruling that the local board must furnish plans for eliminating racial imbalance.

The main statistical evidence of discrimination employed by the Court was that a small number of elementary schools in northwest Washington, where the enrollment was mostly white, spent on the average $100 more per capita than the elementary schools as a whole.

Finances Distorted

It did no good to explain in our testimony that small schools with dwindling enrollments, often of no more than 80 pupils taught by three or four teachers at the top of the salary scale, must inevitably cost more per pupil than growing new schools with staff assigned from the incoming classes of teachers.

It was useless to explain that even in the same building pupils in one class taught by a $10,000 a year teacher would be having about twice as much public money spent on them as the pupils in the class next door who were being taught by a new, first year $5,000 teacher.

It was a waste of our time to explain that we were using vacant rooms in the so-called favored white schools for poor, mentally retarded children bussed in at public expense and that the smallness of these classes also ran up the per capita costs computed for these small schools.

The court ignored clear testimony that in many black, low-income schools the per capita expenditures exceeded those in white high-income schools.

Equally useless was the clear testimony that at the secondary levels, both in the junior high schools and senior high schools, the predominantly white schools in the more affluent areas received less per capita than more than half of the so-called poor black schools.

It proved to be a waste of time to testify that elementary class sizes had been reduced from 38.7 in 1950 for black pupils to 30.2 in 1965 for all pupils, most of whom were black and poor.

And I could say with equal sense of injustice that it was useless to tell the court of increases in special services, special teachers, librarians, counselors, programs for the educable mentally retarded, for dropouts, for girls pregnant out-of-wedlock, all mainly for the benefit of the Negro and the poor.

Or that in a building program costing more than 135 million dollars, all new construction except for an addition of four rooms to a so-called affluent predominantly white school applied mainly to the benefit of the Negro and the poor.

And finally, the court was silent on the testimony that for all operating expenditures the per capita amount more than doubled over a ten-year period, that Washington was second in rank of per capita expenditures among the major cities, and that only one local suburb catering to the white and the affluent spent more money per pupil than did Washington, and that this improving condition applied to a population of 94 percent colored and to a large extent poor.

As I see it, the court could not conclude that the so-called black schools were receiving extra attention, that they were anything but inferior, for otherwise the main argument for *de jure* integration would disappear.

To eliminate the sin of *de jure* segregation does not justify employing the counter-balancing sin of *de jure* integration. Nor does the concept of the integrated man support the democratic theory which recognizes individuality, draws its strength from variety and pluralism, makes progress a result of the contributions of individuals and groups freed of the necessity of living within a limited predetermined cultural framework.

Enforced Integration

And as important as the theoretical flaws in the *de jure* integration doctrine is the built-in pragmatic one, namely that the effort is committed to failure. Without a police state to enforce the movement, as long as people retain a modicum of choice, they will reject enforced integration.

A realistic look at the resegregative effect of state-imposed integration is in order at this point.

White parents tend to remove their children from public schools when the black membership exceeds thirty percent.

Two examples will illustrate: one is the Gould, Arkansas, experience when the small community was ordered by the court to pair two schools.

The number of white pupils fell in less than a year from 250 to 50 pupils. According to the Gould superintendent, the number will fall to 20 in the coming school year.

The other example of severe population change is the District of Columbia. From 1950 to 1967, the over-all white school membership dropped from 46,736 to 11,784 while the black enrollment jumped from 47,980 to 139,364.

A careful statistical study shows that formerly all-white schools invariably moved to 75 percent black enrollment two years after the 50 percent point was reached.

Even a modest amount of speculation on the ultimate prospects for an integrated society can produce some extraordinary possibilities. How long will it be before quotas are set up for neighborhood development that will require the number of poor to be proportionate to their total number in the community? When privately constructed housing must be sold on a schedule determined by the ratio of whites and blacks, Jews and non-Jews, Protestants and Catholics, in a given community? When in achieving a totally integrated society the pluralism that has been one of the strengths of America is erased?

An agency most admirably equipped to keep its eye on this new social development is the American Association of School Administrators.

Although the approach may be open and uncommitted, the Association should make known to its constituents what is going on in all aspects of American life to promote good human relations, the best means of preventing discrimination against any individual or group by reason of race or religion, the extent of the growing state role in the manipulation of school children to achieve the dream of the fully integrated society, and the best ways to achieve acculturation in a pluralistic society rather than assimilation in a monistic social order.

Unless as a group, and as individual citizens, we exercise our full strength to prevent discrimination, whether it be the result of state-imposed segregatory or integrative methods, our cherished dream of a free society will perish.

Alexander M. Bickel

SKELLY WRIGHT'S SWEEPING DECISION

In the following article, Alexander M. Bickel, Professor of Law at Yale University and a noted social commentator, asks how far a judge should go in dictating solutions to serious social injustices. Mr. Bickel feels strongly that the court in *Hobson v. Hansen* overstepped its bounds.

In a long, passionate opinion in the case of *Hobson* v. *Hansen,* Judge J. Skelly Wright of the US Court of Appeals for the District of Columbia, sitting by assignment as a District Judge, has roundly indicted the Washington school system and its superintendent, Dr. Carl F. Hansen, declaring the former, and quite possibly also the latter, unconstitutional. The opinion is a jeremiad and as such commands respect. The inner city of Washington, with its slums, its poverty, its juvenile crime and its schools, is a disgrace. Against this, Judge Wright cries out, from the heart. But Judge Wright is a judicial officer administering the Constitution, and the Constitution does not put at the disposal of judges the resources to prevent, abolish, or even alleviate poverty, juvenile delinquency, slum housing, or rotten schools.

The Constitution forbids segregation enforced by law and requires federal judges to remove its vestiges. This involves no making of educational policy, and certainly no effort to rearrange a deteriorating social and economic environment. It involves removing the coercive force of the state as a cause of segregation, and then neutralizing its lingering effects. But with very few exceptions, federal judges other than Judge Wright have felt unable to tackle situations of massive *de facto* segregation in major urban centers. They have failed to act, because, as Judge Wright unwittingly demonstrates, they have no well-developed body of principles to fall back on in reforming such educational institutions as the neighborhood schools. They enter, in the area of *de facto* segregation, territory that is unfamiliar to them, in which they are not entitled to have special confidence in whatever answers they may evolve, for these are likely to reflect no more than their own personal preference or

From *The New Republic,* July 8, 1967, pp. 11–12. Reprinted by permission of *The New Republic.* © 1967, Harrison-Blaine of New Jersey, Inc.

orders of priority. There was, in contrast, a good bit of history and principle to fall back on in deciding that legal segregation, coerced by the state, was unconstitutional. Judges have failed to act also because, even if they knew some answers, they would still lack the resources—the money, the personnel, the machinery—to put them into effect. This is not a question of being obeyed. Law always runs the risk of being disobeyed, as *Brown* v. *Board of Education* often was. That case, however, was a "stop" order. When courts undertake to issue a "go" order, as Skelly Wright has done, they need resources which are not at their disposal.

Judge Wright's indictment of the superintendent and the school administration is rife with imputations of bad faith, but in the end it comes to rest on a charge of complacency only, not on a charge of intentional segregation. He condemns as unconstitutional the track system, optional school zones, teacher assignment practices, and in some measure the entire neighborhood school policy, but he does not quite come to hold that these features of the Washington school system were instituted or maintained in order to perpetuate segregation in the schools.

It seems quite clear to Judge Wright that the optional zones, for example, operate to allow white children in a relatively integrated neighborhood to escape from a predominantly Negro school into an integrated, but substantially white school. And yet it is far from clear that if the optional feature of the zones were removed, the result might not be more segregation than at present, either because rigid neighborhood lines would have that effect, or because more whites would simply flee. Moreover, the option is available not only to whites but to Negroes, and is availed of in some measure by both. Despite his imputations of bad faith, Judge Wright fails to prove his case concerning the optional zones.

One of the purposes of the track system of ability grouping is the remedial one of helping the slow and disadvantaged student. Another is to permit the quick to advance at their own pace. Judge Wright makes a persuasive case against the system as it operates in Washington. It is too rigid, it tends to validate its own predictions, which in turn are made on the basis of tests that yield much less certain a measure of true ability than is often supposed; and it does not fulfill its remedial purpose, because it is not supported by sufficient remedial resources. No doubt it could be improved and perhaps it should be abandoned. The difficulty comes in declaring a well-intentioned—and debatable—educational policy unconstitutional, either because one deems it wrong, or maladministered, or, for whatever reasons, a failure. If this is the function of the Constitution and of our judges, they have their work cut out for them.

Another portion of Judge Wright's opinion deals with supposed inequalities in facilities and quality of instruction between predominantly Negro schools in the District and the few predominantly white ones. Here there is no doctrinal difficulty. Whatever the intention behind them, demonstrable inequalities in treatment at the hands of government that run along racial lines are unconstitutional. They were well before *Brown* v. *Board of Education.* The prior constitutional doctrine commanded equality in separation. The Constitution now forbids separation, but it has not abandoned the goal of equality. So the issue is a factual one. As to physical facilities, the evidence seems to be neither here nor there. Negroes are vastly in the majority in the Washington school system, and in consequence they occupy some of the oldest and some of the newest buildings. But Judge Wright makes out a persuasive case concerning the distribution of teachers in the District.

The predominantly white schools have apparently had more than their share of experienced, tenured teachers. Whether this is a real advantage may be questionable, and the school administrators in Washington apparently do question it. But since experience is a criterion of competence in most professions, it is not easy to see why it should be discarded in the teaching profession. At any rate, the decisive consideration is that the Washington school system has not discarded it, but has simply tolerated a smaller proportion of experienced teachers in Negro schools.

Judge Wright is also persuaded that there is a substantial disparity in per capita expenditures per pupil among white and Negro schools, with greater expenditures, of course, in the white schools. To the extent that the disparity is real, it seems to be a function of the greater proportion of tenured—and hence higher salaried—teachers in the predominantly white schools. So it scarcely proves anything additional to that.

Finally, though faculties and other school personnel are integrated in Washington, Judge Wright finds that white teachers tend to be assigned to white schools and Negro teachers to Negro schools. It is natural that in a school system with over 90 percent Negro pupils there should be a great majority of Negro teachers; and so there is—some 78 percent. Given these two large percentages, it is a mathematical certainty that there will be great concentrations of Negro teachers in predominantly Negro schools. And many Negroes feel—they made that clear in the dispute about School 201 in Harlem—that Negro pupils *should* have Negro teachers, who should displace as authoritative figures the white teachers who predominated in the past. Be that as it may, the preferences of white teachers for white middle-class schools do seem in some measure to have been informally respected by the Washington school administrators.

Declaring De Facto Segregation Unconstitutional

Judge Wright deals with these matters by forbidding the track system outright, and ordering abolition of the optional zones. As to teachers, he orders the Board to present a plan for teacher assignment which will fully integrate the faculty of each school. Since many of the white schools in the Northwest section are underpopulated, he orders the school administration to provide busing to the Northwest schools for such children in overcrowded, predominantly Negro schools, as volunteer for it.

But all this is, relatively speaking, less important detail. The main and most innovating thrust of Judge Wright's opinion is the proposition, which he adopts more squarely than any court has yet done, that *de facto* segregation as such is unconstitutional. And what does he propose to do about that? "Because of the 10-to-1 ratio of Negro to white children in the public schools of Washington," Judge Wright says, "and because the neighborhood policy is accepted and is in general use throughout the United States, the court is not barring its use here at this time." However he requires the school system to prepare and present to him a plan "to alleviate pupil segregation," and to "consider the advisability" of educational parks, school pairings, "and other approaches toward maximum effective integration." But what kind of maximum effective integration can there be in a school system in which Negroes constitute over 90 percent of the school population, and in which they may well ultimately constitute even more? In tacit recognition of this unanswerable question, Judge Wright adds that he will require efforts at compensatory education, to provide equal opportunities even in predominantly Negro schools. But how is Judge Wright going to see that effective methods of compensatory education are invented, how is he going to produce the trained personnel to apply them, and how, even if he could guarantee success, is he going to see to the financing of these efforts?

Here, then, is the heart of the matter. Judge Wright's remedy for conditions that he found to be unconstitutional is still in an early stage of development, but it is reasonably clear that he, no more than anyone else, has a remedy or can put one into effect. What then is the use of such judgments? What is the use of a hortatory constitutional pronouncement urging Washington, D.C., to solve its social and economic problems? Judge Wright's opinion might have been a document issued by some group of civic leaders, or some foundation or research organization, and whatever disagreement one might have had with this or that aspect of it, one would have welcomed its attention to the school problem. But the Constitution and the judges who guard it have a well-defined role to play, which no one else can play. They are to address themselves to those features of the society with which law can deal by defining rights, obligations and goals. No charitable organization and no study group can do that job, can invoke the power of government to those ends. It is no service to any worthy cause to saddle legal institutions with functions they cannot discharge, and to issue in the name of the law promises the courts cannot redeem.

Ira Marienhoff

THE COURTS AND THE SCHOOLS: A DISSENT

In the next article and in the article following it, Ira Marienhoff, Department Chairman of Social Studies of Hunter College High School, and his colleague Bernard Flicker, of Hunter College in the Bronx, engage in a polemic over the general role the court should play in influencing educational policy-making. Their opposing views leave us with the desire to explore the issue as it has affected school prayer, teacher rights, collective bargaining, and other areas of educational decision-making.

In a recent editorial, *The New York Times* observed that "to apply legal procedures to questions of school discipline introduces a cure that may soon be worse than the disease. Educational institutions, as part of their function and impact, ought to be permitted to evolve their own disciplinary, remedial, and judicial roles and channels." The writer could not agree more, but the *Times* was too detached in its observations about the increasing intrusion of the courts into the educational sphere with pronouncements about professional matters of importance. Were the posi-

From *Social Education*, December, 1967, pp. 719–720. Reprinted by permission of the author and the National Council for the Social Studies.

tions of the courts and the schools reversed, such pronouncements would be justifiably attacked as contemptuous.

To question the propriety of these judicial actions is to run the risk of being branded reactionary, racist, or worse. The net effect of the courts' intrusion, of the educators' reluctance to "put up a fight," and of the community's apparent lack of interest, has been to diminish the stature of the school. It is not improbable that the courts will succeed eventually in immobilizing the school's ability to control conduct, prescribe standards, and set educational goals. It is all the more deplorable that educators should be a party to the process in behalf of some higher morality that only the "elect" can fully comprehend.

What have the courts done? Specifically, they have obstructed the disciplinary function of the school regarding the removal of troublesome students who make it impossible for other students to learn. They have denied the right (some consider it more in the light of an obligation) to prescribe standards of suitable dress. The courts have prevented the training of the young in the awareness of responsibilities that are commensurate with rights and privileges. Most recently, they have mitigated the consequences of cheating on Regents examinations. The courts appear to champion the civil libertarian approach which holds that the wishes of the majority, arrived at in democratic fashion by professional people in specific areas for which they have been trained, are to be disregarded. Seeking to apply to the operations of the schools the judicial restraints devised for limiting the role of government in depriving citizens of their liberty without due process of law, the courts have ruled against the school and for the individual student in a grotesque misreading of the need for restraint in an educational institution. In so doing, they have established themselves as arbiters of discipline, umpires in cheating cases, referees in matters of dress and deportment, and mediators in disputes among educators about matters of professional competence in which nobody's "rights" are involved. Only the rank distortion of the role of the courts in our society could produce such a result.

It is clear that any questioning of the courts' role at present is looked upon with suspicion because of their alleged libertarian influence. The writer dissents from the view that the courts are above criticism and concludes that they have intruded themselves into situations that are sensitive to the survival of the schools as social institutions wherein "infants" (a legal term) have responsibilities as well as rights. It is essential that the function of the school for the good of all must take precedence over the legalisms manufactured in the offices of civil liberties lawyers.

Perhaps it is not amiss to ask of the courts that they refrain from imposing judicial caveats on the schools with the same restraint that has been
exercised in the field of professional sports. Possibly the educational process is at least as important as sports, and some members of the teaching
profession are at least as competent to handle their charges as General
Eckert and Pete Rozelle are in the governing of theirs.

It is important to note that the courts have been successful on all levels of government—federal, state, and local. Standards of dress may not
be prescribed in New York City schools because of a court decision upholding a specific ruling of the Commissioner of Education which local
boards of education have construed as ending their authority in this
field. If a disturber of the peace makes instruction impossible in a classroom, cuts classes repeatedly, reviles his teachers, annoys his classmates,
and after successive warnings is ordered removed from the school when
he has reached the legal age, an ulterior motive must be sought and is
immediately adduced. The rights of those disturbed are as nothing compared to the "right of this child to an education"! Just why the courts
have been more solicitous in this matter than in the rights of those others to their education is a question not answered. Indeed, that question
is not even raised. Counsel for the students must be present, and no
mention is made of counsel for the multitudes that wish to learn but
cannot because the courts have ordered the miscreant to remain.

Do the courts really care about the sanctity of examinations when
they equate the actions of the principal who punishes cheating under
the law with the deprivation of rights under the Fourteenth Amendment?
Where does the responsibility of the school as the protector of the social
values end? What happens when the students understand that no decision of the school is final, that the teachers have no means to enforce
standards of honesty, probity, and integrity that may not be assaulted in
the courts and there find a sympathetic hearing—and an even more
sympathetic judgment? If parents fail to provide a sense of values for
children and schools are judicially restrained from so doing while the
churches are busy with other matters, who will do the job? Supine
boards of education and corporation counsel conclude that there "is no
case," that the end has come, and that the courts have entered the classroom to become determinants of the application of professional competence in a manner no other profession would tolerate.

It is no wonder that education and teachers are being held in increasingly low esteem; it is not strange that it has become difficult to staff
problem schools or that urban schools are fading from the standards of

former glory when the courts conclude that *they* are more qualified to judge the educational function than the licensed professionals. Teachers now understand that they are fighting a losing battle in a society that has abnegated its responsibility for legislation to courts that are only too eager to take up the "burden." The courts intrude with alacrity into areas of which they are ignorant, with rulings that herald the end of restraint and responsibility by the school in deference to the presumed rights of students who will listen to no regulations because the courts have become boards of education as the latter have become debating clubs.

Bernard Flicker

THE COURTS AND THE SCHOOLS: A RESPONSE

Candide finally found out at the end of his long journey that this simply isn't the best of all possible worlds. He accepted this fact and attempted to make his garden grow. I think that Ira Marienhoff should follow Candide's advice and utilize "social learnings" instead of "social status quo."

In the December 1967 issue of *Social Education*, Mr. Marienhoff railed against the probability that the courts would eventually succeed ". . . in immobilizing the school's ability to control conduct, prescribe standards, and set educational goals." I find this probability a note of good fortune if put into proper perspective. If the school were a perfect institution run by a perfect staff and contained perfect students we might not need the courts, a militant union or social studies teachers— we might only need psychiatrists. Sadly, the schools usually contain several emotionally disturbed students, teachers, and supervisors in larger numbers as the total number of students and staff increases. "Disturbed" youngsters are eliminated from most "normal" situations in a variety of ways. Some are bounced from class to class, some suspended, some encouraged to drop out or play truant, some are helped through treatment, and some manage to control their hostility and rage during school hours in order to release it upon a waiting society the moment they are free to do so.

Where do the courts come into this scene? It has occurred to me that

From *Social Education*, May, 1968, pp. 451–452. Reprinted by permission of the author and the National Council for the Social Studies.

we make mistakes with students and fail to allow them recourse to rectify the error. The courts are open to medical negligence suits—why not to educational negligence or malfeasance? Mr. Marienhoff states that we have reached a sad pass when the courts disregard the wishes of the majority ". . . arrived at in democratic fashion . . ." and champion the "civil libertarian" approach. Worst of all, ". . . the courts have ruled against the school and for the individual student. . . ." "Aha! Now we are close to the crux of the issue. The rights of the individual student are absurd when compared to the proper functioning of our proper school in our society, according to Mr. Marienhoff. The only trouble with this reasoning is that history has usually shown that the natural extension of this idea is to uphold "democratic" totalitarian regimes in their suppression of the individual. Of course, the courts and schools functioned in Stalinist Russia and Nazi Germany just as they do in present-day Greece—but what have these courts done for the individual?

Let us separate good intentions from bad theory. One cannot argue against the removal of disturbed youngsters from classrooms where they not only prevent others from learning but continually destroy themselves. Who will be the judge of the definition of "disturbed"? The recently concluded contract between the United Federation of Teachers and the New York City Board of Education sets up a panel of parents, teachers, and child behaviorists to rule on the disposition of behavior problems. This action might possibly prevent future law suits if pursued in good faith by all parties. Let's not con ourselves into thinking that teachers are the gurus of truth, beauty, and wisdom. (Check out the works of Nat Hentoff, Kenneth Clark, Robert Coles, Jonathan Kozol, John Holt, Paul Goodman, and Edgar Z. Friedenberg—to name a few —for confirmation). To err is part of pedagogical humanity and we should be prepared to admit error and seek rectification. We cannot invent a shibboleth like "We do this for the good of all" because it is tragic to mishandle even one human being.

Mr. Marienhoff's contention that the courts have made themselves ". . . referees in matters of dress and deportment . . ." reminded me of a recent issue of *Esquire* magazine in which two pages were devoted to before and after photos of various folk-rock heroes, e.g., Bob Dylan. One would have to be pretty "square" not to admit that the boys with the long hair were much more handsome than their younger crew-cut, hairless, slicked down former selves. Taste aside, who is really disturbed by the dress or hair of students? The "true believer" in "democracy"? I doubt this since some ancient democratic Greeks as well as Washington,

Jefferson, and Jackson—among others—wore their hair rather long. No, those who are disturbed by hair styles and Sgt. Pepper jackets are probably wizards of semantics who define democracy and dissent as conforming to *their* set values. Those whose peace is disturbed by the dissenter have been aptly defined by H. L. Mencken as followers of Puritanism—". . . the impulse to punish the man with a superior capacity for happiness—to bring him down to the miserable level of 'good' men, i.e., of stupid, chronically unhappy men." Mencken went on to call for men who were possessed with a ". . . steady freedom from moral indignation, an all-embracing tolerance."

I would hope that we have come to understand that freedom and responsibility cannot be indoctrinated into our students through edicts from the power structure. True discipline in education is an inner discipline based on a love for learning and respect for the rights of others. Courts of law cannot produce this state of affairs—they can only ascertain whether or not an individual's rights have been abused and try to achieve justice. How can we challenge the right of the courts to rule in favor of the individual only when decisions upset our "professional" rule? Logically, then, we should extend ourselves into other areas and attack the courts for throwing out Bible reading in public schools, outlawing segregated schools, upholding free speech for American Nazis and Communists, and preventing police from using any method deemed necessary at any given moment in carrying out law enforcement. I'm afraid we can't have it both ways—unless our students understand that the name of the course we teach is "Hypocrisy 101."

The school must attempt to give the students the *tools* with which to determine social values; we must protect ourselves from the conception that the school alone knows which values are good and bad. (Wasn't there a fellow called Socrates who constantly questioned values?) Our students should discover for themselves that "honesty, probity, and integrity" have true meaning only when the individual sees through the false values surrounding us and reaches the level of man's humanity for his fellow man. We are only teachers—not philosopher-kings. The schools we teach in are not palace court schools. We have also grown up absurd and should remember that judges can be judged.

Questions for Discussion

1. Is the use of a constitutional pronouncement urging Washington, D.C., or any other large city, to solve its social and educational problems when there are no apparent resources or remedies for the problems likely to create

more problems than solutions? Why? What evidence can you offer to support your conclusions?

2. Should the schools or the courts have the right to legally force parents to send their children to schools which they dislike? Should not parents have the right to send their children to the neighborhood school?

3. What do you think should be done with a vast school system that is, on the whole, segregated by residential housing patterns, not by the force of law? Is busing a reasonable answer to school segregation in such systems?

4. Is it possible that concentration on integration could lead to a neglect of quality education?

Topics for Further Study

1. In this chapter, a deliberate attempt has been made to study the role of the courts in local school decision-making using Northern racial imbalance as an illustration. The issue could also have been illustrated by using *de jure* rather than *de facto* segregation as its example. Can you redo this chapter using as your illustration of local court intervention the literature and cases related to racial imbalance in the South? What new elements enter into the chapter when *de jure* segregation is being considered?

2. After studying this chapter and doing topic number 1, do you think that the following statement is accurate today?

   . . . public schools in the Deep South must be racially mixed under pain of losing Federal funds, while school authorities outside the Deep South are free to follow a color-blind policy or adopt rules aimed at bringing about racially balanced schools. [*]

3. As a part of his well known "Southern strategy," President Nixon was alleged to have made some promises to "go slow" on enforcement of Southern school desegregation. Does his behavior regarding school desegregation seem to indicate that he is keeping this alleged promise? Has the Burger Court shown signs of delaying school desegregation in the South?

4. What has been the Nixon position regarding *de facto* segregated education in the North? Has the Supreme Court yet shown any signs that it may consider a *de facto* segregation case? When examining recent journals and newspaper articles in search of clues to the Nixon position and the future role of the Supreme Court, also look for comment on the role of the Department of Health, Education and Welfare regarding enforcement of desegregation decisions. How does HEW reflect the wishes of the President even when these wishes are not uttered publicly?

5. School administrators and school boards in large school districts have been under severe pressure at various times from community leaders, teachers organizations, students, and even the Justice Department to integrate student bodies and school faculties. One of the most interesting cases has been the Justice Department ultimatum to the Chicago Public Schools to integrate

[*] James Bolner, "The Supreme Court and Racially Imbalanced Public Schools, 1967," *Journal of Negro Education*, Spring, 1968, p. 134.

all school faculties or face loss of federal funds and embarrassing legal action. At the time this book went to press, the Chicago Board of Education and its Superintendent were still struggling to find a solution to the problem that would please the federal government. By use of Chicago newspapers and journal articles available in your library, piece together the story and tell what you would do to solve the problem.

Chapter 3. THE POLITICS
OF SCHOOL CONTROL

AS the character of urban populations has changed, the problems confronting our metropolitan school systems have intensified. Lower-class nonwhites have become the majority in many of the elementary schools in our urban centers. These groups bring to the schools a cultural tradition which differs considerably from the white middle-class traditions upon which school systems have been built. As many people point out, however, most public institutions within metropolitan areas have not changed to reflect the values and meet the needs of their new clients. The school, for one, has been charged with living in the past. Critics contend that school responses to the new urban dwellers are geared to the needs of a long gone white population.* This may also have been the case thirty to fifty years ago, as discussed in Chapter 6, "Ethnicity and the Schools," when city schools were treating large groups of recently arrived white ethnics as if their cultural traditions did not exist. White ethnics seldom challenged the schools although frequently they turned to an alternate system, the parochial school. Until very recently, neither did the new urban dwellers challenge the schools. In fact, the public school was considered by the majority to be a city institution that was off limits for criticism and personal involvement. Critical attention was focused, instead, on big-city political bosses, police brutality, and slum landlords. Most parents simply did not feel that they had a right to attack the public school system or to become involved in it. To them it was a closed system and unapproachable.

There exists a general belief among critics of the public schools that the origins of this attitude can be traced to the school teachers and administrators who work in urban schools. The critics argue that these professionals were trained by educators who considered schooling to be

---

* For a detailed discussion of this observation, see Mack, and Glazer and Moynihan (Chapter 6).

the domain of the professional and certainly not the business of the low-income black, brown, red, or white ethnic parent who, in their opinion, could not possibly understand the philosophies, principles, and methods of teaching. This attitude toward the school client, especially in the ghetto, prevailed and inhibited the residents from becoming questioning partners in school affairs.

During recent years, however, with the increasing effectiveness of local community groups and civil rights organizations, the urban school system has been removed from the nonpolitical, off limits category and has become a major target institution for demands by city residents. In order fully to comprehend the reasons for this challenge to the status quo and the sacrosanct nature of the public schools, it is necessary to understand the operational structure of the typical large-city school system.

Urban school districts, like all school governmental units in the United States, were established by state legislatures. Their legal status is derived from state law, which was carefully conceived to ensure their independence from city government and to encourage the separation of education and politics in general. This tradition of school-system independence is deep-rooted. It is best documented, historically, by the trend toward fiscal independence, which provides schools with the power to tax, thereby freeing them of ties to local and state governments. The effort to separate education from the partisan political system is also evident in a unique governance structure comprised of locally elected (or appointed) school boards, whose members are state officials. School board members are generally nonpartisan, unsalaried, and unrepresentative of the poor.

In the past few years, the schools have been forced to make policy decisions which have drawn boards of education into the center of the political arena. By requiring busing of children to achieve school integration, for example, many big-city school boards have gone beyond the traditional bounds of educational concerns and have dealt with extremely sensitive political questions. Such actions, which have necessitated the allocation of scarce, local resources for essentially noneducational causes, have changed the thrust of school board decision-making and have brought the schools under severe criticism from all sides. The professionals, who have traditionally controlled the schools through a large bureaucracy, have recently been threatened by the emerging power wielded by civil rights groups and community organizations. These new actors on the educational scene have shown a determination to challenge the power of the professional bureaucracy. Their goal is to secure access to the system for lay organizations, which to date have been unable to participate in decision-making because they do not conform to the standards upheld by the meritocracy.

It was during the mid-1950's that educators first became cognizant of the fact that the schools were not adequately serving all youngsters. The *Brown v. Board of Education of Topeka, Kansas* decision in 1954 provided the impetus responsible for the sudden awareness on the part of educators that some form of accommodation must be made by the system if that system itself were to survive. Before long, civil rights leaders began to push for large-scale school integration. This demand can be accurately assessed as a failure simply through a brief reexamination of Chapter 2, in which the legal battle for elimination of *de facto* segregation is traced. As integration was failing, educators tried a new concept: compensatory education for ghetto youth. Large amounts of money were poured into the ghetto for afterschool, preschool, and summer programs. All were designed to raise pupil performance in the various school subjects. Recent research suggests that these new approaches are also failing or have already failed. Many reasons are offered, but a recurrent explanation is that failure can largely be attributed to the fact that such programs are only prep courses for "making it" in a white, middle-class curriculum. In any case, the apparent ineffectiveness of both integration and compensatory education programs has led many to question the underlying organizational and control structure of the school system. Such questioning has created considerable controversy and has given rise to a demand by central city dwellers for shared power in the educational decision-making process. Out of this controversy has emerged the main issue of this chapter: *Should the demands for shared power in educational policy-making be accommodated?* An affirmative answer to this question would necessitate a dismantling of the present public education structure and require the creation of a new social organization to provide education for urban residents. The struggle to resolve this issue will be watched carefully because it is considered by many to have implications for the future of all metropolitan institutions.

The demand by ghetto residents for shared power in educational policy-making has brought the rigid urban school bureaucracy under serious attack. This attack has moved many large-city school systems at least to say something about greater lay participation in school decision-making processes. It is worth noting that the demand for shared power now being voiced in urban areas is exactly the type of school control which historically has been an integral part of small-town life. Rural and sub-urban communities were always able to provide effective local control because of the small numbers and close proximity of their populations.

Lately, central boards of education in such cities as Detroit, Chicago, Philadelphia, and Washington, D.C., have made strong statements expressing interest in studying and experimenting with models for school decentralization and community control. New York City has, however, taken the biggest step toward learning about the problems associated with community control. This step is an experiment being conducted in three areas of the city, the most well known being Ocean Hill-Brownsville. Great controversy and public attention have engulfed this experiment, which was designed to provide shared power between the central board of education and the neighborhoods themselves in the governance of several local schools. The Ocean Hill-Brownsville experiment will be one focus of attention in this chapter. An in-depth exploration of this specific experiment will serve to reveal the subissues underlying the demand for community control. Before beginning an examination of the Ocean Hill controversy, however, we will preview some of the concepts and variables associated with the issue of shared power in school policy-making.

Marilyn Gittell and Alan Hevesi
COMMUNITY CONTROL OF THE SCHOOLS

Marilyn Gittell and Alan Hevesi, both from the Institute for Community Studies at Queens College and leading authorities on urban politics, distinguish between administrative decentralization and community control, as well as summarize the general conflict out of which the shared-power issue has emerged. According to Gittell and Hevesi, "decentralization" denotes an administrative readjustment within the bureaucracy, while "community control" denotes a complete redistribution of power within the local neighborhood. "Community control," furthermore, suggests dispersal of power whereby a whole range of people would sit on boards with influence over professional employees. The phenomena described in this selection transcend most educational, shared-power arrangements—particularly those of the Ocean Hill-Brownsville experiment.

From Marilyn Gittell and Alan Hevesi, *The Politics of Urban Education* (New York: Praeger Publishers, Inc., 1969), pp. 8–12. Footnotes omitted. Reprinted by permission of the publisher.

The failure of integration plans and compensatory education programs has led those concerned to look to a reform of urban educational institutions for solutions; such reform would create new structures, thus providing a new and healthier environment. One group of reformers emphasizes administrative change; its proposals are concerned with readjustment of bureaucratic practices, new recruitment policies, and new systems of organization. The proponents of these concepts are generally professionals who recognize the need for some change but cannot radically revise their own values to accept fundamental change. The other, more vocal, group of reformers is predominantly made up of nonprofessionals living in, or identified with, the ghettos. They are, to a large extent, community leaders and ghetto dwellers who reject administrative reform and demand a complete redistribution of power; to effect such a redistribution, they stress the techniques of decentralization of school systems and community control.

The reformers in this latter group no longer accept the values imposed on educational systems by middle-class reformers of past decades, the purpose of which was the separation of education from partisan politics. They reject the traditional middle-class reform ethos that stressed nonpartisan elections, public authorities, and professional control of public policy. They argue that these values, laudable within the context of their original purpose, answer neither the needs of the 1970's nor the interests of a powerless, uninvolved population. Moreover, the ends sought by middle-class reform tradition—standardized procedures, merit promotions, appointment through objective examinations, specialization of function, and centralized leadership—are now considered instruments of maintaining the system; they are the means whereby ghetto residents are excluded from a role in that system and they are contributory factors in the educational failure of ghetto children.

The frustration that has resulted from professionalization and political insulation stems from the way in which these are used to close off access to the centers of decision-making. The poor, increasingly alienated from the institutions of society that are failing them and finding access routes blocked, turn in frustration either to apathy or to militancy. The educational system is not alone in this trend toward overcentralization and overprofessionalization. It is also evident in many noneducational institutions and groups that, although deeply involved in the policy process, have become less and less receptive to public participation in policymaking precisely at a time when an increasing segment of the population is alienated from these institutions and groups. For example, the medical profession has monopolized public policy with respect to the establishment of health standards, the administration of health institutions, the training of professionals, and even the determination of the extent of government participation in insuring the financial liability of citizens burdened with the financial trauma of illness. The logical response to these circumstances is the call for community control—the means for achieving "a piece of the action."

Community Control: The Controversy

Those who support decentralization criticize centralized control of decision-making because they believe it excludes from participation those elements that are essential to a workable system: the parents and the community. They deny the validity of the concept of professionalism as the absolute and exclusive value upon which a power system should be based. To them, professionalism has come to mean bureaucracy in its most rigid form, and this, in turn, has resulted in the alienation of parents and the community. Community control does not mean an abandonment of professional competence in administering schools. Rather, it means that parents will have policy-making power in broad terms and will participate in determining the general direction of educational policy in their communities. Advocates of this position recognize that professionals will always retain a monopoly of the skills and expertise that are of primary importance in policy determination, but they suggest that professionals should not be allowed complete control over the system, nor should the application of co-optive self-serving standards to school conditions be their first priority. Hence, a central goal of the proponents of decentralization is the revision of existing mechanisms of professional dominance—such as the rigid merit system and the civil service examination—that restrict access to positions of responsibility, barring those who, despite their demonstrated ability to contribute much to the education of slum children, are unable to meet the "objective," culture-laden standards.

Supporters of community control also believe that the administration of education on a centralized city-wide basis automatically prevents the adjustment of educational programs to particular local needs. There are, they suggest, compelling problems growing out of the varying cultures, backgrounds, languages, and levels of deprivation that can no longer be ignored; these problems cannot be approached through educational policies emanating from a single source that is geared to the median level of performance of hundreds of thousands of students.

Opposition to community control comes from several areas and is founded on a variety of reasons. Many have concluded that decentralization and community control constitute the radical proposals of a militant minority intent on challenging American traditions. They do not believe that increased public participation in policy-making will aid in finding solutions to school problems and they remain pessimistic about the stimulation of broader involvement under any circumstances. Studies made by social scientists of the distribution of urban power generally rationalize elitist—that is, professional—control in functional areas as satisfying the demands of democratic theory because the elites are multiple and do not overlap. These studies, abandoning the notion of a participatory system, serve as a continuing reinforcement of the existing system. At no point do they explore the possibility that the failure of our cities to make the necessary adjustments for resolving growing racial problems is related to a failure of the multiple-elite structure.

Within the cities, an increasing number of groups oppose community control because they fear it is a euphemism for black racism. Often these fears are aroused by minority-group efforts to secure increased representation for themselves. In some situations, however, extremism does pose a legitimate threat to established concepts of behavior.

There are many who oppose community control because they believe that it tolls the death knell of integration. This is a position that engenders much sympathy; yet, with every study pointing to both the failure of integration and the intensification of segregation in all major cities, the argument is, at best, well intentioned but invalid and, at worst, specious. Interestingly, many of those who bitterly fought attempts at integration in cities throughout the country now invoke integration as an argument against community control. Faced with this argument, advocates of community control claim that integration is much more likely to occur when the poor are better able to compete in society —that is, when they reach a material level of security on a par with the middle class; then, and only then, will the white middle class begin to accept integration with black people. Nonetheless, supporters of community control do not accept the argument that decentralization is incompatible with effective integration. A central school agency must exercise the power to adjust school-district lines in a manner designed to attain a level of racial balance that conforms to a court order. A decentralized school system, legally, has the same sanction to integrate as has a centralized school system. The key issue still is—as it has always been—the desire and the ability, considering urban population shifts, to integrate.

Opponents of community control and decentralization also fear that it will lead to a damaging parochialism. Proponents of decentralization counter with the argument that localizing decision-making will certainly produce *greater* conflict among groups in the local community; because local control can be a technique for developing community identity and encouraging active participation in the institutions of a community, it is likely to foster greater diversity. Such a development, they suggest, is particularly important for disadvantaged groups who share common feelings of alienation, mistrust, frustration, and helplessness. Parents and community representatives in, for example, New York City's three experimental decentralization districts have taken a much greater interest in their schools since the program emphasizing community participation began. In each of the districts—and all are poverty areas—voter turnout in school board elections has been relatively high, attendance at school meetings is surprisingly large, and an identity with the schools is now voiced by parents for the first time.

The greatest benefit to be reaped from community control, according to advocates of the movement, is the willingness of the community's people to experiment and to innovate in the attempt to find solutions to educational problems that are local in nature. Centralized school systems have been notoriously inflexible in dealing with the overwhelming problems confronting them today. Local control is a more visible alternative that offers greater opportunity for change.

Attempts to restructure any system are likely to meet enormous resistance from those with a vested interest in maintaining the status quo. Since the forces calling for change are generally powerless, they must organize for direct action. This may take the form of the direct vote, political pressure, and/or the formation of alliances with other groups. When these approaches fail, direct confrontations against official power groups become the only recourse of the powerless groups. This has been the case with respect to the politics of reform of urban schools. Community groups have met resistance from administrators, teachers, and those parent groups that fear dramatic change. Elected officials favoring change have had to suffer charges that their actions were "political"— that they were really trying to restore a discredited patronage system.

The crisis over the Ocean Hill-Brownsville experiment in New York City is a classic example of the struggle for inclusion by ghetto residents in the governance of American institutions. This crisis has centered attention on the schools and has made the issue of shared power in local school control one of considerable concern to such diverse people as politicians, social scientists, educators, and citizens of both the ghetto and the more affluent sections of big cities. Indeed, the term "community control" has become household language for most residents. Other than administrative decentralization, with its limited uses, community control offers probably the only option available within public schooling, as we know it, for the ghetto resident to influence his own educational destiny.

Martin Buskin

COMMUNITY CONTROL AT THE CROSSROADS

Martin Buskin, Education Editor of *Newsday* and former president of the Education Writers Association of America, provides a detailed look at the struggle experienced by the Ocean Hill-Brownsville community as it experimented with shared power in the governance of its neighborhood schools. The article illustrates the shared-power issue by focusing on the events before and immediately after the bitter, 1968 New York City teachers' strike, which was triggered by the conflict surrounding the 9000-student, Ocean Hill experimental district. This chronological review of the Ocean Hill dispute places in perspective many of the events and relationships influencing the movement to alter the governance of education. Some of the factors worth noting while studying this article are (1) the role of the mayor, (2) the influence of the governor, (3) the position of the United Federation of Teachers, (4) the central board-local governing board relationship, (5) the role of the local administrator, (6) the demands of the militant, black teachers' association, (7) the role of the state legislature, (8) the intervention of the courts, and (9) the part played by community leaders.

In May, 1968, the Ocean Hill-Brownsville governing board, one of the three locally elected school boards in New York City, decided to assume a basic power that it had never legally been given by the central board of education. It ordered the transfer of 19 teachers and supervisors, arguing that a local board had the power to order such transfers.

The UFT, 55,000 members strong, saw this as a completely unacceptable attack on the job security of its members—an issue that the union ranked ahead of integration, educational improvement and the normal functioning of the entire city. The union demanded an impartial hearing for 10 remaining teachers (the others had transferred out of the district). The hearing acquitted all 10 of charges that they were incompetent or trying to sabotage the decentralization experiment.

The Ocean Hill governing board refused to accept the 10 teachers back and, on the opening day of school this fall, the union struck the entire city system. Two days later, the board and the UFT reached a settlement providing for return of the 10 teachers. But the next day, a struggle broke out in Ocean Hill as bitter residents tried to physically block the return of the UFT teachers.

Charging that the governing board had broken the agreement the union struck again on September 13.

During this period, the city unable to find a solution, called in state education commissioner James E. Allen, Jr. . . . Allen suspended the governing board and worked out a plan that would station neutral observers in the schools to report on any harassment of UFT teachers. On September 30, the second strike ended and the UFT teachers once again returned to Ocean Hill.

Violence broke out again October 1, as supporters of the governing board tried to prevent the return of the union teachers. Ten policemen were injured. Nine persons were arrested. Teachers *supporting* the governing board walked out of one of the two junior high schools in the district.

The central board tried everything to force the local district to accept the returning UFT teachers, whose number, by this time, had dwindled to less than 80. The board:

Suspended the governing board again, since Allen's original suspension had expired.

Suspended the administrator of the district, Rhody McCoy, a calm, philosophical black educator who kept publicly insisting that he worked for the governing board, not the central board, and that only the governing board could suspend him.

Suspended seven of the eight principals in the district, all of whom had been appointed by the governing board.

The whole situation took on a bizarre quality. The suspended governing board kept meeting and making plans for the district. While the suspended principals worked from nine to three at central board headquarters, "reviewing curriculum plans," they continued to meet with their staffs *before* nine and *after* three. And McCoy continued to report to his office every day as usual, and even conferred on the phone about district matters with Superintendent of Schools Bernard Donovan—the same man who had ordered his suspension upon instructions from the board.

Five days after suspending the principals and McCoy, and two days after closing down Junior High School 271 because of chaotic conditions, the board reinstated all the officials, ordered the school reopened —and made a concession that the union would not accept. Donovan, speaking for the board, said that McCoy had the power to assign UFT teachers to duties other than teaching, while the union had consistently maintained that the teachers must be returned to their former duties in the classroom.

Charging that the board had broken its agreement, and declaring that union teachers had been threatened with death at JHS 271, the union struck again October 14. Then came the long, bitter haul.

This time, the union demanded complete dismantling of the Ocean Hill district. It rejected compromises from Dr. Allen and Mayor Lindsay. There was even talk of a special session of the legislature to consider the dispute.

The union had only one weapon to enforce its demands on Ocean Hill—the citywide strike—and it kept pressing the trigger, day after day. Days lengthened into weeks.

The strike continued to remain so effective at least partly because of the enthusiastic support of most of the school system's principals and supervisors, represented by the Council of Supervisory Associations (CSA). For a few days, even the custodians supported the strike, refusing to open those few schools where teachers wished to conduct classes. In Ocean Hill, when a principal complained that his school was locked and the custodian had not reported, McCoy told him to break the lock and hold classes as usual. At another Ocean Hill school, the principal shoveled coal to heat the building when the custodian did not show.

Within the union, black teachers were torn between their union loyalty and what they considered the legitimate demands of the ghetto communities. Within the city, religious and civil groups began to grow increasingly alarmed at the bitter attacks being made by militant blacks against the predominantly Jewish members of the teachers' union. Crowded parochial, private and suburban schools were besieged by parents trying to enroll their children.

Ironically, throughout all of the strikes, classes went on as usual in Ocean Hill and in the Harlem experimental school district, where the UFT lacked the strength to shut down the schools. But by mid-November even the Ocean Hill governing board (still suspended) said it would take back the UFT teachers and try to live with them. The governing board looked on this as a giant compromise—but the union insisted that the governing board could not be trusted.

Finally, a state court ruled that three of the Ocean Hill district princi-pals had been illegally appointed. Negotiations began again and a final "agreement"—denounced by the governing board—was reached, calling for:

Suspension of the three principals, until their case could be appealed.

Return of the union teachers, with guarantees against harassment.

Appointment of a state trustee to oversee the district.

Since that settlement, there have been three state trustees in Ocean Hill, as battles raged over retention of the principals (they have since been reinstated), suspension of two teachers accused of harassing UFT teachers (they, too, have been reinstated), more disruption that tem-porarily closed JHS 271 (the school is now open and calm) and a two-day running boycott of high schools by several thousand students.

Through all of this upheaval, the public kept reading in the newspa-pers and seeing on television a constant parade of white and black leaders, trading insults and angry accusations. Ocean Hill became syn-onymous with angry mobs shouting and pushing against police barri-cades. And the UFT projected a constant warning about the danger to all districts when "irresponsible" black militants are given power—and everyone knew the few places in the city where these so-called militants *had* any real power.

The Will to Live

The upshot of it all: Ocean Hill had taken on, at one time or another, the power and animosity of the entire city, and had emerged more or less intact. There arose in the area, understandably, a new determina-tion to survive.

But the state legislature, which last year ordered that a permanent de-centralization plan be submitted for approval by the central board, was —and is—more concerned with the bitter divisiveness in the city and the breakdown of authority. The union had demonstrated unprece-dented brute power and had made it clear that it would be difficult in-deed to effect any change in the New York City school system without its approval.

Against this background, the city's central school board began formu-lating its permanent decentralization plan for submission to the legisla-ture later this year. The basic elements of the board's plan included 30 local districts, with the power to hire teachers and fire them (with due process and observance of tenure rights); the power to spend a lump sum of money on curriculum; and the power to elect local boards and hire district administrators. The central board would conduct contract negotiations with the union and operate the high schools for almost the entire city. Most significantly, the experimental districts—one in Ocean Hill, one in Harlem and one on the lower east side of Manhattan— would be retained. The 30 local districts could each form one experimental subdistrict, if they desired.

While this plan was attacked by some of the experimental districts for not giving enough power to the communities, the UFT and the supervisors association attacked it for continuing the experimental districts and for granting *too much* local power.

Here and there, a voice of reason was raised, calling for calm consideration of the plan and for compromise that would be acceptable to all groups. But the teachers and supervisors turned up the volume and it soon became simple to locate the trenches in the power struggle. On one side was the central board; on the other the union; in the middle, the legislature.

As plans were made for alternate decentralization schemes, some members of the legislature began theorizing about the type of bill that might finally emerge. A number of legislators mentioned the possibility of a five-district bill. Others foresaw the possibility of putting the entire mess off for another year of study. But all insisted that, whatever plan was finally adopted, it had to be one that would prevent a recurrence of chaos. And some lawmakers were known to be extremely concerned about the possibility of more trouble with the union if something was not done about the unpredictable governing boards of the Ocean Hill and Harlem districts.

It is apparent from the two preceding articles that shared power in the governance of ghetto schools is an emotion-laden topic. In effect, community control—and even administrative decentralization, to a lesser degree —threaten the assumptions about education held by professional educators for generations. Theories of teacher selection, the "right" of tenure, curriculum decision-making, and accepted methods of instruction are challenged whenever the status quo is changed. It seems that just as teachers have finally achieved substantial influence in educational policy-making, they find themselves on a collision course with the community-control movement.

Furthermore, various groups have attempted to capitalize on the vulnerability of the community-control movement to accomplish questionable ends, such as racial separatism. Others sincerely believe that there is a relationship between political power in the governance of education and the educational achievement of children. The latter rationale for community control is based on the theory that parental involvement with the schools and concern for the child's achievement rub off on the child. This theory has been tested in middle-class schools and is now being studied for its transferability to low-income ghetto neighborhoods.

The relationship between achievement and political governance of the schools, and the threat to educational professionalism are critical school problems which have serious practical implications. Needless to say, these particular topics lend themselves well to political-science analysis.

Robert F. Lyke

POLITICAL ISSUES IN
SCHOOL DECENTRALIZATION

Robert F. Lyke is a political scientist who has written about the politics of urban education and has analyzed the basic political concepts implicit in the struggle for control of the schools. In this article he emphasizes (1) the conflict between democratic control and professional autonomy, (2) the conflict between procedural and substantive values in policy-formation, and (3) the conflict between community development and societal integration. Each of these conflicts can be illustrated by reference to the Ocean Hill controversy and, in fact, Lyke often does refer to the New York City situation.

American public education has long been characterized by political decentralization. Until the passage of the Elementary and Secondary Education Act of 1965 the Federal government's involvement in educational policy-formation was generally minimal. Even state governments, which legally bear the primary responsibility for public education, have customarily granted wide discretion in policy-formation to boards of education appointed or elected in over 20,000 separate local school districts. It is true that increasingly state legislatures and state departments of education have established requirements and promulgated regulations that restrict local autonomy, but still most observers would agree with

Roscoe Martin that "the public school is the nation's principal hostage to its ancient tradition of grassroots control over local government."

So pervasive is the ideology of localism in American public education that there has customarily been areal decentralization within individual school districts as well. Although there are exceptions, districts commonly have comprehensive schools serving local attendance areas, so that all public school children, regardless of their ability or interests, attend a school near their home. Elementary schools in particular reflect neighborhood identity by promoting meetings of parents and teachers and encouraging use of school facilities for social events. While the ideology of the neighborhood school generously overestimates the actual extent of community participation, let alone influence, in school affairs, education does have more citizen involvement than do other governmental services.

Areal decentralization in American education is symbolized in the power of the principal. While the board of education and the superintendent set some district-wide policies and maintain a cursory review over school programs, much administrative decision-making is decentralized to the local school. There the principal oversees all programs: there are few personnel in his school who are primarily responsible to someone else. Principals' recommendations about personnel policy and budget allocations help shape the general district policy, and their decisions about hiring and promoting teachers are often automatically approved. Principals have considerable discretion for settling disputes and disciplining students, judging whether the district policy should be applied to particular controversies. Moreover, they generally direct curriculum development within their schools, approving course content and teaching methods.

That the structure of American school systems is generally decentralized does not mean that there are no strong centralizing forces as well. Members of the board of education, the superintendent, and other central staff officials attempt to control the policies and actions of principals and teachers in the individual schools. Using budgetary and personnel powers, they have in places reduced the autonomy of principals and teachers, at times even putting tight controls on the curriculum and teaching methods. Forces of decentralization and centralization are thus set against each other in an uneasy balance, sometimes tipping one way and sometimes the other.

To a great extent public interest in decentralization is due to the bitter dispute in New York City over three demonstration school districts and the proposals of a panel headed by McGeorge Bundy to restructure the City's school system. While the events in that dispute are interesting, they have been adequately described by other writers and will not be dwelled upon here. Instead, this paper will discuss basic political issues underlying school decentralization movements in large cities in general. These movements are a reaction to strong centralizing forces which have come to dominate large urban school systems since the late nineteenth century. It is important to recognize, however, that current disputes are not merely between advocates of centralization and advocates of decentralization. The latter, in fact, are sharply split into two groups, one advocating administrative decentralization and the other community control. By comparing these two types of decentralization with centralization one can understand both the underlying political issues and the strategies of the affected interests.

Centralization in Urban Education

In the middle of the nineteenth century large cities frequently were divided into small, separate school districts or had community boards with extensive control over the local schools. For example, both New York City and Pittsburgh are now composed of cities which were once legally autonomous and maintained their own school systems; as population expanded and problems of intercity cooperation arose, annexation or consolidation occurred, thus creating one common school district. Even those cities which underwent little or no geographical expansion and had but one school district frequently had a weak central board of education and strong local boards. In Philadelphia, for example, the present boundaries of the school district were established in 1854 but the district was divided into twenty-four wards, each with a board of twelve directors. One director from each ward was then selected to sit on the central board of education. Although the central board of education exercised general supervision over the school system, the local boards retained the important powers to erect schools, appoint teachers, and provide supplies. New York City's school district was also decentralized with twenty-four boards of trustees who had similar authority. In Brooklyn there was such a committee for each school building. The local boards in Philadelphia were elected, while those in New York and Brooklyn were, at least after 1871, appointed. The impact in either case was the same: strong, central direction of the schools was discouraged while local influences were strengthened.

During the late nineteenth and early twentieth centuries, however, the structure of large urban school districts became more centralized: local community boards were weakened and then abolished; uniform personnel, purchasing, and curriculum standards were adopted; and a single superintendent, responsible only to the central board of education, was appointed to administer the growing system. In 1905, for instance, the Pennsylvania legislature reduced the size of the central Philadelphia Board of Public Education, gave it most powers formerly held by the local boards, and created three superintendency positions: one for buildings, one for supplies, and one for instruction. The local boards retained only the power to appoint elementary school janitors and to make recommendations to the central board.

Supporters of this centralization made three main arguments. The most prominent one, and the one which may have had the greatest impact on state legislators, was that local school boards were often corrupt. Board members often had connections with local political machines, and they used their influence for personal or partisan ends. A critic in New York City charged that:

some—perhaps many—of the Trustees were illiterate men, who secured their places through political influence; that they considered the appointment of teachers as so much "patronage," which they dealt out in turn; that they displayed marked favoritism in the promotion of teachers, and "pulled wires" in the interest of their favorites; and that in the matter of repairs to school buildings, etc., they assigned the work to favored mechanics, for the purpose of strengthening their position with an eye to political preferment, and the like.

The reformers realized that in the short run political machines would still attempt to place people in school jobs, but they hoped that with centralization higher nonpartisan standards would at least weed out those who were incompetent. In the long run, the reformers thought, removing the schools from the influence of political parties would speed the collapse of the machines themselves.

Centralization also helped middle-class Americans, generally Protestants, maintain their influence over public education at a time when public services in most large cities were coming under the power of working-class political machines. By attempting to remove education from politics by abolishing the local community boards, the reformers were shielding the schools from those organizations through which working-class ethnic groups had the most influence. Moreover, by centralizing hiring and developing professional, nonpartisan standards for teachers, large urban districts became less likely to hire teachers from those families whose children could not afford to attend normal school or college. Centralization also insured that the school curriculum would serve middle-class interests. Immigrant children would be given employable skills and adapted to the prevailing American social culture through a common curriculum. Similarly,

Where the old school had directed its energies, however patronizingly, to all young children in common, the new system was designed to benefit high school graduates, that minority completing a process whose effects presupposed completion. The parents the new schools cultivated were those of at least a comfortable middle class, hopefully mobile, who sought professional assistance in pushing their children up the ladder.

Thus centralization in large urban school districts in the late nineteenth and early twentieth centuries affected social groups differently, and it established conditions against which lower-class groups were later to protest.

The Unsteady Balance

While urban education became more centralized there still remained counteracting pressures for decentralization. Despite the abolition of local community boards, parents kept pressing, sometimes successfully, to influence the schools which their children attended. Parents had access to present their grievances and suggestions through the principal, who interpreted central regulations and supervised the programs in his school. Occasionally community pressure would modify the cultural homogeneity enforced on the school system by central standards: it was not unusual, for example, for a qualified principal to be appointed on the basis of his ethnic or religious identification with the community or for history and literature books to be used which gave favorable treatment to the local nationality groups. Rather than disapprove such community pressures, principals encouraged them, for they used them to bargain for more autonomy from the central administrators. Thus the neighborhood school movement and various parent-teacher associations helped reinforce what strength remained in areal decentralization in urban areas. The balance between centralization and decentralization tipped one way and then the other, depending on the issues and personnel involved, but it never swung back to extensive community control nor toward complete central direction.

Nonetheless, since 1950 there have been renewed pressures within urban school systems for more centralization. During the McCarthy Era

citizens attacked some teachers and programs as subversive, forcing educators to make tedious defenses and to exercise caution in personnel
selection and course design. In the late 1950's urban educators were
caught between civil rights groups and white segregationists, the former
demanding integration and the latter resisting plans that would increase
the number of black students in schools their children attended. That
the community was concerned about subversion or desegregation was
understandable, but educators found themselves poorly prepared to handle the onslaught of court suits, demonstrations, and boycotts. Being
buffeted among groups of active citizens, many educators became convinced that extensive community involvement in the schools would be
disastrous, and they sought refuge behind centralized administrative
structures which could guarantee them autonomy.

Moreover, by 1960 urban school districts were having serious problems within the schools as well. Many students, especially lower-class
blacks and Puerto Ricans, were not learning and were not getting jobs
upon graduation, if indeed they remained in school that long. In the primary grades such children often scored lower on standardized tests than
middle-class white children, and in advanced grades they did even less
well. Upon entering high school the students were channeled into the
bottom academic tracks or vocational courses. Parents complained that
this was due to poor facilities and teaching in the lower grades and that
the school system was perpetuating unequal treatment. Features of
ghetto schools symbolized these distinctions and reinforced the parents'
views: school buildings were older and lacked the facilities found in
white schools; teachers were hard to recruit and often poorly-prepared
when they were hired; and discipline was alternatively lax and repressive. Mounting frustration turned to bitterness when racial integration,
the apparent solution to the disparity in educational achievement, was
never implemented despite repeated promises of both educators and
board members. With tension rapidly rising, changes obviously had to
be made.

The primary response to these problems in the early 1960's was, interestingly enough, more centralization. If urban schools were failing, so
modern reformers argued, the primary cause was the power of entrenched teachers and administrators who, accustomed to teaching
white middle-class children, could not adapt to the changing character
of the student body. These educators had resisted and subverted integration programs out of fear that an increase in minority students would
lower their school averages on standardized tests. The reformers urged

that to educate ghetto children new teachers must be hired and creative programs designed. More money, either from state or Federal sources or from private foundations, would have to be obtained to finance the changes. Most important, the superintendents of schools would have to have more authority and resources to force changes through the recalcitrant principals and teachers. If the superintendents were creative and forceful, the new reformers urged, the system would improve, while if they were conservative and cautious, problems would continue to multiply. Further centralization under the right administrative leadership was said to be the answer.

However, after several years it became apparent that reformed centralization also could not improve ghetto education. Reform-oriented superintendents were hard to find, and those who were hired often discovered they could not institute change. Lacking control over personnel selection and program planning, the new superintendents found themselves hemmed in by state regulations, uncooperative administrators, and tradition-oriented teachers who resented outsiders trying to give advice. Recommendations were diluted or ignored, and the harder the superintendents pressed for reform the less support they received on other projects. Superintendents simply lacked the political and administrative resources to bring about reform.

The problem was not solely financial. Additional money was becoming available from a variety of sources: state grants-in-aid were increased for both general operating expenses and specialized programs and Federal aid was sharply increased under Title I of the Elementary and Secondary Education Act. Private foundations, anxious to stimulate change, provided money for demonstration projects. However, these additional funds were not as significant as the reformers had estimated since much of the increase went directly into educators' salaries, thus reinforcing the very personnel who consistently blocked reform. While obviously in the long run higher salaries would draw more qualified teachers, in the short run they had little impact.

This is not to say that reformed centralization produced no changes, for curriculum experimentation rapidly increased in ghetto schools. However, since many experiments were uncoordinated and poorly planned, it was difficult to know what worked and what did not. Even the successful projects were tried on a scale too small to affect the ghetto as a whole. Children grew confused and few showed real progress, while their parents became cynical about the programs' extensive publicity and inflated promises.

Thus, despite more centralization, black and Puerto Rican children still scored poorly on standardized tests and still had difficulty obtaining jobs or entering college. Rising class and racial tensions magnified these problems and reduced parents' trust of existing administrators. In some schools communication became impossible: parents whom educators asked for advice suspected attempts at cooptation, while educators to whom parents forcefully complained dismissed the critics as irresponsible. Occasional acts of lying, bigotry, and violence by both parents and educators convinced each side of the need for uncompromising firmness. Most important, these disputes occurred in a period when opponents were becoming organized. Parents found in neighborhood associations what teachers found in union locals—protection against personal attacks and encouragement to challenge critics. By the late 1960's education politics in ghettos had become polarized.

Two Models of School Decentralization

Challenges to centralization in urban school systems are now common, and in some places they may be too strong to divert. One group of critics, principally black parents and community leaders, finds the present centralized system unresponsive to the needs of their children and yet too powerful to be reformed. Black people have found they lack the skills and power to influence the central administrators, while at the same time their efforts for local reform are undermined from above. They argue that if the schools are to educate the children they must be controlled by the local community: authority over school policy must be decentralized to lay boards locally selected. Another group of critics, principally teachers and some principals in the individual schools, finds the present centralized system both cumbersome and bureaucratic. They cannot obtain needed supplies and personnel, let alone get better ones, and they are prevented by the central staff from making curriculum and teaching reforms that would improve instruction. According to this group, if the schools are to educate the children they must be controlled by the local educators: authority over school policy must be decentralized within the administration. Thus the controversy involves a choice between two different decentralized models, community control or administrative decentralization, as well as the presently centralized structure. Of course, in practice, an administrative structure need not match one model precisely; most will contain elements of all three. However, to understand the issues and strategies of decentralization disputes one must first recognize the basic demands of different groups.

Proponents of centralization still exist, of course, and in many cities they retain considerable influence. They include educators who would lose authority or their positions under either model of decentralization, such as central supervisors, curriculum specialists, or personnel or budgeting staff members. Moreover, people who now have influence over the central staff or who otherwise agree with its policies will also be likely to oppose decentralization. These will often, though not always, include the superintendent of schools and those board of education members who want to retain the access they would surely lose if decision-making were divided among numerous schools or communities. White parents' organizations interested in preserving current school policies often are firm supporters of the present structure. Finally, educators within the system who presently have good relations with central administrators or who want to be promoted to central positions will continue to favor centralization. Other educators lack these connections or goals but fear that any decentralization will diminish their power: some school principals, for example, worry that under administrative decentralization the teachers might dominate them while under community control the laymen might.

It is wrong to see these proponents of centralization as any more self-interested than proponents of either form of decentralization. While it is true they are concerned about their positions and influence, most are also convinced that educational reform can in the long run come only by centralization. They argue that the failure of urban schools lies not so much with centralized direction as with low pay and depressing working conditions. In the long run there must be more money, while in the short run there can be compromises where advocates of decentralization have valid objections. The school system should indeed devote more resources and personnel to ghetto schools, encourage more blacks and Puerto Ricans to become teachers, and develop a more responsive curriculum. If criticism mounts, then a protracted defense is in order: the bureaucracy can persist longer than the critics can, just as it did in the 1950's.

With administrative decentralization the locus of political authority remains with the single, city-wide board of education. No community boards need be established, and indeed no structural changes may be necessary. In practical terms, however, there is a significant shift of in-

fluence from the centralized administrators to the field administrators
—the district supervisors, building principals, department chairmen
in individual schools, or even the teachers. Field personnel under
administrative decentralization attain the power to make decisions
which formerly were made, or at least cleared, by central administrators. For administrators, decentralization will be significant to the extent
that they can prepare and administer their own budgets and do their
own hiring and promoting. For teachers, decentralization will be significant to the extent that they can design their own curricula. Of course a
central administration must remain to apportion funds among the individual schools, set minimum standards, and promote coordination. However, these centralized limitations are not inconsistent with local flexibility if field personnel are actively involved in policy formation, if they
have wide latitude in applying general policy to particular cases, and if
they have discretionary funds to spend.

Administrative decentralization may, but need not, involve closer cooperation between schools and their communities. Under some versions
local advisory boards may be appointed to convey criticism and offer
suggestions, while under others principals and teachers may have more
citizen contact merely because they have more power and become better access points. Increased cooperation need not occur, however, if educators feel that their newly-won autonomy must be protected from community activists.

The primary proponents of administrative decentralization are field
educators who would gain autonomy and influence. Teachers have long
been concerned with the expanding central staff controls over the curriculum, which not only increase their own paperwork (since they must
verify that they have been following central directives) but also reduce
their professional flexibility. They find it more difficult to assign what
they think best or to vary their schedules and approaches. Worse yet,
teachers have found they have very little influence over, let alone communication with, central staff members: directives and forms descend
more readily than complaints and suggestions ascend. Greater professional autonomy for teachers has been one of the important demands of
teachers' unions in urban areas. Unions, in fact, find it both a good recruiting device and a useful demand to put before the central board of
education.

Principals find themselves divided by proposals for administrative decentralization. On the one hand they are given greater administrative
authority and more influence, but at the same time they are charged

with more responsibility. For some, the trade-off is adequate: having the confidence of their staff and anxious to try new programs, they welcome the greater freedom. Others, however, fear that their increased influence may not be sufficient to handle problems for which they will be blamed. At the present time principals can pass unpopular decisions up to central administrators, or at least say they do, but under administrative decentralization they will have to assume full responsibility themselves. Decentralization may, in short, reduce the extent to which these principals can play central pressures off against local ones.

The community control model of decentralization involves more substantial shifts of formal authority and influence. The single, city-wide board of education transfers authority to boards of education in separate communities throughout the city, which then assume some of the legal responsibility for the schools within their district. The central board remains in a federal relation with local boards, retaining some authority in the various policy areas. The important question obviously is how much authority will be retained centrally and how much will be devolved to the local boards. At the very least, significant decentralization requires extensive local control over budget and personnel policy, since the quality of education depends so much upon who the teachers are and how the scarce funds are apportioned. The central board, on the other hand, would retain authority to raise revenue and divide the funds among the community districts. Moreover, it might operate special schools, provide auxiliary services, settle boundary disputes, and, perhaps, construct new schools.

Furthermore, state and Federal controls over public education, limited as they are, would continue. Thus it is inaccurate to assume that school decentralization will create *autonomous* community schools; it will merely shift policy formation to the local level. The unsteady balance between centralization and decentralization, which we have seen to be long characteristic of urban school districts, is merely to swing in the decentralized direction.

What is critical about the community control model is that authority to shape educational policy rests not with field educators but with laymen serving on district boards. Such boards can be selected in a variety of ways: direct election, indirect election through district assemblies, or appointment by the central school board or by municipal officials. Board seats in turn can be restricted to parents or other local residents, or they could include representatives of community organizations, teachers, or even students. "Community control," however, implies that at least a majority of local board seats will be held by local residents locally selected, and that the selection process will permit some degree of citizen direction and accountability.

The primary advocates of community control of education are parents and leaders in black communities, who are concerned with improving the education given their children and with assuming control of institutions now run by whites but serving primarily blacks. Racial distrust is quite important in the demands for community control: while white parents under similar conditions would have similar complaints, the quickening politicization of ghetto areas provides black leaders with both additional motivation and direction for their reform drive. At the same time, these black leaders are joined by numerous black educators and some young white liberal educators who see that their own influence and effectiveness would be increased. Finally, elected officials who consider these groups their primary constituents are also likely to support community control.

Advocates of decentralization in urban school districts are thus split into two groups, those favoring administrative decentralization and those favoring community control. In general, educators favor the former and parents and community leaders favor the latter, although, as has been mentioned, there are important exceptions. Both members of the board of education and the superintendent play a pivotal role in school decentralization. If they want to maximize their direct personal influence or if they approve of the policies of the central administrators, then they would undoubtedly work to maintain centralization. On the other hand, if they feel that good education requires basic structural changes, then they would prefer a form of decentralization. Even those who prefer centralization, however, may realize the limitations of their own influence over the central staff, and they may recognize the political liability of defending centralization against criticisms of field educators and parents. Advocating a limited form of decentralization which combines both some community control and more discretion for teachers may, in fact, be a useful strategy to prevent either central administrators, teachers, or community leaders from dominating particular issues.

Basic Political Issues

Proponents of continued centralization or of either the two models of decentralization disagree in part because they conflict on basic political issues. Three such issues will be discussed here: the conflict between

democratic control and professional autonomy; the conflict between substantive and procedural values in policy-formation; and the conflict between community development and societal integration.

The most fundamental conflict underlying the dispute over decentralization is between democratic control and professional autonomy. Both
values are important in American political culture; indeed, as was
pointed out above, they have been the source of continual conflict in
public education over the past century. The argument for democratic
control can be simply put: administrators of government services ought
to be accountable to citizens as a whole for the policies they enact and
implement. This should be the case particularly for public education,
which consumes such a large percentage of governmental revenue and
plays such a critical role in preparing children for adult life. Advocates
of community control assert that their model alone insures such accountability by placing educators under the watchful eyes of a local school
board which has the authority to set personnel, budgetary, and curriculum policy. Neither centralization nor administrative decentralization,
on the other hand, clearly permit such accountability. We have already
seen that with the growth of large school systems members of the central
board of education must struggle to direct and control administrators
and teachers. Under administrative decentralization, with more policy-
formation occurring in the individual schools, they would have an even
harder battle. Moreover, even if board members could reasonably control the educators, it is not clear that parents could easily influence the
board members, particularly if they were appointed. While parents
could be placed on local advisory committees, they would still not have
any actual authority to limit the educators.

The argument for professional autonomy asserts that educators, like
doctors or lawyers, cannot perform their tasks well under close supervision of laymen. While the latter may be legitimately concerned about
education, they lack knowledge and experience of what occurs in the
classroom. According to this argument, it is sufficient for citizens to set
broad limits to educational policy, such as what shall be taught or how
much should be spent, but beyond that they are likely to hamper the expertise of teachers. Consequently, either centralization or administrative
decentralization is preferable to community control, since both minimize
the extent to which parents and community leaders can interfere with
educational policy.

How valid are these opposing arguments? If the test for validity were
the vehemence with which the arguments were asserted during the New

York teachers' strikes, one would have to conclude that their validity is unquestionable. Analysis rather than ideological fervor, however, indicates that we can accept the theories of democratic control and professional autonomy only with qualifications.

To begin with, it is unlikely that even under the community control model a community will actually "control" educational policy-making. The often-mentioned analogy is with suburban school districts where, it is argued, white parents are able to run the schools. But this is precisely what does *not* happen in the suburbs: suburban public education, even under a community control model, is by and large shaped by the teachers and administrators. Lay members of suburban boards lack the expertise and the time to shape most policies; occasionally they carefully investigate a particular, controversial matter, but generally they just review educators' own decisions and handle routine, trivial questions. Suburban board members have their greatest influence on revenue and school construction questions, two matters on which local community boards would not even be involved. There is little reason to anticipate that community boards in urban areas would be more influential than suburban boards: while they may be able to change those practices which now produce so much hostility and tension, on the whole they too will have to rely upon their educators.

Moreover, even if laymen could control the educators this control is unlikely to be "democratic" or "community" in any more than a formal sense. In the suburbs, as is likely to be the case in urban communities, laymen who do have some impact on school policy are few in number and only vaguely accountable to the citizens as a whole. Of course suburban board members are elected, as they would be in urban areas, but typically only after a campaign devoid of issues and by a meager percentage of the potential electorate. Most citizens simply do not become involved or have much influence. Thus under community control there is danger that only a local elite of educators and board members will determine school policy.

Similarly, we can accept the argument for professional autonomy only with qualifications. To begin with, educators themselves are divided over the issue of autonomy, with many—especially young blacks and liberal whites—believing that good education can occur only when there is extensive interaction with the community. Teachers trained to educate middle-class white children can be useful in ghetto schools only if their traditional isolation from the community is reduced. To preserve autonomy in the face of confusion and disruption is only to perpetuate the mistakes which cause the problem in the first place.

Furthermore, professional autonomy has often been used to protect practices which are most unprofessional. In New York, for example, giving the educators autonomy in hiring practices has meant that qualified black and Puerto Rican teachers cannot easily obtain key administrative positions. Teachers' organizations, which are often instrumental in shaping professional goals, have long sought tenure laws and automatic salary increases, which both protect and reward poor teachers. Most important, parents who feel they have legitimate complaints about how teachers relate to their children find that "professional autonomy" is used as an excuse to avoid explanations, let alone reforms. Professional autonomy, then, is a strategy with which educators protect their own self interest while thwarting the interests of the children and the community.

Given these qualifications, some validity remains on each side of the two opposing arguments. The community control model of school decentralization will permit more community influence over school policy, even if that influence may not be very democratic or sufficient to overcome the expertise of the educators. Centralization or administrative decentralization, on the other hand, will insure more control over education policy by teachers and principals, even if that control may be used for unprofessional ends. This conflict is both pervasive and insoluble, and it will frustrate attempts to achieve agreement on administrative structure.

The controversy between professional autonomy and democratic control is related to a controversy between substantive and procedural values in policy-formation. Advocates of administrative decentralization argue that a decision-making procedure should yield decisions which are "good," and that any particular procedure is to be judged simply as instrumental toward that end. The substance of a policy is thus more important than characteristics of the procedure by which it is made. Since, the argument continues, over the long run educators make the best decisions about education, then it follows that a procedure which maximizes their influence will over time yield the best policies. Thus administrative decentralization, which grants wide discretion to field educators, is preferable to community control, which permits unknowledgeable interference.

Proponents of this view are the first to admit that ghetto education is poor, and they admit that some ghetto teachers are not doing their job properly. But the main problem, they feel, is not that there is too little contact with the community, but that ghetto schools are poorly financed and managed. If significantly more money were available, then better teachers could be hired, fewer children put in each class, and more auxiliary and remedial services provided. Administrative decentralization by itself will not provide more funds, but it will provide better management: the teachers and principals within the individual schools will have more influence in setting and implementing policy for their school, and the central administrators will be less able to interfere. While it is true that educators as a group disagree about the aims and methods of teaching, administrative decentralization will permit the ordered diversity in which improvements can be made.

Contrary to this argument, however, is the view that decision-making ought not be judged solely by the policy it produces, but that certain procedures are desirable because they have significant side-effects. In particular, extensive citizen participation is valuable: it is argued that only by regular, meaningful participation can individuals become aware of what is occurring in the community and develop the skills and understanding necessary to make a rational contribution. Moreover, it is argued that participation enables an individual to develop his personal values so he can act as his own agent, not unwittingly as someone else's. This theory is currently appealing to black theorists, who feel that only through participation in black communities can black people begin to shed the values and perspectives inculcated into them by white society. Advocates of this theory naturally favor the community control model of decentralization, since it alone permits extensive citizen activity.

The validity of the former argument turns on one critical question: how possible is it to identify "good" educational decisions? Should we really assume that educators make the best choices? While everyone agrees that education involves acquiring some basic skills in reading and mathematics, there is actually little agreement beyond this about what "good" education is. Some people assert equal resources ought to be devoted to all children, while others argue that more ought to be given those who are brighter or more skilled. Some feel schools should concentrate on training in marketable skills while others urge that they should simply develop critical awareness. History, some insist, should be taught to yield knowledge of the past, while others maintain that it should be taught to instill maxims for the future. Disagreement on these and other basic questions indicates that the central methodological assumption of those who support substantive evaluation is false: one cannot judge which decision-making procedure is best by simply referring to the quality of the decisions it produces. Thus it cannot be argued that field educators will necessarily produce good decisions about urban education once influence over policy-formation is decentralized to them. Indeed, an administrative model which grants extensive autonomy to principals and teachers and minimizes the influence of other people raises the danger that a closed elite will come to determine public education policy.

Alternatively, the argument that participation is so critical depends not so much on the extent of citizen participation as on its character. The anticipated advantages of participation—awareness of one's own preferences and of what is occurring in the community, and the acquisition of political skills and understanding—are likely to occur only if the participant is regularly active, if he finds his activity efficacious, and if he is forced to consider opposing points of view. These conditions, however, rarely occur in suburban school politics, and they are unlikely to occur in urban school politics, either. Individual activity is unlikely to be regular because it is so hard to participate in school politics: nonpartisanship precludes the political organizations which could provide advice and support; and election campaigns, which rarely involve issues, are dull. Most activity is left by default in the hands of board members and educators, none of whom want to encourage critical participation. Moreover, what action there is generally is not efficacious: individual citizens find it difficult to have much impact on educational policy, especially given educators' concern for professional autonomy, and they find it equally frustrating to try to rally community support. In the short run ghetto communities may have extensive participation (many do now) as citizens press to have long-standing grievances corrected: in the long run, however, they are unlikely to have any more than suburban areas. Finally, what participation there is rarely forces one to consider opposing points of view. Aside from meetings of board members and educators there are no regular exchanges on policy problems, and the few confrontations that do occur frequently are emotional and tend to reinforce previously-held opinions. Given the likelihood that a community control plan would divide the single urban school district into numerous relatively homogeneous districts, the possibility is small that there will even be divergent social groups to provoke confrontations.

Thus the claims of advocates of each side are vastly overrated. One cannot simply assert that educators make "good" policy choices about public education, nor can one plausibly argue that citizen participation in school politics will be either extensive or beneficial to the participant.

Finally, there is a conflict between community development and societal integration. Advocates of community control often argue that citizen control of the local schools can be the first step toward the community revitalization necessary to solve complex social and economic problems of the ghetto. In the 1960's reformers attempted to use centralized governmental services to tackle some of these problems, but they had little success. In part this was due to bureaucratic resistance and poor funding, but it was also due to inadequate knowledge of local conditions. The solution of ghetto problems, the argument continues, depends upon knowledge that can be obtained only by living in the community and upon inter-agency coordination that must be handled locally. To attack poverty successfully, in other words, policy-formation and implementation must be devolved to the local community. Control over education is seen as the critical step in this transformation because of the salience of the school in the local community: it dominates the lives of the children, it draws deep concern among parents, and, with its extensive personnel and supply needs, it is a potential source for economic rejuvenation. The schools could become social centers for the children and training centers for adults, and they could provide employment for both teachers and para-professionals.

Advocates of centralization or administrative decentralization, on the other hand, argue that community development is illusory and that in the long run the crisis of the ghetto can be solved only by external resources and gradual integration of indigent minorities into the larger society. Internal community development is unlikely, so the argument goes, because ghetto communities have high population mobility and economic and social problems caused largely by outside forces. Increasing the power of the people in the local community is not going to reduce unemployment, for this depends much more upon Federal economic policies and municipal tax levels. Similarly, strengthening the local community is not going to decrease significantly the steady influx of the poor from other areas or prevent crime. Those communities which do not have these problems are not more powerful but only wealthier: it is a matter of money, not power. Advocates of centralization argue that the solution is to provide more money, both directly through increased employment opportunities and national assistance of some sort or other and indirectly through expanded governmental services. Adoption of a national tax-sharing program, for example, could provide substantial revenue for both state and local services. Advocates of decentralization, while agreeing with this argument of the centralists, also feel that the lack of expertise and coordination of centralized governmental services is hampering ghetto reform. To them the solution is not to establish community control but to decentralize policy-formation of the services to field personnel and to promote more decentralized inter-agency cooperation. Advisory committees can build in citizen knowledge without threatening the necessary administrative cohesion. Advocates of both centralization and decentralization feel that community control would balkanize the center city at the very time that problems of governmental services can be met only by planning and decision-making on a wider, metropolitan basis.

This conflict between community development and societal integration is too complex to be adequately handled in a short paragraph or two. Nonetheless, several comments can be made about both arguments. First, and most important, both theories appear to be valid only to the extent that the reforms they urge are thoroughly implemented; *i.e.*, that ghetto dwellers actually do obtain control of important governmental services or that administrators do obtain sufficient revenue and coordinating authority. Halfway measures are unlikely to be successful. Communities will not become revitalized if residents can control public education but not law enforcement or housing policy, nor will government agencies solve social and economic problems if they are not reorganized and refinanced. Recent political experience suggests that none of these other reforms are likely to occur, regardless of what the structure of the school system is. Municipal services are most unlikely to be broken down by separate communities; bureaucracies are quite resistant to reorganization; and more funds for domestic social programs will not be made available. In general, it is best not to cast the debate over administrative reorganization of city schools in terms of general social and economic reform.

However, it is likely that community control of the schools will very quickly change the character of political interaction in ghetto communities. Citizens will no longer trace all problems in the schools to a repressive white society, hostility and tensions are likely to diminish as reforms are made, and future debate over education policy will be less likely to be as ideological as it currently is. Moreover, other governmental agencies, anxious to head off community control of their own services, will probably make minor reforms and adjustments to placate some of their critics. Granting more power to black communities is a quick way to split them into separate factions that will argue with each other. In these senses community control of education could have profoundly conservative implications: the presently mounting anger of ghetto residents may be diverted so that more significant reforms will not occur.

On the other hand centralization or administrative decentralization would prevent the balkanization of public education in urban areas, and they would keep the possibility open that there might be metropolitan solutions to educational problems at some time in the future. Minor cooperative programs already exist in some metropolitan areas, and more will be started. Of course it is unlikely that such areal cooperation will aid ghetto communities unless the political power of blacks and Puerto Ricans continues to grow and racial divisions in the society as a whole become less marked. Advocates of metropolitan solutions, however, must ask themselves whether reforms can be delayed this long without provoking severe political disorder.

Strategies

Participants in a struggle over decentralization follow various strategies to protect and further their interests. Unless a referendum is held on the issue, which is unlikely, very few of those whose interests are affected will be able to determine what structural changes will occur. To influence those who will decide—the superintendent, the board of education, or the state legislature—interested parties appeal for political support and issue threats and sanctions. The manipulation of public images is the most significant strategy, since if people are convinced their interests are going to be adversely affected they will put pressure on the decision-makers. Interest groups manipulated public images for three ends in the New York City dispute: to create solidarity within their own group, to split their opponents, and to build popular support. Thus the United Federation of Teachers characterized the Ocean Hill-Brownsville conflict as a dispute over "teacher rights" and "due process of law," rather than "community control" in an attempt to draw the support of black and young white liberal teachers. To split the potentially wide support for local control, the UFT raised the spectre of black extremism before lower-middle class Catholics and of anti-semitism before Jews. To build broad public support the UFT stressed repeatedly that community control would create turmoil in the schools, citing disruption which has been occurring in the demonstration districts. Black community leaders, on the other hand, stressed "local democracy" and "community control" in an effort to rally community support for the local governing board; they tried to split the UFT by arguing that good education in the ghetto requires extensive participation of black parents. To build popular support the black leaders attempted to manipulate the widespread concern about education and the future of ghetto schools. Indeed, the intense ideological fervor of the New York dispute can be directly attributed to these strong public image campaigns.

Influencing the public commission that recommends a particular decentralization plan is another strategy for attaining political support. This can be done either directly, by placing advocates and supporters on the commission itself, or indirectly, by making clear to the commission what provisions will or will not be acceptable. Experience in New York suggests that the recommendations of a commission will serve more as benchmarks for debate than as proposals that ultimately are enacted. This is partly due to the difficulty of devising a plan that will be acceptable to the numerous interested groups, and it is partly due to the realization of the interest groups that skilled campaigning might win an even better plan. Nonetheless, since the ultimate decision-makers may rely upon the commission's recommendations, it is still useful to attempt to influence them.

Threats and sanctions may be effectively combined with appeals for political support. Customarily the threats assert that dire problems will arise should a particular proposal be adopted: teachers will strike or resign their positions; lecturers will preach white racism or anti-semitism; children will be mis-educated or become unruly; parents will start demonstrations or boycotts; etc. Given the racial and class tensions in cities, most of the threats will be persuasive if they are frequently repeated and supported by "examples." Teachers have the strongest threat that is credible since by striking they could close schools throughout the city, send the children back home, and raise endless problems about schedules, college requirements, etc. Given urban teachers unions' recent militancy, board members and school officials are likely to believe strike threats, even when striking is forbidden by law.

Actually imposing sanctions is more difficult because this could undermine campaigns to create a good public image. However, interest groups are occasionally forced to enact them to keep their threats credible and to satisfy their members' desire for retaliation. In the New York City dispute participants attempted to maneuver their opponents into making minor mistakes so retaliation would then appear justified: local governing boards would seize upon deficiencies common to all teachers as grounds for dismissing union teachers, while the UFT would point to the hostility of black leaders they had frustrated as grounds for abolishing the demonstration districts. Sanctions which destroy a favorable public image may still be successful if, like teachers' strikes, they are strong enough that opponents will sue for peace.

In general, advocates of continued centralization or administrative decentralization have significant strategic advantages. Proponents of centralization need not rally supporters to their side as long as they can split the opposition and defeat proposals for reform; indeed, as long as there is no change their interests will be protected. Administrative decentralization involves only internal administrative changes which school districts can usually enact without obtaining approval from either the state department of education or the state legislature. Alternatively, proponents of community control of schools must appeal to the state legislature to amend the state school code. In general, legislatures have always been reluctant to grant wider local control over governmental services; they will be even more reluctant to do so against the arguments of the professionals and the fears of middle-class whites. After all, the principal proponents of community control are black activists, who have never had much influence in state capitols. The New York State Legislature flatly rejected community control proposals in the spring of 1969; it even failed to protect the three existing demonstration districts. One can predict that community control of urban education will not be widely adopted throughout the country.

The dispute over decentralization of urban schools is in large part a dispute over who is going to run public education in cities. Central board members and central administrators are vying for control against field educators, and in turn both groups are struggling against community leaders and parents, principally blacks. Although none of these groups are unified, most have substantial support from their members or followers. It is wrong to characterize these contestants as primarily concerned with their own positions and influence, though of course that is part of their motivation; instead, what separates them are disagreements over basic educational and political issues. Three of the latter have been discussed in this paper: the conflict between democratic control and professional autonomy; the conflict between procedural and substantive values in decision-making; the conflict between community development and societal integration. These political conflicts, though basically insoluble, will become temporarily settled as one group or another gains influence to determine school policy. Considering the importance of the stakes, one can anticipate bitter fights wherever the dispute occurs.

The probable consequences of the struggle for a change in school governance and the demands for shared power are not yet clear. When projections are made, however, most authorities are convinced that the prosaic urban school governance approach, characterized by bureaucratic decision-making, will not long survive.

Whitney M. Young, Jr.

MINORITIES AND COMMUNITY CONTROL OF THE SCHOOLS

Whitney M. Young, Jr., Executive Director of the National Urban League, until his death in 1971, argued forcefully for community control of the schools. In this article he suggests that shared power is not a revolutionary idea and that it is a workable concept which need not be opposed by either whites or blacks who fear take-over of the ghetto by extremists. He sees the urban financial crisis as the major barrier to local control of the schools.

Minority groups have always been dissatisfied with the quality of education provided in the public schools for their children. Because they have been powerless to determine educational goals and to develop strategies toward attaining these goals, they have been forced to accept the decisions of the larger community. The public schools are so structured that the white middle class is able to exclude the community of the poor and the black from their proportionate share in responsibility for school decision-making. Even in areas where the overwhelming majority of the school population is black, representatives of the white middle class are able, and indeed required by the influence wielded by the white middle class, to administer the schools without regard to the will of the black community—as though not only their most powerful, but their only constituent community were the white one. Until recently little concern was expressed by educational authorities for the low level of

From *Journal of Negro Education*, Summer, 1969, pp. 285–290. Reprinted by permission of the publisher.

educational achievement experienced in ghetto schools. When such concern was finally expressed it took the form of experts condemning the life style of the black family and asserting that the only way for the black child to overcome his cultural handicaps would be through programs of racial integration where he would adopt new values, language patterns, and mores and would assume the culture of the white middle class.

Black parents and community members, while not accepting this rationale knew that all of the educational pluses were found in predominantly white middleclass schools. Therefore for many years they worked desperately to achieve the goal of integrated education for their children. The years of boycotting, demonstrating and negotiating for integration left parents disappointed and frustrated. The quality integrated education desired by so many in reality served very few. White backlash and political opportunism minimized the number of students who participated in this effort. And for those who did, the price paid was great—racial isolation within integrated facilities and educational personnel who were negative or indifferent.

Today ghetto parents are rising up against the educational establishment. Their cry has changed from integration to community participation, decentralization to community control. Out of desperation with existing school systems, community leaders and parents of black children have begun to discuss and develop their own programs and approaches to change. Too often they have found that the overlapping responsibilities within our educational systems leave the majority of professionals more interested in pleasing superiors who control their professional futures than the parents whose children are in their care.

As parents became disillusioned with the reluctance of school systems to integrate their schools, they looked for solutions that would provide quality education within the ghetto schools. They were aware of the inequities in per pupil expenditures, teacher quality and condition of physical plant between ghetto and predominantly white schools. In many urban areas they asked the school board to let them share in the decisions that affected the education of their children. They proposed that school systems be decentralized and funds equitably distributed. In this way the needed physical and human resources could be attracted to low-income minority communities that would upgrade the quality of education. Such requests were either denied or granted with so many qualifications that such programs were rendered totally ineffective.

There is a deep and abiding faith in the black community that in the face of all obstacles a decent education is the ticket to success. Black parents believe a decent education can be obtained if the right decisions are made and those decisions will only be made if they have major control over them. They are weary of being presented new packages that do not reflect the realities of life in the ghetto, the varieties and the beauty of cultural heritages or the complexities of neighborhood life.

Black parents will no longer accept teachers and administrators who do not respect, motivate and teach their children. They know that the atmosphere of a school can either depress or encourage learning. They know that the teacher is essential to the atmosphere which instills confidence in the child's ability, that affection, warmth and understanding are essential if the child is to learn. And also essential to student achievement is parent and community partnership in school programs. There must be maximum opportunity for participation of parents and community members in policy decisions affecting their schools. And, there must be accountability to parents for what occurs in the schools.

A child needs to feel that there is a partnership between school and community if he is to develop a sense of self-worth and an awareness of his heritage. A child needs to know that his school is committed to him, to his success and his future. Black parents and community members have become convinced that only through community control of the schools will these educational benefits accrue to their children.

Community control is not as revolutionary as it sounds. White suburbanites take for granted their control of local school boards and school budgets. When complaints are registered in Cicero, on Park Avenue or Palm Beach regarding school curriculum or lack of public service, community groups are considered to be exercising their constitutional rights. When people in Harlem, Watts or Roxbury assert "these are our schools, this is our community," they are accused of militant propagandizing and making trouble. Community control is essentially a redistribution of power to the people most directly affected by decisions. In large city systems a set of exclusive powers and financial resources essential to effectively implementing the powers are assigned to the local community. Powers that are imperative to effective community control are the allocation of human and material resources. In this way the community has the clout needed to develop an educational structure and process that will be responsive to the needs of the local community and accountable to it for its success.

Community control also fulfills a prime requirement of democracy—maximum citizen participation. As the country becomes larger and more complex, more and more power has been vested in centralized bureau-cracies, relatively immune from citizen control. The creation of new institutions controlled by the citizens whose lives they influence is a step toward the renewal of democratic institutions.

Local control is more than just an external "paper" transfer of power; it could bring about tremendous changes. For example, a central school board might decide that funds for a ghetto district could be used to ex-pand gym facilities, in line with a city-wide decision to stress physical education. If the community disagreed, it could put that money instead into new textbooks or into a program for teacher aides. The point is that parents would make the major decisions affecting their children, just as white middle-class parents do.

Local control will be meaningless unless new ways can be found to finance school expenditures. Voters, bristling under high taxes can be counted on to kill school bond issues. Federal money clearly has to be put into local school systems. The Office of Education should declare a minimum level of per pupil spending and then make up the difference between that level and what local communities can afford to pay for schools. A minimum local school tax rate should be set to prevent locali-ties from simply shifting their responsibilities on to Washington. In ad-dition to providing more funds, this would equalize pupil expenditures between suburban systems that spend $1500 per pupil and ghetto schools that spend $500. Bonus allotments should be made available to low-achievement school districts for reading specialists, teaching ma-chines or other needed programs that would bring them up to standard. Ghetto schools, especially, have to be saturated with special services to overcome the handicaps of the slum environment.

Another solution to these urban fiscal problems is the creation of a metropolitan taxing authority which would collect taxes throughout the region, distributing them on a per capita basis to local governments. Some of the money would be funneled by the cities into the local com-munity councils under a formula based on need. It must be stressed here that this money would be wasted if it were funneled simply through the present bureaucracies that have made the public schools a sanctuary for security-minded people who are indifferent to developing their students' potentials. Little improvement will occur unless school authorities agree to share or transfer control to concerned parents. As the Bundy Report on New York City school decentralization stated, "There is an intimate relation between the community and the ability of public education to function effectively. [If] the community regards the school as an agency in which they have an investment, which acknowledges a responsibility for pupil achievement—in short, as their own—children will enter the school with positive expectations."

This implies a drastic shift in power. School administrators, teachers and unions will have to surrender a part of their power to the parents. Their refusal to do this nearly wrecked New York City in 1968, when the teachers' union called three strikes that demanded elimination of effective decentralization of the schools. Its intentions were clouded by charges of violation of due process, harassment, and anti-Semitism, but the real issue was power. The teachers (or at least the ones who struck —a large minority broke into the schools to teach their pupils) were backed by supervisors and principals fearful that schools controlled by the community wouldn't stick to the old civil service promotion lists in hiring supervisory staff.

Decentralization may represent a threat to the present holders of power, but it represents the hope of a new day for children, parents and teachers. I visited the embattled Ocean Hill-Brownsville school district that was the focal point of the New York strikes. This experimental district was sabotaged from the beginning by forces that wanted it to fail, and it was beset by public controversy. Racial "militants" seeking a confrontation with the police and the striking teachers added to the district's problems. The ability of the teachers and administrators to keep these self-proclaimed "leaders" from speaking for them and the community, as well as what I observed in the schools, confirmed my faith in the concept of community control.

Youngsters were learning as never before. They were reading and learning math and making progress that was unheard of under the old system. They were being taught black history and black culture—but they also got lessons on the meaning of Rosh Hashanah and other Jewish holidays, as well as in the customs of other peoples. They were being educated for an Open Society by a young teaching staff that was eager to work in the district. One teacher told me that he could never again teach under the old system, which made teachers afraid to try something new: "We aren't required to serve the system here—just the kids." Another teacher told me how important it was to her to have the help of concerned parents, and parents told me how important the schools had become to the whole community since the experiment began. For the first time, many parents were involved in the schools and participated in their children's education. The schools I saw were no longer the usual ghetto failure factories—they were schools that met the needs of the children, fulfilled the hopes of their parents, and gave their teachers a strong new joy in their work.

Even with additional funds, and parent participation, public education will fail unless it attracts dedicated teachers like the ones I met in Ocean Hill-Brownsville. As Kenneth Clark has said, "A normal child who is expected to learn, who is taught and who is required to learn will learn."

The teaching profession ought to have the recognition it deserves. The present system of lumping all teachers together—the effective with the ineffective—paying them the same salary, and subjecting them to the same restrictions doesn't make sense. Neither does the licensing system, which assumes that accumulating a certain number of credits in educational theory makes a person qualified to teach a child in the ghetto.

I'd like to see a system of teaching internship. Before a teacher could qualify for a full-fledged position, he should teach under the supervision of a master teacher. Creation of the higher-paid post of master teacher would recognize merit and accomplishment in teaching, just as superior accomplishment is rewarded in other fields. Interns could be recruited from Peace Corps returnees, VISTA volunteers, and others who may not meet present license requirements but who exhibit the compassion and the zeal so noticeably lacking in our schools.

The very best teachers ought to be in the ghetto schools, and, as specialists performing the most exacting and demanding work, they should get the rewards due them. Sending inexperienced or unsympathetic teachers into ghetto schools is too much like having interns perform complex operations, while the specialists treat healthy people for common colds. If we started the schools of the ghetto with master teachers and made these schools accountable to the community we would transform the dying institutions of public education.

Most of the objections to community control I have heard are based on the assumption that black people aren't capable of controlling their own destinies. It's all very reminiscent of Englishmen who claimed their colonies couldn't function without Mother England to control their destiny. Those who seek to perpetuate the colonialism of the ghetto use fancier words, but the meaning is the same.

Many opponents of community control are fearful that "extremists" will take over the ghetto. This ignores the fact that, despite sensational newspaper accounts, "extremists" are a very small part of the total black population. In general, they surface only when it appears that white intransigence is about to crush legitimate black demands. Then they tend to exercise greater influence, capitalizing on the anger within the community.

It is curious, though, that so many people who have tolerated white extremists should suddenly grow fearful at the possibility that black extremists might gain influence. John Birch Society members have been sticking their noses into local school systems and libraries for years, and responsible people have fought them and usually won. Why do some people assume that responsible black citizens will be any less successful? Every poll I've ever seen indicated that black people have little sympathy with the extremists in their midst. Local election results—in Model Cities neighborhood elections, as well as local poverty board elections and polling for state and city representatives—prove this. In fact, when we look at some of the people white districts have sent to Congress or to the State House, there is cause to believe that black people will prove more responsible.

The danger of extremist takeover can be met with built-in safeguards. Community councils would derive their power and their funds from the city, state and Federal governments, and abuses of power would be prevented by the accounting procedures and the guidelines these bodies would set. There is no more justification for allowing ghetto communities to abuse their powers in a system of local control than there is now in allowing communities in the South and elsewhere to ride roughshod over minorities. Community control is not a scheme to get whites out of the ghetto; if anything, it is designed to attract the talents and skills of white people working with the black community. White teachers, policemen, businessmen, and others should all be welcomed, for we need what they can contribute. The only difference is that with community control, their presence will be welcomed by a community that sees them as helpers, not occupiers. It would be senseless for the black community, which has suffered exclusion and the denial of its skills, to turn around and deprive itself of the contributions of others on racial grounds alone.

It has also been charged that community control would perpetuate segregation, but we've never had integration, and so long as black children are denied decent schools, and black families remain imprisoned in rotting tenements and grinding poverty, arguments about segregation take on an aspect of unreality. The fact remains that the overwhelming majority of black people live in racial ghettos, and giving them control over their own lives and their own communities may break the cycle of degradation and powerlessness that crushes so many.

This is not a question of "gilding" the ghetto by bettering conditions there. Our aim is twofold: First, to create new mechanisms that will enable people to exercise democratic control over their own neighborhoods and their own lives; and second, to equip people with the skills, experience and confidence they need to enter the mainstream of our society.

Community control represents a way to give people a choice. They could decide to move into the dominant society—in fact, the better services and education that would be made available to the ghetto would equip them to make such moves. But at the same time, community control would assure that black people who opted to remain in predominantly black neighborhoods would not be forced to pay a penalty in the form of inferior public services and opportunities. Blacks can, and, I think, should move into the large society, but so long as the ghetto exists, its people must be given control over their own lives.

John R. Everett

THE DECENTRALIZATION FIASCO AND OUR GHETTO SCHOOLS

In this selection John R. Everett, President of the New School for Social Research in New York City, criticizes as "educational nonsense" much of the thinking that has guided decentralization efforts to date. He opposes both the rigid bureaucracy of the status quo and attempts at community control of the Ocean Hill-Brownsville type. By so doing, Everett raises questions about the future effectiveness of our urban educational systems. Indeed, he provides a challenge to think about alternatives that will teach children the values necessary "to live together in peace and with mutual respect" while at the same time creating a system responsive to the local community.

Back in 1954 when the Supreme Court made public its historic school desegregation decision I was president of Hollins College in Virginia. Having once been a member of the national board of the ADA, I had enough liberal credentials to qualify for a modest amount of mail from some Southern brethren pointing out that I was a Communist and prob-

From *The Atlantic Monthly*, December, 1968, pp. 71–73. Copyright © 1968 by The Atlantic Monthly Corporation, Boston, Mass. Reprinted by permission of the author and publisher.

ably also a nigger lover since I raised some money for the United Negro College Fund.

When the Supreme Court desegregation decision came out, I promptly lost all of my liberal credentials by giving a speech against desegregation. I even got a letter of commendation from the then governor of South Carolina, James Byrnes.

They, the governor and the other segregationists, had, of course, missed the point. The point was hardly complex—that the simple ordering of desegregation would not help the Negro, it would probably hurt him. It would take unprepared black boys and girls who had been historically given poor educations and put them with white boys and girls who had historically been given better educations. The Negro students would suffer the psychological wounds of sure defeat in an unfair competition, and the Negro teachers would not be hired by the predominantly white school boards.

So, I concluded, this was not really a ruling that would help Negroes, but rather one that would keep them from getting into the American mainstream and would destroy one of their most meaningful areas of employment. The American liberal had concocted a solution that would achieve his enemy's ends because he misunderstood the process of education as well as the function of schools.

This is not to say, of course, that ultimately this nation should not have totally desegregated schools, housing, jobs, and all the rest. All Americans have equal rights in this nation, and certainly no one group has the right to oppress and depress another. And full American equality cannot be achieved until we are all truly color blind and creed blind. But this blindness is not going to be achieved by creating a situation that is as inherently unfair as pre-1954 segregation.

And now, the American liberal has done it again in New York City. This time he has decided that if predominantly Negro sections of the city want to have their own school boards, with authority to hire and fire teachers and influence subject content, then by all means give them the power to do so.

They go even further. The liberal Brooklyn College faculty voted to take into its freshman class two hundred *unqualified* Negro students as a gesture of its concern for their future welfare. Both the decentralization program and the Brooklyn College action again demonstrate that trying to use the schools to gain political solutions for America's race problems will fail and fail miserably. It is almost as though some super-racist is manipulating the American liberal with such ease and grace as to be invisible.

False Analogy

The New York City decentralization program has been so widely reported as a result of the teachers' strike that there is little need to describe it here. The gist of it is that the city would be divided into thirty-three districts, and that each of these districts would have its local school board. These district boards would engage teachers from a central city roster of qualified and certified teachers. If the teachers were not satisfactory to the local board, they would be returned to the roster to be picked up by one of the other districts.

The first experimental district—the Ocean Hill-Brownsville section of Brooklyn—has already produced the city's longest teachers' strike and bared the issues of teachers' rights and the local board's powers. The teachers were back, then out again. Like an underground fire, the trouble would not die out.

It might be instructive to look at the general theory of decentralization. The theory is based upon a false analogy, that the thirty-three proposed school districts in the city of New York are roughly analogous with thirty-three cities that have populations of around 250,000. Cities of this size stretch across the country and appear not to have such large bureaucracies that things get immobilized. They also appear to have responsive school officials who understand the dreams and aspirations of the citizens. Such city systems appear to be large enough to be efficient and small enough to be close to the community.

After all, the city of New York is nothing more than a collection of about 8 million people in a small area. The geography is not important; the number of cubic feet each citizen occupies is a useless statistic. Rather, what is important is to count the number of people. Once 250,-000 or so warm bodies are identified in one area, a line is drawn around it on a map and there is a school district.

What Is a Community?

It is obvious that this does not produce a cross section of population in a city such as New York, or in any other large city for that matter. Cities are a collection of ethnic, religious, and economic communities. When these communities reach certain sizes and have their own school boards, they can then have their boards reflect the aims of the various communities. The "community" is not, of course, the heterogeneous mixture of talent, wealth, poverty, educational level, religious heritage, racial stock, and so on of a normal town of 250,000. In all probability, it is far more homogeneous than heterogeneous.

One of the purposes of the American public school system is to weld people of diverse backgrounds into a nation with common goals, common ideals, and common aspirations. The glory of public education in America is that it was able to take the children of immigrant parents and teach them not only a common language but also to forget the historic hatreds of the bloody battlegrounds of the world. The school boards that helped to accomplish the miracle of making this nation were filled with diversity and heterogeneity. Out of their debates, their clashes of thought and ideals, and their hopes for their children came the programs and attitudes that made America.

If the Negro or Puerto Rican areas of New York are given their own school boards, they will not necessarily bring their young more rapidly into the center of American life. Such a move is far more likely to impede their progress. The schools can easily be turned into local pressure-group battlefields, with teachers and students finding themselves unpleasantly and blatantly cheated. It seems patently obvious that you do not tell the disadvantaged that they are being helped by being allowed to fight out their differences among themselves with no firm direction as to how to use the schools for their advantage.

The kind of thinking that treats the Negro as a fresh immigrant group, as were the Jews, the Irish, the Poles, and all the rest, leads to some of these peculiarly unproductive proposals. The Negroes are Americans in every way. The fact that the majority of white Americans have mistreated them has no bearing on the fact that they are as American as anyone else. The white majority has given them inferior educations, inferior jobs, inferior houses, inferior incomes, but none of these massive discriminatory sins can shake the fact that the Negroes in America are Americans.

The problem is how to redress an enormous historic wrong. If the white community is really serious about wanting to bring Negro Americans into all levels of production and consumption of the goods and services of this society, it is clear that a special case must be made of them and special things must be done for them by the people who have the means to do them.

When it became clear that the farmers of America needed help in modernizing their farms in order to become more productive, to increase their incomes and the food supply, this nation did not say to them, set up your own schools and teach yourselves. On the contrary, there was a clear understanding that special institutions had to be built for them and that highly trained county agents had to be provided to show them how to use machinery and fertilizer and how to use and reuse soil scientifically. Special roads were built for them, subsidized electrification programs were established, and very expensive systems of water conservation were constructed. This was a group of Americans who wanted to become more productive and they knew that they needed help, and the help was provided in a meaningful fashion. Some farmers rioted, spilled milk on the highways, and withheld produce from the markets, but the job was done.

It is now that the Negroes need special help. They do not need to be told to pull themselves up by their own bootstraps. And they do not need to be told that if the whites put them in schools that are predominantly white, they will be able to achieve their desires. This will not work with the Negroes any more than it would have worked with the farmers.

Educational Nonsense

It is strange that liberal white guilt assuages itself by devising programs that say white people and black people start as equals if they start school together. They do not start as equals. By custom and design Negroes have been excluded from building up the body of skills and attitudes which the whites have built for themselves. Without the tradition the Negroes cannot effectively compete with those who have the tradition. The only rapid way of giving Negro Americans this tradition is to design an educational program just for them that will attack the fundamental problem. A decentralized school system and simplistic desegregation are political palliatives and educational nonsense.

The New York City schools will be in a shambles until the citizens of this largest city in the nation finally understand the nature of the problem. Not only is the Negro not to be helped by decentralization, but the job security and morale of the teaching force are placed in serious jeopardy. Like it or not, the teachers of the city are in a union. The union knows full well that thirty-three district boards around the city with the power to engage and dismiss teachers from their schools will produce revolving doors for all kinds of nonacademic reasons. Ethnic considerations that have nothing to do with instructional effectiveness will be introduced by local ethnic politicians, and a teacher's defense against them will be weak indeed. The Ocean Hill-Brownsville situation makes it clear that, justified or not, the teachers are both frightened and worried.

Nothing that has been said here in any way defends the almost immovable bureaucracy of the centralized Board of Education of the city. It is incapable of dealing with the problem of New York City schools, and this fact has been demonstrated time after time. Back in 1961 it was thought that the difficulties could be corrected if the Board of Education were removed and a new one appointed. Governor Rockefeller called a special legislative session and had the board removed. A distinguished group of citizens were empowered to give Mayor Wagner a list of names from which the new board was to be appointed. The mayor appointed an outstanding group. And nothing improved, and the problems of ghetto education continued to worsen. Removing the old board and installing a new board of the city's finest citizens certainly proved that the fault does not lie with the quality of the citizens.

It probably does lie in the encrusted and archaic bureaucratic administrative structure, much of which was developed when the school system was breaking away from political manipulation. The Depression years added their contribution in the form of excessive and intricate formulations of job-security regulations. And it is probably true that a good deal of the unresponsive central bureaucratic power would be broken by decentralization. The only trouble is that decentralization will produce equally bad horrors, perhaps worse.

Local Desires vs. Local Needs

The simple fact is that a school must be responsive to the desires of a local community and to its needs. These two are not the same. The needs of a community are seen in preparing students for further academic work and for places in the productive life of the nation. Most local communities in large cities, or indeed elsewhere, know very little of the literature projecting the nation's work force and professional needs. It is folly to think that the average nonprofessional citizen would have either the time or the inclination to keep up with the mountain of reports, articles, and books that come out on these subjects each year. Here lay boards must trust professionals, and the school system will meet community needs in exact proportion to the skill and effectiveness of the professional and his freedom from local community pressures.

Meeting the desires of a community raises other questions. Sometimes parents want their children taught the same prejudices they hold and insist that the school reinforce the ideas and values they cherish. If mother and father do not believe in evolution, then the child should not be told that Mr. Darwin thought that this idea helped explain a great number of the facts of biological existence. Sometimes parents want racial and religious groups ranked in accordance with their notions of "truth" and acceptability. And so it goes.

There is no question that teachers must often make compromises with their own convictions in order to keep peace in a community. The closer teachers get to attempting to be totally responsive to the local desires the more they must compromise if they are themselves well educated.

The cliché, therefore, that runs through the argument for decentralization—that the board becomes "more responsive to the local community"—is dangerous and requires serious examination in the light of just what people want their schools to do for them and their children. Often, to be responsive is to kill the true function of education.

It is time for this nation to stop being romantic about education. Education is not a mode of salvation; it is an activity of high utility that places people in the production and consumption game and gives them a sufficiently common sense of the values of life so that they can live together in peace and with mutual respect. Ideally, students should not compete against each other in gaining knowledge and skills; they should instead be trying to overcome their own ignorance. Unfortunately, in these United States competition among students for grades and recognition is a greater motivation than the disembodied search for truth and knowledge.

Any educational strategy for helping the disadvantaged must begin with this recognition before it can even start to find workable solutions. Beyond this must come the recognition that school programs should only be constructed to give students the best possible chance in a dangerous and tough world. Without these recognitions schools are misused for political and all kinds of noneducational ends. Simplistic desegregation and decentralization seem to refuse both recognitions.

Questions for Discussion

1. The emphasis in this chapter has been on urban school systems. In which ways do small-town and rural communities exercise control over their

schools? What implications, if any, does the community-control issue in large metropolitan areas have for small-town, rural America?

2. Do you think your schooling would have been better if your parents had had a controlling voice over what went on in your school? Why? Give some examples.

3. Are you bothered by the roles professional educators are called upon to play by community-control proponents?

4. Do you anticipate having special education decision-making expertise upon completion of your formal undergraduate or graduate training? Do you think such expertise, anticipated or not, is treated too lightly by community-control adherents?

5. This chapter has dealt with the struggle for power in educational decision-making. What are the various groups that are vying for power? Which of the groups that you have identified do you think should have the major voice in determining educational policy?

Topics for Further Study

1. Not all educational communities are characterized by as complex a school-politics atmosphere as New York City. All big cities, however, are now experiencing pressures from various groups to bring decision-making closer to those benefiting from it. As you study the newspapers published in the large city nearest your home, try to assay the struggle for shared power that the system is experiencing. Are there any parallels with the New York City crisis? What seem to be the roles of the various actors in the struggle for community control in the city you are studying?

2. No attempt has been made in this chapter to comment directly on the future of the Ocean Hill-Brownsville situation. After a comprehensive review of the literature related to this experiment, make some predictions about its future. On what available evidence do you base your predictions?

3. Study the Coleman Report and *Racial Isolation in the Public Schools.*° Also search for other major studies related to school achievement in the ghetto. From what you are able to learn, do you feel that there might be a relationship between educational achievement and the source of political power controlling the public schools?

4. There seems to be a basic assumption underlying the argument that community control of schools is the best form of governance for the ghetto school. The assumption is that teachers, principals, and other school officials will be more accountable to the community they serve after decision-making has been transferred to the community. Interview a number of teachers, principals, and other school officials in an attempt to ascertain whether their professional obligations and responsibilities would be influenced by a change in political control of the schools.

° James Coleman *et al., Equality of Educational Opportunity.* Washington, D.C.: U. S. Office of Education, 1966.

Racial Isolation in the Public Schools, A Report of the U. S. Commission on Civil Rights. Washington, D.C.: U. S. Government Printing Office, 1967.

5. Interview a number of teachers' union members in the large city near your home in order to learn whether they would have supported the union stand in the Ocean Hill controversy. Develop the items for your interview schedule from a reexamination of the union stand portrayed in selections from this chapter.

Chapter 4. TEACHER POWER

A FEW short years ago, Americans viewed their public school teachers as timid but dedicated public servants. A teacher was a kindly soul, committed to a job which paid lowly wages and offered trying working conditions—someone whose psyche was soothed through rewards found in the noble pursuit of service to the young. Teachers were the protectors of the status quo. They could be counted upon to transmit to their charges, with little variation, that which had been transmitted to them. When one reflected upon the teachers encountered in schooling, the reflection revealed a nostalgic picture of a benevolent, maidenly Miss Jones or the outwardly gruff but essentially sensitive teacher-coach—to whom all sorts of magical, life-changing powers were attributed. The power associated with militancy was conspicuously missing.

This perception of teachers still lingers in many parts of the country. Teachers themselves have played no small part in contributing to and sustaining it. They have tended to acquiesce to anachronistic norms governing their private and public lives (except while away from the community, as the often-repeated story about the vacationing teacher tells us), and have willingly accepted an impotent role in educational-policy matters.

Many people have looked for the causes of the stereotype and teachers' contributions to it. Some would have us believe that the overriding cause is the fact that teaching has been a woman's profession, comprised of too many people who looked upon it as an interval between undergraduate studies and marriage. Others argue that teaching has been used as a vehicle for upward social mobility and that status seekers, however small the climb, are willing to put up with all sorts of conditions while making their climb. Still others point out that teachers are the most poorly educated of our crucial professions—that they know it or sense it and have therefore been inclined to accept a second-class professional citizenship.

The real causes probably lie in a combination of the above and many

193

other factors. But today, these explanations are merely academic or the purview of historians. During the last ten years—and particularly in the last five—a dramatic change has taken place in how society views teachers and in how teachers view themselves. Increasingly, teachers are renouncing the old stereotype and, in the process, destroying it.

The move away from traditional perceptions began in teacher efforts to improve their salaries and in related money matters. It soon spread to an expression of deep concern over working conditions, teacher training, and demands for a more influential role in school-policy matters. Today, teachers are expressing their collective concern and, hence, influence, over larger social issues such as civil rights and the war in Vietnam. Only a minority of teachers are militantly involved in these issues. But few people are willing to deny that teacher activism is laying to rest the old stereotype of teachers.

Local school boards, city councils, state departments of education, and state legislatures—individually and collectively—have been the major targets of teacher militancy. This is easily understood. Much of teacher dissatisfaction is a function of decisions bearing upon educational matters in which these agencies played a major part. Teachers are dissatisfied with their salaries, the percentage of revenue for public schools, per capita state expenditures for education, working conditions, certification requirements and procedures, the public servant role ascribed to them, and the quality of the professional training they received and are expected to engage in continually for purposes of tenure and salary increases.

What accounts for the dramatic and rapid change within the teaching profession? What underlies teacher militancy? Are teaching conditions really substandard? Is teacher militancy merely a function of interorganizational jealousy and rivalry? What is the forecast for teacher power? How does it relate to the growing interest in community control of schools? Will the National Education Association and the American Federation of Teachers merge? Is teacher militancy truly aimed at improving the quality of education for all youngsters? Are teachers ready and capable of setting performance standards by which teachers should be judged? No one answer to any one of these questions would suffice. But there are several social forces which may help us to understand why teachers have become militant: the increased awareness of all members of society regarding the problems of education; the increased level of consciousness regarding social problems in general; the increased affluence of America and the readiness of those who do not share in it—or who think their share is not commensurate with their contributions—to protest militantly against what they perceive to be oppressive conditions; and the rivalry between the National Education Association and the growing American Federation of Teachers. The questions above and those factors which play upon any answers to them are the substance of this chapter and the issue therein: *Is teacher militancy aimed at, and a necessary condition for, improving the teaching profession and bettering education for all children and youth?*

Lester S. Vander Werf

MILITANCY AND THE PROFESSION OF TEACHING

In the first descriptive selection, Lester S. Vander Werf identifies some of the major professional questions which surround the present militancy of teacher groups. He notes that the issue of teacher militancy is not appropriately dealt with if one merely debates the "professionalism" of unions vs. professional organizations, the ethics of strikes or other work stoppages, or the extent of teacher dedication. Vander Werf points out that the essence of the teacher militancy issue involves the nature and functions of a profession. Accordingly, he describes three major areas of professional responsibility and cites some emerging pressures which may move the teaching profession to handle these professional responsibilities more effectively than has been the case in the past.

Lester S. Vander Werf is Dean of the Graduate School of Education at Long Island University.

As one who has gone on record advocating, over many years, increasing responsibility for, and corporate autonomy of, teachers, this writer views the present militancy of teacher groups with strangely mixed feelings and even alarm. The issue is not unions vs. professional organizations, since it is difficult at best to validate the differences between them. The worst of the semantic quibbling is suggested by the question: Can a union member call himself professional? The United Federation of College Teachers uses the phrase "professional unionism." Nor is the issue one of strikes or other work stoppages, although both the American Federation of Teachers locals and the National Education Association affiliates recently have been responsible for several of them. Finally,

From *School and Society*, March, 1970, pp. 171–173. Reprinted by permission of the publisher.

it is not a matter of dedication, for who would attempt to measure the statistically significant difference between the average dedication index of NEA members as opposed to AFT members.

The real issues involve what a profession is and does. While the term profession has been defined variously, nearly all definitions suggest specialized knowledge, a high degree of autonomy, admission by other professionals according to standards set by professionals, protection from those who fail to meet the standards, educating the public to its service importance as well as the standards, and others.

Traditionally, teachers' organizations have paid little attention to any of these except perhaps in a small way to specialized knowledge and only recently to autonomy. It is the nature of the growing autonomy as exemplified by negotiated agreements that we should examine and seek to draw some inferences. In order to do this it would not be improper to use as an example New York City, whose Board of Education and United Federation of Teachers negotiated, in the fall of 1968, with national impact, the most sophisticated and hard-nosed contract in the country.

As one reads the contract with its 600 odd items, one is impressed with the way the whole thing is put together, with only a smidgen of mutual trust shining through, and with as little as possible left to chance. Furthermore, there is the clearest bending of diction to purpose. One can "excess" a class by the number of students over the contracted limit. In this context, excess is a power word, a hard, brutal word, especially when a class is *excessed* administratively. Every category of teacher is listed and provided for by class size, teaching periods, relief from non-teaching chores, transfers, and similar matters. For example, a teacher can apply for transfer every five years, but those longest in service, of course, always have seniority. Nearly every category of school and special class is mentioned—each with its own vagaries, class limits, and restrictions on personnel.

A cluster teacher has a program of 20 45-minute teaching periods a week, with some non-preparation periods assigned by the principal. A teacher of the homebound works a six-and-a-half-hour day; a teacher of industrial arts or home economics in special service schools has 23 teaching, seven preparation, and five administrative periods; while one in a regular junior high school has 26 teaching, five preparation, and four administrative periods. One could go on about a dozen more examples of hardening of the categories.

How is this to be viewed? The first inference is that what is numeri-

cally limiting is likely to become maximum. A teacher's work is described as so many periods, period. Any commitment beyond this will
be viewed as harmful to all teachers, as suspected ingratiation, and,
therefore, unpopular with union leaders as very "unprofessional." There
is evidence that this happens rather frequently. If it seems commendable
to set limits on class size—the first New York City contract set a precedent for this—does a profession set limits on everything else? Traditionally, professions have used service, not gain, as the ordering principle.
Nor can service be measurable in hours. Could it not be argued that the
more detailed the contract, the more the agreement is sprayed with mi-
nutiae, the farther removed from "professional" everybody gets? For, by
virtue of the spelling out of detail, general principles are defined and,
thus, restricted. This very restriction cramps professional style and flexibility.

Quite a different view was possible by observing the picket lines
while the negotiations were being carried on during the strike. It is
common knowledge that, when on strike, teachers tend to mimic the
overt behaviors often cited for laborers on strike: the purple language
hurled at non-striking colleagues, the slashing of automobile tires, and
other quite unprofessional activities. Pressed for objective statements describing events, teachers will admit these things, but union officialdom
rarely will. In free discussion, this nub appears like a club. Many teachers simply do not want to be associated with these behaviors or run the
risk of being so associated.

What is it about strikes that seems to bring out the worst in some people? Perhaps the condition is just another reminder of how thin the line
is that we all walk between our human and animal natures. None of
these remarks should be interpreted as necessarily anti-strike, for there
are times when teachers' perceptions reveal no alternative. In the past,
teachers often were intimidated by boards of education and administrators. Yet, it seems unfortunate that our politics so prescribe our perceptions as to make misunderstanding—to say nothing of outright warfare
—necessary.

There is still another item worth mentioning. Following the release of
the Bundy report on school decentralization for New York City, the
UFT, predictably and typically, supported the Board of Education in a
negative response. With a common enemy, the parties of agreement
often band together. Liberal perhaps in some ways, the union leadership
became hidebound conservative on this issue for quite obvious reasons:
if there were, in fact, to be 30 to 60 independent districts with authority

to appoint, there would be powerful forces working against a monolithic union structure. However, the point is that a profession should attempt to thaw the frigidities of a system rather than to freeze in support of them.

It may be too early for teachers to question the results of this attitude. It is, of course, true, particularly in large cities, that teachers function in strong bureaucracies with their hierarchies of leadership, strict protocols of authority, and unbending, carefully defined structures. Under such an array of pigeon-holes within tightly varnished boxes, teachers are discouraged from making waves, stepping up innovations, or developing imagination. Yet, now that teachers have forced themselves into power positions to effect the processes of decision-making, they find that, while in some ways their security is enhanced, freedom or independence is even less possible than formerly.

Because the AFT forced the NEA to a more aggressive stance, "professional" attitudes are placed in limbo for another eon. The "unity" of the profession has all but disappeared, what with the labor-management dichotomy blazing like a fiery cross on all hillsides. Educational administrators and teachers belong to different "professions." There are many signs that administrators will go it alone. Altogether, I am not at all sanguine that teaching will arrive in our time at anything like professional status. But, it is fair to ask what it would take to do so.

Ideally, it would take a deliberately planned relationship among the length of preparation, the ability to complete the preparation, and the salary the preparation would demand. This relationship does not exist presently, but would be a natural relationship in the sense that if the preparation were long enough and difficult enough, salaries would be higher. As it is, we have tended to develop salary schedules based on credit accumulation.

The first professional responsibility is preparation for the profession. Teachers now work at several different levels of preparation: teacher aides; substitutes, both temporary and permanent; and teachers with bachelor's degrees, master's degrees, sixth-year advanced certificates, and doctorates. While all of them do not apply in all school systems, there is no generally accepted notion of what a teacher's preparation ought to be either in length or content, although there is a trend among the 50 states to require five years (master's) of preparation for permanent certification. One of the first items then is for teachers to decide the guidelines for preparation. Once this professional responsibility is assumed, teachers could call an agency like the National Council for Accreditation in Teacher Education (NCATE) to help them firm up programs and eliminate the weak institutions.

If teachers can not agree on what kind of people they wish to have as colleagues, they are not likely to set up criteria for admission to teaching nor assume the responsibility for admission. This, however, is the second major professional responsibility. Here we must distinguish between professional licensure and state certification. Certification is a civil service function and should concern itself with citizenship, health, age, applicability of tenure, etc. Certification should follow admission into the profession because if one can not be admitted, the civil service items are obviated. Admission to the profession suggests graduation from an approved school and the passing of examinations, either state or national. Admission by examination is the practice of many other professions now. Teaching is not a trade.

The third major professional responsibility is the elimination of incompetents. No college, however superior, will guarantee the character of its graduates forever. People do vary markedly in their responses to a code of ethics. Nor, for that matter, will the completion of a doctor's degree guarantee first-rate teaching. While teachers are loath to meet these issues, it seems odd that a group which spends its life making judgments about students seems most reluctant to judge its peers or to have its peers in the seat of judgment. If teachers want power, they could use it no more effectively than here. From the public's view, however, unless teachers go about this in a planned and determined fashion, there will be increasing resistance to across-the-board salary increments.

A profession should assume, of course, more than these three basic responsibilities. Yet, there is little indication, aside from an occasional small voice, that teachers will take these seriously. However, there are three "movements" that will be interesting to watch. The first is a possible merger of the NEA with the AFT. Overtures have been made and so far rejected; yet, the energies now expended in the competition could be used more fruitfully elsewhere. The second is the noise being made by NEA affiliates. The American Educational Research Association has left the NEA fold, while the American Association of School Administrators and the Association for Supervision and Curriculum Development, both large and powerful, have discussed separation and will do so again. The third is the behavior of state legislatures. States increasingly have permitted or demanded negotiation between teachers and school boards.

With added contradictory pressures from many sides, American citizens will want to know if this trend is halted, reversed, or extended, and they may wish to add some pressures of their own.

Peter A. Janssen

THE UNION RESPONSE TO
ACADEMIC MASS PRODUCTION

The advent of teacher militancy is directly related to the rapid growth of the American Federation of Teachers. A few short years ago the AFT was virtually unheard of among teachers. Today, it symbolizes teacher power. Peter Janssen, Education Editor of *Newsweek*, offers an in-depth look at the AFT. He discusses its history, traditional and emerging loyalties, and influence upon teacher activism. An understanding of these matters is crucial to an understanding of the nature, functions, and likely eventualities of teacher militancy.

As you read this article, recall the three major responsibilities of a profession as described by Vander Werf. Do you see any possible contradictions or conflicts between these responsibilities and the role of the AFT as described by Janssen?

Ten years ago, the American Federation of Teachers (AFL-CIO) was so limp it employed—and could afford—only one organizer to recruit new members in the entire United States east of Lincoln, Nebraska. Today, the AFT is powerful enough to shut down many of America's largest school systems—and often does. In the idiom of the cities where it musters its strength, the AFT is "what's happening, baby." Now its very success begins to raise serious questions about the applicability of trade union techniques to the classroom—and, beyond that, about the possibility that the AFT itself will become as rigid and hierarchical as the school systems in which it operates.

The AFT is enjoying a period of almost frantic growth. Its membership has doubled in the last four years, reaching more than 146,000 today. In a series of chain-fire victories, it has beaten the established 1,000,000-member National Education Association in elections to represent teachers in collective bargaining with school boards in New York,

From *Saturday Review*, October 21, 1967, pp. 64–66, 86–88. Copyright © 1967 Saturday Review, Inc. Reprinted by permission of the author and publisher.

Chicago, Detroit, Boston, Philadelphia, Cleveland, Providence, Gary, and Washington, D.C.

The federation's growth is a direct product of the malaise of big-city schools with their all-too-familiar litany of problems: crowded classes, deteriorating buildings, overwhelming bureaucracy, irrelevant curriculum. In these conditions, teachers have more often been wardens than instructors. Suffering under mounting clerical and disciplinary chores, they are rewarded with subsistence-level pay. Last year, the average pay for teachers was $6,821; for construction workers, $7,525. Only 6.5 per cent of all teachers made more than $10,000. To dissatisfied teachers, the AFT promised a change, playing the theme that the NEA was so tied in with the existing system that it somehow was responsible for the deterioration. Above all, the AFT stresses that it is a teachers' organization. "Teachers want to do things for themselves," says Charles Cogen, diminutive (5 feet, 2 inches) AFT president. "They want the freedom and the power to control their own professional destiny."

The AFT gave teachers a clear chance to break with the past by separating them from their administrators, urging them to band together to protect their interests from oppressive bosses. AFT leaders even stepped out of the gentlemanly schoolteacher mold to emphasize the point. "Martinets, authoritarians, petty tyrants—these are too often the characteristics of administrators," Cogen has said. In too many cases his charge rang true. The AFT constitution prohibits anyone with the rank of principal or higher (or any organization of such persons) to become members. Union organizers point out, meanwhile, that the American Association of School Administrators is a branch of the NEA.

The secret ballot has become a key to the AFT's success. Significantly, in almost all its elections with the NEA, the federation is the decided underdog. The fact that it often wins—receiving far more votes than it has members—supports Cogen's assertion that teachers feel coerced into joining the NEA by supervisors who for decades have moved through a series of NEA departments. In November 1964, for example, the Philadelphia federation did not even have a representative in 40 per cent of the city's schools. Three months later, in a secret ballot election, it handily defeated the NEA affiliate which had twice as many registered members.

The union, of course, doesn't win all its bargaining contests. The NEA has beaten it in Rochester, Buffalo, Denver, and twice in Milwaukee—where it is still weak—and Newark, where the AFT was licked at its own game. Both the New Jersey Education Association and its Newark affiliate are among the most militant in the NEA. The Newark teachers association has even walked out on strike, with the support of the NJEA —exercising a form of protest frowned on by the NEA. And the federation's chances in Newark weren't helped when labor leaders there lobbied publicly against the state's sales tax to help support education.

Usually the AFT manages its power more effectively. Catching the public sympathy with the early tactics of the civil rights movement, it has often broken state laws by taking to the streets to win a point. In the last school year alone, the AFT sponsored twenty-two strikes across the country, from New York and Baltimore to the Camp Parks Job Corps Center in California. "If teachers don't fight for better schools," Cogen asks, "who will?" The growing number of male teachers, and the declining enchantment with being merely a white-collar "professional" —regardless of pay and working conditions—have helped the AFT carry the battle. In general, its appeal is to younger teachers who have seen the dark realities of urban schools and are persuaded that a romantic attachment to "dedication" is not enough, either for them or their pupils.

The strikes have been helped substantially by $250,000 grants in each of the last three years from the Industrial Union Department of the AFL-CIO. Strikes further have given the AFT's growth a snowballing effect, advancing its image as a militant fighter for teachers' rights, destroying the picture of the teacher as a silent partner in the educational process. Nothing kills the Mr. Chipps fantasy faster than a picture of striking teachers being loaded into police vans in Baltimore.

Most of the AFT's strikes have paid off as teachers sit at negotiating tables as equals with their school boards. Such collective bargaining usually produces higher salaries and smaller class size in rapid order. The United Federation of Teachers, the AFT's New York local, achieved an average pay increase of $750 per teacher in 1962, when it negotiated the city's first contract. That document also contained thirty-four fringe benefits and guaranteed teachers a duty-free lunch period for the first time in memory. Contracts also often emphasize straight labor items. The contract which went into effect last January 1 in Chicago, for instance, stipulates that "the high school day may begin and end at different times from school to school but shall not exceed 406 minutes in length for a high school teacher"—establishing a nice round number. Philadelphia teachers were ecstatic when the federation won a contract guarantee of $7.50 an hour for extracurricular duties—particularly since the previous rate was $2.75.

Such victories, and the battles that precede them, have raised serious questions about the use of trade union techniques in the educational process. The questions have to do not only with the right of public employees to strike or with the philosophical problem arising from definitions of "professional conduct," but also with the issue of power itself. The traditional union aims—shorter hours, more pay, protection of members—are not necessarily consistent with the improvement of education, and a union contract which stipulates the maximum number of hours a teacher can work is not likely to reduce the dropout rate. Stamping out fenders in an automobile plant requires a different set of incentives and different organization from the process of teaching children to read, and the critics of the union have not been slow to point out the difference. Yet, not surprisingly, the AFT has been most successful in exactly those school systems which look and operate like factories. The big-city administrations and the public have created the factory school; the teachers' union is the employees' response.

If the AFT acts like an industrial union, its traditional loyalties—and its current public relations efforts—tend to place it with the liberal wing of the labor movement. The organization promotes its image of currency by aligning itself with the civil rights movement and by borrowing some of its techniques. In 1951, three years before *Brown v. Topeka,* it ordered its Southern locals to desegregate or get out. (This was not a costly decision. It had only seven.) The AFT provided teachers and $50,000 to set up Freedom Schools in 1964 for more than 4,000 Southern Negro pupils. Last year it created a civil rights department and then sponsored a "Racism in Education" conference in Washington. More than 1,000 teachers there resolved to drop the "slave name" of "Negro" from the curriculum and use "Afro-American" instead. Finally, on the first day of the recent New York strike, Bayard Rustin, the movement's philosopher and leader of the 1963 March on Washington, was out walking the picket lines with UFT President Albert Shanker. Estimates are that as many as one-fifth of the AFT's members are Negroes.

In practice, however, the federation's commitment is less certain. The union and the movement have developed divergent interests. The UFT, for example, did not support the Reverend Milton Galamison's massive school boycott to promote integration in 1964. As a result, many disgusted New York teachers formed their own organization, the African American Teachers Association, which now claims half the city's 4,800 Negro teachers as members—and has its offices in Bedford-Stuyvesant. (The UFT's offices are on Park Avenue.) "The UFT," says the association's president, Albert Vann, "is concerned with teachers' rights and salaries, but not so much with community problems." At a time when ghetto parents are asking for year-round schools, the union demands shorter hours; while black parents ask for local control, as at Intermediate School 201 last year, the union adopts as protective a response as does the Board of Education hierarchy. AFT locals also often work against civil rights by vetoing plans to integrate faculties, insisting that teachers have the right to transfer to any school. This insistence places large numbers of inexperienced teachers in ghetto schools, but it doesn't disturb federation members who have seniority.

The AFT was founded by four teachers' groups in Chicago in 1916 and affiliated with the American Federation of Labor. Its first charters went to locals in Chicago, Gary, Oklahoma City (Oklahoma), Scranton (Pennsylvania), New York, and Washington, D. C. The new union's growth was slow. By 1934 it had fewer than 10,000 members (including professors from Harvard, Yale, Princeton, Chicago, and Wisconsin—a clientele the AFT would like to renew). Throughout the Thirties the federation was split bitterly by internal Communist problems. In 1941 its members voted to expel locals in New York and Philadelphia (which subsequently reorganized) after investigations found too much Communist influence.

The federation remained fairly dormant until the Sputnik era started the public thinking that something might be wrong with the schools. Dave Selden, an early AFT organizer, recalls that by the mid-Fifties "we probably had a net gain of 100 teachers a year. There were too many issues. The federation wanted to get involved in everything— religion, politics, you name it. It didn't even have a clear policy on strikes."

But AFT leaders then made a policy decision to concentrate on New York, where teachers were split into scores of competing and overlapping organizations. Cogen, then president of the UFT, led a one-day strike (the first in the city's history) in November 1960, to force the New York school board to hold a teacher-representation election. When the election was granted the next year, the UFT beat a hastily organized Teachers Bargaining Organization supported by the NEA and kept its momentum by staging a one-day strike during its first contract negotiations the next spring. More than half the system's 40,000 teachers stayed home, and the AFT had arrived almost overnight as a power.

To a large degree, the federation's growth is due to Cogen and Selden. Cogen, sixty-four, is from Brooklyn, an economics honors graduate of Cornell (where he won the intramural wrestling championship in the 115-pound class) who went on to Fordham law school and tried his hand as a lawyer in 1930. By 1933 he had started his career as a teacher with a $25-a-week job in Brooklyn. Soft-spoken in person, he is a bull-horn on the platform. But it is Selden, a former Dearborn teacher who organized the UFT, who takes care of the details. It is Selden who briefs reporters at AFT conventions, and it was Selden who was working in a corner of Shanker's office the first day of September's New York strike. Selden is personable, blond, and casual (coming on at a recent press conference in blue blazer, olive pants with white stripes, madras shirt, and loafers). Both Cogen and Selden are firmly committed to militancy and collective bargaining.

When Cogen was elected president of the AFT by a margin of thirty votes in 1964, he brought Selden along as his assistant. At the time, the AFT was divided into two parties—or caucuses. The National Caucus, with its strength in Chicago, was not sure it indorsed collective bargaining or even a strict union identification. Cogen's Progressive Caucus has been more militant and thoroughly committed to working within the AFL-CIO. In 1966 Cogen was re-elected easily, carrying the entire progressive slate of sixteen AFT vice presidents with him. The Progressive Caucus's aims are unmistakable. The very first goal of its platform states that it will "work closely with those forces in the labor movement to organize those workers presently unorganized." The National Caucus was all but eliminated when many Chicago teachers defected to the progressives at the AFT's convention last August in Washington.

The AFT's president and sixteen vice presidents are elected at large by delegates to the convention for two-year terms, forming the union's executive council. The current vice presidents are from all sections of the country. Three are Negroes. The council, which sets AFT policies between conventions, is almost as large as its staff. The federation's headquarters consists of about ten professional staff members and clerks with another ten organizers coming and going from the field. The national budget is just under $2,000,000 and contains modest salaries ($18,300 for Cogen, compared with $50,000 for the NEA's executive secretary).

But the headquarters services are minimal. The research department exists on $68,832, yielding dubious documents like the one on the need for an immediate $5,000 raise for every teacher in the United States. The research on this particular item was so poor that many reporters at a press conference where it was announced refused to write a word about it. Other departments are hardly more impressive. The AFT's federal relations staff consists of Carl Megel, past AFT president, and a secretary. "We always go along with labor," Megel told me. "That's our strength and prestige." The federation's twenty-two state organizations are similarly weak. The AFT just got around to hiring a coordinator of state federations last year.

A member of a teachers' local automatically belongs to the AFT, but dues vary from city to city. In Philadelphia, for example, a starting teacher pays $42 in annual dues. The AFT constitution says each local must pay $1 per month for each member into the national treasury. Two cents is set aside in a defense fund.

The support of labor is crucial to the AFT. "The labor affiliation is a great help to us," Cogen says. "There've been a number of situations— New York, Detroit—where unions have helped us out, organizing a strike, putting moral pressure on the board of education." In smaller communities the teachers' local often uses AFL-CIO staff and facilities.

The teachers also are important to organized labor. The UFT, with more than 50,000 members, is the largest local in the AFL-CIO. And Nick Zonarich, director of organization for the Industrial Union Department, says that "the teachers have been the greatest inspiration in instilling new life in the labor movement." The work force is changing— from blue-collar, private employment to white-collar, public employment—and the IUD hopes that teachers can set the pattern for other fields to follow. To keep pace with the shift, the AFL-CIO earlier this year formed a Council of Unions for Scientific, Professional, and Cultural Employees to help organize the new workers. Cogen is vice president.

The AFT's programs, meanwhile, are geared directly to the present of the urban schools, particularly the schools of the poor. The major program (Cogen calls it the "AFT's most important contribution to our profession") is the More Effective Schools campaign. The New York federation first proposed MES three years ago during contract negotiations after the school board offered $1,000 "combat pay" to lure experienced teachers to slum schools. The federation countered with MES to provide intensive educational, remedial, and counseling services to the ghetto. MES is now in twenty-one New York schools, costing $10,000,000 a year. A teacher's dream, it limits class size to twenty-two pupils in elementary grades and establishes a guidance team of a social worker, psychologist, and part-time psychiatrist in each school. To make sure all this attention filters down to the child, four teachers are assigned to every three classes.

Despite the increased manpower, MES is far from an unqualified success. For one thing, the Center for Urban Education, evaluating MES for the New York school board, found that many teachers didn't know how to work with all the program's special help. The Center cited "little evidence that materials or teaching techniques had been adapted to capitalize on the smaller classes," while there was a "general absence of creative or innovative teaching practices." Still, teachers, principals, and pupils were enthusiastic about the program. More startling, however, was the conclusion that MES produced disappointing gains in pupil achievement. MES pupils scored only slightly higher on reading achievement tests than did children in non-MES control schools, and MES was not strong enough to pull its pupils up to grade level. Indeed, even MES pupils fell farther behind the longer they stayed in school, starting only a month below grade level in the second grade but dropping more than a year behind in the fifth grade. As a result of these findings, the board was reluctant to expand the program this fall as the federation desired, producing a major issue in the September strike. The AFT, however, hopes to export MES to Boston, Detroit, Los Angeles, and New Orleans.

Another major federation goal is to persuade the federal government to expand its categorical aid to city schools and to set national standards which systems must meet to qualify for federal aid. The AFT also supports a national assessment to measure pupil performance, a testing opposed by many elements of the NEA. Occasionally the federation's policies take a quixotic turn. At the recent convention, Cogen urged President Johnson to call a "national educational strategy conference" to be attended by many classroom teachers. The proposal drew no comment from the White House. And Cogen, with a straight face, also suggested at the convention that the federal government set $8,500 as the minimum pay for a teacher with a bachelor's degree.

The federation has brought an explosive impact to the cities where it represents teachers. It has awakened school boards, shaken bureaucracies. Its impact also can be quite tangible. The Philadelphia federation sent its own recruiters throughout the East last spring, helping to cut teacher vacancies in the city from more than 1,000 to a handful. So far, however, the AFT has demonstrated little influence on national policies. Recognizing the void, the union moved its national offices during the summer from Chicago to two floors in the Continental Building, about five blocks from the White House. (The move precipitated a short strike by AFT employees who didn't want to leave the Midwest.)

What happens next? As the AFT grows larger, it faces the danger of institutionalization. There are indications it already is joining the Establishment. A recent study of change in big-city schools by two professors from the City University of New York and one from Teachers College said that in the few areas where the New York federation has taken a public position "it appears to have been motivated largely by a desire to maintain the status quo." The study added that "in interviews conducted with union leaders, there was some expressed concern that their own positions of power might be threatened if they violated the narrower interests of their membership. Thus, the New York teachers' union acts as an obstacle to change in the system rather than as an innovator."

The AFT, however, undoubtedly will continue to grow, although perhaps at not as rapid a rate. It has no large organizing drive planned this year, but hopes to move to the smaller cities and the suburbs. Union leaders are sanguine about the future. Cogen, riding the crest of the wave, predicts, "We'll continue our growth at the expense of the NEA —certainly among the million or so teachers who are unorganized." Unless school conditions change dramatically, the AFT probably will remain where the action is. Increasingly, though, the action will have to do not with wages or working conditions, but with power. The union thus becomes not merely a bargaining agent or an organization of professionals, but a political force that will represent a major element in the operation of city schools. It is thus a major new entry in the political equation that determines the future of public education in America.

Arthur E. Salz

FORMULA FOR INEVITABLE CONFLICT: LOCAL CONTROL VS. PROFESSIONALISM

Teachers have not enjoyed much influence in the making of educational policy. Indeed, unlike most if not all professionals, teachers have had little to say about matters directly or indirectly bearing upon the enterprise for which they have been educated. It is because of this situation that many observers of professions have been reluctant to characterize public school teaching as a profession. Nevertheless, the AFT and, in recent years, the NEA have set about to rectify the situation. Paralleling the growth of teacher militancy, however, has been an increased consciousness and vociferousness among citizens at large about their role in

From *Phi Delta Kappan,* February, 1969, pp. 332–334. Footnotes omitted. Reprinted by permission of the author and publisher.

educational decision-making; and the emergence of these two phenomena, teacher militancy and community control, suggest not only continuing controversy in education but the very likely possibility of conflict between teachers, as a group, and community-control advocates.

In the following descriptive article, Arthur E. Salz, Assistant Professor of Education at Queens College, discusses possible points of conflict between community-control advocates and teachers who are demanding more power. He notes that any optimism about cooperation between the community and its teachers must be guarded since the two movements are on a "collision course." (See also Chapter 3, on "The Politics of School Control.")

The Ocean Hill-Brownsville controversy, which apparently has been settled for the time being, will be viewed in retrospect as merely the opening round in what is destined to become a long and protracted struggle for control of public education in the United States. What has begun as a local conflict in one small district in the nation's largest urban area will spread to urban areas throughout the country. What is now essentially a city problem will, in the not too distant future, be a major concern of teachers and laymen in our suburbs. Albert Shanker, president of the United Federation of Teachers, realized this when he planned to go on a national speaking tour during last fall's teacher strike. Dave Selden, national president of American Federation of Teachers, understood the sweeping implications of the controversy when he entered into the negotiations which eventually settled the third strike of the 1968 school year. For while the burning issue will not be settled in either-or terms, it is best to pose it that way to see what is at stake. Thus, who shall control our schools, laymen or professionals? Ten years ago the question was never raised; today it cannot be avoided. For in the past decade two major trends in the history of educational, social, and political thought have been on a collision course which was not discernible until quite recently: on the one hand, the movement toward self-determination for minorities in urban areas, focusing on community control of various institutions; on the other hand, the growth of teacher professionalism.

Self-determination is a very old notion. One needn't be reminded that it was the prevailing ideology of our own revolution, and supposedly the fundamental principle governing the settlement of World War I. Of even greater import, it has been the basic underlying concept of the post-World War II nationalism that has swept Africa and Asia, and it is not merely coincidental that Stokely Carmichael, Charles Hamilton, and others have applied the colonial model to the plight of the black man in the United States. For if the analogy holds, then self-determination is an appropriate antidote for the oppressed black man here, as it was for the disease of colonialism on the continent of Africa in the past two decades. Interestingly enough, the thrust toward an integrated American society in the 1950's muted this concern for self-determination. However, with the failure of either school or housing integration in the 1960's (or was it never attempted?), the trend toward community control has developed momentum. Anti-poverty legislation and the Office of Economic Opportunity formalized and sanctioned the concept of self-determination by calling for maximum feasible participation by those affected by the legislation. The movement was strengthened considerably when blacks in Harlem, realizing that the new Intermediate School 201 was not to be integrated as promised, shifted tactics and demanded control of their community school. Also of great importance was Mayor John Lindsay's appointment of a high-powered committee, headed by McGeorge Bundy, to study school decentralization. The trend is obvious. Whatever is finally implemented by way of legislation, the idea of self-determination and community control of institutions is now soundly imbedded in the conscience of blacks and Puerto Ricans in the urban areas.

Professionalism, on the other hand, is not an easy concept to define. Nevertheless, while some may differ as to definition, there is general agreement that the Milquetoast teacher who came hat in hand begging for salary increases, who had to wade through piles of low-level clerical work, who had to take lunch duty, lavatory duty, and the like throughout the school day, was hardly being treated as a professional. It has also become unprofessional for teachers to provide their services in situations which seriously militate against success, e.g., where there are huge classes, outdated textbooks, and inadequate facilities. To the extent that teacher militancy and collective negotiations have improved this situation they have contributed to furthering the professionalization of teachers. But these tend to be bread-and-butter matters, and while certainly not unimportant, they do not clearly distinguish the teacher unionist from other unionists.

On the matter of educational policy, however, a trend has developed which portends a major breakthrough. Heretofore, policy matters in education have been in the domain of the school board, as representative of the public. While one can argue with some validity that any collectively negotiated contract that calls for smaller class size, more remedial reading teachers, more guidance counselors, etc., has involved teachers in policy making, these items still can be viewed as being in the area of improved working conditions. However, in the negotiations between the UFT and the Board of Education in 1967, the union pressed for expansion of the More Effective Schools program, which it has been instrumental in developing. The MES, begun in 1964, was an attempt to provide quality education to children with educationally deficient backgrounds by means of smaller classes and a host of remedial and supportive services. While the research as to its success had been mixed, the UFT pressed vigorously for additional appropriations for the program. What was at stake here, apart from the money, was the UFT's right to negotiate policy. Out of the settlement came an appropriation of $10 million for experimental programs involving smaller class sizes. Also significant was the fact that the committee to plan these programs was to be made up of two members of the board, two from the UFT, and two more community people chosen jointly by the board and the UFT. Based on proposals made by this committee last year, four different types of experimental schools are in operation during the current year. The importance of this is clear. Not as advisors, consultants, or suppliants, but as an equal voice at the negotiating table, the teachers of New York, through their union, have been involved in making policy for the entire school system. This is the trend toward professionalism which is of vital significance.

A professional, as Myron Lieberman has pointed out, does the following:

1. Practices a unique, definite and essential social service.
2. Emphasizes intellectual techniques in performing his service.
3. Requires a long period of specialized training.
4. Possesses a broad range of autonomy for both himself and for his occupational group as a whole.
5. Accepts broad personal responsibility for judgments made and acts performed within the scope of professional autonomy.
6. Places an emphasis upon the service to be rendered, rather than the economic gain to the practitioner, as the basis for the organization and performance of the social service.
7. Is a member of a comprehensive self-governing organization of practitioners.
8. Adheres to a code of ethics, developed by his occupational group, which has been clarified and interpreted at ambiguous and doubtful points by concrete cases.

While teachers, individually and as a group, exhibit many of these characteristics, the glaring omission has been the lack of autonomy that has existed within the profession. As noted above, this weakness is obviously being rectified as teachers become increasingly militant and achieve collective negotiations arrangements. However, what has generally been overlooked is that when teachers act professionally, i.e., with the necessary autonomy to define the conditions within which they will provide their services, they come into direct conflict with those traditionally in control of education: the public. The professionalization of teachers and local, lay control of education are on a collision course. No matter how optimistic we are about cooperation between the community and its teachers, many issues will arise which will inevitably pit the desires of the professional teacher against the wishes of the community.

This analysis holds for education in general in the United States. The problem, however, is considerably more critical in New York City, where the public has never felt it truly controlled its schools. Under massive pressure from civil rights leaders and others, the Board of Education began a tentative decentralization program in order to eventually place control of the schools in the local communities. By the summer of 1968 the board had broadened its program by giving all local districts the power to select district superintendents and to hire and fire teachers under city-wide standards. Currently the city is operating under an interim decentralization plan, pending passage of legislation in Albany this spring. The crux of the problem, then, is that at the very moment local leaders are, for the first time, insisting upon and achieving increased power in educational decision making, the teachers, as professionals, are exerting their right to determine policy. Until very recently both teachers and minority groups have been quite impotent in determining their destinies. Suddenly they are getting a taste of power; unfortunately they both have their spoons in the same bowl.

The Ocean Hill-Brownsville dispute, which is still smoldering, is an example of the type of confrontation which will become more and more common. The issue, initially, was whether a community board of education could circumvent procedures established by the central Board of Education and remove teachers and supervisors from that district. The UFT, caught in the middle, obviously supported the interests of the teachers. Job security has historically been the prime concern of trade unionism. But in reality the issue merely centered around the question of who had the power to remove the teachers, the local *lay* board or the central *lay* board. No one was questioning the right or the advisability of laymen performing this function.

A more significant development will come in the future when teachers are powerful enough to seek a voice in determining entrance into the profession, establishment of tenure procedures, and methods of policing these procedures. At our current point in history the only thing teachers can insist upon is that due process be followed and justice be meted out. This is not unimportant. But of far greater moment will be the confrontation that develops when teachers are ready to take a stand in determining who enters and remains in the profession. On this and many other issues like curriculum control, use of paraprofessionals, academic freedom, etc., professional autonomy will be pitted against lay control. Conflict must follow.

Obviously, there are serious racial overtones that exacerbate the current issue in New York. Nevertheless, it serves to sharpen the focus of the problem by indicating that where laymen feel intensely about the functioning of their schools, and teachers feel strongly about their professionalization, there will be areas of dispute. This would be true with or without the racial issue. That this condition has not erupted before can be attributed to a lack of public control in the cities, lack of strong feeling among local communities concerning their schools, and, most important, lack of real power among the ranks of the teachers. Once we remove our heads from the sand and acknowledge that there are areas of inevitable conflict between teachers and local communities over education, we can begin to deal with them. What will emerge in New York City in the future is not so much the concept that lay control and professionalization don't mix; rather, that a new form of relationship taking into account the growing autonomy of teachers *and* the growing urban concern for local control will be hammered out through negotiations and other forms of channeled conflict. This relationship will hardly be tension-free. The teachers of New York, who have taught their colleagues throughout the country so much concerning militancy, collective bargaining, and professionalism, will be forging a curriculum on the topic of realistic relations between the community and the professional teacher. It is important that those concerned with education in our cities watch carefully the events in New York; they may portend the future in our nation's other urban areas.

Preceding articles in this chapter make clear some of the major questions involved in the teacher militancy issue. As already noted, questions concerning professionalism, unionism, self-determination, teacher rights, the ethics of strikes and work stoppages, the futures of the AFT and NEA, their relationship to each other, and the place of professionals and lay citizens in educational decision-making all pervade this issue. Accordingly, it is not surprising that both a vast amount and a wide range of materials exist from which one can choose to illustrate the complexities and very real consequences of teacher activism. One need only turn to recent newspaper accounts of teacher strikes, for example, to encounter the life drama, as it were, of this issue.

We have selected two illustrative accounts which are addressed, in the main, to the educational problems—as perceived by teacher groups—which lead to teacher militancy, and the real and potential points of conflict between "professional rights" of teachers and a particular public policy directed at public schools. The first selection reports on the role of a state NEA affiliate. As such, it offers insight into how that organization operates in representing the interests of teachers. Although both selections report on matters emerging out of particular school systems, they nevertheless serve to illustrate some of the complexities of the issue as a whole.

Gayle Norton

THE FLORIDA STORY

"The Florida Story" reports on an educational situation which rocked Florida in 1967 and shocked the nation into an awareness of how powerful teachers had become. Although teachers had closed down individual schools and even individual local school systems before, in Florida, teachers throughout the entire state walked out of their classrooms. Norton reports on some of the major problems which led to this statewide walkout. His account manifests the need for better communications between teachers and the different "publics" to which they are accountable. This selection also makes clear that politics, as such, is not something divorced from the teacher-militancy question.

Mr. Norton is the Editor of the *Edpress Newsletter*. Edpress represents more than 600 editors of education publications in the United States and Canada.

Hidden somewhere in the wordy morass now labeled "The Florida Story" lie all the facts of the nation's largest public school crisis.

The full story probably will never be known.

It is doubtful that any journalist, however ambitious or objective, could ever wade through the tons of news clippings, editorials, film clips, speeches, photographs, telegrams, private letters, legislative records, education periodicals, and confidential memorandums which de-

From *Phi Delta Kappan*, June, 1968, pp. 555–560. Reprinted by permission of the author and publisher.

tail what National Education Association Executive Secretary Sam M. Lambert has called "one of the most significant victories in the history of American education."

Among the hundreds of publications received by the Educational Press Association of America during the last year, there have been few which have not mentioned "The Florida Story." Those periodicals which carried detailed information on the walkout had been published by state and local education associations closely affiliated with the NEA. Of these, the majority religiously reproduced NEA and FEA handouts. In a few instances, enterprising editors filled considerable space with research and editorial copy in an attempt to explain to their readers what this "militant" business is all about.

Others used Florida's school problems to illustrate "what cannot and must not happen to *our* teachers." The more sophisticated publications (e.g., the *Saturday Review,* in "Politics and Education in the Sunshine State," James Cass, April 20, 1968) inferred that most of the answers to Florida's school crisis lie buried in a huge pile of neglected legislation ignored year after year by unconcerned governors and legislators elected by an apathetic public, none of whom gives a tinker's dam about Florida's public schools or those who teach in them.

Such inferences thrill most teacher leaders. They make self-justification easier and require less hard analysis of past action than do such things as weak communications, bad public relations, and poorly planned political tactics.

Until Florida's teacher leaders admit to themselves that they have failed miserably in getting their story across to the taxpayers; until they are willing to put as much energy, money, and effort into down-to-earth programs aimed at educating the parents of the children they teach as they have spent in the last 18 months failing to make their points with sanctions, walkouts, crisis Sundays, and moneyless paydays, they can expect continued apathy and spurts of hostility from the public.

It has become clear to even the casual reader that no single person, no one organization (including the NEA and Florida Education Association), no representative of any mass medium, and certainly none of the publications which go regularly to America's school teachers has sufficient information to answer all questions which have arisen over the Sunshine State's education dilemma.

There are parts of "The Florida Story" which I feel qualified to report. As a member of the Florida Education Association staff from 1963 to 1967, I had a first-hand opportunity to watch and listen as a new group of teachers made plans to take control of Florida's largest professional organization. I knew what was going to happen. And I didn't like it. I knew how it would happen. I liked that less. So I quit. Others on the staff knew, too. My resignation had been preceded by that of the FEA director of research. A long-time field representative resigned shortly thereafter. In recent weeks, the FEA's director of legal and personnel relations and its director of finance and lay relations have resigned.

In the last 12 months I have talked to and corresponded with literally hundreds of my colleagues in education journalism. I have discussed Florida's school crisis with news reporters, magazine editors, book publishers, and experts in public relations. I have spoken to teachers, both individually and in groups, including the county superintendents of one state who meet regularly in special classes designed to help them strengthen their relationship and improve their communications with the teachers who look to them for administrative guidance.

These people all want to hear *now* direct answers to questions like those asked by Editor Barbara Krohn in a recent issue of *Washington Education:*

How many Floridas can the NEA afford? [The NEA reportedly spent nearly $3 million in cash and manpower in Florida.] If the NEA won in Florida, what had Floridians won? If the NEA did not pull it off, why not? Was it, despite all of the massed power, a failure of technique? Or was it a miscalculation of the disposition of teachers toward work stoppages—and of the public toward government by crisis? What do we do if there's a next time?

FEA leadership has one set of answers to these questions. Many FEA members have others. NEA staff members report strong disagreement among high-level NEA officials on actions taken in Florida. Different answers come from Florida's State Department of Education. Still others are offered by Florida's legislators and the governor's office.

The result of these varying points of view is that spokesmen for each group have become so defensive about their own positions they have found it difficult to communicate with each other.

The question I am asked most often by teachers is, "Did the FEA leadership really believe that by walking out they could get what they wanted and still hold the confidence of the governor's office and the public?"

The answer is simple. Whatever hopes the FEA had of working more closely with their governor in 1966 were dashed in November when Republican Claude Kirk, a relatively unknown Jacksonville investment banker, soundly defeated his FEA-endorsed Democratic opponent, Robert King High of Miami. Politically unsophisticated teachers, certain they had a winner in the Democratic nominee, had so completely isolated themselves and their support from Kirk that they couldn't find their way back to him.

The FEA was *never* able, during the years I lived in Florida, to get their message across to the voting public.

They made an honest attempt in the spring of 1966 when they asked for and received some special help from the NEA to outline a program of communications and public relations.

A detailed four-page proposal for an FEA public relations program was carefully outlined and presented to an FEA ad hoc strategy committee.

"Since we are blessed with time—it is on our side," the report began. "It is not feasible to have a sustained attention-grabbing campaign to last for a full year. Instead, we should start with a slow, deliberate, low-pressure campaign in the fall with teachers in the vanguard.

"It is important for teachers to sell themselves—it is their image that needs to be improved. And there is no better way to accomplish this objective than to have teachers help improve their own image. We must involve teachers in the campaign—a campaign aimed at spelling out the association's objectives. Based on a program aimed at mustering the total resources—cooperating educational agencies and business, industrial, civic, and fraternal organizations among others—this campaign should not cost a lot of money or give the public the impression that it is expensive. That is why we have emphasized a self-help campaign involving teachers and the total resources of the community on a voluntary basis to tell the education story.

"This is good, honest public relations," the report concluded, "and it's a lot of hard work. And it can be effective if everyone pulls together."

Everyone didn't pull together. Part of the program was eventually adopted by the FEA Board of Directors. But to the dismay of the NEA staff members and others who had worked on it, it never got off the ground.

In the fall of 1967, when its public image was at one of its lowest ebbs in years, the FEA heard the results of this public relations negligence in an address by Daytona Beach newsman George Allen, who said, "You do not, in my opinion, have the wholehearted backing of the general public. More importantly, you do not have the backing of the voters. Finally, you do not have the backing of the taxpayer. Somewhere along the line you have not been able to get your message across. The lines of understandable communications have been clogged. If you think you have been understandable, I beg to differ. I haven't understood a damn thing you've been talking about during the past year."

Neither, apparently, had Governor Claude Kirk nor the Florida legislature.

One central figure in the Florida school crisis whom the governor and the legislature had little trouble understanding was Floyd T. Christian, state superintendent of public instruction and a former FEA president.

Maligned at times by both Governor Kirk and the FEA, Christian nevertheless held firm to his initial commitment to keep Florida's schools open during the walkout at any cost.

I talked with Christian in mid-April and asked him for a general appraisal of the FEA's directed work stoppage. He gave me a talk he had prepared for a speech downstate.

"I believe the walkout represented poor timing and poor judgment," he said. "It was an uncalled for action on the part of the FEA leadership. I hope that the leadership of the FEA, and the teachers and administrators who walked out, have learned their lesson."

Christian said he believes many of the teachers who walked out "sincerely, but mistakenly, believed they were doing something to help the children of Florida."

He also said there is "no question" in his mind that the NEA is competing for teacher members with the AFT.

"Action was needed to show the NEA's strength in order to prevent defections of teachers to the AFT, whose national membership is increasing dramatically," he said.

Christian quickly added that he "much prefers having the professional organization represent Florida's teachers than a union."

Christian believes the FEA lost public support in their walkout because it was "not possible for the public to understand how our teachers could leave their jobs after the special session had provided more than $200 million additional dollars for education, as well as the highest teacher salaries in the South and one of the highest in the nation. For comparative purposes, note that last biennium the state spent $571.5 million in general revenue funds for the public schools (kindergarten through junior college). This biennium the figure is almost double—$998 million—nearly a billion dollars."

Asked why he thought the teachers walked out in the face of such dramatic increases, Christian said, "I believe they were misinformed. In one FEA bulletin, teachers were told the special session provided one amount for education. In the next bulletin, another figure was used. And on a television program still another figure was used. The bill as finally passed by the legislature was complicated. But despite its complications, there was no need for the teachers to be as misinformed as they were on this issue."

Christian said changes in position by both the governor and the FEA added to the confusion.

"At first, the governor wouldn't talk to the leadership of the resigned teachers. He thought the 25,000 who left their classrooms should be run out of Florida. Then his mail began to change, and he changed with it —now he wanted school boards to show compassion, and to take the teachers back.

"His position on the education package changed, too. At one time or another he took every position open to him: He threatened to veto the legislation. He told me he was going to sign it. Then he announced he would let it become law without his signature, because the FEA didn't like the measures.

"There were also several changes in the FEA's posture. At first, the legislation was branded as unacceptable. But, finally, the FEA took credit for the governor not vetoing the bill."

There is no new way to retell the details of the war between the FEA, the 1967 Florida legislature, and Florida's flashy governor, Claude Kirk. There are, however, some incidents which have not been widely described outside Florida. One involves the resignation of a member of the FEA board during the legislative session.

John R. Clark had been elected to the Florida House of Representatives from Polk County in 1966. He had been an elementary principal for 12 years, was past president of the Okaloosa County Education Association, the Okaloosa County Principals Association, the Polk County Classroom Teachers Association, and the Polk County Education Association. He also had served as co-chairman of the FEA Organization and Functions Committee and as a member of several other important FEA committees. No one knew the FEA's legislative program better than he.

But Clark, in a move which drew thunderous applause from his legislative colleagues and abject dismay from his fellow FEA board members, stood in the Florida House chambers and strongly defended education legislation then under severe attack by the FEA. He said, in effect, that if the FEA could not accept the legislation, he would resign his FEA board position. The FEA didn't. Clark did.

Much debate has centered on the number of teachers who were reported out of the classroom at the peak of the walkout. The following are figures taken from *official* files kept by the Florida State Department of Education:

Date	In	Out	Total
2/19/68	33,873	24,811	58,684
2/20	32,951	25,712	58,663
2/21	33,348	24,895	58,243
2/22	33,838	24,313	58,151
2/23	34,393	23,824	58,217
2/26	36,073	22,812	58,885
2/27	36,743	22,302	59,045
3/4	39,713	19,378	59,091
3/5	40,714	18,318	59,029
3/6	41,037	17,855	58,892
3/7	41,470	17,539	59,009

Another set of education statistics which varies in size with where it appears is one showing average teacher salaries, average per-pupil expenditures, and total state allocation of funds for the K-12 program. Again, these are official figures from the Florida State Department of Education.

During the 1965–66 school year, the average K-12 Florida teacher's salary was $6,538. Average expenditure per pupil was $447. Total state allocation of funds was $271,717,258.

For the 1966–1967 school year, average K-12 teacher salaries were $7,114. The average per-pupil expenditure remained the same. Total state allocation was $288,489,141.

The 1967–68 figures showed the average K-12 salary at $7,500, with average per-pupil expenditures at $554 and total state allocations of $305,722,412. These figures were estimated, since they do not include money (from the special session) which will be held until July.

Following the 1968 special legislative session, the average 1968 teacher salary in Florida jumped to $8,000. Increases ranged from $431 (which covers about 37 percent of all teachers) to $2,681. An additional $146,036,513 was tagged for K-12 education.

Nationally, Florida now ranks 29th in per-capita income. With money from the special session, per-pupil expenditures moved from 30th to 17th. Teacher salaries moved from 24th to 12th.

Another lightly reported incident related to the walkout was the defection of two of the FEA's strongest and most colorful teacher leaders to the American Federation of Teachers shortly after the teacher walk-out ended. Mrs. Louise Alford, a former FEA board member and past president of the Classroom Teachers Department of the FEA, and Joe Whelpton, former CTD director, announced that they had been hired by the AFT to help organize teacher unions in Florida.

At an April 16 press conference, Mrs. Alford predicted the AFT locals would be strong enough "in a year or two" to be a bargaining power. She also said the AFT "never would have called a state-wide teacher strike as the FEA did in March when less than half the FEA member-ship participated."

Mrs. Alford said she believes the FEA will "lose its members in large numbers next year. Many of these people have approached us about AFT."

She labeled FEA's walkout a "failure" and criticized the organization for being a "staff-run organization, with decisions handed from the top down rather than made at the grass-roots level."

Her decision to bolt the FEA for the AFT apparently had not been a hasty one. Nor did it come as a great surprise to the FEA's leadership. On September 18, 1967, David Bustin, assistant executive secretary for the Maine Teachers Association, wrote a letter to Gary Watts, director of NEA's urban and field services. The letter read, in part, "I met a gal named Louise Alford. . . . Towards the end of the clinic she told me that she favors a merger of the NEA and AFT as soon as possible. My own feeling is that such a merger should be on the NEA's terms and I would like to see the urban teachers back in the fold if it could be worked out. What concerns me, however, is that she told me she had been offered $18,000 a year to organize Florida for the union and that she told them to come back to see her in a few months."

Watts, of course, sent a copy of the letter on to the FEA.

What lies ahead for the FEA? What are the plans if Florida's teachers face another showdown with their legislature and their governor? An FEA officer told me he believes his organization will simply call a three-day strike with no advance notice. A no-strike resolution intro-duced at this year's FEA convention in Miami Beach was never voted out of committee.

"One of the mistakes we made in our first walkout," said this FEA leader, "was announcing our plans and then waiting so long to put them into effect. That won't happen again."

This year's Miami convention provided FEA Executive Secretary Phil

Constans, Jr., and his staff with the incentive they need to push FEA membership to its highest peak.

Some 4,000 delegates representing all 50,000 FEA members overwhelmingly approved a 100 percent increase in dues ($20 to $40), with an additional $10 to be added next year.

Constans was jubilant. "The fact that our delegates voted to hike the annual dues by 100 percent proves that the organization was not crippled. Essentially, what the delegates told us was 'full speed ahead.' And they put their money where their mouths were."

With the additional $1,000,000 in its kitty, the FEA board plans to triple its professional negotiations staff from three to nine, double the communications staff from three to six, and hire an outside public relations firm for $100,000. Another $100,000 has been earmarked for legal defense and $300,000 more to open an FEA branch office in Fort Lauderdale, to expand the Orlando office, and to set up a field operation in North Florida. Another $250,000 will go toward paying off the mortgage and adding on to the present FEA headquarters building.

Whether the 4,000 delegates who attended the Miami Beach meeting truly spoke for the pocketbooks of the other 46,000 dues-paying members FEA must enroll before schools open next fall remains to be seen. Historically, the FEA has operated on reserves until dues, deducted from payrolls in most of the larger counties, begin coming in near the end of the calendar year.

Delegate approval of a unified dues structure effective in 1969–70 also means that some teachers will be paying close to $100 annually for local, state, and national memberships.

Time will also test the sincerity of plans to use money allocated to public relations and communications. Will it be invested wisely in salaries for skilled professionals who'll be given latitude to organize and direct the programs without unnecessary direction from amateur committee members? Or will these teacher committee members finagle their way on to the staff as they have done in the past and be allowed to dabble in the FEA's most serious staff responsibility?

Another significant action of this year's FEA Delegate Assembly was the elimination of all departments within the FEA. Gone are the Classroom Teachers Department, the Department of Supervisors, the Department of Higher Education, and the Departments of Elementary and Secondary School Principals. Florida's school superintendents voluntarily withdrew their affiliation from the FEA shortly after the walkout ended. They formed their own association.

Taking over as FEA president on July 1 will be Miss Jane Arnold, a former president of the FEA's Department of Classroom Teachers. Miss Arnold has been among the last few Florida teachers whom local school boards have refused to rehire.

FEA's president-elect, Robert Pearson, is a cigar-chewing, divorced bachelor who for 10 years was head of the Department of Behavioral Sciences at Pensacola Junior College. He also left his teaching post during the FEA walkout and now has lost his $13,500 job. In early May he said, "I read in the local paper that the committee had recommended that my contract be terminated June 12."

Pearson said it appeared that his being allowed to come back to the PJC campus after the walkout had been "some sort of an accident."

"I was given no preliminary hearing, had no official notice, nor heard any reasons for my dismissal," Pearson said. "But it is a beautiful picture for me to present to my colleagues around the state who are already steaming mad over similar treatment that's been given other teachers."

A member of Pearson's college advisory board confirmed that the seven-man group had unanimously voted to terminate Pearson's employment.

"He had done nothing but hold little FEA meetings in the hallways. His students had complained that he continually harangued over the teacher strike. We simply cannot tolerate that type of conduct," the board member said.

There's little doubt that Pearson intends to teach somewhere in Florida so that he can begin preparing for the FEA presidency he'll assume July 1, 1969.

He ought to be one of the strongest presidents the FEA has had in several years. And his empathy with university staffs should help greatly in attracting college and university faculties to FEA's membership rolls. University faculties and college staffs have been poorly represented in the FEA in the past.

"College faculties have believed that they had nothing in common with the elementary and secondary teacher," said Pearson. "But during our recent donnybrook they seemed to develop strong sympathies for our cause. And I am confident that within the next two years we can make strong inroads into universities where we've never made any headway before."

Pearson is also optimistic about the FEA's growth. He predicts 60,000 members by 1969 and does not view the AFT as a serious threat to the FEA.

Like some FEA leaders, Pearson has matured politically since 1966. "We got bogged down in the idea that we had to endorse somebody running for public office," he said. "That endorsement idea is not worth two cents. We are going to keep active in politics, but we are going to keep our mouths shut. We have discovered that the way people win elections is by winning votes. This seems like such a simple solution, but we surely wandered away during the last two elections."

The FEA surely did. And Pearson could be the one to put the FEA back on its track.

Emanuel Hurwitz

THE JUSTICE DEPARTMENT ULTIMATUM

Our second illustrative selection is a case study of the Chicago school system's response to an order from the Justice Department calling for an end to racially motivated discriminatory practices in the placement of teachers. Emanuel Hurwitz illustrates the complexities of the teacher-power movement, particularly concerning points of conflict between policy which teachers perceive as beneficial to them and policy which others perceive as beneficial to the community as a whole.

As you read this account, reflect upon the manner in which the Chicago Teachers Union and the Board of Education worked with each other. Do you think that cooperation on this matter was greater than it would have been, let us say, over teacher salaries and other economic benefits? If so, why?

On July 9, 1969, Chicago Board of Education President, Frank Whiston, and Superintendent of Schools, James Redmond, each received the following ultimatum from the U.S. Attorney General's Office.

Mr. Frank Whiston, President
Chicago Board of Education

Dear Mr. Whiston:

The Attorney General has received complaints in writing from Negro parents living in Chicago, Illinois, complaining that their children have been deprived of the equal protection of the laws, on account of race, in the operation of the public schools in that city. . . .

In accordance with our responsibilities under Title IV of the Civil Rights Act of 1964, we have completed an examination of the Chicago Board's policies and practices of faculty and staff assignments. . . . This examination compels the conclusion that the school system's practices with respect to the assignment and transfer of faculty has had the effect of denying to Negro students in the Chicago Public Schools the equal protection of the laws in violation of the Civil Rights Act of 1964 and the Fourteenth Amendment to the United States Constitution.

We are writing this letter to advise you of the results of our examination of the facts and to provide you with an opportunity to take appropriate steps to eliminate voluntarily the racially discriminatory practices we found in the operation of your school system. . . .

Sincerely,

Thomas A. Foran   Jerris Leonard
United States Attorney   Assistant Attorney General
Northern District of Illinois   Civil Rights Division

This ultimatum came as no real surprise to President Whiston, Dr. Redmond, or the Board. But it did hit them just as they were in the midst of trying to solve a serious financial crisis. Redmond, especially, was understandably shaken. He had visions of the ultimatum making front-page news. Since he is a man who is keenly conscious of the public relations image of the Chicago educational community, he sensed that the ultimatum had all of the ingredients of a major controversy and would get out of hand unless he devoted full attention to it immediately. He knew that if not handled properly this Justice Department intervention could lead not only to an embarrassing lawsuit and loss of federal funds, but it could conceivably trigger another teacher strike and possibly cause a total collapse of public education in Chicago.

Normally, the well-liked Superintendent functioned self-effacedly as a behind-the-scenes mediator and conciliator, making all decisions appear as though they had stemmed from the Board. But Redmond reflected that this might be one time when he would have to step forward to provide overt leadership. He knew that if he chose that alternative he would be setting precedent for superintendents of the nation. Until then, no big-city school administrator had ever taken a public stand on faculty integration. Most administrators had been avoiding leadership responsibilities in this vital area, just as they had in the area of student integration. Redmond knew that his role in resolving the faculty integration problem in Chicago was going to be one of the biggest challenges of his career in school administration, which began in Chicago and which has taken him successfully to both New Orleans and suburban New York City.

Redmond lost no time in consulting with Whiston, and together they issued a joint statement to the press, making an uncompromised denial of the government's allegations. This is how they put it:

We have never practiced segregation of faculty in Chicago, but we have permitted seniority choice of schools by our teachers. Race has never been made a basis for assignment or transfer in Chicago.

While Redmond awaited reactions from the Chicago Teachers Union, the Governor, the local political leaders, the black community and others, he worked feverishly to piece together all of the past and present factors which might have led to the Justice Department ultimatum. He and the Board had been given just two weeks in which to reply to the federal government.

On the surface, the facts in the case spoke clearly for themselves. Faculty segregation was real. In 1966, 35 percent of the city's schools had integrated faculties. In 1967, the figure went up to 43 percent, but in 1968 it dropped back to 40 percent. (The Chicago Board of Education defines a school as being integrated when at least 10 percent—but no more than 90 percent—of its teachers are white.)

The following table shows the faculty racial makeup of all Chicago schools for the last three years.

Percent of white teachers	Number of schools		
	1966	1967	1968
100	292	209	214
90 to 99	65	85	64
10 to 90	217	250	238
1 to 10	34	31	70
0	15	10	12

The problem of faculty racial imbalance was first noted publicly in a 1967 U.S. Office of Education Report, now called the "Redmond Plan." In that study it was noted that "the teaching staff in the Chicago schools is highly segregated by race; for the most part, Negro teachers teach in predominantly Negro schools." Immediately following publication of the Redmond Plan, its author sought broad teacher-transfer power. But his gallant attempt to gain this power was at that time vigorously opposed by the Teachers Union and the objective was dropped.

After disclosure of the ultimatum, the press was quick to point out that other big cities were able to join with their teachers' unions to achieve teacher desegregation as far back as 1966. Why had Chicago not been able to do so? For example, in Philadelphia, new teachers were assigned explicitly for the purpose of integrating teaching staffs. The result: only 15 of 272 schools in Philadelphia had racially imbalanced faculties, compared with 156 in 1966.

While Redmond's administrative staff studied the issues and collected data on Chicago and other cities, he confided to his closest colleagues his belief that much of the crisis was politically motivated from the White House. Usually calm and statesmanlike in his approach to crises, Redmond was noticeably upset by this unanticipated intrusion in a local school problem. He let it be known that he resented what he labeled "blanket harassment from the federal government."

Redmond recalled vividly a 1965 threat by the Department of Health, Education and Welfare to withhold funds for a similar reason. That crisis was averted by the intervention of Mayor Richard Daley, who prevailed upon President Lyndon Johnson to order his Commissioner of Education to retreat. Because Mayor Daley's influence in Washington had evaporated, however, no such simple solution was possible now.

Furthermore, Redmond suspected that President Richard Nixon might be using the Chicago ultimatum to begin a campaign to stake out new ground in the broad field of civil rights enforcement. Some astute political observers, such as John Dreiske of the *Chicago Sun Times*, noted that just prior to the Chicago confrontation, Nixon had ordered what appeared to be a slowdown in school desegregation in the South. Liberal critics, like *New York Times* columnist James Reston, had charged the Administration with a "wavering commitment" to civil rights as a result of this seemingly abortive desegregation action. Because the Chicago ultimatum was issued on the same day as a similar Georgia order, some felt, as Redmond did, that the President was now trying to dispel the notion that he might be tolerant of delay in school integration cases. Anyway, Redmond could do nothing more than conjecture about any hypocritical strategy adopted by the Chief Executive.

Despite what the Superintendent felt personally about this unpleasant diversion of his energies, the fact remained that he had to move ahead aggressively in preparing an answer to the Justice Department. In so doing, Redmond was donning a new look. This action would clearly place him in an overt leadership role rather than his usual passive, sub-ordinate, and professional advisory role in relation to the Board. Thus, he would be shouldering some of the responsibility for the Board and easing the squeeze between it and the federal government, on the one hand; between it and the Union, the black community, and special in-terest groups, on the other.

While the faculty segregation issue was still in the news headlines, Chicago Teachers Union President John Desmond was invited to the Superintendent's office for a private talk. Desmond's remarks were pre-dictable, as was his mood. "Teacher transfer is a sacred right and it must not be tampered with," he thundered. He placed the blame for fac-ulty segregation squarely on the Board of Education by arguing that the Board had the power to appoint 10 percent of the teachers in each school and that it had not used this power to achieve integration. Des-mond was referring to Article 42-2 of the Union-Board Agreement of 1970, an article which has been in effect many years and which states:

Any regularly appointed teacher who is eligible to transfer shall take prece-dence over newly appointed teachers or substitute teachers in filling a vacancy, except that no regularly appointed teachers will be transferred if 90 percent or more of the positions on the staff of the school to which transfer is desired are already filled by regularly appointed teachers.

In practice, this provision allows the Board to assign, to any individ-ual school, teachers selected because their background and training rep-resent a culture different from the majority of the children in the school. "The Board had five years in which to implement this article," Desmond emphasized to Redmond—"five years during which it could have as-signed 12,000 teachers by this method and, thus, could have integrated all of the school faculties." Desmond continued in an angry tone: "If the Board had done so there would not now be 214 Chicago Schools—or one out of every three—with all white faculties. The Board has failed and we will not sacrifice our transfer right under any circumstances to correct a failure that is the Board's, not ours!"

Nothing could be gained by arguing with Desmond. But, in defense, Redmond spoke of the many deterrents to faculty integration which had precluded the use of the 10 percent Board assignment solution in the past: (1) housing patterns, which find teachers opposed to transfer to avoid long commuting trips; (2) racial isolation, which causes teachers to lack experience and knowledge of unfamiliar cultures; (3) black con-sciousness, which causes many Negro teachers to consider the act of transferring to be "deserting the black cause"; (4) riots, demonstrations, and boycotts, which tend to reduce progress toward integration; and (5) the Illinois School Code, which outlaws the consideration of race in teacher assignment. Implicit in the Justice Department ultimatum, of course, was an order to the Board and Superintendent to somehow overcome all of these obstacles so as to provide an equal educational opportunity for all the children.

Even though he recognized the validity of Desmond's arguments, Redmond began to wonder about the legitimacy of the Union in the controversy. He could see that the Union and the Justice Department were on a collision course and that the Justice Department was not going to recognize the Union as a legitimate party to the controversy. He was certain that the federal government would deal only with the Board of Education.

Redmond was right. During the two-week period provided for the Board to develop a desegregation plan, the Justice Department announced that the Union could not be a party to the initial talks. This angered the Union to a point where the leaders began to threaten a strike if they were not included. United States Attorney, Thomas Foran, in announcing his decision, declared: "By law the responsibility for the proper conduct of the school system is with the Board of Education. The Union does not run the school Board." Vivian Gallagher, vice president of the Union, retorted sharply:

The Board cannot integrate its faculties without the cooperation of the Union. When the Justice Department meets with the Board to discuss the Board's response to the ultimatum, the Union will also need clarification of the proposed plan. There is no question that the Union will be dissatisfied with any plan worked out by the Superintendent and the Board, and it behooves the Justice Department to include us in their initial meetings.

The rejection of the Union by the Justice Department drew criticism even from Board members. Mrs. Lydon Wild asked, "Why don't the federal officials ask for the cooperation of the Union? Have they forgotten labor? Without the teachers, how can we operate?" Mrs. Carrey Preston argued that the "petty technical principles involved with denying participation to the Union would not justify the serious consequences of a probable strike." Even Redmond found himself supporting the Union in its demand to be included in the early stages of the talks.

But the Union fight was doomed to failure because, regardless of the technical reasons offered for keeping the Union out, the real reason apparently was the determination on the part of U.S. Attorney Foran to avoid what he knew would be fruitless talks. Foran was convinced that

equal distribution of qualified teachers was synonymous with equal educational opportunity. He insisted that the Union position on retaining
control of teacher transfer policy was going to be a barrier to equal educational opportunity and would probably be found in violation of the
equal protection clause of the Fourteenth Amendment.

This hard-line policy on the part of the federal government made bed-
fellows of Redmond and Desmond. As long as Foran would not consent
to include the Union in the talks, these two leaders were united in a
common stand. But whether or not this type of Superintendent-Union
relationship could be a real factor in preventing a strike remained to be
seen.

About the time that Redmond and the Board began to feel squeezed
by both the Justice Department and the Union, several newspaper editors and political leaders began to question the intervention of the federal government in this local school problem. "Just how much will the
concerned citizens of Chicago tolerate?" asked one editorial.

This focus on federal intervention was triggered by a sharply worded
letter released by Republican Governor Richard Ogilvie's office to Attorney General John Mitchell, in which the Governor said that the "premature" ultimatum would block action that he hoped would be taken voluntarily. More specifically, the Governor said:

Arbitrary deadlines and hasty decrees, which must be modified later by the
dictates of common sense to achieve effective solutions, do a disservice to all
involved. I am deeply concerned over the demands with which the Justice Department confronted the Board of Education. I should hope that all would
agree that federal intervention, asserting the federal legal force in the details of
local school matters, is undesirable and should be used only as a last resort
when local initiatives have failed.

Surprisingly, a well-known Democratic state legislator supported the
Justice Department's threat to file suit. Much to Redmond's irritation, he
said:

Hard as it may be on the Board and Dr. Redmond, some such external push
had to be supplied; without it, the Board might never have been able to
change the pattern of teacher segregation. Too many forces—including the
Teachers Union, the wishes and rights of teachers both black and white, and
long-established habit—are at work to keep things as they are. It is unlikely to
be changed without outside pressure, so I am glad the federal government is
supplying the pressure.

Another opinion on the ultimatum was voiced by Representative
Roman Pucinski of Chicago, who is now chairman of the House Educa-

tion subcommittee. The Congressman alarmed the public by saying that the threatened suit could result in "chaos." His contention was that the federal government was inviting a mass exodus of teachers from the Chicago school system. He also questioned whether the courts would even order mandatory assignment of teachers because it would mean breaking of a written contract between the Union and the Board.

Finally, before setting out to draft his response to the ultimatum, Redmond sought clarity of the black position. Despite the seriousness of the problem and the widespread press coverage, Redmond found that, ironically, there was little interest in the faculty integration crisis on the part of black teachers and the black community. The apparent reason was that the majority of the 6500 black teachers in the Chicago system felt that they were most effective in black schools, and they had no interest in being transferred to white schools merely to integrate the teaching faculties. The *Daily Defender,* the biggest black newspaper in the city, did take the occasion, however, to attack the Union by claiming that "its [the Union's] main objection is the preservation of segregation." The paper then called for a separate black teachers' union. None of this seemed particularly relevant to the teacher-integration question except the absence of real interest in the problem by the black community.

This absence of interest baffled Redmond because many major studies, including the 1964 Hauser Report and the 1967 Redmond Plan—both done in Chicago—showed beyond question that teachers in black schools and in schools in low socioeconomic neighborhoods were less experienced, had less formal training, were less qualified, and were subject to higher turnover than was the case with their colleagues in predominantly white schools and in schools in more favored socioeconomic areas. The failure of the black community to consider this important and the seeming lack of interest in teacher integration, signaled to Redmond that any plan to change the status quo in the black community was destined for severe resistance.

Redmond decided that his strategy would be to go it alone. He prepared an initial draft of his report to the Justice Department without consulting directly with Board members, Union officials, or Justice Department representatives. He was determined to include in his plan a proposal which would require the federal government to share in the costs of disestablishing the segregated pattern of faculty assignments. On July 21, 1969, two days before the deadline, Redmond submitted his Fifteen-Point Plan to the Board, which adopted it virtually unaltered. The following are some highlights of the plan:

1. Maintain, as vacancies occur, a minimum of 10 percent temporarily certificated teachers in each school, until September, 1969, and then maintain, as vacancies occur, a minimum of 15 percent temporarily certificated teachers.

2. Assign to the 10 percent or 15 percent of vacancies in each school temporarily certificated teachers who are about to begin their first year of teaching, providing such persons are available who possess a background of training and/or experience with a different culture from that of the majority of the children in the school.

3. Assign temporarily certificated teachers in the Chicago public schools to the school in which they taught last year unless their services are necessary in order to accomplish item no. 2 above.

4. Permit a regularly certificated teacher to place his name on the list for transfer to another school only after he has served one full year, rather than five months, in the school to which he is currently assigned. Announce that, effective September, 1969, transfer will not be considered until after the teacher has served in a school a minimum of two years as a regularly certificated teacher, rather than one year.

5. Seek to staff newly established schools so that they reflect the citywide ratio of experienced and inexperienced teachers.

6. Require participation in in-service education programs at the district level by all temporarily certificated teachers and regularly certificated teachers who have not previously taught children of the same culture group as those in their present assignment. Federal funds are requested in the amount of $340,000 per year for each 1,000 teachers.

7. Establish an experimental program for the transfer between inner-city and peripheral schools of experienced, mature teachers of a different culture from that of the children in the receiving school to work with children, teachers, and parents to create an understanding of the culture about which the teacher is knowledgeable. Federal funds are requested in the amount of $1,650,000 per year to staff 150 selected schools in this manner.

8. Improve the teaching-learning opportunities in selected inner-city schools by providing, on an experimental basis, additional experienced teachers to act as team leaders in the development of instructional teams which, in addition to professional staff, would include teacher aides and other non-professional personnel. (The team leader would receive a monthly increment over his basic salary.) Federal funds are requested in the amount of $955,800 per year to provide two teams, consisting of one team leader and two teacher aides for each of nine schools overall.

9. Restate and clarify for students, teachers, parents, and community the policy of the Board of Education to integrate school faculties in order that they may reflect a racial and ethnic diversity and thus better prepare students for today's world.

10. Seek the assistance of the federal government in instances where integration is impeded or made difficult because of harassment of teachers and other staff by teachers or other adults or by students.

11. Work with the federal authorities to correct problems or complaints of an

individual nature, related to integration, of which the federal authorities have knowledge.

12. Provide security protection for faculty parking lots in 200 schools. Federal funds are requested in the amount of $1,280,000 to implement this program.

The plan ended with the following recommendation:

The Chicago Teachers Union, on the basis of its contract with the Board of Education and the provisions therein requiring notice of consideration and mutual agreement on any modification or amendment thereto, has requested that it be made a party to a three-way conference involving the Board, the Union, and your office to discuss this entire subject. The Board of Education joins in this suggestion with the hope and expectation of full agreement by all parties.

On the day following the Board's adoption of Redmond's Fifteen-Point Plan, the Union was invited to meet with the Board and the Superintendent. The Justice Department was not involved in this meeting. As Redmond expected, the main objections from the Union were directed at the proposed changes in negotiated transfer procedures. Instead of a teacher being able to put his name on a transfer list after five months, he would now have to wait a full year and could not transfer until he has been teaching two years instead of the presently required one year. This provision was designed to correct the uneven distribution of experienced faculty. The Union also felt threatened by Redmond's proposal to raise the Board-controlled positions in each school from 10 percent to 15 percent. The Union protested that both of these provisions violated their transfer rights and the entire concept of seniority and tenure. Surprisingly, the Union did not object to the incentive program designed to make inner-city schools more attractive through salary bonuses. And, furthermore, the Union gratefully acknowledged the sincere effort that the Board was making to try to alleviate the serious parking lot security problem, which was a major reason why many otherwise willing teachers refuse inner-city assignments.

On the morning of July 23, 1969, exactly two weeks after the Justice Department ultimatum was received, the Fifteen-Point Plan was made public and dispatched to Washington. There was encouraging public acceptance of the Plan as it underwent scrutiny in Chicago's newspapers. The only mild objection came from the *Daily Defender,* in an editorial which claimed that so-called combat pay to white teachers in ghetto areas would be just another form of discrimination. The *Defender* further suggested that there were "too many whites" in the inner-city schools already.

Redmond and the Board waited anxiously for three months before the Justice Department reacted to the proposed plan. The response was a shattering setback for Redmond and the Board. The entire plan, *in toto*, was rejected. These were the final paragraphs of the rejection letter:

. . . we have concluded that the plan does not promise to adjust the conditions giving rise to the denial of the equal protection of the laws. . . . We would, therefore, make the following suggestions for obtaining an educationally feasible plan which promises realistically to correct these conditions.

Title IV, Section 403, of the Civil Rights Act of 1964 authorizes the Department of Health, Education and Welfare to render technical assistance to school districts in the preparation, adoption, and implementation of plans for the desegregation of public schools. Upon receipt of the following assurances we will forego any legal action until the Board has had an opportunity to review the recommendations of the United States Office of Education, Department of Health, Education and Welfare.

(i) The Board shall request HEW to prepare an educationally feasible faculty desegregation and equalization plan without placing any restrictions on HEW with regard to the formulation of the plan. Such a plan should be submitted by the end of this calendar year.

(ii) The Board agrees that implementation of any plan to overcome the constitutionally impermissible faculty assignment patterns shall not be contingent upon ratification of the plan by the Teachers Union.

(iii) The Board shall immediately compile centrally located records reflecting, by school, the name, address, and race of all teachers and professional staff personnel.

The dictatorial implications of this total rejection of the plan outraged Redmond and the Board members. Mrs. Carrey Preston revealed her anger by asserting that "the federal government is deliberately setting the Board eyeball to eyeball with the Union. The only way to settle this," she said defiantly, "is to let them file suit."

Mrs. Louise Malis attacked the federal intervention issue head-on. She said: "The Justice Department is guilty of outright coercion and intimidation of our local school board by its willingness to accept even a small part of our plan. The implications of this action are far-reaching for all big-city school boards. In my opinion, local school control has been seriously challenged."

During the summer of 1970, it became clear that the Justice Department was determined to pressure the Chicago Schools into faculty desegregation. In fact, the Chicago Board was ordered to transfer 1,000 teachers effective at the beginning of the new school year. As of September, 1970, it was not yet evident how the Union might respond, but most observers believed at that time that a real test of union strength was imminent. But the anticipated confrontation never really occurred. Instead, during the 1970–71 school year, the Justice Department in conjunction with the Office of Education modified its original order and proposed a reasonable plan for faculty integration which was readily approved by the Board of Education. After a minimal amount of protest the Union also accepted the plan which was quite similar to the ten percent assignment policy already agreed to by the Board and the Union. Thus, for the immediate future at least, the faculty integration problem in Chicago seems to be settled.

Much of the political and social power of professional groups is a consequence of their monopolistic control over a body of knowledge and practice deemed vital to society. The tighter the control and the greater the influence over who shall have access to it, the greater is the power wielded by the group in affecting legislation which concerns it. The influence of the AMA on Congress and state legislatures is an excellent case in point. So too is that of the ABA. The body of knowledge about teaching and learning which is the exclusive province of teachers, on the other hand, is limited. And the influence of teachers over who has access to the profession is almost nonexistent (see Vander Werf's article, p. 195). Although these are not the only criteria which define the nature of a professional, many people have argued that without satisfying them, teachers are destined to remain on the fringes of a profession as such. The teacher-power movement reflects a recognition of this situation and is an attempt, in part, to rectify it.

James Cass and Max Birnbaum

WHAT MAKES TEACHERS MILITANT

The sources of teacher militancy are analyzed in the following article. In it the authors contend that many of the most crucial variables bearing on teacher militancy have been obscured by the exaggerated emphasis which observers give to salary questions. It is to these neglected variables that the article is particularly addressed. James Cass and Max Birnbaum are convinced that in light of them, forces contributing to teacher militancy are going to increase in the years ahead. James Cass is Education Editor of the *Saturday Review*. Max Birnbaum is Director of the Human Relations Laboratory at Boston University.

From *Saturday Review*, January 20, 1968, pp. 54–56. Copyright © 1968 Saturday Review, Inc. Reprinted by permission of the publisher.

Last September the American school teacher served notice on the public that old stereotypes have changed—kindly Mr. Chips and the meek schoolmarm are dead. On the day that schools were scheduled to open in New York City and Detroit—and in smaller districts in Michigan, Illinois, Maryland, and Kentucky—schools remained closed. Teachers were on the picket line, not in the classroom. Florida's teachers, meanwhile, were threatening to close all the schools in the state if the Governor refused to call a special session of the legislature to act on their demands for increased support for education.

To date, the growing militancy of teachers has been explained primarily in terms of the mounting competition for members and power between the small but rapidly growing American Federation of Teachers (AFT), an AFL-CIO affiliate, and the larger, professionally oriented National Education Association (NEA). It is true that in the competition for selection as teacher representative in contract negotiations, the largely urban-based AFT (146,000 members) has scored a number of notable successes in the nation's larger cities over the small-town-based NEA with its million-plus members. It is true, too, that as a result the NEA has been prodded into an unaccustomed aggressiveness in representing its members—a new stance that is virtually indistinguishable from that of its trade union competitor. But the competition between the two organizations is only one part—albeit an important part—of a complex of forces that have caused the teachers to shed their traditional middle-class behavior.

Many of the factors that have an important bearing on teacher militancy have been obscured by the emphasis on salaries in contract negotiations. The question of take-home pay is an important one, to be sure, but equally crucial for many teachers is the issue of job satisfaction.

The rewards of teaching are complex and subject to a variety of local influences. There is no doubt an element of truth in the traditional rhetoric about "love of children" and "dedication to the future of society." It seems clear, however, that there are more fundamental factors that contribute to job satisfaction. Over the years, for instance, teaching has offered a large number of capable individuals a reasonably independent professional career. It has provided a substantial degree of community status which, although often limited, was almost always present. And for an occupation dominated by women, relatively few of whom were heads of families, teaching has offered salaries that usually have been adequate—if not much more. As a larger number of men entered teaching after World War II, salaries took on added importance, but teachers also sought a stronger hand in determining their own professional fate. Therefore, in recent years there has been a growing emphasis in contract negotiations on the demand for a more influential voice in developing school policy, as well as on conditions of teaching, and the facilities available for instruction.

Once a "reasonable" salary level is reached, it appears that substantial numbers of teachers today will accept lower salaries if other job satisfactions are high. By the same token, it seems clear that when other professional rewards are lacking, the emphasis on salaries rises. What has happened in recent years is that teacher salary levels in general have risen materially—but at the same time, especially in urban areas, a number of other forces have converged on the schools that have reduced job satisfaction precipitately. It is these forces and the context in which they developed that merit more careful scrutiny.

As the crucial role of education in modern society has been more widely recognized, the schools have developed a new political potency. The National Defense Education Act of 1958 and the Elementary and Secondary Education Act of 1965 made vast new federal funds available to the schools for the first time. The level of both state and local support increased materially during the same period. New horizons for education were appearing as it was recognized as the nation's major "growth industry." Thus teachers, along with other members of society, were caught up in what has been called the revolution of rising expectations. But it soon became clear that rising expectations are not fulfilled automatically.

Many occupational groups in America have learned that it is not the justice of individual demands that wins increased salaries and higher status from society, but the economic and political power of organized groups. The nation's doctors—long the teachers' ideal professional model—demonstrated a generation or more ago the tangible returns that can be derived from a strong organization and group solidarity. But physicians constitute a relatively small, elite professional group; teaching is a mass profession. And doctors, typically, are not public employees; most schoolteachers are. Therefore, teachers had to seek elsewhere for a realistic model for professional organization and action. But the obvious examples of other public employee groups presented special problems for them.

Those groups with education equal or superior to teachers—librarians, social workers, and engineers, for instance—seldom were highly organized and, lacking the teachers' numbers or the critical nature of their function, usually received lower salaries. Those civil service groups that have developed strong organizations—police, firemen, and sanitation workers, for example—have, typically, functioned close to the center of local political power and could be counted on for a high degree of loyalty and cooperation at election time. Teachers have not. Rarely have they been willing to compromise what they considered to be their professional commitment by becoming entangled in the realities of practical politics.

Faced with the competition of other civil service groups that shared their rising expectations, and unwilling to ally themselves with the political establishment, teachers often sought, and received, the support of another major power group in the city—organized labor. For many years, nevertheless, even as they benefited from the support of labor, few teachers were willing to affiliate as union members. But it became increasingly plain that rising expectations could be satisfied only through strong organizations and direct group action. No matter how reluctant teachers might be to desert their traditional professional posture, the imperative was clear.

Given these circumstances, and lacking realistic alternatives, teachers have joined for collective action in the AFT—and, more recently, in a newly militant NEA—which could offer the power of a labor union while allowing members to retain their traditional self-image of independent professionals. Neither organization, despite the AFT's affiliation with the AFL-CIO, is solely a trade union in the traditional sense, but each can act like one when the negotiating chips are down. At other times, members and leaders can step forth as bona fide professionals.

Yet it would have been inconceivable a decade ago for the American schoolteacher, with so long a history of conformity and conservatism, to desert the professional classroom for the trade union picket line. Such action denies too directly the deeply ingrained values and attitudes of traditional middle-class behavior. So dramatic a shift in teacher attitudes was made possible only by the radical change in the etiquette of social protest that has been so visible a part of the national experience in the 1960s. The wide acceptance of civil disobedience as an appropriate means for protesting social wrongs heralded a profound change in national perspectives which were reflected in teacher attitudes.

The nonviolent action of the civil rights movement in the South during the 1950s dramatized for the public the way in which civil disobedience might be used to protest the persistence of unjust laws or the reluctance of society as a whole to take positive action to redress social inequities. During the 1960s, home television screens repeatedly carried reports of the arrest, and sometimes violent treatment, of respected national figures as they registered their rejection of social injustice. The hundreds of college students who flocked to Mississippi to work in voter registration drives in the summer of 1964 were widely applauded. And, perhaps symbolically, the most telling event occurred when the head of the United Presbyterian Church in the U.S.A., accompanied by the white-haired mother of the Back Bay governor of Massachusetts, went south to register their protest against inequality—and were arrested and jailed.

Clearly, large numbers of Americans had come to accept direct action as an appropriate means for challenging the status quo—if the cause is just. The lesson was not lost on the nation's teachers. All that remained was to translate teacher demands into social imperatives.

But the sources of teacher militancy go far deeper than merely a revolution of rising expectations and a new acceptance of direct action as a legitimate means of achieving tangible rewards when expectations are frustrated.

Teachers have always occupied an equivocal position in our society —and society has always been ambivalent about its teachers. Many individuals and agencies in the community "teach," and it has become progressively more difficult to define the unique role of the classroom teacher in an age when the mass media provide so much and such diverse kinds of information. Even more specifically, it has never been possible to establish a direct correspondence between high salaries and "good teaching"—or, more particularly, high pupil achievement. Therefore, society has felt quite comfortable in paying its respects to teachers in the loftiest rhetoric while refusing adequate support for the schools for either salaries or facilities. Americans have found both Mark Hopkins and Ichabod Crane valid representatives of the profession. And Shaw's facile dictum—"He who can, does. He who cannot, teaches"— has haunted teachers for a half century or more. Other factors, too, have conspired to reinforce society's ambivalent attitude toward the profession—and the teachers' own traditional feeling of self-doubt or— in the social psychologist's term—self-hate. As a result, teachers have been undergoing a process of progressive alienation both from the school as an institution and from the community it serves.

A major factor in the alienation of teachers has been the growing im-

personality of the school as it has become larger and more highly structured. As enrollments swelled in the postwar years, education took on
more and more of the features of a mass production process. Administrative and supervisory positions grew in number and importance, and the
classroom teacher was progressively more removed from the central
functioning of the school. It became more difficult, then, for the teacher
to identify closely with the school as an institution. The problem was intensified as the management function became more complex and time-
consuming, and the school principal became less the traditional senior
teacher and colleague than the resident representative of absentee management.

(It appears that the recent dissolution of the Educational Policies
Commission, sponsored jointly for many years by the American Association of School Administrators and the National Education Association,
reflects the growing division between the interests and objectives of administrators and teachers. The NEA and AASA have always contended
that the professional interests of their respective members were identi-
cal, but there are strong indications that the AFT's insistence upon the
distinction between management and labor in education is more
realistic—especially in the light of the growing acceptance of collective
negotiations as an appropriate means for settling teacher disputes.)

Even as teachers were finding it more difficult to identify with the
schools in which they taught, they were also feeling increasingly divorced from the communities served by their schools. Few grew up in
the communities in which they taught, and many did not even live
there. A growing number of teachers today, it appears, do not feel an integral part of the community in which they teach. In the affluent suburbs they sometimes cannot afford to live in their school's high tax district, and in the anonymity of the great city their school may serve no
identifiable community or neighborhood. Therefore, the teacher's relationship to both the school and the community is changing rapidly as
the sense of belonging is lost.

The alienation of teachers has been stimulated, too, by the increasing
—and sometimes unrealistic—demands that have been made on the
schools. Americans have always looked to education as the ultimate
corrective for social ills or the means for meeting society's needs. Two or
three generations ago, for instance, the schools were assigned the task of
Americanizing our immigrant fathers and, at a somewhat later date,
were asked to develop a pool of skilled manpower through vocational
education. More recently, they have been charged with a variety of as-

signments from teaching the evils of alcohol to exploring the intricacies of sex education.

In the past, teachers were expected to introduce the rising generation to the knowledge and skills that were considered appropriate for the development of competent citizens and civilized men. Some children learned more readily than others, but this was expected. Those who lacked academic talent or motivation simply disappeared from the classroom to return to the farm or to find unskilled work in the community. But today no such simple solutions to the problem of the nonlearner are possible; everyone must succeed—and the definition of success varies with the community.

In the suburbs, with a high level of education among parents, it is no longer enough to shepherd the children of the middle class through high school and into college. The revolution of rising expectations functions in many contexts, and increasing numbers of parents demand that their children be prepared to compete successfully for admission to the most selective institutions.

At the other end of the scale, in the inner city, teachers are expected to induce learning among children who are imperfectly prepared by background or experience for the discipline of classroom work. Often lacking special training for the task, the teacher may have an equally imperfect understanding of the child and his special learning problems. At the upper grades, "education" often becomes a mere exercise in custodial care, and not infrequently the teacher has reason to be physically afraid of the students. Yet, increasingly, inner-city parents and their representatives refuse to remain silent. They demand that the schools succeed in their assigned task—and charge that the teacher has failed when their children do not learn.

At the same time, education is attracting a new breed of teachers. Better educated than in the past, they are less "dedicated" and more pragmatic than their predecessors. They have a surer sense of their own professional competence, and consequently resent assignment to nonprofessional duties and have less patience with the traditional inadequacies of time, facilities, and administrative support. At home with the new etiquette of social protest and faced with the growing impersonality of the educational environment, today's teachers respond in predictable ways.

Old loyalties have crumbled, and new allegiances are emerging. Lacking the old devotion to school and community, and threatened by new demands on the schools for which neither experience nor training have prepared them, today's teachers are turning inward. It is to the group—either the trade union or the professional organization—that they look for support and security.

In *The Secular City*, Harvey Cox writes: "Urbanization means a structure of common life in which diversity and the disintegration of tradition are paramount. It means a type of impersonality in which functional relationships multiply." The massive changes in our society to which Professor Cox refers have precipitated major shifts in the values and attitudes of many individuals and groups. But few, if any, have been more fundamental or more dramatic than those of teachers. Traditional patterns of association are disintegrating, and teachers are seeking new "functional relationships" not only with administrators and school boards, but even with their staunchest supporters in the past, the parents.

The forces that have contributed to teacher alienation, and, consequently, to militancy, almost certainly are going to increase rather than diminish in the years ahead. And the virus of change is already spreading from its point of origin in the city to the suburbs and beyond. We can expect that as the forces reducing job satisfaction for many teachers increase, the demands for higher salaries will become more intense. And each time the teachers win one more bitterly fought contest for higher pay and improved working conditions, their sense of group solidarity will be increased—and their feeling of alienation from the community will grow.

Any realistic appraisal of teacher militancy today seems to indicate that we have seen only the beginning.

In 1960 Myron Lieberman wrote that "the foremost fact about teacher organizations in the United States is their irrelevance in the national scene. Their futility in protecting the public interest and the legitimate vocational aspirations of teachers is a national tragedy, much more dangerous to our democratic institutions than the excessive power wielded by such familiar bogeys as 'Madison Avenue,' 'labor bosses,' 'captains of industry,' 'military high brass,' and the like. Because their organizations are weak, teachers are without power; because they are without power, power is exercised upon them to weaken and corrupt public education." (*The Future of Public Education*, 1960)

Whether today's teacher organizations protect the public interest or the *legitimate* vocational aspirations of teachers is open to question. But today's teacher organizations are very much *on* the national scene and clearly and increasingly powerful. How this power is likely to be used and how it should be used is the focus of the following projective article.

Myron Lieberman

IMPLICATIONS OF THE COMING NEA-AFT MERGER

Myron Lieberman contends that rivalry between the AFT and the NEA has played a crucial role in the dynamics of teacher militancy. Accordingly, he argues that failure to consider such rivalry in any examination of the teacher-militancy issue would lead to a distorted picture of this question.

In the following article, Lieberman assumes a merger between the rival teacher groups. In projecting such a merger, he discusses the points of conflict between the two groups, the benefits which he believes would follow from merger, and the implications for collective negotiations.

Myron Lieberman is the author of numerous books and articles which are mainly addressed to the profession of education. He is a leading national authority on collective negotiations in education.

A merger of the National Education Association and American Federation of Teachers will probably be negotiated in the near future. Such a move will have far-reaching national implications for teacher militancy. Perhaps because very few educators realize how imminent merger is, our professional literature is virtually devoid of any consideration of the likely conditions and consequences of merger. Inasmuch as organizational rivalry plays such an important role in teacher militancy, it would be unrealistic to consider the dynamics of teacher militancy without serious attention to the effects of merger upon it.

In the following comments, I am going to assume that merger will take place within a few years. This assumption is based largely upon what appears to me to be the practical logic of the situation. My purpose here, however, is not to demonstrate what appears obvious to me, i.e., that the merger will take place in the next few years at most, but to call attention and scholarly inquiry into what is problematical, the conditions and consequences of merger. These are the crucial problems, not whether or when the merger will occur.

Without question, the organizational rivalry between the NEA and AFT has been an important stimulus to teacher militancy. At all levels,

From *Phi Delta Kappan*, November, 1968, pp. 139–144. Reprinted by permission of the author and publisher.

the two organizations and their state and local affiliates have come under much more pressure to achieve benefits than would be the case if there were only one organization. A representation election almost invariably causes the competing organizations to adopt a more militant stance in order to demonstrate their effectiveness in achieving teacher goals. For the same reason, any failure to press vigorously for teacher objectives becomes a threat to organizational survival. State and national support are poured into local elections and negotiation sessions in order to protect the interests of the state and national affiliates. Thus at the local level organizational rivalry has led to a vastly greater organizational effort to advance teacher objectives. This development is consistent with the experience of competing organizations in other fields.

The crucial importance of the NEA-AFT rivalry in stimulating teacher militancy raises the question of whether the merger of the two organizations will reduce such militancy. Probably, the merger will simultaneously encourage some tendencies toward greater teacher militancy and some toward less militancy; the overall outcome is likely to vary widely from district to district and time to time. To see why, it will be helpful to review the issues involved in merger.

Historically, two major organizational issues have divided the NEA and AFT. One was the fact that local, state, and national education associations typically permitted all-inclusive membership, i.e., these associations enrolled administrators and supervisors (hereafter referred to as "administrators" or "administrative personnel") as well as teachers. The other issue was the AFT's affiliation with the AFL-CIO. It is becoming evident, however, that these issues no longer divide the organizations as they did in the past.

In the first place, a number of teacher negotiation laws and/or state administrative agencies have settled the issue of administrator membership substantially along the lines advocated by the AFT. True, in a few other states, such as Connecticut, Washington, and Maryland, state negotiations legislation permits or even mandates the inclusion of administrative personnel in a teacher bargaining unit; but this aspect of the statutes is either ignored in practice or is creating too many practical difficulties for all parties. In any event, the Michigan experience is likely to be the predominant pattern. In that state, many superintendents withdrew from, or did not join, local associations after passage of the Michigan negotiations statute in 1965. In 1966, the Michigan Association of School Administrators withdrew from the Michigan Education Association and joined with the Michigan School Boards Association and Michigan School Business Officials to form a new organization. In 1967, the state organizations of elementary and secondary school principals pulled out of the Michigan Education Association.

It should be noted that in the collective negotiations context, administrator membership in the teacher organization (which is not the same thing as membership in the same negotiating unit as teachers) is dangerous for the school board as well as for the teacher organization. Such membership, especially if the administrative personnel are active in the teacher organization, could lead to charges of employer support or domination of the employee (teacher) organization or to other unfair labor practices. In other words, administrator membership may jeopardize both the organization's right to represent teachers and the legitimacy of the board's approach to teacher bargaining.

The Michigan pattern concerning administrative membership in teacher organizations is still a minority one in the country as a whole. Nevertheless, it is likely to prevail eventually because of the difficulties inherent in maintaining all-inclusive membership in a negotiating organization. School boards will increasingly resist situations in which personnel assigned to administrative duties are represented by an organization controlled by the teachers they administer.

At the present time the issue of administrative membership is being debated at all organizational levels. In some districts the issue is seen as pertaining only to local organizations; it is assumed that administrative personnel can and should retain membership in state and national teacher organizations. In other places it is already accepted that administrative personnel cannot continue as regular members of local and state teacher organizations, but it is thought they should continue as members of NEA. Nevertheless, it is clear that even at the national level all-inclusive membership poses many sticky problems; the American Association of School Administrators, National Association of Secondary-School Principals, Department of Elementary School Principals, and Association for Supervision and Curriculum Development are some of the NEA departments already considering the need for modifying their relationships with the NEA in the near future.

The existence of these different approaches is understandable only in terms of intra-organizational perspectives. A state association leader might reluctantly accept the demise of all-inclusive membership at the local level but seek desperately to retain it at the state level. For one thing, he will naturally be unhappy at the prospect of losing dues revenue from administrators and supervisors. And if, as is often the case, such personnel play important roles in recruiting teachers to state membership, the loss of administrative personnel involves much more than the numbers of such personnel. In this situation the state association leader easily convinces himself that all inclusive membership in the state association is still desirable. After all, he tells himself and others, the local association, not the state, is the negotiating organization. Furthermore, both teachers and administrators have a common interest in more state aid, an improved retirement system, and so on.

As plausible as these arguments are, they ignore the pressures toward separation at the state as well as at the local level. How will administrators be represented in the state association, if not through local associations? What will happen to administrators in districts too small to establish local organizations of administrators? Since the state organization will invariably support teachers in showdowns at the local level—to do otherwise would be organizational hara-kiri—how will administrators be able to work vigorously for their objectives inside the organization? How will school boards react to administrative membership in organizations supporting teachers' strikes or other militant action against the board and its representatives? Will administrators be willing to pay dues to state organizations that support teachers in militant anti-administration activities?

In their frantic efforts to maintain the status quo, some state association leaders have overlooked these hard questions relating to administrative membership in state teacher organizations. Nevertheless, administrators are taking the initiative in withdrawing from the state associations as often or more often than they are being excluded from them by militant teachers.

The same kind of wishful thinking characterized the outlook of NEA leaders until the recent past. For several reasons, NEA leaders did not want to adopt a position on administrative membership at local and state levels. There was concern that the exclusion of administrators from NEA would be damaging in terms of NEA membership, and again, the fear was related to administrative help in recruiting teacher members as well as to the loss of administrators per se. There was an emphasis upon the common interests of teachers and administrators at the national level, e.g., in getting more federal aid. There was also a failure to grasp the interdependence of local, state, and national organizations in a negotiating context.

An even more difficult problem was the tremendous regional, state, and local differences relating to negotiations. Association experience in

Michigan or Massachusetts meant nothing to association leaders in Alabama or Mississippi. A membership policy vis-à-vis administrators that would have seemed sensible in Michigan would have horrified association members in Alabama.

The resolution of this difficult organizational problem was deceptively simple. The NEA's *Guidelines to Professional Negotiation* (1965) proposed that the inclusion of administrators in the negotiating unit and the negotiating organization be left to local option. This was not very helpful to local associations who wanted guidance on what their policy should be, but it was probably the only feasible way to avoid the issue until the pro-negotiation forces were stronger and there was a wider understanding of the problem throughout the association structure. Certainly, some NEA leaders realized from the outset of the negotiations movement that local option on administrator membership, without limits or guidelines, was a hopeless long-range policy; but a realistic policy had no chance of acceptance in the early 1960's.

A merger between the NEA and AFT will unquestionably accelerate the flight of administrative personnel from the merged organizations at all levels. First, the very fact that merger talks are taking place will confirm the feelings of many administrators that the associations are becoming "just like the union"—if not worse—and hence that administrators have no business in the association, with or without a merger. A more important point is that the AFT will demand some type of administrative exclusion as a condition of merger. Such a demand would actually make more sense from a propaganda than from a substantive point of view. The reason is that the inclusion of AFT membership in a new organization would tip the organizational balance in favor of administrative exclusion. Thus even if the exclusion of administrators were not a condition of merger, such exclusion would be organizational policy anyway within a year or two after merger. I suggest this independently of any conclusion about the desirability of excluding administrators from teacher organizations; the point is that a sincere belief in the importance of such exclusion does not necessarily justify setting it as a condition of merger.

Note that the issue here is not whether administrators have or should have the right to join teacher organizations. Most assuredly, they do have the right and will continue to have it, insofar as teachers permit it. The real issue is whether a teacher organization which includes administrators should have the legal right to represent teachers on terms and conditions of employment. Teachers and administrators have a constitutionally protected right to join the same organizations, but organizations enrolling both teachers and administrators do not have a constitutionally protected right to represent teachers in negotiations with their employers. Organizational rights to represent teachers are conditioned by law upon a number of public policy considerations. One such consideration is whether the organization can represent employees effectively. In private employment, this consideration has led to the mandatory exclusion of managerial personnel if the organization is to retain negotiating rights. The alleged differences between public and private employment, professional and nonprofessional employment, and between education and other fields are not likely to weaken the public policy arguments for exclusion of administrators from organizations seeking to represent teachers.

Experience in other fields strongly suggests that administrative membership in state and national teacher organizations will probably not survive collective negotiations by teachers. If such membership is to survive, which is doubtful in any case, it is essential for the NEA and its affiliates to examine the issue by some sort of high-level task force in which teachers and administrators alike could have confidence. Such a task force would have to include experts in collective negotiations and public administration who clearly had no vested interest in the outcome and who could propose a feasible structure for all-inclusive membership. Otherwise, the forced exclusion or voluntary withdrawal of administrators from state associations and the NEA will increase rapidly, and the makeshift arrangements to hold everyone together will continue to ignore important practical considerations. One comprehensive study of the problem, adequately staffed and financed, would have served better than the hasty and improvised studies that have been made thus far. In any event, no task force of the kind envisaged has been or is in prospect; since such a group might well conclude that the separation is desirable and inevitable, perhaps little has been or will be lost by the absence of such an effort.

We should recognize, however, that many of the arguments for or against separation are oversimplifications of a complex problem. Teachers and administrators do not have to be in the same organization in order to communicate and cooperate with each other. Likewise, the fact that they are in the same organization would not necessarily reduce tensions or disagreements or conflicts between them. In other words, equating all-inclusive membership with cooperation, or separate organizations with conflict, is an oversimplification. In any case, the most probable outcome is a sort of confederation of educational organizations, in which each controls its own membership, budget, and policies. There could be joint financing and support of activities commanding the support of all organizations while the organizations go their own way in areas where their views or interests clash. Obviously, we can expect such clashes in the areas of collective negotiations and teacher militancy.

The upshot seems to me to be this: Regardless of the formal membership structure of the merged organization, teachers will control the state and national organizations that merge. The emerging organizations will put great pressure on teachers to join, and we can expect a dramatic increase in teacher organizational membership at all levels. With greatly increased membership and resources—none of which are needed to fight a rival teacher organization—and without the internal constraints inherent in administrator membership or control, the new organization will probably pursue more militant policies in behalf of teacher interests and views than anything we have experienced thus far in either NEA or AFT.

I say "probably" because some aspects of merger will tend to reduce teacher militancy. Thus it is often thought that merger will reduce teacher militancy by eliminating competition between the two organizations. So long as two organizations are competing for members, there is great pressure on each to achieve significant results. With merger, this pressure, and the militancy it generates, will disappear. Interestingly enough, many leaders in both organizations, as well as experienced observers familiar with experience in other fields, share this expectation.

Undoubtedly, organizational rivalry typically results in greater organizational militancy. Even if this were not the case in other fields, it is clear that the recent sweeping changes in the NEA and its state and local affiliates would not have occurred (at least not so soon) except for the challenge of the AFT. This conclusion is not questioned, privately at least, by many NEA leaders.

Nevertheless, although organizational rivalry increases teacher militancy, it does not necessarily follow that merger will reduce such militancy, or that every aspect of merger will have this effect. For example, in many school districts, neither the local association nor the federation can afford full-time local leadership. With merger, the teachers may be able to support full-time local leadership with adequate facilities; much of the time and resources that were devoted to fighting the other teacher organization may now be directed at the school board. One of the certain consequences of merger will be a substantial increase in full-time representation of teachers and in their organizational resources, facilities, and support at all levels.

The increase in organizational capability may not fully offset the loss of dynamism inherent in two competing organizations. The crucial point, however, is that merger will not necessarily end the kind of competition and rivalry that has undergirded so much recent teacher militancy. In short, we must consider the possibility that competition *within* the merged organization will result in as much teacher militancy as competition between the present separate organizations.

I have noted that enrolling everyone in the same organization does not automatically eliminate differences or conflicts of interest among the members. In negotiations where there are rival organizations, the minority organization may criticize the results in order to persuade teachers to vote for and join the minority organization and give it a chance to become the bargaining agent. With one organization, the objective is to persuade teachers to change the leadership of the organization instead of to change their organizational affiliation. However, from the standpoint of teacher militancy, the dynamics of the situation can be much the same. In both situations, there is pressure on organizational leadership to achieve results, and there is also a leadership need to arouse teacher militancy for the same purpose.

The crucial difference between competition between two organizations and competition within a single organization relates to the capacity of those not in control of the organizational machinery to wage an effective campaign against the incumbents. To be specific, NEA publications are controlled by persons independent of AFT control, and vice versa. Thus, regardless of which organization is the bargaining agent in a given school district, there is a rival organizational apparatus not controlled by the bargaining agent. This rival apparatus constitutes a source of information, criticism, and opinion whose very existence places greater pressure on the bargaining agent to achieve every possible gain.

If, however, there is a merger and therefore only one organization, how will critics and opponents of the incumbent leadership get their views publicized? They will no longer have an official organizational publication for this purpose. They will no longer control organizational conventions, conferences, news releases, and other means of disseminating their views. As a result, the incumbent leadership comes under less pressure to achieve results, with a consequent diminution of teacher militancy.

Merger per se will tend to weaken effective capacity to oppose incumbent leadership, and such weakening will inevitably lessen teacher militancy. However, appropriate action could be taken to insure that this does not happen. The appropriate action would be the introduction of the caucus system in the merged organization. Because the long-range effects of the merger will depend on how soon and how effectively caucuses are established in the new organization, and because the existence and effectiveness of caucuses will be the major influence on teacher militancy in the merged organization, it is necessary to analyze their role in some detail.

A caucus system is essentially a system of political parties within the organization. Organization members may join a caucus, pay dues to it, attend its meetings, participate in its deliberations, and perhaps represent it in official organization proceedings. It is essential that caucuses be financed and operated independently of the organizational machinery; otherwise there is the danger that the caucus will lose its ability to function as an independent source of information, criticism, and leadership. The crucial point is that in the absence of a caucus, individual members or convention delegates are helpless before the organizational machinery. To change organizational policy or to launch a campaign to change organizational leadership, collective action is needed. First, there must be a forum not controlled by incumbent leadership in which the opposition has full opportunity to state its case and generate support. Floor fights (hopefully, only verbal ones) must be organized, fall-back positions established, and strategy coordinated. Signs, posters, and other literature may have to be printed and disseminated, and so on. These and other essentials of effective organizational leadership or influence cannot be initiated effectively by ad hoc committees or organizations, which are formed—usually over one issue—at a particular convention and then wither away. At all times there must be an organizational mechanism which can serve all the constructive purposes served by a rival organization. Such a mechanism, however, must be as independent of control by incumbent leadership as is a rival organization.

The incumbent leadership will also need a political mechanism independent of the organizational machinery. The elected officers of the organization should not be able to use organizational funds to finance their election campaign. As in most such situations, the incumbents will have certain political advantages accruing from their incumbency, but they too will have political needs which cannot legitimately be met by using official organizational machinery. It would, therefore, be erroneous to regard caucuses solely as a means for helping the "out's" clobber the "in's." Neither democracy nor militancy will flourish in the merged organization unless there exists practical means of exerting organizational influence and leadership which are not dependent upon the official organizational structure. Policies and leaders must be forged in the caucuses, and thence into the official organizational structure. If this is done, and I believe it can and must be done, we can be optimistic about the level of internal democracy in the merged organization. We can also expect a continuing high level of teacher militancy under these conditions.

Affiliation As a Merger Issue

For all practical purposes, the forthcoming merger will end teacher affiliation with the AFL-CIO. The AFT will need some face-saving concession on this issue, such as a national referendum on the question within the merged organization or local option to affiliate with the AFL-CIO; but the issue is already a dead horse for all practical reasons. The fact that AFT leaders are already proposing a referendum, knowing full well that it would be overwhelmingly defeated in the merged organization, ought to be signal enough for anyone to see. There is even reason to doubt whether such a referendum confined to the present AFT membership would support affiliation. Certainly there is very little sentiment in the AFT to insist upon affiliation at the cost of preventing merger.

Allowing local option to affiliate with the AFL-CIO might be a viable solution, since it would ease the transition problem, support the principle of local autonomy, and quickly lead to disaffiliation anyway. Affiliation with the AFL-CIO is not important to most AFT members, but it is important to some AFT leaders in some large urban centers. If local option is permitted, only a few locals will affiliate with the AFL-CIO, and the impracticalities of such a relationship will lead to their disaffiliation soon afterward. Furthermore, it is doubtful whether the AFL-CIO would find it advantageous to enroll a few teacher locals, even a few relatively large ones.

Since the teacher organizations choosing to be affiliated with the AFL-CIO would not be a rival to the merged teacher organizations, affiliation would not constitute an organizational issue as it does now. Actually, there is no constitutional reason now why an NEA local affiliate cannot affiliate with the AFL-CIO. Such affiliation would probably lead to expulsion by the NEA Executive Committee under present circumstances, but such a reaction would be overkill if there were only one teacher organization. At any rate, despite the enormous importance of the issue in the propaganda war between NEA and AFT, it is not a very important substantive issue, and it will not hold up merger as long as it takes to read this paper.

What will be the impact of disaffiliation on teacher militancy? A popular view is that AFT militancy is due to its affiliation with the AFL-CIO. This seems very questionable. Affiliation has contributed to AFT militancy, in specific communities under specific circumstances; likewise, affiliation has often been a conservative influence in many situations. The teacher stereotype of labor bosses inciting teachers to strike is far removed from the facts, as is the notion that the AFT depends largely upon the AFL-CIO or the IUD [Industrial Union Department, whose main function is recruitment] for support. The AFL-CIO did play an important role in the early stages of the AFT's drive for collective bargaining, but it is not a decisive factor now. Surely, there have been enough teacher strikes, boycotts, sanctions, and other pressures by associations in recent years to end the fallacy that affiliation with the AFL-CIO underlies or is an essential ingredient of teacher militancy. In fact, nonteacher members of the AFL-CIO at any level may view teachers' strikes more critically as parents and taxpayers than favorably as the justified efforts of fellow wage earners. Realistically, there is no strong reason to believe that disaffiliation will reduce teacher militancy in any significant way.

The major problems of merger are not philosophical or ideological; they are practical, such as who gets what job in the merged organization. The practical problems will be complicated more by the political implications of any settlement than by the equities from a strictly organizational or employment point of view. To be candid, there are enough resources to take care of everybody reasonably well. The more difficult problems will arise over the inevitable efforts by the negotiators on both sides to place their political supporters in as many of the key positions as possible. These efforts will create internal problems on each side which may be more difficult to resolve than the issues dividing the negotiators along organizational lines.

It would be naive to underestimate the importance of this problem. Beyond the broad social factors affecting teacher militancy, the quality of teacher leadership is necessarily a crucial factor in the dynamics and future of teacher militancy. For this reason, my concluding comments will relate to this matter.

The most immediate effects of merger upon leadership will be at the state level. In a number of states, federation locals dominate the large urban districts, whereas other districts are largely association-dominated. Especially where the AFT-dominated districts include greater proportions of all the teachers in the state, the impact of merger may be truly traumatic at the state level. In fact, there are states where federation members have no significant reservations about affiliation at the national level but object strenuously to state association leadership. This is especially true in states like California and Minnesota, where state association leadership—to the obvious chagrin of many NEA leaders—has vigorously opposed effective negotiation legislation.

Another point here is that the NEA's national staff is much more oriented to collective negotiations and teacher militancy than is the leadership of many state associations. Many state associations are oriented more to lobbying in the state legislature than to effective support of locals at the bargaining table. It appears that the NEA has had to establish regional field offices to assist local associations in negotiations partly because of state association slowness in responding to the negotiations movement. The state associations in Massachusetts, Michigan, New Jersey, and Rhode Island were the quickest to adapt effectively to negotiations, but in many states the local associations must still look to the NEA rather than the state association for significant help in negotiations. Indeed, this is still necessary occasionally in the states mentioned as having made the most rapid adjustment. The point is, however, that merger will sometimes change the constituency of the state organization more than it will the national; hence changes in leadership and policy in some of the state organizations may emerge rather quickly.

At the national level, full-time leadership in the merged organization will be largely as it is now in the NEA, at least for the near future. This is not only due to the arithmetic of the situation, i.e., the NEA's much greater membership and national staff. It will also be due to the fact that most of the NEA's present leadership is negotiation-oriented. Merger, therefore, will not be seen as a threat but as a step forward toward a more militant organization. On this score, it must be conceded that changes in the NEA within the past few years, and especially since its top leadership changed in 1967, have been truly remarkable.

In the early 1960's, one New York City law firm (Kaye, Scholer, Fierman, Hays, and Handler) provided the national leadership and the expertise which saved the NEA and its affiliates from organizational catastrophe in its competition with the AFT. It is a little known but singular fact that a New York City law firm, which ordinarily represents management in its labor practice, negotiated the first association agreements, trained the association staff, and guided the NEA to an acceptance of, and commitment to, collective negotiations. Ironically, corporation lawyers succeeded in convincing NEA leadership (correctly, it appears) that the NEA had to cease rejecting collective negotiations and demonstrate its determination to negotiate better agreements for teachers than those negotiated by the AFT. As this view prevailed, those who supported it became more influential in the NEA; today, NEA leadership is clearly committed to collective negotiations and includes a capability in this area which is not inferior to the federation's.

Without getting into personalities, therefore, it seems to me that one of the most encouraging aspects of the present situation is the tremendous improvement in the quality of teacher leadership and in the likelihood that merger will strengthen the tendencies in this direction. If this is the case, teacher militancy will continue to increase and will be increasingly devoted to constructive public policy as well as teacher objectives.

Questions for Discussion

1. In which ways do you see teacher militancy as an expression of true concern for quality education?
2. Which aspects of the teacher-power movement do you perceive as lying outside the realm of concern for quality education?
3. What kinds of questions would you raise about the professionalism of teacher affiliation with a labor union?
4. In which ways do you think teachers could be made more influential in the control of their profession?
5. Review the Burnett article in Chapter 1. In which ways do you think the readings in this chapter support some of Burnett's conclusions?
6. Has the increasing militancy of teachers been a motivating factor in your choice to become a teacher?

Topics for Further Study

1. Teacher power is one of the major components of the community-control controversy discussed in the Salz article and in Chapter 3. Review the Ocean Hill–Brownsville case and try to determine the influence of the UFT in this situation. In order to accomplish this assignment, it will probably be necessary to review the case by tracing its chronology week by week in the *New York Times*. Has the community-control threat to the professionals caused a united professional front which can prevent experimentation in educational politics?

2. This chapter takes cognizance of the fact that teacher militancy is on the rise. Has the movement in this direction affected your local community? Interview the officers of the local NEA and AFT chapters. Are they militant? Do the representatives of the two organizations seem to espouse the same ideas? If so, why are there two different organizations? What arguments does the AFT officer give for being associated with the AFL-CIO?

3. What do you think is the stereotype of the teacher in your community? Try to find out by talking to people in various walks of life. What questions should you ask in order to acquire data related to community attitudes and expectations about teachers?

4. Teachers are demanding a role in all local school district decision-making. They want to have a voice in hiring of new teachers and in determining the school curriculum. Use your local system as a case study to determine the success of these attempts. Do these efforts make teaching more respectable as a profession? What are the criteria for qualification as a profession?

5. Study the influence of the black militants on the policies of public school systems and, particularly, on the unions in those systems. Interview the black leaders in the city school system near your home. What do their goals seem to be? How do their objectives differ from those of the white union leaders? What are your predictions for the future role of the black teacher in urban school policy-making? What effect would the adoption of community control have on your predictions?

6. School administrators have been caught off guard by the rapidly increasing teacher militancy. Furthermore, the superintendent in many schools has found himself in a situation where he may be forced to redefine his role. Many people even feel that there is no longer any need for the superintendency in the traditional sense. What would be the reasoning behind the latter argument? What new role is the superintendent now expected to play as a result of the increased militancy of teachers? Discuss the role of the chief school administrator with various school and community leaders.

Chapter 5. STUDENTS IN REBELLION: UNREST IN THE SCHOOLS

IN recent years one of the most cherished of all American institutions—the public school—has become enveloped in the growing wave of student dissent which has been sweeping through the nation's college campuses. The filtering down of this rebellion into the secondary schools was expected. Indeed, even in the middle 1960's educators knew that its arrival was imminent. The determinants underlying the changing mood of America's youth are not merely related to the arbitrary matriculation date between high school and college; they are closely tied to the sub-cultures of adolescence and young adulthood, both of which cut across levels of education.

The increase of student dissent in the public schools leads us to think seriously about the role of the school in our society—a question which has taken on new meaning as the mood of students increasingly becomes one of disdain for the prevailing school-society relationship. The exact nature of this student mood is essential background for study of the specific issue selected for examination in this chapter. Before examining the issue, let us try to capture the spirit of the students who are attempting to reshape our society.

The "turned-on" youth sub-culture expresses its concerns in the form of its own struggle for a place in a society whose values it finds difficult to accept. In the eyes of student dissenters, our society has created a generation of boredom and a people whose lives are filled with emptiness and material things. It is a society built on human understanding and respect for individual expression that the young critics are seeking. They cite particularly what they consider to be the immoral acts of big business as a major reason for societal decay. Big business is blamed for converting our schools from domains of free thought to factories producing individuals concerned only with profit, competition, and the business ethic.

Even though this mood is felt only by a minority of students, values are changing and society may be undergoing a significant cultural shift. The students whose feelings are reflected, strongly believe that student unrest is the beginning of a real revolution to change society. They reject the notion, suggested by Bruno Bettelheim and others, that their unrest is merely a mass temper tantrum brought on by a combination of irritations such as racial discrimination, war, infatuation with sexual freedom, and the changing attitude toward drug use.

The effects upon education of the apparent cultural shift and its accompanying shift of values constitute the major concerns of this chapter. It would be helpful at this point if the student would return to the Spindler hypotheses in Chapter 1 in order to explain the value conflicts encountered by the emerging youth subculture as it questions the status quo. It would also be worthwhile to examine, in light of the educational philosophies summarized by Pounds and Bryner in Chapter 1, the contrasting views of the majority who seek to maintain the present system and the new breed of students who demand change. In philosophical terms, does the new breed reflect a reconstructionist point of view or does it reflect a somewhat more radical one? The reconstructionist approaches the development of a new social order with a strong attachment to science and its techniques. Does the emotional nature of the present student mood preclude the categorization of this new breed of students as reconstructionist? Is the rationalism of the reconstructionists at odds with the dissenting students' values?

This discussion suggests that some of our youth see the need for a vast revision in the school-society relationship. Furthermore, it suggests that these students, representing a very active and influential group within the adolescent and youth subculture, may be about to give up on the present system and those who lead it. Thus a school-society role dilemma is emerging. Inherent in this dilemma is the issue which will be the focus of this chapter: *Must the structure and the underlying philosophy of the American education system be reconstituted in order to accommodate the needs and demands expressed in recent student dissent?* Or, to put it another way, is it possible under the present public school system for a significant portion of young Americans to realize the goals, values, and ideals expressed in its protest activities? This issue has far-reaching implications not only for the future of American education but, more importantly, for the viability of our society.

This chapter proceeds on the assumption that youth is a force to be reckoned with and that the concerns and demands of youth must be considered in any discourse regarding the overall question of the school-society relationship. Needless to say, this assumption is vulnerable to criticism from large segments of society. Conservative elements have always viewed youth as an ineffective force in societal change. Furthermore, they might argue that a nonparticipatory role in societal decision-making is appropriate for late adolescence and, therefore, demands by students need not be taken seriously. On the other hand, as the preceding pages have implied, the new breed of student, buoyed by increasing dissatisfaction with society among numerous segments of the adult population, has begun to take an active role in challenging what it believes to be a general societal resistance to change. It perceives the schools as reflecting and perpetuating this resistance. This new breed notes that numerous attempts have been made by federal commissions, distinguished individuals, and even professional organizations to bring more relevance to the school curriculum. In the opinion of the students, few if any of these attempts have been successful. Thus, these activist forces promise to break what they consider to be the barrier to change. This growing activism places the increasingly more powerful student bodies of our public schools in direct opposition to those of conservative leanings, who are anxious to defend the status quo.

Even though it is only a manifestation of the real problem, student protest has become a major subissue surrounding the emerging issue of student power. The protest, or student activism, is a symptom which in many communities has become the focus of attention detracting from the power issue itself. For the purposes of this chapter, the subissue of student protest provides an excellent tool for revealing the root causes of the controversy associated with the issue of student power. We will, therefore, examine the causes of student unrest enunciated by spokesmen of various philosophical positions.

HIGH SCHOOL ACTIVISTS
TELL WHAT THEY WANT

This collection of viewpoints by four student leaders of militant organizations captures the feelings of discontent held by many adolescents disenchanted with the "system." Explicit throughout the article is the perception that the educational system is phony in that it pretends to prepare students to live and participate fully in our society. This seems to be the element that student radicals react to most in our educational system. They contend that if the schools were achieving this end, students would not have to resort to protest in order to be an effective power in our society.

MDS: We're organizing at Shaker because
white students need to be doing things

Cleveland MDS, or Movement for a Democratic Society, got off the ground this summer, expanding from a small group of hard-core young adult organizers to a broad movement composed of SDS chapters in many local colleges and high schools, several medical students' organizations, a welfare workers' union, the Cleveland Draft Resistance Union, and a group called Radicals in the Professions.

The high school students, who hold weekly meetings together, published an underground newspaper this summer. We see the potential power of a citywide student union, but have decided to gain a broader base in our individual schools first.

We're organizing at Shaker Heights because affluent, unoppressed white kids in a 15 per cent black school with a liberal administration need to be doing things. To let apathy reign at Shaker is to let the system renew itself. Kids whose parents are corporation executives, and who attend a high school where 98 per cent of the students will go on to college, are the ones who will *be* the system in our future. We must reach these kids before they are engulfed by that which they neither need nor understand. However, the seemingly liberal stand of the school is rooted in the affluence of a traditionally conservative community. The power over the administration is largely handled by those who represent

From *Nation's Schools*, December, 1968, pp. 29–31, 84. Reprinted by permission of the publisher.

the reactionary force. At the elementary school and neighborhood level, segregation exists and thus isolation from the "big bad world" is prevalent as in much of suburban America.

Those of us organizing at Shaker must recognize and deal with these community forces. It is our job to educate students at our high school about the present political situation and the New Left alternatives. The issues of the war, the draft, racism, corporation influence, and distribution of wealth must be discussed within the context of the existing suburban power structure situation.

We have sensed the need of students for a voice other than that which the faculty-censored school paper provides. We have taken the widespread apathy for school functions and activities to mean a passive discontent with school life. Therefore, our primary goal is that of education—turning kids on to what school is doing to them, and to the "outside" issues that directly affect them—of which they are pathetically unaware. Students are not oppressed at Shaker—but they must not let themselves get totally involved with simply *school*. In the pressured atmosphere of "Get good grades—go to college—be a success," a questioning and redefinition of values is necessary. In the uncomfortable setting of a structured classroom, students may lose their feelings as *persons*. Our second goal, then, is to emphasize the *human* aspect of relationships between people—students with students, students with teachers, students with parents, and to stop the gradual dehumanization by the institutions of this society.

We hope as individuals and as a group to bring about a new awareness of the political situation existing in our society. Through organization we hope that action for radical changes of the system and deeper understanding in human relationships will occur.

Lynn Szwaja and Susan Pennybacker
for Cleveland's Movement
for a Democratic Society

N. Y. Student Union: High schools pacify us with values for a future we reject

Students, like many other Americans, understand that at present we have no power to affect the decisions that are made in this country. The education industry has been revealed as a channeling institution for the military, and a training ground for future functionaries. High schools are an important part of the present American system, pacifying us with values that are dishonest, for futures we reject.

Schools are major instruments for the perpetuation of the racism and inequalities of our society. They inculcate the beliefs and behavior that support and preserve the status quo. This serves two functions—it simultaneously teaches us to conform and obey, to take orders without question, and through its mealy-mouthed history instills bigotry and fear in white pupils, and in black pupils a belief in their inferiority. Typical of history-text politics is this quote: "Though the Indians did help the early settlers, and have made some cultural contributions, on the whole, their effect has been bad because they hindered western expansion." We reject an educational system that feels one of its primary functions (to quote a history curriculum) is to see that we are "strengthened with democratic values and the finest ideals of American life," especially when we find that we are fed these values and ideals in their perverted forms, the racist and imperialist forms that exist today, not the democratic forms that are expressed in our Constitution. It is lessons in these forms that rationalize wars like Vietnam. And it is systems like this that speak of our right to dissent but beats us on the streets of Chicago, and the streets of the ghetto, when we exercise it. All our actions, in some form, will demand that our schools become institutions of learning and discussion, not factories for turning out mindless slaves and robots.

Laurie Sandow
for the Union

USM: Students must have a voice in determining what is a relevant education

The United Student Movement is the organized high school movement now present in Palo Alto. The USM is a radical organization formed to promote change in the schools and in the community. Members of the movement believe some sort of revolution must come about to bring the necessary reforms to the systems that control our lives. How this is to be done has not yet been resolved.

The student movement's first commitment is to the student. Apathy and ignorance of the outside world are very much a part of the high school campus. The movement's role is to bring some degree of awareness to the student. A second goal is to give the student a voice in the school. We find it necessary that the student be given the right and responsibility of determining what is a relevant education. We feel we deserve the right to say how our lives are to be lived.

In the community, the movement can act as a voice of the student and as a catalyst for involvement in community issues. The role of the police in our community is one issue that is being studied. The movement has become involved in the fight of the workers and supports such actions as the California grape boycott. By this type of involvement, we hope to make life better for ourselves and others.

The need for establishing a student movement stems from the fact that there are no adequate or efficient channels for student expression and action. Student government in its present form has no responsibility designated to it and therefore can make no decisions on matters of importance. Any kind of radical study or theory expressed inside the school is quickly dampened or discontinued by the school administration or by pressure from the community. Basically, the student movement has been formed to give the student a strong voice in the school and the community.

The movement is growing. New faces and new ideas are coming. Hopefully, what is now a minority will become a majority in the future. Many of our present ideals will need testing and these ideals may change as the environment and circumstances we face change.

We will no longer sit back while another generation attempts to control our lives. If this generation which is now in the position of authority cannot see where it is going wrong, then it is our duty to make these people aware of their mistakes. We will have the strength to resist their control if no sign of change develops.

Joe Pickering
for the United Student Movement

Chicago Black Students: Basic changes will have to come in education

The black youth of today is different from any other previous generation of his race in the sense that he has the advantage of previous generations setting up premises beforehand and that he is an educated person, mostly self-taught through living experiences he has observed taking place all over America. This youth sees the injustices of the white power structure, knows it either has to be changed or destroyed, knows about social patterns and trends of mass movements. He has learned that neither total passiveness nor total aggressiveness is advisable for the black man's predicament in America. With this knowledge the black youth of America has embarked on a journey to determine his destiny. This journey will determine his future life and that of any future black man in America. Although most white Americans and some blacks refuse to admit it, the black youth of today will also determine America's future—whether she will change and all will prosper, or resist and all be destroyed.

One of these basic changes will have to come in education. The black youth of Chicago have taken it upon themselves to initiate this change. We recognize the importance of an education that is important to us in helping our struggle towards black manhood and womanhood. Because our parents and teachers for numberable reasons (but mostly because of fear and conditioning by the white power structure) have been inept at making progress toward this goal—a better and more relevant education—we feel that it is our duty to see what we can do to achieve these goals. We are working on a local as well as a central scale. Through our observations we found that basically all problems stem from no community control of schools. We realize the problems of incapable administrators, of teachers certified by the board yet proven unqualified by students, counselors that suggest to black students that they drop out and get jobs.

All these problems and others come from the ineptness of the board of education due to the lack of communication and acknowledgement of the black community. These elite board members cannot possibly know what the black communities need and what they want. There are too many uneducated guesses made by the board of education on these issues. The board of education could be much more successful and beneficial in the realm of education if it would realize the importance of collaboration with the communities on such things as specific needs, wants, criterias used for certification, and qualifications for administrators.

The board is set up as the people's servant. We, as black youth, demand that the board start serving us. We demand that they listen to us when we say, "The teachers you send us, the administrators you appoint, the counselors you give us are not qualified. Talk to us, discuss these problems before you spend our money. Collaborate, find out what we need, what is relevant, what is important to us."

This plea as yet has fallen upon deaf ears. We, the black students of Chicago, will not wait much longer for a positive response from the board of education. We have been working on three levels with the students, as well as teachers, and most importantly, the community. We are prepared to set up our own educational functions if necessary. If the white educational structures in Chicago can not see fit with its blind eyes to start teaching the black youth of Chicago properly we will teach ourselves.

Sharron Matthews
for Chicago black students

Jane Hunt

PRINCIPALS REPORT ON STUDENT PROTEST

It would be reasonable to assume that this article, which is a report of a survey by the National Association of Secondary School Principals and is written by a member of the Association staff, would present a striking contrast to the previous descriptive selection. But such is not actually the case. For this reason, one should note carefully the similarities and differences between the causes of unrest offered by the student activists and those identified by the principals, who of course are spokesmen for the "system."

To be a principal in times like these is not for the fainthearted—and we're just getting started on this protest business.

Thus spoke a high school principal and, according to a survey conducted early this year by the National Association of Secondary School Principals, his feeling is shared by most of his colleagues.

The survey was sent to every fifteenth high school principal in the United States, including those at private or parochial schools. Three out of five respondents reported some form of protest in their schools. What's more, 56 percent of the junior highs had such activity as compared with 59 percent of senior high schools. The table shows how widespread were the reports of protest.

Because of term "protest" was not defined, each principal could draw his own line between normal adolescent restlessness and genuine protest activity. Behavior that might go unnoticed in one school could be a turning point somewhere else.

So many reasons for protest were named that one wonders if protest

From *The Education Digest*, December, 1969, pp. 49–51. (Article appeared originally in *American Education*, October, 1969.) Reprinted by permission of the publisher, Prakken Publications, Inc.

Percentage of Surveyed Schools with Student Protest

	Large (over 2,000)	Medium (801–2,000)	Small (801 or less)	All
Urban	74	62	60	67
Suburban	81	72	56	67
Rural	67	67	50	53

isn't sometimes a desire on the part of young people to assert themselves rather than to express any real grievance. Again and again the target of protest was referred to as "authority," "society in general," "the system." Eighty-two percent of the principals of schools with protest said that school regulations were under attack; 45 percent found the school's instructional program being criticized; and 25 percent reported activism concerning national issues.

Personal appearance is the big problem with school regulations—mainly boys' long hair and girls' short skirts. The next most frequent targets among school regulations are smoking rules and the cafeteria—the quality of food, its cost, and service. The cafeteria is the only issue often protested by student boycotts.

Censorship also inspires protest, as when a principal vetoes assembly programs or speakers for club meetings. Underground newspapers are on the rise, put out by students and often teachers who are irked by censorship of the regular school paper.

Some students complain that the scheduling of sporting events is inconvenient. Others want more school dances and want to be able to invite outsiders. Another source of much dissent is the school's approach to discipline, especially the use of suspension as punishment. Many other matters under the heading of regulations were mentioned occasionally: the need for new student organizations, inadequacy of the student council, student desire for more voice in rule making, motor vehicles, senior privileges, cheerleader elections, the use of lockers. Only one-half of one percent of the schools with protest mentioned restrictions on the use of marijuana or other drugs as a topic of protest.

Protest School Program

Next to the issues of dress and behavior, high school students are most likely to protest the education they receive. Almost half of the schools with protest named teachers, curriculum, class schedules, grades, homework, and exams as a source of dissatisfaction. Many students want to select their teachers and some of their courses. Mentioned, but less often, were free study time instead of supervised study halls, class size, extracurricular activities, academic programs for low achievers, sex education, improved teaching methods for languages and sciences. Catholic schools reported dissatisfaction with their religion courses.

Protest about the instructional program is evenly distributed through schools and communities of all sizes, with one exception: Among the large (more than 2,000 pupils) urban senior high schools that have protest, more than 80 percent have experienced this kind of criticism.

One-fourth of the principals of schools with protest reported activism regarding controversial national issues, with racial tension cited by 10 percent. Though occurring most often in cities, it is a problem in communities of every size and in every part of the country. There were no charges of official discrimination by schools, although parents often accuse individual teachers. Most principals in racially troubled schools believed they had found constructive methods of easing the tension.

Protest against the Vietnam war and the draft is rare: Vietnam or the peace movement were named by only 3 percent of the schools with protest, the draft by 2 percent. All these were in senior high schools. A few other issues appeared, such as the vote for 18-year-olds, the need for political clubs in school, central versus local school boards, welfare programs, and opportunities for work experience for students. There was a little clamor against the police, the church, and "authority in general."

Individual students are the source of dissent, said the vast majority of respondents. Individual parents and student or community organizations were the next most frequently named. Asked if Students for a Democratic Society (SDS) was a source of protest, 5 percent answered yes. SDS ranges from California to New York state, where it seems most active. Schools with SDS were both large and small, junior and senior highs, in towns of any size. Several were Catholic schools. The favorite SDS targets were dress and rules of conduct.

How, in general, was a protest expressed? The vast majority of principals replied that protesters simply talked to them or, sometimes, to faculty members. The school paper offered a means of expression in some cases, as did local newspapers and radio and TV stations. A few schools reported black power salutes; one mentioned refusal to stand for the national anthem. When Martin Luther King, Jr., was assassinated, there were several walkouts in schools that did not close. The only mention of violence came from a few schools where fights between individuals occurred.

Coping with Protest

The principals also offered suggestions for coping with their problems: Move with the times, they say. ("Since the home and community have more or less emancipated the youth, is it any wonder they rebel at being completely regimented six hours a day?") Let students update the rule book. Establish a student court. Use a student-faculty advisory council. Anticipate problems. Build good community relations. ("The most devastating weapon a principal can employ with dissidents is the force of the community and its leaders poised against unreasonable demands.") Be firm and candid. ("Some areas must be handled democratically, others dictatorially. Don't try to make people believe you are democratic if you are going to make the decision.")

Despite the principals' deep concern, a strong thread of optimism ran through their answers. The comment of one was, "The students, to our utter despair, are exhibiting—at long last—the very kinds of behavior that we say we want to encourage, nourish, and develop as responsible educators. The requirement for—and agonies of—change are on our doorsteps more than on theirs. We must change or foster total revolution in our schools, public or private."

The preceding articles raise serious questions concerning the structures of public education. These structures are the links between school and society. They are the school boards, community organizations, and other formal agencies affecting education. When a significant portion of our population believes that the bridges between school and society are functioning inadequately, a definite potentiality is developed for total collapse of the public school system. The crisis now manifesting itself in student protest is a threat to the status quo that is unparalleled in recent decades.

Johns Harrington

L.A.'S STUDENT BLOWOUT

In this illustrative selection, Johns Harrington shows how the second largest school system in the country was dramatically influenced by a student walkout. Of significance here is the fact that student activists had a

From *Phi Delta Kappan,* October, 1968, pp. 74–79. Reprinted by permission of the author and publisher.

direct effect on the policy-making structure of the Los Angeles public schools. Furthermore, the structure seemed to respond to this student pressure.

Johns Harrington is Editorial Coordinator for District Publications in the Los Angeles Unified School District.

A new kind of monster raised its head in Los Angeles last spring when the city school district faced its first student walkouts in a 113-year history. Whatever happens to the 13 grand jury indictments for conspiracy that are still pending as this is written, the repercussions of the events during the week of March 5 are likely to produce shock waves that will affect schools and minority groups in urban areas throughout the country. Certainly there are lessons to be learned from the "student blowout" that should be helpful to public school teachers and administrators elsewhere.

Five Mexican-American high schools on the east side were involved, but the primarily Negro Jefferson High School also closed its doors for three days. In two predominantly Negro junior high schools as well, pupils left classes for a time. Some set fires in trash cans and broke windows. As a side effect, 800 white students and non-students clashed with police in Venice some 18 miles across the city on the west side.

In addition to its large Negro population, Los Angeles is unique in that it has 800,000 citizens of Mexican descent—the greatest concentration outside Mexico itself. The city is also the most popular "port of entry" in the southwestern United States for immigrants from Mexico.

The extent of participation in the blowout is difficult, if not impossible, to measure accurately. Estimates vary with the point of view and knowledge of the observer. School spokesmen report that some 2,500 students joined in the walkouts, and another 1,000 stayed away from classes because of apparent fear of violence. In the main, however, demonstrations were nonviolent. Demands of demonstrators, agitators, and the few teachers who joined with them ranged from sweeping educational changes to abolishment of corporal punishment and permission to wear miniskirts.

Although the district staff said that newspapers exaggerated the extent and nature of the disorders, an indication of events during the week-long demonstrations can be gleaned from such reports as the following:

"Police and school authorities today are probing possible underground agitation as the cause of disorders Tuesday and Wednesday at four Los Angeles high schools. . . .

"One school official attributed the walkouts and rock-throwing, bottle-throwing demonstrations to editorials in an 'underground magazine' which urged students to 'rise up' and protest any conditions they did not like. Two policemen dispersing students at Roosevelt High were hit by flying bottles yesterday. One was hospitalized for treatment of an eye cut. . . . At Lincoln High about 400 young persons refused to attend classes. They were urged, a school official said, to attend a rally at a nearby park by a bearded youth who wore the uniform of the 'Brown Berets,' a militant Mexican-American group. . . ." (*Los Angeles Herald-Examiner*, March 7)

"Police Chief Tom Reddin warned today that 'professional agitators' are in for trouble for inciting school walkouts like the one at Belmont High School yesterday, where fires were set, police cars stoned, and six persons arrested." (*Los Angeles Herald-Examiner*, March 8)

"Two hundred young persons broke up a meeting of the City Board of Education and sent most board members fleeing out a rear door Thursday as a climax to a day of boycotts, arson, and the stoning of police cars at schools attended by minority groups.

"Mrs. Georgiana Hardy, board president, pounded her gavel and adjourned the meeting as a bearded member of the Brown Berets strode down the aisle and took over the guest speaker's microphone.

"'If you walk out today, we will walk out tomorrow,' shouted the youth." (*Los Angeles Times*, March 8)

In a statement to the press issued March 8, Jack Crowther, city schools superintendent, declared:

"Every effort is being made to maintain an orderly and normal educational process in the Los Angeles city schools. Representatives of the Board of Education and Secondary Division staff are meeting today with student representatives of protest groups to discuss grievances which have been raised regarding some of the high schools.

"It is important to note that, despite the many disturbances at these schools in the last few days, the overwhelming majority of students have remained in class and continued their studies. . . ."

On the following Monday, Crowther addressed a letter to teachers in the schools concerned and asked that they read a message to students. It included:

"Let me emphasize that all of us agree with the desperate need to improve the educational program, buildings, and equipment in your schools. These are the very things which we are fighting for—and indeed on the very day that classes were being disrupted, I and members of the Board of Education were in Sacramento making a desperate plea to the State Legislature for more money to improve our schools.

"I think we can all agree that your viewpoint has been heard—and has been made known dramatically during the last four days of last week. Today your representatives will present their views to the Board of Education.

"Therefore, I am asking each one of you from this moment on to remain in school and continue your class work. Nothing further can be gained by leaving your classes, and the only result of such action will be further harm to your education. *Time lost from classes is gone forever and cannot be regained.* We know that your parents are anxious and eager for school to continue without further interruption."

Shortly after the first walkouts, the Board of Education took the following actions:

1. Agreed to hold a special meeting at Lincoln High School to discuss educational problems in the East Los Angeles area.

2. Granted amnesty to the students who boycotted classes since March 7.

3. Appointed a Negro principal, vice principal, and head counselor at Jefferson High School. (These assignments were already in process, however, when the demonstrations at Jefferson took place.)

But the board refused to order removal of police from the high school campuses or to ask for release of students who had been arrested during the demonstrations.

The demands and recommendations with which the board and staff were deluged both for and against the walkouts came from a wide variety of sources, including the Educational Issues Committee, a community group in East Los Angeles; the California Association of Educators of Mexican Descent; the East Los Angeles Coordinating Council; the Broadway-Central Coordinating Council; the Citizens' Compensatory Education Advisory Committee; the Los Angeles Teachers Association and the American Federation of Teachers; faculty and student groups, both official and unofficial; the community press; and "underground" newspapers.

The demands themselves covered almost the entire spectrum of the educational program, including:

Free press
Free speech
Bilingual school personnel
Bilingual instruction

School buildings
Cafeteria service
Community relations
Corporal punishment
Counseling ratio
Electives
Fences around campuses
Reading
Reallocation of R.O.T.C. funds
Suspension policies
"Community parents" as teacher aides
Dress and grooming
Homogeneous grouping
Mexican-American contributions to U.S. society
Administrators of Mexican-American descent
Teachers of Mexican-American descent
Nonacademic assemblies   I. Q. tests
Library facilities
Academic courses
Prejudice of school personnel
Open restrooms
Eligibility for student body office
Swimming pools
Dismissal or transfer of teachers because of political or philosophical views

Ironically, some of the demands were direct quotations from statements by Crowther or Stuart Stengel, associate superintendent, Division of Secondary Education, regarding improvements in the educational program that they were seeking. Objectives that have been emphasized by Stengel as "imperative" include:

1. Development of practical testing instruments which will measure the disadvantaged pupil's true potential

2. More counseling services to provide continuous encouragement of pupils to fulfill their potential

3. Full elective programs available in all schools or within a reasonable geographic area, despite comparatively low enrollments in such electives

4. An expanded program for educable mentally retarded pupils

5. Improvement of vocational education programs which will train non-college-bound pupils for gainful employment and the increased development of placement services

6. Improvement of textual and supplementary additional materials which are at both the pupil's ability level and the pupil's interest level

7. An expanded program of English as a second language

8. Provision for experimental classes taught in Spanish in various subject fields

9. Provision of sound human relations training for teachers and administrators

10. Provision for continuous follow-up studies to determine what's happening to the high school graduate

"It is my belief that the staffs of East Los Angeles secondary schools are doing an outstanding job, within the limitations of what is financially feasible," Stengel said. "I think that our program constantly improves, although not as rapidly, of course, as school personnel and community would like it to ideally."

Since the student blowout, the Board of Education and staff have been working on responses to the 36 major demands that were presented. As a barrage of scathing criticism from militant groups continued, Crowther told the board:

"It needs to be emphasized that, in the main, many of the items [demands] are essentially the same as projects which staff has, from time to time, presented to the board for its consideration. The list of demands has created two erroneous implications: 1) that little, if anything, has been attempted by the board and the district in trying to carry out educational improvements demanded by the students and community; and 2) that improvements have been carried out in other schools throughout the district, particularly in more affluent areas, at the expense of East Los Angeles schools.

"One other impression also needs to be clarified: that funds are available to carry out the list of demands. The fact is that no such funds are available without cutting elsewhere. The facts are that a major share of funds is already being allocated to minority area schools (an average of $53 more annually per student than in so-called advantaged areas). . . ."

When the Board of Education granted amnesty to students and appointed Negro administrators at Jefferson High School, the actions were criticized by demonstrators as not going far enough and also by some teacher and other groups for yielding to pressure.

A statement signed by 101 teachers from Roosevelt High School read in part:

"Let it be clearly understood that no teacher whose name appears on this petition wishes to leave Roosevelt. On the contrary, this petition is intended to reflect our loyalty to our school and our deep concern for our students.

"Under the present circumstances, however, we feel that, by submitting to the intimidation of a small militant faction, the Board of Education has acted in error.

"The board's lack of firm action, its display of divided authority, and

its nonsupport of local administrators and teachers in their efforts to uphold the provisions of the Education Code and the Administrative
Guide of the State of California have made teaching virtually impossible.

"Because of the board's vacillation, teacher morale is depressed, student attitude is confused, and administrative authority is undermined."

Despite the crisis and conflicts of views, however, within a week after
the boycott school programs were resumed as Superintendent Crowther
and his staff continued to seek additional funds to strengthen the educational program and made both immediate and long-range plans to heal
the wounds.

Observers within and without the school system attributed the walkouts to a wide range of causes. Obviously, some were related to recent
incidents, such as dissatisfaction with local policies, cancellation of a
local high school play, and unrest on college campuses. Others, however, concerned problems that have been growing in intensity for years.
Although all agreed that additional help is needed for pupils in East
Los Angeles—as in many other urban areas throughout the nation
where students should have better educational opportunities and there
has been an influx of new residents—some have claimed that the blowout was spontaneous while others have contended that the "rabble-
rousers always present" somehow had managed to gain enough momentum to enlist widespread student and community support. Another
version was that political opportunists saw a power vacuum and seized
the opportunity to cut a niche for themselves. In referring to the blowout in the *Los Angeles Times* for March 17, 1968, Dial Torgerson
wrote, "It was, some say, the beginning of a revolution—the Mexican-
American revolution of 1968."

Whatever the cause, or combination of causes, there were many advance indications that storm clouds were reaching threatening proportions. In its February 11 issue—nearly a month before the crisis—the
East Los Angeles Gazette carried a banner on page one which read,
"Walkout by Students Threatened at Garfield, Five Other Schools." The
story began as follows:

"The threat of a student walkout, dramatizing overcrowded conditions
and alleged disregard of cultural heritage in Eastside high schools,
which may be staged May 3 (or sooner), is presently hanging over the
heads of school administrators.

"The original area of concentration was considered to be Garfield, Roosevelt, Lincoln, and Wilson high schools, but it was learned this week

that planners are now trying to encompass both Huntington Park and Bell high schools in the proposed mass absence. . . ."

Julian Nava, Mexican-American member of the Board of Education and a history professor at San Fernando Valley State College, was quoted in the February 25 issue of the *East Los Angeles Gazette* as saying, "It is 'a healthy sign that [East Los Angeles] students are finally speaking up' in regard to educational demands and threats of a walkout if the student's voice goes unheeded." The story added:

"The Board of Education member made it clear he did not favor any form of student violence but, rather, regarded the complaints of local students as a major step for the Mexican-American people."

In contrast with Nava's position, "underground newspapers" published many inflammatory articles for months prior to the walkout. For example, in the December 25, 1967, issue of *La Raza*, one of the militant community publications that have recently been established, a columnist said:

"I almost vomited in the Belvedere auditorium recently. The place was jammed with people when some guy . . . leader of some Daddy Club spouted nonsense. He gave a talk about the group and then fell apart saying that his group are good guys. WE ARE NOT AGITATORS, he said over and over.

"All he had to say was something like this: 'I'm a good Mexican. I keep my mouth shut. I don't make waves. I keep my blind followers doing the same. Please don't criticize this school or any other or I won't get a chance to speak at things like this. I'm in with all the Gringos here and they all like me so don't ruin anything. I like this even though the strings on my back itch and the top of my head aches from getting patted so much by my blue-eyed friends. Please join us but only if you don't bring up anything important like changing the schools so they do a better job. Just come to the meetings, keep your mouth shut, and come to our dances. Oh Goodie!' . . ."

This item appeared in *Eastside Inside* on December 8, 1967:

"The boys' vice principal would make an excellent night watchman and the registrar could always tag along and help with the flashlight or keys or something.

"The principal should remain at home. I mean, really, he doesn't do anything. He could always telephone or write a letter once every two or three weeks and I'm sure he could accomplish as little as he has by being present. Why be only ninety percent ignorant of the school's problems when you could be completely ignorant. . . ."

The *Free Student,* another underground newspaper, carried an attack labeled "Student Gov't a Farce," which read in part:

"There are basically two ways of ending the administrative control of student government. Different schools may find one or the other more effective. . . . By acting and not talking, we can end the farce of student government."

These excerpts are mild compared with other items in the underground press, many of which ridiculed individual members of school staffs. In spending a few hours scanning a sampling of the papers, a reader gets the impression that the writers consider nothing right with the educational program—including personnel, facilities, and governing policies.

Since the educational blowout, many steps have been taken to help meet the needs it dramatized. Most of the measures, however, were already on the drawing boards before the shrill voice of dissent shattered the educational calm. Among innovations have been:

1. Appointment of James Taylor, a Negro, to the newly created post of assistant deputy superintendent of instruction (with the rank of an assistant superintendent).

2. Assignment of John Leon, a Mexican-American, as head of a new instructional planning center in East Los Angeles.

3. Authorization by the Board of Education of two highly "innovative" educational "complexes," to be located in East Los Angeles and the Watts area. (Plans for the complexes were initiated long before the blowout.)

"This project is an approach to provide a real breakthrough in the education of minority-group young people by doing an all-out job of providing a variety of services and programs in a concentrated area and by using the newest ideas to put them into effect," Crowther commented. "A flexible, specific program for each school in the complexes will be developed. Our plan is to have ideas come from the school community— by involving parents, other community members, teachers, and administrators."

4. Appointment of Edward Moreno as supervisor of bilingual education in the Instructional Planning Branch and issuance of a study report on what has been done, is being done, and is planned in the Elementary Curriculum Bilingual-Bicultural Program.

5. Conduct of the largest summer school in the history of the Los Angeles city schools, involving 149,000 pupils at 259 locations.

Both elementary and secondary schools offered special classes of various types. One program included five educational enrichment centers for elementary school pupils of varying socioeconomic backgrounds.

6. Teaching of conversational Spanish to 210 teachers in summer workshops.

7. Establishment of the Eastside Bilingual Study Center for approximately 1,800 adults at Salesian High School.

8. Employment of 88 bilingual clerks.

9. Provision of workshops for school personnel to develop greater understanding of the Mexican-American culture and community.

10. Establishment of a classified personnel office for the school system on the east side.

Although instructional materials had already been designed especially to help minority group students, more have been developed and others are on the way. An instructional guide on Mexico was published in 1959, and *Angelenos—Then and Now, Californians—Then and Now,* and *Americans—Then and Now* were issued in 1966. The latter series consists of pupil materials for elementary schools which describe the contributions and achievements of members of minority groups. Spanish editions of various pupil materials have been printed or are now being translated. A leaflet called "Blending of Two Cultures" focused on services for Mexican-American pupils.

Reference lists for teachers and pupils include "A Selected List of Books on American Ethnic Groups for Secondary School Libraries," "Recommended Books on American Cultural Minority Groups for Elementary School Libraries," and "Bibliography of Books in Spanish Compiled from Recommended Titles for Secondary Libraries."

Although it is too early to say whether L.A.'s student blowout has been properly patched up or what organizers may think of next, it must be evident to most observers that a heavy thrust is being made by the Los Angeles city schools to provide the kind of education that all pupils need. Many would agree with John Leon, director of the new instructional planning center in Los Angeles, when he recently said:

It seems to me that in American education we have three major phases. In the first, the schools blame the homes for the failures of children. In the second, the parents and other citizens blame the schools. Now we must enter the third phase, in which schools and homes share the blame for educational problems and work together toward their solution.

Unlike a Grade B movie, however, the story does not necessarily have a happy ending. In fact, for the time being, at least, there seems to be no ending at all. An article in the *Los Angeles Times* for August 4 reported that the Educational Issues Coordinating Committee of East Los Angeles had "rejected" the Board of Education's handling of the 36 "student" demands for educational reforms. The coordinating committee also has requested status independent of the board and asks that the committee and the district staff choose an independent group of educators to investigate East Los Angeles problems.

"We are not going to be put off," the *Times* quoted the Rev. Vahac Mardirosian, chairman of the committee, as saying. "We are not going to go away."

The student blowout and its aftermath in Los Angeles have dramatically illustrated the need for better communications between schools and community, more financial help, and greater emphasis on minority group culture. Perhaps the most important lesson, however, is the urgency of decentralization in urban areas to encourage local participation and to assure provision of an educational program that meets local needs. In the future, community influences undoubtedly will have a greater impact on curricular offerings and other aspects of individual school programs.

Sociologists, psychologists, anthropologists, and even psychiatrists have studied the nature of student unrest in our country. Most of their study has focused on college unrest but is applicable also to the growing activism problem in the public schools. Because of their scientific approach to the study of this problem threatening the traditional educational system, social scientists have been able to develop numerous theories and hypotheses to explain emerging patterns of student dissent. The sociologists have concerned themselves with the concept of radicalism while the psychologists have explored the nature of rebellion. Political scientists have examined the protest movement because of its implications for overall power relationships and its conflict-producing potential in local communities.

Richard Flacks

THE LIBERATED GENERATION: AN EXPLORATION OF THE ROOTS OF STUDENT PROTEST

In this sociological study, Richard Flacks identifies and analyzes several trends in our society related to radicalism. Although this study was made just as the public school student protest movement was taking shape, it is not, however, geared solely to the college activist. Instead, it is a general

From *Journal of Social Issues*, July, 1967, pp. 52–63. Footnotes and internal notes omitted. Reprinted by permission of the author and publisher.

examination of the student generation. Professor Flacks is uniquely qualified to write on the topic of radicalism because he was one of the original
organizers of the Students for a Democratic Society (SDS). He is presently Professor of Sociology, University of California at Santa Barbara.

As all of us are by now aware, there has emerged, during the past five
years, an increasingly self-conscious student movement in the United
States. This movement began primarily as a response to the efforts by
southern Negro students to break the barriers of legal segregation in
public accommodations—scores of northern white students engaged in
sympathy demonstrations and related activities as early as 1960. But as
we all know, the scope of the student concern expanded rapidly to include such issues as nuclear testing and the arms race, attacks on civil
liberties, the problems of the poor in urban slum ghettoes, democracy
and educational quality in universities, the war in Vietnam, conscrip-
tion.

This movement represents a social phenomenon of considerable significance. In the first place, it is having an important direct and indirect
impact on the larger society. But secondly it is significant because it is a
phenomenon which was unexpected—unexpected, in particular, by
those social scientists who are professionally responsible for locating and
understanding such phenomena. Because it is an unanticipated event,
the attempt to understand and explain the sources of the student movement may lead to fresh interpretations of some important trends in our
society.

Radicalism and the Young Intelligentsia

In one sense, the existence of a radical student movement should not
be unexpected. After all, the young intelligentsia seem almost always to
be in revolt. Yet if we examine the case a bit more closely I think we
will find that movements of active disaffection among intellectuals and
students tend to be concentrated at particular moments in history. Not
every generation produces an organized oppositional movement.

In particular, students and young intellectuals seem to have become
active agents of opposition and change under two sets of interrelated
conditions:

When they have been marginal in the labor market because their numbers
exceed the opportunities for employment commensurate with their abilities
and training. This has most typically been the case in colonial or underdevel-

oped societies; it also seems to account, in part, for the radicalization of European Jewish intellectuals and American college-educated women at the turn of the century.

When they found that the values with which they were closely connected by virtue of their upbringing no longer were appropriate to the developing social reality. This has been the case most typically at the point where traditional authority has broken down due to the impact of Westernization, industrialization, modernization. Under these conditions, the intellectuals, and particularly the youth, felt called upon to assert new values, new modes of legitimation, new styles of life. Although the case of break down of traditional authority is most typically the point at which youth movements have emerged, there seems, historically, to have been a second point in time—in Western Europe and the United States—when intellectuals were radicalized. This was, roughly, at the turn of the century, when values such as gentility, laissez faire, naive optimism, naive rationalism and naive nationalism seemed increasingly inappropriate due to the impact of large scale industrial organization, intensifying class conflict, economic crisis and the emergence of total war. Variants of radicalism waxed and waned in their influence among American intellectuals and students during the first four decades of the twentieth century.

If these conditions have historically been those which produced revolts among the young intelligentsia, then I think it is easy to understand why a relatively superficial observer would find that new wave of radicalism on the campus fairly mysterious.

In the first place, the current student generation can look forward, not to occupational insecurity or marginality, but to an unexampled opening up of opportunity for occupational advance in situations in which their skills will be maximally demanded and the prestige of their roles unprecedentedly high.

In the second place, there is no evident erosion of the legitimacy of established authority; we do not seem, at least on the surface, to be in a period of rapid disintegration of traditional values—at least no more so than a decade ago when sociologists were observing the *exhaustion* of opportunity for radical social movements in America.

In fact, during the Fifties sociologists and social psychologists emphasized the decline in political commitment, particularly among the young, and the rise of a bland, security-oriented conformism throughout the population, but most particularly among college students. The variety of studies conducted then reported students as overwhelmingly unconcerned with value questions, highly complacent, status-oriented, privatized, uncommitted. Most of us interpreted this situation as one to be expected given the opportunities newly opened to educated youth and given the emergence of liberal pluralism and affluence as the characteristic features of postwar America. Several observers predicted an intensification of the pattern of middle class conformism declining individualism, and growing "other-directedness" based on the changing styles of childrearing prevalent in the middle class. The democratic and "permissive" family would produce young men who knew how to cooperate in bureaucratic settings, but who lacked a strongly rooted ego-ideal and inner control. Although some observers reported that some students were searching for "meaning" and "self-expression," and others reported the existence of "subcultures" of alienation and bohemianism on some campuses, not a single observer of the campus scene as late as 1959 anticipated the emergence of the organized disaffection, protest and activism which was to take shape early in the Sixties.

In short, the very occurrence of a student movement in the present American context is surprising because it seems to contradict our prior understanding of the determinants of disaffection among the young intelligentsia.

A Revolt of the Advantaged

The student movement is, I think, surprising for another set of reasons. These have to do with its social composition and the kinds of ideological themes which characterize it.

The current group of student activists is predominantly upper middle class, and frequently these students are of elite origins. This fact is evident as soon as one begins to learn the personal histories of activist leaders. Consider the following scene at a convention of Students for a Democratic Society a few years ago. Toward the end of several days of deliberation, someone decided that a quick way of raising funds for the organization would be to appeal to the several hundred students assembled at the convention to dig down deep into their pockets on the spot. To this end, one of the leadership, skilled at mimicry, stood on a chair, and in the style of a Southern Baptist preacher, appealed to the students to come forward, confess their sins and be saved by contributing to SDS. The students did come forward, and in each case the sin confessed was the social class or occupation of their fathers. "My father is the editor of a Hearst newspaper, I give $25"! My father is Assistant Director of the ——Bureau, I give $40". "My father is dean of a law school, here's $50"!

These impressions of the social composition of the student movement are supported and refined by more systematic sources of data. For example, when a random sample of students who participated in the anti-Selective Service sit-in at the University of Chicago Administration Building was compared with a sample composed of non-protesters and students hostile to the protest, the protesters disproportionately reported their social class to be "upper middle", their family incomes to be disproportionately high, their parents' education to be disproportionately advanced. In addition, the protesters' fathers' occupations were primarily upper professional (doctors, college faculty, lawyers) rather than business, white collar, or working class. These findings parallel those of other investigators. Thus, the student movement represents the disaffection not of an underprivileged stratum of the student population but of *the most advantaged* sector of the students.

One hypothesis to explain disaffection among socially advantaged youth would suggest that, although such students come from advantaged backgrounds, their academic performance leads them to anticipate downward mobility or failure. Stinchcombe, for example, found high rates of quasi-delinquent rebelliousness among middle class high school youth with poor academic records. This hypothesis is not tenable with respect to college student protest, however. Our own data with respect to the anti-draft protest at Chicago indicate that the grade point average of the protesters averaged around B-B+ (with 75% of them reporting a B- or better average). This was slightly higher than the grade point average of our sample of nonprotesters. Other data from our own research indicate that student activists tend to be at the top of their high school class; in general, data from our own and other studies support the view that many activists are academically superior, and that very few activists are recruited from among low academic achievers. Thus in terms of *both* the status of their families of origin *and* their own scholastic performance, student protest movements are predominantly composed of students who have been born to high social advantage and who are in a position to experience the career and status opportunities of the society without significant limitations.

Themes of the Protest

The positive correlation between disaffection and status among college students suggested by these observations is, I think, made even more paradoxical when one examines closely the main value themes which characterize the student movement. I want to describe these in an impressionistic way here; a more systematic depiction awaits further analysis of our data.

Romanticism: There is a strong stress among many Movement participants on a quest for self-expression, often articulated in terms of leading a "free" life—i.e., one not bound by conventional restraints on feeling, experience, communication, expression. This is often coupled with aesthetic interests and a strong rejection of scientific and other highly rational pursuits. Students often express the classic romantic aspiration of "knowing" or "experiencing" "everything."

Anti-authoritarianism: A strong antipathy toward arbitrary rule, centralized decision-making, "manipulation". The anti-authoritarian sentiment is fundamental to the widespread campus protests during the past few years; in most cases, the protests were precipitated by an administrative act which was interpreted as arbitrary, and received impetus when college administrators continued to act unilaterally, coercively or secretively. Anti-authoritarianism is manifested further by the styles and internal processes within activist organizations; for example, both SDS and SNCC have attempted to decentralize their operations quite radically and members are strongly critical of leadership within the organization when it is too assertive.

Egalitarianism, populism: A belief that all men are capable of political participation, that political power should be widely dispersed, that the locus of value in society lies with the people and not elites. This is a stress on something more than equality of opportunity or equal legal treatment; the students stress instead the notion of "participatory democracy"—direct participation in the making of decisions by those affected by them. Two common slogans—"One man; one vote"; "Let the people decide".

Anti-dogmatism: A strong reaction against doctrinaire ideological interpretations of events. Many of the students are quite restless when presented with formulated models of the social order, and specific programs for social change. This underlies much of their antagonism to the varieties of "old left" politics, and is one meaning of the oft-quoted (if not seriously used) phrase: "You can't trust anyone over thirty".

Moral purity: A strong antipathy to self-interested behavior, particularly when overlaid by claims of disinterestedness. A major criticism of the society is that it is "hypocritical". Another meaning of the criticism of the older generation has to do with the perception that (a) the older generation "sold out" the values it espouses; (b) to assume conventional adult roles usually leads to increasing self-interestedness, hence selling-out, or "phoniness". A particularly important criticism students make of the university is that it fails to live up to its professed ideals; there is an expectation that the institution ought to be *moral*—that is, not compromise its official values for the sake of institutional survival or aggrandizement.

Community: A strong emphasis on a desire for "human" relationships, for a full expression of emotions, for the breaking down of interpersonal barriers and the refusal to accept conventional norms concerning interpersonal contact (e.g., norms respecting sex, status, race, age, etc.). A central positive theme in the campus revolts has been the expression of the desire for a campus "community", for the breaking down of aspects of impersonality on the campus, for more direct contact between students and faculty. There is a frequent counterposing of bureaucratic norms to communal norms; a testing of the former against the latter. Many of the students involved in slum projects have experimented with attempts to achieve a "kibbutz"-like community amongst themselves, entailing communal living and a strong stress on achieving intimacy and resolving tensions within the group.

Anti-institutionalism: A strong distrust of involvement with conventional institutional roles. This is most importantly expressed in the almost universal desire among the highly involved to avoid institutionalized careers. Our data suggest that few student activists look toward careers in the professions, the sciences, industry or politics. Many of the most committed expect to continue to work full-time in the "movement" or, alternatively, to become free-lance writers, artists, intellectuals. A high proportion are oriented toward academic careers—at least so far the academic career seems still to have a reputation among many student activists for permitting "freedom".

Several of these themes, it should be noted, are not unique to student activists. In particular, the value we have described as "romanticism"—a quest for self-expression—has been found by observers, for example Kenneth Keniston, to be a central feature of the ideology of "alienated" or "bohemian" students. Perhaps more important, the disaffection of student activists with conventional careers, their low valuation of careers as important in their personal aspirations, their quest for careers outside the institutionalized sphere—these attitudes toward careers seem to be characteristic of other groups of students as well. It is certainly typical of youth involved in "bohemian" and aesthetic subcultures; it also characterizes students who volunteer for participation in such programs as the Peace Corps, Vista and other full-time commitments oriented toward service. In fact, it is our view that the dissatisfaction of socially advantaged youth with conventional career opportunities is a significant social trend, the most important single indicator of restlessness among sectors of the youth population. One expression of this restlessness is the student movement, but it is not the only one. One reason why it seems important to investigate the student movement in detail, despite the fact that it represents a small minority of the student population, is that it is a symptom of social and psychological strains experienced by a larger segment of the youth—strains not well understood or anticipated heretofore by social science.

If some of the themes listed above are not unique to student activists, several of them may characterize only a portion of the activist group itself. In particular, some of the more explicitly political values are likely to be articulated mainly by activists who are involved in radical organizations, particularly Students for a Democratic Society, and the Student Non-violent Coordinating Committee. This would be true particularly for such notions as "participatory democracy" and deep commitments to populist-like orientations. These orientations have been formulated within SDS and SNCC as these organizations have sought to develop a coherent strategy and a framework for establishing priorities. It is an empirical question whether students not directly involved in such organizations articulate similar attitudes. The impressions we have from a preliminary examination of our data suggest that they frequently do not. It is more likely that the student movement is very heterogeneous politically at this point. Most participants share a set of broad orientations, but differ greatly in the degree to which they are oriented toward ideology in general or to particular political positions. The degree of politicization of student activists is probably very much a function of the kinds of peer group and organizational relationships they have had; the underlying disaffection and tendency toward activism, however, is perhaps best understood as being based on more enduring, pre-established values, attitudes and needs.

Social-Psychological Roots of Student Protest: Some Hypotheses

How, then, can we account for the emergence of an obviously dynamic and attractive radical movement among American students in this period? Why should this movement be particularly appealing to youth from upper-status, highly educated families? Why should such youth be particularly concerned with problems of authority, of vocation, of equality, of moral consistency? Why should students in the most advantaged sector of the youth population be disaffected with their own privilege?

It should be stressed that the privileged status of the student protesters and the themes they express in their protest are not *in themselves* unique or surprising. Student movements in developing nations—e.g., Russia, Japan and Latin America—typically recruit people of elite background; moreover, many of the themes of the "new left" are reminiscent of similar expressions in other student movements. What is unexpected is that these should emerge in the American context at this time.

Earlier theoretical formulations about the social and psychological sources of strain for youth, for example the work of Parsons, Eisenstadt, and Erikson, are important for understanding the emergence of self-conscious oppositional youth cultures and movements. At first glance, these theorists, who tend to see American youth as relatively well-integrated into the larger society, would seem to be unhelpful in providing a framework for explaining the emergence of a radical student movement at the present moment. Nevertheless, in developing our own hypotheses we have drawn freely on their work. What I want to do here is to sketch the notions which have guided our research; a more systematic and detailed exposition will be developed in future publications.

What we have done is to accept the main lines of the argument made by Parsons and Eisenstadt about the social functions of youth cultures and movements. The kernel of their argument is that selfconscious subcultures and movements among adolescents tend to develop when there is a sharp disjunction between the values and expectations embodied in the traditional families in a society and the values and expectations prevailing in the occupational sphere. The greater the disjunction, the more self-conscious and oppositional will be the youth culture (as for example in the situation of rapid transition from a traditional-ascriptive to a bureaucratic-achievement social system).

In modern industrial society, such a disjunction exists as a matter of course, since families are, by definition, particularistic, ascriptive, diffuse, and the occupational sphere is universalistic, impersonal, achievement-oriented, functionally specific. But Parsons, and many others, have suggested that over time the American middle class family has developed a structure and style which tends to articulate with the occupational sphere; thus; whatever youth culture does emerge in American society is likely to be fairly well-integrated with conventional values, not particularly self-conscious, not rebellious.

The emergence of the student movement, and other expressions of estrangement among youth, leads us to ask whether, in fact, there may be families in the middle class which embody values and expectations which do *not* articulate with those prevailing in the occupational sphere, to look for previously unremarked incompatibilities between trends in the larger social system and trends in family life and early socialization.

The argument we have developed may be sketched as follows:

First, on the macro-structural level we assume that two related trends are of importance: one, the increasing rationalization of student life in high schools and universities, symbolized by the "multiversity", which entails a high degree of impersonality, competitiveness and an increasingly explicit and direct relationship between the university and corporate and governmental bureaucracies; two, the increasing unavailability of coherent careers independent of bureaucratic organizations.

Second, these trends converge, in time, with a particular trend in the development of the family; namely, the emergence of a pattern of familial relations, located most typically in upper middle class, professional homes, having the following elements:

(a) a strong emphasis on democratic, egalitarian interpersonal relations

(b) a high degree of permissiveness with respect to self-regulation

(c) an emphasis on values *other than achievement;* in particular, a stress on the intrinsic worth of living up to intellectual, aesthetic, political, or religious ideals.

Third, young people raised in this kind of family setting, contrary to the expectations of some observers, find it difficult to accommodate to institutional expectations requiring submissiveness to adult authority, respect for established status distinctions, a high degree of competition, and firm regulation of sexual and expressive impulses. They are likely to be particularly sensitized to acts of arbitrary authority, to unexamined expressions of allegiance to conventional values, to instances of institutional practices which conflict with professed ideals. Further, the values embodied in their families are likely to be reinforced by other socializing experiences—for example, summer vacations at progressive children's camps, attendance at experimental private schools, growing up in a community with a high proportion of friends from similar backgrounds. Paralleling these experiences of positive reinforcement, there are likely to be experiences which reinforce a sense of estrangement from peers or conventional society. For instance, many of these young people experience a strong sense of being "different" or "isolated" in school; this sense of distance is often based on the relative uniqueness of their interests and values, their inability to accept conventional norms about appropriate sex-role behavior, and the like. An additional source of strain is generated when these young people perceive a fundamental discrepancy between the values espoused by their parents and the style of life actually practiced by them. This discrepancy is experienced as a feeling of "guilt" over "being middle class" and a perception of "hypocrisy" on the part of parents who express liberal or intellectual values while appearing to their children as acquisitive or self-interested.

Fourth, the incentives operative in the occupational sphere are of limited efficacy for these young people—achievement of status or material advantage is relatively ineffective for an individual who already has high status and affluence by virtue of his family origins. This means, on the one hand, that these students are less oriented toward occupational achievement; on the other hand, the operative sanctions within the school and the larger society are less effective in enforcing conformity.

It seems plausible that this is the first generation in which a substantial number of youth have both the impulse to free themselves from conventional status concerns *and can afford to do so.* In this sense they are a "liberated" generation; affluence has freed them, at least for a period of time, from some of the anxieties and preoccupations which have been the defining features of American middle class social character.

Fifth, the emergence of the student movement is to be understood in large part as a consequence of opportunities for prolonged interaction available in the university environment. The kinds of personality structures produced by the socializing experiences outlined above need not necessarily have generated a collective response. In fact, Kenneth Keniston's recently published work on alienated students at Harvard suggests that students with similar characteristics to those described here were identifiable on college campuses in the Fifties. But Keniston makes clear that his highly alienated subjects were rarely involved in extensive peer-relationships, and that few opportunities for collective expressions of alienation were then available. The result was that each of his subjects attempted to work out a value-system and a mode of operation on his own.

What seems to have happened was that during the Fifties, there began to emerge an "alienated" student culture, as students with alienated predispositions became visible to each other and began to interact. There was some tendency for these students to identify with the "Beat" style and related forms of bohemianism. Since this involved a high degree of disaffiliation, "cool" non-commitment and social withdrawal, observers tended to interpret this subculture as but a variant of the prevailing privatism of the Fifties. However, a series of precipitating events, most particularly the southern student sit-ins, the revolutionary successes of students in Cuba, Korea and Turkey, and the suppression of student demonstrations against the House Un-American Activities Committee in San Francisco, suggested to groups of students that direct action was a plausible means for expressing their grievances. These first stirrings out of apathy were soon enmeshed in a variety of organizations and publicized in several student-organized underground journals—thus enabling the movement to grow and become increasingly institutionalized. The story of the emergence and growth of the movement cannot be developed here; my main point now is that many of its characteristics cannot be understood solely as consequences of the structural and personality variables outlined earlier—in addition, a full understanding of the dynamics of the movement requires a "collective behavior" perspective.

Sixth, organized expressions of youth disaffection are likely to be an increasingly visible and established feature of our society. In important ways, the "new radicalism" is *not* new, but rather a more widespread version of certain subcultural phenomena with a considerable history. During the late 19th and early 20th century a considerable number of young people began to move out of their provincial environments as a consequence of university education; many of these people gathered in such locales as Greenwich Village and created the first visible bohemian subculture in the United States. The Village bohemians and associated young intellectuals shared a common concern with radical politics and, influenced by Freud, Dewey, etc., with the reform of the process of socialization in America—i.e., a restructuring of family and educational institutions. Although many of the reforms advocated by this group were only partially realized in a formal sense, it seems to be the case that the values and style of life which they advocated have become strongly rooted in American life. This has occurred in at least two ways: first, the subcultures created by the early intellectuals took root, have grown and been emulated in various parts of the country. Second, many of the *ideas* of the early twentieth century intellectuals, particularly their critique of the bourgeois family and Victorian sensibility, spread rapidly; it now seems that an important defining characteristic of the college-educated mother is her willingness to adopt child-centered techniques of rearing, and of the college educated couple that they create a family which is democratic and egalitarian in style. In this way, the values that an earlier generation espoused in an abstract way have become embodied as *personality traits* in the new generation. The rootedness of the bohemian and quasi-bohemian subcultures and the spread of their ideas with the rapid increase in the number of college graduates, suggests that there will be a steadily increasing number of families raising their children with considerable ambivalence about dominant values, incentives and expectations in the society. In this sense, the students who engage in protest or who participate in "alienated" styles of life are often not "converts" to a "deviant" adaptation, but people who have been socialized into a developing cultural tradition. Rising levels of affluence and education are drying up the traditional sources of alienation and radical politics; what we are now becoming aware of, however, is that this same situation is creating new sources of alienation and idealism, and new constituencies for radicalism.

Bruno Bettelheim
STUDENT REVOLT: THE HARD CORE

This selection analyzes student protest from Bruno Bettelheim's perspective as a social psychologist. The noted scholar allows his personal animosity toward student rebels to creep in as he takes a close professional look at some of the causes of student unrest. He then examines the psychological characteristics of students involved in rebellious activities. The remarks below are taken from a speech delivered by Dr. Bettelheim to a U.S. House of Representatives subcommittee studying the turmoil in our educational system.

The problems to society which originate in the students' rebellions are so manifold and have such far reaching implications that in a short presentation only a very small selection of them can be alluded to, I shall, therefore, concentrate . . . [1] on a few of the factors which contribute to the widespread unrest among relatively large numbers of students, black and white; [2] on the small group of leaders who, by making skillful use of the general unrest, succeed in doing damage way beyond the importance of this group because of their tactics of intimidation and coercion and due to the publicity they receive. . . .

[1] In order to understand this discontent one has to realize that so many more go to college than ever before, and hence many more are much less well prepared for this experience. Taking advantage of college and being satisfied with this experience rather than being defeated

From *Vital Speeches of the Day*, pp. 405–408. Reprinted by permission of the author and publisher.

by it, requires a considerable amount of self-discipline, and a high degree of satisfaction with what can be derived from developing one's intellect. Present day education both in home and school teaches very little self-discipline compared to even very recent times. The expectation
is that education can hand over knowledge and skills, and this nearly
instantly. There is widespread feeling that if students do not do well in
school, this is the failing of the educational system, not due to their lack
of application. With each year in school, this feeling becomes stronger
in those who do not do well academically. And with it, the system becomes the enemy which deliberately withholds from them which they
believe could so easily be given to them by it, hence the hatred of the
system.

To understand why pressures erupt in adolescence on a growing scale
nowadays, and why controls seem to grow weaker, we must recognize
that adolescent revolt is not a stage of development that follows automatically from our natural makeup. What makes for adolescent revolt is
the fact that a society keeps the next generation too long dependent in
terms of mature responsibility and a striving for independence.

Years ago, when schooling ended for the vast majority at fourteen or
fifteen, and thereafter one became self-supporting, got married and had
children, there was no need for adolescent revolt. Because while puberty
is a biological given, adolescence as we know it with its identity crises, is
not. All children grow up and become pubertal. By no means do they all
become adolescents. To be adolescent means that one has reached and
even passed the age of puberty, is at the very height of one's physical
development—healthier, stronger, even handsomer than one has been,
or will be, for the rest of one's life—but must nevertheless postpone full
adulthood till long beyond what any other period in history has considered reasonable. And their educational experiences in the home and
school prepare only a small minority well for such a prolonged waiting,
for being able to control their angry impatience while engaged in such
waiting.

And it is this waiting for things—for the real life to come—which creates a climate in which a sizeable segment of students can, at least temporarily, be seduced into following the lead of the small group of militants. It seems to give them a chance to prove themselves as real men.
Thus it is an empty waiting for real life to come, which makes for student rebellions. This can be seen from the fact that most rebellious students, here and abroad, are either undergraduates, or those studying the
social sciences and humanities. There are no militants among students of

medicine, engineering, the natural sciences. They are busy with doing things that are important to them, they are working in the laboratory and at their studies. It is those students who do not quite know what they are preparing themselves for, and why, the students who sit around waiting for examinations rather than doing active work, which form the cadres of the student rebellion.

One example may stand for many: In a class I am presently teaching, a student was close to the activists. He gave me a very hard time in class at first. Two months later he was one of the most interested, cooperating students. I asked him what happened. He answered: "A few weeks ago I got a job which interests me, and I also began to be interested in my classes, that did it."

In my opinion there are, today, far too many students in the colleges who essentially have no business to be there. Some are there to evade the draft, many others out of a vague idea that it will help them to find better paying jobs, though they do not know what jobs they want. And again many go to college because they do not know what better to do and because it is expected of them. Their deep dissatisfaction with themselves and their inner confusion is projected against the institution of the university first, and against all institutions of society secondarily, which are blamed for their own inner weakness.

To make matters worse, our institutions of higher learning have expanded much too fast, have under public pressure for more education for everybody increased enrollment beyond reason. The result is far too large classes. Many classes in our large universities are taught by teaching assistants some of whom, out of their own inner dissatisfaction and insecurity, tend to side with the rebellion. All this led to the anonymity, the impersonal nature of student faculty contacts about which many students rightly complain. And since many of them are essentially not interested in the intellectual adventure, the knowledge which the faculty can convey to them is not what they want. They want essentially group therapeutic experiences which will help them to become mature, secure, to find themselves. But colleges are not mass therapeutic institutions, and hence disappoint the students where the greatest need lies.

In addition because of such vast expansion in numbers, the old methods to give coherence to the college experience and to offer students a life geared to the needs of the late adolescent age group have disintegrated. This the fraternities and sororities used to do, which were group homes easing the transition from home to society at large. They no longer can contain the vast number of students. And here the demands of some black students for separate black housing, etc. has to be understood as the consequence of their feeling lost in the anonymous mass of students. Only most of the white students are similarly lost until such time as they find themselves in their work and study experience.

Also, the old rituals which enhanced student life and bound them to each other, and to their college, such as football rallies, homecomings etc., all have lost most of their meaning and have not been replaced by anything but the excitement the sit-ins and rebellions provide. The spirit of intimate comradeship that used to prevail in a fraternity house is now found by all too many students in their sit-ins, where they feel closely bound together, important as at no other time, doing things together which they deep down know they do also for the emotional satisfactions they derive from such being together, whatever high sounding issues they think are motivating their actions.

In this context, the symbolic meaning should not be overlooked of students' invading the dean's or president's office, violently, or by means of sit-ins, big in age and size, who inwardly feel like little boys, and hence need to play big by sitting in papa's big chair. They want to have a say in how things are run, want to sit in the driver's seat, not because they feel competent to do so, but because they cannot bear to feel incompetent.

I think it is unnatural to keep a young person for some 20 years in dependency, and attending school. This might be a way of life for that small elite which always in the past went to universities. They were those who could go to school for 20 years. But they were never more than a small percentage of the population. In the past, the vast majority of young people were actively meeting life, proving themselves as men or women. And in this way they found themselves as real, strong human beings. Now the tremendous push that everybody should go to college has brought an incredibly large number into the university who do not find their self-realization through study, or through the intellectual adventure. But they still need to find their early manhood. They try to change the university to something where they can find it through engaging in an active, sometimes even violent battle against the existing order or all of society. Only that would change the university so that it would be no longer an institution dedicated to the intellectual virtues, to the frontiers of knowledge, but one dedicated to a belligerent reshaping of society. And this is exactly what the militants want—not to engage in study and research, but in political battles.

The reason we didn't have student revolts before is partly because only those went to college who wanted to be educated, and partly because those students who had to put themselves through school, by the very fact that they could do that, of their own strengths, could prove their early manhood—at least to some degree.

I think many of the rebellious students are essentially guilt-ridden individuals. They feel terribly guilty about all the advantages they had. And there's also the guilt of their exemption from the draft, which is a serious guilt. Only again, they cannot bear to live with their guilt. They try to destroy society or certain institutions rather than deal with their own inner guilt, because they have it so good. . . .

[2] I feel I can be shorter about the very small group of leaders of the student rebellion because were it not for the widespread student discontent which I discussed above, they would find scant following, and if they should break the law, without such followers, they could be readily dealt with. It is the mass following they can arouse because of the widespread discontent which alone makes them dangerous. I therefore think we should concentrate in our thinking and planning not on these very few, but on what needs to be done so that they won't find ready followers.

There were always a small percentage of persons bent on destroying society, and on fomenting a revolution. In previous generations they were the Wobblies, later there were the campus communists. The reason why the present brand of campus revolutionaries, who are of anarchist and nihilist persuasion, are so much more dangerous is that they can point to success after success of their disrupting tactics. Here, too, nothing succeeds like success. As early as 200 years ago Immanuel Kant warned that we shall never be able to control violence if it is rewarded. "It is far more convenient," he wrote, "to commit an act of violence, and afterwards excuse it, than laboriously to consider convincing arguments and lose time in listening to objections. This very boldness itself indicates a sort of conviction of the legitimacy of the action, and the God of success is afterwards the best advocate." The greatest danger, then, is presently the readiness with which violence is afterward excused, and the seemingly convincing arguments which are brought forth to justify it before and after the act. Worst and most dangerous of all, there seems to be a tendency in our society to legitimize the results of violence so that, as Kant puts it, the God of success afterwards serves as advocate for the violent action that preceded it and suggests its future use. On our campuses those committed to violence (to quote Kant again), "lose no time on considering arguments, or on listening to objections." They simply refuse to be rational about their grievances and through using violent means insist on having their way, no matter what. And if they get their way, as Kant already knew, their success then legitimizes their disruptive actions.

And they gain their success by arousing a sizeable number of students through the tactics of confrontations, and by universities' fear of such confrontations. Confrontations have one important aim—to use the reaction of those they provoke to generate a feeling of new unity among the demonstrators. This has been used in its most direct form by militants, who stand in front of policemen and denounce them as pigs and wait until the man in uniform hits out. The art of demonstrating then lies in seeing that the blows are directed against the less committed demonstrators and, if possible, against completely uninvolved persons. This then provides the mass following that they need for their success. A whole system of provocations has been worked out for this purpose.

Speaking of the small group of leaders of the radical left, it has been observed that most of them come from well educated, very liberal families. From my own observations I would like to add that those whom I got to know might be characterized by having had their intellectual abilities developed very highly at much too early an age, but at the expense of their emotional development. Very bright as they often are, emotionally some of them remained fixated at the age of the temper tantrum. It is this descrepancy between great intellectual maturity and utter emotional immaturity which is so baffling, often even to the universities, where some members of the faculty fail to see behind the obvious intelligence the inability to act rationally, and most of all, the inability to act responsibly. It is one of the weaknesses of university faculties that, as persons committed to value most highly intellectual abilities, they are captivated by the intelligence of these students to the degree as to be ready to excuse, or make little, of their disruptiveness and intellectual arrogance.

As for these students themselves, psychologically I always found them hating themselves as intensely as they hate the establishment, a self-hatred they try to escape by fighting any establishment. Obviously they need help in overcoming their emotional difficulties, and punishing them is hardly the way to do it. If we bring them to the universities, we should provide facilities for helping them. I believe it is their emotional immaturity that explains both their call for immediate action, and the retreat of the dropout and the hippy into utter nonaction, because each one masks an inability of these very intelligent young people to take time to think things out first. Essentially these militants must want to destroy the universities because they do not want to be students. Because to be a student means to prepare oneself to do something more worthwhile in the future. The militant student's cry is for action now, not preparation for action later. In this real sense he is no longer a student at all, since he clearly rejects knowledge as a precondition of any meaningful activity. Truth, moreover, is no longer sought, but "revealed"; the contempt for free speech and free thought is demonstrated as much in his actions as in his words. Were he ever to capture the university, it would cease to be a university at all.

In their inability to think things out because they cannot delay action for thought, both right and left extremists, the militants of all colors, are brothers under the skin. This is among the reasons why in history it happened that the young followers of the extreme right can very easily become those of the extreme left, or the other way round. Because the mainspring of their action is their wish to prove themselves strong, and less any particular political conviction, which is super-imposed on their self-doubt and a hatred of a society that they feel left them out in the cold. There were reasons why, in Germany, the National Socialists and the Communists voted together, worked together to bring down the democratic Weimar government. There is a reason why former Nazis could easily become active in the Communistic government of eastern Germany.

But there is also reason why mainly the children of leftist parents become hippies, or student revolutionaries in our society, as in other places or times the children of conservative parents, when the similar emotional conditions prevailed in their families, spearheaded rightwing radicalism. It was the children of conservative German parents, for example, who first embraced the Emperor's War and enthusiastically went to their death, because they felt a need to lay "their bodies on the line," as it were, for ideas their parents had only lukewarmly held. This way they could prove themselves strong, while at the same time proving their parents weak, wishy washy, not worthy of true respect. They felt, too, this was a rebirth, a way to revitalize an ossified society, to create a new society, one of true authenticity and confrontation. All these were the main tenets of academic Hitler youth, as they are now those of our student left.

Thus, while the emotional constellations which make for very different student revolts are strangely familiar, the specific political content of a student revolt depends to a very large degree on the beliefs of their parents. Because in many ways, it is a desperate wish to do better than the parent, exactly where he seemed weak in his beliefs. In this sense it is also a desperate desire for parental approval. But even more it is a desperate wish that the parent should have been strong in his convictions that motivate many of their actions. This is the reason why so many of our radicals embrace Maoism, why they chant in their demonstrations "Ho Ho Chi Minh" exactly as another generation of students chanted at their football rallies. These are strong fathers, with strong convictions, who powerfully coerce their children to follow their commands. While consciously they demand freedom and participation, unconsciously their commitment to Mao and other dictatorships suggests their desperate need for controls from the outside, since without it they are unable to bring order into their inner chaos.

Thus while these militant students need controls, such controls must not be imposed punitively, nor for the benefit of others. They must be controls that clearly and definitely benefit the person himself, so that he will eventually make them become his own inner controls.

It is this, their inability to wait and work hard for long range goals, which marks these militants as emotionally disturbed, as does their hatred for their parents who failed to give them direction, set them against the world, by exposing their immature minds to criticism of all that could have given meaning to their lives.

It is their hatred of society that makes it so easy for the small group of militant leaders to make common cause with another small group that provides temporary leadership for some of the rebellions: outright paranoid individuals. I do not believe the number of paranoids among students is greater than their number would be in any comparable group of the population. They become dangerous again because of their high intelligence, which permits them to hide more successfully the degree of their disturbance from the nonexperts. Having worked professionally with some of them for years, I know that student revolt permits them to act out their paranoia to a degree that no other position in society would permit them. How understandable, then, that all paranoids who can, do flock into the ranks of these militants. Unfortunately, most nonexperts do not know how persuasive paranoiacs can be, at least for a time, until they are recognized as such. The persuasiveness of a Hitler or Stalin is now recognized as the consequence of their own paranoia, and their unconscious appeal to the vague paranoid tendencies that can be found among the immature and disgruntled. I have no doubt that the ranks of the militants contain some would-be Hitlers and Stalins, hence again their dangerousness. . . .

A number of individuals from various walks of life have been moved by the recent public school unrest to comment upon ways of sharing with youth some of the decision-making power in our society. Hard-core revolutionaries and representatives of the "system" alike have speculated about possible changes in our educational structure that might serve to accommodate the needs and demands of dissident youth. Needless to say, however, the true revolutionary has as his goal the total destruction of the educational system, while the less extreme commentators and activists offer alternatives to the present system. Some of these latter alternatives still threaten the traditional structures. Others are designed to reconstruct the present system utilizing its underlying philosophical assumptions.

Peter Marin

THE FIERY VEHEMENCE OF YOUTH

Peter Marin, a fellow at the Center for the Study of Democratic Institutions and formerly director of an experimental high school near Palo Alto, provides a provocative, searching essay on the role of the school during these times of student unrest. The author finds himself in a quandary over whether the existing school system should be maintained in its present form.

Swept by energies that are tidal, unfamiliar, unyielding, the adolescent is once more like an infant. He is in a sense born again, with a fresh identity beset inside and out by the rush of new experience. What is growing within him demands expression, requires it, and must, in addition, be received by the world and given form. Otherwise it will wither or turn to rage.

The adolescent must test within social reality the new power within himself. He needs to discover himself as a bridge between inner and outer, a maker of value, a vehicle through which culture perceives and transforms itself. Yet it is just during this period in his life that we adults seem compelled by a persistent lunacy to isolate him.

The adolescent knows at first hand, through his own energies, the pos-

Reprinted, by permission, from the January 1969 issue, pp. 61–74, of *The Center Magazine*, a publication of the Center for the Study of Democratic Institutions in Santa Barbara, California.

sibilities of life—but he knows these in muddled, sporadic, contradictory ways. The rush of his pubescent and raw energy seems at odds with public behavior, the *order* of things, the tenor of life around him, especially in a culture just emerging—as is ours—from a tradition of Victorian, puritanical evasion, repression, and fear.

The contradictions within the culture itself intensify the young person's individual confusion. We ourselves are at the moment torn between future and past in the midst of a process of transformation we barely understand. The development of adolescent energy and ego—difficult at any time—is complicated in our own time by the increase in early sexuality, the complicated messages of the media, and the effects of strong and unfamiliar drugs. These three elements are, in themselves, salient features of a culture that is growing ever more permissive, less repressive. The adolescent tries—partly as a form of self-defense against the pressure of his own energies—to move more freely, to change his style of life, to "grow." But it is then that he finds he is locked into a culture, trapped in a web of ideas, law, and rituals that keep him a child, deprive him of a chance to test and assimilate his newer self. It is now that the culture turns suddenly repressive.

Schools, rooted as they are in a Victorian century and seemingly suspicious of life itself, are his natural enemies. They don't help, as they might, to make that bridge between his private and the social world; they insist, instead, upon their separation. Indeed family, community, and school all combine—especially in the suburbs—to isolate and "protect" him from the adventure, risk, and participation he needs.

The same energies that relate at this crucial point to nature result in a kind of exile from the social environment. The problem is that our institutions are geared to another century, another set of social necessities, and cannot change quickly enough to contain, receive, or direct adolescent energies—and as we suppress or refuse these energies they turn to rage. Thus the young, in that vivid confrontation with the thrust of nature unfolding in themselves, are denied adult assistance.

Primitive cultures, through dramatic, symbolic initiation rites—the rites of passage—legitimized and accepted these energies and turned them toward collective aims. The young men were merged with the life of the tribe and in this way acknowledged, honored, and domesticated —but not destroyed. The rites provided for a liturgized merging of the individual with shared sources of power. They were, in a sense, a social contract—one occurring specifically, profoundly, on a deep psychic level.

Our public schools educate and "socialize" their students by depriving them of everything the rites bestowed—drama, release, and support. They manipulate them through the repression of energies. They isolate them and close off most parts of the community. They refuse to make use of the individual's private experience. They are organized to weaken the student so that he is forced, in the absence of an outlet for his energies, to accept the values and demands of the institution. To this end we deprive the student of mobility and experience. Through law and custom we make the only legal place for him the school, and then, to make sure he remains dependent, manipulable, we empty the school of all vivid life.

When I think of adolescents, none of the proposed changes in our schools make sense to me: revision of curriculum, teaching machines, smaller classes, encounter groups, redistribution of power. All of these are stop-gap measures, desperate attempts to keep the young in schools that are hopelessly outdated. The changes suggested and debated don't go deep enough. For what needs changing is not the methods of the school system but its aims, and what is troubling the young and forcing upon their teachers an intolerable burden is the *idea* of childhood: the ways we think about adolescents, their place in the culture itself. More and more one comes to see that changes in the schools won't be enough. The crisis of the young cuts across the culture in all its areas and includes the family and the community. The young are displaced; there seems no other word for it. They are trapped in a prolonged childhood almost unique in the world.

In few other cultures have persons of fifteen to eighteen been so uselessly isolated from participation in the community, or been deemed so unnecessary, or so limited by law. Our ideas of responsibility, our parental feelings of anxiety, blame, and guilt—all these follow from our curious vision of the young. This is what needs changing: the definitions we make socially and legally of the role of the young. They are trapped in the ways we see them, and the school is simply one aspect of the whole problem.

We can no longer imagine learning outside the schools, or child-adult relationships in the community. We can no longer imagine what children will do outside schools. We regard the young as monsters who will, if released from adult authority or help, disrupt the order of things.

But mass schooling is a recent innovation. Children in the past seem to have learned the ways of the community or tribe through constant contact and interchange with adults. It was taken for granted that the young learned continually through their place close to the heart of the community.

We seem to have lost all sense of that. The school is expected to do what the community cannot do, and that is impossible. In the end, we will have to change far more than the schools if we expect to create a new coherence between the experiences of the child and the needs of the community. We will have to rethink the meaning of childhood. We will begin to grant greater freedom *and* responsibility to the young. We will drop the compulsory-schooling age to fourteen, perhaps lower. We will take for granted the "independence" of adolescents and provide them with the chance to live alone, away from parents and with peers. We will discover jobs they can or want to do in the community—anything from mail delivery to the teaching of smaller children and the counseling of other adolescents.

At some point, perhaps, we will even find that the community itself—in return for a minimum of work or continued schooling—will provide a minimal income to young people that will allow them to assume responsibility for their own lives at an earlier age and learn the ways of the community outside the school. Finally, having lowered the level of compulsory schooling, we will find it necessary to provide different kinds of schools, a wider choice, so that students will voluntarily continue the schooling that suits their needs and aims.

All these changes, of course, are aimed at two things: the restoration of the child's "natural" place in the community and lowering the age at which a person is considered an independent member of the community. Some of the needed changes can, to be sure, be made in the schools, but my sense of things, after having talked to teachers and visited the schools, is that trying to make the changes in schools *alone* will be impossible.

The education system breeds obedience, frustration, dependence, and fear: a kind of gentle violence that the student usually turns against himself, one that is sorrowful and full of guilt, but a violence nonetheless. We don't teach hate in the schools, or murder. But we do isolate the individual. We empty him of life by ignoring or suppressing his impulse toward life. We breed in him a lack of respect for it, a loss of love. And thus we produce gently "good" but threatened men, men who will kill without passion, out of duty and obedience, men who have in themselves little sense of the vivid life being lost or the moral strength to refuse.

From first to twelfth grade we acclimatize students to fundamental deadness and teach them to restrain themselves for the sake of "order." We insist that they separate at the most profound levels their own experience from institutional reality, self from society, objective from subjective, energy from order—though these various polarities are precisely those which must be made coherent during adolescence.

The end of education is intelligent activity, and that demands a merging of opposites, a sense of process. But instead of intelligent activity we produce immobility, insecurity, an inability to act without institutional blessing or direction. Or, at the opposite pole, we induce a headlong rush toward motion without balance or thought. The young learn to "behave" at the expense of themselves. Or else—and you can see it happening now—they turn with a vengeance and may shout, as they did at Columbia, "Kill the adults," for they have allied themselves with raw energy against reason and balance.

What is at stake, I suppose, is the freedom of volition. This is the basic condition with which people must learn to deal, and the sooner they achieve within that condition wit, daring, and responsibility, the stronger they will be. It seems absurd to postpone the assumption of that condition as long as we do. In most other cultures, and even in our own past, young people have taken upon themselves the responsibility of adults and have dealt with it as successfully as most adults do now. The students I have seen can do that, too, when given the chance. What a strain it must be to possess that capacity, to sense in oneself a talent for adventure or growth or meaning, and have that sense continually stifled or undercut by the role one is supposed to play!

Thus it seems unmistakably clear that our first obligation to the young is to create a place in the community for them to act with volition and freedom. They are ready for it, certainly, even if we aren't. The students I have worked with seem strongest and most alive when they are in the mountains of Mexico or the Oakland ghetto or out in the desert or simply hitchhiking or riding freights to see what's happening. They thrive on distance and motion—and the right to solitude when they want it. Many of them want jobs; they themselves arrange to be teachers in day-care centers, political canvassers, tutors, poolroom attendants, actors, governesses, gardeners.

They returned from these experiences immeasurably brightened and more sure of themselves, more willing, in that new assurance, to learn many of the abstract ideas we had been straining to teach them. It was not simply the experience itself that brought this about. It was also the feeling of freedom they had, the sense that they could come and go at will and make any choice they wanted—no matter how absurd—if they were willing to suffer what real consequences followed.

We considered them free agents and limited our own activities to advice, to what "teaching" they requested, and to support when they needed it in facing community, parents, or law. What we were after was a "guilt-free" environment, one in which the students might become or discover what they were without having to worry about preconceived ideas of what they had to be. What students learned was the sense of themselves as makers of value, the realization that the environment is at best an extension of men and that it can be transformed by them into what they vitally need.

When we permitted students freedom of choice and gave them easy access to the community, we found that ideas acquired weight and value to the extent that students were allowed to try them out in action. It was in practical and social situations that their own strength increased, and the merging of the two—strengthened self and tested knowledge—moved them more quickly toward manhood than anything else I have seen.

Running through my mind is a line I read in a friend's first published story, "The Idea in that idea is: there is no one over you." *There is no one over you.* Perhaps that signifies the gap between today's children and their parents. For the children it is true; they sense it. There is no one over them; believable authority has disappeared; it has been replaced by experience. The parents still believe in "someone" over them. They insist upon it—in fact, demand it for and from their children. The children themselves cannot believe it. It means nothing to them.

Adults see the school as the principal vehicle for value, for "culture." But just as men of the Reformation rebelled against the established church as the mediator between God and man, students now rebel against the school (and its version of things) as the intermediary between themselves and experience and the making of value. This is, then, a kind of Reformation—the same reformative shift that occurred in religion, a shift from the institutional (the external) to the individual (the internal), and it demands, when it occurs, an agony, an apocalyptic fury, a destruction of the past itself. I believe it is happening now. One sees and feels it everywhere: a violent fissure, a kind of quake.

A sense of faceless authority pervades our schools and colleges, driving the young to rebellion or withdrawal. The young want to have the masks of authority, all its disguises, removed—and to see it plain. That is in large part what lies behind the riots in the schools. The specific grievances are incidental; the real purpose is to make authority show its face, to have whatever pervasive and oppressive force makes them perpetual children reveal itself, declare itself, commit itself. It is biblical; it is Freudian. It reminds me of the primitive initiation rites: the effort to unmask the gods and assume their power, to become an equal— and to find in that the manhood one has been denied.

The schools seem to enforce the idea that someone is over you. They induce alienation from oneself, dependence, insecurity. They are the means by which we deprive the young of manhood. And we must not be surprised when youth seek that manhood in ways that must of necessity be childish and violent.

But this troubles me, for there is little choice between mindless violence and mindless authority, and I am just enough of an academic, an intellectual, to want to preserve much of what will be lost in the kind of rebellion that is approaching. And yet, the rapidity of events leaves me with no clear idea, no solution, no sense of what will be adequate change. I know only that the problem now seems to be that our response to crisis is to move away or back rather than forward, and that we will surely, for the sake of some imagined order, increase in number and pressure the very approaches that have brought us to this confusion.

So I have no easy conclusions, no startling synthesis with which to close. What I am after is an alternative to separation and rage, some kind of connection to things to replace the system of dependence and submission—the loss of self—that now holds sway, slanted toward violence. What I have been trying to articulate for adults is a way of seeing, of feeling that will restore to the young a sense of manhood and potency without at the same time destroying the past. What I know is that there is a necessity for each young person to experience himself as an extension and maker of culture, and to feel the whole force of the world within himself—not as an enemy, but as himself.

As I write I think of myself as an observer at a tribal war—an anthropologist, a combination of Gulliver and a correspondent sending home news by mule and boat. By the time you hear of it, things will have changed. And that isn't enough, not enough at all. Somebody must step past the children, must move into his own psyche or two steps past his own limits into the absolute landscape of fear and potential our children inhabit. That is where I am headed. So the ideas I have set forth, in effect, are something like a last message tacked to a tree or tucked under a stone. I mean, we cannot *follow* the children any longer; we have to step ahead of them. Somebody has to mark a trail.

Scott D. Thomson

ACTIVISM: A GAME FOR UNLOVING CRITICS

An administrator's point of view is represented in this selection by Scott D. Thomson, Superintendent of Evanston, Illinois, Township High School. Mr. Thomson feels that the present structures are outmoded and that students cannot emerge from their isolation unless schools provide channels to outside organizations for those students who want an active involvement in the promotion of societal causes.

Student activism, were it any ordinary mortal movement, would be immobilized beard-deep in a sea of words. Rhetoric, edicts, essays, and research studies flow forth unrelentingly. It is time, however, to step back and get a broader overview of our present posture and the options for the immediate future. This is, then, in essence, an older generation's essay on student activism, an attempt to gain general perspective to guide us with particular problems.

We all know of at least four different alienated student groups: the New Left activists, the advocates of Black Power, the hippies, and the Third World Liberation Front. Each is unique. Hippies flee from power, dropping out from a society considered hopelessly materialistic, while New Left activists plan to reshape that society by assaulting schools and gaining power. Black Power groups stress black initiative and accept assistance with skepticism, while the Third World Liberation Front has resulted from a partnership of the more radical black and white students.

Always there has been and will be a generation gap, because, as Eric Sevareid points out, youth have a one-dimensional vision—a view of the present as contrasted to the ideal, whereas adults have a three-dimensional vision gained by living in the past, by possessing broader views of the present, and by also seeing the ideal ahead.

What, then, makes the current problems of student unrest so different and so difficult? The answer can be found in two areas: (1) the peculiar nature of youth today as affected by historical forces, and (2) the open-

From *The Education Digest*, September, 1969, pp. 1–4. (Article appeared originally in *The Bulletin of the National Association of Secondary School Principals*.) Reprinted by permission of the author, *The Education Digest*, and NASSP.

ing up of schools beyond their essentially intellectual function to a direct and reciprocal contact with society and conflict.

One peculiar quality of today's alienated youth as contrasted to past generations is the *level* of hostility directed toward existing institutions. The distressing emotionalism found today probably arises first from an alienation from liberal ideals (data indicates that the parents of most activists have themselves been critical of social problems), followed by a brief nihilism and then, in a search for security, radicalism. This process results in commitment to a world unborn and, in actuality, unknown. That is why activists have such difficulties describing the society they desire. Note that the radical revolutionist's point of departure is his alienation from traditional democratic liberalism.

The radical activist's belief that he possesses the foolproof antidote for the defects of liberalism obviously disassociates him from being the reformist liberal that he is seen as being by some commentators. The activist's contempt for liberals as fuzzy-headed functionaries unsure of Truth and the activist's obsession with gaining goals by any means at hand, including intimidation and force, illustrate his alienation not only from the routine institutions of democratic liberalism but from its central political values as well.

As a result of this new level of alienation, some interesting traits occur in the personalities of activists—for instance, the disgust of the alienated with the social consequences of technology. Activists feel that today's world is dehumanized and destructive, and that technology must be tamed. A corollary is the alienation of many activists from the future as they see it. Most are uninterested and unsuccessful in math and science. Aware that an increasing prestige goes with success in technology, they tend to feel threatened by a future in which their own personal worth could be questioned, and fear being surplus and discredited.

Schools unwittingly abet the alienation process. An emphasis on "problem solving," inductive thought, and experimental technique provides pupils with "super skills" for seeing and questioning the observable. They become brilliant analysts. Every defect in the fabric of life becomes clearly observable. But dedication to finding solutions for these problems within democratic values is missing. Ridiculing society's awkwardness in dealing with injustice but lacking solutions except those based on impatient force, the activist has an overriding obsession with goals. He replaces a commitment to democratic process with a commitment to self and to his personal concept of the future. And since process is the lifeblood of democracy, the implications are serious.

The task for schools, then, clearly is to show that reform through a thorough understanding and a vigorous application of traditional democratic values to changing institutions is more constructive than revolution. This will require all the imaginative leadership and courage that teachers, administrators, and parents can muster.

A second main point in this overview of activism is the relationship of schools to community problems, and especially the opening up of schools as centers of overt action. This strikes at the heart of our present difficulties, which to a large degree are caused by an intimate involvement of the school campus with political and social forces whirling about the general community.

Ideas and Action

Obviously, students should become involved in discussion of crucial issues, the military draft for instance. But should they organize on campus with the objective of affecting politically this law? Students should debate thoroughly the race question, environmental pollution, foreign policy, the adequacy of party primaries, the Electoral College, and other pressing issues. But should not a delicate line exist between discussion and action? And should not this line be placed between the school and the community? As Bruno Bettelheim of the University of Chicago states, "The purpose of a university is to *study* revolt, not to engage in it; to *examine* how peace may be won and maintained, not to crusade against war; to *investigate* and plan for social reforms, not to carry them out." The central objective of a school or a university is to study every possible question, but to fight for only one cause: freedom of inquiry and openness of thought.

We must find this fragile line between talking and doing, between ideas and action. Then we must nurture this line into healthy vigor and explain its centrality to the community. Finally, we must step forward and provide channels to outside organizations for those students who want an active involvement in the promotion of causes in the broader community, the actual working for any ideal ranging from tutoring the underprivileged to influencing foreign policy.

Schools cannot be separated from society, nor am I advocating that. And schools must be relevant. We do at school—to reinterpret George Counts—"dare to build a new social order," but one of ideas, not of implementation. That is the job of the larger community, and a task with which schools cannot become involved and still maintain their special atmosphere of free thought, their security from political pressures, their contemplation devoid of immediate conflict, and their privilege of partial self-government.

Those zealots who want students to play at school all the games of the adult world, under the aegis of civil rights, simply do not understand the Pandora's Box they are attempting to unlock. To assign to the school campus open programs of action could result in a disastrous sequence of events against reflective thought, and would give opportunity for manipulating youth for any cause.

During a California hearing on student activism last spring, American Civil Liberties Union representatives argued that a broad involvement with society by students at school is essential to modern education. But in reality, is political activism the safeguard of freedom, or is advocacy? Might not, therefore, the chief safeguard of the preservation of democracy be unfettered ideas and lively debate? And the best safeguards for free debate are schools where young people may explore ideas in the best possible intellectual environment, apart from emotionalism, activism, and intimidation.

One feature of American public education has been its freedom from political control. Remove the delicate line between thought and action, and you invite eventual control by partisan bodies. Then youth can be used more easily. And youth is an impressive political force, as history illustrates from the ancient Spartans to the modern Mao.

Believing this, I also feel strongly that schools have a direct responsibility, especially today, to help interested students to become involved actively in the community off the school campus. Each school should have a community counselor who works with community agencies and makes certain students have easy and immediate access to these groups.

Schools may have little to do with the appearance of alienated activists; the home, the mass media, modern literature, affluence, and mobility are beyond our schoolmaster's rod. But educators slip into the position of sponsoring activism if they allow it on campus.

Schools are for ideas, for nourishing intellectual growth. Schools are the custodians of a precious commodity, the fragile flask of academic freedom. Too much heat and pressure can pop the cork and shatter the container. Charles Frankel of Columbia University writes that the supreme obligation of educators is to protect the freedom to teach and to learn. Teachers and administrators must be "intolerant of intolerance," according to Frankel. If we lose the struggle for rational discourse in the schools, how will we maintain it in the larger society? "If we lose this struggle, what will the youth of the future say to us? Youth will not thank us for equivocating about the values of civilized conduct. I think most youth know this. It is for teachers and administrators to make it plain that we know it too, and we mean to make it work."

Richard Basciano

THE PERSPECTIVE OF STUDENT RADICALISM

Richard Basciano argues that the future for public education looks bleak because of the strong hold on society of the business and corporate ethic. In an essay written expressly for this chapter, Mr. Basciano, one of the editors' own students at the Chicago Circle Campus of the University of Illinois, contends that the schools cannot succeed in their present form because they are given over to serving the big corporations and, in fact, are merely corporations in their own right.

The recent history of the United States has been one of nearly limitless change. Since 1918 America has been a creditor nation; since 1946 she has been the most powerful nation on earth. The trend toward economic growth in the United States has become so familiar that it is taken for granted. Although the overt territorial expansion which formed the background for the ideology of "manifest destiny" in the nineteenth century has now practically ceased, the enormous zest and naive aggression of the American people have been turned inward—the slogan is no longer "54-40 or fight" but "production means progress."

Production also has meant concentration of wealth. At the same time, the growth of mass production has entailed the concurrent growth of productive units. Thus, the liberal vision of an economy in which supply and demand—outside the control of any single man or any single institution—regulated the economic life of the nation is dead. Concentration of wealth, in other words, brought with it concentration of power. The power of the corporate employer over a large segment of the working-class population triggered government regulation of job conditions and, ultimately, federally sanctioned trade unions. While the success of these reformist measures in the alleviation of working-class misery took much of the edge off the Marxist criticism of American capitalism, it also fundamentally changed the structure of society and

Printed by permission of the author.

redefined the prerogatives of government. Corporate life is the new American reality. No aspect of life has been left untouched by it. The employer is a member of a corporation (for instance, General Motors); the employee is a member of a corporation (the Teamsters Union), as is the government official (the State Department) and the student (the University of Illinois). By corporation, I mean any institution in which there has been a concentration of productive, distributive, or administrative capacity for the purpose of producing or distributing goods, administration of an organization, or the dispensing of specialized services. The usefulness of this unusually broad definition of corporation lies in the fact that it indicates that American life has become both more complex and more homogeneous. In a very real sense, the president of General Motors lives an experience similar to that of the assembly-line worker. There is, in modern life, a natural tendency toward the elimination of social distinctions. The rigid class society of Marxist diatribe has given way to a society where differences (there are still many) are less obvious and concentrated power stays in the background while center stage in American life is occupied by a vast middle class comprised of bureaucrats, scientific and social technicians, and skilled laborers. Electorally their power is significant; collectively as consumers they wield considerable, if largely unused, influence; but their control over productive units is negligible. Generally, they are economically secure, socially paranoid, and politically pragmatic. Many are second-generation Americans who have risen socially either through individual effort or a moderate education. In a sense most were swept into the middle class by the wave of postwar prosperity. They preach the "tried and true" American virtues of individual initiative, relentless work, and spiritual frugality. Their acquaintance with liberal dogma came late in life and has taken only a superficial hold upon them. Emotionally, many are still of the working class. The chief hope and pride of this new class is their children and, more specifically, the possibility that their children will rise both socially and economically. The key to socioeconomic progress in the United States is public and higher education. No generation in history has been more convinced of the godly qualities of education.

The many excellences of American education is one subject upon which there has existed complete agreement between middle-America and the directors of the major corporations. The rapid growth of American business and government created a nearly insatiable demand for highly trained technicians and bureaucrats. The result was the equally rapid growth of the educational establishment in America. A new complex of public schools and state universities was erected, and established institutions streamlined to meet modern needs. The function of these institutions has been to create an educated elite of technically specialized bureaucrats, and the destiny of this potential elite has been the assumption of positions of administrative power within corporate America. The entire process of education, beginning with high school, has been reshaped to meet this increasing demand for highly educated functionaries. High school has been transformed into an intensely competitive "weeding out" period in which the academically talented are propelled toward their destined bureaucratic niche and the academically unfit are cast aside. The tenor of both high school and college life has thus been altered.

The public schools function in much the same manner as modern industry. The faculty turns out a product (knowledge) to be purchased by a group of consumers (students). The critical independence of education in the school system has been undermined by the fact that most superintendents and chancellors are little more than political appointees. Their ability to represent the desires of faculty and students is challenged by their political obligation to unenlightened local board members or state legislators. The result has been that the schools are run "from the top down" in the same authoritarian way as the modern corporation. The task of the university, for example, to process as many students as rapidly as possible, brings the inevitable consequence of drastic overcrowding. The worst effect of the deterioration of the modern university is the lack of a coherent philosophy of education. The liberal assumptions no longer fit the present situation, yet they are mouthed daily in an unending "credo" of little meaning. The modern university is as bizarre and contradictory an institution as any in America. The same might be said even more emphatically about the lower-level public schools.

With this background in mind, we ask how the student radical might look at America. He does so from the perspective of the need for complete change. In this, he differs from the majority of so-called middle-Americans who, while disgruntled with certain aspects of life, are satisfied with the general direction of society. However, he is not alone. He represents only the forefront of a rapidly growing segment of educated American youth. The two major issues around which this discontent grows are institutionalized racism and the war in Vietnam. These issues don't exhaust the discontent but merely provide axes around which a profound revulsion for the foundations of corporate America can turn. In short, the student radical is in revolt against a society which benignly neglects major domestic social problems while engaged in costly economic gangsterism abroad.

The radical student rejects both the goals and life style of middle-America. To him, the life of corporate man represents a hysterical flight from the social responsibilities inherent in life in a democratic state. He believes that the social and political decadence of modern America demands a militant corrective response. Student radicals will not play middle-America's games. Honor-the-flag chauvinism, the Communist Crusade, "biggest car, bustiest broad," barbecuing on the front lawn, and "leave me alone I pay my taxes" are the hallmarks of a life he has turned from in disgust. Radicalism calls for a return to personal responsibility, a reaffirmation of the principles outlined in the Constitution, a movement beyond corporate America toward socialist America.

The American society described above has produced a student elite to meet the needs of an expanding economy. A significant proportion of these students at the secondary and higher education levels are preparing themselves to render a specialized service for society. Fewer students than ever before are becoming individual entrepreneurs. The result has been a subtle shift in attitudes. The social technicians see their services within the context of society. Only a minority of these social technicians have become openly critical of American society. The vanguard of this new social criticism, as implied above, is the student radical movement. The radical is repelled by the modern corporation with its strict, hierarchical structure, venomous personal corruption, and heavy emphasis upon private profits. He seriously questions the educational institutions which are designed to train him to "fit into" the corporate schema. The policies of the American government, both foreign and domestic, controlled by the rich for the rich, alienate him from participation in the traditional party system. American aggression in Vietnam is complemented by "benign neglect" of domestic poverty. To the radical, these policies represent the antithesis of enlightened governmental action. Radicals demand not only political liberty but also economic justice. The traditional socialist principle—"From each according to his ability, to each according to his need"—summarizes their view of wise foreign and domestic policy. To realize this principle, radicalism calls for the complete restructuring of American society. This social revolution will entail redistribution of income, a broad extension of economic planning, the abolition of corporate private property, the institution of local political control of federal funds, provisions for socioeconomic equality for all races, and a complete reversal of the present trend in

American foreign policy. The radical movement will lead the American people toward these changes through extensive educational programs, participation in electoral politics, and nonviolent political agitation.

Although the central purpose of this essay has been to voice the radical viewpoint on the present state of American society, an attempt has also been made to demonstrate that radicalism represents but a small segment of those discontented with modern American life. This darkly critical stance toward the United States has become an important sociopolitical reality, however; and the radical student movement at the high school and university levels must take full advantage of it. Those discontented with their lot in America provide a cross section of the national life: radicals, blacks, moderate students, a significant minority of the managerial class, professionals, and a large part of the working class. The causes of this discontent are encountered daily. They have become a part of the fabric of American life. Some of these causes are Vietnam, racism, violence in the cities, inflation combined with recession, and a gradual lessening of individual freedom. The depth and extent of this national frustration indicate that the radical movement should concentrate this suppressed rage on the major institutions which have caused this unstable situation—the private corporation, the military-industrial complex, the business-dominated government, and the public schools. Destructive criticism of these institutions must be closely bound to the advocacy of constructive alternatives. The ultimate goal of student radicalism must be the establishment of democratic socialism in America within this century.

Discontent within America is deep and is growing daily. In order to mobilize this dissatisfaction the radical movement must not use tactics which will completely alienate large segments of liberal opinion. The aim of radicalism must be to demonstrate provocatively the inequities of American life without isolating the movement from other progressive forces within the society.

In certain segments of the movement today, it is *de rigueur* to vastly overestimate the failings of political democracy in America. This is a mistake: the radical criticism of American institutions should be incisive but not misleading. Political democracy, if tarnished, is still operative in America. Radicalism must use democratic methods to win the support of the people. The modern world offers two vastly different types of government best exemplified by Cuba and the United States. Cuba offers mankind economic equality under an authoritarian regime, while the United States offers political freedom without economic equality. The goal of the student radical movement must be to offer the American people the best of both worlds: democratic socialism.

If the ends of radicalism are to be attained, long-range organization must be attempted. The present fluid status of the movement must be transformed into a substantial coalition of progressive forces. Radicals must build alliances with sympathetic liberals, black leaders, professionals, and union officials in an attempt to reach all sources of discontent within America. The war in Vietnam, racism, and urban problems must be used to criticize the structures of present American society. The movement must not only use the electoral process to effect change, but also those protest tactics which have proved useful: nonviolent confrontations with authority, pamphleteering and picketing, strikes and national marches to dramatize an issue. The tactics of the movement must be controversial but democratic. The aim of the movement must be the formation of a tightly knit coalition for the radical reconstruction of American society.

The formation of a strong progressive front in America depends upon the ability of radical students to work in a militant yet disciplined manner toward the goal of democratic socialism in America. Change in the most complex modern state is, of necessity, gradual. Radicalism must develop the patience which only long-range dedication and organization can bring. Radicals, rightly critical of the provincial values of middle-America, must nevertheless use the needs of the middle and working classes as a central dynamism of their movement. The possibility of a New America depends upon the ability of radicals to turn the explosive energies of the antiwar movement into the controlled force of a new leftist coalition.

Questions for Discussion

1. Many people contend that teacher-education students are one of the most conservative of student groups. What do you think about this contention? Whether it is an accurate observation or not, why do you think it has been made?
2. Do the values and beliefs expressed in student dissent lead you to question your motives for choosing teaching as a profession? Do you think the radical or critical views represented in several of the selections in this chapter suggest that public school teaching is a "respected" or honored profession?
3. Do you sympathize with the radical views expressed in the first article in this chapter or with the views expressed by Basciano? Have you ever protested in support of these or other such views? Why? If you did, what do you feel was gained?

4. The demand of black students for a relevant curriculum is in many ways a microcosmic example of the larger student protest movement. Do you think the black-power drive was a breakthrough for student dissent as a whole? In other words, how much of the student movement as a whole do you think would have developed if there had been no black-power or civil rights drive?

5. Assuming an end to American involvement in the war in Indochina, how vital will student protest be then? Will it fade away or are there other comparable sustaining issues?

6. Do you disagree with the bleak picture of American society as painted by the student dissenters? Why?

Topics for Further Study

1. The underground newspaper is the mouthpiece for student activists in the high schools. After reading John Birmingham's *Our Time Is Now* (1970), visit the editorial offices of an underground newspaper in your area. Do the editors of the newspaper you visited seem to be concerned with the issues highlighted by Birmingham or has the several-year interval since the publication of *Our Time Is Now* made that book irrelevant to the concerns of today's youth? What are the concerns of today's youth?

2. It is apparent from several of the readings in this chapter that today's student activists reject established role-patterns and seek outlets for their creative abilities. They rebel both against "corporate man" and predetermined organization of society. Survey your peers in order to ascertain what values they hold relative to this anti-establishment attitude.

3. One means of measuring the success of the student protest movement in any particular locale is to study the changes that have been brought about in the governance of the school system. Return to your own high school and try to determine whether there is a real shared power relationship developing among faculty, administrators, parents, community organizations, and students. What criteria might you use to examine this question? Use your own experience as a point of departure in this study.

4. This chapter has not provided a selection which represents the "corporate man" point of view so vehemently opposed by radical students. Make arrangements to interview a number of people whom you feel reflect the corporate man image. Then try to articulate this point of view in your own terms. Do you feel that the student activist has or will have an influence on big business and its leaders? What economic, social, and political conditions must prevail for the radical position to influence the corporate point of view?

Chapter 6. ETHNICITY AND THE SCHOOLS

SINCE the 1950's, Americans have been made dramatically aware that a significant portion of our population is both unhappy with its lot in our society and unwilling to accept it. First through the civil rights movement and then through the black-power movement, the black American revealed for all to see a malignant social disease in America. The discovery of that malignant disease not only awakened us to the problems of race and racism as such, but has given rise to numerous issues and controversy related to ethnicity.

Few thinking people would deny that ethnicity as a racial phenomenon constitutes a major social problem of our time. There is much disagreement over how the school should deal with this problem, but that it should deal with it—administratively and in terms of curriculum, teacher training, etc.—*is* generally agreed. There is no such agreement relative to ethnicity as a phenomenon apart from race. But there are different sides; there is heat and controversy; and the schools are caught in the middle of the conflicting views. There are those, for instance, who argue that ethnicity is no longer a vital influence in our society, that this is the way our philosophy of life and government meant it to be, and that we should, therefore, let sleeping monsters lie. Others claim that there has been a sharp decline in the significance of European ethnic groups and that particular attention ought to be given to "new" ethnic minorities which have come to populate our large urban centers: Puerto Ricans, Southern white mountaineers, and blacks. Taking the opposite point of view, many persons contend that a larger ethnicity (i.e., including European ethnic groups) has been and indeed still is a crucial factor in American society and that to ignore this is to insure the creation of all kinds of individual and associative problems. And still others argue that whether or not a larger, more inclusive ethnicity is influential and crucial to progress in our society, it should be. If it is not, they argue, this is due to the fact that our society has intentionally set out to deny and thereby destroy ethnic differences. They point out that our vital pluralistic tradition is in danger of extinction and that public institutions, particularly the school, should provide for and enrich—and use as an enrichment resource—all the cultural differences which flow from ethnic group identification.

The current debate over the general question of ethnicity has many causes. One major cause, as we have already suggested, has been the civil rights movement in general and the black-power movement in particular. These movements which, among other things, call for recognition of and due credit for the role of black culture in American life, have reawakened interest in the phenomenon of ethnicity. Moreover, they have stirred a residue of discontent not only with regard to the way blacks have been treated in our schools and society at large, but also with regard to the ways in which schools responded to problems occasioned by the mass wave of immigration to this country around the turn of the century.

From 1880 to 1914, about ten million people from southern and eastern Europe entered the United States. This massive wave of immigration was to result in long-term social problems for developing America. The immigrants who came here during this period were attached to cultural and ethnic traditions quite different from those of earlier immigrants. And it was this difference which caused people to ask: What will happen to America with all these diverse peoples? How should old-world and ethnic traditions be handled? How should they be Americanized? What kind of education should be given to them? Some of the readings in this chapter, particularly in the descriptive section, are addressed to the ways in which these questions were answered and to some of the consequences. Some people believe that the educational answers, particularly, which prevailed were wrongheaded and produced long-term problematic consequences in which we are now enmeshed—consequences which have been intensified by the struggles of black Americans.

In any case, the important point is this: new problems are arising in regard to the integration of all Americans—whatever their ethnic background—into the mainstream of American life. And the basic question which permeates these problems is that of the need and desirability of cultivating many forms of ethnic and/or group identification.

The increasing awareness of ethnicity as an important phenomenon in our society, and the fury kicked up in the recent debate over how to deal with it should not blind us to the universality—indeed the eternalness—of this phenomenon and the basic problem attached to it. And the problem is this:

The shared symbols, interests, affections, and real or imagined traits which draw some men together into the group or community are the walls which separate these men from others. Hence, the communion that nurtures intra-group cohesion is often the first condition for intergroup conflict. To state it more tersely, for there to be "brothers" there must also be "others." Boundaries, whether they be geographical or psychological have a way of being both cohesive and divisive. °

That the ethnic question is a universal one does not diminish its cruciality in our society. On the contrary, this reality suggests that ethnicity may be—or at least possesses the potential for being—a greater problem in this country than elsewhere. The United States has been populated by more numerous and widely divergent ethnic groups than has any country in modern times, if not in all man's history. Furthermore, the vastness of this country has permitted some groups—Southern white mountaineers, for example—to live in virtual isolation from the larger society: in a form of isolation which has permitted these groups to create and perpetuate life styles quite distinct from those in the larger society.

The problem of ethnicity, then, has added new significance to such age-old questions in our country as:

1. What constitutes integration in a society with a vital pluralistic tradition?

2. Does integration demand assimilation?

3. How can we insure equality of opportunity to all peoples?

4. Is assimilation of ethnic tradition inevitable?

These questions, basic to the phenomenon of ethnicity, are important for all social institutions. But they are crucial for the school. It is *the* major public institution through which children and youth are socialized into the larger society. Hence, we come to the central issue of this chapter: *How should schools deal with ethnicity?* This is not an easily answered question. It is compounded in difficulty by the fact that it incorporates—but is not limited to—the major problems of race, racism, and prejudice. Moreover, it is not a merely academic question. Answers to it have consequences for the very fabric of American life. Finally, it is related to the school-society relationship issue discussed in Chapter 1. If ethnicity is a social problem, should the schools become embroiled in

° Edgar Litt, *Beyond Pluralism: Ethnic Politics in America* (Glenview, Ill.: Scott, Foresman and Company, 1970), p. 4.

the problem? Should they ignore it? Or should they become active agents for social change by attempting to study the ethnicity problem and come up with solutions to it?

James W. Vander Zanden
SOURCES OF AMERICAN MINORITIES

The first descriptive selection provides an overall view of American minorities through an account of their origins. Although the article does not provide an adequate up-to-date account of the influx of Latin-Americans into this country since the late 1960's, the selection does offer an excellent general perspective on the number, origins, and ethnic backgrounds of immigrants to this country.

James W. Vander Zanden has contributed numerous articles to leading professional and sociological journals and is the author of several books. He is Professor of Sociology at The Ohio State University.

American Indians

In 1492 there were about 700,000 to 1,000,000 Indians in that area which now comprises the United States. In the regions of earliest contact with Europeans, the area along the Atlantic seaboard and the Gulf of Mexico, the tribal territories of the Indians were appropriated and the aborigines were either annihilated or driven inland. Some made their way into the swamps, coves, and wooded mountains of these regions. Following the American Revolution, the new government followed a policy of negotiating treaties of land cession with the Indians. Where the Indians failed to agree, they were confronted with military force. Local groups of whites often moved on their own against the Indians. When the Indians resisted white encroachments upon their lands, warfare ensued, the Seminole War in Florida and the Black Hawk War in the Illinois Territory being among the better known of the wars fought east of the Mississippi. Eventually, with the exception of portions of the Iroquois nations, the tribes signed treaties of cession and moved westward. Some went resignedly, others at bayonet point.

West of the Mississippi, similar patterns prevailed. Against the Plains

Indians, a policy of systematic annihilation was pursued. The slaughter of buffaloes was deliberately encouraged as a war measure to force the Indians into capitulation. In 1871, Congress made the Indians wards of the United States, and a reservation policy was followed. It was a program directed at destroying Indian cultures and forcing the assimilation of the Indians as individuals within the American way of life. The policy had devastating consequences for the Indians, a fact recognized in 1933 with the reorientation of Indian policy toward a program of pluralism. In 1924, Indians were finally granted American citizenship, a right denied them for nearly 150 years.

Negroes

In 1619 twenty Negroes were purchased from a Dutch man-of-war by the settlers at Jamestown. Since there was no precedent in English law regarding slaves, it appears that Negroes initially assumed the status of indentured servants, much in the fashion of whites. However, the Negroes' distinctive physical characteristics doubtless furthered their differential treatment from the beginning, and in time facilitated their enslavement. The growth of Negro slavery was closely tied with the development of the plantation system of agriculture that evolved within the South. Prior to the invention in 1793 of the cotton gin, slaves were primarily used in commercial agriculture based upon tobacco, rice, indigo, and naval stores. To supply the considerable demand for slaves, an elaborate trade system emerged. The voyage of the slaves from Africa to America, often referred to as the "Middle Passage," was a veritable nightmare. Overcrowding and epidemics were common.

At the time of the first federal census, taken in 1790, there were 757,208 Negroes in the country, of which more than 90 per cent were concentrated in the South. However, it was not until Eli Whitney solved the problem of separating the cotton seed from the close-adhering lint that cotton became the major crop of the South. By 1815 the production of cotton had increased at a phenomenal rate. This expansion of the cotton economy was accompanied by the growth of the slave population. Although by 1808 England and the United States had outlawed the traffic in slaves, the slave trade persisted, merely having been driven underground. Nevertheless, by far the chief source of growth in the slave population was natural increase. The growth in the Negro population of the United States since 1790 can be seen in Table 1.

Table [1]. Growth of the Negro Population Since 1790

Census Year	Number of Negroes	Percentage of Total Population	Percentage Increase of Negroes During Decade	Percentage Increase of Whites During Decade
1960	18,871,831	10.5	25.4	17.5
1950	15,044,937	9.9	17.0	14.4
1940	12,865,518	9.8	8.2	7.2
1930	11,891,143	9.7	13.6	15.7
1920	10,463,131	9.9	6.5	15.7
1910	9,827,763	10.7	11.2	21.8
1900	8,333,940	11.6	18.0	21.2
1890	7,488,676	11.9	13.8	27.0
1880	6,580,793	13.1	34.9	29.2
1870	4,880,009	12.7	9.9	24.8
1860	4,441,830	14.1	22.1	37.7
1850	3,638,808	15.7	26.6	37.7
1840	2,873,648	16.8	23.4	34.7
1830	2,328,642	18.1	31.4	33.9
1820	1,771,656	18.4	28.6	34.2
1810	1,377,808	19.0	37.5	36.1
1800	1,002,037	18.9	32.3	35.8
1790	757,208	19.3		

SOURCE: U.S. Bureau of the Census, *Negroes in the United States, 1920–1932,* 1–2; *Sixteenth Census of United States, Population,* II, 19.

Immigration to the United States

The total number of immigrants admitted to the United States throughout our history is not known. In 1820 the government began maintaining a record of immigration, but until 1907 the enumerations suffered from serious limitations. Accordingly, only a rough approximation of total immigration to this country can be gained from federal sources. These data are presented in Figure 1. Until the depression years of the 1890's, the volume of immigration generally increased each decade. Immigration remained high until the passage of restrictive legislation in the 1920's, which set ceilings upon the number of migrants to be admitted from each nation. Many immigrants to the United States eventually returned home. Between 1907 and 1930 the ratios of outflow to inflow for total alien migration ranged from 23.7 to 32.0 per cent, with the exception of the World War I period when it rose to 55 per cent.

During the depression years of the 1930's emigration exceeded immigration, but, since World War II, there has been a sharp decline in outflow relative to inflow.

The data on the number of immigrants to the United States from particular countries suffer from an even greater number of limitations than the data on immigration generally. Owing to the changes in the list of countries separately reported and to changes in boundaries, data for a number of nations are not comparable throughout. Furthermore, prior to 1906, the enumeration was made with reference to the country from which the alien came rather than the country of the alien's last permanent residence. Table 2 . . . gives a rough approximation of the total immigration to the United States from various nations since 1820.

The Period from 1783 to 1830. In 1790 the white population of the United States was predominantly of English stock. There were comparatively few Germans, Irish, and Dutch, and even fewer French, Canadians, Belgians, Swiss, Mexicans, and Swedes. Between 1783 and 1830 about 10,000 immigrants came to the United States each year.

Table [2]. Immigrants, by Country of Origin: 1820–1963

Country	Total, 144 Years 1820–1963	Country	Total, 144 Years 1820–1963
All countries	42,702,328	Portugal	293,420
		Spain	188,974
Europe	34,896,219	Sweden	1,255,296
Austria ⎱	4,280,863	U.S.S.R.	3,344,998
Hungary ⎰		Yugoslavia	69,834
Belgium	191,981		
Czechoslovakia	129,704	Asia	1,160,758
Denmark	354,331	China	411,585
Finland	28,358	Japan	338,087
France	698,188	America	6,218,631
Germany	6,798,313	Canada and	
Great Britain	3,844,058	Newfoundland	3,697,649
Greece	499,465	Mexico	1,291,922
		West Indies	684,175
Ireland	4,693,009		
Italy	5,017,625	Africa	53,186
Netherlands	338,722	Australia and	
Norway	843,867	New Zealand	84,468
Poland	451,010	Pacific islands	22,332

SOURCE: U.S. Bureau of the Census, *Statistical Abstract of the United States*, 1964, 94.

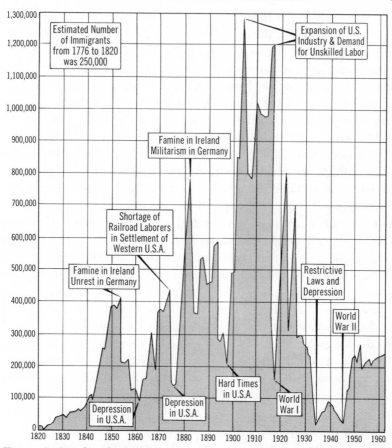

Figure 1. One hundred and forty-one years of immigration into the United States. (SOURCE: *Philadelphia Inquirer*, William Streckfuss, Staff Artist. By permission.)

The Period from 1830 to 1882. The next period, from 1830 until 1882, was marked by a great increase in immigration. The great land areas beyond the Mississippi served to induce many foreigners to come to America. Rapid industrialization created major demands for unskilled labor to build canals, railroads, and roads, to work in factories, and to carry on many non-mechanized tasks. During these fifty-two years, English, Irish, Germans, and Scandinavians predominated among the migrants. The Irish came in especially large numbers after 1840 when the failure of their one crop, the potato, caused famine and resultant widespread suffering throughout Ireland. More than 1,350,000 Irish were recorded as having arrived in the United States during the eight years from 1847 to 1854. For the most part the Irish settled in the tenements of American cities, under slum conditions similar to those found among the southern and eastern Europeans of later date. In contrast with the Irish, the Germans and Scandinavians clung less tenaciously to the cities, many of them settling on farms in the Midwest. The German immigration reached its peak between 1880 and 1892 when more than 1,770,000 Germans were admitted; the Scandinavian immigration, between 1881 and 1890 when more than 656,000 were admitted.

The period from 1830 to 1882 was characterized by varied attitudes toward immigrants. Since organized labor was still struggling to secure recognition as an integral ingredient within the American system of labor-management relations, opposition from the trade unions on economic grounds had as yet not reached its full strength. Manufacturers generally eagerly sought the cheap labor provided by successive waves of immigrant groups and were not anxious to see this flow impaired. However, considerable objection was raised to the admission of paupers, criminals, and other "undesirables" among the aliens, as well as to the increase of the Catholic element within the population. In particular, considerable opposition was directed against the Irish. Prior to the Civil War, the Know-Nothing movement gained widespread support, as nativistic sentiment was spurred on by economic competition and apprehension over the increasing number of culturally different Irish and German immigrants. The party blossomed from a splinter group into a political force that elected nine governors and displayed a striking measure of strength in state legislatures and Congress.

1882—A Turning Point. The year 1882 represents a turning point in the history of American immigration. It marked the climax of the movement of migrants from northern and western Europe to the United States and the beginning of the large-scale movement of migrants from southern and eastern Europe. It was also the time of the passage of the Chinese Exclusion Act, and it inaugurated the beginning of federal control of immigration in general. Included in the so-called new migration (as opposed to the "old" migration from England, Germany, Scandinavia, France, Holland, etc.) were the Italians, Poles, Jews, Greeks, Portuguese, Russians, and a varied assortment of other Slavs. Within the span of some twenty years there was a complete reversal in the proportions of immigrants from northern and western, and southern and eastern Europe. Whereas, in 1882, 87 per cent came from the former area and only 13 per cent from the latter, by 1907 the corresponding figures were 13 per cent and 81 per cent, respectively. In the decade from 1901 to 1910

Italy's 2 million immigrants alone exceeded the 1.9 million from all the countries of northern and western Europe combined. By virtue of significant cultural differences between the "new" immigrants and the native American population, as well as a variety of other factors, the "new" immigrants were considered less desirable than the "old." Whereas the "old" migration had been predominately Protestant except for Irish Catholics and some Catholic Germans, an overwhelming percentage of the new immigrants were Catholic, Jewish, or Greek Orthodox in religion.

With the turn of the twentieth century, public sentiment in favor of restricting immigration became intense and widespread. The farmlands of the Midwest had all been homesteaded, and the settlement of the West and Southwest was well underway. The great railroads had been built, and great industries were flourishing. The "new" migration flowed into the large cities where ethnic islands emerged. New York, Chicago, and other large cities each came to have its "Little Italy," "Little Poland," etc. Within these separate neighborhoods and communities, the native languages and customs were kept alive.

With the influx of the large-scale immigration from eastern and southern Europe and a marked increase in ethnic antipathies, Congress in 1907 authorized an immigration commission to make "full inquiry, examination, and investigation of immigration." Clearly, the United States was moving in the direction of a policy aimed at regulating and restricting immigration. As early as 1882, Congress had enacted a law prohibiting Chinese from entry, save for a small group of scholars, ministers, and merchants. In the same year, legislation was also passed excluding paupers, criminals, "lunatics," and other undesirables, and imposing a head tax. In 1884, contract labor was outlawed; in 1903, insane persons, beggars, and anarchists were added to the exclusion lists; between 1907 and 1910, new types of mental "defectives" and persons involved in crimes of "moral turpitude" were included; and in 1917, a literacy test was added. The inflow of Japanese had been curtailed in 1907 by an agreement between Japan and the United States.

Numerical Restriction of Immigration. Following World War I there occurred an upsurge in American isolationist sentiment, a wave of antipathy for immigrants and foreigners, and a mass fear of aliens as "Reds" and "radicals." Within this context Congress was finally persuaded to take direct action toward the numerical restriction of immigration, the result being the act of 1921. The purpose of the act was to curtail the total volume of immigration and to favor migrants from western and northern Europe. It provided for a quota system under which each nation was allocated an annual immigration allowance equal to 3 per cent of the number of its foreign-born in the United States as reported by the 1910 Census. As the quotas of 1921 still gave to the nations of the "new" migration a large share of the persons to be admitted each year, the law was revised in 1924. The act of 1924 established a new formula for computing a country's quota, based on 2 per cent of the number of people born in that country who were residing in the United States in 1890. In 1890 the flow of "new" immigrants had not been large enough to build up a large foreign-born population of southern- and eastern-European origin. The 1924 act also provided that beginning July 1, 1929, the quota of any country would have the same ratio to 150,000 as the number of persons of that national origin living in the United States had to the total population living in the United States, as determined by the 1920 Census. Table 3 lists the quotas under these acts and clearly suggests how they discriminated against immigrants from southern and eastern Europe. Under the quota system, an estimated 84 per cent of the quotas went to northern and western Europe and only 14 per cent to southern and eastern Europe. The act of 1924 also barred Orientals from migrating to the United States. However, these restrictions were largely removed during World War II, and under the act of 1952 Orientals were assigned a token quota.

Post World War II Legislation. A more recent step in legislation was the passage of the Immigration and Nationality Act of 1952. The act simplified the national-origins formula of the 1924 act by basing the annual quota on a flat $\frac{1}{6}$ per cent of the population according to the 1920 Census. By presidential action, new quotas were established in 1953 for each quota area, totaling 154,657. These quotas have been periodically revised. Congress has also passed a number of acts relating to the admission of displaced persons and refugees. The Displaced Persons Act of 1948 authorized the entry of certain displaced persons and refugees, without regard to the availability of quotas, but subject to charges against future quotas. The act expired in 1952, but in 1953 Congress authorized the issuance of 214,000 special non-quota visas until the end of 1956 to refugees from Communist-dominated nations. Similarly, special legislation was enacted in 1958 which permitted Hungarian refugees from the abortive 1956 revolution to enter the United States. It is important to note that the quota system actually provides only one-third of the yearly immigration into the United States. These supplementary laws have authorized the entry of hundreds of thousands of displaced

Table [3]. Annual Immigration Quotas, by Country, Under Successive
Immigration Laws and Amendments: 1921–1963

| Country | 1921 Act (3%, 1910) | 1924 Act | | 1952 Immigration and Nationality Act (as amended) |
		Effective 1924 (2%, 1890)	Effective 1929 (national-origin ratio)	
Total	356,995	164,667	153,714	156,987
Asia	1,043	1,300	1,323	3,290
Africa and Oceania	481	1,420	1,400	3,900
Europe	355,406	161,546	150,591	149,597
Northern and Western Europe				
Belgium	1,563	512	1,304	1,297
Denmark	5,694	2,789	1,181	1,175
France	5,729	3,954	3,086	3,069
Germany	68,059	51,227	25,957	25,814
Great Britain	77,342	34,007	65,721	65,361
Ireland		28,567	17,853	17,756
Netherlands	3,607	1,648	3,153	3,136
Norway	12,202	6,453	2,377	2,364
Sweden	20,042	9,561	3,314	3,295
Switzerland	3,752	2,081	1,707	1,698
Total, Northern and Western Europe	197,990	140,799	125,653	124,965
Southern and Eastern Europe				
Austria	7,451	785	1,413	1,405
Bulgaria	302	100	100	100
Czechoslovakia	14,282	3,073	2,874	2,859
Finland	3,921	471	569	566
Greece	3,294	100	307	308
Hungary	5,638	473	869	865
Italy	42,057	3,845	5,802	5,666
Poland	25,827	5,982	6,524	6,488
Portugal	2,520	503	440	438
Romania	7,419	603	295	289
Spain	912	131	252	250
Turkey	656	100	226	225
U.S.S.R.	34,284	2,248	2,784	2,697
Yugoslavia	6,426	671	845	942
Total, Southern and Eastern Europe	154,989	19,085	23,300	23,089

SOURCE: U.S. Bureau of the Census, *Statistical Abstract of the United States,* 1964,
91.

persons, political refugees, and others without regard to the quota system. In addition, Congress yearly approves thousands of individual "private" laws to permit the entry and naturalization of named individuals.

1965 Legislation. Critics charged that America's immigration laws judged persons by race and place of birth rather than personal worth to society. In response to this criticism Congress enacted new legislation in 1965 which provided for the abolishment of the old national-origins quota system after June 30, 1968. After this date an annual ceiling of 179,000 immigrants will apply on a basis of strict equality to all nations of the world outside the Western Hemisphere. There will be no country-by-country quotas, and the national of an Asian or African country will receive the same consideration as a citizen of Great Britain or France. No country, however, will be allowed more than 20,000 immigrant visas in a single year.

After June 30, 1968, an overall ceiling of 120,000 annually will apply to the Western Hemisphere, but without the 20,000 country-by-country limitation. This will be the first time that such a restriction has been placed on immigration from Canada and the independent nations of Latin America and the Caribbean. The new legislation gives preference to applicants chiefly on the basis of (1) family ties to Americans and (2) occupational skills in short supply in the United States. Whereas the Statue of Liberty bears the inscription "Give me your tired, your poor, your huddled masses yearning to breathe," the immigration pattern that will ensue under the new legislation will be "Give me chiefly your skilled workers and trained professionals."

Internal Migration

In both urban and rural areas of the United States the proportions of foreign-born are steadily declining. Foreign-born persons who die are simply not being replaced by other foreigners. The immigrants' place in the social and economic life of American cities is being taken by migrants from rural areas within the United States. The major rural groups migrating to American cities are Negroes, Puerto Ricans, Mexican-Americans, and white southern "hillbillies." These groups differ from the immigrants in that they are American citizens and, except for some Puerto Ricans and Mexican-Americans, their native language is English. The migrants have taken over many of the unskilled, low-paying, low-status jobs vacated by the immigrants who are declining in numbers and ascending the status ladder. As did the bulk of the immigrants before them, these migrants from rural America face the dual burdens of poverty and urban inexperience.

The so-called "hillbillies" present a good example of the norms, values, beliefs, and general habits that lower-class rural groups bring to the urban environment. Although Protestant, native white descendants of early Anglo-Saxon Americans, these migrants from the Southern Appalachian and Ozark regions constitute a minority group within a number of our large cities. Their way of life often conflicts with that of other urban dwellers:

Settling in deteriorating neighborhoods where they can stick with their own kind, they live as much as they can the way they lived back home. Often removing window screens, they sit half-dressed where it is cooler, and dispose of garbage the quickest way. . . .

Their children play freely anywhere, without supervision. Fences and hedges break down; lawns go back to dirt. On the crowded city streets, children are unsafe, and their parents seem oblivious. Even more, when it comes to sex training, their habits—with respect to such matters as incest and statutory rape—are clearly at variance with urban legal requirements, and parents fail to appreciate the interest authorities take in their sex life.[1]

The rural background of the "hillbillies" has ill-prepared them for the highly formal, circumscribed behavior required by American industrial life. The "hillbillies," used to individual work on farms or in hunting and fishing, carry over into the factory the habit of working at their own pace, a practice incompatible with highly coordinated industrial operations. As yet not fully committed to the city, workers often quit their jobs and fall back upon their rural kin for support or take weekends to go "home" for family occasions. Some even limit their city sojourn to the winter months when they are not needed on the farm. Absenteeism and unreliability lead to low seniority and little advancement. Within the city, the migrants, many of whom are young adults, are freed from traditional moral codes; sexual transgressions and general demoralization are a frequent result. The difficulties experienced by the "hillbillies" are all the more distinctive because the group has no "strikes" against it in terms of race, religion, or national origin.

[1] Albert N. Votaw, "The Hillbillies Invade Chicago," *Harper's Magazine*, February, 1958, p. 65.

James W. Vander Zanden

STRATIFICATION BASED UPON RACIAL
AND ETHNIC MEMBERSHIP

Most of us are familiar with sociological analyses which examine social stratification through socioeconomic criteria. Seldom do we come into contact, however, with analyses which are addressed to stratification based upon religious, ethnic, and racial membership. Still less often do we encounter accounts of the relationship between these modes of stratification.

In the following selection, James W. Vander Zanden offers a brief descriptive account of the distinction between these two patterns of stratification. He points out why and when it is essential to keep these distinctions in mind.

Within American life there is, in addition to the stratification structure based upon social class, that based upon religious, ethnic, and racial membership. These two sets of stratification structures crisscross. A general formulation of this principle is found in Hollingshead's statement that a social structure may be "differentiated *vertically* along racial, ethnic and religious lines, and each of these vertical cleavages, in turn, is differentiated *horizontally* by a series of strata or classes that are encompassed within it. . . ." [1] Thus religious, ethnic, and racial groups are not arranged in a simple higher and lower ranking with respect to the class stratification system. Each of the religious, ethnic, and racial groups tends to span a range of higher and lower positions within the class structure, sometimes from the top to the bottom, sometimes within a narrower range. The most critical consequence of these two stratification structures is that members of a minority group who achieve mobility into a higher class are not accorded many of the benefits bestowed upon members of the dominant group of the equivalent class.

From James W. Vander Zanden, "Stratification Based Upon Racial and Ethnic Membership," *American Minority Relations, The Sociology of Race and Ethnic Groups,* Second Edition (New York: The Ronald Press Company, 1966), pp. 269–271. Some footnotes omitted. Copyright © 1966 by The Ronald Press Company and reprinted with their permission.

[1] August B. Hollingshead, "Trends in Social Stratification," *American Sociological Review,* 18 (1952), 679–686.

The two systems need to be kept conceptually separate in order to discover the nature of their interrelationships. An illustration will help to clarify the matter. How does A, member of the old-American group and the "working class," articulate his status attitude toward B, a member of the Jewish (or Italian or Polish or Negro) group who has a high "middle class" status? In terms of the class hierarchy, the minority-group member would outrank the member of the old-American group. But, in terms of the ethnic or racial structure, the reverse situation would hold true. Reciprocally, the question becomes: How does B articulate his status attitude in relation to A? Do the attitudes of one stratification structure, either the ethnic and racial or class structure, tend to prevail? Do confusion and tension ensue from the crisscrossing of the two sets of patterns within specific behavior situations?

The answers to these questions in part depend upon whether individual B is a member of the Jewish, Italian, Polish, or Negro group. The resolution of the matter would quite probably be reversed in some circumstances in the case of an Italian, on the one hand, and a Negro, on the other—the attitudes of the class structure tending to prevail in the former case, the attitudes of the racial and ethnic structure in the latter. Everett C. Hughes points to the dilemma of the Negro professional man: "The dilemma, for those whites who meet such a person, is that of having to choose whether to treat him as a Negro or as a member of his profession." [2] Similarly, within this situation the Negro professional faces a dilemma as to the choice of his proper role. In the realm of social organization, such matters are likely to be avoided by an "elaboration of social segregation," where the Negro professional man may serve only Negro clients. Where a white client makes use of a Negro's professional services, the contact is likely to remain purely professional and specific, rarely extended into a general social relationship.

The importance of keeping these two systems conceptually separate is seen in still another connection. It is known that family, clique, associational, and social relationships tend to be confined to members of one's own or closely adjoining classes. To what extent does the ethnic or racial factor divide the intimate group life of members of the same social class? By way of illustration, do middle-class Jews have more intimate social contacts with middle-class gentiles or with lower-class Jews? The same question can be asked of Italians, Poles, and Negroes in relation to the old-American group. The matter again depends to a considerable ex-

[2] Everett Cherrington Hughes, "Dilemmas and Contradictions of Status," *American Journal of Sociology*, L :1945), 357.

tent upon the ranking of the ethnic or racial minority on the social-distance scale.

The distinction between the two systems is similarly of importance in considering social mobility, that is, the movement of people up and down the stratification hierarchy. In situations where the accent falls on democratic relations, status ideally is determined by what an individual can *do,* not by what he *is.* A distinction can be made between these two types of status, that is, between *achieved* status and *ascribed* status. Ascribed statuses are assigned to individuals, without reference to ability, on the basis of such characteristics as sex, age, and family membership. Achieved statuses are acquired by individuals through competition and individual effort. Within the ethnic and racial structure of stratification, status is ascribed to the individual by the society; it is not rooted in his own competitive or individual effort. On the other hand, within the class structure, there is greater room for the achievement of status, although complete achievement often is limited by inheritance and unequal access to opportunities, both of which tend to be associated with family membership. To the extent to which status is ascribed (e.g., on the basis of religious, ethnic, and racial membership), social mobility within a social order is impaired; to the extent to which status is achieved, social mobility is facilitated.

David B. Tyack

BECOMING AN AMERICAN: THE EDUCATION OF THE IMMIGRANT

From 1815 to 1915, over thirty-five million people of very diverse ethnic origins came to this country. During this period the public schools were expected to make these diverse peoples into one people. David B. Tyack presents an historical overview of the response of the schools to this enormous task and points out some of the dysfunctions this response engendered involving the child and his family. What Tyack describes as taking place in the schools several decades ago is not unlike what is taking place today concerning ethnicity.

David B. Tyack is Associate Professor of History and Education at Stanford University.

The rolling waves of immigrants to the United States posed a sharp challenge to the common school. During the hundred years following

From David B. Tyack, *Turning Points in American Educational History* (Boston, Mass.: Copyright © 1967 by Ginn & Company), pp. 228–234. Reprinted by permission of the publisher.

1815 over thirty-five million people came to this country in the greatest migration in history. Germany contributed the largest number, followed in order by Italy, Ireland, Great Britain, Austria-Hungary, Russia, and scores of other nations. Facing public education was the task of transforming these millions of newcomers—speaking dozens of languages, clinging to diverse folkways, owing multiple loyalties—into one people: *e pluribus unum.*

Although Americanization occurred in countless ways outside the classroom, a special burden rested upon the common school, for it was one institution which reached most of the young. In concert with other social agencies, formal and informal, schools accelerated the process of assimilation. German farmers who had retained their language and customs for centuries when transplanted to Russia became Americanized in one generation when they settled in Eureka, South Dakota. Children of parents who spoke a babel of tongues in the iron mines of the Mesabi range were taught meticulously correct English in the Minnesota grammar and high schools. Urban school systems prodded some young men and women to climb out of the ghettoes to positions of affluence and influence.

Naturally, assimilation of ethnic groups proceeded at different paces in different environments, and immigrants adapted to American mores often only in a grudging and superficial manner. Americanization normally meant discarding old customs and values. Hence successful assimilation often disrupted families and sowed doubt and recrimination between the generations. Some of these conflicts of cultures still reverberate in American society.

In order to Americanize, schoolmen first had to decide who was this new man, the American. In 1782 Crèvecoeur had asked this question and concluded that "this promiscuous breed, that race, now called Americans" had been the oppressed of Europe who had been regenerated in America by "new laws, a new mode of living, a new social system." These attitudes and institutions shaped the newcomer from the moment he stepped off the boat. Thus Crèvecoeur and DuPont de Nemours, Frenchmen, and Thomas Paine, Englishman, could become instant Americans. Although native Americans like Noah Webster might be self-conscious and nervous about the nature of "Americanism," Paine and Crèvecoeur could describe it confidently. As time passed, native citizens came increasingly to believe that American beliefs and folkways should be fixed not fluid, homogeneous not pluralistic. In 1835 the Ohio reformer Calvin Stowe warned teachers that "it is altogether essential to our national strength and peace, if not even to our national existence, that the foreigners who settle on our soil, should cease to be Europeans and become Americans. . . ." The schools must create a national feeling, a unity of thought and action, for "nothing could be more fatal to our prospects . . . than to have our population become a congeries of clans, congregating without coalescing, and condemned to contiguity without sympathy." Only deliberate effort "to shape the rising generation to our own model" in schools common to all could prevent this disaster. Though foreign adults might resist assimilation, their children might "re-act on the parents, and the young become the teachers of the old."

The process of uprooting and transplantation awoke immigrants to their own distinctiveness; for the first time they learned what it meant to be an "Italian" or "Polish" by living in a land where their mores were not self-evident and unquestioned. And in turn, Americans were forced to define their own values more self-consciously in the process of teaching them to the newcomers. In the textbooks American heroes and history were glorified, often at the cost of other nations. The English language taught in the schools was largely prescriptive, its grammar artificial and usage canonical, as if to build barriers against foreign corruptions. And as Sara O'Brien demonstrated in her *English for Foreigners*, Americanization required clean hands, regular use of the tooth brush, a balanced diet, patient industry, neat dress, and an idyllic middle-class family life. The version of politics she taught was the Mugwump-Progressive ideal: immigrants should vote for the trained and disinterested public servant. If the strangers were dirty, ignorant of proper dress and food, linguistically barbaric, prone to elect corrupt bosses and to listen to demagogues, they must be taught otherwise. Often the most ardent Americanizers in the schools were teachers who came from second or third generation immigrant families.

In the middle of the nineteenth century hope ran high that the schools could unify the nation and that the hybrid people would be stronger than the native stock alone. "Let them be like grafts which become branches of the parent stock," said Stowe of the immigrants, "improve its fruit, and add to its beauty and its vigor; and not like the parasitical mistletoe, which never incorporates itself with the trunk from which it derives its nourishment, but exhausts its sap, withers its foliage, despoils it of its strength, and sooner or later, by destroying its supporter, involves itself in ruin."

Despite the usual reverence expressed toward the family in the textbooks and in the official culture of the school, teachers were in effect telling children that they must change their ways and not emulate their parents. The public schools became a wedge splitting immigrant children from their parents. When children entered the doors of the public school, they passed into a world unfamiliar to their elders, one which seemed to teach them to scorn inherited traditions. "Well, look what happens when we send our children to school," one immigrant mother exclaimed. "All they learn is to despise us. Look how they talk back to us!" Parents turned to their children for interpretation of the new society; their authority undermined, they lamented that the young were disrespectful and unmanageable. One boy was haled into court for resisting his Italian father's discipline and retorted "Well, Judge, honest now, do you think an American ought to let himself be licked by a foreigner?" Although pained by the disintegration of the family and the frequent contempt of the children for foreign folkways, parents were ambivalent about the school. Like Mary Antin's father, many also hoped that education would open a door for their sons and daughters into the privileges of American society.

The child, caught in a conflict of cultures, could not often conform to the expectations of both the public school and the immigrant family. In a city ghetto the public school might simply be an unreal world whose rituals bore little meaning within the ethnic island. When the immigrant child was in a minority, adult pressures to conform to American customs were powerfully assisted by the child's peers. Ridicule was a rapid Americanizer. The Chinese boy's pigtail, the Mexican girl's tortilla, the Italian child's baroque accent—these often disappeared as a result of belittling comments or schoolyard scuffles. And sometimes even kindness cut; Elizabeth Stein recalled that her schoolmates pitied her when she opened her lunch of gefüllte fish—thinking that she had squashed her lunch—and offered her their own sandwiches and dessert.

Now and then stalwarts stood up to the homogenizers. A teacher asked the Armenian Bagdasar Krekor Bagdigian what his name was. She replied in dismay "Oh, give that up and change your name to Smith, Jones, or a name like that and become Americanized. Give up everything you brought with you from the old country." Furious, Bagdigian refused, thinking to himself, "The Turkish sword did not succeed in making me a Turk and now this hare-brained woman is trying to make an American out of me." For some children the street gang became a means of identity apart from the orthodoxy of the home and the orthodoxy of the school. It was a group where adolescents might determine their own system of status and recognition.

Many immigrant groups supported, often at great sacrifice, their own private schools designed to perpetuate their religious and ethnic heritage. Norwegian Lutherans in Minnesota, Polish Catholics in Chicago, Russian Jews in Boston created their own educational systems, sometimes to supplement the public schools and sometimes to compete with them, but always to preserve their own culture. They juxtaposed their own ethnocentrism against American ethnocentrism, but by the second or third generation Americanism partially won: the children spoke English, preferred American folkways, blended with the general population at work, and retained ethnic peculiarities chiefly in their private lives and in their social circle (and sometimes in their religious and political associations as well).

The common school changed the immigrant, but the immigrant altered the school, too. The teacher in a ghetto classroom could not take familiar skills and attitudes for granted; now it was essential to take over a whole realm of duties formerly performed by the family. Teachers often gave children baths, taught them manners, proper dress, names for familiar objects. The teacher could no longer assume that a child knew how to speak English; in one school in New York, for example, there were twenty-five different nationalities. These difficulties staggered even the most dedicated and energetic teacher. In the large and heterogeneous classes—often containing fifty or more children of a half-dozen nationalities—strict routine reigned. Teachers were trained to believe that the school should start from scratch in implanting correct ideas and behavior; the children's background and environment were not to be trusted.

To the child the school might have meant bells clanging, seats bolted in long rows, silent marches in lines down dark corridors, books full of unfamiliar people and strange imperatives, an omniscient power structure represented by the Principal. But it was also one of the few places where there were no quarreling adults, roving gangs, or smells of leaking gas or rotting garbage; one of the few places where he could sit in a clean, warm, well-lighted room, secure in the routine, though probably a bit bored. Often school was the main contact a ghetto child had with the wider society, and on the quality of this experience depended much of his desire to defy or to become a part of that society.

The community expected the school to be policeman as well as parent-surrogate. One principal, Angelo Patri, heard all sorts of complaints from people who thought the schools should *do* something about children's misbehavior: a candy peddler whose beard was pulled by some boys; a sign painter who charged that rogues had stolen his ladder and left him perched high over the sidewalk; a delicatessen owner complaining that Rachel was in the habit of stealing dill pickles. Patri accepted the notion that the teacher was "responsible for what the child does out of school." How otherwise, he asked, "can the teacher ever know that her world counts in the life of the child?"

Anxiously, Americans turned to the common schools to solve problems larger than stolen pickles and yanked beards. A fear of ethnic diversity, of corruption, of class conflict led one superintendent of schools to conceive of public education as a para-military organization. "Its army of half a million teachers, sustained by popular devotion to the cause, must in times of peace and through peaceful measures fight this continuous battle for the perpetuity of national life," he declared. "This army stands today holding the hands and hearts of tomorrow's nation. To make a citizenship whose intelligence, moral rectitude, and steadfast virtues will counteract . . . disintegrating forces and social disorders is the function and mission of our public schools."

In the late 1880's and 1890's, especially after panic over the Haymarket riot, schoolmen worried increasingly about teaching patriotism. They grew lyrical over flag rituals and patriotic badges. They held nationalistic ceremonies in the schools, inviting parents to attend. Teachers began to pay more and more attention to civics and United States history. In Frontenac, Kansas, a mining town where almost 88 per cent of the parents were foreign born, pupils studied American history in the sixth, seventh, eighth, and ninth grades, in addition to learning about American heroes in the lower grades. The climax of patriotic instruction came in the years of World War I, when many citizens feared the "hyphenated Americans" as a domestic fifth column and sought to stamp out, in particular, the German language and vestiges of German culture. "What kind of American consciousness can grow in the atmosphere of sauerkraut and limburger cheese?" asked one super-patriot.

Although the schools reached most of the children of the foreign born —and thereby indirectly influenced the parents—little attention was paid to formal schooling of adult immigrants until the early twentieth century. Voluntary associations of native Americans, such as the Daughters of the American Revolution, the Y.M.C.A., and employers' groups, as well as the immigrants' own mutual benefit associations and charities, did accomplish a good deal in introducing foreigners to American ideas and institutions, but haphazardly in comparison with the public schools.

By the second decade of the twentieth century, however, the federal, state, and local governments became interested in Americanizing the adult immigrant. The resulting adult education was not very successful. In Passaic, New Jersey workers explained that they were too tired to go to school after ten or more hours of labor and said that they had to work at night when the classes were held. Adults complained of the teaching methods and condescension of the instructors: "They treat you like a child because you don't know English." In time teachers became better trained and public funds flowed into the work more freely. But compulsion was lacking, and only a small percentage of the adult immigrants attended schools.

In the period of the common school crusade schoolmen had been hopeful that the hybrid but uniform American produced by public education and social assimilation would surpass both native and immigrant stock. Toward the end of the nineteenth century, however, racist myths about the inferiority of the "new immigrants" undermined faith in schooling as well as belief in the value of ethnic mixture. Bogus anthropologists divided the peoples of Europe into "races" and popularizers were quick to brand the "Teuton" or "Nordic" race superior to the "Alpine," "Mediterranean," and Jewish breeds. Immigration during the three decades before World War I consisted largely of people from southern and eastern Europe. These "new immigrants" were "illiterate, docile, lacking in self-reliance and initiative, and not possessing the Anglo-Saxon conceptions of law, order, and government," the educator Ellwood Cubberley complained in 1909. "Their coming has served to dilute tremendously our national stock, and to corrupt our national life." Cubberley believed that the only hope was to break up the ghettoes, for the nation was "afflicted with a serious case of racial indigestion."

While educated men began to doubt the possibility of Americanizing these new "racial" groups—with their inferior hereditary characteristics—red-neck nativists were unequivocal about the menace. "Ominous statistics proclaim the persistent development of a parasitic mass within our domain," said the Imperial Wizard of the Ku Klux Klan. "Our political system is clogged with foreign bodies which stubbornly refuse to be absorbed, and means must be found to meet the menace. We have taken unto ourselves a Trojan horse crowded with ignorance, illiteracy, and envy." Xenophobia in the postwar years, resurgence of strong nativist feeling, fear of economic competition from cheap foreign labor, and racist ideology combined to produce the climate of opinion in which Congress passed two immigration restriction bills in 1921 and 1924. The latter, especially, was based on the premise of the inferiority of the southern and eastern European immigrants. Not until 1965 was the quota system based on "racial" origins abolished. The restrictive laws represented, among other convictions, a decline of faith in assimilation through the common school, a fear that ethnic differences defied eradication through education.

Especially in the twentieth century a number of Americans questioned the wisdom of trying to eradicate ethnic differences. Diversity, said these pluralists, was a blessing, not a curse. What should the United States be, asked Horace Kallen, "—a unison, singing the old Anglo-Saxon theme 'America,' the America of the New England school, or a harmony, in which that theme shall be dominant, perhaps, among others, but one among many, not the only one?" The cultural pluralists quarreled with the social worker who reported "not yet Americanized; still eating Italian food." The children of immigrants should be taught to respect their parents' traditions, said a student of the *Social and Religious Life of Italians in America:* "When I discuss the matter with teachers in the public schools, I become aware that they possess a holy terror of teaching the language and history of Italy." Was it not the American nativist who was most guilty of clannishness?

From the time of the Revolution forward, substantial numbers of Americans supposed that the free citizen was the uniform man, that diversity somehow endangered the promise of American life since it threatened cohesiveness. Others saw a free society as a place where it was safe to be unpopular, comfortable to be different. The common school in successive decades expressed both points of view in differing degrees, seeking to strike the precarious balance of ordered liberty. The task of Americanizing the immigrant posed in all its complexity the problem of unity within diversity.

There is no shortage of illustrative material for the issue dealt with in this chapter. One need only turn to black studies or to those demands for alternatives to the public schools occasioned by a desire to enrich cultural and ethnic differences. The reader is invited, therefore, to search the literature and draw from it information which illustrates the ethnicity issue. The issue "How should the schools deal with ethnicity?" is illustrated here in some very early as well as recent writings.

Jane Addams

THE PUBLIC SCHOOL AND
THE IMMIGRANT CHILD

This selection focuses on some of the difficulties, particularly familial, which follow from educating ethnics without regard for their ethnic values and traditions. Published in 1908, Jane Addams' paper argued—way back then—for what many persons concerned with the question of ethnicity are arguing for now: to rely upon ethnic traditions and cultures to enhance and enrich formal schooling experiences. Those who would agree with Miss Addams' suggestions would also agree that few if any educators have listened to her perceptive insights. Jane Addams, of course, was the founder of Hull House in Chicago and the "mother" of modern social work.

I am always diffident when I come before a professional body of teachers, realizing as I do that it is very easy for those of us who look on to bring indictments against results; and realizing also that one of the most difficult situations you have to meet is the care and instruction of the immigrant child, especially as he is found where I see him, in the midst of crowded city conditions.

And yet in spite of the fact that the public school is the great savior of the immigrant district, and the one agency which inducts the children into the changed conditions of American life, there is a certain indictment which may justly be brought, in that the public school too often separates the child from his parents and widens that old gulf between fathers and sons which is never so cruel and so wide as it is between the immigrants who come to this country and their children who have gone to the public school and feel that they have there learned it all. The parents are thereafter subjected to certain judgment, the judgment of the young which is always harsh and in this instance founded upon the most superficial standard of Americanism. And yet there is a notion of culture which we would define as a knowledge of those things which have been long cherished by men, the things which men have loved because thru generations they have softened and interpreted life, and have endowed it with value and meaning. Could this standard have been given rather

From *NEA Addresses and Proceedings* (1908), pp. 99–102. Reprinted by permission of the National Education Association.

than the things which they see about them as the test of so-called success, then we might feel that the public school has given at least the beginnings of culture which the child ought to have. At present the Italian child goes back to its Italian home more or less disturbed and distracted by the contrast between the school and the home. If he throws off the control of the home because it does not represent the things which he has been taught to value he takes the first step toward the Juvenile Court and all the other operations of the law, because he has prematurely asserted himself long before he is ready to take care of his own affairs.

We find in the carefully prepared figures which . . . sociologists have published that while the number of arrests of immigrants is smaller than the arrests of native born Americans, the number of arrests among children of immigrants is twice as large as the number of arrests among the children of native born Americans. It would seem that in spite of the enormous advantages which the public school gives to these children it in some way loosens them from the authority and control of their parents, and tends to send them, without a sufficient rudder and power of self-direction, into the perilous business of living. Can we not say, perhaps, that the schools ought to do more to connect these children with the best things of the past, to make them realize something of the beauty and charm of the language, the history, and the traditions which their parents represent. It is easy to cut them loose from their parents, it requires cultivation to tie them up in sympathy and understanding. The ignorant teacher cuts them off because he himself cannot understand the situation, the cultivated teacher fastens them because his own mind is open to the charm and beauty of that old-country life. In short, it is the business of the school to give to each child the beginnings of a culture so wide and deep and universal that he can interpret his own parents and countrymen by a standard which is world-wide and not provincial.

The second indictment which may be brought is the failure to place the children into proper relation toward the industry which they will later enter . . . [C]hildren go into industry for a very short time. I believe that the figures of the United States census show the term to be something like six years for the women in industry as over against twenty-four years for men, in regard to continuity of service. Yet you cannot disregard the six years of the girls nor the twenty-four years of the boys, because they are the immediate occupation into which they enter after they leave the school—even the girls are bound to go thru that period —that is, the average immigrant girls are—before they enter the second serious business of life and maintain homes of their own. Therefore, if they enter industry unintelligently, without some notion of what it means, they find themselves totally unprepared for their first experience with American life, they are thrown out without the proper guide or clue which the public school might and ought to have given them. Our industry has become so international, that it ought to be easy to use the materials it offers for immigrant children. The very processes and general principles which industry represents give a chance to prepare these immigrant children in a way which the most elaborated curriculum could not present. Ordinary material does not give the same international suggestion as industrial material does.

Third, I do not believe that the children who have been cut off from their own parents are going to be those who, when they become parents themselves, will know how to hold a family together and to connect it with the state. I should begin to teach the girls to be good mothers by teaching them to be good daughters. Take a girl whose mother has come from South Italy. The mother cannot adjust herself to the changed condition of housekeeping, does not know how to wash and bake here, and do the other things which she has always done well in Italy, because she has suddenly been transported from a village to a tenement house. If that girl studies these household conditions in relation to the past and to the present needs of the family, she is undertaking the very best possible preparation for her future obligations to a household of her own. And to my mind she can undertake it in no better way. Her own children are mythical and far away, but the little brothers and sisters pull upon her affection and her loyalty, and she longs to have their needs recognized in the school so that the school may give her some help. Her mother complains that the baby is sick in America because she cannot milk her own goat; she insists if she had her own goat's milk the baby would be quite well and flourishing, as the children were in Italy. If that girl can be taught that the milk makes the baby ill because it is not clean and be provided with a simple test that she may know when milk is clean, it may take her into the study not only of the milk within the four walls of the tenement house, but into the inspection of the milk of her district. The milk, however, remains good educational material, it makes even more concrete the connection which you would be glad to use between the household and the affairs of the American city. Let her not follow the mother's example of complaining about changed conditions; let her rather make the adjustment for her mother's entire household. We cannot tell what adjustments the girl herself will be called upon to make ten years from now; but we can give her the clue and the aptitude to adjust the family with which she is identified to the constantly changing conditions of city life. Many of us feel that, splendid as the public schools are in their relation to the immigrant child, they do not understand all of the difficulties which surround the child—all of the moral and emotional perplexities which constantly harass him. The children long that the school teacher should know something about the lives their parents lead and should be able to reprove the hooting children who make fun of the Italian mother because she wears a kerchief on her head, not only because they are rude but also because they are stupid. We send young people to Europe to see Italy, but we do not utilize Italy when it lies about the schoolhouse. If the body of teachers in our great cities could take hold of the immigrant colonies, could bring out of them their handicrafts and occupations, their traditions, their folk songs and folk lore, the beautiful stories which every immigrant colony is ready to tell and translate; could get the children to bring these things into school as the material from which culture is made and the material upon which culture is based, they would discover by comparison that which they give them now is a poor meretricious and vulgar thing. Give these children a chance to utilize the historic and industrial material which they see about them and they will begin to have a sense of ease in America, a first consciousness of being at home. I believe if these people are welcomed upon the basis of the resources which they represent and the contributions which they bring, it may come to pass that these schools which deal with immigrants will find that they have a wealth of cultural and industrial material which will make the schools in other neighborhoods positively envious. A girl living in a tenement household, helping along this tremendous adjustment, healing over this great moral upheaval which the parents have suffered and which leaves them bleeding and sensitive—such a girl has a richer experience and a finer material than any girl from a more fortunate household can have at the present moment.

I wish I had the power to place before you what it seems to me is the opportunity that the immigrant colonies present to the public school: the most endearing occupation of leading the little child, who will in turn lead his family, and bring them with him into the brotherhood for which they are longing. The immigrant child cannot make this demand upon the school because he does not know how to formulate it; it is for the teacher both to perceive it and to fulfil it.

A person even with a minimum of interest in current events as they relate to education will be aware that there is a great controversy over ethnicity and the role of the school concerning this phenomenon. Yet, other than a substantial body of literature dealing with the pathology of inter-ethnic relations, very little has been published on the retention of ethnic orientations, the present situation of ethnic groups, and the role of education in relation to them. This lack of published material may very well reflect the deemphasis on ethnicity which many knowledgeable people claim has contributed to the controversy with which we are now faced. We hope that the following analytical selections will contribute to a better understanding of ethnicity in American society.

Andrew M. Greeley

WHAT IS AN ETHNIC?

The first selection is intended, as the title suggests, to get at the meaning of "ethnic." The author points out that any definition of the word is bound to have its shortcomings and to raise several questions. He is convinced, however, that attempts at definition and attempts to deal conscientiously with the questions that follow are both necessary if ethnic issues are to be taken seriously.

Andrew M. Greeley is the author of over a dozen books and numerous articles. He is a Roman Catholic priest, Director of the National Opinion Research Center at the University of Chicago, and Professor of Education at the University of Illinois, Chicago Circle.

It is very difficult to speak precisely about what an ethnic group is, but it is possible to develop a working definition somewhat empirically and to describe ethnicity by showing how contemporary ethnic groups came into existence. While . . . there is some broad equation possible between ethnic groups and immigrant groups, it is not enough merely to say that the ethnic groups are immigrant groups. Whatever definition we emerge with is likely to leave us with some very embarrassing questions. For example: Does everyone belong to an ethnic group? Is a white Anglo-Saxon Protestant an ethnic? Are Texans or Kentuckians, for example, ethnics? And what about American intellectuals, particularly those who are not Jewish and who seem to be quite cut off from any trace of nationality background? Do they constitute a new ethnic

From Andrew M. Greeley, *Why Can't They Be Like Us?* (New York: Institute of Human Relations Press, 1969), pp. 15–30. Some footnotes omitted. Copyright 1969, The American Jewish Committee. All rights reserved. Reprinted by permission of Institute of Human Relations Press.

group? Such questions do not admit of quick answers; yet we must address ourselves to them if only because there are a number of Americans who are not prepared to take ethnic issues seriously unless responses to those questions are provided.

The ancestors of the immigrants to the United States were, for the most part, peasants living in the agricultural communities of European post-feudal society. This society was post-feudal in the sense that the peasants either owned some land of their own, or at least had been emancipated from the worst rigors of the feudal system. The peasant villages of Ireland, Germany, Italy, Poland or the Balkans were not the most comfortable places in the world, and the nostalgia bordering on romance over them that is to be found in the works of some 19th-century sociological writers is misleading. Granted that post-feudal peasant society provided a great deal of stability, it did so at the price of stagnancy; and granted also that it provided a great deal of social support, it did so by imposing a great deal of social control. A man was, indeed, sure of who he was and where he stood and what he might become in such societies, but most men were in inferior positions and had no expectation of becoming anything more than inferior.

Nevertheless, there was a warmth and intimacy and closeness in these peasant communities. A person could be sure of the pattern of relationships and be sure that while he might have enemies, he also had friends, and the friends and enemies were defined by historic tradition. Society indeed controlled individual members, but it also rallied support, strength and resources when help was needed. It was a highly personal world, not in the sense that the dignity of the human person was respected more than it is today, but in the sense that relationships were, for the most part, between persons who knew each other, understood their respective roles, and knew what kind of behavior to expect. Family, church and community were all fairly simple and overwhelmingly important, and though mankind had evolved beyond the all-pervading intimacy of the tribe or the clan, life was nonetheless quite personal and intimate in a stylized and highly structured way.

Some time after 1800, European peasant society began to break up, partly because, as the population increased, there were more people than jobs in the agricultural communes, and partly because the emergent industrialization in the cities desperately needed new labor. Those who made the move from commune to metropolis in hope of finding a better life began a number of social trends which actually meant a better life, if not for them, at least for their children or their grandchildren.

The pilgrimage from peasant village to city, and later to the cities of America, brought to many the wealth of the affluent society.

But something was also lost: the warmth and intimacy, the social support of the commune was gone. Gabriel Le Bras, the famous French sociologist of religion, remarked that there was a certain railroad station in Paris which apparently had magical powers, because any Breton immigrant who passed through that station never set foot in a Catholic church again. The church, the family, the commune which had provided the parameters of the ordinary person's life were all either destroyed or so substantially altered as to be unrecognizable. The peasant migrant was forced to spend most of his waking day with people who were strangers. This is an experience which does not seem peculiar to us at all, but to a man who had encountered few strangers ever before in his life, it was frightening and disorienting.

"Our Own Kind"

In the strangeness of the new environment, the individual or his battered and bedraggled family looked around for someone with whom he had something in common—hopefully a place in the big city where previous migrants from his village had settled. Because such settlers were "his kind of people," he could trust them; they knew their obligations to him and would help him to adjust to this new world in which he found himself. Thus, in the Italian neighborhoods of New York's lower east side in the early 1920's it was possible to trace, block by block, not only the region in Italy but also the very villages from which the inhabitants had come. Indeed, it is no exaggeration to say that some of these blocks were nothing more than foreign colonies of Sicilian villages.

If you weren't able to find someone from your own village, then you searched for someone from your area of the country; even though you may never have met him before, you could depend on him to have some of the same values you had, and you shared some sort of common origin. He may not have been from Palermo, but at least he was a Sicilian; he may not have been from Ballyhaunis, but at least he was from County Mayo; and these village or regional groupings, based especially on family and kinship relationships, in their turn sought protection and some power against the strange world in which they found themselves by banding together, one with another. So that for many groups, as Glazer has pointed out, the nationality became a relevant factor only when the necessities of adjusting to American experience forced the village and regional groups to band together.

The ethnic group provided a pool of preferred associates for the intimate areas of life. It was perhaps necessary in large corporate structures to interact with whomever the random possibilities of the economic system put at the next workbench or desk. But when it came to choosing a wife, a poker (and later on, bridge) partner, a precinct captain, a doctor, a lawyer, a real estate broker, a construction contractor, a clergyman and, later on, a psychiatrist, a person was likely to feel much more at ease if he could choose "my kind of people."

So then, as Max Weber defines it, an ethnic group is a human collectivity based on an assumption of common origin, real or imaginary; and E. K. Francis, supplementing the Weber definition, has argued that the ethnic collectivity represents an attempt on the part of men to keep alive, in their pilgrimage from peasant village to industrial metropolis, some of the diffuse, descriptive, particularistic modes of behavior that were common in the past. The ethnic group was created only when the peasant commune broke up, and was essentially an attempt to keep some of the values, some of the informality, some of the support, some of the intimacy of the communal life in the midst of an impersonal, formalistic rationalized, urban, industrial society.

That the immigrants tried to associate with their own kind was understandable enough in the early phases of immigration, but we are still faced with the necessity of explaining why ethnic groups have persisted as important collectivities long after the immigration trauma receded into the background. Why was not social class the membership around which American city dwellers could rally, as it was in England? Why have the trade unions rarely, if ever, played quite the fraternal role in American society that they have in many continental societies? Granted that urban man needed something to provide him with some sort of identification between his family and the impersonal metropolis, why did he stick with the ethnic group when there were other groupings to which he could make a strong emotional commitment?

First of all, one must acknowledge the fact that other groups have, on occasion, provided the same enthusiasm that ethnic groups do. Some men need more of this enthusiasm than others, and by no means all who need it seek it in a nationality group. As a matter of fact, it is probably likely that for many, at least at the present stage of acculturation, religion is more important than ethnicity as a means of social definition and social support, a means of identifying ourselves in relation to others.

However, religion and ethnicity are so intertwined in the United States that it is extremely difficult to separate them; an attempt to sort out this relationship is one of the major challenges facing social theorists who become concerned with ethnic groups.

Pluralism and Group Survival

It seems to me that there were two factors which made for the survival of ethnic communities after the immigration trauma was over. First of all, the United States is a society which has demonstrated considerable ability in coping with religious and racial pluralism, one way or another. A nation which was, in effect, religiously pluralistic before it became politically pluralistic, the United States had to learn a sufficient amount of tolerance for religious diversity merely to survive. It was necessary only to expand this tolerance when the new immigrant groups arrived on the scene with their own peculiar kinds of religious difference. It also seems that, even before the Revolutionary War, nationality differences were important, so the Germans and the Irish (usually meaning the Scotch Irish) were considered as a group quite distinct from the Anglo-Saxon majority. Furthermore, even though the racial relationship had deteriorated into tyranny and slavery, there was, at least until the invention of the cotton gin, apparently some possibility that even this might be peacefully settled. In other words, by the time the large waves of immigrants came, in the early and middle 19th century, America was already acquiring some skills in coping with the religiously and ethnically pluralistic society. The immigrants were not welcome, and considerable pressure was put upon them to become Anglo-Saxons as quickly as possible. Yet the pressures stopped short of being absolute; the American ethos forced society to tolerate religious and ethnic diversity even if it did not particularly like it. Under such circumstances, it was possible for the ethnic groups to continue and to develop an ideology which said they could be Irish, German, Polish or Jewish, and at the same time be as good Americans as anyone else—if not better.

But why is it still important to be an Italian, an Irishman, a German or a Jew? Part of the reason, I suspect, has something to do with the intimate relationship between ethnicity and religion. But another element, or perhaps another aspect of the same element, is that presumed common origin as a norm for defining "we" against "they" seems to touch on something basic and primordial in the human psyche, and that, as we pointed out in the previous chapter, much of the conflict and strife that persists in the modern world is rooted in such differences. If anything, the separatist nationalisms within the major nation states seem stronger today than they were a quarter of a century ago: Catholics rioting in Londonderry, Ireland; Scots electing nationalist members to Parliament; the mutterings of Welsh separatism. The Basques, and even the Catalonians, grumble about being part of Spain; the Flemings and the Walloons are at odds with each other over Louvain; the Bretons wonder if it might be possible for them to escape from France; and the French Canadians are not at all sure they want to remain part of the Canadian nation, even if they could have their own prime minister.

Most of these separatist movements make little sense in terms of economic reality. The Province of Quebec would be hard put to go it on its own; Wales and Scotland would very quickly have to form a political and economic union with England, not much different from the one that already exists; and Brittany would have to do the same with the government in Paris. Maybe tribal loyalties and tribal separatism ought not to continue in a rational, industrial world—but they do, and it is a threat to the fabric of almost any society large enough to be made up of different ethnic communities. One is almost tempted to say that if there are no differences supposedly rooted in common origin by which people can distinguish themselves from others, they will create such differences. I suspect, for example, that if Scotland did become independent of England, there would be conflict between the Highlanders and the Lowlanders as to who would run the country. Ethnic diversity seems to be something that man grimly hangs on to, despite overwhelming evidence that he ought to give it up.

Edward Shils has called these ties primordial and suggests that, rooted as they are with a sense of "blood and land," they are the result of a pre-rational intuition. Such an assumption seems to make considerable sense, but is difficult to prove empirically. It is certainly true, however, that family, land and common cultural heritage have always been terribly important to human beings, and suspicion of anyone who is strange or different seems also to be deeply rooted in the human experience. Ethnic groups continue, in this hypothesis, because they are a manifestation of man's deep-seated inclination to seek out those in whose veins he thinks flows the same blood as flows in his own. When blood is also seen as something intimately related to belief, and both blood and belief impinge strongly on what happens to a man, his wife and his children, he is only too ready to fight to protect the purity of that belief, or the purity of his blood, or the purity of his family when it is threatened by some strange outside invader.

This view of ethnicity, it must be confessed, is essentially a negative one. But one can make a more positive case for it. It could be said that the apparent inclination of men, or at least of many men, to consort with those who, they assume, have the same origins they do, provides diversity in the larger society and also creates sub-structures within that society that meet many functions the larger society would be hard put to service. And while the demons of suspicion and distrust prove very hard to exorcise from inter-ethnic relationships, such suspicion and distrust are not, I am convinced, inevitable. If they can be eliminated, ethnicity enriches the culture and reinforces the social structure. . . .

The Functions of Ethnicity

[Our answer to the question, "What is an ethnic?" raises several questions.] First of all, is everyone an ethnic? In one sense, of course, the answer to such a question is an obvious yes. It is true that all our ancestors at one time did migrate to the American continent. But does national origin seem important to everyone? Here the response must be no. For some people ethnic background is very meaningful both because it affects their behavior and is an important part of their self-definition. For others, ethnic identification may be completely unimportant and ethnic background may have little influence on their behavior. In other words, ethnicity is one of a number of ways in which Americans may identify themselves and which they may use as part of their self-definition. At the social-psychological level, then, not everyone is an ethnic. But the relevant question seems to be—under what sets of circumstances do which people express what sort of ethnic identification? When is ethnicity relevant, and for whom? Unfortunately, American behavioral science cannot answer that question at the present time.

One suspects, however, that ethnicity becomes very important in three sets of circumstances: 1) When an ethnic group is very large and has great actual or potential political and economic power. It is probably far more meaningful to say that someone in Chicago is Polish than to say that Senator Muskie of Maine is Polish. And to be Irish probably means much more in Boston than it does in Tallahassee, Florida. 2) When one is a member of a small but highly visible or well-organized minority. To be Mexican, or black or Jewish is probably always important because these background characteristics are almost always highly visible. 3) When a sophisticated group suddenly becomes conscious that it has become a minority and is surrounded by many other well-organized ethnic communities. Thus, to be a white Anglo-Saxon Protestant in, let us say, Nebraska may not be nearly as meaningful as to be the same thing in New York City, when one suddenly discovers that one is, indeed, a member of a minority group—and a minority group which, for all its economic power and social prestige, enjoys (or at least enjoyed, until recently) very little in the way of political potential. Visibility, sudden recognition of minority status, or being a large group in an environment where ethnic affiliation is deemed important—these three variables may considerably enhance social-psychological and social-organizational influence of ethnic groups. . . .

Perhaps the most critical issue that can be raised about ethnic groups is the nature of their relationship to religious groups. Will Herberg's answer was simple enough—the ethnic groups are dissolving into the super-ethnic community provided by one of the three major American religious groupings. But it is apparent that Herberg was somewhat premature in his judgment. To be a Norwegian Protestant is by no means the same as to be a Southern Baptist; nor is it the same as to be a Missouri Synod Lutheran. Similarly, Irish Catholicism and Polish Catholicism are very different phenomena and provide very different kinds of identification. The mutual resentment between Poles and Irish is, in many instances, far more serious than are their feelings toward any of the heretics, schismatics, infidels, agnostics and apostates (all currently called separated brothers) outside the Church. The lines among the various Catholic ethnic groups may be growing a bit more blurred, but they are still there, and any bishop who forgets it and sends an Irish priest to a Polish parish, or vice versa, is not going to be able to forget it for very long.

I would make two assertions about the relationship between religion and ethnicity.

1) The ethnic groups provide subdivisions and subdefinitions within the various religious communities. Catholicism is, for example, still too big a category to be completely satisfactory—at least for everyone—as a quasi-communal identification.

2) There is a two-way flow of influence between religion and ethnicity. From one point of view it can truly be said that the Irish are Catholic because they are Irish. That is, the identification of Catholicism with Irish nationalism—the biggest favor that Mother England ever did for

the Catholic Church—has helped to make the Irish the strong, if not to say militant, Catholics that they are. On the other hand, the fact that the Irish in the United States are Catholic and are linked to the Catholic Church through the Irish tradition probably makes them more likely to be conscious of their Irish origins than they would be if religion and ethnicity were not so intimately linked in their cultural experience. Whether it is religion or ethnicity that is celebrated during the St. Patrick's Day parade is anyone's guess, but I think we can say, with some degree of safety, that it is both, and that the nature of the relationships and of the mix between the relationships is likely to vary from individual to individual.

Ethnic groups—even if they are not sub-cultures (and I suspect they are)—are at least sub-structures of the larger society, and in some cities, comprehensive sub-structures. The Polish community in Chicago, for example; the Jewish community in New York; the Irish community in Boston; the black community of Harlem all represent a pool of preferred associates so vast and so variegated that it is possible, if one chooses, to live almost entirely within the bounds of the community. One can work with, play with, marry, attend church with, vote with and join fraternal organizations with people who are of exactly the same ethnic background. One can choose fellow ethnics to perform all the professional functions one requires, from interior decorator to psychiatrist to undertaker. One can belong to ethnic organizations, read ethnic newspapers, seek counsel from ethnic clergymen, play on ethnic baseball teams and vote for ethnic candidates in elections. While some of us may lament the exclusiveness in such ethnic communities, it is nonetheless true that the pattern of ethnic relationships constitutes an important part of the fabric of the larger community, organizing the amorphous population of the city into a number of clearly identifiable and elaborately structured subgroups.

Sub-Structures and Life Styles

From the viewpoint of those responsible for the larger social structure, these organizations are particularly convenient because the leadership is readily identifiable and is generally willing to negotiate for the advantage its own community members with an eye on the political realities in which it finds itself. (In Los Angeles, for example, citizens of different ethnic backgrounds are not organized into ethnic communities, and this is one reason Los Angeles is quite ungovernable. In Chicago, on the other hand, it is the ethnic sub-structures that make it still possible—though difficult—to govern.)

These same sub-structures also provide a greater degree of stability in personal and professional relationships, because those who are one's "own kind of people" are considered to be substantially more trustworthy and may, in fact, actually be more trustworthy than the members of out-groups. (By trustworthy here I do not mean that an Irish psychiatrist would cheat a German client: I simply meant that a German psychiatrist might much more easily understand what his German client was talking about.)

Ethnic groups also serve as bearers of distinctive cultural reactions. Some of the research on the relationship between medicine and ethnicity, for instance, indicates that Italians are much more likely to give free expression to feelings of pain than are Irish, and thus are likely to be a considerable trial to hospital personnel. The Irish, on the other hand, bear their pain grimly and bravely and may cause less trouble, but it is harder to discover how sick an Irishman really is, because he's not likely to tell you.

There are also differences in political style. Professor James Q. Wilson, of the Department of Political Science at Harvard, reports that when an Irish police officer has a choice between formal, official channels of communication and informal, unofficial channels, he will almost always choose the latter. It was said of the Kennedy administration that, in addition to the titular head of the various administrative agencies, there was always someone at a slightly lower level who was "Kennedy's man" and had special contact with the White House on the affairs of that agency.

Some researchers have suggested that there is a great deal more fatalism and lack of achievement orientation among Italians than there is among white Anglo-Saxon Protestants. Blacks insist that "soul," and all the word implies in the black community, is not to be found among most white ethnic groups. And, as we shall point out in a later chapter, ethnic background also correlates strongly with occupational choice. Jews are more inclined to be doctors than anyone else, while Germans, both Protestant and Catholic, overchoose engineering careers and the Irish overchoose law, political science and, more recently, the foreign service.

I would like to make two not altogether facetious suggestions for research. First of all, we might take a serious look at debutante balls. In a city like Chicago there is a complex and elaborate hierarchy of debu-

tante cotillions. The most important and best publicized is the Passavant cotillion which is sponsored allegedly to support one of the city's
famous hospitals. It is basically a debutante party for the Protestant ar-
istocracy, though occasionally a Catholic girl may make it if her father
is rich enough or important enough. (One of Mayor Daley's daughters
was a Passavant deb.)

The second ranking cotillion, sponsored by the Irish Catholic aristoc-
racy (although certain non-Irish Catholics are permitted into it in much
the same fashion the Passavant cotillion tolerates an occasional Catholic), is known as the Presentation Ball, and is named after the presentation of the young ladies supposedly to the Chicago Archbishop or one of
his hapless auxiliaries.

But then the fun begins. There are Polish, Czech, Slovak, Ukrainian,
German (Protestant and Catholic), Scandinavian, Puerto Rican and
black cotillions, and by no means just one for each ethnic community. In
fact, a researcher eager to find the similarities and the differences in
such critically important social events could well keep himself busy for
weeks on end, were his stomach and his nervous system strong enough.

It would be easier, I suspect, to study the culture of wedding celebrations. On this subject I can claim to be somewhat more of an expert
than on debutante balls, since for weal or woe I never was fortunate
enough to make one of the latter, but at one time in my career I was required professionally to show up at an almost infinite number of wed-
dings. My impressions, subject to confirmation or rejection by further research, were that Irish wedding receptions were marked by drinking
(and eventually, frequently by singing); Polish receptions by endless
dancing; Bohemian receptions by prodigious consumption of food; and
Jewish receptions by much food, and prodigious and interminable conversation.

I cite these two areas for research not merely because there is a certain amount of humor in debutante balls and different kinds of wedding
celebrations, but also because I suspect that they will strike a familiar
chord in the reader's memory. It seems fairly obvious, even though we
have little empirical data to confirm it, that the ethnic communities, particularly in areas where they are relevant for their members, do indeed
maintain traditions of their own. What some of these traditions would
mean to their cousins in the old country may perhaps be another matter.
Whether the County Mayo or the County Clare Irish, for example,
would make any sense out of the Presentation Ball seems highly questionable.

Mobility Pyramids and Mobility Traps

One final point needs to be made about the social functions of ethnic groups: They provide mobility pyramids that may turn into mobility traps. Because the ethnic sub-community is, at least if it's big enough, a comprehensive sub-structure, it is possible for an upwardly mobile professional and businessman to build his career almost entirely within its confines. Not only a general practitioner, but even a surgeon, can have patients almost all of his own ethnic background; a Catholic academician can achieve a position within the system of Catholic colleges (which are, for the most part, Irish Catholic colleges) that he would not enjoy in the larger academic system; a political leader can gain far more power as the head of an ethnic faction within the party than he would if he tried to operate without such a power base; a contractor or an undertaker may do very well indeed servicing the needs of his ethnic colleagues, where he might be considerably less successful competing beyond the bounds of the ethnic group; even a racketeer, though he may be viewed with contempt by the larger society, may be respected for his success and affluence within his own sub-structure.

These mobility pyramids are, of course, very helpful for those who manage to achieve influence, affluence and prestige that might well be less possible for them in the larger society. And such substructural mobility probably adds to the satisfaction and morale of the members of an ethnic community. On the other hand, there is the risk of a mobility trap. A promising academician who accepts his first major appointment at a Catholic college may move up very rapidly within the Catholic system, but find the door closed to him for more meaningful mobility outside the system. Similarly, a doctor who has built his clientele within the ethnic community may feel that he has great prestige there, but when he goes to medical association meetings and finds himself outside the power elite of these associations, he may wonder if he might not have had even greater success beyond his own ethnic group.

A few individuals manage to avoid the ethnic trap, moving from positions within their own group to similar positions in the larger structure; with increased influence and prestige. Thus, certain journalists whose careers originally were established within Catholic publishing journals have been able, because of their success on these journals, to switch over to important positions with secular newspapers and magazines. And the Kennedys, whose power roots lie in the ward politics of Boston, were able—with the aid of large sums of money and great personal dedication—to break out of the Irish Catholic political mold and make it in the big time. But the mobility pitfalls persist, and many ethnics eager for upward mobility are faced with Caesar's choice—whether to be first in the small pyramid or run the risk of being second (or much lower than second) in Rome.

In summary, then, the functions of ethnic groups in American society are multiple. They keep cultural traditions alive, provide us with pre-ferred associates, help organize the social structure, offer opportunities for mobility and success, and enable men to identify themselves in the face of the threatening chaos of a large and impersonal society. On the other hand, they reinforce exclusiveness, suspicion and distrust, and, as we have already noted, serve as ideal foci for conflict. Finally, ethnic groups are something like the Rocky Mountains or the Atlantic Ocean —whether we like them or not really doesn't matter very much; they are concrete realities with which we must cope, and condemning or praising them is a waste of time.

Milton M. Gordon

ASSIMILATION IN AMERICA: THEORY AND REALITY

In this selection, Milton M. Gordon analyzes three ideologies or con-ceptual models which have been relied upon to explain the manner in which numerous ethnic groups have been molded into American society. The three ideologies are called "Anglo-conformity," "the melting pot," and "cultural pluralism." Gordon traces the historical background of these ideologies and then offers an analysis in which he suggests that while ac-culturation has taken place on a very large scale, the United States is still structurally pluralistic.

Milton M. Gordon is Professor of Sociology at the University of Massa-chusetts. He is the author of Social Class in American Sociology (1958) and Assimilation in American Life (1964).

Three ideologies or conceptual models have competed for attention on the American scene as explanations of the way in which a nation, in the

From Daedalus, Journal of the American Academy of Arts and Sciences, Spring, 1961, pp. 263–285. Some footnotes omitted. Reprinted by permission of the pub-lisher.

beginning largely white, Anglo-Saxon, and Protestant, has absorbed over 41 million immigrants and their descendants from variegated sources and welded them into the contemporary American people. These ideologies are Anglo-conformity, the melting pot, and cultural pluralism. They have served at various times, and often simultaneously, as explanations of what has happened—descriptive models—and of what should happen—goal models. Not infrequently they have been used in such a fashion that it is difficult to tell which of these two usages the writer has had in mind. In fact, one of the more remarkable omissions in the history of American intellectual thought is the relative lack of close analytical attention given to the theory of immigrant adjustment in the United States by its social scientists.

The result has been that this field of discussion—an overridingly important one since it has significant implications for the more familiar problems of prejudice, discrimination, and majority-minority group relations generally—has been largely preempted by laymen, representatives of belles lettres, philosophers, and apologists of various persuasions. Even from these sources the amount of attention devoted to ideologies of assimilation is hardly extensive. Consequently, the work of improving intergroup relations in America is carried out by dedicated professional agencies and individuals who deal as best they can with day-to-day problems of discriminatory behavior, but who for the most part are unable to relate their efforts to an adequate conceptual apparatus. Such an apparatus would, at one and the same time, accurately describe the present structure of American society with respect to its ethnic groups (I shall use the term "ethnic group" to refer to any racial, religious, or national-origins collectivity), and allow for a considered formulation of its assimilation or integration goals for the foreseeable future. One is reminded of Alice's distraught question in her travels in Wonderland: "Would you tell me, please, which way I ought to go from here?" "That depends a good deal," replied the Cat with irrefutable logic, "on where you want to get to."

The story of America's immigration can be quickly told for our present purposes. The white American population at the time of the Revolution was largely English and Protestant in origin, but had already absorbed substantial groups of Germans and Scotch-Irish and smaller contingents of Frenchmen, Dutchmen, Swedes, Swiss, South Irish, Poles, and a handful of migrants from other European nations. Catholics were represented in modest numbers, particularly in the middle colonies, and a small number of Jews were residents of the incipient nation. With the exception of the Quakers and a few missionaries, the colonists had generally treated the Indians and their cultures with contempt and hostility, driving them from the coastal plains and making the western frontier a bloody battleground where eternal vigilance was the price of survival.

Although the Negro at that time made up nearly one-fifth of the total population, his predominantly slave status, together with racial and cultural prejudice, barred him from serious consideration as an assimilable element of the society. And while many groups of European origin started out as determined ethnic enclaves, eventually, most historians believe, considerable ethnic intermixture within the white population took place. "People of different blood" [sic]—write two American historians about the colonial period, "English, Irish, German, Huguenot, Dutch, Swedish—mingled and intermarried with little thought of any difference." [1] In such a society, its people predominantly English, its white immigrants of other ethnic origins either English-speaking or derived largely from countries of northern and western Europe whose cultural divergences from the English were not great, and its dominant white population excluding by fiat the claims and considerations of welfare of the non-Caucasian minorities, the problem of assimilation understandably did not loom unduly large or complex.

The unfolding events of the next century and a half with increasing momentum dispelled the complacency which rested upon the relative simplicity of colonial and immediate post-Revolutionary conditions. The large-scale immigration to America of the famine-fleeing Irish, the Germans, and later the Scandinavians (along with additional Englishmen and other peoples of northern and western Europe) in the middle of the nineteenth century (the so-called "old immigration"), the emancipation of the Negro slaves and the problems created by post-Civil War reconstruction, the placing of the conquered Indian with his broken culture on government reservations, the arrival of the Oriental, first attracted by the discovery of gold and other opportunities in the West, and finally, beginning in the last quarter of the nineteenth century and continuing to the early 1920's, the swelling to proportions hitherto unimagined of the tide of immigration from the peasantries and "pales" of southern and eastern Europe—the Italians, Jews, and Slavs of the so-called "new immigration," fleeing the persecutions and industrial dislocations of the day—all these events constitute the background against which we may consider the rise of the theories of assimilation mentioned above. After a

[1] Allan Nevins and Henry Steele Commager, *America: The Story of a Free People* (Boston, Little, Brown, 1942), p. 58.

necessarily foreshortened description of each of these theories and their historical emergence, we shall suggest analytical distinctions designed to aid in clarifying the nature of the assimilation process, and then conclude by focusing on the American scene.

Anglo-Conformity

"Anglo-conformity" is a broad term used to cover a variety of viewpoints about assimilation and immigration; they all assume the desirability of maintaining English institutions (as modified by the American Revolution), the English language, and English-oriented cultural patterns as dominant and standard in American life. However, bound up with this assumption are related attitudes. These may range from discredited notions about race and "Nordic" and "Aryan" racial superiority, together with the nativist political programs and exclusionist immigration policies which such notions entail, through an intermediate position of favoring immigration from northern and western Europe on amorphous, unreflective grounds ("They are more like us"), to a lack of opposition to any source of immigration, as long as these immigrants and their descendants duly adopt the standard Anglo-Saxon cultural patterns. There is by no means any necessary equation between Anglo-conformity and racist attitudes. . . .

Anglo-conformity received its fullest expression in the so-called Americanization movement which gripped the nation during World War I. While "Americanization" in its various stages had more than one emphasis, it was essentially a consciously articulated movement to strip the immigrant of his native culture and attachments and make him over into an American along Anglo-Saxon lines—all this to be accomplished with rapidity. To use an image of a later day, it was an attempt at "pressure-cooking assimilation." It had prewar antecedents, but it was during the height of the world conflict that federal agencies, state governments, municipalities, and a host of private organizations joined in the effort to persuade the immigrant to learn English, take out naturalization papers, buy war bonds, forget his former origins and culture, and give himself over to patriotic hysteria.

After the war and the "Red scare" which followed, the excesses of the Americanization movement subsided. In its place, however, came the restriction of immigration through federal law. Foiled at first by presidential vetoes, and later by the failure of the 1917 literacy test to halt the immigrant tide, the proponents of restriction finally put through in the early 1920's a series of acts culminating in the well-known national-origins formula for immigrant quotas which went into effect in 1929. Whatever the merits of a quantitative limit on the number of immigrants to be admitted to the United States, the provisions of the formula, which discriminated sharply against the countries of southern and eastern Europe, in effect institutionalized the assumptions of the rightful dominance of Anglo-Saxon patterns in the land. Reaffirmed with only slight modifications in the McCarran-Walter Act of 1952, these laws, then, stand as a legal monument to the creed of Anglo-conformity and a telling reminder that this ideological system still has numerous and powerful adherents on the American scene.

The Melting Pot

While Anglo-conformity in various guises has probably been the most prevalent ideology of assimilation in the American historical experience, a competing viewpoint with more generous and idealistic overtones has had adherents and exponents from the eighteenth century onward. Conditions in the virgin continent, it was clear, were modifying the institutions which the English colonists brought with them from the mother country. Arrivals from non-English homelands such as Germany, Sweden, and France were similarly exposed to this fresh environment. Was it not possible, then, to think of the evolving American society not as a slightly modified England but rather as a totally new blend, culturally and biologically, in which the stocks and folkways of Europe, figuratively speaking, were indiscriminately mixed in the political pot of the emerging nation and fused by the fires of American influence and interaction into a distinctly new type?

Such, at any rate, was the conception of the new society which motivated that eighteenth-century French-born writer and agriculturalist, J. Hector St. John Crèvecoeur, who, after many years of American residence, published his reflections and observations in *Letters from an American Farmer*.[2] Who, he asks, is the American?

He is either an European, or the descendant of an European, hence that strange mixture of blood, which you will find in no other country. I could point out to you a family whose grandfather was an Englishman, whose wife was Dutch, whose son married a French woman, and whose present four sons have now four wives of different nations. *He* is an American, who leaving be-

---

[2] J. Hector St. John Crèvecoeur, *Letters from an American Farmer* (New York, Albert and Charles Boni, 1925; reprinted from the 1st edn., London, 1782), pp. 54–55.

hind him all his ancient prejudices and manners, receives new ones from the new mode of life he has embraced, the new government he obeys, and the new rank he holds. He becomes an American by being received in the broad lap of our great *Alma Mater*. Here individuals of all nations are melted into a new race of men, whose labours and posterity will one day cause great changes in the world.

Some observers have interpreted the open-door policy on immigration of the first three-quarters of the nineteenth century as reflecting an underlying faith in the effectiveness of the American melting pot, in the belief "that all could be absorbed and that all could contribute to an emerging national character." [3] No doubt many who observed with dismay the nativist agitation of the times felt as did Ralph Waldo Emerson that such conformity-demanding and immigrant-hating forces represented a perversion of the best American ideals. In 1845, Emerson wrote in his Journal: [4]

I hate the narrowness of the Native American Party. It is the dog in the manger. It is precisely opposite to all the dictates of love and magnanimity; and therefore, of course, opposite to true wisdom. . . . Man is the most composite of all creatures. . . . Well, as in the old burning of the Temple at Corinth, by the melting and intermixture of silver and gold and other metals a new compound more precious than any, called Corinthian brass, was formed; so in this continent,—asylum of all nations,—the energy of Irish, Germans, Swedes, Poles, and Cossacks, and all the European tribes,—of the Africans, and of the Polynesians,—will construct a new race, a new religion, a new state, a new literature, which will be as vigorous as the new Europe which came out of the smelting-pot of the Dark Ages, or that which earlier emerged from the Pelasgic and Etruscan barbarism. *Le Nature aime les croisements.*

Eventually, the melting-pot hypothesis found its way into historical scholarship and interpretation. While many American historians of the late nineteenth century, some fresh from graduate study at German universities, tended to adopt the view that American institutions derived in essence from Anglo-Saxon (and ultimately Teutonic) sources, others were not so sure. One of these was Frederick Jackson Turner, a young historian from Wisconsin, not long emerged from his graduate training at Johns Hopkins. Turner presented a paper to the American Historical Association, meeting in Chicago in 1893. Called "The Significance of the Frontier in American History," this paper proved to be one of the most influential essays in the history of American scholarship, and its point of

[3] Oscar Handlin, ed., *Immigration as a Factor in American History* (Englewood, Prentice-Hall, 1959), p. 146.
[4] Quoted by Stuart P. Sherman in his Introduction to *Essays and Poems of Emerson* (New York, Harcourt Brace, 1921), p. xxxiv.

view, supported by Turner's subsequent writings and his teaching, pervaded the field of American historical interpretation for at least a generation. Turner's thesis was that the dominant influence in the shaping of American institutions and American democracy was not this nation's European heritage in any of its forms, nor the forces emanating from the eastern seaboard cities, but rather the experiences created by a moving and variegated western frontier. Among the many effects attributed to the frontier environment and the challenges it presented was that it acted as a solvent for the national heritages and the separatist tendencies of the many nationality groups which had joined the trek westward, including the Germans and Scotch-Irish of the eighteenth century and the Scandinavians and Germans of the nineteenth. "The frontier," asserted Turner, "promoted the formation of a composite nationality for the American people. . . . In the crucible of the frontier the immigrants were Americanized, liberated, and fused into a mixed race, English in neither nationality nor characteristics. The process has gone on from the early days to our own." And later, in an essay on the role of the Mississippi Valley, he refers to "the tide of foreign immigration which has risen so steadily that it has made a composite American people whose amalgamation is destined to produce a new national stock." [5]

Thus far, the proponents of the melting-pot idea had dealt largely with the diversity produced by the sizeable immigration from the countries of northern and western Europe alone—the "old immigration," consisting of peoples with cultures and physical appearance not greatly different from those of the Anglo-Saxon stock. Emerson, it is true, had impartially included Africans, Polynesians, and Cossacks in his conception of the mixture; but it was only in the last two decades of the nineteenth century that a large-scale influx of peoples from the countries of southern and eastern Europe imperatively posed the question of whether these uprooted newcomers who were crowding into the large cities of the nation and the industrial sector of the economy could also be successfully "melted." Would the "urban melting pot" work as well as the "frontier melting pot" of an essentially rural society was alleged to have done?

It remained for an English-Jewish writer with strong social convictions, moved by his observation of the role of the United States as a haven for the poor and oppressed of Europe, to give utterance to the broader view of the American melting pot in a way which attracted

[5] Frederick Jackson Turner, *The Frontier in American History* (New York, Henry Holt, 1920), pp. 22–23, 190.

public attention. In 1908, Israel Zangwill's drama, *The Melting Pot*, was produced in this country and became a popular success. It is a play dominated by the dream of its protagonist, a young Russian-Jewish immigrant to America, a composer, whose goal is the completion of a vast "American" symphony which will express his deeply felt conception of his adopted country as a divinely appointed crucible in which all the ethnic divisions of mankind will divest themselves of their ancient animosities and differences and become fused into one group, signifying the brotherhood of man. In the process he falls in love with a beautiful and cultured Gentile girl. The play ends with the performance of the symphony and, after numerous vicissitudes and traditional family opposition from both sides, with the approaching marriage of David Quixano and his beloved. During the course of these developments, David, in the rhetoric of the time, delivers himself of such sentiments as these: [6]

America is God's crucible, the great Melting Pot where all the races of Europe are melting and re-forming! Here you stand, good folk, think I, when I see them at Ellis Island, here you stand in your fifty groups, with your fifty languages and histories, and your fifty blood hatreds and rivalries. But you won't be long like that, brothers, for these are the fires of God you've come to—these are the fires of God. A fig for your feuds and vendettas! Germans and Frenchmen, Irishmen and Englishmen, Jews and Russians—into the Crucible with you all! God is making the American.

Here we have a conception of a melting pot which admits of no exceptions or qualifications with regard to the ethnic stocks which will fuse in the great crucible. Englishmen, Germans, Frenchmen, Slavs, Greeks, Syrians, Jews, Gentiles, even the black and yellow races, were specifically mentioned in Zangwill's rhapsodic enumeration. And this pot patently was to boil in the great cities of America.

Thus around the turn of the century the melting-pot idea became embedded in the ideals of the age as one response to the immigrant receiving experience of the nation. Soon to be challenged by a new philosophy of group adjustment (to be discussed below) and always competing with the more pervasive adherence to Anglo-conformity, the melting-pot image, however, continued to draw a portion of the attention consciously directed toward this aspect of the American scene in the first half of the twentieth century. In the mid-1940's a sociologist who had carried out an investigation of intermarriage trends in New Haven, Connecticut, described a revised conception of the melting process in that city and suggested a basic modification of the theory of that

[6] Israel Zangwill, *The Melting Pot* (New York, Macmillan, 1909), p. 37.

process. In New Haven, Ruby Jo Reeves Kennedy [7] reported from a study of intermarriages from 1870 to 1940 that there was a distinct tendency for the British-Americans, Germans, and Scandinavians to marry among themselves—that is, within a Protestant "pool"; for the Irish, Italians, and Poles to marry among themselves—a Catholic "pool"; and for the Jews to marry other Jews. In other words, intermarriage was taking place across lines of nationality background, but there was a strong tendency for it to stay confined within one or the other of the three major religious groups, Protestants, Catholics, and Jews. Thus, declared Mrs. Kennedy, the picture in New Haven resembled a "triple melting pot" based on religious divisions, rather than a "single melting pot." Her study indicated, she stated, that "while strict endogamy is loosening, religious endogamy is persisting and the future cleavages will be along religious lines rather than along nationality lines as in the past. If this is the case, then the traditional 'single-melting-pot' idea must be abandoned, and a new conception, which we term the 'triple-melting-pot' theory of American assimilation, will take its place as the true expression of what is happening to the various nationality groups in the United States." [8] The triple-melting-pot thesis was later taken up by the theologian, Will Herberg, and formed an important sociological frame of reference for his analysis of religious trends in American society, *Protestant-Catholic-Jew*. But the triple-melting-pot hypothesis patently takes us into the realm of a society pluralistically conceived. We turn now to the rise of an ideology which attempts to justify such a conception.

Cultural Pluralism

Probably all the non-English immigrants who came to American shores in any significant numbers from colonial times onward—settling either in the forbidding wilderness, the lonely prairie, or in some accessible urban slum—created ethnic enclaves and looked forward to the preservation of at least some of their native cultural patterns. Such a development, natural as breathing, was supported by the later accretion of friends, relatives, and countrymen seeking out oases of familiarity in a

---

[7] Ruby Jo Reeves Kennedy, "Single or Triple Melting-Pot? Intermarriage Trends in New Haven, 1870–1940," *American Journal of Sociology*, 1944, 49: 331–339. See also her "Single or Triple Melting-Pot? Intermarriage in New Haven, 1870–1950," *ibid.*, 1952, 58: 56–59.

[8] ——— "Single or Triple Melting-Pot? . . . 1870–1940," p. 332 (author's italics omitted).

strange land, by the desire of the settlers to rebuild (necessarily in miniature) a society in which they could communicate in the familiar tongue and maintain familiar institutions, and, finally, by the necessity to band together for mutual aid and mutual protection against the uncertainties of a strange and frequently hostile environment. This was as true of the "old" immigrants as of the "new." In fact, some of the liberal intellectuals who fled to America from an inhospitable political climate in Germany in the 1830's, 1840's, and 1850's looked forward to the creation of an all-German state within the union, or, even more hopefully, to the eventual formation of a separate German nation, as soon as the expected dissolution of the union under the impact of the slavery controversy should have taken place. Oscar Handlin, writing of the sons of Erin in mid-nineteenth-century Boston, recent refugees from famine and economic degradation in their homeland, points out: "Unable to participate in the normal associational affairs of the community, the Irish felt obliged to erect a society within a society, to act together in their own way. In every contact therefore the group, acting apart from other sections of the community, became intensely aware of its peculiar and exclusive identity." [9] Thus cultural pluralism was a fact in American society before it became a theory—a theory with explicit relevance for the nation as a whole, and articulated and discussed in the English-speaking circles of American intellectual life.

Eventually, the cultural enclaves of the Germans (and the later arriving Scandinavians) were to decline in scope and significance as succeeding generations of their native-born attended public schools, left the farms and villages to strike out as individuals for the Americanizing city, and generally became subject to the influences of a standardizing industrial civilization. The German-American community, too, was struck a powerful blow by the accumulated passions generated by World War I—a blow from which it never fully recovered. The Irish were to be the dominant and pervasive element in the gradual emergence of a pan-Catholic group in America, but these developments would reveal themselves only in the twentieth century. In the meantime, in the last two decades of the nineteenth, the influx of immigrants from southern and eastern Europe had begun. These groups were all the more sociologically visible because the closing of the frontier, the occupational demands of an expanding industrial economy, and their own pov-

[9] Oscar Handlin, *Boston's Immigrants* (Cambridge, Harvard University Press, 1959, rev. edn.), p. 176.

erty made it inevitable that they would remain in the urban areas of the nation. In the swirling fires of controversy and the steadier flame of experience created by these new events, the ideology of cultural pluralism as a philosophy for the nation was forged.

The first manifestations of an ideological counterattack against draconic Americanization came not from the beleaguered newcomers (who were, after all, more concerned with survival than with theories of adjustment), but from those idealistic members of the middle class who, in the decade or so before the turn of the century, had followed the example of their English predecessors and "settled" in the slums to "learn to sup sorrow with the poor." [10] Immediately, these workers in the "settlement houses" were forced to come to grips with the realities of immigrant life and adjustment. Not all reacted in the same way, but on the whole the settlements developed an approach to the immigrant which was sympathetic to his native cultural heritage and to his newly created ethnic institutions. For one thing, their workers, necessarily in intimate contact with the lives of these often pathetic and bewildered newcomers and their daily problems, could see how unfortunate were the effects of those forces which impelled rapid Americanization in their impact on the immigrants' children, who not infrequently became alienated from their parents and the restraining influence of family authority. Were not their parents ignorant and uneducated "Hunkies," "Sheenies," or "Dagoes," as that limited portion of the American environment in which they moved defined the matter? Ethnic "self-hatred" with its debilitating psychological consequences, family disorganization, and juvenile delinquency, were not unusual results of this state of affairs. Furthermore, the immigrants themselves were adversely affected by the incessant attacks on their culture, their language, their institutions, their very conception of themselves. How were they to maintain their self-respect when all that they knew, felt, and dreamed, beyond their sheer capacity for manual labor—in other words, all that they *were*—was despised or scoffed at in America? And—unkindest cut of all—their own children had begun to adopt the contemptuous attitude of the "Americans." Jane Addams relates in a moving chapter of her *Twenty Years at Hull House* how, after coming to have some conception of the extent and depth of these problems, she created at the settlement a "Labor Museum," in which the immigrant women of the various nationalities crowded together in the slums of Chicago could illustrate their native methods of

[10] From a letter (1883) by Samuel A. Barnett; quoted in Arthur C. Holden, *The Settlement Idea* (New York, Macmillan, 1922), p. 12.

spinning and weaving, and in which the relation of these earlier techniques to contemporary factory methods could be graphically shown.
For the first time these peasant women were made to feel by some part
of their American environment that they possessed valuable and interesting skills—that they too had something to offer—and for the first
time, the daughters of these women who, after a long day's work at their
dank "needletrade" sweatshops, came to Hull House to observe, began
to appreciate the fact that their mothers, too, had a "culture," that this
culture possessed its own merit, and that it was related to their own
contemporary lives. How aptly Jane Addams concludes her chapter with
the hope that "our American citizenship might be built without disturbing these foundations which were laid of old time." [11]

This appreciative view of the immigrant's cultural heritage and of its
distinctive usefulness both to himself and his adopted country received
additional sustenance from another source: those intellectual currents of
the day which, however overborne by their currently more powerful opposites, emphasized liberalism, internationalism, and tolerance. From
time to time, an occasional educator or publicist protested the demands
of the "Americanizers," arguing that the immigrant, too, had an ancient
and honorable culture, and that this culture had much to offer an America whose character and destiny were still in the process of formation,
an America which must serve as an example of the harmonious cooperation of various heritages to a world inflamed by nationalism and war. In
1916 John Dewey, Norman Hapgood, and the young literary critic, Ran-
dolph Bourne, published articles or addresses elaborating various aspects of this theme.

The classic statement of the cultural pluralist position, however, had
been made over a year before. Early in 1915 there appeared in the
pages of *The Nation* two articles under the title "Democracy *versus* the
Melting-Pot." Their author was Horace Kallen, a Harvard-educated philosopher with a concern for the application of philosophy to societal affairs, and, as an American Jew, himself derivative of an ethnic background which was subject to the contemporary pressures for dissolution
implicit in the "Americanization," or Anglo-conformity, and the melting-pot theories. In these articles Kallen vigorously rejected the usefulness of these theories as models of what was actually transpiring in
American life or as ideals for the future. Rather he was impressed by the
way in which the various ethnic groups in America were coincident

[11] Jane Addams, *Twenty Years at Hull House* (New York, Macmillan, 1914),
p. 158.

with particular areas and regions, and with the tendency for each group to preserve its own language, religion, communal institutions, and ancestral culture. All the while, he pointed out, the immigrant has been learning to speak English as the language of general communication, and has participated in the over-all economic and political life of the nation. These developments in which "the United States are in the process of becoming a federal state not merely as a union of geographical and administrative unities, but also as a cooperation of cultural diversities, as a federation or commonwealth of national cultures," [12] the author argued, far from constituting a violation of historic American political principles, as the "Americanizers" claimed, actually represented the inevitable consequences of democratic ideals, since individuals are implicated in groups, and since democracy for the individual must by extension also mean democracy for his group.

The processes just described, however, as Kallen develops his argument, are far from having been thoroughly realized. They are menaced by "Americanization" programs, assumptions of Anglo-Saxon superiority, and misguided attempts to promote "racial" amalgamation. Thus America stands at a kind of cultural crossroads. It can attempt to impose by force an artificial, Anglo-Saxon oriented uniformity on its peoples, or it can consciously allow and encourage its ethnic groups to develop democratically, each emphasizing its particular cultural heritage. If the latter course is followed, as Kallen puts it at the close of his essay, then,[13]

The outlines of a possible great and truly democratic commonwealth become discernible. Its form would be that of the federal republic; its substance a democracy of nationalities, cooperating voluntarily and autonomously through common institutions in the enterprise of self-realization through the perfection of men according to their kind. The common language of the commonwealth, the language of its great tradition, would be English, but each nationality would have for its emotional and involuntary life its own peculiar dialect or speech, its own individual and inevitable esthetic and intellectual forms. The political and economic life of the commonwealth is a single unit and serves as the foundation and background for the realization of the distinctive individuality of each *natio* that composes it and of the pooling of these in a harmony above them all. Thus "American civilization" may come to mean the perfection of the cooperative harmonies of "European civilization"—the waste, the squalor and the distress of Europe being eliminated—a multiplicity in a unity, an orchestration of mankind.

[12] Horace Kallen, "Democracy *versus* the Melting-Pot," *The Nation*, 18 and 25 February 1915; reprinted in his *Culture and Democracy in the United States*, New York, Boni and Liveright, 1924; the quotation is on p. 116.
[13] Kallen, *Culture and Democracy* . . . , p. 124.

Within the next decade Kallen published more essays dealing with the theme of American multiple-group life, later collected in a volume.[14] In the introductory note to this book he used for the first time the term "cultural pluralism" to refer to his position. These essays reflect both his increasingly sharp rejection of the onslaughts on the immigrant and his culture which the coming of World War I and its attendant fears, the "Red scare," the projection of themes of racial superiority, the continued exploitation of the newcomers, and the rise of the Ku Klux Klan all served to increase in intensity, and also his emphasis on cultural pluralism as the democratic antidote to these ills. He has since published other essays elaborating or annotating the theme of cultural pluralism. Thus, for at least forty-five years, most of them spent teaching at The New School for Social Research, Kallen has been acknowledged as the originator and leading philosophical exponent of the idea of cultural pluralism.

In the late 1930's and early 1940's the late Louis Adamic, the Yugoslav immigrant who had become an American writer, took up the theme of America's multicultural heritage and the role of these groups in forging the country's national character. Borrowing Walt Whitman's phrase, he described America as "a nation of nations," and while his ultimate goal was closer to the melting-pot idea than to cultural pluralism, he saw the immediate task as that of making America conscious of what it owed to all its ethnic groups, not just to the Anglo-Saxons. The children and grandchildren of immigrants of non-English origins, he was convinced, must be taught to be proud of the cultural heritage of their ancestral ethnic group and of its role in building the American nation; otherwise, they would not lose their sense of ethnic inferiority and the feeling of rootlessness he claimed to find in them.

Thus in the twentieth century, particularly since World War II, "cultural pluralism" has become a concept which has worked its way into the vocabulary and imagery of specialists in intergroup relations and leaders of ethnic communal groups. In view of this new pluralistic emphasis, some writers now prefer to speak of the "integration" of immigrants rather than of their "assimilation." However, with a few exceptions, no close analytical attention has been given either by social scientists or practitioners of intergroup relations to the meaning of cultural pluralism, its nature and relevance for a modern industrialized society, and its implications for problems of prejudice and discrimination—a point to which we referred at the outset of this discussion.

[14] Op. cit.

Conclusions

In the remaining pages I can make only a few analytical comments which I shall apply in context to the American scene, historical and current. My view of the American situation will not be documented here, but may be considered as a series of hypotheses in which I shall attempt to outline the American assimilation process.

First of all, it must be realized that "assimilation" is a blanket term which in reality covers a multitude of subprocesses. The most crucial distinction is one often ignored—the distinction between what I have elsewhere called "behavioral assimilation" and "structural assimilation." The first refers to the absorption of the cultural behavior patterns of the "host" society. (At the same time, there is frequently some modification of the cultural patterns of the immigrant-receiving country, as well.) There is a special term for this process of cultural modification or "behavioral assimilation"—namely, "acculturation." "Structural assimilation," on the other hand, refers to the entrance of the immigrants and their descendants into the social cliques, organizations, institutional activities, and general civic life of the receiving society. If this process takes place on a large enough scale, then a high frequency of intermarriage must result. A further distinction must be made between, on the one hand, those activities of the general civic life which involve earning a living, carrying out political responsibilities, and engaging in the instrumental affairs of the larger community, and, on the other hand, activities which create personal friendship patterns, frequent home intervisiting, communal worship, and communal recreation. The first type usually develops so-called "secondary relationships," which tend to be relatively impersonal and segmental; the latter type leads to "primary relationships," which are warm, intimate, and personal.

With these various distinctions in mind, we may then proceed.

Built on the base of the original immigrant "colony" but frequently extending into the life of successive generations, the characteristic ethnic group experience is this: within the ethnic group there develops a network of organizations and informal social relationships which permits and encourages the members of the ethnic group to remain within the confines of the group for all of their primary relationships and some of their secondary relationships throughout all the stages of the life cycle. From the cradle in the sectarian hospital to the child's play group, the social clique in high school, the fraternity and religious center in college, the dating group within which he searches for a spouse, the marriage partner, the neighborhood of his residence, the church affiliation and the church clubs, the men's and the women's social and service organizations, the adult clique of "marrieds," the vacation resort, and then, as the age cycle nears completion, the rest home for the elderly and, finally, the sectarian cemetery—in all these activities and relationships which are close to the core of personality and selfhood—the member of the ethnic group may if he wishes follow a path which never takes him across the boundaries of his ethnic structural network.

The picture is made more complex by the existence of social class divisions which cut across ethnic group lines just as they do those of the white Protestant population in America. As each ethnic group which has been here for the requisite time has developed second, third, or in some cases, succeeding generations, it has produced a college-educated group which composes an upper middle class (and sometimes upper class, as well) segment of the larger groups. Such class divisions tend to restrict primary group relations even further, for although the ethnic-group member feels a general sense of identification with all the bearers of his ethnic heritage, he feels comfortable in intimate social relations only with those who also share his own class background or attainment.

In short, my point is that, while *behavioral assimilation* or acculturation has taken place in America to a considerable degree, *structural assimilation*, with some important exceptions, has not been extensive. The exceptions are of two types. The first brings us back to the "triple-melting-pot" thesis of Ruby Jo Reeves Kennedy and Will Herberg. The "nationality" ethnic groups have tended to merge within each of the three major religious groups. This has been particularly true of the Protestant and Jewish communities. Those descendants of the "old" immigration of the nineteenth century, who were Protestant (many of the Germans and all the Scandinavians), have in considerable part gradually merged into the white Protestant "subsociety." Jews of Sephardic, German, and Eastern-European origins have similarly tended to come together in their communal life. The process of absorbing the various Catholic nationalities, such as the Italians, Poles, and French Canadians, into an American Catholic community hitherto dominated by the Irish has begun, although I do not believe that it is by any means close to completion. Racial and quasi-racial groups such as the Negroes, Indians, Mexican-Americans, and Puerto Ricans still retain their separate sociological structures. The outcome of all this in contemporary American life is thus pluralism—but it is more than "triple" and it is more accurately described as *structural pluralism* than as cultural pluralism, although some of the latter also remains.

My second exception refers to the social structures which implicate intellectuals. There is no space to develop the issue here, but I would argue that there is a social world or subsociety of the intellectuals in America in which true structural intermixture among persons of various ethnic backgrounds, including the religious, has markedly taken place.

My final point deals with the reasons for these developments. If structural assimilation has been retarded in America by religious and racial lines, we must ask why. The answer lies in the attitudes of both the majority and the minority groups and in the way these attitudes have interacted. A saying of the current day is, "It takes two to tango." To apply the analogy, there is no good reason to believe that white Protestant America has ever extended a firm and cordial invitation to its minorities to dance. Furthermore, the attitudes of the minority-group members themselves on the matter have been divided and ambiguous. Particularly for the minority religious groups, there is a certain logic in ethnic communality, since there is a commitment to the perpetuation of the religious ideology and since structural intermixture leads to intermarriage and the possible loss to the group of the intermarried family. Let us, then, examine the situation serially for various types of minorities.

With regard to the immigrant, in his characteristic numbers and socio-economic background, structural assimilation was out of the question. He did not want it, and he had a positive need for the comfort of his own communal institutions. The native American, moreover, whatever the implications of his public pronouncements, had no intention of opening up his primary group life to entrance by these hordes of alien newcomers. The situation was a functionally complementary standoff.

The second generation found a much more complex situation. Many believed they heard the siren call of welcome to the social cliques, clubs, and institutions of white Protestant America. After all, it was simply a matter of learning American ways, was it not? Had they not grown up as Americans, and were they not culturally different from their parents, the "greenhorns"? Or perhaps an especially eager one reasoned (like the Jewish protagonist of Myron Kaufmann's novel, *Remember Me to God*, aspiring to membership in the prestigious club system of Harvard undergraduate social life), "If only I can go the last few steps in Ivy League manners and behavior, they will surely recognize that I am one of them and take me in." But, alas, Brooks Brothers suit notwithstanding, the doors of the fraternity house, the city men's club, and the country club were slammed in the face of the immigrant's offspring. That invitation was not really there in the first place; or, to the extent it was, in Joshua Fishman's phrase, it was a "'look me over but don't touch me' invitation to the American minority group child." [15] And so the rebuffed one returned to the homelier but dependable comfort of the communal institutions of his ancestral group. There he found his fellows of the same generation who had never stirred from the home fires. Some of these had been too timid to stray; others were ethnic ideologists committed to the group's survival; still others had never really believed in the authenticity of the siren call or were simply too passive to do more than go along the familiar way. All could now join in the task that was well within the realm of the sociologically possible—the build-up of social institutions and organizations within the ethnic enclave, manned increasingly by members of the second generation and suitably separated by social class.

Those who had for a time ventured out gingerly or confidently, as the case might be, had been lured by the vision of an "American" social structure that was somehow larger than all subgroups and was ethnically neutral. Were they, too, not Americans? But they found to their dismay that at the primary group level a neutral American social structure was a mirage. What at a distance seemed to be a quasi-public edifice flying only the all-inclusive flag of American nationality turned out on closer inspection to be the clubhouse of a particular ethnic group—the white Anglo-Saxon Protestants, its operation shot through with the premises and expectations of its parental ethnicity. In these terms, the desirability of whatever invitation was grudgingly extended to those of other ethnic backgrounds could only become a considerably attenuated one.

With the racial minorities, there was not even the pretense of an invitation. Negroes, to take the most salient example, have for the most part been determinedly barred from the cliques, social clubs, and churches of white America. Consequently, with due allowance for internal class differences, they have constructed their own network of organizations and institutions, their own "social world." There are now many vested interests served by the preservation of this separate communal life, and doubtless many Negroes are psychologically comfortable in it, even though at the same time they keenly desire that discrimination in such areas as employment, education, housing, and public accommodations be eliminated. However, the ideological attachment of Negroes to their

[15] Joshua A. Fishman, "Childhood Indoctrination for Minority-Group Membership and the Quest for Minority-Group Biculturism in America," in Oscar Handlin, ed., *Group Life in America* (Cambridge, Harvard University Press, forthcoming).

communal separation is not conspicuous. Their sense of identification with ancestral African national cultures is virtually nonexistent, although Pan-Africanism engages the interest of some intellectuals and although "black nationalist" and "black racist" fringe groups have recently made an appearance at the other end of the communal spectrum. As for their religion, they are either Protestant or Catholic (overwhelmingly the former). Thus, there are no "logical" ideological reasons for their separate communality; dual social structures are created solely by the dynamics of prejudice and discrimination, rather than being reinforced by the ideological commitments of the minority itself.

Structural assimilation, then, has turned out to be the rock on which the ships of Anglo-conformity and the melting pot have foundered. To understand that behavioral assimilation (or acculturation) without massive structural intermingling in primary relationships has been the dominant motif in the American experience of creating and developing a nation out of diverse peoples is to comprehend the most essential sociological fact of that experience. It is against the background of "structural pluralism" that strategies of strengthening intergroup harmony, reducing ethnic discrimination and prejudice, and maintaining the rights of both those who stay within and those who venture beyond their ethnic boundaries must be thoughtfully devised.

Richard O. Ulin

ETHNICITY AND SCHOOL PERFORMANCE: AN ANALYSIS OF VARIABLES

In the final analytical selection we turn to an examination of the influence of ethnicity on student performance. Ulin, in comparing the academic performance of two groups of high school male students, one "Yankee" and one "Italo-American," shows the relationships which he believes to exist between the students' academic performance and some variables which may be functions of their ethnicity.

Richard O. Ulin is Associate Professor of Education at the University of Massachusetts.

One problem which continues to plague American educators is that of determining conditions which enable children of ethnic minority groups

From *California Journal of Educational Research*, September, 1968, pp. 190–196. Reprinted by permission of the author and publisher.

to derive maximum benefit from the American school experience. Since ethnic groups, ethnic heritages, and school situations all vary widely, obviously no single answer or set of answers will do. The question, therefore, must be answered piecemeal. Addressing himself to one facet of the problem, this researcher has focused on the case of Italo-American boys in a suburban American high school.

Considerable evidence now exists to indicate that in recent years the old stereotypes of the Italo-American as laborer-racketeer-musician have tended to recede. Displacing them, however, has arisen another image of the second- and third-generation Italo-American as a fully acculturated member of the U.S. body politic. His unusual energy and obvious success in the arenas of business, entertainment, and politics contribute strongly to this impression, an impression which, nevertheless, warrants serious questioning.

Demographic data show that Italo-Americans are moving out of our urban little Italys into the more heterogeneous and comfortable suburbs. This is a trend which reflects not only their increasing affluence but also their desire to fit into the wider community. It reflects also their assumption that suburban schools with relatively well-paid staffs, small classes, elaborate facilities, and college orientation will accelerate the upward mobility of their children. However strongly it may be held, this is a premise which the results of this report suggest is unreliable.

A significant body of research has already been done on the problem of Italian acculturation in the United States, but these investigations have dealt almost exclusively with congested urban centers (Child, 1943; Williams, 1938; Whyte, 1956). As yet, however, almost no empirical attention has focused on Italo-Americans in middle-class metropolitan suburbs. Nevertheless, the presence of a sizable Italo-American block in predominantly Yankee suburban communities is a common phenomenon today, and it is with Italo-American high school boys in such a town that this investigator is concerned. Here he will report on two facets of a more comprehensive study. First, he will compare the academic performance of two groups of boys, one "Yankee" and one Italo-American; and second, he will make an analysis of the relationships which appear to exist between the boys' academic performance and such variables as their intelligence, their socio-economic status, and their adherence to particular values.

The study was carried out in a quiet bedroom community eight miles from Boston, Massachusetts. Among its 22,050 inhabitants, one out of six would classify himself and/or be classified as an Italo-American. Actual subjects of the study were the 41 Italo-American and 141 Yankee boys in the town's high school on whom complete data were available. A boy was considered *Italo-American* if all four of his grandparents were born in Italy. A boy was labelled non-ethnic or *Yankee* if he was a white Protestant who traced his lineage on both sides to Northern Europe, and all his great-grandparents were born in the United States or Canada.

Second- and third-generation Italians and at least third-generation Yankees, the boys ranged in age from fourteen to nineteen. All 41 Italo-American subjects traced their antecedents to the provinces of *Southern* Italy, a fact which at this point calls for cautionary comment. The wide cultural gulf between the two Italys, North and South, a well documented matter, makes it unwise for one to assume that the findings of this research obtain as well in the case of those Italo-Americans, far fewer in number, who are of North Italian background (Azimonte, 1936; Foerster 1919). The study's so-called *Yankee* subjects might have been labelled "non-ethics," those to whom no nationality label applies. They were all at least third-generation, white, Protestant "Old Americans" who perceived of themselves and were so perceived by their neighbors as "Yankee."

A preliminary analysis of the data confirmed the writer's first hypothesis, namely that Yankee boys outstrip their Italo-American classmates in quality of academic performance. By all measures and in all courses, the grades made by Yankee students he found do surpass those made by Italo-American students. The mean Yankee grades stanine (5.26) contrasts sharply with the Italo-American mean (3.85), a difference significant at the .0001 level. If anything, the figures probably underplay the real difference, in that Italo-American boys congregate strongly in courses and curricula where grading standards are comparatively lenient. A discrepancy of similar proportions appears on available measures of intelligence. The mean Yankee Otis IQ stanine (6.25) surpasses the mean Italo-American score (3.95), a difference significant at the .0005 level. Again, in socio-economic status levels (SES) the same sort of imbalance appears. Judged on a six category format similar to that used by the U.S. Bureau of the Census (High 1—Low 6), Yankee boys show a mean index of socio-economic status (1.88) markedly above that of their Italo-American classmates (4.05), again significant at the .0005 level.

At this point let us note the degree of association the data reveal among the four variables so far discussed: ethnicity, grades, intelligence, and socio-economic status. As one might predict, the highest of the correlations is that between *Grades* and *IQ* (.62); the two lowest those between *Grades* and *Ethnicity* ($-$.32) and *Grades* and *SES* (.34). All six

Correlations (Zero Order) Among Major Variables

	IQ	SES	Grades
Ethnicity °	− .40	− .61	− .32
IQ		.55	.62
SES			.34

° Coefficients in which Ethnicity is involved are point biserials in which Italo-Americans are coded 1 and Yankee 0.

correlations, however, are highly significant statistically. When no variables are held constant, therefore, the correlations suggest that, in schools such as this, one can predict that those students who have high IQ scores, whose background is Yankee rather than Italian, and whose fathers work at high status jobs will make the best grades. This is interesting and useful empirical evidence, but these are not startling findings.

One question which they raise, however, is the degree to which IQ operates as an independent variable in the situation. Previous studies indicate that the observed IQ difference between these Yankee and Italo-American boys may be only an artifact of their sharply contrasting socio-economic statuses. And such, indeed, does prove to be the case. When the investigator neutralized the effects of socio-economic status (i.e., held SES constant), the correlation between IQ and Ethnicity lost its significance. With SES held constant, the correlation between IQ and Ethnicity is − .11 (non-significant at the .05 level). What residual bias remains in favor of Yankee IQ's can perhaps be attributed to the verbal and abstract nature of the tests. Thus it may be said that independent of socio-economic status, these Yankee and Italo-American boys do not differ appreciably in intelligence, at least as intelligence is measured by IQ tests.

This finding led to a further question: Could SES alone account for the significant variance the two groups showed in academic achievement? Could the overwhelming discrepancy in the socio-economic levels of the two groups by itself account for the significant variance in Yankee and Italo-American grades? Previous studies (Coleman, 1940; Davis, 1948; Warner, 1944; Warner, 1949) have indicated this possibility. Therefore, to test this hypothesis, the investigator held SES constant and found that the zero-order correlation between the grades the boys made and their ethnicity did indeed drop sharply (from .32 to .18). But the .18 figure still indicated a significant relationship. Thus, although SES could be held to account for a major share of the difference, a significant residual share still remained unaccounted for. Even with the effects of *IQ* and *SES* neutralized, the academic performance of Italo-American boys still showed itself inferior to that of Yankee boys.

Values and Ethnicity

Other factors were apparently operative. In an attempt to pinpoint some of them, the investigator considered it reasonable to posit that, other things being equal, people generally exert greater effort and hence are more productive in those areas where they care most; that men's efforts and hence their results are often determined by their scale of values; that in this case something in the value orientations of the two groups of boys could account for the stubborn residual variance in their grades. He hypothesized that the two groups held contrasting value patterns and that it was this difference in value-orientations which reflected itself in the contrasting academic grades the boys received.

No cataloguing of a group's values can be definitive, but on the strength of his ten years as a participant-observer in the school and community, this researcher felt in a position to posit that among the values on which these students operated he could identify seven as critical: Peer Group, Family Allegiance, Athletics, Dating, Financial Security, Upward Mobility Urge, and Respect for Academic Achievement. In order to measure adherence to these values, he then devised and administered a *Values Profile* of 42 situations of the forced-choice type, in each of which, by choosing, the subject reveals something of his value structure.

As might have been predicted, the instrument disclosed that while Italo-American and Yankee boys share certain values, they do not share others. In their concern for *Peer Group, Athletics, Dating,* and *Financial Security* and in their *Respect for Academic Achievement,* Italo-American boys show no significant differences from their Yankee classmates. Of pronounced significance, however, are the differences which appear between the two groups in the strength of their *Family Allegiance* and their *Upward Mobility Urge.* Italo-American boys prove to be far more family-centered than their Yankee classmates while the latter show a decidedly stronger desire to move up the socio-economic ladder.

Values and Grades

Still unanswered, however, was the crucial question of whether there exists a demonstrable linkage between the students' values and their academic performance. If so, what is the nature and extent of the linkage? In point of fact the data did reveal that several significant correlations do exist between the boys' grades and their values. In the case of four of the seven values the correlations proved of marked import: boys who get good grades not only have a relatively high respect for academic achievement, but they are less concerned with girls, less responsive to family concerns, and more eager to move up the occupational ladder. The *Values Profile*, in fact, does demonstrate that a significant relationship exists between the quality of the boys' scholastic performance and their value patterns.

At this point let us return to our earlier findings, namely that Italo-American boys are distinguishable from Yankee boys in at least five dimensions: in academic performance, in IQ, in socio-economic status, in the strength of their family ties, and in their urge for upward mobility. On the strength of the fact that of all the dimensions he had considered, these were the five which showed significant zero-order correlations with "Yankee-ness" and "Italian-ness," the investigator chose to include them in a multiple correlation designed to predict ethnicity. This combination did, indeed, serve to distinguish Italo-American from Yankee boys (Ry. 12345 = .67; F = 9.05; p < .01). Of the five factors, the single most important one again proved to be *SES*. In fact the extremely high correlation between *SES* and *Ethnicity* (Beta weight − .52) again raised the question of whether it was of such magnitude that it *per se* accounted for the significant difference between Italo-American and Yankee boys. Further examination, however, revealed that even when *SES* was held constant, a significant portion of the variance still stems from the remaining fourfold combination of *IQ*, *Grades*, *Family Allegiance*, and *Upward Mobility Urge* (F = 10.89; p = .01).

Next, when each of the four remaining variables was tested individually, with the effects of *SES* neutralized, each of them—again with the single notable exception of *IQ*—showed that the specific portion of the variance it accounted for between Italo-American and Yankee boys is in itself a significant portion. Individually *Grades*, *Family Allegiance*, and *Upward Mobility Urge*, independent of *SES*, actually do serve to differentiate between Italo-American and Yankee boys.

Grades, Socio-Economic Status, and Values

One question still remained to be answered: What is responsible for that significant variance between Yankee and Italo-American grades which is still unaccounted for even when the boys are of comparable socio-economic status. Having eliminated *IQ* as a possibility, the investigator turned next to each of the two values which have the power to discriminate between the boys: *Family Allegiance* and *Upward Mobility Urge.*

. . . [First] he found that neutralizing the effects of *Upward Mobility Urge* does, in fact, reduce the correlation between *Ethnicity* and *Grades* but only inconsequentially so. As was the case with *SES*, even when the two groups are equated on this variable, Italo-American boys still show significantly lower grades. Next, equating the boys on the strength of their *Family Allegiance* produces a similar situation. The correlation between *Grades* and *Ethnicity*, while dropping slightly, still remains significant. It can thus be said that neither the low *Socio-Economic Status* of Italo-American boys, nor their low *Upward Mobility Urge,* nor their high degree of *Family Allegiance* is a strong enough factor *alone* to account for their inferior scholastic performance. In fact, even when the investigator lumped both values together, when he equated the boys for both *Upward Mobility Urge* and *Family Allegiance,* Italo-Americans continued to show significantly poorer grades. To this point in the analysis, therefore, the significant zero-order correlation initially discovered between *Ethnicity* and *Grades* stubbornly has resisted any effort to reduce it to a level of non-significance.

The picture, however, changes radically when we consider *SES* in combination with either or both of the discriminating values. With *SES* as well as *Upward Mobility Urge* held constant, the *Ethnicity-Grades* correlation $(-.13)$ drops sharply and loses its significance. It does also when *SES* and *Family Allegiance* $(-.14)$ are held constant. And finally, when *SES* and both values are neutralized, the correlation practically disappears $(-.09)$. The data thus suggests that while one *can* predict with some assurance that among Yankee and Italo-American boys of comparable socio-economic status, Yankee boys will get better grades, one *cannot* make this prediction if the boys also show comparable adherence to at least one of the two values, *Family Allegiance* and *Upward Mobility Urge.*

Discussion

The present study does not presume to have measured *all* the factors which contribute to school achievement. What it does do, however, is cut through the surface connection between "Italian-ness" and school performance. It does so in the process of reducing the highly significant zero-order correlation between *Ethnicity* and *Grades* to a level of non-significance. On the basis of the data, it now can be said with some confidence that in any discussion of the inferior scholastic performance of Italo-American boys, their socio-economic status *must* be taken into account, but then so, too, must *other* significant correlates. While socio-economic status must be considered as a *necessary* condition to explain the inferior scholastic performance of Italo-American students, socio-economic status is not, in and of itself, a *sufficient* condition. In accounting for the low grades of these boys, one must point not merely to their underprivileged social status but also to their distinctive value-orientations.

As yet no researcher has made a thorough-going analysis of the distinctively Italo-American value structure. But the present study indicates that at least two important constituents of it, two which do have a significant relationship with school performance, are strong *Family Allegiance* and a lack of *Upward Mobility Urge*. If we wish to see these values in a context of the total Italo-American value pattern, we must look to the philosophic approach these boys have to life, to the basic attitudes, orientations, and predispositions which distinguish them from their Yankee classmates. Many of these attitudes, orientations, and predispositions have discernible roots in their cultural inheritance. As would be the case with any ethnic group that displays differential behavior, if we seek to probe further for concomitants as well as antecedents of the Italo-American students variant performance, that culture-complex and its antecedents in South Italy will require more probing and systematic analysis than they have yet had.

Up to this point the readings have taught us that although there may be a decline in the influence of European minority ethnic groups upon the general fabric of American life, the "melting pot" has failed to completely eradicate ethnic differences. Moreover, the presence of new "ethnic" immigrants in the city is giving cause to new questions about the nature and functions of ethnicity. What about the future of ethnicity? What new ethnic groups, if any, will emerge in the years ahead? Will ethnic groups survive? Will interethnic conflicts continue? And what about the schools? Should they cultivate ethnic ties and, thus, ethnic differences? Or should they make more diligent efforts, if that is possible, once and for all to eradicate the influence of ethnicity? These questions are not easily answered; and because of the speculative and normative nature of answers to them, it is unlikely that the answers will attract uniform agreement. Such questions are dealt with in the projective selections which follow.

Raymond W. Mack

THE CHANGING ETHNIC FABRIC
OF THE METROPOLIS

In this selection Raymond W. Mack discusses two important changes
in the distribution of minorities in the American social structure: the
declining significance of European ethnic groups and the emergence of
three new minorities in our metropolitan areas—Negroes, Puerto Ricans,
and Southern white mountaineers.

The author is Professor of Sociology and Director of the Urban Studies
Center at Northwestern University.

All dwellers in cities must live with the stubborn fact of annihilation. . . . The
city at last perfectly illustrates both the universal dilemma and the general solution, this riddle in steel and stone is at once the perfect target scraping the
skies and meeting the destroying planes halfway, home of all people and all
nations, capital of everything, housing the deliberations by which the planes
are to be stayed and their errand forestalled.[1]

E. B. White's characterization of the metropolis as "the universal dilemma and the general solution" is perhaps as true of ethnic conflict as
of nuclear warfare. Today eight out of every ten Americans live in or
within twenty-five miles of a city of at least 25,000 people, and the cities
house in their concrete canyons the Little Italies, the Harlems, the Chi-
natowns, and the ghettos. At the same time that the city shows us these
ethnic pockets of segregated, unassimilated minorities, it boasts—in what
we often disparage as the anonymity of urban life—an acceptance of
difference unknown in primitive or rural societies, but evidenced in the
uncritical acceptance of one another's right to exist, which is typical of a
milling city crowd. . . .

A number of people may be defined as a minority by the dominant
population on grounds of race (i.e., that they are physically different) or
of ethnicity (i.e., that they are culturally different, that they share a set
of learned behaviors, such as language, religion, dress, or diet, that set
them off from the other members of the society). Despite the noble ef-

From *Education in Urban Society*, B. J. Chandler, L. J. Stiles, and J. I. Kutsuse, editors (New York: Dodd, Mead and Company, 1962), pp. 54–69. Reprinted by permission of the publisher.
[1] E. B. White, *Here Is New York* (New York: Harper & Row, 1949).

forts of social scientists to set up logical, meaningful, analytic concepts, the whole issue is dreadfully confounded by two facts: (1) Defining a race as a minority isolates them from the main stream of the culture to such an extent that they tend to become ethnic, that is, to develop patterns of behavior peculiar to the race; and (2) defining an ethnic category as a minority leads the dominant people to attempt to justify their discrimination by imputing some immutable characteristics to that minority; it is not unusual, therefore, for dominant people to refer to ethnic minorities as "races." In short, the treatment that they receive tends to make minority races ethnic, and people tend to call ethnic minorities races. Therefore, in the following discussion of the changing ethnic structure of metropolitan America, the word "ethnic" is used to connote both racial and cultural minorities. . . .

Any consideration of the ethnic fabric of the metropolis must be essentially nationwide in scope for two reasons: (1) As has been pointed out in earlier chapters, the United States is rapidly becoming an urban society. (2) Historically, American minorities have, for the most part, been city-dwellers. The Negro was in the past an exception, but today a higher and higher proportion of Negroes is moving to urban areas. Analyzing the changing ethnic composition of the metropolis, then, involves examining the changing face of America.

The United States remains today a nation in which minorities comprise a significant proportion of the social structure. However the ethnic fabric of the society is undergoing extensive alterations. Who our minorities are, where they fit into the social structure, the rate at which they are encouraged to assimilate, and their impact upon such major institutions as education and government are all variables in a rapidly changing situation. We shall examine here what seem to be the two most important changes in the distribution of minorities in the American social structure. We shall then project four trends which seem to be a likely consequence of these changes.

The Waning Importance of European Minorities

One striking change in the composition of American society is the declining significance of European ethnic groups. There are two reasons for this change: the number of Europeans entering the United States has decreased markedly, and those already here and their descendants are becoming assimilated.

Most of the people who became members of a minority in the United

States did so as a result of voluntary migration. The primary source of voluntary migrants has been Europe—northern Europe before 1890, southern and eastern Europe since that time. Over 37 million immigrants have entered the United States in the past century. Fewer than one million of these came from Asia and Africa. In short, for the past century most of the country's minority population has been comprised of foreign-born immigrants of European extraction. This is no longer true. The children born in the coming decades will be the first in the history of the United States to be reared amidst a population that is over 95 percent native born. . . .

The rate of assimilation of an immigrant into the dominant population is influenced by how recently he arrived, how different his native culture is from his adopted one, how concentrated he and his fellows are in one part of his adopted city or country, and whether or not he is physically different from the dominant population. All four of these assimilation-deterring factors add up to one thing: *How visible is he?* The more recently he has arrived, the less time he has to learn the language, mode of dress, and other culture patterns of the dominant group, and the more identifiable he is. The similarity of the culture in which he was reared to the one to which he has immigrated is a factor in his rate of assimilation for the same reason: the more different he is, the more identifiable he is. A large number of "different" people in one area are considerably more noticeable than a few would be. Because they are different and noticeable, they seem to be even more numerous than they really are. They are more likely to inspire fear, to be singled out as a threat to "our way of life," to have stereotypes built up about them, and to become objects of prejudice and discrimination. Concentration in the population makes them visible; visibility slows their rate of assimilation.

European immigrants have not been as visibly different as other minorities; consequently, they have been assimilated faster. The next generation of their descendants—native-born, playing in American city streets, attending American public schools, exposed to movies and television which explicitly and implicitly teach the ways and the desirability of American culture—are assimilated at an even faster rate than their parents and grandparents were. They are less concentrated in the population; they carry little of the burden of cultural differences; they are natives, not new arrivals; they are in most ways, not visibly different from the dominant people, and they therefore assimilate.

Does this combination of rapidly increasing assimilation with drastically curtailed immigration mean the end of ethnic minorities as a significant feature of the American metropolitan social structure? It does not. The waning of European immigration and the assimilation of the immigrant generation serves only to focus our attention more pointedly on our three new urban minorities.

The New Minorities in the Metropolis

The second major change involving the place of ethnic groups in the social structure is the emergence of three new minorities in our metropolitan areas. The first of these are the Puerto Ricans. Legally the Puerto Ricans are not immigrants; they can pass freely from the island to the mainland without a passport, just as one would cross a state line. Sociologically, of course, they fall into the category of voluntary migrants, becoming a minority as they move out of the culture in which they were reared and appear—concentrated, newly arrived, culturally different, and visible—in a new land.

The Puerto Ricans are not widely distributed on the mainland, but are a peculiarly metropolitan problem. They are concentrated in a few large cities, most notably New York. By 1960 there were over 600,000 Puerto Ricans in New York City; to use a journalistic cliché, there were more Puerto Ricans in New York than in San Juan. Of the new minorities, the Puerto Ricans are the most like their European predecessors as immigrants in that they are marked off from the dominant population by language and religion. They have one difficulty, however, with which few of our previous minorities have had to cope: racial ambiguity. Some Puerto Ricans have physical characteristics considered in the United States to be white; others would be classed on the mainland as Negroes.

The second of the new minorities are not only English-speaking, they are also native-born. Furthermore, they are white. They are nonetheless an ethnic minority, unprepared by their upbringing, by the values and patterns of behavior they have learned, to be readily assimilated into the life of the metropolis. Southern white mountaineers, more commonly known as "hillbillies" or "Okies," are recent migrants to northern industrial cities and constitute an ethnic minority in several of them.

Like the Puerto Rican, the Southern white mountaineer has all the characteristics of an ethnic minority except the technicality of foreign birth. He comes from an area where the culture is different from that of the city, where different behaviors are rewarded and punished. He has recently arrived. He has come from a poor environment seeking economic opportunity, and hence will be found concentrated in an old, run-down section of the city. Both his speech and his behavior make him visible, and many people in the dominant population consider him inferior and undesirable.

The third new minority deserves most of our attention, since it is by far the largest. Everything we have said about the Southern white mountaineer as a minority applies to him, with one exception: he is more visible, and his visibility is not so easily shed, because he is Negro. It may be contended that the Negro is not a new minority; this is true, but he is a newly *urbanized* minority and hence is of concern to us here. To see that the Negro as an urban dweller is a new minority one need only note how ill-equipped our metropolitan areas are to deal with him. He compounds the problems of being racially visible with those of the rural person attempting to be integrated into an urban milieu.

Throughout the three centuries of Negro residence in the United States, most Negroes have dwelt in rural areas. As recently as 1900, 90 percent of the Negroes in the United States lived in the South, and over 80 percent of all Negroes in the United States lived in rural areas in 1900. By 1960, 73 percent of the Negroes were urban dwellers; [2] outside the South, over 90 percent lived in cities, which is to say that Northern Negroes are more urban than whites.

The change in the distribution of minorities in the metropolitan social structure can, then, be summarized as follows. For 150 years, European immigrants comprised most of our minority population; their most important learning task on the road to assimilation was the exchange of their native culture patterns for the ways of the Americans. Now, and for the foreseeable future, most of our minority population is composed of citizens of the United States: Negroes, Puerto Ricans, and Southern whites. Their assimilation depends upon adjustment to urban life, upon the exchange of rural values and behaviors for city ones. The overwhelming majority of them face the added block to assimilation of a visibly different skin color—a topic we shall pursue further in our discussion of the consequences of the changing ethnic fabric of the city.

We should note one other characteristic of these new minorities that is of importance in considerations of public policy. During the past few years, our newspapers and magazines have bombarded their readers with editorials and feature articles posing the frightening question of the impact on Northern city schools, neighborhoods, churches, governments, and other institutions of the flood of ignorant, unschooled, Southern mi-

[2] U.S. Department of Commerce, Bureau of Census, *Statistical Abstract of the United States* (Washington, D.C.: U.S. Department of Commerce, 1961), p. 30.

grants, both Negro and white. Such a rapid flow of uneducated migrants as the journalists deplore would create serious problems if it were to occur. However, the actual situation, like so many other "facts" about minority populations, is directly contrary to popular belief about it. As it happens, the in-migrants have a higher level of educational attainment than the resident urban population they are coming to join.

Of the resident population of the Chicago metropolitan area in 1950, for example, less than 15 percent had attended college. Of the in-migrant population to the Chicago area that year, over 30 percent—more than twice as many—had attended college. In-migrants present this favorable contrast with the resident population whether the data are considered as a total or broken down by race. That is, the Negroes who are arriving in the city have a higher level of educational attainment than the Negroes already there; the whites arriving have a higher level of educational attainment than the whites already there; all migrants arriving average more formal education than the present residents.

This is not startling information to a sociologist, because migrants are notoriously clustered in the younger age groups, and, in our society, younger people average more formal education than older people. It is apparently so startling to some of our journalistic friends as to be unthinkable, since they present us with thoughtful analyses of the magnitude of the problems which these uneducated migrants create without bothering to examine the 1960 Census.

The slowing of foreign immigration, the assimilation of European ethnic minorities, and the rise of a new, relatively well-educated urban minority most of whose members are racially visible—this drastic revision in our social structure should have some interesting sociological consequences. Let me state as propositions several reasonable hypotheses regarding the ethnic structure of American cities in the 1960's and 1970's.

Hypotheses Regarding the Ethnic Structure

If the members of a society are to exclude some of their fellows from full participation in the culture and define them as a minority, the people who comprise the minority must have some visible characteristics by which they can be identified. The Negroes of the Ituri Forest can treat the pygmies as a minority because they can tell by a man's stature that he is a pygmy. New England Yankees can treat local French-Canadians as a minority because the latter's speech and family names set them off from the dominant people. A minority's identifiability may result from its members' speaking a different language, having a different skin color, possessing different eye color, or attending a different church from the people in the dominant category. In other words, minority populations can be different physically or they can behave differently, but one or the other is necessary if they are to be identifiable. And they must be identifiable if they are to be discriminated against as a minority; this is why the Nazis forced the German Jews to wear arm bands.

If it is his behavior that makes him identifiable, the member of a minority group can become socialized into a new culture and be assimilated. But physical differences are more permanent; if it is one's skin color that identifies him, no amount of socialization into the culture of the dominant category will remove him from minority status. So-called racial minorities are therefore less able than are ethnic minorities to lose their separate identity and escape their minority status.

Racial minorities, unlike ethnic ones, have been discouraged from total assimilation. Some states have laws against intermarriage between whites and Negroes or Orientals. All the culture patterns that keep racial minorities separate from the dominant category—segregated housing, schools, churches, and so on—are a deterrent to total assimilation, because total assimilation means that one is no longer identifiable as different. That would mean biological amalgamation and intermarriage.

The Rate of Assimilation of the Three New Metropolitan Minorities Will Vary According to Their Visibility. Identifiability is the key to the rate of assimilation and the degree of assimilation of a minority. The basic difference between European ethnic minorities and Asiatic and African racial minorities is the degree to which their identifiability is readily changeable. The Polish immigrant who learns English and changes his name will rear children who will not only not be identifiable as Polish, they will not *be* Polish. Their visibility as a minority depends upon culture patterns; if American culture patterns are substituted for Polish ones, their visibility as a minority is reduced to the vanishing point. But no matter how completely a Negro is American in his thoughts, language, religion, name, and behavior patterns, he is identifiable as a member of a minority because his visibility depends upon his physical features, not his learned behavior.

The Southern white mountaineers who currently seem such a problem to Chicago and Detroit are therefore the most easily dismissed from our discussion of the new urban minorities. They are visible only because they are rural people from one region come to dwell in the cities of another region. As soon as they have learned the behaviors that are Northern and urban, and substituted these for the culture patterns that are Southern and rural, they will be assimilated.

Those among the Puerto Ricans whose racial ancestry allows them to be considered white will be the next fastest to assimilate. They have a little more to learn, a few more changes to make, than the Southern whites. Where the Southern white needs only to change his accent, the Puerto Rican must learn a new language. But so long as he does not look Negro, only the need to learn new ways of behavior blocks him from total assimilation.

The dark-skinned Puerto Rican, however, like the Southern Negro migrant to the city, remains a visible member of a minority no matter how complete his cultural assimilation. It seems safe to predict that those defined as racial minorities will be the last to assimilate, and that they will not do so in our lifetime or, for that matter, in our children's.

Since those socially defined as Negroes constitute our relatively permanent minority, the rest of my predictions will focus upon them.

The Social Distance Between Dominant and Minority Populations Will Diminish. Already we see evidence of a decrease in social distance between whites and Negroes. Polls by the National Opinion Research Center indicate that the views of white Americans on the intelligence and educability of the Negro have changed considerably in fifteen years. People were asked: "In general, do you think Negroes are as intelligent as white people—that is, can they learn things just as well if they are given the same education and training?" [3] In 1942, 50 percent of the Northern whites queried answered "Yes" to this question; by 1956, the proportion of Northern whites answering "Yes" had risen to 83 percent. Perhaps even more significant, the proportion of "Yes" answers among Southern whites increased from 20 percent in 1942 to 59 percent in 1956.

A recent Gallup poll asked: "If your [political] party nominated a generally well-qualified person for President and he happened to be a Negro, would you vote for him?" Thirty-eight percent of the respondents answered this question in the affirmative, with the "Yes" percentage running as high as 51 in the New England states. Even in the South, 22 percent of the voters say that they would support a Negro for President.

A great deal of sociological research indicates that social distance declines with increased socioeconomic status. The higher a person's occupational prestige, or the higher his income, or the more formal education he has, the less likely he is to be an ardent segregationist, or to

[3] Herbert H. Hyman and Paul B. Sheatsley, "Attitudes toward Desegregation," *Scientific American* (December, 1956), pp. 35–39.

condone violence as a weapon in dominant-minority relations. Social distance is least where both Negro and white have high socioeconomic status; social distance is greatest where both Negro and white have low socioeconomic status.

Given the constantly increasing educational attainment of our population, both Negro and white, our steadily rising level of living, and the fact that the cities are drawing as in-migrants the better-educated members of the Negro minority, it seems reasonable to predict a decrease in social distance between the races in the coming decades. Most of the rationalizations justifying our treatment of the Negro as a minority are descriptions of lower-class behavior: poverty, disease, ignorance, irresponsibility, poor property upkeep, and so on. Most American Negroes must, at the present time, be objectively rated as occupying a low socioeconomic status. As more and more of them achieve the education, income, and behavioral prerequisites of middleclass "respectability," they will not automatically escape from their minority position, but the beliefs which justify keeping them at a caste-like distance will be greatly weakened.

This greater acceptance will, however, be one part of a paradox, opposed to our third proposition.

The Rapid Change in the Status of the Negro Will Be Accompanied by an Increase in Interracial Conflict. All that we know of the sociology of revolution indicates that—contrary to the popular fiction that people rise up against their masters when they are too downtrodden to bear further oppression—a group is most amenable to revolution when its status has been improving. Galley slaves do not revolt; they have neither the opportunity nor the strength. The French *bourgeoisie* overthrew the social structure not because they were a crushed and miserable minority, but because they had gained so many concessions and were doing so well that it seemed to them that their world might be an even better place if they took it over and ran it. The Thirteen Colonies which united to throw off the yoke of English oppression in the 1770's were probably the best and most generously governed colonies in the world at that time. The Russian serf lived for centuries under conditions of political and economic subjugation almost impossible for us to imagine, and was too busy just staying alive to question the justice of his lot, much less initiate any effective protest against it. But a series of political and economic reforms in the late nineteenth and early twentieth centuries vastly improved the status of the Russian peasant and culminated in the bloodiest revolution of this century.

Three conditions are necessary for intergroup conflict: the groups must be (1) in contact with each other, (2) in competition with each other, and (3) visible to each other. All three of these conditions will obtain in Negro-white relations in the United States in the coming years. Visibility we have discussed. The very conditions that define city life—crowding and rapid movement, for example—will throw the groups into a closer and more frequent contact than was customary when the Negro was a rural dweller. Every improvement within the status of the Negro throws him into more direct competition with the white. Visibility, contact, competition—all are intensified in the urban environment.

Add to these the uncertain definition of the situation, the ambiguity of role expectations that is a concomitant of urban life and of rapid social change, and you have an almost ideal situation for engendering conflict.

Because of the decreased social distance mentioned in our second proposition, it seems unlikely that this conflict will manifest itself in interpersonal violence, such as lynchings. It seems much more likely to occur as true intergroup conflict, for example, as street gang warfare. If we face the likelihood of conflict realistically, we may, with skill and care, be able to channel it into socially acceptable channels. One such channel—the political arena—seems likely to be used, whether or not for this deliberate purpose. It is with this that our fourth proposition is concerned.

The Cultural Lag in the Definition of Metropolitan Political Boundaries Will Enable Minorities to Seize Considerable Political Power. The pattern of urban growth which we so often refer to as new is, in several sociological essentials, the same pattern of urban growth which we have always had in this country. The oldest, least desirable housing has customarily been located in or near the centers of American cities; the newest, most desirable housing has been located beyond the city limits. We speak with wonder of man's newest social invention, the suburb. The new thing about having desirable housing away from the center of the city is that unrealistic political boundaries in metropolitan areas are separating the wealthier, better-educated citizens from control of their central city.

The fact that an increasing proportion of middle-class housing falls outside the city limits in most metropolitan areas has an obvious corollary: an ever-increasing proportion of the people inside the city limits are members of minority populations. Whereas only 12 percent of the people in the Chicago metropolitan area are Negro, 24 percent of the people within Chicago's city limits are Negro, and the percentage will probably increase in the future. This sort of trend makes speculation about a Negro mayor for Chicago more realistic, if no less startling, than it would be without the cultural lag in city boundary lines. Indeed, a mayor of New York who is either Puerto Rican or Negro, or both, seems very likely within the next twenty years. If this seems fantastic today, consider the probable reaction of a resident of New York City in 1920 had he been told that three candidates for mayor in 1950 would be the Messrs. Pecora, Impellitteri, and Corsi.

The four propositions reinforce each other. The variable rates of assimilation and the lessened social distance will allow increased political power for the Negro minority. Increased political power will make them more visible, hence retarding assimilation, but will confer higher prestige, thus decreasing social distance. At the same time, the bid for political power will intensify interracial competition and provide a fertile field for conflict, which in turn will interfere with assimilation, and so on.

Social Class Differences Will Become More Noticeable as Class Becomes Less Easily Mistaken for Ethnicity. From the sociologist's point of view, the bulk of the traits which most people cite as typical of a minority are actually characteristics of people in lower socioeconomic statuses. This is precisely why people are so frequently forced to defend their stereotypes by consigning some specific case to the category of "an exception to the rule." When someone who is convinced that Negroes do not take care of their property is driven west on Emerson Street in Evanston, Illinois, he has to concede that these Negroes are exceptions to the rule. When he tours West Madison Street in Chicago, he is forced to the conclusion that the whites there live like Negroes—but not like the Negroes in Evanston. A much simpler way to interpret these data is to note that lower-class people do not take as good care of their property as middle-class people.

Many class distinctions of this variety are bound to become more obvious as the social distance between dominant and minority categories decreases, and as people become less accustomed to viewing one another through race-colored glasses. Not the least of these is the strong tendency of public schools in metropolitan areas to be segregated—not necessarily by race, but virtually always by social class.

We are a long way from, but on the road to, grappling with the problem that where factory laborers' sons go to one school and company executives' sons attend another, separate facilities are inherently unequal.

Nathan Glazer and Daniel P. Moynihan

THE FUTURE OF ETHNICITY
IN NEW YORK CITY

Nathan Glazer and Daniel P. Moynihan discuss the increasing and future importance of religion and race—as opposed to national origins—as ethnic factors. Although their paper deals specifically with New York City, Glazer and Moynihan's projective observations can be generalized to indicate the future of ethnicity in the country as a whole.

Mr. Glazer is Professor of Education and Social Structure at Harvard. Mr. Moynihan is Professor of Education and Urban Politics at Harvard.

Religion and race seem to define the major groups into which American society is evolving as the specifically national aspect of ethnicity declines. In our large American cities, four major groups emerge: Catholics, Jews, white Protestants, and Negroes, each making up the city in different proportions. This evolution is by no means complete. And yet we can discern that the next stage of the evolution of the immigrant groups will involve a Catholic group in which the distinctions between Irish, Italian, Polish, and German Catholic are steadily reduced by intermarriage; a Jewish group, in which the line between East European, German, and Near Eastern Jews is already weak; the Negro group; and a white Protestant group, which adds to its Anglo-Saxon and Dutch old-stock elements German and Scandinavian Protestants, as well as, more typically, the white Protestant immigrants to the city from the interior.

The white Protestants are a distinct ethnic group in New York, one that has probably passed its low point and will now begin to grow in numbers and probably also in influence. It has its special occupations, with the customary freemasonry. This involves the banks, corporation front offices, educational and philanthropic institutions, and the law offices who serve them. It has its own social world (epitomized by, but by no means confined to, the *Social Register*), its own churches, schools, voluntary organizations and all the varied institutions of a New York

From Nathan Glazer and Daniel P. Moynihan, *Beyond the Melting Pot* (Cambridge: M.I.T. Press, 1963), pp. 314–315. Copyright © 1963 by The Massachusetts Institute of Technology. Reprinted by permission of the publisher.

minority. These are accompanied by the characteristic styles in food, clothing, and drink, special family patterns, special psychological problems and ailments. For a long while political conservatism, as well as social aloofness, tended to keep the white Protestants out of the main stream of New York politics, much in the way that political radicalism tended to isolate the Jews in the early parts of the century. Theodore Roosevelt, when cautioned that none of his friends would touch New York politics, had a point in replying that it must follow that none of his friends were members of the governing classes.

There has been a resurgence of liberalism within the white Protestant group, in part based on its growth through vigorous young migrants from outside the city, who are conspicuous in the communications industry, law firms, and corporation offices of New York. These are the young people that supported Adlai Stevenson and helped lead and staff the Democratic reform movement. The influence of the white Protestant group on this city, it appears, must now grow as its numbers grow.

In this large array of the four major religio-racial groups, where do the Puerto Ricans stand? Ultimately perhaps they are to be absorbed into the Catholic group. But that is a long time away. The Puerto Ricans are separated from the Catholics as well as the Negroes by color and culture. One cannot even guess how this large element will ultimately relate itself to the other elements of the city; perhaps it will serve, in line with its own nature and genius, to soften the sharp lines that divide them.

Protestants will enjoy immunities in politics even in New York. When the Irish era came to an end in the Brooklyn Democratic party in 1961, Joseph T. Sharkey was succeeded by a troika (as it was called) of an Irish Catholic, a Jew, and a Negro Protestant. The last was a distinguished clergyman, who was at the same time head of the New York City Council of Protestant Churches. It would have been unlikely for a rabbi, unheard of for a priest, to hold such a position.

Religion and race define the next stage in the evolution of the American peoples. But the American nationality is still forming: its processes are mysterious, and the final form, if there is ever to be a final form, is as yet unknown.

Thomas C. Hogg and Marlin R. McComb

CULTURAL PLURALISM:
ITS IMPLICATIONS FOR EDUCATION

Thomas C. Hogg and Marlin R. McComb argue that to the extent that cultural pluralism continues to be an important variable in the life of this country, the school must continue to educate itself about such pluralism. Thomas C. Hogg is Associate Professor of Anthropology at Oregon State University. Marlin R. McComb is an Instructor in the Department of Sociology at Baylor University.

Cultural pluralism has been a dominant feature in man's very recent history; and, yet, there has been a general failure to consider its meaning and to examine its implications for American culture in general and the field of education in particular. The persistence of antecedent cultural traditions and successive migrations of vast numbers of people accounts, in very large measure, for the present cultural pluralism existing in the United States and specific settings therein.

The processes of cultural survival and migration contribute to a diverse and conflictive sociocultural condition to which all institutions, including schools, must adapt. Today, the very spatial and social mobility of populations, both in terms of their urban concentration around the city core and their subsequent flight and extension to the city's more rural environs, has created many new problems for the schools and the educational process.

American Cultural Pluralism and Education

As a society, America has come to enshrine education with the idealism, hope, and missionary qualities that characterize other American systems and the value system as a whole. Equally, and typically, there is a growing recognition that the professions of idealism do *not* match the practices of reality for *many,* including children, in our society.

America's educational system has long been held up as a model, free

From *Educational Leadership,* December, 1969, pp. 235–238. Internal notes and footnotes omitted. Copyright © 1969 by the Association for Supervision and Curriculum Development and reprinted with their permission and the authors'.

and open to children from all social and economic levels, all religious and cultural backgrounds. Also, the educational system has been pointed to with pride by those who see it as an enculturation mechanism whereby such diverse backgrounds would be changed so that individuals might be made culturally capable and able to function in American society and would be offered through education an invaluable means for self-realization and social mobility. Looking beyond the enculturation, social mobility, and self-realization processes, the school has been pictured as a force for social change—a source of innovation and a laboratory for bold experimentation.

In fact, however, the end product of the educational process has now been recognized by educators and public alike to be something less for those children who came from different cultural backgrounds. For the poor black, Indian, Puerto Rican, Mexican-American, or white child, the American educational process has been inadequate, and it has systematically devalued and attempted to destroy their cultural uniqueness. This educational inadequacy has been assaulted through massive public expenditures to accelerate the process of "better" education, but in its train has also come cultural devaluation.

Deviations from the posited cultural norm have been labeled as manifestations of "cultural deprivation or [of being] disadvantaged" in the educational world. Exemplars of such diversity in America have been poked at, probed, and diagnosed *ad infinitum* by a bewildered educational profession, utilizing a string of euphemisms that change as the problems they fail to conceptualize remain. For too long the educational profession has been content to place the blame on the culturally different for failing to be compatible with and malleable to the school environment. Perhaps even more important is the implication that the culturally different offer an appearance, in poverty and lifeway, of what America should not be—culturally heterogeneous and socially disintegrated.

Such cultural examples are seen as being different, but it has been held that they can and should be made the same, that they, too, can become a part of the American mainstream and melting pot. How to bring this state into being was the difficult question that plagued past American educators, and it continues to vex us in our time.

The fundamental premises of assimilationist approaches to education have seldom been seriously questioned, even though many of the sources of our past and present assimilation dilemmas appear to stem from two fundamental fallacies about the American social and cultural situation.

First, is the notion that there is occurring and has occurred a proper melting-pot effect in assimilating the culturally different; and second, is the notion that American society *should be,* and therefore *is,* a homogeneous cultural system. It is becoming more apparent in other cultures around the world that there exists a wide range of pluralistic structures and cultures. The same appears to hold for the United States, a culture often held to be a prime example of the "melting pot" thesis. Even here, contrary to many existing beliefs, assimilation has been more myth than fact. It appears that only now, after we have come to recognize cultural diversity within other nations of the world, not only in Africa, but in Europe as well, have we dared to apply realistic frameworks to the American cultural milieu.

Indeed, pluralism in America stems from earliest colonial days, appears again in the debates and compromises surrounding the Constitution, and is associated with the cultural separatist features of the Westward Movement. It also looms large in the causes of the Civil War, multiplies due to urban-industrialism, European immigration, and internal migrations by Afro-Americans, accelerates during World War I, the Depression, and World War II as mobile Americans discover new cultures at home and abroad.

In more recent years, the demand for "Black Power," "Red Power," and other additional evidences of a new cultural awareness on the part of many American cultural categories are becoming more manifest for all Americans to see. Many of these manifestations are part and parcel of the urban crisis, the context for which is cultural pluralism and social non-articulation. Similarly, even now we are slowly coming to recognize, contrary to the ideas expressed in literature but a decade or two ago, that the small towns of rural America are not, and probably never were, as homogeneous as we thought.

Our own recent researches in Sweet Home, Oregon, for example, have revealed the survivals of antecedent traditions as well as a situation of cultural conflict for small and rural settings. Nestled as it is in the foothills of the Cascade Mountains of western Oregon, Sweet Home has served as the base for bands of hunting and gathering Indians, early settlers seeking escape from religious discrimination, robust loggers or "timber beasts" exploiting the forest by brawn and individual ability, the modern logging and milling industries, and now, water reservoirs promising recreation and new abundance. This local setting has gone through a series of adaptive stages as new immigrants and new modes of subsistence, both carrying distinctive forms of human organization and world view, have replaced the old. Though largely superseded, early stages of Euro-American cultural adaptation continue to be manifest in Sweet Home, not only in terms of values and norms, but also in terms of behavioral patterns.

We have found that the multiple orientations of townsmen toward schools and government are more, much more than a stubborn adherence to conservatism. Their views constitute values which have served well in other cultural challenges, values to which others, those lacking that experience and socialized in still other idioms of thought, behavior, and things, cannot relate. It is in this persisting conflict situation that institutions try to maintain themselves, and yet it is also the type-situation which most severely threatens the existence of institutions, particularly those designed to accomplish basic social processes like education.

In Sweet Home, as in America more generally, the fundamental question appears to be, education for what? To what value system, to what form of cultural adaptation does an educational system structure itself when no clear trends of cultural substitution are apparent, when many cultures are manifest, and when a setting still possesses an ecology which permits a number of technical, social, and ideological choices? More critically, can our schools survive the game of cultural roulette? Which tradition is to be given educational legitimacy? Which bearers of what culture are to be ignored and therefore destroyed?

Cultural pluralism and its attendant conflicts in America are increasing under the impact of industry; pluralism plus conflict appear to be part of the new quality of industrial, social, and cultural life. Thus, a condition which in eras only recently past was viewed as a strain in the social system now appears to be the system. The new adaptation is not a matter of choosing one of many cultures, it is to succeed with many cultures.

Cultural Adaptations for Education

It is our view, then, that the school in the American setting, and the educational process more generally, must adapt to cultural conditions. Given the existence of varying cultural traditions, and assuming that a setting's institutions are formal and enduring manifestations of local culture, then the school and the educational process must formally adjust to extant pluralism, if they are to retain their institutional character. Moreover, not only must education itself adapt to cultural pluralism, it must educate the young for cultural pluralism. This latter task necessarily involves revision of not only educational technology and organization, but the ideology as well.

In this process of change the following considerations must be given due weight. First, in cultural terms, the school must provide each student with a set of relevant cultural experiences so that successful and meaningful cultural adaptations might be made. In accomplishing this task, it must work within and tolerate multiple ranges of interaction and ideology, providing reasons for expression of and respect for distinctive behaviors and thoughts. Basic to the task is the necessity for the school to go through the process of a fundamental redefinition and redirection of assumptions presently made about our society, the purpose of the school, and the school's organization and external relationships in culturally pluralistic settings.

Failing this, the school is encouraging the range of social problems afflicting all culturally different youth—dropping out of school, unemployment, deteriorated self-image, hostility toward authority, and withdrawal from social involvement. Moreover, by a failure to recognize cultural pluralism, the school discourages innovation and syncretism of conflictive cultural elements, thereby increasing conflict and public apathy. What education has done *to* the American Indian, it is also doing to those of a different culture not recognized through skin color and tongue.

Second, in educational terms, through a premise of individual "cultural worth" the school must establish means for cultural expression in the widest variety of school contexts—classrooms, assemblies, clubs, and curricula. This could mean a revision of curriculum including redirection of language and other art programs as well as technical *expression* (rather than training) programs, an expansion of the technical concept beyond training simply for placement in economic technology. Such means as these require special training and recruitment of teachers and administrators and their sensitization to cultural pluralism. In order to ensure its community future, the school must maintain constant contact with community members in family and organizational contexts. This means cooperation with and study of other private and public agencies. Through consciously sought "cultural feedback" the school must restructure its organization and activities and attempt to become a center of community interaction.

Finally, the school must go beyond just becoming a reflection of cultural diversity. It must participate in, and prepare youth for, a culturally pluralistic life and society; and such an educational strategy must become a major and clearly articulated set of goals in the educational process. The extent to which these challenges can be met in culturally pluralistic settings depends ultimately upon the extent to which the school is sensitized to cultural differences within the setting. So long as cultural pluralism is a factor, the school's role must be to educate itself.

Questions for Discussion

1. Has your college experience included any required formal study of ethnicity as it operates in American society? If not, has this chapter in any way led you to believe that such study should be required for prospective teachers? Why?
2. Do you think that cultivation of ethnic differences through our schools will lead to greater intergroup conflict?
3. How much do you know about your ethnic background? Has the school contributed to this knowledge? If not, why?
4. What kinds of educational changes must take place if our public schools are to accommodate the ethnic diversity of their students? Are such changes warranted? Why?

Topics for Further Study

1. Study several detailed accounts of public school student protest in the black, brown, and white ethnic communities of our big cities. One especially good account is that of Russell J. Spillman in the May, 1969, issue of *Contemporary Education*. How does black protest over the schools reflect concern about the development and maintenance of a black cultural identity? Are there differences between black, brown, and white ethnic student protests along ethnic lines? Use examples from your study of student protest activities to illustrate your assertions.
2. There is very little material that has been published on the question of ethnicity and the schools. Why do you think this is the case? Survey material which has been published on this question. What has been the major thrust of the material? Does this major thrust reflect attachment to any one of the three major ideologies discussed by Gordon? Support your assertions with material uncovered in your survey.
3. Construct a questionnaire the purpose of which is to collect data on teacher and administrator attitudes toward the melting pot theory (review Gordon's paper). After administering this questionnaire to a number of teachers and principals in your community, draw some inferences about their attitudes toward the issue discussed in this chapter.
4. Survey some recent issues of newspapers and magazines which are directed to the black community. Draw some inferences about the status of the black separatist movement. What is it? How strong is it as reflected in the material you found in these newspapers and magazines?

Chapter 7. THE CRISIS IN URBAN SCHOOL FINANCE

THE American public school system is in deep and growing trouble with the taxpayer. In one local election after another, voters are turning down proposed issues of school bonds. Pleas for increases in school-tax levies and budgets are falling upon deaf ears. Local taxpayers have simply lost patience with the schools, which they feel have become blotter-like in their ability to absorb funds. One case after another can be cited to illustrate the increasing unwillingness of citizens to support their schools at a time when education is under growing pressure—from the courts, the federal bureaucracy, and civil rights groups—to move into costly programs aimed at social change. The experience of the Los Angeles school system, the second largest in the country, exemplifies the mounting crisis. The fiscal plight of the system is growing worse as enrollments steadily increase, costs continue to rise, and the relevative amount of state aid remains constant. In addition, the Los Angeles Board of Education is under court order to integrate its schools. At a time when money is not available to maintain the present level of education, the Los Angeles Board is forced to use its scarce resources for new and costly programs aimed at social and educational reforms.

The Los Angeles situation is dramatic but by no means more critical than the Philadelphia and Chicago situations. In Philadelphia, the Board of Education declared that it was about to run out of money two months before the close of the 1968–1969 academic year. Even in Chicago, neither the influence of the Governor of Illinois on the state legislature nor the magic of Mayor Richard Daley could find a way to bail the schools out of a ten million dollar deficit in 1969. But it is not only the large school systems that are experiencing financial upheaval. Youngstown, Ohio, taxpayers allowed their public schools to remain closed from Thanksgiving, 1968, to January, 1969, because of a financial deficit.

Only five years ago, United States voters were approving 75 percent of the school bond issues submitted. Now these same voters are turning down one out of every two issues. In seeking reasons for this relatively sudden change in voter attitude, some authorities note that school bond issues are the only vehicle remaining through which voters can express their anger at a seemingly endless spiral of rising taxes. With government bureaucracy growing in all areas, school issues remain as the only target subject to direct control at the polls. Not all of the changed voter attitude can be attributed to simple determination not to increase taxes. Experts also observe that there is a growing resentment against the "frills" of education. This usually translates into opposition by white voters against special programs for the economically deprived who, in the big cities, are mainly black.

There is little question that the large urban areas suffer most as the pressures for money converge. This fact is attributable to the recent redistribution of population in the United States. Poor, insufficiently educated, nonwhite Americans are remaining in the inner city, as higher-income, white families are moving to the suburbs and taking the tax base with them. This is a sharp departure from recent history, when the cities had the solid tax bases and were the rich school districts with money for special programs and high quality staffs. Despite the obvious need for more resources in the city schools, they are now spending less than their suburban counterparts. In 1968 the average per-student expenditure in the inner city was $449, compared with $573 for the suburbs. The disparity between the two figures is distressing, but even more striking is the fact that the difference between city and suburban expenditures seems to be widening. It is impossible for the inner city to compete with the suburbs. One major reason is that resource allocation on a statewide basis discriminates against the city. Many observers are of the opinion, however, that increased state aid is one real answer to the financial crisis. The states do have the power to restructure the school support system and, in fact, to readjust totally the boundaries of local governments in order to favor urban school systems. Such state powers have seldom been used, however, and are not likely to be used now that reapportionment has given suburban areas added strength in the legislature.

As local governments have become helpless and the states unwilling, or unable, to solve urban school problems, the federal government also seems to have turned its back on education. President Nixon has severely curtailed the funds available for education and the Congress has not recently made education a high priority. Federal programs which had promise originally, such as Head Start and others, have not been provided with sufficient funds to make a significant contribution to urban education. Thus we are in the midst of a crisis in urban school finance.

We have touched briefly upon some of the inequities now existing among urban, suburban and, by implication, rural school systems. The problem confronting us is whether the present structures can provide the necessary funds to eradicate the inequities that we have cited. The specific issue we are concerned with is: *How can the distribution of financial resources be adjusted to ensure that schools will receive the support required to achieve the goals expected of them by society?*

Nearly every layman as well as every educator has his own pet solution to the urban education financial crisis. One group of supporters of the status quo has challenged the present state and local governments to find new sources of revenue. These people have faith in the present financial system and attribute its failure to a temporary diversion of funds dictated by international conditions. They feel that the tax structures will again be adequate to support urban education when national priorities reestablish education as a top recipient of funds.

Another group of critics has given up on the imagination of state and local government and has turned to the federal courts for guidance in the crisis. This group claims that school aid formulas shortchange urban children and deny them equal protection of the laws. Numerous court tests have been made of this hypothesis, the most well known being *McInnes v. Ogilvie* in 1969. In this case, the U. S. Supreme Court upheld a lower-court decision that the solution suggested for correcting the distribution of fiscal resources was unworkable. The plaintiffs in the case had asked that state funds be allocated to local districts on the basis of educational need. The court held that "educational need" was a vague term that could not be defined and that this rendered the proposed solution unworkable. Further court tests can be expected in the future. (It is interesting to note that the courts are about to become involved in another significant area of influence regarding educational decision-making. At this point the reader may wish to review the chapter on the courts in order to recall the historical role of the courts in relation to education.)

Still another group of critics has given up entirely on the present school system and what they consider to be its outmoded tax structure. This group has called for alternatives to the present systems. In Chapter 8, we introduce several of the alternatives proposed by this group. One, for example, is the tuition voucher plan offered by the conservative economist Milton Friedman. This plan has generated much public support because it appeals to those who believe that the "free market" principle ought to be applied to social services, such as the schools. Another example of the type of alternative called for by this group of critics is the "free school" being established by black organizations frustrated with the city schools.

Finally, a group of educators led by former Secretary of Health, Education and Welfare Wilbur J. Cohen has recommended severe modifications of the property tax and eventual replacement of it with federal funds. Specifically he has suggested a 5 percent surtax on the income tax to be earmarked for education.

Each of the solutions recommended above is designed to alleviate the financial crisis now being experienced by the public schools. Though all of the solutions have obvious deficiencies, they illuminate the need for increased attention to the problem of finances. Numerous variables affecting the issue of redistribution of resources were apparent in the above solutions. Other variables inherent in the issue are suggested by the following questions: (1) To what degree can the cities be expected to solve their own school problems without the help of other levels of government? (2) Can municipal overburden be reduced by new concepts of local government in order to free money for use in urban schools? (3) Can the inner-city child be offered an equal educational opportunity without altering the entire housing-job-education cycle in our country? (4) To what extent does the taxpayer rebellion reflect a growing concern by urban parents about the declining quality of public education?

Thomas P. Wilbur

FINANCING URBAN SCHOOLS: A CONTINUING CRISIS

The crisis in urban school finance is described vividly in this article, which cites recent national studies to dramatize the plight of big-city education. Thomas P. Wilbur is pessimistic about the future of public education in lower economic-class neighborhoods because he observes that society is really not willing to change its priorities regarding ghetto education. Wilbur discusses the challenge to city schools from a vantage

From *School and Society*, Summer, 1969, pp. 286–288. Some footnotes omitted. Reprinted by permission of the publisher.

point of Consultant in the Bureau of Research, Michigan Department of Education.

The most important demographic fact of 20th-century America has been the population explosion in her metropolitan areas. Automation and technology have combined with healthy birth and longevity rates to transform our rural, small-town society into an increasingly urban one. What Jean Gottman called "megalopolis" is clearly with us and spreading rapidly. It has been estimated that, by 1970, two-thirds of our people will be living in metropolitan areas,[1] and the Regional Plan Association predicts that the New York City area alone will contain 11,000,000 additional people by the year 2000.

The big cities are the centers of our populous metropolitan areas. They provide home for a large number of Americans and work, recreation, and cultural space for a great many more. Because quality education is a presumed necessity for entrance into contemporary American society and because of the vast number of people involved, it is important that large cities offer excellent public educational opportunities. Our central cities have more educational problems to solve than affluent districts and less money to solve them with. At present they are not meeting this challenge.

Large cities, with their concentration of wealth and talent, were once the educational leaders of the nation; but no longer. Their educational decline partially has resulted from increasing demands and problems: large numbers of "educationally disadvantaged" children and those with special problems; teacher shortages and militancy; and rising school site and construction costs.

As the demographic revolution in America sends large numbers of rural poor to the cities and large numbers of the rising middle classes to the suburbs, city schools are being given a greater number of problem children to work with than more socio-economically favored school districts. A related factor in this population shift is that city schools increasingly are dominated by non-white youngsters, which might not be bad except that, as Miller has pointed out, "All figures collected in the census . . . on housing, education, occupation, income . . . show that the Negro still ranks among the poorest of the poor."[2]

---

[1] Catherine Baer Wurster, "Framework for an Urban Society," in *Goals for Americans* (Englewood Cliffs, N.J.: Prentice-Hall, 1960), p. 255.

[2] Herman P. Miller, *Rich Man Poor Man* (New York: New American Library, 1965), p. 97.

A typical study of achievement related to social status conducted in Pennsylvania showed that "A significantly larger proportion of urban school children achieve one half grade level or more below the 1963 standard achievement test scores examined. . . ." [3] We see, thus, the effects of an increasing racial and socio-economic imbalance on city schools. To counter these disadvantages, urban districts will have to provide more educational help and excellent teachers. Obviously, this will require immense expenditures.

Another group of expenditure-raising children who are treated in urban schools more often than elsewhere are those that require trade, vocational, and technical schooling or other special services. The Research Council of the Great Cities has shown that ". . . the higher costs of special and vocational educational programs are largely concentrated in major cities." [4] The financial implications of these statements should be clear. If urban children need, on the average, more and better educational services than children in other areas, we must either raise expenditure levels or we will fail to provide them with what they need.

Because of the difficult classroom problems faced by teachers in many urban schools and the attractiveness of teaching in suburban systems, central-city personnel administrators face a more serious teacher shortage than their fellows in more-favored circumstances. In addition, central-city teachers have been more militant and demanding than their suburban and rural brethren. Teacher shortages and militancy have combined to drive teacher salaries in the cities to high levels. Usually, 55–70% of a school district's budget is spent on professional salaries, and these factors have compounded the urban financial dilemma.

Another factor in the cost of education in cities has been the skyrocketing cost of some non-personnel budget items. City boards of education have been hit especially hard in the area of school site and building construction costs. The Research Council of the Great Cities notes that ". . . substantial differences in school site costs between the large cities and other districts constitute a handicap in providing adequate facilities in the districts with higher costs. Construction costs and restrictive building codes are additional factors which contribute to the high cost of school plants in large cities." [5]

One side of the financial crisis in large cities, then, is the existence of

---

[3] *Special Education and Requirements of Urban School Districts in Pennsylvania* (Philadelphia: Fels Institute of Local and State Government, 1964), p. 6.

[4] *The Challenge of Financing Public Schools in Great Cities* (Chicago: Research Council of the Great Cities Program for School Improvement, 1964), p. 6.

[5] *Ibid.*, p. 9.

more costly problems than experienced by most school districts. As needs and prices have risen in the cities, unfortunately, available resources have not kept pace. Three major factors contribute to the comparative reduction of available resources: the available tax base in the cities has not kept up with educational demand; "municipal overburden" robs schools of money in large cities; and state aid formulas do not consider urban education problems effectively.

While the past few years have witnessed a tremendous growth in metropolitan regions, all parts of these areas have not been affected in the same way. The middle classes, with their affluent tax base, are concentrating largely in the burgeoning metropolitan suburbs as the poor inherit the central city. This unequal diffusion of people not only has made city problems more acute, but is ". . . removing to inaccessible suburbs the very resource base which is necessary to solve city problems." [6]

Two other factors cripple the tax base in large cities. First, many valuable city properties belong to church and educational institutions and are, therefore, tax exempt. Secondly, cities, in general, have been lowering their rates of assessment. James, Kelly, and Garms have shown that average property assessment in cities has dropped from 72% of market value in 1930 to 51% in 1960. Expansion of property values, thus, is ". . . undercut by limiting the exposure of property to taxation." [7]

Big cities have tremendous financial problems in areas other than education. They often feature air and water pollution, poor transportation facilities, and substandard and overcrowded housing. In addition, they must supply costly amounts of police, fire, health, and welfare services. These difficult problems and necessary extra services cost a great deal of money. The Fels Institute has described the result of this municipal overburden on city education: "The high cost of municipal services which produce much higher total tax burden in the urban districts significantly reduces the ability of urban districts to provide comparable fiscal support for educational services." [8]

State government provides a large amount of the financial base to

[6] Alan K. Campbell, "Financing Education: Matching Resources to Needs," in *Leadership for Education* (Washington, D.C.: National Committee for Support of the Public Schools, 1967), pp. 29–30.

[7] H. Thomas James, James A. Kelly, and Walter L. Garms, *Why City Schools Need More Money* (Chicago: Research Council of the Great Cities Program for School Improvement, 1967), p. 5.

[8] Fels Institute, *op. cit.*, pp. 6–7.

local school districts in many states and the urban school difficulties mentioned above would lead us to expect that city districts would receive proportionately more of this money than their wealthier neighbors. Because state legislatures usually are dominated by rural and suburban interests, however, the distribution is not what we logically would expect. "As recently as 1957," writes Campbell, "annual expenditures in 35 of the largest metropolitan areas were roughly equal in the cities and their suburbs. By 1963, the suburbs were spending, on the average, $145 more per pupil than the central cities. This differential is primarily a reflection of the fact that during those years the disparity in wealth between suburbs and cities was growing. The shocker, however, is that state aid to the schools, which one might think would be designed to redress this imbalance, somewhat discriminates *against* the cities. On the average, the suburbs receive $40 more in state aid than the cities." [9]

The studies presented in this brief essay are typical of those that have been made on the financing of urban public school systems. They indicate beyond a doubt that these districts have proportionately more demands made of them and fewer available resources to meet these demands than most other districts. The urban districts' financial position appears to be especially poor in comparison with its suburban neighbors. This obvious educational differential, along with the knowledge that great numbers of children are involved, and the central city's proven capability for socially disruptive violence have led to much discussion by educators and other professional commentators as to what courses of action best will "solve," or at least "alleviate," the urban educational crisis. Not all of these plans involve more money. Socio-economic and racial integration, school decentralization, the employment of computers and system analysis techniques, and so on would cost nothing and might even save money in the large district. Assuming a significant relationship between educational quality and school system expenditure level, however, it is doubtful that we can improve the quality of city schools without more money. Most educators argue, therefore, for more state and Federal aid to the cities along with an expansion of the urban tax base.

While the proposal for more money is, thus, a rational one and theoretically could create an equitable American school system, past experience forces us to be doubtful that the actual flow of new money even can keep pace with the social decay of our inner cities, let alone conquer it. Given the competitive nature of our culture and its formal sys-

[9] "The Rich Get Richer and the Poor Get Poorer . . . Schools," *Carnegie Quarterly* 14:1.

tem for socializing young people, we would have to spend substantially more money on the disadvantaged city child than his suburban peers if we were to offer him anything approaching an "equal" education. So long as we persist in extending the ideal of free enterprise into our public school system, however, there is little hope of dramatically narrowing the gap between what we spend on city and suburban children.

Our society and its leadership does not appear eager to redistribute educational and other public dollars radically or, equally necessary, to mount a concerted drive for socio-economically and racially integrated schools. This reticence on the part of the majority does not offer much comfort to the parents of disadvantaged children. Nor does it comfort those Americans of every class who would have their children educated into a multiracial egalitarian society.

> The crisis in school finance can be illustrated by the problems of almost any city in the country. Each city is struggling with most of the problems of urban America—exodus of whites to the suburbs and consequent high concentration of blacks in the inner city, the decline of the downtown area and resultant drop in the tax base, and the increasing burden on the city's services created by the poor, the aged, and the deprived. With such internal difficulties, it is not surprising that several major cities are now confronting head on a critical problem that seems certain to face hundreds of cities in the next few years—bankruptcy of the school system.

Pete Sheehan

WHY THE MONEY RAN OUT IN YOUNGSTOWN

Journalist Pete Sheehan has selected Youngstown, Ohio—a formerly prosperous steel-milling city—as a perfect example of a community suffering from urban ills. Youngstown is plagued by labor problems, vexed by uneasy relations between the school board and the voters, and troubled by an increasing number of black and Puerto Rican students who need special—and expensive—programs. For these and other reasons cited by the author, the Youngstown schools have been caught in a severe political and financial bind.

Dan Rowan: "It's time now for the Flying Fickle Finger of Fate Award."
Dick Martin: "Who gets the goodie this time?"

From *Phi Delta Kappan*, November, 1969, pp. 118–121. Reprinted by permission of the author and publisher.

Rowan: "The voters of the city of Youngstown, Ohio. For the sixth time in two years, they voted down an increase in school taxes."
Martin: "So? A lot of cities do that."
Rowan: "Yes, but in Youngstown, they don't even have enough money to keep the schools open."

Youngstown, O.—Residents of this steel center lived down labels like "Murdertown, Ohio," "Sin City," and "Crimetown, U.S.A." They winced over publicity about an unprecedented teachers' strike, a nurse walkout, and a "no-work seminar" by police and firemen.

Then they got a "don't care" reputation when they turned down school levies with regularity and were given a "Fickle Finger of Fate Award" by TV comedians Rowan and Martin just to rub it in. After the sixth straight levy defeat in 23 months, public schools were shut for 15 days last year. In the end, the lost days were made up in June to fulfill a state requirement.

Following a long Christmas holiday—from Thanksgiving Eve to January 2, 1969—school officials decided to wait until the May primary to try No. 7. During the intervening period a series of events reshaped the school board structure and took the steam out of some of the opposition to the levies.

Youngstown is a basic steel town, consequently a strong labor area. For several years James P. Griffin, as director of District 26, United Steelworkers of America, and Al Shipka, a Griffin aide and president of the Greater Youngstown AFL-CIO Council, supported public school levies and provided vital leadership for their success.

The first school levy to fail in about 25 years was a new 4.8-mill levy in November, 1962, when labor quietly backed away. The next year labor gave full support to a 3-mill levy which carried 55 percent of the vote. Another renewal of 6.7 mills won by a greater majority in November, 1965.

Then the break with labor became more apparent. The Youngstown Federation of Teachers AFL-CIO was gaining membership, especially in the junior high and high school buildings, and seeking recognition. Leaders went to Shipka and Griffin and got their support.

Later, J. H. Wanamaker, then superintendent of Youngstown public schools, told a press conference there was a concerted effort by both individuals and groups to undermine confidence in the city school system. He wouldn't name names.

Griffin had served as a hard-driving vice chairman of the Citizens Advisory Committee for Youngstown Schools until November 17, 1966, when he resigned because, he said, the board did not set a secret ballot between the YFT and the YEA.

Within a week the YFT struck for recognition. Teachers set up picket lines the Monday of Thanksgiving week, marking the first teacher strike in Ohio. A few weeks before, the board had recognized the Youngstown Education Association, and members of this organization did not respect the YFT picket lines.

Attorney Edward Roberts, representing the YEA, scored the striking teachers. He declared, "The YEA wants the parents and pupils of this community to know that this is an illegal strike under Ohio law. It's a sad day when the law is broken, when an illegal act is used to try to coerce members of the professional staff of Youngstown's public schools who are dues-paying members of the YEA."

During the short strike of one week (but only three school days), Griffin issued this statement to all officers and stewards of locals in District 26, as he urged support of the striking teachers' union:

Basically, the strike is caused by the absolute refusal of the board to give attention to the needs and problems of the classroom teachers down through the years. Complaints have been ignored; grievances denied; suggestions shelved; assignments and promotions used as weapons of discipline, discrimination, and rank favoritism.

The classroom teachers were herded into a "company dominated" association which is under the control and guidance of the "foremen," the "general foremen," and "superintendent." This is a 1966 version of the "unions" that the steel, auto, and other basic industries attempted to shackle on us 30 years ago when our basic wage was 47 cents an hour. It took the historic 1937 strikes of the auto and steel workers to bury our company "unions" and to give us a voice in determining our wages and working conditions.

Griffin indicated that the only issue in the Youngstown strike was:

Shall classroom teachers be allowed to have a democratic, bona fide AFL-CIO union of their own choice to speak for them on wages, hours, and working conditions, or shall they be denied this right by connivance of the board and a stooge company union?

All you need to do to reach a judgment on whether YEA is a company union or the honest voice of teachers is to read the statements of their spokesmen. They are exposed for what they are by their frantic shouting against the strike aims and for the discharge of their fellow teachers by the invocation of the vicious Ferguson Act. [The Ferguson Act forbids public employees to strike.]

Criticizing the school board for "stacking the election by insisting on their supervisors and administrators being allowed to vote," Griffin asked, "Can you imagine our allowing the foremen, general foremen, superintendents, and company officials to decide whether we should have a union, to hold office in our union, establish our policies, to attend our meetings, and to be on our grievance committee?"

As the strike neared the end of its first week, a group of irate citizens went to court and the judge ordered teachers to return by Monday. Over the weekend the YFT worked out an agreement with school officials which assured them of an election late in 1968 and separate bargaining units for classroom teachers and supervisors-principals.

Eugene Green, counsel for the YFT, argued that the YEA, with 10 percent of its members belonging to the supervisory group, "cannot possibly get free expression of its members."

Less than two weeks after classes were resumed, Youngstown voters gave the school levy only 29.1 percent affirmative votes—the worst licking in the long series, and this levy was for only five mills.

Griffin's refusal to support the levy did not get as much comment or blame as the union teachers did. They were called the killers because "good law-abiding citizens would not tolerate their action."

Austerity then became the word of the school board and school officials. Board members decided to go for 7.5 mills in May, 1967, and said there would be loss of athletics, all extracurricular activities, and kindergarten if the levy failed. Despite the scare tactics, only 35.3 percent of the electorate voted for the levy.

The board carried out its threats. School reopened in September, 1967, without kindergarten and most extracurricular activities. Football coaches worked without the extra pay they receive under contract for gridiron work. The six public schools played all season without the benefit of their school band support. Woodrow W. Zinser had come from Mansfield to replace Superintendent Wanamaker, who retired and went into college teaching. One high school, Chaney, did not have basketball because its coach refused to work without pay.

The austerity didn't bother Youngstowners too much. In November, 1967, they again turned down a 6.1 levy, but the affirmative vote did climb to 43.6 percent, making backers hopeful the fourth time would be lucky.

By spring, 1968, there were rumblings about "quality education" and how public school standards had fallen. There was criticism of the antiquated books, which had no treatment of the developments of the past 10 years. The YEA was talking about more money despite the levy defeats. The board put a 12-mill levy on the ballot in May, 1968, to ensure quality education. It got 41.9 percent of the vote.

Further cutbacks and closings were forecast as the 12-mill issue was resubmitted the next month. Backers used a soft sell. Little was said about the levy, in the hope that opponents would stay home. The vote total was 8,300 fewer than it had been the previous month, but the affirmative portion also was smaller—37 percent.

The YEA got busy and demanded pay raises or no school in September. Ohio Federation Association officials came to town to express their support of seminars for teachers instead of classes for children. The pressure was heavy.

Just before reopening day, the school board yielded on the recommendation of Superintendent Zinser, granting a 7.7 percent pay increase for all employees and a program of quality education. Kindergarten was restored, up-to-date textbooks were purchased, and a full extracurricular program including high school athletics with fully paid coaches was reestablished.

Superintendent Zinser admitted his recommendation for raises and restoration of programs "may not be good management, but I think it's good education."

The board voted for the pay raises and the rest of the package four to three, with Abe Harshman, Robert Murphy, and William Holt representing a new "liberal" faction which declared that the raises and the restored programs should wait until there was sufficient money.

The vote was to close the schools when the money ran out if the next levy didn't pass. Probate Judge Charles P. Henderson, former mayor and probably the most respected political figure in town, was named to head a special citizens' committee for the schools. It staged a broad, intelligent campaign, obtaining endorsement from virtually every segment of the community except the AFL-CIO Council.

Griffin was relatively silent, but Shipka attacked the board's "anti-labor policy" and its knuckling down to the YEA by giving them a wage increase and then announcing an election. He also claimed that the board had reneged on the agreement to have separate bargaining units. The YFT withdrew from the election under these conditions, but the voting was held and considered legal, and the YEA was given bargaining rights for three years.

The new citizens' committee adopted the slogan "Give a Damn." Even this shock attempt backfired in some areas. Many parents objected to the effect "such language" might have on their children.

The local *Catholic Exponent* and *Jewish Times* carried ads with "Give a Damn" in large type. Signboards throughout the area had the message.

The city's big daily, the *Vindicator*, revised the ads to read "Give One."

The levy failed again. This time, with 53,008 persons voting, it got 48.7 percent or 25,821 for to 27,187 against. Oddly, there were 5,028 persons who voted but did not pull the lever on the school issue.

People asked, "Why did the school board increase expenses in the face of another defeat, virtual bankruptcy, and school closing?"

The tactic of forcing teacher pay raises that the school board cannot afford is called a "reverse strike." Under this plan the board keeps running with higher costs and taxpayers get the message—"raise the taxes or we close the schools." The closing of the schools is called a "shock tactic" and was used by other affiliates of the Ohio Education Association in some Southern Ohio districts as the OEA became more militant. The tactic appeals to teachers, who get their higher pay at once. Salary increases do not depend on strike action or on future tax votes which might fail.

One Youngstown board member said, "It is better to run a quality program until the money runs out than to run crippled schools."

Merle Huffman, president of the OEA, said that it was a move toward quality education on a broad front. He said the message was being spread around the nation and that school administrators were beginning to move away from trying to deal with teacher militancy in a labor-management sense and instead were joining with teachers to demand voter support for quality education.

Roy Fisher, then president of the YEA, said, "We were hoping we would run out of money by October 15, and close a few weeks before election. Large industries rescued the schools by paying their property taxes early."

In reply to criticism that the 12-mill increase requested was too high, Zinser said that board members polled various organizations, both political parties, business, industry, and Negro leadership, asking how much they felt schools should have. He said he was encouraged to ask for what he thought was needed. Then the board turned to a group of 23 persons, mostly company auditors and treasurers, for a financial projection. Their figures indicated that the 12-mill increase would be required.

The state gives Youngstown schools 22 percent of their total budget but no additional aid in an emergency. The city's tax rate was $36.30 per thousand valuation, with $22.30 going to schools. The school rate was second lowest in Mahoning County.

The only group to speak out against the board was the YFT. Officers demanded that the school board confer with them about school conditions before classes resumed in January.

This brought a scathing attack from the board president, Dr. Earl Young, a prominent obstetrician and long-time board member.

He put all the blame for the YFT attack and the levy defeats on Griffin. Dr. Young claimed Griffin was retaliating against the board because of its refusal to endorse a levy for a proposed Mahoning County Community College, a project Griffin spearheaded. The county-wide levy failed by an overwhelming vote, as the college was closely tied with labor.

Griffin said Dr. Young would do well to look into his own house instead of trying to find scapegoats among ethnic, religious, and labor groups. The YFT demanded Dr. Young's resignation. He ignored this demand but several weeks later did announce he would not seek reelection in the fall.

Abe Harshman, who succeeded Dr. Young as president, is a certified public accountant who was endorsed by labor when he ran for his first term two years ago. He is a past chairman of the Ohio Civil Liberties Union. Attorney Robert Murphy, another member of the new liberal board faction, is a labor lawyer.

The *Vindicator,* in a page one editorial on New Year's Day, dedicated itself to passage of the levy and staged a broad campaign to fulfill its commitment.

During the winter months Griffin was upset in his bid for a sixth term as director of the 26th district of the U.S. Steelworkers Union. His successor, Frank Lesegnaich, did not take office until after the primaries.

Griffin took no stand on the new levy attempt. The AFL-CIO Council under Shipka voted to let each member local make its own decision. Al DeVico, president of the Youngstown Building Trades Council, came out for the levy even before Shipka released locals. Presidents of the biggest Steelworkers locals appealed to their members for support.

A group of high school girls designed a red armband which was adopted as a campaign badge. This time there was a different slogan: "Join the Arm Band."

Parents canvassed door-to-door throughout seven wards, because in several sections of the city support had lagged in every prior election. They discussed the issues intelligently with persons who at first refused to sign their names and give permission to use the signatures in a newspaper advertisement for the levy. Eventually there were nine full pages of signatures. The *Vindicator* ran a separate story on every one of the 42 schools in the system, with picture layouts.

Voters were warned before the election that the only way to save the system was by passage of the levy. Spokesmen said the system would close at the end of the 1968–1969 year in mid-June and could not reopen before new tax money was available the first of next year. The board voted to ban teacher raises for a year.

And No. 7 turned out to be the lucky one for Youngstown. The levy received 57.11 percent of the vote, winning by a 7,000-vote margin.

Now another crisis faces the board. A 7.3-mill renewal comes before the voters this month and is vital to the continued operation of the school system. The 12-mill addition last spring was a continuing levy (something new under Ohio law); the renewal would also continue. If it passes, the Youngstown schools will be back on course—at least for awhile.

WHERE SCHOOL TAXES SPARKED A REVOLT

The plight of big-city school systems is illustrated again in this brief report of the Los Angeles situation. It is clear that property owners, rebellious over rising taxes, are now prepared to reject rate boosts earmarked for educational programs. This article also intimates that the relationship between local and state governments may be in a period of transition as a result of the pressures for more school money.

A taxpayer revolt of major importance appears to be showing itself in this city, stemming from the outcome of the voting in last November's elections.

The one chance that taxpayers had to register their reaction in a clear-cut way was on two measures to raise more money for schools. Both were defeated.

Something like a crisis is facing Los Angeles schools as a result.

Voters rejected a proposed increase of 47 cents in the present tax limit of $2.65 per $100 of property valuation for support of the city's elementary and secondary schools.

Also voted down was a proposal to increase by 15 cents a 35-cents-per-$100 property valuation in taxes for six junior colleges operated by the city.

School system suffers. The upshot is that the school system here—largest in the country next to New York City's—must cut expenses by as much as 19 million dollars in the next school year.

Reprinted from *U.S. News & World Report*, February 27, 1967, p. 64. Copyright 1967 U.S. News & World Report, Inc.

Says School Superintendent Jack P. Crowther: "Los Angeles city schools are faced with the most critical financial situation of modern times."

About 1,500 school employes could either lose their jobs or be transferred to other duties.

Among the moves Mr. Crowther is considering are an end to free bus transportation, cuts in maintenance and custodial operations, fewer nurses, doctors and clinic personnel, an end to such high-school courses as driver training, art appreciation and music, and a shortening of the class day by one period for high-school freshmen and sophomores.

What's behind the revolt against higher taxes for schools in Los Angeles?

Chiefly, it appears to be a feeling among property owners that they have shouldered as big a burden as they want to bear for school costs.

"The message of last November was very clear," says a school-board executive. "Property owners were saying: 'We've had it. We don't think we should carry the major share of the burden. Money to run the schools from here on will have to come from other sources, not just from property owners.' "

Adds Superintendent Crowther: "The voters . . . have given us a mandate not only to seek new sources of revenue, but to move toward a reduction of the load on property owners."

Reagan: a stumbling block? Mr. Crowther sees the answer to the financial problems of Los Angeles schools in getting more money from the State legislature. But here he could run head-on into the economy program of Governor Ronald Reagan.

Governor Reagan already has called for budget cuts for State-operated colleges and the State university, and for the imposition of tuition charges for the first time.

Many officials here view the Los Angeles school situation as the latest example of growing taxpayer resistance to rising costs of education.

They note that in the November elections, many special issues of school bonds were defeated throughout the State. The one major exception was a 230-million-dollar measure to improve State college and university facilities.

A recent survey by the California Poll discloses that 52 per cent of those questioned favor a budget cut, although not to the full amount proposed by Governor Reagan. About 51 per cent favor charging some tuition at the State colleges and university.

Another pollster, Don Muchmore of Opinion Research of California, says:

"The whole attitude about tuition-free higher education has changed. Not more than eight months ago, the idea was supported by a margin of 3 to 1. Today, it's nip and tuck."

Mr. Muchmore adds that the typical voter does not appear to be disturbed about higher liquor or cigarette taxes. "Somehow," he says, "voters have tied education to the property tax. If there could be a reduction in property taxes, the public probably would support more educational problems."

A local issue. The point stressed by officials here is that the higher property taxes rejected by Los Angeles voters were the only school tax proposals where the public had a chance to veto the ideas. Other school taxes are authorized by the California legislature, not by local citizens, and thus are not subject to direct voter reaction.

The present limits on school taxes on which voters have a direct say were set many years ago. In addition to these levies, local property owners pay additional school taxes for such costs as teachers' retirement funds, health and medical programs, adult education, and school construction.

All told, the 1966–67 school tax rate totaled $4.33 per $100 of assessed valuation, up 8.2 cents over the preceding year and 46 per cent higher than the 1956–57 rate of $2.90.

As early as last July, the Los Angeles Chamber of Commerce urged a broad cost-reduction program for the city's school system. Says attorney Leslie G. Tupper, chairman of the committee that drew up the program:

"On the one hand, the school system wants to provide the best education it can to everyone. On the other hand, the public feels that, when costs are so great and money so tight, you have to evaluate programs more closely."

Developments in this key State are seen as signaling an important shift in public attitudes on the whole issue of taxes and education—a change that may be reflected in many other parts of the country.

The Youngstown and Los Angeles illustrations have served to point up the seriousness of the public school financial problems. Needless to say, not all big cities are faced with the imminent closing of their schools. But all are faced with the challenge of finding new sources of revenue. One major reason the big cities are prevented from acquiring all of the school funds they need is the unequal distribution of state aid to local school districts. Because there is more than average competition for the tax dollar in the inner cities, a smaller proportion of collected taxes is given to the schools. The role of the states should be to equalize this disproportionate situation. Unfortunately, the states do not. Recently, educators and legal experts have begun to draw attention to these inequities in school finance. As mentioned earlier, numerous law suits have been brought against states to determine whether the states can be compelled to correct these discrepancies in tax support. Even if the courts eventually decide clearly in favor of the cities, the victory would only be a partial one because the money would merely be redistributed within the state. But this prospect for more big-city funds is the most promising on the horizon at this time.

Arthur E. Wise

THE CONSTITUTIONAL CHALLENGE TO INEQUITIES IN SCHOOL FINANCE

According to Arthur E. Wise and a growing number of educational finance experts, the disparities between rich and poor districts within each state are unconstitutional. In this selection, the author provides a scholarly, analytical argument to support his conclusion. Professor Wise, of the University of Chicago, became instantly controversial with the publication of his book, *Rich Schools, Poor Schools: The Promise of Equal Educational Opportunity* (1969).

Within nearly every state there are wide disparities in the amounts of money spent for the education of children in the public schools. Some children receive the benefits of an education costing several times that received by others. For example, in 1967 per pupil expenditures in California ranged from $274 to $1,710 and in Michigan from $394 to $915. These dollar differences measure rather directly the quantity and quality of services which schools provide. As early as 1965, it had become clear that a constitutional challenge to inequities in school finance could be made.

Variation in educational opportunity arises from the way states finance public education. In nearly all states, statutes place primary reliance for financing schools on the local property tax. The local school district is empowered to levy taxes on the local tax base. Within limitations, the local school district is free to raise as much in taxes as is politically feasible. Educational opportunity is, then, very largely a function of the local assessed valuation per pupil.

From *Phi Delta Kappan*, November, 1969, pp. 145–148. Footnotes omitted. Reprinted by permission of the author and publisher.

Indeed, it is generally true that poor school districts tax themselves at a higher rate than do rich school districts. However, these higher tax rates do not compensate for the deficiencies in the local tax base. Moreover, state aid equalization disbursements fail by design to compensate for the differences in local taxable capacity.

In short, the operation of school finance programs fails to provide even an approximation to equality in school support. And, it may be argued, the least is being provided where it is needed most. Equality of educational opportunity in the United States is a myth.

The question we raise is whether the Equal Protection Clause of the Fourteenth Amendment to the Constitution of the United States compels a state to afford equal educational opportunity to all students attending the public schools within that state without regard to where they live or the wealth of their local community.

Because state legislatures have refused to confront the problem, the issue is ripe for judicial action. The situation is directly comparable to that which led the Supreme Court to assume jurisdiction over legislative apportionment. For at least 50 years prior to reapportionment, state legislatures struggled with the periodic reapportionment which was mandated by their own constitutions. These attempts failed for a variety of political reasons. Similarly, for at least 50 years, state legislatures have struggled with the equalization of educational expenditures. State legislatures are generally charged by their own state constitutions with the responsibility for establishing "a uniform system of public schools." To expect state legislators to vote for programs which do not yield direct benefits to their own constituents is unrealistic, as can be seen in the fact that few equalization programs are passed which fail to provide some revenue to even the wealthiest districts.

In effect, a state's school finance statutes embody a de facto classification of the students in the state on the basis of the school district where they happen to reside. This classification, explicitly on the basis of school districts and implicitly on the basis of local assessed valuation per pupil, largely determines the quality of educational opportunity the student is to receive.

The U.S. Constitution allows states to classify. Generally, however, the Supreme Court has ruled that a classification to be reasonable must be related to the purpose of the law. The question becomes: Is the classification of students according to the tax base where they live sufficiently related to the purpose of the law to be considered reasonable?

The logic of the case for equal educational opportunity is to be found in three lines of Supreme Court decisions. These cases enunciate general principles which, while not controlling in the present instance, at least indicate how the Court might approach the problem of inequality in education. Limitations of space do not permit the full development of the legal argument; we will only show the framework within which it can be developed.

The school desegregation cases, especially *Brown* v. *Board of Education* in 1954, began to define public education as a constitutional right which fell within the scope of the Equal Protection Clause:

Today, education is perhaps the most important function of state and local governments. Compulsory school attendance laws and the great expenditures for education both demonstrate our recognition of the importance of education in our democratic society. It is required in the performance of our most basic public responsibilities, even service in the armed forces. It is the very foundation of good citizenship. Today it is the principal instrument in awakening the child to cultural values, in preparing him for later professional training, and in helping him to adjust normally to his environment. In these days, it is doubtful that any child may reasonably be expected to succeed in life if he is denied the opportunity of an education. Such an opportunity, where the state has undertaken to provide it, *is a right which must be made available to all on equal terms.*

Of course, the Court was here attempting to establish the proposition that discrimination in education by the state may not be based on color. In an attempt to avoid desegregation, officials of one county in Virginia closed the public schools and supported private, segregated schools. At the same time, public schools in all the other counties of the state were being maintained. In *Griffin* v. *County School Board,* the Court held:

Whatever nonracial grounds might support a state's allowing a county to abandon public schools, the object must be a constitutional one, and grounds of race and opposition to desegregation do not qualify as constitutional.

The state cannot permit differences among school districts when the basis for that difference is race.

The proposition that geography alone cannot form the basis for quantitative differences from one part of a state to another emerges from the reapportionment cases. Here the Court was establishing the principle that historical accidents associated with the boundary lines of local governmental units could not be used to dilute the value of some votes [*Reynolds* v. *Sims*].

The concept of equal protection has been traditionally viewed as requiring the uniform treatment of persons standing in the same relation to the governmental action questioned or challenged. With respect to the allocation of legislative representation, all voters, as citizens of a state, stand in the same relation regardless of where they live. Any suggested criteria for the differentiation of citizens are insufficient to justify any discrimination as to the weight of their votes, unless relevant to the permissible purposes of legislative apportionment. Since the achievement of fair and effective representation for all citizens is concededly the basic aim of legislative apportionment, we conclude that the Equal Protection Clause guarantees the opportunity for equal participation by all voters in the election of state legislators.

By implication, there may be some criteria which justify differentiation among persons within a state; at least in the case of voting, geography is not one of these.

The third general proposition concerns the irrelevance of wealth to social justice and is based on cases in the area of the administration of one of a state's services—criminal justice. These cases confronted one kind of discrimination between the rich and the poor in the application of state laws. The landmark case was *Griffin* v. *Illinois*. The Supreme Court held that an indigent defendant cannot be denied the same opportunity to appeal an adverse judgment that is available to others simply because he cannot afford the price of a transcript of the trial proceedings:

> It is true that a state is not required by the federal Constitution to provide appellate courts or a right to appellate review at all. . . . But that is not to say that a state that does grant appellate review can do so in a way that discriminates against some convicted defendants on account of their poverty.

The *Griffin* rule has been extended to include a wide range of services which the state must make available to indigent defendants. It has become increasingly clear that governmental discrimination may not be based upon wealth, at least in the area of criminal justice.

The general propositions which have emerged from these three lines of cases create a climate within which one can question whether the absence of equal educational opportunity within a state constitutes a denial by that state of the equal protection of its laws.

Of great importance to the present problem, these cases develop the concept of reasonable classification. The concept of equal protection requires the uniform treatment of persons standing in the same relation to the governmental action in question. It does not require that persons different in fact be treated in law as though they were the same. It does require that those who are similar be similarly treated.

While the method for allocating educational funds must be changed, there must be a rational basis for allocating these funds. *What is clear is that the amount of money spent on a child should not depend upon his parents' economic circumstances or his location within the state.* Any particular plan for financing public education in a state must meet this criterion. The traditional rhetoric of equal educational opportunity is not helpful. We simply cannot afford to spend enough on every child until he reaches the maximum development of his individual potentialities. There are a variety of approaches to defining equality of educational opportunity. In general, they have as their objective the reduction of the high correlations among socioeconomic status, local assessed valuation per pupil, expenditures per pupil, level of educational services, and student achievement.

If the current system of school finance were declared unconstitutional, it is to be supposed (indeed, hoped) that the Court would develop only a broad standard of equal protection in education. With a broad standard such as "the quality of a child's education should not depend upon his wealth or location," state legislatures would be free to experiment with a wide range of plans. It may be supposed further that this would be a period of intense political activity, with the advocates of various interest groups vying for a favored place in the new scheme. Undoubtedly, a variety of plans would emerge from the interactions among political, legislative, and educational forces. Finally, it may be supposed that these plans would be subject to judicial review to ascertain the extent to which they meet the broad standard.

Equality of educational opportunity is a philosophical abstract. A working definition of this term must be administratively feasible. Let me propose one definition which I believe is both administratively feasible and which should satisfy the requirements of equal protection and reasonable classification.

The basic rule would require that there be an approximately equal per pupil expenditure throughout the state. The application of the rule would require that educational resources be allocated so that the maximum discrepancy in per pupil expenditures does not exceed a specified ratio. This approach would be similar to the approach employed in the reapportionment decisions. The courts might require that the maximum variation in per pupil expenditure be no more than two-to-one or one and a half-to-one. Variation can be justified as an accommodation to educational needs, price-level differences, differences in the economies of scale, or, indeed, political expediency.

An adjunct to this rule could be a mechanism to channel additional resources to school districts with high concentrations of students with low academic achievement. This could be accomplished in one of two ways. The first would be to provide an additional sum, say X percent in excess of the basic per pupil amount, to those districts which have a high concentration of families on relief or with earnings below the poverty line. This method is similar to that employed under Title I of the Elementary and Secondary Education Act. The second method would be to provide an additional sum, say X percent in excess of the basic amount, to those districts which have a large number of students who score below the norm on achievement tests.

Equality of educational opportunity—however it is defined—demands revision in school financing. One form of revision would be a plan in which the state collects all school revenues and distributes them to local school districts. These revenues could be collected by means of a state-wide property tax or, as is currently the case with state-aid revenues, by means of a sales tax or income tax. A state-wide system of property taxation would probably release new funds for schools, since districts with high expenditures tend to have low tax rates. In addition, gerrymandering of school districts over the years has resulted in industrial enclaves free from high local taxes.

A second form of revision would be a plan to equalize the tax bases of local school districts by redrawing district lines. As the size of school districts increases, the tax base tends to become equalized; that is; poorer and wealthier residential and industrial areas are brought within the same school district. This kind of plan would involve a reorganization of school control, since smaller districts would necessarily have to be consolidated. Reorganization of school control is a by-product of this plan only and is not a necessary consequence of expenditure equalization. Moreover, it is not clear that substantial equalization of tax bases would occur even with substantial gerrymandering, since, in some states, wealth is widely dispersed geographically.

A third form of revision would involve manipulation of equalization formulas. The reformulation of equalization plans could be made to conform to whatever standards are required. The larger the permissible deviations, of course, the less the equalization that is required.

The prognosis for the proposed suit is not clear. The cases undertaken to date have been notably unsuccessful. At the present time it is not unconstitutional for states to spend more money on rich children than on poor children in the public schools. So apparently did the United States Supreme Court conclude on March 24, 1969. The case was *McInnis* v. *Ogilvie*, on appeal from the United States District Court for the Northern District of Illinois. The Supreme Court's holding came in its affirmation of the lower court's ruling. In the history of this litigation we are perhaps at the point today that legislative apportionment was in 1946 when the Supreme Court denied that it could entertain jurisdiction over reapportionment. In 1962, the Supreme Court chose to interject itself vigorously into the problems of reapportionment. My own prediction is that we will see a decision in favor of the equalization of educational opportunity after a lengthy period of litigation. It behooves educators to prepare for this eventuality before lawyers step into the vacuum.

David L. Kirp

A CRITIQUE OF WISE'S THESIS

In an analysis as persuasive as Arthur E. Wise's, David L. Kirp refutes much of the equal protection of the laws argument offered in the preceding article. Mr. Kirp, Acting Associate Professor of Public Policy and Lecturer, School of Law, University of California at Berkeley, is a recognized authority on equal educational opportunity questions as seen from the legal perspective.

The "opportunity" for education, the Supreme Court asserted in *Brown* v. *Board of Education,* "is a right which must be made available to all on equal terms." Although the Court was clear in saying that dual school systems segregated by race did not meet this test, no further attempt to define equal educational opportunity appears in the decision. Was de jure racial discrimination the sole measure of equal educational opportunity? Certainly a great deal more than de jure segregation has come to be included in discussions of equal educational opportunity since *Brown.* Despite the impression given in Arthur Wise's article for the *Kappan,* equal allocation of resources is only one of many approaches to defining equal opportunity. Others include compensatory education, decentralization of schools, community control of schools, racial balance, a quest for equal achievement, competing alternate school systems, and attacks on the constitutionality of tracking. Although there is some overlap in these considerations, there is also considerable incompatibility. The present discussion, however, will focus largely on Wise's case for equal allocation of resources within states.

From *Phi Delta Kappan,* November, 1969, pp. 148–150. Footnotes omitted. Reprinted by permission of the author and publisher.

Wise develops a new and potentially revolutionary view of the state's constitutional obligation to provide equal educational opportunity. He rejects the prevailing assumption that, with respect to resource allocation, inequality is the norm and equality the rare exception. Instead, Wise makes equality a constitutional requirement and would oblige a state to justify deviations from an equality standard. He cites a variety of equal protection decisions—notably those concerned with school desegregation, voting rights, and criminal due process—as judicial support for his view.

Wise sees the Supreme Court eventually deciding that "the quality of a child's education should not depend upon his wealth or location." This, he says, is a "broad standard" that will leave the states "free to experiment with a wide range of plans." Wise, however, sets out only one plan that would work: approximately equal per pupil expenditures throughout the state, with variations permitted only for differences in educational needs, in price levels, in economies of scale, and (curiously and capriciously) for political expediency.

Wise's thesis, while exciting in its potential, nonetheless raises some serious questions. One concerns his approach: Are the courts more likely to develop a workable and enforceable standard of equal educational opportunity than the state legislatures? Another deals with theory: What criteria of equal educational opportunity can and should be applied? Others bear on the propriety and feasibility of the action Wise suggests: Will an equalization of educational resources bring about equal educational opportunity? Will a scheme that apparently requires shifting resources from rich to poor communities be beneficial? Or will it preserve (or create) mediocrity at the expense of a few well-to-do school districts which now, it is said, stimulate excellence? What are the likely political consequences of Wise's approach?

Philip Kurland, a noted student of the Supreme Court, has taken up the question of judicial versus legislative solutions to the problem of equal educational opportunity in his essay, "Equal Educational Opportunity, or the Limits of Constitutional Jurisprudence Undefined." Kurland doubts the Court's ability to foster support for this new foray into social engineering, and he questions whether it has adequate means to enforce decisions requiring financial disbursements. Yet as Kurland himself notes, the Court has had considerable success in implementing its indigent criminal and reapportionment holdings. Legislators generally have not resisted implementing these decisions. Where resistance has been threatened, the Court has found ample means to force compliance, including staying elections and enjoining state tax collections and disbursements.

Kurland also questions the desirability of resolving the equal educational opportunity issue through equalizing resources, which he terms "the problem of the wrong problem."

"The real problem," Kurland writes in his essay, "is either that there are too many of our school systems that are undernourished or that the desegregation problem is not subject to solution so long as local governmental units exercise autonomy over their school systems. In either case, I don't expect the solution to be found in a simple rule of equality of educational opportunity on a state-wide basis."

Wise, however, assumes that "equal resources" is not only a permissible measure of equality, but also that it is the most significant. When discussing "variations" from this standard, he does not mean other possible interpretations of equal educational opportunity which don't depend on resources, but merely variations which lead to unequal resources. He then proceeds to construct a legal framework to support his constitutional position.

Wise lacked space to develop the legal arguments in his *Kappan* article. But it is not that simple for an audience of non-lawyers to infer his reasoning from the cases he has cited and quoted. He has set forth the legal arguments in his essay in *The Quality of Inequality* and in his book, *Rich Schools, Poor Schools*. In *The Quality of Inequality*, he offers the legal syllogism: Discrimination in education on account of race is unconstitutional. Discrimination in criminal proceedings on account of poverty is unconstitutional. Therefore, discrimination in education on account of poverty is unconstitutional. These premises, he states, reflect "the law of the land." Yet Wise's premises so oversimplify the "law of the land" as to render any conclusion based on them almost meaningless. Consider the syllogism noted above. Is discrimination in education on account of race always unconstitutional, or only when such discrimination represents declared public policy? Does the safeguard against discrimination in criminal proceedings always guarantee the poor man an attorney when charged with an offense? Does that safeguard assure him expert witnesses as proficient as those that more affluent defendants can afford? Does it guarantee him a lawyer as well versed in criminal practice as one he might hire if he had unlimited resources? These questions are unanswered in the decisions Wise has cited; all of them have been brought back to the courts for an answer. And thus far the answers have generally been negative, revealing that the courts have a standard of equality more fragile, a view of discrimination more ambiguous, than Wise's formulations suggest.

Furthermore, Wise's insufficient attention to the complexities of defining a measure of equality leaves him vulnerable to the argument (which Kurland makes) that "equalization" could be constitutionally required with respect to any public service. But courts have permitted communities to choose between different services and have permitted states to give communities unequal financial support for a particular public service; it is doubtful that all of these cases will be overturned. Wise attempts to distinguish other services from education on the ground that "state constitutions have placed the responsibility for education on the state. The same cannot be said for the other services." This response is both inaccurate (for some state constitutions do vest responsibility for other public services in the state) and beside the point, for it assumes that the Equal Protection Clause can be applied to enforce state constitutional mandates, an assumption that the Supreme Court has never shared. Kurland's argument can be answered only by understanding what the common elements are that relate the seemingly disparate rights—to equal educational opportunity, to counsel for an indigent criminal defendant, to an equal vote—and that do not apply to all governmental activities. Wise has not undertaken this task. He declares that three lines of Supreme Court decisions "enunciate general principles which, while not controlling in the present instance, at least indicate how the Court might approach the problem of inequality in education." Nowhere does he elucidate the parallels between the diverse cases he discusses. Yet the parallels and the distinctions need to be analyzed, the limiting characteristics of what have been termed *fundamental* rights need to be determined, if the courts are to be persuaded of the soundness of analogies drawn from such diverse cases. If a definition of equal educational opportunity is carefully developed from these cases, the courts might favorably consider the constitutional argument based on that definition. Otherwise, courts might well regard the constitutional argument as merely an egalitarian impulse, which they would be obliged to pursue with regard to *all* public services. Without a carefully constructed definition, the courts are likely to declare that equality of educational opportunity is a constitutional "thicket" still too tangled to penetrate.

This is in fact what the Supreme Court did in *McInnis* v. *Ogilvie*, the one resource allocation case that it has decided. The Court, obliged to pass on the lower court's decision, affirmed that decision in a one-sentence *per curiam* opinion. This form of opinion permits the Supreme Court to accept the ruling of the lower court without necessarily accepting its reasoning. Thus, all the Court did in *McInnis* was agree that the plaintiffs should have lost the case. The Supreme Court did not, and did not have to, give its own reasoning. It may have agreed that the state law was constitutional. It may have agreed that there was presented no constitutional standard on which the Court could rule. It may have felt that the particular facts in *McInnis* were not appropriate for a Supreme Court ruling on equal educational opportunity. What matters is that the decision gives us no basis for choosing between these readings.

This is a most important "technical" point to bear in mind. It suggests that a successful *McInnis*-type lawsuit remains a real possibility. It should also give pause to those district court judges (and district school superintendents) who have uncritically accepted Wise's assertion that, after *McInnis*, states may discriminate in financial support for the schools on the basis of wealth without fear of judicial rebuke.

Wise's own difficulties in attempting to establish a standard clearly demonstrate the problems that face a court in such cases. "What is clear," he tells us, "is that the amount of money spent on a child should not depend upon his parents' economic circumstances or his location within the state." This standard, however, is no solution. A few paragraphs after Wise states his standard he moves away from it. He would encourage states to "provide an additional sum . . . to those districts which have a high concentration of families on relief or with earnings below the poverty line." The impulse is admirable, but here Wise is advocating a formula which allocates resources according to location within the state and community wealth and therefore—by Wise's single standard—is unconstitutional. Since the courts rarely allow us to have things both ways, we must question Wise's "clear" standard. Does a constitutional rule which effectively, if inadvertently, rules out compensatory education make any sense?

Wise does set forth a corpus of case law and statutes that could be used to develop compelling constitutional objections to the way public education is presently financed. But would a reallocation of a state's educational resources in accordance with such a standard lead to a measurably better education for children who are presently underschooled? Or would shuffling resources only continue to provide what Eldridge Cleaver has termed a "higher uneducation"?

Wise does not respond directly to this question. He sets forth three methods by which states could finance education. Yet all three methods assume that the state will continue to support a single, uniform system of public schooling which children are obliged to attend. What about a state financing scheme which gives money for schooling directly to children and not to school districts, which permits children to buy the kind of education they—and their parents—want rather than the kind of education their community prefers? Perhaps Wise would not object; perhaps he would; he does not address the issue. Nor does he discuss any other possibilities beyond his three rather minor variations on what we already have.

In a colloquium at the University of Chicago Center for Policy Study at which his proposals were considered, Wise was moved to comment, "I began with a rather limited objective. That was to propose an attack on the current method of public school financing. We seem to be bringing the whole of the educational enterprise into the picture. I am not sure this is necessary." This limitation of the issues to be considered is regrettable. It allows Wise to insist, as he does in *Rich Schools, Poor Schools*, that "questions of desirability" and "values" are outside his competence. Yet he does have ideas about desirability and values, which are clearly set forth in the preface to *Rich Schools, Poor Schools:* "I was impelled in this endeavor by the *belief* that there is no justification . . . for permitting the circumstance of parental wealth and geography to determine the quality of a child's education in the public schools of a state." More importantly, the limitation prevents him from considering the political impact of his scheme. Wise is prescribing a "professional" solution to an educational problem. But in many communities there exists real doubt concerning the feasibility of any educational policy making undertaken *by* professionals *for* communities, policy making which carries with it assumptions about what is important in schooling (that children be equipped to fit into the society's middle class) and how to measure the success or failure of schooling (through standardized verbal and arithmetical achievement tests).

There are sound reasons for bringing the kind of judicial action that Wise proposes. The threat of such a suit might prod a legislature into developing a different, and hopefully better, resource reallocation scheme. Were the suit to succeed, it is likely (given predictable political pressure) that the result would not be merely a reallocation of existing resources but an absolute increase in state educational expenditures. Furthermore, the consequences of spending more money for schools attended predominantly by poor and black children—another likely result of such a suit—would undoubtedly benefit them and their community.

The Coleman Report's measure of the effect of increased expenditures on education is based on a relatively narrow range of expenditures; it does not consider what would happen if the state spent two, three, or four times more for public education than it has traditionally spent. And increases in expenditures of these magnitudes will probably be necessary to enable the states to move toward providing equally effective educational opportunity for all children.

Determining the bounds and meaning of equal educational opportunity is a most critical theoretical question for educators and for the community. Any successful challenge to conventional notions would doubtless produce massive shifts in the deployment of public resources (broadly conceived, dollars and textbooks, teachers and schoolchildren); political upheavals of volcanic proportion; not-so-quiet revolutions in society's expectations concerning the value of an education. While Wise heralds the revolution, he leaves unanswered questions that revolutionaries must answer.

Much speculation about the future funding of education has been engaged in by educators, lawyers, city planners, politicians, and others from all walks of life. School support is an issue of universal interest because if it does not affect a citizen directly through his work, it certainly reaches him when he pays his rent or property taxes. Much evidence has been gathered to date in an effort to predict the future of the urban school financial crisis. Clearly, though, prediction is difficult because of the present diverse opinion surrounding solutions to the problem of big-city school finance. Its potential implications for all society make this issue one of immediate concern and speculative interest to both lay citizens and scholars of all disciplines.

William P. McLure
FINANCING EDUCATION
AT THE FEDERAL LEVEL

Noted school-finance authority William P. McLure, Director of the University of Illinois Bureau of Educational Research, in this article shows the changing relationship among the federal, state, and local levels of government in educational decision-making. He has used his observa-

From *Federal Policy and the Public Schools*, edited by the American Association of School Administrators (Washington: The Association, 1967). Number six of nine essays, no pagination. Reprinted by permission of the author and the AASA.

tions of trends in the interaction among governmental levels as bases for his prediction that a tax-sharing plan between the state and federal governments will provide the eventual solution to the problem of distributing fiscal resources.

The Elementary and Secondary Education Act of 1965 has led to an intervention of the federal government in the direct management of public schools to an unprecedented extent, resulting in extensive confusion and disunity throughout the educational system. The approach to massive federal support through categorical aids is proving what most leaders and students of education predicted: a cumbersome method that does violence to long-established principles of administration by an enlightened profession.

The root of the problem lies in the method of distributing federal funds for specific purposes with concomitant controls. More than 80 types of grants are in force, a scale of operation that has produced an unbelievable amount of frenetic activity throughout the educational system. The proven methods of evaluating, weighing alternatives, and establishing criteria for balancing related programs and services, have been turned upside down. There has been a disturbing shift of decision making from the state and local levels to the federal level of government.

It is time to examine the fruits of recent experience, to place the positive results in proper perspective, and to offer constructive alternatives to the present approach to federal financing of education.

Why?

What were the conditions that led to the present state of federal participation in financing education? To name the chief ones will help one to understand the present dilemma and to see the logic of the alternative to be described later.

The most fundamental fact to consider is the progressive income tax system which the federal government has developed. This is perhaps the most powerful fiscal system that any national government has ever devised. The power of Congress under the Tenth Amendment to the Constitution to levy taxes for any purpose deemed in the national welfare, coupled with the power to budget expenditures and to control the supply of money and credit, gives the federal government the essential tools for responsible leadership in the maintenance of a healthy economy.

The states have relatively weak tax systems. They rely mainly on sales and property taxes, both of which are regressive in character. In theory they could utilize a progressive income tax to go far toward balancing the equity of the total system. While two-thirds of the states have a state income tax, none uses this form extensively for two logical reasons. First, no state wants to get very far out ahead of others for fear of adverse business effects. Second, the concentration and complexity of economic activity would make a large amount of tax avoidance possible unless all states levied a uniform tax.

Thus, the states have the responsibility for education and the expenditure need but inadequate tax systems. The federal government has the only tax system which can tap the national economy as equitably as can be devised. This gap between the fiscal power to raise revenue on the one hand and the expenditure need on the other constitutes the basis for federal participation in financing education.

A number of forces gained momentum in recent years to increase the costs of education faster than revenue potential. For a time the birth rate increased faster than state and local tax bases. The farm revolution sent millions of persons to the cities. This movement accelerated the flight of big-city dwellers to the suburbs. These changes occurred at a time when most states failed to make commensurate changes in the organizational structure of their school systems, their local tax systems, county governments, and other agencies of government. Thus, states have not put their houses in order to administer adequately and economically the modern needs of government.

These needs have not gone unnoticed by educators, students of government, and economists. The shelves of libraries are heavy with reports of studies on all of these problems. Many members and groups of the educational profession, for example, have proclaimed repeatedly the needs of various educational improvements to the public at large, to state legislatures, and to the Congress of the United States.

Sputnik should have come as no surprise to any student of American education. It caused panic among some leaders in education and government. It precipitated federal fiscal policies which under other circumstances might have been different. The long, deliberative route of pursuing general aid, with roadblocks of opposition from private and parochial schools and other sources, was abandoned. Instead the action was based on categorical aid, an approach which some of the ardent opponents finally accepted in the hope that this method would be followed only temporarily.

Categorical Aids

There are some gains from the recently expanded program of special aids. Perhaps most important of all, the program is highlighting the complexity of needs of the schools. It should be amply clear by now that there has been a tendency in recent years to oversimplify education. There has been too much tendency to find simple answers to very complex problems. Recent events may have aroused a public awareness of the size of the educational task facing this nation. There is evidence coming to indicate that citizens are beginning to understand the inadequacies in tax structures, local school districts, archaic intermediate districts, the multiplicity of educational agencies at the state level, lack of highly talented teachers, and shortages of facilities as they take advantage of federal funds.

There are dangers of continuing these procedures with myriads of categorical aids beyond a temporary period of stimulation and exploration that also are becoming apparent. The dangers are very real and deep. Some of the most serious ones are as follows:

Categorical aids have a divisive effect on the profession. They arbitrarily elevate particular instructional fields and services and thus directly downgrade other fields of equal validity and value. They proliferate programs and build structures that are difficult to change. Staff members are divided into special-interest groups which inevitably develop insular tendencies.

They reduce the rigor of choice among alternatives. Surplus equipment from special grants is all too frequently found because of "making the most of the opportunity while it is available."

An inordinate amount of professional time is required to prepare proposals and evaluations to meet the guidelines of decision makers outside the system.

They restrict the freedom of cooperation within school systems. For example, the teachers of language arts may contribute as much, if not more, to the vocational competence of a high school graduate than the teachers of "vocational" courses. To put the latter on special salary schedules with other perquisites and to deny these to the former is difficult to justify to the persons intimately involved.

They oversimplify by spurious definitions programs and services in the "national interest." Just what values are there in educational programs and services that contribute to the development of every individual that are not in the national interest?

They hinder the development of rational emphases in education. Educational purposes have to be defined in functional components known as instructional fields and services. Changes and adaptations should result from indigenous needs and requirements based upon the best and widest use of human intelligence in society rather than from decisions of a few administrative agents of government.

By their nature they require a system of external control that is antithetic to American values of government and to psychological principles of effective human behavior.

These disadvantages likewise overshadow advantages of categorical aids to institutions of higher education.

General Aids

General aids have far more advantages than categorical aids as a means for distributing federally collected revenues to school systems. Some of the chief advantages are:

They promote a more defensible system of control and administrative responsibility to pursue educational objectives worthy of a free society.

They promote an intellectual disposition of creativity rather than compliance.

They strengthen the capacity of local school systems to study, to plan, to take responsible action, and to evaluate.

Certainty and stability of support are more easily assured than is possible to establish for special aids.

General funds are more suitable to tie school support to the economic capacity of the nation. School systems need the fiscal capacity that permits flexibility to cope with fluctuations in the composition of the school population and the attendant educational requirements.

School systems are responsive, if not arbitrarily handicapped, to the basic drive of the American people for excellence. The oft-repeated question of political leaders, "Can we be sure that the funds will yield the best educational results?" is certainly legitimate. But it deserves to be answered adequately rather than to be used rhetorically.

The Alternative

There are responsible scholars and leaders in education, as in other fields of endeavor, who believe that there is overwhelming evidence in the experience of public education in America to favor the superiority of general federal funds over categorical aids for education. This idea is an old one, dating back at least a half century. The first classic statement of basic theory and operational structure to describe this idea was made by the late Professor Paul R. Mort in 1936 in *Federal Support for Public Education*. Since that time there have been any number of proposals embodying the same basic idea with variations in structural detail. A recent advocate with national recognition is Walter W. Heller, former chairman of the Council of Economic Advisers to the late President Kennedy and during one year of President Johnson's administration. He has championed general funds in the form of shared revenues rather than general grants-in-aid.

Proponents of general aid believe that this type of support can be devised to accomplish the best that is known about federal-state-local relations in the governance of education; the soundest fiscal policy; the greatest degree of adaptability of the school system to future needs of every individual and society; the soundest principles to promote creativity, scholarship, and responsibility among teachers and other educational leaders; and the safest principle to ensure the highest quality of education.

This idea has been expressed in two forms: (1) general grant-in-aid, and (2) tax or revenue sharing. The author prefers the latter because it comes closer to expressing the fundamental role of the federal government; namely, to restrict its action to purely fiscal relationships with the states. Tax sharing would serve as the means to gear a basic support of education to the total economy of the nation. The states would be responsible for administering the schools and providing additional support from state and local taxes. Each state would have responsibility for developing a fiscal structure with refinements to meet various adjustments, including the extra costs in cities of dense population and the most sparse areas, equity among districts of variable local taxable wealth, incentives to improve local district structure, and other factors. The fiscal structure of each state should encompass the funds collected from all levels of government.

The alternative proposal for federal financing would be as follows:

Definition of educational revenues into large blocks: (1) elementary and secondary schools, and (2) higher education.

Gradual consolidation of present categorical aids and transfer of most of them to general payments after a specified date. Exceptions would be a few special aids such as GI educational scholarships, payments in lieu of local property taxes in federally impacted areas, educational programs in the armed forces, and other similar functions best centralized in the federal government.

Designation of a given percentage of the total federal income tax collections to be distributed to the states for education. The federal government could prorate the funds between elementary and secondary schools and higher education, or it could leave this decision to the state legislatures. (Heller has an excellent suggestion for a trust account to handle these funds, a mechanism which would take them out of the federal budget and expedite the flow of funds to states.)

Distribution of educational revenues to the states should be made as follows:

Higher education. Since comparable cost units are virtually nonexistent in higher education, the most feasible basis would be a given percentage of the educational and general expenditures, with a normative overage for capital outlay.

Elementary and secondary schools. The basis for distribution would be one of the following: (a) A given percentage of school expenditures, including expenses of current operation and capital outlay. (b) School-age population if the decision is made to support that portion of education which private and parochial schools may share with the public schools; otherwise pupil membership (enrollment) in the public schools would be used as the distribution unit.

Adjustments in distribution of federal revenues to states. Two adjustments are proposed for revenues to elementary and secondary education. The principles are applicable to higher education, and the same corrections might be applicable to both areas of education. (1) The first one is an adjustment for differences in relative ability of the states. In this case the writer has chosen the index, *average personal income per pupil ages 5–17.* (2) The second one is an adjustment for extra costs necessary in sparse and dense areas. In the former areas schools have extra costs of transportation and some low pupil-staff ratios due to small schools. The large cities constitute the other extreme where a disparate school population with high rates of retardation, emotional maladjustment, and mobility call for extra staff and resources to meet individual needs.

Estimated Adjustments

For many years advocates of general federal aid to education argued for the principle of equalization in relation to the average tax ability of each state. In recent years studies have revealed that the costs of education in the great cities are greater than would be necessary in smaller cities. These extra costs have been referred to as compensatory expenses. They result not from density per se but from fundamental characteristics of the school population such as just mentioned. The extent of these deviate characteristics which cost extra money seems to be greatest in the large cities of greatest density. There are some exceptions in smaller cities, but usually these are suburbs of larger cities. The question has been raised as to whether the extra costs of the great cities, most of which are in the wealthiest states, might not offset the justifiable correction for low wealth.

The writer has explored this question in recent years. The base of reference for estimating extra costs is a city with about 10,000 pupils in 12 grades, composed of a normally distributed school population. Larger size has little if any effect on cost because of economies of scale. However, there are extra costs that creep into large, densely populated cities when the proportions of retardation and social maladjustment go up. Also, increased land prices and labor rates affect costs of capital outlay.

In some recent studies with 15 of the large cities the writer found a needed correction of 16 percent for identifiable programs and services. He estimated an additional 17 percent for programs in experimental stages, giving a total correction of 33 percent. This is about the limit which he found to be necessary in the most sparse areas in previous studies in West Virginia, New York, Mississippi, and Illinois. Therefore, using these limits, interpolating in between, and aggregating corrections for the school population as it was dispersed in 1965, a correction was computed for each state.

The following table shows the density-sparsity correction, the wealth correction, and the net correction for each state.

While the density-sparsity corrections would be substantial in some communities within states, the state averages, when spread over the

Corrections for Density-Sparsity-Wealth

State	Density-Sparsity Correction	Wealth ° Ratio 1965	Net Correction	State	Density-Sparsity Correction	Wealth ° Ratio 1965	Net Correction
Alabama	12%	2.05	1.85	Nebraska	19	1.40	1.36
Alaska	24	1.17	1.21	Nevada	14	1.05	1.01
Arizona	19	1.66	1.53	New			
Arkansas	17	2.00	1.85	Hampshire	10	1.40	1.23
California	14	1.08	1.04	New Jersey	3	1.05	.92
Colorado	18	1.40	1.35	New Mexico	18	1.98	1.85
Connecticut	3	1.02	.90	New York	17	1.00	1.00
Delaware	4	1.10	.98	North Carolina	7	1.88	1.67
Florida	11	1.40	1.29	North Dakota	22	1.74	1.67
Georgia	12	1.75	1.60	Ohio	7	1.33	1.20
Hawaii	13	1.34	1.26	Oklahoma	17	1.57	1.49
Idaho	20	1.68	1.61	Oregon	20	1.30	1.28
Illinois	15	1.07	1.04	Pennsylvania	9	1.29	1.09
Indiana	6	1.32	1.18	Rhode Island	4	1.20	1.06
Iowa	14	1.39	1.31	South Carolina	7	2.22	1.95
Kansas	16	1.38	1.32	South Dakota	21	1.81	1.73
Kentucky	11	1.86	1.69	Tennessee	12	1.84	1.68
Louisiana	13	1.94	1.77	Texas	16	1.63	1.44
Maine	15	1.63	1.52	Utah	18	1.80	1.70
Maryland	8	1.23	1.21	Vermont	16	1.59	1.50
Massachusetts	5	1.12	1.00	Virginia	9	1.53	1.38
Michigan	12	1.27	1.19	Washington	17	1.28	1.23
Minnesota	15	1.44	1.36	West Virginia	9	1.91	1.71
Mississippi	14	2.58	2.32	Wisconsin	13	1.38	1.21
Missouri	16	1.32	1.27	Wyoming	22	1.57	1.53
Montana	22	1.62	1.57	United States	16	1.35	1.29

° Ratio of average personal income per person ages 5-17 in wealthiest state (New York) to the average in each respective state.

total school population, are small compared to the needed corrections to adjust for differences in average state ability. According to these estimates, Mississippi would receive $2.32 of federal revenue for each $1 distributed to New York.

Summary

What assurance can the federal government have that the revenues distributed by this proposed procedure will be spent most effectively? The only technical assurance needed is a proper audit certifying that the funds have been spent for the general purpose as designated. In addition, states should be expected to publish reports of far more evaluative rigor than they have prepared in the past. Such reports are needed not merely to justify use of federal funds but as a matter of public responsibility irrespective of sources of financial support. The state of knowledge is reaching the point where comprehensive evaluations of deployment of input resources can be made and related to some dependable data on educational results (benefits). These evaluations can go beyond the current limited and oversimplified approaches to national assessment. Furthermore, the techniques and results can be made a matter of public information so that researchers are challenged to advance the science of evaluation.

What incentive will states have to continue state and local effort to support education? In the past the states of low wealth have made a greater tax effort than states of high wealth. There is no evidence to indicate that educational aspirations in any state will decline. The demands for improvements of various kinds are so great that there is no foreseeable reduction in educational costs. An increase in federal funds would permit many communities at high tax-effort levels to slow down the rate of increase in local tax burden. This condition would permit some local tax relief in efforts to reach educational goals, but not reduction except in rare instances.

What should be the limits of federal participation? The goal should be to establish an axiomatic level of support that would be modified as often as necessary to keep the states of lowest wealth within reach of an adequate level of expenditure after placing a reasonable burden on state and local tax sources.

Would this general tax-sharing plan call for some means of communication between the policy-making agencies of state and federal governments? It would seem that some means of communication are needed. At present they appear to be working independently, if not competitively, in some instances.

Theodore R. Sizer

THE CASE FOR A FREE MARKET

In this selection, Theodore R. Sizer, Dean of the Harvard Graduate School of Education, introduces a new concept to the solution of urban

Reprinted from *Saturday Review*, January 11, 1969, pp. 34 ff., a special issue produced in cooperation with the Committee for Economic Development, by permission of the author and publisher.

education finance problems. He proposes that the money crisis can best be resolved by creating a competitive marketplace in the cities for various types of schools. Much attention has been given to proposals of this nature in recent years by politicians and local community organizations. Needless to say, numerous lay and professional groups refuse to take this type of plan seriously. If a struggle for a "free market" system of education should develop in the future, it will have serious consequences for the public schools as we now know them.

Competition is the newest old panacea for the reform of American schools. The argument for it is simple: The public schools are a monopoly and monopolies offer neither variety nor high quality. As America needs both varied and excellent schools, competitive pressure is clearly required. A marketplace must be created for education, with children and their parents as the choice-making consumers. The consumers, the argument continues, will pick the better schools most of the time and, in so doing, will force the quality of all to improve.

Like all panaceas, this one suffers from oversimplification. Nonetheless, it has considerable merit, particularly if a "competitive" scheme were conceived as a part of a larger, comprehensive effort at school reform. The marketplace should not be the total arbiter of educational quality. Children are, on the whole, poor judges of the "product" they are buying; their parents' judgment is very uneven; and empirical evidence on the quality of schooling is meager and confusing. Still, the "consumer" should have some influence over the school he attends, enough to shape it in appropriate ways, but not enough to terrorize it. In a field where values are paramount—schools are places designed to *influence* children and as such are supremely moral enterprises—no group, students, parents, teachers, or government, should have total control. There should be a balance. Many of today's school systems do not permit sufficient diversity among individual students and individual schools. In doing so, they foster a dull conformity. Competition among schools must be added to the balance.

Despite evidence to the contrary, particularly that cited in James S. Coleman's report *Equality of Educational Opportunity,* a change in control *can* lead to a change in the quality of children's learning. Some changes in control, such as turning the schools in black communities completely over to black educators, are essentially political maneuvers, provoked by a general dissatisfaction rather than by any specific theory about the means of educational reform. Some possibly inevitable shifts in control may be pedagogically harmful. But changes in control can be significant for children. Many significant things that children learn are untestable, and may be affected by the political structure of a school or school system. The attitudes of teachers, the pride (or lack of it) that parents have in a school, the extent of accountability of the staff—all may have subtle but important effects on learning. No one yet has documented this, but anyone who has taught in different schools knows that it is true. Those who say that the manner of a school's governance has little effect on pupil achievement and learning are deluded. New forms of control, including those that forward concepts of competition, will touch children.

There are various means to encourage competition, some essentially political and some fiscal. The one most in the public eye at present is decentralization, an effort to give more power over a particular school or school district to those in the immediate community served by that school. The arguments for decentralization usually do not originate in a belief in competition per se, but rather from the conviction that a minority group within a large community has been disregarded by the monopolistic system and will continue to be unless that group can influence the schools it uses. The Ocean Hill-Brownsville community in New York City wants more control over its schools because its leaders believe that their children are getting not only an inferior education but also one dominated primarily by white rather than black values.

Decentralization will create competing schools only in the sense that people unhappy with the schools in one district can move to another, and this possibility is unlikely in many communities due both to the large numbers of people involved and the restriction of lower-class Negroes from most suburban, middle-class white communities. Decentralization will give a small, relatively homogenous community—whether white or black, rich or poor—a school or schools over which it has monopolistic control. It would Balkanize big-city districts and return them, more or less, to the way they were organized seventy-five years ago. The variety in the city would be reflected by the variety in the schools. Each geographical group, more or less, would have its own public school enclave.

For political reasons, drastic and total decentralization may now be essential and inevitable. The black community in particular has been frustrated too long to weigh heavily the debits of such a move. It wants to control what its children learn and it wants to hire and fire the teachers who teach them. It will achieve this goal, but much tension and violence will precede it.

Apart from political realities, total decentralization has little to commend it. The biases of a tiny geographical minority will hold sway over children who, if present patterns continue, will almost certainly not remain in the community where they were schooled. Little village bigotries will get disproportionate attention; teachers will find local pressures difficult to work under (ask anyone who has taught in a small, fundamentalist Protestant town); and pedagogical reform, which rarely arises from the grass roots, will be even more difficult to achieve than it is now.

Nonetheless, the political claims of the black community have become more persuasive than these educational drawbacks. It remains to be seen if a form of decentralization that minimizes pedagogical reaction can be evolved; early reports from the Ocean Hill-Brownsville experiment were hopeful.

While decentralization is primarily a political scheme, a second, more radical plan would employ public money to create separate, private school systems for minorities. This approach would decentralize by persuasion rather than geography. An area with a mixed population could have, cheek by jowl, several public schools—for example, one run by the city (PS 121), one by the Catholic Church (St. Mary's School), and one by the black community (the Martin Luther King Freedom School). Under this scheme, all would receive public financial support in varying measures and in varying ways, perhaps in patterns similar to those used in the United Kingdom or, closer to home, in American private universities. In England, for example, some independent schools receive state aid for each student assigned to that school by a public authority; the school holds places open for such students. Some American private universities receive between 40 and 60 per cent of their annual operating funds from federal sources; they are, in Clark Kerr's term, "federal grant universities." "Public" and "private" are increasingly meaningless terms in U.S. higher education. Perhaps they should be in elementary education, too.

Many who gasp at the prospect of publicly financed black private schools fail to see the extent of the precedent set by Catholics in many large cities. Between a quarter and a third of all school-age children in New York City are educated in Catholic schools, saving the taxpayer (if not the Catholic parents) a very large sum indeed. Their schools were created in the early part of the century to keep Catholic traditions strong and to counteract the implicitly but unmistakably Protestant teaching found in the public schools. They are *segregated* schools— segregated by religion, though open to all.

Catholic schools are facing a financial crisis that can only be solved by some form of public aid to their system. Public aid to their schools may be cheaper in the long run than the costs of absorbing their youngsters into an expanded public system and, if this is true, the pragmatic American will willy-nilly get over his church-state hang-up. Taxes now seem to be a more telling issue than theology.

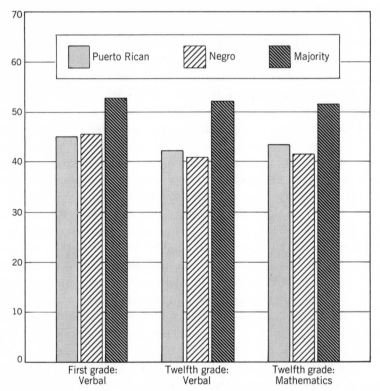

Existing schools appear to provide little opportunity for minority groups to overcome initial deficiencies. (Scores are based on nationally standardized tests for which the median score would be 50.)

—*Data based on U.S. Office of Education Report, "Equality of Educational Opportunity."*

But a black school system? Such a plan would segregate—as did the Catholic schools. Clearly racial, religious, and economic integration must remain a fixed goal, and a central one for the society, but integration in a practical, short-term sense may be in some cities an impossibility now. The best solution, some say, may be a system responsive to and for the black community. This is sad, a measure of the galling failure of integration over the last fifteen years.

Competition in this scheme, then, would be among public systems of special persuasions—white, Protestant-liberal; Jewish; Catholic; black; and others. The competition would be essentially ideological, and children would attend one or another school because of their religion or race or some other persuasion. In many ways such a system would exalt bigotry, separatism, and apartheid. It could be as cloistered and as narrow as geographically decentralized districts. But, as with decentralization, it may be politically inevitable.

Widely differing public and private schools will inevitably have some goals in common. All might agree on some product—the skills of reading for example. Many existing schools, public and private, teach these skills poorly. One way to improve the product would be to create competition, say, among purveyors of reading skills, private companies who would contract for a program within a school, or even of an entire school. The consumer could state the product desired—competence at reading to some definable level—and the contractor would be obliged to reach it. The contractor which did so most cheaply and quickly would prosper—and so would the youngsters being taught.

This third competitive scheme most resembles the industrial sector. Private concerns contract and compete. But the industrial sector requires a *specific*, measurable product, and much of education is unspecific and unmeasurable. Feeling, joy, love, appreciation, candor, and compassion should all be "taught" in school; but how can we measure these in a way suitable for a contract? All must be judged subjectively or taken on faith. Competitive industry has no useful place here. However, it may well have a place in skill training, as the text-book industry has demonstrated. Schools might now contract for more than texts alone, for teams of teachers and pedagogical equipment to come along with the materials. And schools might start insisting that both texts and teachers deliver what they promise. In certain well defined areas, competition among contractors might have considerable merit. Other areas are so ill defined that a contractor could too readily slight them. Such areas need support on faith.

A fourth scheme to increase competition is a classic like those preceding: Give public money *directly* to the children and let them and their parents choose their own school. This idea has deep roots. Its best-known present advocate is economist Milton Friedman.

One version of this scheme gives to poor children a voucher which can be cashed by the particular school that the child and his parents select. The poorer the child the more valuable the voucher: A child from a severely restricted background will require more expensive services than one from a wealthier family.

A major virtue of this plan is that it concentrates resources directly on the particular school, public or private, that a poor youngster attends. No money gets creamed off as it passes through intervening bureaucracies, and a public school with a large number of children from very poor families might obtain through vouchers a sum several times as great as its central budget.

Competition would be forwarded in several ways. The scheme would allow private schools in the slums to survive. If an "open enrollment" policy existed among the schools of a system, it would provoke competition by making a poor child a financial asset: A school with a significant number of poor children—and thus a significantly enlarged budget— could mount a program for *all* youngsters which was notably richer than that found in other schools. Principals of schools might thus compete for poor students. In communities where inter-city pupil transfer plans such as Boston's METCO and Hartford's Project Concern were in effect, wealthy suburban schools might be particularly persuaded to enroll poor inner-city youngsters, thus forwarding class, and perhaps racial, integration. Put boldly, they might be bribed into taking many poor youngsters. Idealism spiced with cash has been a typical American recipe for action.

By giving power to poor parents to choose schools for their youngsters, such a plan provides some of the real freedom of choice enjoyed by the middle class. Some of this freedom will surely be abused, as it was and is under higher education's GI Bill, but it remains a lesser evil than the total monopoly over ghetto education now held by political leaders and professionals. It will distribute power, and give parents some options, some clear leverage on their neighborhood school (the leverage of removing their child and his voucher), and some "desirability" (a poor child brings money with him).

Total free enterprise cannot be tolerated, of course. As with the GI Bill, only accredited schools could cash vouchers, and to be accredited a school would be required to admit students of any race, color, or creed. Public money through vouchers could help schools started with black (or white) initiative, but they could not be used to forward deliberate segregation. Competition, as we have said, may reward bigotry; competition has this risk inherent within it. But bigotry and racism can be held in check if there are adequate civil rights restrictions written into the laws launching and establishing such a program and adequate resources appropriated for policing it. A voucher scheme without such safeguards could undermine the small, but important steps toward integration in places where it is possible. Furthermore, a voucher plan for all children (not just poor children) that replaced some existing sources of public aid would cripple the public schools and would give excessive power to middle-class parents. A voucher scheme must be a supplement to the present system—better yet, a part of a new comprehensive funding plan—and *must discriminate in favor of poor children.*

Such, in admittedly oversimplified outline, are four devices to extend competition among schools. All four will loosen up the present system by changing the power structure. The public monopoly in education would either have within it competing parts or would be pressed to high quality service by publicly financed private schools (in much the same way as our private universities, now heavily supported with public funds, compete with public higher education).

There are, of course, problems with competition as a means to improve the schools. As soon as one gives power of choice to parents, one must provide sound information about the several available options in a community. Accreditation by the state or regional authorities must be strengthened and made relevant, a staggering intellectual and practical task. Evaluation must be extended and improved, on a large scale. The National Assessment Program, launched two years ago, is a small step in this direction. The strengths and weaknesses of schools should not be left wholly to gossip and unsupported assertions.

A problem of equal complexity will come as schools become more varied and hold sharply differing ideologies. The states will have to allow for diversity, but prevent destructive extremism. In a society made increasingly homogeneous by the mass media, education carries a new responsibility for this diversity and for nurturing cultural identities of great variety. The school should no longer be the melting pot, if it ever was. It should be the vehicle for individual and group identity within a broad American system, but not a slave to it. While it is obvious that the state must prevent obvious extremists of any persuasion from dominating any school, it must recognize and honor responsible diversity. The need for the common school has largely passed; television has seen to that. We need more critical, culturally dissenting, and intellectually vigorous people. Today's schools must produce these.

Finally there is the political problem. The public school is Mom and apple pie. The facts that it is a monopoly and that all children with few exceptions are *forced* to submit to *communal* schooling rarely dissuade July Fourth orators. The notion of deliberately creating entities to compete with Mom is jarring indeed, and will be lost on more than a few Washington lobbyists.

However, in context and as part of a large, careful scheme for the reform of American education, one or more schemes to abet competition among schools have considerable promise. Perhaps American educators and politicians are mature enough to see the promise as well as the problems. Curiously these radical notions may be more congenial to the Republican than to the Democratic party.

Policies encouraging competition will only have effect if embedded in a larger plan for educational reform. Decentralization or any other scheme simply added to the present muddle will merely increase the muddle. The system as a whole must be overhauled, and the place of competitive programs carefully arranged within it.

I can do no more here than to sketch an example of what I mean. The following interconnected policies, if adopted together, might appreciably improve the education of children:

1) Drastically decentralize certain educational decisions—curricula, the hiring of teachers, the expenditure of funds—to individual schools or small clusters of schools. The principal of the school would be appointed jointly by a parents' council and the central metropolitan authority and would serve at their pleasure. He would have great power and would receive advice from the parents' council and the central authority. Through this policy, most of the decisions directly affecting a youngster will be made by those who know him as an individual and who are accessible to his parents. Such a plan may make his education more relevant than at present, and certainly more flexible.

2) Centralize to metropolitan authorities responsibilities for: raising local taxes and distributing block operating grants to schools; planning, siting, and building school houses; assigning pupils and arranging for a meaningful open enrollment policy; evaluating individual schools and widely publishing for the general public the results of such studies; operating special schools for the blind and other handicapped groups; providing supporting services, such as instructional television and in-service teacher training.

3) Require that the states license teachers and accredit public and private schools; provide grants to equalize and supplement resources for each metropolitan region; provide incentive grants to particularly de-

serving individual schools; and serve as an agent for mediation between individual schools and their central districts. In addition, states should set teacher salaries; the unions or teachers' associations should bargain at the state rather than the local level.

These three policies are hardly radical: versions of all have worked successfully in the United Kingdom since 1944.

4) Discriminate in favor of poor children with a federal Poor Children's Bill of Rights. Public and private schools for the poor would thereby be given a major and needed boost.

5) Discriminate in favor of racial and class integration with a federal school building program which supports construction *only* of buildings designed to handle diverse student populations within metropolitan authorities.

6) Equalize through federal grants the financial resources available for education in each state.

7) Discriminate in favor of imaginative schools and school districts with federally administered incentive grants, such as those embodied in the original Title III of the Elementary and Secondary Education Act of 1965.

8) Radically increase federal support of research and evaluation in education; and develop and support national, but independent, "consumers' unions" for education to evaluate school materials and industrial contractors' plans, and to publicize widely and in popular form the findings of such evaluations.

Within such a plan, several competitive plans have desirable play, and an improved balance of power is approached. There is decentralization of certain educational functions. Open enrollment within the metropolitan region is possible, and poor children, with their vouchers, are mobile and possibly even sought after by wealthy districts. With vouchers, private schools for the poor are financially possible. Evaluation of individual schools, of school materials, and of private contractors' services are provided for at several levels. The narrowness of total decentralization is guarded against through central evaluation, and the political need for new, mass, private school systems is lessened by significant decentralization.

These suggestions are in many respects drastic. Yet today they may be realistic because school systems are, particularly in many large cities, close to collapse. At such times panaceas may evolve into practical possibilities.

Biloine Young

REQUIEM FOR A SCHOOL LEVY

Biloine Young, an ex-newspaper reporter married to George Young, former Superintendent of Schools in Canton, Ohio (now Superintendent of
Schools in St. Paul, Minnesota) offers an opinion on who might be the
real culprit in the urban school-finance issue. She zeros in on the middle-
class citizen as one who has the most to gain from education but who, at
least in her community, does not support the schools. She also cites other
reasons why she thinks existing school systems have not been successful in
raising needed tax dollars. But the important contributions of this selection are its implied suggestions for needed changes in community school
attitudes which lead to speculation regarding the future of local educational finance structures.

Today another school tax levy bit the dust—one of those minor trage-
dies of civic life mourned by the PTA, the teachers, and a few school
children. On a community disaster scale it ranks somewhere near the
loss of a family pet.

Failures of levies for schools have become such common occurrences
that newspaper stories of their defeat and the resultant school closing
are lumped together on the back pages under small headlines: "Ohio
Schools Face Closings" or "Voters Decide Fate of 103 Ohio Districts."

My husband is the embattled superintendent of one of those school
districts. He finds himself presiding over a bankrupt city school system
for which the voters have twice, within a month, refused to vote additional monies. Barring a political miracle (such as a special session of
the legislature to appropriate more state funds) this city's schools will be
closed from June until around November 23, 1970—almost five months.

Sitting in the wreckage, as it were, of the second levy campaign, one
gains a certain perspective on the attitudes of many citizens toward
public education. These attitudes come as a shock to educators who assume that everyone still believes, as they do, the civics class rhetoric
about education: the last best hope of civilization, creator of enlightened
citizens (and, incidentally, good for a leg-up on the mobility ladder).

Who defeats school levies? Why do parents vote against what appears

From *Phi Delta Kappan*, May, 1970, pp. 472–475. Reprinted by permission of the author and publisher.

to be the clear self-interest of their own children? Here are some observations about our small city, so fearsomely typical of Eastern industrial communities.

The levy was passed by the community's wealthiest precincts and by its poorest. The black community supported the levy, despite a recent acrimonious school board contest involving a defeated black candidate. Everyone between the rich and the poor, from the upper-lower class through the middle and into the upper-middle class, voted it down. The group with the most to gain, if indeed education does enable one to move more freely from one social stratum to another, rejected the schools.

Also, those school areas in which the district had invested most heavily in building improvement showed the greatest margin of defeat for the levy. One principal, greeting parents at the door of his school as they came in to vote, watched their gazes wander over the carpeted Learning Resources Center room and became convinced they all voted "no" on the basis of the rug on the floor. Another neighborhood, where parents had enthusiastically participated in the dedication of a long-awaited addition to their school, overwhelmingly rejected the levy.

The schools, for the past three years, have had excellent newspaper coverage of their new programs, ranging from courses designed to help the high-ability student to work-study programs, new vocational offerings, and dramatic progress in reducing the dropout rate. Strangely, these articles, it is feared, may have hindered rather than helped passage of the levy.

Something has eroded old attitudes that said, "My kids have got to have it better than I did." Now there is a feeling that kids have it too good. Educators who expect to be supported in their efforts to make improvements, whether in buildings or in better programs, should be careful not to run afoul of the attitude that says, "What was good enough for me is good enough for the kids."

The continual complaints about unspecified "frills" in the schools may be code language for parents' fears and rationalizations that innovative schools are responsible for the general lack of control over youth which much of the adult generation believes it is experiencing. One senses a pathetic belief that if the schools would only return to their one-room-with-heating-stove simplicities and virtues, the present problems would evaporate.

The levy campaigns disclosed a surprising credibility gap, not just among the determinedly ill-informed but among those individuals who should know better. Despite statements by the superintendent and members of the Board of Education that the schools would be forced to close if the levy failed, many voters refused to believe it.

The night before the second attempt to pass the levy, I attended a committee meeting at the local Jewish Community Center, certainly the bastion of upper-middle-class attitudes and rationality. As I went in, the chairman of the meeting was assuring the other members that he had it on good authority (his Rotary Club luncheon companion) that the schools would not close if the levy failed. He had no sooner finished than another member of the committee, an attorney active in community affairs, announced in authoritative tones that "the schools won't close regardless of what happens to the levy."

This exchange, representative of the head-in-the-sand attitude of many of the upper-middle-class voters in the city, is made incredible by the fact that the community has had a succession of nonpolitical Boards of Education marked by probity, candor, and straightforwardness. There has been no history here of double-dealing or deceit on the part of the Board of Education or school administrations.

An odd feeling a superintendent has as he shouts in his special wilderness for help for the community's expiring institution is, "Is anybody there?" The PTA is there, to be sure, and the staffs of the schools. But these people have already identified themselves with the schools. In a sense they, and he, are special pleaders. "Where is everybody?" the superintendent wonders as he looks at the unions, the clubs, the churches, the other institutions that compose the decision-making network of a city, and tries to rally support for the institution he believes to be the religion of a democracy.

Shortly before noon on election day number two, a local radio broadcaster called to offer an hour of his mid-day broadcast time for the superintendent to answer levy questions phoned in by listeners. The superintendent and a high school principal dropped everything and rushed to take advantage of the offer. Pleased as they were by the free time (they had already purchased advertising time as part of the levy campaign) and gratified to find that someone else had become panicky over the thought of 23,000 children with no schools to attend, they could not help but wonder what the outcome would have been if such offers had come before election day was half over.

"Where is everybody?" At 11 A.M. on election day the precincts were checked. At one precinct, of 300 registered voters, only nine had been in to vote. More than half of the parents of all of the children in the schools were not even registered to vote. This was true despite two levy campaigns within weeks, during both of which canvassers had visited every home in the city, left literature, posted ads, and distributed bumper stickers and signs.

The rapid growth of higher education has had the effect of relegating elementary and secondary public education to the status of a forgotten stepchild. This is best illustrated by comparing monies appropriated by state legislators for public education and higher education.

In Ohio, the state invests $154 per year per pupil in education for its public school students. (An additional $396 is raised by property taxes to cover the total cost of $550.) When a student goes to college, however, the state contribution jumps to $510, plus an additional $540 paid as tuition by his parents. Ohio citizens and their lawmakers assume that a high school senior can be educated for $550 per year; yet three months later, when that youth enters a state university in the same community, his education for his freshman year will cost $1,050.

The inequities do not end there. In high school teachers are responsible for their students 27½ hours a week. In college they meet with them 15 or 16 hours a week. In high school the school board buys the books; in college the student buys his own. The state requires public schools to average no more than 25 students per class to be eligible for the $154 per student financial aid, and classes may be taught only by certificated personnel. In college classes may range in size from 75 to 200 or more and may be taught by television or a student assistant. Finally, the state requires communities to tax themselves for school buildings for public schools. College buildings, for the most part, are built by the state and in recent years increasingly with federal help.

Few parents, though they may grumble, are unwilling to make the sacrifice to buy higher education for their capable children. Why are they, then, by and large, not willing to make the minimal gesture required to support the lower schools? Are we dealing with a situation in which we only value what we have to pay the most for? Those who vote against the school levies are themselves alumni of these very schools. The majority terminated their formal education with graduation from high school. Why do they now turn against their *alma maters?*

Part of the answer may be traced to an unexpected by-product of our compulsory education laws. Children have no choice about attending school. In most states they must go until they are 16. Even our good students, in the fine schools, at times find this an onerous burden. Learning is not easy. It involves effort and frustration and pain. In the public schools a youth is subjected to this frustration involuntarily—not by choice.

Even the most benevolent dictator, one who rules in his subjects' best interests, is still a dictator and resented as such. When education becomes an obligation, enforced by law and threats of punishment, then it is no longer a treasured right and privilege—at least in the subconscious of a great many citizens. Passive support they will give, the kind of socially acceptable approval one reserves for motherhood, but the commitment is not deep enough to cause one to vote against his pocketbook in the privacy of the polling booth.

This may explain one of the puzzling outcomes of the recent levy campaign. There is convincing evidence that some of the PTA volunteers who canvassed door-to-door in support of the levy actually voted against it. They did not have the courage to come out against the schools in public and so gave their apparent support, only to express their true feelings where it counted.

I do not intend to argue against compulsory education laws, but it is necessary to point out that where school budgets are subject to a direct vote, various deep-seated attitudes beyond the control of administrators and endemic to the system may adversely affect the outcome.

The usual explanation given for the defeat of school levies is that people are tired of increased taxation and schools are the most vulnerable target for the taxpayers' revolt. While this is certainly true, the tax burden argument is also the easiest and most plausible for an individual to invoke in rationalizing a vote against a school levy. The truth is that the public schools are the biggest bargain left in the country.

The schools of this city spend $550 per year to educate each child. A parent's share of this depends on the value of the property he owns. If he rents, he pays nothing directly. The owner of a $10,000 home currently pays $116.40 annually in school taxes. The Canton levy would have added $34.40 to that tax bill. For a direct cost of $150.80 a year, a family could send an unlimited number of children through a fine school system. It is hard to imagine a bigger bargain than that, or to see this as the basis of a taxpayers' revolt. And yet, because of the low value placed on public education, this is precisely what is happening.

At a luncheon with teachers following the second defeat of the levy, two dedicated elementary school teachers offered to teach without pay from September through November if it would help to get the schools open. In a similar vein, a custodian wrote to my husband, in pencil on ruled tablet paper, offering to forgo the custodians' promised salary increase if it would help resolve the current crisis. He added that this would involve sacrifice on the part of his family, as they were supporting a son in a private college.

Unfortunately, such generous offers of help are precisely the wrong approach. The same teacher who would not dream of giving a student an unearned "A" is offering to give a wealthy community unearned services. Teachers, by accepting low salaries, have too long subsidized public education; and by going along with public assumptions of their status as subprofessionals, they have contributed to the general low opinion of public education—as the failure of school levies dramatically illustrates. The low esteem in which public school teachers have traditionally been held now damages not only the educators themselves, but threatens the life of the institution they serve.

At such times it is difficult to refrain from endorsing confrontation politics. A community nearby has also been facing a financial crisis which threatened to close the schools unless a levy were passed. A week before the election the teachers called a two-day "study day," giving the community an example of what it would be like not to have school in session. The levy in that community passed.

The most curious of the reasons advanced for the failure of the Canton levy is the fact that this city, alone of the eight large cities in Ohio, has had no student violence, no teacher strikes, no custodian walkouts, no black-white confrontations, no controversy over busing, lunch programs, or sex education. The implication is that if less restraint had been used, less administrative finesse and reasonableness, less wisdom and imagination brought to bear on the crushing problems of a city school system, the public would be more supportive.

Civil rights activists blame the defeat of the levy on latent racism. They point to the increased efforts of the schools to develop the skills of all the children, particularly those from poor homes, black or white, and claim this has alienated middle-class supporters. It probably is true that some middle-income white citizens, already overburdened by the problems of society and their own static position in it, may believe that the gains of minority groups have been made at their expense.

These vague feelings of unease, of worry that something is wrong, that someone else is getting something they are not, have found a devastating voice in the radio talk shows. On these programs, callers who do not identify themselves are given free use of the microphones to spread spurious information, innuendo, and malicious gossip. ("Did you know the superintendent's wife is secretly on the payroll? . . . There is a hidden swimming pool in one of the high schools.") Hiding behind their anonymity, these callers make charges and create attitudes which are impossible for the schools to counteract, using conventional methods of responding to their critics.

A mild example is the woman who phoned a radio talk program to complain that the Board of Education never revealed how it spent community monies. She claimed to have attended Board of Education meetings and had never been able to get any financial information. Anyone listening to her could be convinced that schools, indeed, did not make an accounting to the public of their use of tax funds. By accident, a school staff member later discovered the caller's identity and asked her what board meetings she had attended. It turned out that her one visit to a Board of Education meeting had occurred over 20 years ago.

Those who seek solutions to the problem of how to finance the public schools adequately and fairly look to a restructuring of the tax laws to ease the burden on the property owner. This is certainly necessary and should have highest priority. I would hope, however, that means could also be found to change the present civil service image of the schools. For all of their faults, they do not deserve the slings and arrows they are presently receiving. I keep remembering the speaker at a Harvard seminar for school administrators who attributed the decline of the Washington, D.C., school system not to the influx of children who needed massive help from the schools in order to survive, but to the withdrawal of confidence and support by the community.

The irony of the whole thing is that there are individuals and groups who really do want to destroy the public school system. These include both the far left and far right, groups which reject the idea of reform and change in favor of the concept of destroying the institution in order to rebuild. City school superintendents are familiar with the ideas and tactics of both groups, and have been most on their guard against the assaults of those who openly attempt to destroy the institution superintendents are committed to preserve.

Now, it appears, the enemy is approaching from another flank. For while superintendents have kept schools open in the face of riots, arson, and the demands of the militant, they are now being closed by the law-abiding citizens who withhold their support. It is a sad commentary that what rocks and attacks and burnings have failed to do, the unconcerned citizen has accomplished with ease.

Questions for Discussion

1. Do you think that special programs for the economically deprived should be minimized in order to reduce financial problems?
2. Can you think of any programs, course offerings, physical plant facilities, etc., which should be eliminated in order to reduce educational expenditures?
3. Some observers have suggested that schools ought to run on a full-year schedule in order to make more efficient use of facilities and, hence, get more use out of presently available funds. What do you think? How about a 24-hour school operation?
4. Review the chapter on teacher power (Chapter 4). Are teacher demands for economic benefits realistic in light of the financial plight of schools?

Topics for Further Study

1. Some scholars argue that education is an investment in human capital which has profitable returns for society. The problem is that they have not yet figured out how to test the validity of this assertion. In other words, we do not really know how to measure the quality of the product the schools are producing. Can you develop a questionnaire for studying the effectiveness of our schools? What elements would you definitely wish to include? Why?
2. Did you ever wonder why politicians seldom fail to support education bills even though they have no real proof that our educational system is effective? Confront a number of public officials with this question. What seems to be the motive behind the politician's belief that education is sacred? Should it be?
3. Usdan, Minar, and Hurwitz have argued that the competition for the tax dollar has become so acute that overt conflict for funds is emerging among the various levels of education.° Until recently, education competed with the other legitimate public services for funds but now even the different levels of education find that they must compete with themselves for the scarce tax dollar. Do your local educational leaders and public officials recognize this approaching conflict? If so, what steps are being taken in your state to counteract overt conflict? Is there any effort toward statewide coordination of educational lobbying?
4. Throughout this chapter, attention is repeatedly drawn to the fact that urban schools, in particular, are experiencing a financial crisis. Attend a school board meeting in the urban center near your home. What are the major concerns appearing on the board agenda? Do they reflect the financial crisis discussed in this chapter?
5. Visit an inner city school. Is the financial crisis in evidence at this school? If so, how does it manifest itself?

° Michael Usdan, David Minar, and Emanuel Hurwitz, *Education and State Politics* (New York: Teachers College Press, 1969).

6. Is there a taxpayers' rebellion in your community? In order to answer this question, study the voting patterns over the last decade on school bond issues. What seems to be the trend? Is it consistent with the generalizations made in this chapter?

7. Many experts believe that the only way to save the schools from financial disaster is to encourage broad federal support of education. Study the history of federal aid to education. Is there any indication that the local control tradition will give way to greatly increased federal support in the near future? What seem to be the basic arguments for and against such general federal aid? What are the attitudes of your local school board members toward acceptance of federal funds?

Chapter 8. ALTERNATIVES
TO THE PUBLIC SCHOOL

THE American common school movement has been hailed by many as second only to the "Great American Experiment" itself. Yet, today the common school is in deep trouble and its future, indeed its very survival, is much in doubt. Crises over financing, the control of schools, the melting pot ideology, bureaucratic resistance to change, institutional racism, student unrest—all these, sustained if not created by the urban mess, complexities of population growth and technological change, the war in Indochina, and the evils of racism and poverty—have resulted in strident demands for alternatives to the public school.

Alternatives called for range from new kinds of school models and systems—such as "free schools" controlled and staffed by parents and community groups, schools supported by philanthropic foundations, schools designed and controlled by business—to alternative patterns for financing, controlling, and evaluating schools within the present public school framework. The alternatives go far beyond those already existing in prevailing parochial and typical private schools. However, the alternative movement does not urge the abolition of the latter options. On the contrary, it calls for increased public support for such schools so that low-income families could avail themselves of these alternatives. In short, the cry for alternative schools is a move for new school patterns, in and out of the prevailing system. And the basic principle of the movement is that every family should have *equal* access to *every* school, public or private, and that no family should be forced to send a child to a school which he dislikes.

The alternative movement has many motivating ideas. Two overriding ones are the notions that parents and youngsters ought to have the freedom to choose their educational services and that the prevailing school system constitutes an undemocratic school monopoly which is accountable not to the consumer but to the monopolistic system itself.

The value conflicts discussed by Spindler (see Chapter 1) are bound to exist in an institution which both brings together persons of many diverse cultural backgrounds and purports to meet their pluralistic needs. Many people believe, however, that the public school operates as if these varied needs do not exist or consciously denies the pluralism in which they are based. As a consequence, people from all walks of life— from the college professor and affluent suburbanite to the white ethnic and ghettoized black—are now loudly proclaiming their refusal to support an educational institution which they claim seeks to compromise, if not deny, their pluralistic needs and values. This refusal is evidenced in many school-related matters. The school's financial crises (see Chapter 7) and the politics of the school-control issue (see Chapter 3) are two obvious illustrations, in part, of loud renunciations of school support. The demand for alternatives is another, and these refusals bring us to the issue of this chapter: *Should alternatives to public schools, either in the form of completely new institutions, or organizationally altered public schools, be established with the sanction of society?* This is, of course, a complex issue, calling into question the deep emotional and intellectual commitment which Americans have made to the public school idea. The complexity of the issue is compounded by the fact that sanction of alternative schools could lead to a situation wherein racists and separatists, as well as "well-intentioned" groups, would be free to establish their own schools. The articles which follow provide the reader with some basic descriptive information concerning this issue.

John Hardin Best

PUBLIC AND PRIVATE EDUCATION

Many who advocate alternatives to public schools argue for public support of those alternatives. For example, some of these people argue for public support of private schools, and some of the alternative proposals themselves call for public support of private schools. Indeed, some alternatives look very much like new kinds of private schools. It is no wonder that the alternatives issue is clouded by the different meanings attached to the concepts "public" and "private."

John Hardin Best, an educational historian, offers an essentially descriptive account of the past and emerging meanings surrounding these terms

From *Educational Leadership,* December, 1968, pp. 250–253. Some footnotes omitted. Copyright © 1968 by the Association for Supervision and Curriculum Development. Reprinted by permission of the author and the ASCD.

as they relate to education. He looks at these meanings in the perspective of this question: "Can the conception of public education be reinterpreted to stress the interests of the individual in American society?"

The idea of "public" as distinguished from "private" education in America has undergone considerable shift in past years. Perhaps an idea as complex as "public education" is continually changing along with the society and its values. But certainly at the present time we are in an era in which the idea is undergoing a fundamental shift with certain important new elements emerging as part of the definition.

For the past one hundred years, or at least since the Progressive Era of the late nineteenth century, "public education" as an idea in America has had several generally agreed upon components: first, it has meant systematic public support, i.e., annual budgets coming from tax monies; second, public control by officials either directly or indirectly responsible to the taxpayers; and third, schooling in the service of the public interest which in large terms meant the building of a united America wherein individuals could advance themselves within the democratic framework. Public schooling under this conception was considered to be enormously successful, its triumph seen as the essence in fact of the triumph of American democracy.

The historian of this burgeoning public school was of course Ellwood P. Cubberley who took it as his calling not only to chronicle the rise of public education but also, as has every good historian since Thucydides, to make his history serve his cause. Cubberley promoted this burgeoning by every historical means and, one must conclude, with considerable effect. Generations of American educators shared the pride of Cubberley's position, such as this one, a summary statement from his monumental textbook, *The History of Education:*

By 1860, we find the American public school system fully established, in principle at least, in all our Northern States. Much yet remained to be done to carry into full effect what had been established in principle, but everywhere democracy had won its fight, and the American public school, supported by general taxation, freed from the pauper school taint, free and equally open to all, under the direction of representatives of the people, free from sectarian control, and complete from the primary school through the high school, and in the Western States through the university as well, was established permanently in American public policy.[1]

---

[1] Ellwood P. Cubberley, *The History of Education.* Boston: Houghton Mifflin Company, 1920, p. 708.

Cubberley as a historian has in recent years fallen upon evil days, a victim perhaps inevitably of new generations of historians with new causes. His fate, however, need not concern us here, though of course his decline and fall within the past decade may indicate a geologic fault below the seemingly firm surface of the conception of public education.

The distinction of "public" and "private" education during this hundred years, however, was plain and unambiguous. The private school meant privilege, the institution of the rich and high-born. Or it meant schools controlled by the churches which were at the least narrow, i.e., parochial, or at the worst no more than a sink of superstition. Insofar as private education posed a threat to the public school it was seen as fundamentally not in accord with democratic institutions and practices.

The contrast was clear: nonpublic education did not and should not have public support, was not under public control, and could not serve the democratic public interest. Schoolmen at all levels, from elementary schools to the university, shared this conception and defended the distinction of public and private. Perhaps the century from 1860 to 1960 could rightfully be called, with Cubberley's blessing, the "Era of Public Education."

A New Era

In our society it seems that change itself is the only certainty. By the 1960's the idea of public education which had stood so long, reflected in the great system of American public schools, appeared to shift in basically important ways. The immediate background of the change, however, was a series of attacks on the public school during the decade of the 'fifties. These attacks, though fearsome enough, were not really fundamental in that they never struck at the idea of public education.

The various special interest groups, such as the Council for Basic Education, were engaged mainly in efforts to gain influence over the public schools. Their attacks may have damaged certain principles of support and control of public education. Yet the more forceful and effective of the critics were those who set out to bend the principle of service to the public interest in pursuit of "cold war" victories. The public school was to pursue excellence which in turn would pursue Russians which, it was understood, was the national interest.

Such cold-warriors as Rickover and Conant may have bent the principle a bit, but in essential ways they concurred with Cubberley's conception of the public school serving what appeared to be the public interest. The furies of the 'fifties left the public school undeniably shaken, but now it seems clear they were no more than precursors of a reexamination of the basic idea of public education beginning in the 'sixties.

The question being raised today is: Can the conception of public education be reinterpreted to stress the interests of the individual in American society? It is a question in a sense of redefining the idea of the public interest, and with it the ideas of support and control of public education along pluralistic lines, to bring them into accord with current ideas of democracy and individual freedom.

Clearly the old distinction, Cubberley-style, of public *vis-à-vis* private education has become so confused as to be dangerously misleading: historically it has been the private school which stressed the individual interest in contrast to the approach used in the public school. Yet beyond that confusion is a more basic criticism: the public interest as it was spelled out by Cubberley, or the national interest in the terms of the 'fifties, seemed to coincide with the interests of white, middle-class, Protestant America, with very little room for diversity within the consensus.

The public school seemed to find no place for the values of the non-white, non-middle-class, non-Protestant child; in fact, the public school had become the truly parochial school. Hence, under this criticism, the idea of the public school and the public interest needed considerable expanding to meet the demands of this new America of the 'sixties.

New Demands

Several situations, urban and suburban, will illustrate this demand for expansion of the idea of public education. In one city with an approximate 50 per cent nonwhite public school population, there is a massive system of Roman Catholic schools which enrolls less than five per cent of nonwhite children. Several of these Catholic elementary schools, however, are almost entirely nonwhite. And in these latter schools a first-grade teacher expects at least 50 children as the normal class size—50 pupils with no aides and no assistants. The problems of racial integration in this city's public schools are made difficult indeed by the racial makeup of the Catholic system of schools. Yet the interests of the child who is learning to read, or more likely failing to learn to read, under seriously overcrowded conditions would seem to cloud the question of the public interest in any effort to make a clear division of public and private schools.

Uptown in the black ghetto with its black public schools similar questions, too, are being raised regarding what the public school is. The ghetto residents demand direct and complete control of their community schools, an end to the management of their schools by a centralized administration and by a city school board which, they maintain, cannot possibly understand what is needed in the black schools. In New York City these demands have been endorsed of course by the so-called Bundy Report, the prestigious Report of the Mayor's Advisory Panel on Decentralization of the New York City Schools.

To dismantle the structure of the city's public schools with all the ramifications to the professionals in regard to hiring practices, "white" certification requirements, contracts with the teacher organization, and the like, as well as the implication of fundamental curriculum revisions, may well mean the opening wedge for the public schools of the city to become "public" in ways quite different from what public schools have been in the past. Local community control in the interests of the health of the black community would seem to be a long way from the "national interest" days of the 'fifties.

Even in white suburbia a new wave of criticism of the public schools is rising. A Bruner-Gardner sort of school system may be beautifully attuned to the suburban majorities, the upwardly-striving, college-oriented, middle class. The excessive burden of school taxes, given the antiquated tax structure in most areas, brings forth a predictable economy-based criticism of the local schools. Yet of more fundamental importance is the rise of critics who denounce the public school mediocrity, who find the pursuit of excellence never quite rigorous enough, and who advocate, with William Buckley, that we "take education away from the bureaucrats and the egalitarians and the politicians and return it to the teachers and to the parents." [2] Or on the other hand, there are those who concur with Edgar Friedenberg or Paul Goodman that the suburban child must be freed from the repressive regimentation of the "universal trap," who would reorient the public school toward the style and spirit of a Summerhill. These critics from both the left and the right agree on one point, the traditional idea of the public school, the *via media*, will not do today.

The hue and cry over educational establishments in recent years is directly related, it seems, to this reinterpretation of the idea of public edu-

---

[2] William F. Buckley, Jr. "The End of the Public Schools." In a syndicated column, "On the Right." *The Home News.* New Brunswick, New Jersey, January 13, 1968.

cation. The 'sixties have seen the struggle in almost every state's department of education as well as in Washington, in which the old "educationist" establishment has been ousted only to be replaced by the new "reform" establishment. The similarities, in the contest for power, for control over the public schools, between the old and new establishments seem much stronger than any dissimilarities. The effect of these struggles is the demand for an end of this public school bureaucratizing entirely, and the rise of what might be called an educational disestablishmentarianism.

New Formulation of Issues

Given this setting, it seems clear that a new formulation of the issues in American education is needed which abandons the confusions of the traditional, narrow interpretations of public versus private education. Discussion needs directing to the questions of what is the public interest in the pluralistic American society of the 'sixties. In a sense, of course, any educational enterprise is public in that it serves some aspect of the public. How today can the public school (as traditionally defined) become more private (as traditionally defined)? That is, how can the public school serve more adequately the interests of all the varieties of individuals and groups who *are* America, and thereby truly come to serve the public interest?

New discussion of the support and control of education leads to the tangle of problems of feasible ways and means for providing this broadened, reinterpreted public education. Can America move toward a kind of open market of publicly-supported and privately-supported schools as the extremes, with every conceivable arrangement of support and control in between? For example, should stipends be paid to parents for each child, or to small groups of parents to organize a school as in the Netherlands? Arrangements such as these need to be examined.

Bonnie Barrett Stretch

THE RISE OF THE "FREE SCHOOL"

Demands for alternatives have resulted from many different perceived wrongs in the public schools. Most demands, however, are concerned es-

From *Saturday Review*, June 20, 1970, pp. 76–79, 90–93. Copyright 1970 Saturday Review, Inc. Reprinted by permission of the publisher.

pecially with the monopolistic control over education exercised by the public school "establishment," the lack of competition faced by public schools, and the few choices open to parents and students when they encounter aspects of public schooling which they do not like or which do not meet their needs.

Many different types of alternatives, planned for within or outside the prevailing system, are being called for. One such alternative falls under the rubric of "free and independent schools." In the past two to four years there has taken place a rapid increase in the number of parents, teachers, and students who have set out on their own to develop free and independent schools which they see as serving needs which the public schools cannot or will not serve. Bonnie Barrett Stretch traces the development of these new schools and describes a number of them in terms of their educational philosophies and programs.

Miss Stretch is the Associate Education Editor for *Saturday Review.*

For the past five years, critics have been telling parents and teachers what is wrong with the public schools. Such writers as John Holt, Herbert Kohl, Jonathan Kozol, George Dennison, and Paul Goodman have described the authoritarianism that structures many classrooms, the stress on grades and discipline at the expense of learning, and the suppression of the natural curiosity and instincts of the young. Many parents and teachers have begun to see for themselves the boredom, fear, and grievous lack of learning that too often accompany schooling—not only for the poor and the black, but for suburban white youngsters as well—and they have begun to ask what can be done about it.

The revolt is no longer against outdated curriculums or ineffective teaching methods—the concerns of the late Fifties and early Sixties. The revolt today is against the institution itself, against the implicit assumption that learning must be imposed on children by adults, that learning is not something one does by and for oneself, but something designated by a teacher. Schools operating on this assumption tend to hold children in a prolonged state of dependency, to keep them from discovering their own capacities for learning, and to encourage a sense of impotence and lack of worth. The search is for alternatives to this kind of institution.

In the past two years, increasing numbers of parents and teachers have struck out on their own to develop a new kind of school that will allow a new kind of education, that will create independent, courageous people able to face and deal with the shifting complexities of the modern world. The new schools, or free schools, or community schools— they go by all these names—have sprung up by the hundreds across the

country. Through a continuous exchange of school brochures and newsletters, and through various conferences, the founders of these schools
have developed a degree of self-awareness, a sense of community that
has come to be called "the new schools movement."

The new schools charge little or no tuition, are frequently held together by spit and string, and run mainly on the energy and excitement
of people who have set out to do their own thing. Their variety seems
limitless. No two are alike. They range from inner-city black to suburban and rural white. Some seem to be pastoral escapes from the grit of
modern conflict, while others are deliberate experiments in integrated
multicultural, multilingual education. They turn up anywhere—in city
storefronts, old barns, former barracks, abandoned church buildings,
and parents' or teachers' homes. They have crazy names like Someday
School, Viewpoint Non-School, A Peck of Gold, The New Community,
or New Directions—names that for all their diversity reflect the two
things most of these schools have in common: the idea of freedom for
youngsters and a humane education.

As the Community School of Santa Barbara (California) states in its
brochure: "The idea is that freedom is a supreme good; that people, including young people, have a right to freedom, and that people who are
free will in general be more open, more humane, more intelligent than
people who are directed, manipulated, ordered about. . . ."

The Santa Barbara Community School is located in a converted barracks on a hill above the town. The fifty or so children (ages three to
fourteen) almost invariably come from wealthy, white, fairly progressive
families who want to give their children "the nicest education possible,"
as one teacher put it. Inside the building are a large meeting room;
some smaller rooms for seminars, discussions, and tutorials; a wood and
metal shop; classrooms for the younger children; and a small library.
Classes for the younger children are based on the Leicestershire model.
Rooms are organized by activity centers—a math corner here, a reading
corner there. Parents' money has helped provide a remarkable amount
of creative learning materials. Children are free to move from one thing
to another as their interest shifts, and children of all ages frequently
work and play together. For the older kids, the method is largely tutorial: one, two, or three youngsters working with a teacher. Although
there is a "core curriculum" of literature, science, and social studies, the
classes follow the interests and preferences of the students.

Outside and behind the building is enough space for a large playground, a pile of wood and lumber, a large pile of scrap metal including

bicycle and car parts, and an old car, whose motor the older children are dismantling as a lesson in mechanics or physics (depending on whom you talk to). Children of all ages use the wood and metal to carve or weld into sculpture, as well as to fix bikes and build toys. "It's important for kids to learn about tools," explained a teacher. "Most kids don't know how things work. You really have to see a six-year-old in goggles with a welding torch to appreciate what it means."

The parents like the school, although they sometimes worry about how much the children are learning. By "learning" they mean the three Rs, social studies, etc. Parent pressure has led the Community School to place more emphasis on traditional subject matter than many free schools do. Teachers, on the other hand, are more concerned about another kind of learning. They would like to help these white middle-class youngsters develop a better sense of the world, to expose them to styles of life and work besides those of their families. There are frequent trips to ranches, factories, local businesses, and other schools. But these experiences, being interludes, remain essentially artificial to children. What are real are the comforts and concerns that inform their daily lives and that are shared with their friends.

In contrast to this isolation is the Children's Community Workshop School in New York City. Situated in an economically and racially integrated neighborhood, the school makes a conscious effort to keep its enrollment one-third white, one-third black, and one-third Puerto Rican. Because it is intended specifically as an alternative to the public schools, the Community Workshop charges no tuition. It is supported primarily by foundation grants and private donations, but the scramble for money is a continuous one that taxes a great deal of the energy of the school's director, Anita Moses.

Like the Santa Barbara Community School, the Community Workshop bases its structure on the Leicestershire method. And, again like Santa Barbara, it does not hold strictly to that method. There is a great deal of emphasis on the children's own interests, and new directions and materials are being tried all the time. A visitor to the school may find one group of children at a table struggling to build arches out of sugar cubes; another two or three children may be working with an erector set, others with tape recorders and a typewriter. In the midst of all this independent activity may be found one teacher helping one child learn to write his name.

Except for the use of Leicestershire techniques, there is little similarity between the Children's Community Workshop and the school in

Santa Barbara. The heterogeneity of the student body makes the educational and human problems far more complex. Where achievement levels and cultural backgrounds vary widely, there is a great deal of accommodation necessary on the part of teachers and parents. At the same time, there can be no question that the children are learning more than the traditional three Rs.

Both the Community Workshop and the Santa Barbara Community School, however, have more structure than many free schools. The tendency in these schools is not to stress conventional intellectual training, to offer it if and when the children want it, and in general to let the youngsters discover and pursue their own interests. The new schools agree fully with Piaget's statement that "play is the serious business of childhood," and a child may as easily spend whole days in the sandbox as in the reading center. The lack of structure, however, leads to a lot of noise and running around, and all this activity may seem like chaos to a visitor. Often that's exactly what it is. It is a difficult skill to attune oneself to individual children, and to build on their individual needs and concerns, and few teachers have mastered it. Often, too, older youngsters, suddenly released from the constraints of public school, will run wild for the first few weeks, or even months, of freedom. But gradually, as they work the pent-up energy out of their system, and as they learn that the adults really will allow this freedom, they begin to discover their own real interests and to turn their energy to constructive tasks.

"The longer they've been in public school, and the worse their experience there is, the longer it takes for them to settle down, but eventually they all do," says Bill Kenney, who has taught at Pinel School in Martinez, California, for ten years. Pinel is an essentially Summerhillian school were classes in subjects such as reading and arithmetic are offered, but the children are not compelled to attend. Based on his experience at Pinel, Mr. Kenney believes that in a school that is solidly middle-class it can be expected that any happy, healthy child will eventually learn to read, write, and do basic arithmetic, whether or not he is formally taught. The experience of other middle-class free schools tends to corroborate this assumption.

The appeal of this philosophy is enormous, judging from the number of students and teachers applying to the new schools—all these schools report more applicants than they can handle—and from the constant flow of visitors who come to watch, ask questions, and sometimes get in the way. A few schools have had to set up specific visiting days in an effort to stem the tide. Three major conferences on "alternatives in education" took place this spring—in Cuernavaca, Mexico; in Santa Barbara, California; and in Toronto, Canada—and people flocked to them by the hundreds to talk to such "heroes" as John Holt and George Dennison, and to talk to one another and learn who's doing what and how. Representatives from foundations, universities, and the U.S. Office of Education also came, eager to know whether the critics' ideas can be given life.

Through the conferences and through correspondence and exchanges of school newsletters, a self-awareness is developing among the new schools, a sense of themselves as part of a growing movement. Much of this increased consciousness is due to the work of the New Schools Exchange, an information clearinghouse that grew out of a conference of 200 schools a year ago. During its first year, the exchange set up a directory of new schools, put teachers and kids in touch with schools, and schools in touch with teachers, kids, materials—and even, occasionally, money. In that year, too, 800 new names were added to the exchange list, and the exchange helped many through the labor pains of birth by offering nuts-and-bolts information about how to incorporate a school, and ways to get through the bureaucratic maze of building, fire, and health regulations.

But the mortality rate among these new schools is high. Harvey Haber of the Exchange estimates about eighteen months in the average life span. This includes those that endure for years and those that barely get off the ground. Money is universally the biggest hassle and the reason most commonly cited for failure. Even those schools that endure are seriously hampered by the constant struggle for fiscal survival that too often must take precedence over education. Most schools are started by people who are not rich, and charge little or no tuition, in an effort to act as an alternative for the common man (the rich have always had alternatives). Teachers work for pennies, when they are paid at all. "How do I survive?" one teacher laughed a bit anxiously. "I found a nice landlord who doesn't bug me about the rent. I dip into my savings, and get my parents and friends to invite me to dinner—often. Then, there are food stamps, of course. Mostly we rely on each other for moral support and help over the really rough places."

This kind of dedication, however, is too much to ask of anyone for any length of time. Working with children in an open classroom with few guidelines makes tremendous demands on teachers, Anita Moses of the Children's Community Workshop points out. Furthermore, teachers must often give their time for planning, for parent conferences, or for Saturday workshops with new teaching techniques and materials. There are intrinsic rewards for this, of course, but extrinsic rewards are also necessary, Mrs. Moses stresses, and those rewards should be in terms of salary.

There are other hurdles besides money—red tape, harassment by various state and city bureaucracies, and hostility from the community at large. In Salt Lake City, for example, a citizens committee tried to close a new Summerhill school on the grounds that the school was immoral and the teachers were Communists.

But perhaps the most fundamental factor for survival is the degree of commitment on the part of the teachers and parents. For brochures, newsletters, and other public pronouncements, it is possible to articulate the concept of freedom and its importance to the emotional and intellectual development of the child. But basically the appeal is to a gut-level longing for love, joy, and human community, and often the schools are run on this romantic basis. "If you stop putting pressure on the kids, the tendency is to stop putting pressure on the staff, too," one teacher observed. Schools that fail within a few months of opening tend to be those begun by people merely interested in trying out a new idea. When the idea turns out to be more complex, and its implementation more difficult than anticipated, the original good feeling evaporates and a deeper determination is required.

Parents and teachers who have worked out their ideas together, who have similar goals, who know what they want for their children and why, have a better chance of keeping their school alive. Nonetheless, almost every school follows a similar pattern. If they make it over the physical hurdles of getting money, finding a building, and meeting bureaucratic regulations, they run into the spiritual struggle. Usually, somewhere in the first three to six months, according to Harvey Haber, comes the first great spiritual crisis: "structure" vs. "nonstructure." Having experimented with the idea of freedom, and having discovered its inherent difficulties, many parents and teachers become impatient and anxious. Are the children learning anything, they wonder, and does it matter? Frequently there is a slowdown in the acquisition of traditional academic skills. Children, it turns out, would rather play than learn to spell, and the blossoming forth of innate genius in a warm, benevolent atmosphere fails to occur. Anxious adults begin to argue for more structure to the school day, more direction for the kids, more emphasis on the familiar three Rs. Others insist upon maintaining the freedom, and upon learning to work with children on a new freer basis that really tests its limitations and possibilities.

As Robert Greenway, whose sons were enrolled in the Redwood Association Free School in Sonoma County, California, wrote:

It seems to me that this anxiety that gets aroused about "what's happening to our kids" is understandable and inevitable. In a public school, we turn our children over to the wardens; there is no illusion about the possibility of influence to torture us. . . . But a truly cooperative venture arouses every possible hope about involvement in the growth of our children—and probably every latent frustration about what we think *didn't* happen to us as well. . . . I suggest that, unless we find a way of dealing with the real anxieties and concerns that this type of enterprise arouses, then we'll fail before we've hardly started (I'm responding to my own growing sense of frustration and anxiety, and to the sign of sudden and/or premature withdrawals from the school, and to the growing hue and cry for "more organization").

The Santa Fe (New Mexico) Community School went through this crisis in the middle of its second year, a bit later than most. Parents were willing to go along with the school as long as the teachers seemed confident about what was happening with the children. But when one teacher began to articulate the fears many parents had tried to suppress, the situation came to a head. There was a period of trying to impose more order on the kids, and the kids rebelled and refused to take it. Some staff members were fired, and parents demanded more teachers with bachelor's and master's degrees, but found they could not get them for a salary of $200 a month. There were endless pedagogical debates, and finally some of the parents simply took their kids back to the public school. "Unfortunately, those who left were the ones with the most money," sighed one teacher. "We're poorer now, but the people here are here because they're dedicated."

After the crisis, the school was reorganized. Previously ordered by age clusters, it is now divided into activity centers, and children of all ages move freely from one center to another. On a bright Southwestern day a visitor may find a couple of boys sitting in front of the building, slumped against a sunwarmed wall, eating apples and reading comic books. Inside, in the large front room, a group of children may be painting pictures or working with leather or looms. In a quiet, smaller room, someone else is having a guitar lesson. A room toward the back of the building is reserved as the math center; a couple of teachers are math enthusiasts, and many of the older children pick up from them their own excitement for the subject.

In the playground behind the building is an Indian kiva built by students and teachers learning about the culture of local Indian tribes. The Southwest is a multicultural area, and the Community School has tried to draw on all these cultures. There are Indian and Spanish children enrolled, as well as white, and each is encouraged to respect and learn from the cultures of the others.

But despite its efforts to reach into the Indian and Spanish communities, the Santa Fe Community School remains essentially a white middle-class school. The Chicanos and Indians, mainly poor or working-class, tend to shy away from such experiments, partly because their cultures are traditionally conservative with highly structured roles for adults and children, and partly because the poor cannot afford to take a chance on the future of their young. Middle-class whites can always slip back into the mainstream if they choose. But for the poor, neither the acquisition of such intellectual tools as reading and writing nor a place in the economy is guaranteed.

These fundamental differences show up clearly in the community schools operated by and for black people. Black people on the whole bring their children to these schools, not merely because they believe in freedom for self-expression or letting the child develop his own interests, but because their children are not learning in the public schools, are turning sullen and rebellious by the age of eight, and are dropping out of school in droves. The ideology in many of these schools is not pedagogical, but what one school calls "blackology"—the need to educate the children in basic skills and in pride of race. In the black schools there is much more emphasis on basic intellectual training and much more participation on the part of parents. By and large, parents are the founders of these schools; they are the main source of inspiration and energy. They have the final say in selecting both teachers and curriculum, and their chief criterion is: Are the children learning?

As in the white schools, classrooms for the younger children are frequently patterned after the Leicestershire model. But the approach is deliberately eclectic, providing closer guidance and more structured activities for youngsters who need it. The academic progress of the children is carefully observed and quietly but firmly encouraged. "We want teachers who will try a thousand different ways to teach our children," said one mother.

Equally important is a teacher's attitude toward race. Although some schools would like to have all-black faculties—and in a number of cities, parents are in training to become teachers and teacher aides—they must still hire mainly whites. "When I interview a teacher," said Luther Sea-brook, principal of the Highland Park Free School in Boston, "I always ask, can you think of a community person as an equal in the classroom?" Many teachers cannot, either because of racial bias, or because of no-tions about professionalism. Even after a teacher is hired, the going is still rough where feelings run high on the part of blacks and whites, but there is a determination to confront these problems directly through open discussion and group sessions.

The same approach applies to daily work in the classroom. Teachers and aides are encouraged to talk openly about their successes and prob-lems in weekly planning sessions, to admit mistakes, and to try out new ideas. Such sessions are frequently the keystone of the teaching process in these schools. They are the times when teachers can get together and evaluate what has been happening in the classroom, how the children have responded to it, and how the teachers have responded to the chil-dren. "It's a tremendous place to grow," one teacher remarked. "You're not tied to a curriculum or structure, and you're not afraid to make mis-takes. Everyone here is in the same boat. We get support from each other and develop our own ways of handling things."

There is little doubt that the youngsters prefer the community schools to traditional schools. The humane and personal atmosphere in the small, open classrooms makes a fundamental difference. The children work together writing stories or figuring math problems, working with Cuisenaire rods or an elementary science kit. They are proud of their work and show it eagerly to visitors. There is virtually no truancy, and many youngsters hate to stay home even on weekends, according to their mothers.

But perhaps the greatest achievement of these schools is with the par-ents. They develop a new faith, not only in their children but in them-selves. "Now I know," said a New York City mother, "that, even though I didn't finish high school, it is possible for me to understand what they are teaching my child." In changing their children's lives, these parents have discovered the power to change their own lives, as well. Parents who are not already working as aides and coordinators in the classrooms drop by their schools often to see how Johnny is doing. At the East Har-lem Block Schools in New York, stuffed chairs and couches and hot cof-fee put parents at ease, while teachers talk with them as equals and draw them into the education of their children.

Nonetheless, black schools share many of the problems with the com-munity that white schools have. People are suspicious of new ways of teaching, even though their children obviously are failing under the old ways. Parents who enroll their children out of desperation still grow anxious when they see the amount of freedom allowed. In integrated schools, like Santa Fe or the Children's Community Workshop, there is the added problem of race and class, as middle-class parents learn that all the children are not necessarily going to adopt middle-class values and life-styles, that cultural differences are valid and must be accepted.

Some schools are fed up with "parent education"; it takes too much time away from the children. A number of schools already are taking only children whose parents are in sympathy with their aims, parents who won't panic if the child doesn't learn to read until he is eight or nine.

But as a school grows more homogeneous, it faces the danger of becoming an isolated shelter against the reality of the outside world. Instead of educating kids to be strong and open enough to deal with a complex world, the schools may become elitist cloisters that segregate a few people even further from the crowd.

Once again the free schools must ask themselves what they are all about. If one assumes (as many free schools do) that any healthy, happy youngster will eventually learn to read and write, then what is the purpose of school? Is it enough simply to provide one's children with a school environment more humane than the public schools, and then stay out of nature's way?

At a California high school in the Sausalito hills, teachers and students think that that in itself is quite a lot. After going through a typical cycle of kids getting high on freedom and doing nothing for six months, getting bored, and finally facing the big questions—What am I doing? Where am I going?—students and teachers think they have learned a lot about themselves and each other. But as the youngsters return to studying and start to seek answers to those questions, they find the teachers have little to offer besides a sympathetic ear. Some kids return to the public school feeling better for their experience with freedom. (Feeling, too, perhaps, that it didn't work, that they really do need all the rules and discipline their parents and teachers demanded.) Gradually, those who remain have forced the teachers back to the traditional textbooks as the chief source of knowledge.

The humane atmosphere remains, but missing is a curriculum that truly nurtures the independence of thought and spirit so often talked of and so rarely seen. It takes extraordinary ingenuity to build on students' needs and interests. A few brilliant teachers, such as Herbert Kohl, can turn kids on, meet them where they are, and take them further—can, for example, take a discussion of drugs and dreams and guide it through the realms of mythology, philosophy, and Jungian psychology. But what do you do if you're not a Herb Kohl? According to Anita Moses, you "work damn hard." There are other things, too: You can hire a master teacher familiar with the wide range of curriculum materials available. Little by little you can change the classroom, or the school itself, to make it do the things you want it to do. And little by little, through working with the children and hashing out problems with help from the rest of the staff, you begin to know what it is you want to do and how you can do it.

But even this does not answer the deeper questions—questions that are implicit in every free school, but that few have faced. Is it only a new curriculum or new ways of teaching that we need? Or do we need to change our ideas about children, about childhood itself, about how children learn, what they learn, what they need to learn, from whom or from what kinds of experience? It is clear that our ideas about teaching are inadequate, but is it possible that they are simply false? For example, children can often learn to read and write without any formal instruction. This is not a miracle; it is a response of an intelligent young being to a literate milieu. It is also clear that children learn many cognitive as well as social abilities from their peers or from children but a few years older than themselves. What, then, is the role of the adult in the learning of the child?

In simpler times, children learned from adults continually, through constant contact and interchange, and through their place close to the heart of the community. Today, the society has lost this organic unity. We live in times when children often see their fathers only on weekends. We live in a world that separates work from play, school from the "real" world, childhood from personhood. The young are isolated from participation in the community. They seem to have no integral place in the culture. Too often schools have become artificial environments created by adults for children. How is it possible to forsake these roles?

Young people are trying. Many will no longer accept without question authority based solely on tradition or age. They are seeking alternatives to The Way Things Are. But the venture into unfamiliar territory generates enormous anxieties. The young are painfully aware of their own inexperience; they lack faith in themselves. But who can help them in their conflicts both within themselves and with the outside world? Surely, this is a function of education. But in today's world there are few adults who can do this for themselves, far less for their children. For who can respond with assurance to the anxieties of young people over sex, drugs, and the general peril in which we live? Who knows how to deal with others when the traditional roles are gone?

And yet it should be possible for adults to relate to young people in some constructive way. It must be possible because the young, in their alienation and confusion, and the culture, in its schizoid suffering, demand it. In the words of Peter Marin, former director of the Pacific High School, a free school in California:

Somebody must step past the children, must move into his own psyche or two steps past his own limits into the absolute landscape of fear and potential these children inhabit. . . . I mean: we cannot *follow* the children any longer, we have to step ahead of them. Somebody has to mark a trail.

Is this what the free schools are all about? Few of them have asked these questions. Few will ever want to. But the questions are implicit in the movement. The free schools offer alternatives—alternatives that may be shaped to meet new needs and aims. At least, they offer a first step. At least, the possibility is there.

Of the several different alternative proposals and schools that are in existence, one general category that has received much attention of late is that which involves partnerships between the business world and public schools. Partnerships are varied, but at base involve an exchange of commitments among schools and businesses. The articles in this section serve to illustrate the entry of business and industry into education in this new way, and to reflect some of the benefits, problems, and issues which surround this kind of alternative to prevailing modes of educating children and youth.

The reader is encouraged to seek out accounts which could serve to illustrate other alternative patterns.

Stanley Elam

THE AGE OF ACCOUNTABILITY DAWNS IN TEXARKANA

"Performance contracting" is the label used to identify a process whereby a school district contracts with a business firm for certain types

From *Phi Delta Kappan*, June, 1970, pp. 509–514. Some footnotes omitted. Reprinted by permission of the author and publisher.

of educational services. If the firm fails to live up to its delivery promise, then money it would have received if it had been successful is deducted proportionate to its failure. A school district, for example, may sign a contract with a firm which promises to raise the reading levels of a given number of students within a specified time. Upon completion of the contract, the firm will deduct from its original salary agreement an agreed-upon amount of money for each child who does not attain the specified level.

Stanley Elam, Editor of the *Phi Delta Kappan*, reports on the Texarkana experiment in performance contracting with private industry for rapid improvement in pupil achievement. This experiment has started a nationwide interest in this kind of alternative. Elam's account illustrates some of the potential benefits and pitfalls in performance contracting.

On April Fool's Day, Mrs. Elam and I headed southwest for Arkansas, where teachers say, "Thank God for Mississippi."

Without Mississippi, Arkansas would rank lowest among the states on several traditional indicators of educational potential: teacher salary levels [1]; per capita personal income; percent of educationally deprived children eligible under Title I, ESEA; etc.

The goal of our pilgrimage was to find answers to such questions as this: Why is Texarkana, a small city (50,000) with a precarious economy (now bolstered by nearby defense plants) currently the center of attention for alert school policy makers? What are the unique features of the Texarkana schools' performance contract with private industry? How successful is the Texarkana project in raising achievement levels of potential dropouts in reading and math? What are its strengths and weaknesses? Can the plan be successfully adopted and adapted elsewhere? How?

We must confess that our short visit with the courteous, helpful, and intelligent people who run the Texarkana Project did not answer the key question about achievement boosts. No one will know the full answer, we suspect, until much later. As has been widely publicized already, preliminary tests are "encouraging." However, the private contractor, Loyd Dorsett of Dorsett Educational Systems, Norman, Oklahoma, won't even know whether he is a financial winner or loser until the first year's testing is analyzed sometime this month.

[1] Actually, at $6,155 Arkansas ranked 45th in 1968–69, ahead of North Dakota, Alabama, South Carolina, South Dakota, and Mississippi, in the estimated average salaries of all teachers in public schools. The national average was $7,908. (Half of Texarkana is in Texas, which ranked 38th in teacher salary averages at $6,619.)

Unfortunately, an "evaluation" report completed in late March by a third party who tried to compare the Texarkana experimental and control groups is seriously flawed. Its basic flaw was a failure, because of the late start, to match the control group properly with the treatment group.

One of our early disappointments in Texarkana was the discovery that the schools' contract with Dorsett does not include a clause, discussed at the negotiations stage, which would have provided penalties should initial gains disappear after six months. Thus temporary achievement spurts so familiar to educational researchers—usually due to all those factors we lump together as the Hawthorne effect—may fade away without anybody noticing.

If all this is true, why have an estimated 25 U.S. school systems, including those in major cities like Detroit, Dallas, San Diego, and Portland (Ore.), already jumped on the performance contract-accountability bandwagon? Why is an entire state, Virginia, about to contract with private industry for public school instruction? Obviously, it is because of the hope Texarkana holds for demonstrating what the economists call low labor-intensive production, and it may be a chimera. As we look back on our investigation of the Texarkana phenomenon, this appears to be *the* major question, and perhaps an answer, or at least a warning against over-optimism, will emerge from what follows.

It soon became apparent to us, upon examining the most up-to-date materials on performance contracting, that there is one towering figure among the many individuals and companies who would like to see this new educational panacea sweep the country. He is not Leon Lessinger, although the movement probably would not have begun when it did without Lessinger's influence. As associate commissioner of education at the USOE for a year, Lessinger pushed hard for the principle of accountability. He said, "The fact that many results of education are not subject to audit should not deter us from dealing precisely with those aspects that lend themselves to precise definition and assessment."

But Lessinger left the USOE last January for the relative obscurity of the university (Georgia State). Before he did he had met a young man who was thinking on similar lines but emphasizing the notion of performance contracts. The result was the funding of the Texarkana Project in April, 1969.

Today this young man is the real leader of the performance contracting-accountability movement. He is Charles L. Blaschke, president of Education Turnkey Systems, Inc., of Washington, D.C. He represents a special breed, a scholar with the drive and persuasiveness for entrepreneurship. Only three years ago, Blaschke was finishing doctoral requirements at Harvard with a case study of the educational technology industry. At the same time, he was on active duty in the Army with the rank of lieutenant and was teaching graduate courses in political economy and educational technology at Catholic University. (We don't know how he did it all either.)

The question that bothered Blaschke most at that time was, "Can we create the political innovations to effectively develop, evaluate, and utilize the technology which is capable of being produced for public education?" It still bothers him, but he now thinks he has many of the answers. A number of them appear in Volume I, Number 1, of *Education Turnkey News*, dated April, 1970. It is published by his company. Interested educators may secure a copy by writing Education Turnkey Systems, Inc., 1660 L St., N.W., Washington, D.C. 20036—which is only a few doors from National Education Association Headquarters, where the outlook is generally quite different from Blaschke's.

Blaschke had an early hand in the Texarkana Project. Texarkana's city government had secured Model Cities Demonstration Agency money from the Department of Housing and Urban Development late in 1968. The project included a small education component for dropout prevention, and this is where Blaschke came in.

At the time—early spring, 1969—the Nixon Administration had just added Title VIII (dropout prevention) to the Elementary and Secondary Education Act. It provided money for exactly the kind of project Blaschke had in mind, and he was instrumental in getting a five-year $5 million dropout prevention proposal approved by the U.S. Office of Education. The Texarkana Project was in business, and Blaschke went about developing a program plan, evaluation procedures, and a request for proposals.

In the first *Education Turnkey News* there is a special interim report on "Texarkana—First." What follows immediately is taken primarily from this report, with some added facts secured from Loyd Dorsett's representative in Texarkana, C. J. Donnelly; from Martin Filogamo, the local school system representative; and from Ed Trice, superintendent of Arkansas District 7.

On September 9, 1969, the boards of Arkansas District 7 and the Liberty-Eylau District of Texas selected Dorsett Educational Systems from a group of 10 companies—including RCA, QED (Quality Education Development of Washington, D.C.), and McGraw-Hill—to operate

Rapid Learning Centers (RLC's) on a guaranteed performance basis. Their major goal was to prevent dropouts, primarily by raising achievement levels in reading and mathematics.

The RLC's were opened on October 15. By November 1, four were fully operational, with over 100 students enrolled. Centers were established in mobile 900-square-foot classrooms adjacent to junior and senior high schools and, in two cases, were put into vacant classrooms in junior highs. Between October 15 and March 2, over 300 students enrolled in the RLC's, for an average of two hours per day, while participating in extracurricular activities and other school studies during the rest of the school day. All participants were diagnosed as potential dropouts. At the ninth-grade level, Texarkana's black students on the average were 70 percentiles below the white students in reading and math. About 30 percent of the junior high children in the two districts are black; about 50 percent of the RLC children are black.

A letter of intent was agreed upon and signed by Dorsett and the local education agency (Arkansas District 7) on September 15. The actual subcontract, based on the letter of intent, was submitted in late November to the USOE for final approval.[2] USOE contract officials recommended the deletion of several conditions agreed upon by the school and Dorsett in the letter of intent. These included a clause specifying that students could be re-tested some six months after "graduation" from the RLC's to determine whether retention rates were equal to those of the average student within the system. Less than average retention rates would have been the basis of contract renegotiation.

At present 20 local teachers and administrators have been hired as "expert consultants" working part-time (on their own time) to assist the contractor in refining his program. At the same time, these people are being exposed to the RLC instructional system in order to facilitate adoption by the schools during the turnkey phase, which will begin this fall. Training sessions will be held during the summer, once individuals have realized their need for training.

The typical RLC has one paraprofessional and one professional working with 15–25 students each hour. (The goal is 25 students next year.) All of the instructional personnel were hired by Donnelly, who as Dorsett's director in Texarkana has all the duties of a principal without some of the restraints. For example, he fired one teacher a few months

[2] By and large, Texarkana's participating schools were not desegregated until last September [1969], when the all-black high school was closed. Token efforts had been made at the ninth-grade level during the previous two years.

after she was employed because the performance of students under her tutelage was not up to expectations. The reason for this? "She just didn't like children."

(Arkansas has no tenure law, and anyway, the State Department of Education has suspended certification and certain other requirements in the interest of promoting Texarkana's "innovations." Nevertheless, Donnelly was careful to hire only certifiable people as teachers, most of them applicants who had not gotten jobs in the city before. All are paid the same as teachers hired by the school board, except for bonuses paid to compensate for their longer day.) [3]

The RLC instructional program consists of programmed reading and math materials presented largely (about 90 percent) through the Dorsett AVTM-86. A $200 film strip and record teaching machine, relatively simple to operate, it uses mostly Dorsett-developed software. Students log in their time on their punch cards, move through the material at their own rate, and record test results on a punch test card which is later processed to determine progress and branching needs. Science Research Associates reading labs, Portal Press (John Wiley) "Springboards," Job Corps reading programs, Grolier reading labs, and other programmed materials are used in various branching patterns on an as-needed basis. Through student feedback indicated on tests, critical learning points are determined and programs are modified.

These procedures are old hat to educators familiar with school-operated dropout programs. One feature of the RLC programs is not old hat, however. This is a special motivation technique employed by Dorsett. It is frankly extrinsic, but it seems to work. For each lesson successfully completed (100 percent correct) by an RLC pupil, 10 Green Stamps are awarded, at least in one of the centers. For one grade-level advancement in math or reading, the pupil gets a small transistor radio. ("Some of the kids think they're worth $10. Actually, we get them in quantity for $2.98 each. Since by contract we get $80 per grade-level advance, it's a paying proposition to spend $6 on rewards," one teacher told me.) And this is not all. The youngster who makes the greatest advance in grade

---

[3] I found out later that this is not the whole story. If Dorsett's "learning managers" and "associate managers" produce high achievement among the children in their charge, they will be rewarded with stock and stock options in Dorsett's company. Donnelly revealed in a phone conversation that at the end of the project "some kind of efficiency formula will be applied for making differential awards." (At Christmas time all RLC managers received equal stock bonuses.)

Will Texarkana's public school teachers accept the public school counterpart of bonuses: merit rating? We'll have to wait and see.

levels, as measured by the Iowa Tests of Educational Achievement, wins a portable television set. One winner advanced 8.3 subject grade levels—5.1 in math, 3.2 in reading—in just three months of instruction.

There are still other forms of reward. Games, puzzles, popular magazines, and free time to "rap" with friends are part of the RLC philosophy of motivation. When a child has successfully completed a day's assignment, he can employ his spare time in any way he likes. Often the teacher or paraprofessional will play a game of checkers or chess with an early finisher. Superintendent Trice says this procedure may actually bring students and teachers into personal contact for greater lengths of time than traditional group instruction permits, despite the emphasis on technology.

Trice's description of what happens in RLC's is graphic and makes sense: "The role of the teacher in the RLC is altogether different from the role of the teacher in the traditional classroom. She could be called an instructional manager. She programs each individual's assignment. At the end of her school day she goes to the main center and picks up her material for the next day—that is, the film, records, and other software she needs. She takes this back to the school, where each child has his assignment in a folder. He knows exactly where he finished the day before and where he needs to start today. And so when the child comes into the room he doesn't take a seat and wait for roll call or the tardy bell. He goes directly to his folder, picks up his material, gets his record and film, goes to his machine, and threads it himself (unless he runs into some difficulty, when the teacher will help). Then he puts his headset on and he's in business.

"He couldn't care less about what others are doing; he can't even see or hear them, for one thing. Then he starts his program. If he makes a mistake, there's no one to laugh at him. Most of these people have come out of a classroom with group instruction where first of all they've been timid about reciting because they realize by now that they don't know the answers. They've been completely frustrated and humiliated. If they make a wrong answer, then the whole class will laugh at them. Children are just that way. And usually the teacher will not call on them because she too knows they can't answer. But here in the lab they're working at their own level, and if they make a mistake only the machine knows about it.

"As you know, there are incentives built into the process. We have found out that tangible incentives have real value until the youngsters begin to achieve. After a while, according to Mr. Filogamo, and it makes sense to me, achievement is itself an incentive. Children enjoy actually achieving and they forget about the material incentives. But until they enjoy achievement, the incentives are built in."

Trice takes little credit for planning the RLC's, but is proud of one contribution. It was his recommendation that the phrase "dropout prevention" be eliminated from the project vocabulary and that the units where children are taught be called "rapid learning centers." This change has had much to do with the apparent lack of any stigma attached to attendance at the RLC's. As Trice says, "No one is opposed to 'rapid learning.'"

Students were selected for the program, for the most part, on the basis of grade-level deficiencies. However, because of the larger number of volunteers (57 students volunteered last summer for the program, and a waiting list of 200 existed by March), a third of the target population was chosen from the volunteers, so long as they were two grade levels behind. Another third (many of whom were much more than two grade levels behind and came from deprived—often broken—homes) were selected by teachers and counselors. The remainder of the students were selected on a random basis, if they met the entry level criterion of two grade levels behind in math and reading. No children with measured I.Q.'s lower than 70 (in one system) or 75 (in the other) were to be admitted. But some got in anyway, usually at the request of counselors.

It was not until January that the local education agency contracted with the Magnolia (Arkansas) Education Service Center, operated by Dean C. Andrew, to perform the "internal evaluation," using funds from Title III, USOE. In developing the evaluation design, ESC undertook to test and report monthly.

On February 2, 51 students were post-tested with the Iowa Tests of Educational Achievement (which the schools had used in pre-testing) to determine extent of progress. Results indicated that in a total of 89 hours of instruction, the average student had achieved an increase of .99 grade levels in math and 1.50 in reading. In vocabulary subtests even better results were realized.

A second post-test, involving 59 students, was conducted on March 2. Results indicated that in a total of 120 hours, equally distributed between reading and math instruction, students were achieving, on the average, 2.2 grade-level increases in reading and 1.4 in math.

These, remember, are averages. It was somewhat surprising to note that as many as 32 percent of the pupils had made *no* progress—had even slipped back by from .1 to between three and four grade levels in one or another subject. This was true even after 60 hours of instruction in a given subject. For example, of 51 pupils taking the March 2 test of reading comprehension, 13 had slipped from .1 to one grade level and four had slipped between one and two grade levels.

Donnelly had several explanations for this phenomenon. For one thing, several of the poorest performers were not members of the original target population but were less than a grade level behind to begin with. Then there is testing error, both pre-test and post-test. Donnelly also points to the unexpected unreliability of Form I of the Iowa tests (admitted by Houghton Mifflin, the publisher, who pleads that the tests were never intended to determine whether a contractor is paid for instruction). Finally, there is the desire of some youngsters to remain in the program and the fact that the teaching machines just may not suit the learning style of some children.

Blaschke reports that there have been significant behavioral changes as a result of the project: Only one of the 301 participants has voluntarily dropped out of school. Meanwhile, the dropout rate among other high school students, especially in grades 11–12, has increased.

Only five percent of the teachers and administrators have indicated slight or no interest in the RLC program or an unwillingness to use it in the schools. Teachers from two of the junior highs have already requested that the RLC equipment be integrated into their classes immediately. (There is money in the government contract to pay for substitute teachers while regular teachers visit and learn about the RLC program. One teacher who was taking advantage of this opportunity while we visited cheerfully reported that she had learned the Pythagorean Theorem from helping one of the youngsters with his slide-tape math program.)

Vandalism in the cooperating schools has been cut in half. Cost of window replacement is down by one-third. Only one of the Rapid Learning Centers has been burglarized.

Community support and participation is reportedly good. As an early illustration, to save the program, voters who elected four "freedom of choice" proponents to the Texas Independent District board in April, 1969, went back to the polls in a referendum the next month and voted against this segregation-saving device. The issue had been put to them as follows: In order to insure the district's participation in a program which "guaranteed" to raise performance in deficient children, so that upon full-time integration these children could compete educationally without lowering the overall quality of instruction, it would be necessary to vote down freedom of choice. Despite the fact that Texarkana is the home of Freedom, Inc., the national advocate of the so-called freedom of choice plan, the margin was 7–1 against it.

On March 12, 1970, another school board election was held for Arkansas District 7. Even in light of an apparent reversal of federal policy with respect to freedom of choice at that time, and despite growing opposition to busing to achieve desegregation, no board member was replaced by a freedom of choice advocate.

In early February, 1970, the Texarkana schools entered into a contract with Blaschke's organization to conduct program planning and analysis for turnkey operations. ETS, Inc., is now working with the Texarkana Education Service Center and the project management staff to analyze the relative cost-effectiveness of the RLC Program and the existing math and reading programs within the school systems. Filogamo believes that the RLC Program will work out to be about $100 a year cheaper per pupil than the others, on a time-equated basis. But no official figures are yet available.

Once cost-effectiveness has been analyzed, the next step will be to determine the changes required within the existing school system for it to adopt the RLC math and reading programs "to realize a large percentage of the actual potential efficiency demonstrated during the year," to use Blashke's words. Cost will include actual purchase of equipment required, staff development, implementation of performance budgeting and accounting systems, etc. Administrative changes will probably include a movement to individualize scheduling, computer-based student monitoring, and the like. Preliminary analyses indicate that cost savings may be realized, especially in the math area, through a doubling or tripling of students throughout, by better use of facilities, and by hiring paraprofessionals.

These analyses, plus others, will be part of Phase II of the five-year Texarkana Dropout Prevention Program. It is presently expected that, in addition to the turnkey operation, RLC's will be established for grades 4–6 and grades 7–12, especially for those students who will require maintenance as well as accelerated learning due to the vast difference between their present grade level achievement and that of their peers. An integral part of Phase II will be a special project funded through the local Model Cities Demonstration Agency for grades K-3. At present, ETS, Inc., is helping develop a list of bidders and a request for proposals to be sent to various firms, including, of course, Dorsett.

The implications of performance contracting do not seem to disturb

the teachers in Texarkana, although they have disturbed teachers elsewhere. I talked with Mrs. Norma Shaddox on this subject. She is executive secretary of the Arkansas Dist. 7 Classroom Teachers Association
which recently became one of the five such associations in Arkansas
(which has no collective negotiation law) to negotiate a written contract with the local Board of Education. Mrs. Shaddox said Texarkana
teachers, on the whole, view the RLC's very favorably, certainly not as a
threat. "The consensus has been, 'If I had 10 students and 10 machines, I
could do this too!'

"A few teachers are afraid the machines will take their jobs; I'm not,"
Mrs. Shaddox said.

She doesn't agree with the Dorsett reward system, however. "I would
stand on my head if that would make them learn, but I wonder if the
children are *really* learning or just storing a little knowledge for long
enough to get the reward."

We discovered later that Mrs. Shaddox is one of the 20 paid consultants employed to advise the district with respect to the RLC's.

What can one say in summing up the Texarkana experiment? First, it
must be reemphasized that it is still an experiment. Only a few of the
original objectives have been reached, if one insists on definitive proof.
Mr. Donnelly, a scientist who has an engineering degree and not one
hour of academic credit in education (although he has been working
for 17 years with learning materials, including several years in educational publishing) expressed impatience with some of the accolades already showered on the Texarkana Project. Though by no means poor-
mouthing the project, he squirms when people like Jim Wright, associate editor of the *Dallas Morning News,* say, "Private organizations,
business or otherwise, are far more capable of experimenting to find the
best methods to solve the problems than our public agencies [are]. That's
because they can abandon an experiment that fails and try another
approach—remember the Edsel?—while government tends to perpetuate its failures."

Donnelly is sophisticated enough to recognize and admit that private
organizations can cover up their mistakes too. What about Ralph Na-
der's revelations, Mr. Wright?

Donnelly believes that the performance contract and the Dorsett techniques constitute a very powerful instructional program. But he is disturbed by at least two aspects of the RLC Program in Texarkana. He
talked freely about the faults of the instruments that now must be used
to measure pupil progress. He is aware that they don't accurately reflect

the school's instructional program. He also knows that articulation of RLC programs with the school curriculum is poor. Although an effort is made to avoid conflicts, it is inevitable that a student will sometimes miss a regular math, English, or other class in order to fit into the RLC Program. When he goes back to the traditional program next term, the student may find he has missed important concepts. "So he succeeds in the Dorsett program, but his math teacher doesn't see much transfer. He gives the youngster a D."

Donnelly regards the essential purpose of the project as demonstration of a low labor-intensive system; he believes this goal is being realized, but he is aware of the problems involved in achieving some of the other goals of instruction.

It may yet turn out that Texarkana-style multi-media projects are suited best for exactly what they are doing: boosting achievement of potential dropouts on nationally normed reading and arithmetic achievement tests. Wholesale acceptance of the procedures for other purposes, at least in the present state of our ignorance, will not serve American education well. To the extent that Texarkana-style programs do not meet the instructional objectives of a school, we will continue to have problems with them. Loyd Dorsett himself says, "Broad-scale contracting with private industry for the exclusive operation of schools, like the Job Corps contracts, would probably be unwise. But to contract with business firms on a performance basis to install educational innovations in educational procedures now appears to be useful."

Certainly the power of the performance contracting-accountability concept is real. It must be explored further—carefully.

Elliot Carlson

EDUCATION AND INDUSTRY: TROUBLED PARTNERSHIP

In several cities throughout the country companies have entered into contractual relationships with schools whereby the companies agree to provide sums of money, resources, and organized projects and programs which are intended to benefit children. Other companies have entered the educational arena—in particular, publishing—simply to make money. Elliot Carlson reports on some of the problems encountered by businesses

From *Saturday Review*, August 15, 1970, pp. 45–47, 58–60. Copyright 1970 Saturday Review, Inc. Reprinted by permission of the author and publisher.

and the schools as business begins to enter the quagmire of public education.

Mr. Carlson is a reporter for *The Wall Street Journal.*

After a wave of student violence, the Illinois Bell Telephone Company removed all its personnel from Chicago's Crane High School. The Continental Can Company last fall phased out a much-publicized education course in Harlem after Harlemites, apparently bored by the project, became harder to recruit. And the Insurance Company of North America this school year found itself with no takers when it offered a course on insurance to students in an experimental Philadelphia high school.

These are but a few of the woes afflicting companies that have pitted themselves against the tough problems of urban education. After the summer riots of 1967, many large concerns decided they could no longer stay outside the educational world and participate at a distance—through making financial contributions or hawking educational wares. Instead, they decided to enter the educational arena actively and, at least to some extent, apply the problem-solving techniques of business to vexations that have long plagued educators.

In a little more than two years, some thirty companies "adopted" high schools in about twenty cities; in one case, several companies—including Avco, Ford, Procter and Gamble, and General Electric—adopted the entire school system of Lincoln Heights, Ohio, a predominantly black suburb of Cincinnati. The "partnerships"—a word some executives prefer to avoid the paternalism suggested by "adoption"—usually involve an exchange of commitments between the school and the firm. For the most part, companies agree to provide resources and organize projects that they hope will benefit financially hard-pressed school systems.

Also, dozens of firms have forged programs that go beyond relationships with particular schools. A number of companies have fashioned work-study programs in which students from ghetto high schools spend half their day at school and the other half at jobs, while others have developed work-release policies that permit key employees to work with possible school dropouts in hopes of keeping them in school. A few industrial and commercial concerns have established schools outside the public school system that provide training in basic skills for dropouts and potential dropouts.

There's no doubt that a good many of these partnerships—and/or adoptions—are working out well. General Electric has provided two high schools in Cincinnati with modern washing machines and other equipment, enabling the school for the first time in years to fashion a realistic "appliance technology" course. Michigan Bell Telephone and Chrysler have established more than a dozen programs in two Detroit high schools, ranging from part-time jobs and special vocational courses to remedial tutoring and professional counseling.

For educators traditionally wary of outsiders, such efforts represent a significant departure from age-old classroom practice. Predictably, some critics have denounced these ventures as public relations gambits; others argue the ventures constitute a new form of white paternalism. And some observers see many of the programs as simply unimpressive in content. They note that the efforts have produced few innovative activities in schools, and that, in some cases, the very notion of partnership has been overestimated.

"Several of the partnerships now a year old report that they have not developed past the announcement stage," a 1969 study of the Institute for Educational Development, a New York-based research group, pointed out. "The act of reaching an agreement to cooperate did not solve the problem of what to do next. For them and for everyone the burden of inventing efficient ways to bring on bona fide improvements in urban institutions will remain heavy and will not be moved easily."

To a considerable degree, woes plaguing companies that tried to develop educational projects in the ghetto resemble those afflicting firms that recently entered the educational arena to make money. In both cases, there were blissful expectations of immediate results. And in both cases, corporate hopes frequently were shattered when the complexities of the educational world proved more baffling than foreseen.

In the mid-1960s, such corporate giants as IBM, Xerox, RCA, CBS, Time, and General Electric plunged into the so-called knowledge industry with a great deal of fanfare. Executives spoke of mobilizing industrial resources and brain power to solve the age-old problems of overloaded and understaffed schoolrooms, and, at the same time, to exploit what was believed to be a $50-billion-a-year education market. But it hasn't worked out that way. Indeed, these ventures have been plagued by management shakeups, scuttled plans, skimpy profits, and, in some cases, prolonged losses.

Critics charge these big companies entered the educational field without knowing what products to sell or how to sell them. Most industry sources now believe these concerns, among other things, misjudged the size of the market. Also, they are said to have overestimated the readiness of schools to adopt new educational techniques and install expensive new machines. Finally, it has been theorized that the big firms simply misjudged the extent to which their national reputations would open educational doors.

Just how badly a company can miscalculate was demonstrated by Raytheon, the big defense contractor that in 1965 acquired a number of education-related firms. Among them were a closed circuit television and language lab manufacturer, a teaching machine outfit, a maker of science equipment, and, finally, D. C. Heath, an old textbook house that was added in 1966. Behind these acquisitions was something called the "systems approach" to the educational market. In effect, the company sought to merge educational materials (software) and fancy educational systems (hardware) into a "fully integrated" marketing approach.

It didn't work. Right off, Raytheon erred by failing to take into account the importance of tradition in the education market. The company took the Heath name off the textbooks, and the upshot was nearly disastrous. The new Raytheon label impressed far fewer educators, and, as a result, the original name was restored. Despite such troubles many industry observers nonetheless were shocked late last year when the firm announced a major retreat from earlier staked-out territory: Raytheon's education subsidiary said it planned to sell its electronic learning systems business and stick exclusively to publishing.

A number of other corporations now readily admit making errors. "The theory was that the future of education is a marriage of software and hardware. The theory is still right, in my estimation, but it's going to be a long time coming," James A. Linen, Time president, last year told *The Wall Street Journal*. Trade sources note that the General Learning Corporation, a Time-General Electric joint enterprise formed in 1965, lost $5-million during its first three years and, in fact, lost money again in 1969 (the venture, however, is expected to show its first profit in 1970). General Learning officials concede that many of the original ideas behind the marriage of GE and Time were wrong. Among them: misconceptions about the level of federal funding and the pace at which the education market would change.

Underpinning many of these ventures has been the assumption that educational problem-solving was somehow compatible with the profit motive. Nowhere was this view more pervasive than at MIND, Inc., a small learning company that CPC International, Inc. (then Corn Products), set up as a wholly owned subsidiary in 1967. Formed to help companies upgrade the skills of low-level employees and to train the hard-core unemployed, MIND seemed to have a bright future. Indeed, for a time it appeared as though the new firm would have no trouble developing and selling innovative education programs, while at the same time returning profits to Corn.

"I think it is significant that MIND is a profit-making business owned by one of our nation's blue-chip corporations. After all, where does one find better problems-solvers than in business," Charles F. Adams, founder and until last year president of MIND, enthused in early 1968. By that time the learning concern already had 130 companies as clients and was negotiating with 200 others. To serve these customers—and find new ones—MIND's staff grew to 150 in seven branch offices scattered across the country. In mid-1968, Adams confidently predicted that the firm's revenues that year would multiply fivefold to $1.5-million from $300,000 in 1967, and would more than triple to about $5-million in 1969.

For its part, Corn seemed enthusiastic about the prospects of its fledgling subsidiary. "Dissemination of knowledge will soon be the largest single effort in our economy, and if a company wants to hook on to the future it has to get out of traditional businesses. One day, Corn Products will have a bigger position in education than in foods," Bennett E. Kline, a Corn vice president, intoned in 1968. This was a staggering prediction for a company whose revenues that year topped $1.1-billion.

But in April of 1969 the balloon burst. Adams suddenly resigned as president of MIND and took with him a number of the firm's key executives, programmers, and salesmen. In fact, the only people left on the job were about a dozen secretaries and bookkeepers. The split-up followed a bitter wrangle between Adams and officers of Corn over how far and how fast MIND was to develop. In the early months of 1969, Adams says his eyes were opened as to the real nature of MIND's relationship with the parent company.

One thing is sure: The MIND experience reveals just how difficult it is for profit-minded giants and education-oriented subsidiaries to prosper under the same corporate umbrella.

"We found that Corn had no plans to make a major financial commitment to develop MIND," growls the thirty-four-year-old Adams, a thinly thatched dynamo who glares owlishly from behind thick-rimmed eyeglasses. "In point of fact, Corn had done no planning on how we might be integrated into their overall marketing strategy and corporate structure."

According to Adams, Corn had neither objectives for MIND nor the willingness to support the subsidiary's officers in their goals (Adams had hopes of turning MIND into a $167-million firm by 1975).

For its part, Corn seems to have become disenchanted with MIND— or at least with its outspoken president. Even though MIND's 1968 sales —just about as predicted—soared 474 percent to $1.4-million, the company nevertheless continued to lose money. After earlier having projected a profit of $151,000 for 1968, the new firm ended up losing $139,000. Arguing that MIND's operations actually were profitable, Adams says the loss was the result of last-minute expenditures required to expand the sales staff, and thus guarantee even greater growth in 1969. Two other factors apparently conspired against MIND's—or Adams's—ambitions inside Corn. First, Corn's profits had leveled off in the first quarter of 1969, which, according to Adams, reduced its willingness to take risks with capital. Also, Corn named a new chief executive officer, who, reputedly, was less sympathetic to innovative ventures such as MIND.

Whatever the reasons, Adams and Corn parted company with a great deal of bitterness on both sides. The question is raised as to what CPC International's interest was—and continues to be—in maintaining MIND as a subsidiary. Not surprisingly, some "knowledge industry" critics belittle MIND as little more than a gesture that permits Corn to say, "We're doing our part in solving tough social problems." Says Adams: "Corn unquestionably got millions of dollars' worth of publicity out of MIND."

Corn officials reject this view as "absolutely false." Vice President Kline observes simply: "The size of the market didn't warrant the tremendous overhead that had been built up. There were a lot of people on the MIND payroll that just shouldn't have been there." Thus, in the wake of Adams's departure, it was necessary to trim the 150-man staff down to about thirty-five and to reduce branch offices from seven to one, he says. Denying that MIND's woes have alienated clients, Kline notes that the firm now has contracts with about 100 businesses and, at the same time, is solidly in the black. Still, MIND's growth has slowed considerably. According to Kline, MIND's 1969 sales rose no more than 50 per cent, which would have placed them slightly above $2-million— well below the $5-million forecast by Adams in 1968.

How does the MIND program actually work? Put simply, MIND does away with both the classroom and the teacher as educational instruments. In their place are conference tables (around which trainees sit informally) and monitors (nonprofessionals who serve as classroom helpers, but do not provide information). Students learn by hunching over fat basic-education workbooks, and by listening to tapes on earphones plugged into tape machines. Lessons frequently are accompanied by soft music to lull students into a relaxed mood. Theoretically, students are supposed to work at their own speed.

MIND's courses are designed to raise a trainee's math and literacy skills from three to five grade levels to as high as the tenth-grade level in about 160 hours of instruction. Typing courses are designed to train beginners to type forty-five to sixty words a minute after fourteen hours of instruction, and MIND's stenography course is supposed to enable a secretary who can take fifty words of dictation a minute at the start to triple her speed after sixty lessons of fifteen minutes each.

The cost of MIND's basic education course ranges anywhere from $94 per trainee for a class size of seventy students to $562 per trainee for a class size of twelve. Either way MIND officials maintain their program costs less than the expense of searching for prospective employees who already possess the skills that MIND teaches.

Many big outfits, such as IBM, American Express, Consolidated Edison, Continental Can, and Xerox, have used MIND materials, although with a variety of results. Indeed, the experiences of some of these firms suggest just how hard it is to hit upon the right educational formula for the disadvantaged groups. Generally, companies have been most successful when they haven't felt bound to any particular system.

Beginning its education efforts with a heavy emphasis on the MIND program in 1968, Consolidated Edison dropped this approach early last year, and since that time has turned to more conventional methods. "MIND did some good, but we ended up being unhappy with it," says Bruce Wittmer, Con Ed's director of personnel. The trouble, he notes, was that the tape-recorded materials raised trainees' educational standing only about three-fourths of a grade level after 150 hours—instead of the three to five levels claimed by MIND. "This simply wasn't good enough. They wouldn't have been promotable," he adds.

The problem, according to this executive, lies with both the premises on which MIND is based and some of its newfangled techniques. For one thing, he notes, MIND presupposed that dropouts are in revolt against society and the formal educational system—attitudes that presumably would require a novel kind of educational response. In fact, they are nothing of the kind, according to an extensive Con Ed survey of its trainees. "Most dropouts leave school for personal reasons, such as pregnancy or the need to support their families," says Wittmer. Thus, he observes, conventional methods are perfectly appropriate.

"We found nothing replaces the teacher," says Wittmer. "The MIND people said my secretary could be a monitor. It didn't work."

Consequently, Con Ed hired eight professional teachers who now are teaching more than 300 trainees—"dropouts" from seventeen to twenty-three years of age, and men and women over thirty-five—in basic mathematics and English. These courses are part of a twenty-six-week program consisting of one week of orientation and four weeks of "pre-job" training, nine weeks of educational courses (four hours daily of classes and four hours of skills training), and twelve additional weeks of full-time skills training. At the end of the twenty-six weeks, the trainees will become regular employees of Con Ed.

The New York utility says the program—now in its third year—is working, but not always as smoothly as it would like. One trouble is that normally about 40 per cent of all trainees drop out of the program for one reason or another. Con Ed officials say a 60 per cent retention rate is not all that bad and attribute this modest success to the prospect of employment that spurs most trainees to continue. "The trainee needs something at the end of the rainbow to keep him going," observes Wittmer.

Continental Can, also of New York, learned this lesson the hard way last year when it phased out its highly touted educational course begun in Harlem in 1968. Billed as the first company-sponsored school for basic educational skills in the heart of a city, the venture sought to upgrade the English and arithmetic skills of Harlemites whose educational levels were so low they had little or no chance of finding a decent job. In fact, most of those recruited for the first twelve-week cycle in early 1968 tested at about the fourth-grade level.

At first, the effort seemed to work; forty-five Harlem residents graduated after the first cycle amid a great deal of fanfare. But later the program—administered by MIND, Inc.—faltered and, last fall, was terminated (although Continental says it might resume the effort some time in the future). From the beginning, the venture was plagued by dropouts and recruitment difficulties, which, eventually, became the main headache. MIND monitors would recruit on street corners, in bars, and where people congregated, but fewer and fewer Harlemites seemed interested.

Company spokesmen concede the chief reason for this was that the education course wasn't plugged in to Continental Can's—or any other company's—hiring program. Of 200 graduates from at least one of the four cycles MIND conducted during the two-year period, only twenty-two secured jobs with Continental. The others received neither the guarantee of a job nor job counseling. To be sure, many education course grads by themselves found jobs that normally would have been beyond their reach. Others, however, were disgruntled.

One Harlemite complained: "I thought for sure that if I couldn't get a job with anybody else I could at least get a job with Continental Can. The program didn't even give me that much. I need a job." This young lady also was unhappy that the program didn't give her a chance to take a high school diploma equivalency test, which, she added, "would have helped me with something I need and want."

Just the same, Continental Can officials insist the program was far from worthless. They note that the MIND materials helped trainees raise their academic achievement in arithmetic almost three grade levels and in word meaning almost two grade levels. Nonetheless, Continental Can is, as one official put it, "taking a breather" from its Harlem project. At the same time, the firm is trying to isolate the various factors that contributed to their woes. Spokesmen observe, for example, that trainee motivation was lowered by factors other than the absence of a firm job commitment.

"No stipend was offered trainees, and many of them didn't like meeting in hot buildings that weren't air conditioned," says one unhappy company official.

Occasionally, corporate efforts are beset by woes over which they have little control. A case in point is provided by Illinois Bell, which in 1968 offered its personnel, equipment, and facilities to three Chicago high schools. Under the program, the big utility was to provide teacher aides and substitute typists, bookkeepers, mechanics, and engineers to help fill emergency vacancies at the schools. The venture was slowed several months at the start by a strike that greatly limited Illinois Bell operations. While the program gradually got under way in two schools, it folded early this year at Crane High School in a predominantly black neighborhood. The reason: a wave of student violence. Windows were smashed, fires were set, and, finally, several students tried to carry the principal, James P. Maloney, from the building. While the school's regular teachers were demanding more guards, Illinois Bell decided to pull its staff out of Crane altogether. "Our overriding concern was the fear for the safety of our personnel," said Fred Felton, the company's coordi-

nator for the program. "We haven't given up on Crane. We're just looking for ways to establish a relationship with the place."

Another Illinois Bell official added: "We were in a losing situation
from the start. The educational environment was so far gone there that
we couldn't contribute a thing. The school was not functioning as a
school in the traditional sense. It was just a place where kids gathered."

But even before the disorders some Illinois Bell officials frankly
doubted whether their program was correctly shaped to be effective.
"Actually, we didn't get much beyond the physical fix-it-up stage. We
repaired a few shower heads and mended a couple of broken movie
projectors. And we provided a bus for field trips and even gave an
award luncheon for the school's athletes. But these were small, meaningless things," admits a spokesman. "We had hoped we might reach a
point where we could make a contribution to curriculum—and help
ghetto youngsters close the reading gap."

According to Donald E. Barnes, vice president of the Institute for Educational Development, programs often run into trouble when companies are motivated primarily by guilt and a vague desire to do "something for the poor." "The motives and attitudes that go with charity
must be avoided," says Barnes. "The result frequently is that executives
end up offering something pretty silly and then congratulate themselves
for their Christian spirit." Equally dangerous, he notes, is the tendency
of some companies to impose programs of their own making on schools,
which, he adds, resemble organisms that can't easily be tampered with.

For programs to succeed, Barnes suggests observance of a few basic
maxims:

Executives in charge of programs should have enough authority to
make their decisions felt on all corporate levels, even the lowest, where
projects often are stymied through lack of follow-up efforts by the men
at the top.

Executives must develop a tolerance for risk and ambiguity. Frequently, they lapse into a mechanistic view of social change, and think
that developing a good educational program is like manufacturing something automatically on an assembly line.

Accordingly, officials must reconcile themselves to a certain amount of
formlessness that is inherent in schools, and, at the same time, attempt
to aid programs that grow naturally out of the school community.

Finally, businessmen must get physically inside the school building—
and stay there a full school day. "If business is to make a contribution,

its men must eat with the faculty and mingle with the students," says Barnes. "This is the only way they can learn the school's problems."

When these maxims are followed, he claims, the results can be impressive. He cites as an example the Economic Development Council of New York City, a group of about eighty-five companies that recently "adopted" two of the city's ghetto high schools: Monroe and Brandeis.

He recalls that recently a Bell Labs systems analyst stationed at Monroe found that excessive manpower and time were devoted to preparing post cards for parents of absent students. But with so many youngsters normally absent (sometimes as many as a third of the student body a day) and with a highly antiquated filing system that kept information dispersed in various cubbyholes, this was slow and tedious work for the handful of people assigned to the task. Indeed, only a fraction of the parents whose children were absent were ever notified of the fact. The Bell Labs expert made a simple suggestion: Install an addressograph machine. This done, Monroe was able to do the job more quickly and efficiently, since with the new machine the school no longer needed a large staff to handle post cards. Thus, Monroe expects to save annually about $18,000—money that now can be diverted to substantive educational programs.

Generally, companies find they're most successful when they emphasize jobs—and job training—over academic content. For instance, Chase Manhattan Bank, in its widely respected training program for the hard-core unemployed, last year found it was meeting some resistance from trainees because of an excessive concern with academic subjects. The program—known as JOB—was formed in late 1967 to train workers who normally wouldn't qualify for employment. Most of the JOB trainees are young, black dropouts who read at the fifth-grade level. The program is open to any young man or woman who can meet the bank's bonding requirements (which exclude felons and narcotics addicts, but not purse-snatchers or former addicts).

Bank officials say the effort to make these individuals into reliable employees is working. But, at the same time, they concede many zigs and zags and blind alleys were followed before the bank hit upon a workable program. At present, JOB trainees get four weeks of full-time study and then spend five months working and studying on alternate weeks. During the program—for which trainees are paid $1.60 an hour— lessons cover mathematics, business fundamentals, reading, and other language skills. Trainees completing the six-month program automatically become full-time Chase employees; at the end of last year, JOB had graduated 255 workers, 128 of whom were still with the bank.

Despite JOB's seeming success, Chase drastically revised the program in mid-1969, because "we found we just weren't doing it right," says Art Humphrey, Jr., JOB's white director. Until that time, JOB was force feeding its trainees heavy doses of black and Spanish culture and other highly abstract offerings. In fact, trainees frequently found themselves sent to museums, Afro-American exhibits, and—to acquire a little white, middle-class culture—plays such as *Hello, Dolly!* A central idea of the effort was to prepare trainees for the high school equivalency test. "This turned out to be impossible," says Humphrey, noting that only about 20 per cent of JOB graduates were found sufficiently prepared to take the test. Also, many trainees became bored and dropped out.

Then Chase finally got around to surveying the trainees themselves. "They told us all this cultural stuff was a waste of time," the official recalls. "Instead, they said they wanted to know about the bank." Not long thereafter Chase shortened the overall program from a year to six months, eliminated many of the "cultural awareness" programs, and even did away with such old academic stand-bys as algebra and English grammar. The program now emphasizes material needed for success inside the bank rather than for passage of a high school equivalency test. "You'll never use algebra in a banking career," explains Humphrey.

And while trainees still grapple with academic material, they do so in a way that is constantly related to a prospective job inside the bank. For example, trainees learn world geography for use in the bank's international department. "We don't teach geography with maps," notes Humphrey. "We teach it by having students think of the world in terms of zones where the bank does business. This way they learn, say, that Cairo is in the Middle East." Also, trainees still must learn communication skills, although no longer must they wrestle with conjugations and other technicalities of grammar. Instead, they learn bank terminology; for instance, they learn that a "platform" isn't a raised area, but simply a designated space for certain bank officials.

Humphrey vigorously denies the charge some critics have made that JOB's orientation makes trainees useful only for Chase Manhattan Bank, thereby limiting their job mobility. For one thing, he notes that JOB's dropout rate has declined to 20 per cent from 35 per cent as a result of the change. "You don't improve a person's position in the job market by giving him six months of book learning," claims the official. "What makes him mobile is the experience he acquires. We think we help him by giving him what he immediately needs for success."

Other firms have made similar discoveries. In Detroit, both Chrysler and Michigan Bell Telephone have established at two different high schools mock employment centers that test, interview, and tell students where they are weak. In the sessions, youngsters study application forms and learn certain techniques of job interviewing, grooming, employment testing, deportment, and other factors essential to entrance into the job world.

Unhappily, companies have made much less progress reshaping curriculums and developing education innovations. To be sure, some modest contributions have been made. Detroit's Northwestern High beefed up its shorthand program after a number of its graduates did poorly on Chrysler's entry-level tests. Michigan Bell each summer sponsors a six-week remedial program for underachieving students from Northern High that, among other things, uses games, painting, photography, and moviemaking to teach math, English, and science courses.

Companies most often are successful when they stick to their own areas of expertise. A notable case in point is General Electric's appliance technology curriculum, developed for use in Cincinnati public schools. Begun in Courter Technical and Withrow high schools, the program includes a closed-circuit television system, instructional material, and appliances supplied at a substantial discount by GE. The company also provided an initial $10,000 grant in 1968 to get the program going.

Now in its third year, the venture seeks to train appliance repairmen for placement at graduation in GE and other corporate service centers across the country. Aim of the effort is two-fold: develop competent repairmen, and change the image of the appliance repair profession. To do this, GE shaped the program in a way that would have been impossible without its presence. First, it encouraged students at the two schools to wear ties "so they would resemble what technicians look like after employment," says Warren G. Rhodes, a GE educational consultant.

More important, GE yanked out of the two schools all the obsolete equipment—such as twenty-year-old Bendix washing machines mounted on concrete blocks—on which students previously tried to learn this technical craft. In place of the old machines, GE installed sparkling new washers complete with solid-state wiring and transistorized controls. "The old appliances were unrepairable," recalls Rhodes. "It was like trying to train auto mechanics for today's cars on Model Ts."

With the gleaming new equipment, youngsters are flocking to the course and the dropout rate has dipped (GE doesn't guarantee employment to students, but it does have first crack at the brighter ones). In fact, GE feels this particular curriculum is working so well it may attempt to have it installed elsewhere.

Granted, companies aren't always successful when they seek to base educational efforts on their own products or business activities. One failure occurred last fall when the Insurance Company of North America offered a course in insurance to high school students in Philadelphia's new experimental Parkway Program. The program is unique in that students do not attend set classes in a regular school building but, instead, show up for courses held in a variety of downtown institutions. The students wander around town on their way to courses of their choice (selected from a catalogue similar to the type college students use).

Competing with courses on protest literature, adolescent psychology, and various off-beat subjects, INA offered a course on the workings of the insurance industry. But on opening day not a single student showed up for it. "Most teen-agers just don't give a damn about insurance," one official plaintively put it.

But from such experiences executives are gradually learning what makes for a workable program: commitment at the top that makes itself felt throughout the company, appointment to the school of full-time company representatives who can learn the school's problems from the inside, willingness to tolerate experiments and programs that may seem formless to the executive eye, and, perhaps most important of all, a disposition to link educational efforts with job opportunities or job counseling.

At this point, it is too early to tell whether businessmen will overcome the difficulties they have encountered and make a permanent contribution to the nation's school systems. Equally uncertain is whether executives will be any more successful developing education as a lush market for new and fancy products. Some are frankly doubtful. "Big business seems unable to change old habits of mind," snorts Charles Adams, founder of MIND. "They insist on looking at the education market the same way as they would look at, say, the peanut butter market. They're trying to force feed the schools the things they know how to produce. You can neither solve human problems nor develop this particular market in this way."

Meantime, even some big outfits remain unflinching in the face of troubles that have plagued other concerns in the educational arena. The other day, RCA was hired by the Camden, New Jersey, Board of Education as the prime contractor in a joint effort to reform Camden's entire public school system.

Whatever the outcome of this and other ventures, it is clear that the traditional relationship between businessmen and schools is changing. No longer do executives think it is sufficient merely to provide jobs for students; they're beginning to realize they must take an active role in working with schools to help develop this manpower resource. Yet, it is also clear this is turning out to be a much tougher task than expected.

Existing alternative schools, such as those described in the Stretch article, do not receive public financial support; and most are operating without official sanction by appropriate governmental agencies. Students at some of these schools, therefore, run the risk of having their unaccredited education written off when they seek entrance to publicly sanctioned schools. Moreover, they and their parents could incur the wrath of compulsory education laws. The very existence of such schools, however, is providing additional momentum for the increasing demands for alternatives to the public schools and for alternative patterns within the prevailing system. These are demands which, for the most part, hold to the view that schooling is a public function and a social rather than individual financial responsibility. As such, most of these demands call for public approval, as well as public financial support.

Articles in this section analyze the need for alternative patterns to the existing system, as well as some of the problems in one of the most popular ideas for publicly supported alternatives, the voucher plan.

Kenneth B. Clark

ALTERNATIVE PUBLIC SCHOOL SYSTEMS

Kenneth B. Clark, widely known psychologist and author of the well-received *Dark Ghetto* (1965), examines why American public education has been grossly inefficient, particularly in schools serving black and economically underprivileged youngsters. Clark discusses barriers to "effective, nonracially constrained" education, and proposes a strategy for providing quality education in ghetto schools. He argues that the prevailing patterns of public school organization are major obstacles in attempts to improve the quality of education. It will be necessary, he contends, to find "realistic, aggressive, and viable competitors" to the present public

From *Harvard Educational Review*, Winter, 1968, pp. 100–113. Copyright © 1968 by President and Fellows of Harvard College. Reprinted by permission of the *Harvard Educational Review*.

schools. The paper concludes with a discussion of alternatives to existing urban public school systems, including such possibilities as schools operated by the Department of Defense.

It is now clear that American public education is organized and functions along social and economic class lines. A bi-racial public school system wherein approximately 90 per cent of American children are required to attend segregated schools is one of the clearest manifestations of this basic fact. The difficulties encountered in attempting to desegregate public schools in the South as well as in the North point to the tenacity of the forces seeking to prevent any basic change in the system.

The class and social organization of American public schools is consistently associated with a lower level of educational efficiency in the less privileged schools. This lower efficiency is expressed in terms of the fact that the schools attended by Negro and poor children have less adequate educational facilities than those attended by more privileged children. Teachers tend to resist assignments in Negro and other underprivileged schools and generally function less adequately in these schools. Their morale is generally lower; they are not adequately supervised; they tend to see their students as less capable of learning. The parents of the children in these schools are usually unable to bring about any positive changes in the conditions of these schools.

The pervasive and persistent educational inefficiency which characterizes these schools results in:

(1) marked and cumulative academic retardation in a disproportionately high percentage of these children, beginning in the third or fourth grade and increasing through the eighth grade;

(2) a high percentage of dropouts in the junior and senior high schools of students unequipped academically and occupationally for a constructive role in society;

(3) a pattern of rejection and despair and hopelessness resulting in massive human wastage.

Given these conditions, American public schools have become significant instruments in the blocking of economic mobility and in the intensification of class distinctions rather than fulfilling their historic function of facilitating such mobility. In effect, the public schools have become captives of a middle class who have failed to use them to aid others to move into the middle class. It might even be possible to interpret the role of the controlling middle class as that of using the public schools to block further mobility.

What are the implications of this existing educational inefficiency? In the national interest, it is a serious question whether the United States Government can afford the continuation of the wastage of human resources at this period of world history. Although we cannot conclusively demonstrate a relation between educational inefficiency and other symptoms of personal and social pathology such as crime, delinquency, and pervasive urban decay, there is strong evidence that these are correlates.

Increasing industrialization and automation of our economy will demand larger numbers of skilled and educated and fewer uneducated workers. The manpower needs of contemporary America require business and industry to pay for the added burden of re-educating the miseducated. This is a double taxation. The burdens of the present inefficient public education include this double taxation in addition to the high cost of crime and family stability and the artificial constriction of the labor and consumer market.

Beyond these material disadvantages are the human costs inherent in the failure to achieve equality of educational opportunity. This dehumanization contributes significantly to the cycle of pathology—poor education, menial jobs or unemployment, family instability, group and personal powerlessness. This passive pathology weakens the fabric of the entire society.

Obstacles to the Attainment of Efficient Education

The obstacles which interfere with the attainment of efficient public education fall into many categories. Among them are those obstacles which reflect historical premises and dogmas about education, administrative realities, and psychological assumptions and prejudices.

The historical premises and dogmas include such fetishes as the inviolability of the "neighborhood school" concept which might include the belief that schools should be economically and racially homogeneous. The administrative barriers involve such problems as those incurred in the transportation of children from residential neighborhoods to other areas of the city. Here again the issue is one of relative advantages of the *status quo* versus the imperatives for change.

The residual psychological prejudices take many forms and probably underlie the apparent inability of society to resolve the historical and administrative problems. Initially the academic retardation of Negro children was explained in terms of their inherent racial inferiority. The existence of segregated schools was supported either by law or explained in terms of the existence of segregated neighborhoods. More recently the racial inferiority or legal and custom interpretations have given way to more subtle explanations and support for continued inefficient education. Examples are theories of "cultural deprivation" and related beliefs that the culturally determined educational inferiority of Negro children will impair the ability of white children to learn if they are taught in the same classes. It is assumed that because of their background, Negro children and their parents are poorly motivated for academic achievement and will not only be unable to compete with white children but will also retard the white children. The implicit and at times explicit assumption of these cultural deprivation theories is that the environmental deficits which Negro children bring with them to school make it difficult, if not impossible, for them to be educated either in racially homogeneous or heterogeneous schools. This point of view, intentionally or not, tends to support the pervasive rejection of Negro children and obscures and intensifies the basic problem.

There are more flagrant sources of opposition to any effective desegregation of American public schools. White Citizens' Councils in the South, parents' and taxpayers' groups in the North, and the control of boards of education by whites who identify either overtly or covertly with the more vehement opposition to change are examples of effective resistance. School officials and professional educators have defaulted in their responsibility for providing educational leadership. They have tended, for the most part, to go along with the level of community readiness and the "political realities." They have been accessories to the development and use of various subterfuges and devices for giving the appearance of change without its substance and, in doing so, have failed to present the problem of the necessary school reorganization in educational terms. This seems equally true of teachers and teachers' organizations. In some cases, teachers, textbooks, and other teaching materials have either contributed to or failed to counteract racism.

Within the past two years another formidable and insidious barrier in the way of the movement towards effective, desegregated public schools has emerged in the form of the black power movement and its demands for racial separatism. Some of the more vocal of the black power advocates who have addressed themselves to the problems of education have explicitly and implicitly argued for Negroes' control of "Negro Schools." Some have asserted that there should be separate school districts organized to control the schools in all-Negro residential areas; that there should be Negro Boards of Education, Negro superintendents of schools,

Negro faculty, and Negro curricula and materials. These demands are clearly a rejection of the goals of integrated education and a return to the pursuit of the myth of an efficient "separate but equal"—or the pathetic wish for a separate and superior—racially-organized system of education. One may view this current trend whereby some Negroes themselves seem to be asking for a racially segregated system of education as a reflection of the frustration resulting from white resistance to genuine desegregation of the public schools since the *Brown* decision and as a reaction to the reality that the quality of education in the *de facto* segregated Negro schools in the North and the Negro schools in the South has steadily deteriorated under the present system of white control.

In spite of these explanations, the demands for segregated schools can be no more acceptable coming from Negroes than they are coming from white segregationists. There is no reason to believe and certainly there is no evidence to support the contention that all-Negro schools, controlled by Negroes, will be any more efficient in preparing American children to contribute constructively to the realities of the present and future world. The damage inherent in racially isolated schools was persuasively documented by the comprehensive study [*Racial Isolation in the Public Schools*] conducted by the United States Commission on Civil Rights.

Furthermore, the more subtle and insidious educational deprivation for white children who are required to attend all-white schools is furthered by both the black and the white advocates of racially homogeneous schools.

Attempts at Remedies

In spite of these obstacles in the path of genuine desegregation of American public schools and the attainment of effective, nonracially constrained education for all American children, there have been persistent attempts to compensate for the deficits of racial isolation in the American public schools. A tremendous amount of energy and money has been expended in the attempt to develop special programs designed to improve the academic achievement of Negro children, who are the most obvious victims of inferior, racially segregated public schools.

The United States Commission on Civil Rights report, *Racial Isolation in the Public Schools,* has presented facts which raise questions concerning the long range effectiveness of these programs. There is some evidence that these special programs do some good and help some children; but they clearly underline the inadequacy of the regular education these children receive. In addition to the fact that they obscure the overriding reality that underprivileged children are being systematically short-changed in their regular segregated and inferior schools, these programs may also be seen as a type of commitment to the continuation of segregated education.

If one accepts the premise which seems supported by all available evidence, and above all by the reasoning of the *Brown* decision, that racially segregated schools are inherently inferior, it would seem to follow that all attempts to improve the quality of education in all-Negro and all-white schools would have necessarily limited positive effects. All programs designed to raise the quality of education in racially homogeneous schools would therefore have to be seen as essentially evasive programs or as the first stage in an inferior approach to a serious plan for effective desegregation of public schools. Given the resistance to an immediate reorganization of the present system of racially organized schools so as to create a more effective system of racially heterogeneous schools, however, one may be required to attempt to increase the efficiency of education in all-Negro schools as a necessary battle in the larger struggle for racially desegregated schools.

The problem of the extent to which it is possible to provide excellent education in a predominantly Negro school should be re-examined thoroughly in spite of the basic premise of the *Brown* decision that racially segregated schools are inherently inferior. Some questions which we must now dare to ask and seek to answer as the basis for a new strategy in the assault against the inhumanity of the American system of racial segregation are:

(1) Is the present pattern of massive educational inferiority and inefficiency which is found in predominantly Negro schools inherent and inevitable in racially segregated schools?

(2) Is there anything which can be done within the Negro schools to raise them to a tolerable level of educational efficiency—or to raise them to a level of educational excellence?

If the answer to the first question is *yes* and to the second question is *no,* then the strategy of continued and intensified assault on the system of segregated schools is justified and should continue unabated since there is no hope of raising the quality of education for Negro children as long as they are condemned to segregated schools—there is no hope of salvaging them. If, on the other hand, the answers to the above questions are reversed, it would suggest that a shift in strategy and tactics, without giving up the ultimate goals of eliminating the dehumanizing force of racial segregation from American life, would be indicated. This shift would suggest that given the present strong and persistent resistance to any serious and effective desegregation of our public schools, that the bulk of the available organizational, human, and financial resources and specialized skills be mobilized and directed toward obtaining the highest quality of education for Negro students without regard to the racial composition of the schools which they attend. This attempt would demand a massive, system-wide educational enrichment program designed to obtain educational excellence in the schools attended by Negro children.

Recent experiences in New York City, Boston, Chicago, Philadelphia and other northern cities reveal that this temporary shift in the battleground will not in itself lead to any easier victory. School boards and public school officials seem as resistant to developing or implementing programs designed to improve the quality and efficiency of education provided for Negro children in segregated schools as they are deaf to all requests for effective desegregation plans and programs. The interests and desires of white middle-class parents, and the interests of the increasingly powerful teachers' federations and professional supervisory associations are invariably given priority over the desire of Negro parents for nonsegregated quality education for their children. The interests of the white parents, teachers, and supervisors are often perceived by them as inimical to the desires of the Negro parents. Furthermore, the capture and control of the public schools by the white middle-class parents and teachers provided the climate within which the system of racially segregated and inferior schools could be developed, expanded and reinforced and within which the public schools became instruments for blocking rather than facilitating the upward mobility of Negroes and other lower-status groups. One, therefore, could not expect these individuals and groups to be sympathetic and responsive to the pleas of Negro parents for higher quality education for their children. Negro parents and organizations must accept and plan their strategy in terms of the fact that adversaries in the battle for higher quality education for Negro children will be as numerous and as formidable as the adversaries in the battle for nonsegregated schools. Indeed they will be the same individuals, officials, and groups in different disguises and with different excuses for inaction but with the same powerful weapons of evasion, equivocation, inaction, or tokenism.

An effective strategy for the present and the future requires rigorous and honest appraisal of all of the realities, a tough-minded diagnosis of the strengths and weaknesses of the Negro and his allies. We cannot now permit ourselves to be deluded by wishful thinking, sentimental optimism, or rigid and oversimplified ideological postures. We must be tough-mindedly pragmatic and flexible as we seek to free our children from the cruel and dehumanizing, inferior and segregated education inflicted upon them by the insensitive, indifferent, affable, and at times callously rigid custodians of American public education.

In developing an appropriate strategy and the related flexible tactics, it must be clearly understood that the objective of improving the quality of education provided for Negro children is not a substitute for or a retreat from the fundamental goal of removing the anachronism of racially segregated schools from American life. The objective of excellent education for Negro and other lower-status children is inextricably linked with the continuing struggle to desegregate public education. All of the public school, college, and professional school civil rights litigation instituted by the legal staff of the NAACP arose from recognition of the obvious fact that the segregated schools which Negroes were forced by law to attend were inferior and therefore damaging and violative of the equal protection clause in the 14th amendment of the United States Constitution.

The suggested shift in emphasis from desegregation to quality of education is not a retreat into the blind alley of accepting racial separation as advocated by the Negro nationalist groups, nor is it the acceptance of defeat in the battle for desegregation. It is rather a regrouping of forces, a shift in battle plans and an attempt to determine the most vulnerable flanks of the opposition as the basis for major attack. The resisting educational bureaucracies, their professional staffs, and the segment of the white public which has not yet been infected fatally by the American racist disease are most vulnerable to attack on the issue of the inferior quality of education found in Negro schools and the need to institute a plan immediately to raise the educational level of these schools. The economic, political, military, social-stability, international democratic, humane, and self-interest arguments in favor of an immediate massive program for educational excellence in predominantly Negro schools are so persuasive as to be irrefutable. The expected resistance should be overcome with intelligently planned and sustained efforts.

The first phase of an all-out attack on the inferior education now found in racially segregated schools should be coordinated with a strategy and program for massive and realistic desegregation of entire school systems. This more complicated phase of the over-all struggle will continue to meet the resistances of the past with increased intensity. It will be necessary, therefore, to break this task down into its significant components and determine the timing and phasing of the attack on each or combinations of the components. For example:

The evidence and arguments demonstrating the detrimental effects of segregated schools on the personality and effectiveness of white children should be gathered, evaluated, and widely disseminated in ways understandable to the masses of whites.

The need to reorganize large public school systems away from the presently inefficient and uneconomic neighborhood schools to more modern and viable systems of organization such as educational parks, campuses, or clusters must be sold to the general public in terms of hard dollars and cents and educational efficiency benefiting all children rather than in terms of public-school desegregation.

The need to consolidate small, uneconomic, and relatively ineffective school districts into larger educational and fiscal systems in order to obtain more efficient education for suburban and exurban children must also be sold in direct practical terms rather than in terms of desegregation of schools.

The need to involve large metropolitan regional planning in the mobilization, utilization, and distribution of limited educational resources on a more efficient level must also be explored and discussed publicly.

The movement toward decentralization of large urban school systems must be carefully monitored in order to see that decentralization does not reinforce or concretize urban public school segregation—and to assure that decentralization is consistent with the more economically determined trend toward consolidation and regional planning allocation of resources and cooperation.

A final indication that phase one, the struggle for excellent education for Negro children in ghetto schools, is not inconsistent with phase two, the struggle for nonsegregated education for all children, is to be seen in the fact that if it were possible to raise the quality of education provided for Negro children who attend the urban schools to a level of unquestioned excellence, the flight of middle-class whites to the suburbs might be stemmed and some who have left might be attracted back to the city. Hence, phase one activity would increase the chances of obtaining nonsegregated education in our cities. Similarly, some of the program suggestions of phase two such as educational parks and campuses and the possibilities of regional planning and educational cooperation across present municipal boundaries could lead to substantial improvements in the quality of education offered to inner-city children.

The goal of high quality education for Negro and lower-status children and the goal of public school desegregation are inextricable;

the attainment of the one will lead to the attainment of the other. It is not likely that there could be effective desegregation of the schools without a marked increase in the academic achievement and personal and social effectiveness of Negro and white children. Neither is it possible to have a marked increase in the educational efficiency of Negro schools and the resulting dramatic increase in the academic performance of Negro children without directly and indirectly facilitating the process of public school desegregation.

Problems of Educational Monopoly

It is possible that all attempts to improve the quality of education in our present racially segregated public schools and all attempts to desegregate these schools will have minimal positive results. The rigidity of present patterns of public school organization and the concomitant stagnation in quality of education and academic performance of children may not be amenable to any attempts at change working through and within the present system.

Until the influx of Negro and Puerto Rican youngsters into urban public schools, the American public school system was justifiably credited with being the chief instrument for making the American dream of upward social, economic, and political mobility a reality. The depressed immigrants from southern and eastern Europe could use American public schools as the ladder toward the goals of assimilation and success. The past successes of American public education seem undebatable. The fact that American public schools were effective mobility vehicles for white American immigrants makes even more stark and intolerable their present ineffectiveness for Negro and Puerto Rican children. Now it appears that the present system of organization and functioning of urban public schools is a chief blockage in the mobility of the masses of Negro and other lower-status minority group children. The inefficiency of their schools and the persistence and acceptance of the explanations for this generalized inefficiency are clear threats to the viability of our cities and national stability. The relationship between long-standing urban problems of poverty, crime and delinquency, broken homes—the total cycle of pathology, powerlessness, and personal and social destructiveness which haunts our urban ghettos—and the breakdown in the efficiency of our public schools is now unavoidably clear. It is not enough that those responsible for our public schools should assert passively that the schools merely reflect the pathologies and injustices of our society.

Public schools and their administrators must assert boldly that education must dare to challenge and change society toward social justice as the basis for democratic stability.

There remains the disturbing question—a most relevant question probably too painful for educators themselves to ask—whether the selection process involved in training and promoting educators and administrators for our public schools emphasizes qualities of passivity, conformity, caution, smoothness, and superficial affability rather than boldness, creativity, substance, and the ability to demand and obtain those things which are essential for solid and effective public education for all children. If the former is true and if we are dependent upon the present educational establishment, then all hopes for the imperative reforms which must be made so that city public schools can return to a level of innovation and excellence are reduced to a minimum, if not totally eliminated.

The racial components of the present crisis in urban public education clearly make the possibilities of solution more difficult and may contribute to the passivity and pervading sense of hopelessness of school administrators. Aside from any latent or subtle racism which might infect school personnel themselves, they are hampered by the gnawing awareness that with the continuing flight of middleclass whites from urban public schools and with the increasing competition which education must engage in for a fair share of the tax dollar, it is quite possible that Americans will decide deliberately or by default to sacrifice urban public schools on the altars of its historic and contemporary forms of racism. If this can be done without any real threat to the important segments of economic and political power in the society and with only Negro children as the victims, then there is no realistic basis for hope that our urban public schools will be saved.

The hope for a realistic approach to saving public education in American cities seems to this observer to be found in a formula whereby it can be demonstrated to the public at large that the present level of public school inefficiency has reached an intolerable stage of public calamity. It must be demonstrated that minority group children are not the only victims of the monopolistic inefficiency of the present pattern of organization and functioning of our public schools.

It must be demonstrated that white children—privileged white children whose parents understandably seek to protect them by moving to suburbs or by sending them to private and parochial schools—also suffer both potentially and immediately.

It must be demonstrated that business and industry suffer intolerable financial burdens of double and triple taxation in seeking to maintain a stable economy in the face of the public school inefficiency which produces human casualties rather than constructive human beings.

It must be demonstrated that the costs in correctional, welfare, and health services are intolerably high in seeking to cope with consequences of educational inefficiency—that it would be more economical, even for an affluent society, to pay the price and meet the demands of efficient public education.

It must be demonstrated that a nation which presents itself to the world as the guardian of democracy and the protector of human values throughout the world cannot itself make a mockery of these significant ethical principles by dooming one-tenth of its own population to a lifetime of inhumane futility because of remediable educational deficiencies in its public schools.

These must be understood and there must be the commitment to make the average American understand them if our public schools and our cities are to be effective. But it does not seem likely that the changes necessary for increased efficiency of our urban public schools will come about because they should. Our urban public school systems seem muscle-bound with tradition. They seem to represent the most rigid forms of bureaucracies which, paradoxically, are most resilient in their ability and use of devices to resist rational or irrational demands for change. What is most important in understanding the ability of the educational establishment to resist change is the fact that public school systems are protected public monopolies with only minimal competition from private and parochial schools. Few critics of the American urban public schools—even severe ones such as myself—dare to question the givens of the present organization of public education in terms of local control of public schools, in terms of existing municipal or political boundaries, or in terms of the rights and prerogatives of boards of education to establish policy and select professional staff—at least nominally or titularly if not actually. Nor dare the critics question the relevance of the criteria and standards for selecting superintendents, principals, and teachers, or the relevance of all of these to the objectives of public education—producing a literate and informed public to carry on the business of democracy—and to the goal of producing human beings with social sensitivity and dignity and creativity and a respect for the humanity of others.

A monopoly need not genuinely concern itself with these matters. As long as local school systems can be assured of state aid and increasing federal aid without the accountability which inevitably comes with aggressive competition, it would be sentimental, wishful thinking to expect any significant increase in the efficiency of our public schools. If there are no alternatives to the present system—short of present private and parochial schools which are approaching their limit of expansion—then the possibilities of improvement in public education are limited.

Alternative Forms of Public Education

Alternatives—realistic, aggressive, and viable competitors—to the present public school systems must be found. The development of such competitive public school systems will be attacked by the defenders of the present system as attempts to weaken the present system and thereby weaken, if not destroy, public education. This type of expected self-serving argument can be briefly and accurately disposed of by asserting and demonstrating that truly effective competition strengthens rather than weakens that which deserves to survive. I would argue further that public education need not be identified with the present system of organization of public schools. Public education can be more broadly and pragmatically defined in terms of that form of organization and functioning of an educational system which is in the public interest. Given this definition, it becomes clear that an inefficient system of public systems is not in the public interest:

—a system of public schools which destroys rather than develops positive human potentialities is not in the public interest;
—a system which consumes funds without demonstrating effective returns is not in the public interest;
—a system which insists that its standards of performance should not or cannot be judged by those who must pay the cost is not in the public interest;
—a system which says that the public has no competence to assert that a patently defective product is a sign of the system's inefficiency and demands radical reforms is not in the public interest;
—a system which blames its human resources and its society while it quietly acquiesces in, and inadvertently perpetuates, the very injustices which it claims limit its efficiency is not in the public interest.

Given these assumptions, therefore, it follows that alternative forms of public education must be developed if the children of our cities are to be educated and made constructive members of our society. In the development of alternatives, all attempts must at the same time be made to strengthen our present urban public schools. Such attempts would involve re-examination, revision, and strengthening of curricula, methods, personnel selection, and evaluation; the development of more rigorous procedures of supervision, reward of superior performance, and the institution of a realistic and tough system of accountability, and the provision of meaningful ways of involving the parents and the community in the activities of the school.

The above measures, however, will not suffice. The following are suggested as possible, realistic, and practical competitors to the present form of urban public school systems:

Regional State Schools. These schools would be financed by the states and would cut across present urban-suburban boundaries.

Federal Regional Schools. These schools would be financed by the Federal Government out of present state aid funds or with additional federal funds. These schools would be able to cut through state boundaries and could make provisions for residential students.

College- and University-Related Open Schools. These schools would be financed by colleges and universities as part of their laboratories in education. They would be open to the public and not restricted to children of faculty and students. Obviously, students would be selected in terms of constitutional criteria and their percentage determined by realistic considerations.

Industrial Demonstration Schools. These schools would be financed by industrial, business, and commercial firms for their employees and selected members of the public. These would not be vocational schools—but elementary and comprehensive high schools of quality. They would be sponsored by combinations of business and industrial firms in much the same way as churches and denominations sponsor and support parochial or sectarian schools.

Labor Union Sponsored Schools. These schools would be financed and sponsored by labor unions largely, but not exclusively, for the children of their members.

Army Schools. The Defense Department has been quietly effective in educating some of the casualties of our present public schools. It is hereby suggested that they now go into the business of repairing hundreds of thousands of these human casualties with affirmation rather than apology. Schools for adolescent drop-outs or educational rejects could be set up by the Defense Department adjacent to camps—but not necessarily as an integral part of the military. If this is necessary, it should not block the attainment of the goal of rescuing as many of these young people as possible. They are not expendable on the altar of anti-militarism rhetoric.

With strong, efficient, and demonstrably excellent parallel systems of public schools, organized and operated on a quasi-private level, and with quality control and professional accountability maintained and determined by Federal and State educational standards and supervision, it would be possible to bring back into public education a vitality and dynamism which are now clearly missing. Even the public discussion of these possibilities might clear away some of the dank stagnation which seems to be suffocating urban education today. American industrial and material wealth was made possible through industrial competition. American educational health may be made possible through educational competition.

If we succeed, we will have returned to the dynamic, affirmative goal of education; namely, to free man of irrational fears, superstitions, and hatreds. Specifically, in America the goal of democratic education must be to free Americans of the blinding and atrophying shackles of racism. A fearful, passive, apologetic, and inefficient educational system cannot help in the attainment of these goals.

If we succeed in finding and developing these and better alternatives to the present educational inefficiency, we will not only save countless Negro children from lives of despair and hopelessness, and thousands and thousands of white children from cynicism, moral emptiness, and social ineptness—but we will also demonstrate the validity of our democratic promises. We also will have saved our civilization through saving our cities.

Henry Levin

MAKING PUBLIC SCHOOLS COMPETITIVE

One of the best known alternative proposals calling for public support for new kinds of educational patterns is known as the voucher plan. There are many variations of the voucher plan, and the idea itself is not necessarily new. But it is receiving wide attention today. The basic idea calls

From *Current*, October, 1968, pp. 25–32. This is an abridged and edited version of the article that originally appeared in the June, 1968 issue of *The Urban Review*, a publication of the Center for Urban Education. Reprinted by permission of *The Urban Review* and *Current*.

for legislation which would identify a required minimum level of education. This minimum level would be financed by the government through giving parents vouchers redeemable for a specific maximum sum per child per year if spent on "sanctioned" educational services. Parents would be free to spend their allowance, and any additional sum, on educational services provided by approved institutions of their choice.

Henry Levin outlines the voucher plan, examines the benefits and disadvantages, and discusses some of the questions and problems which would have to be reconciled in order to put the plan into operation. He is convinced that the plan would have greater private benefits than does the present system, but he does not believe such benefits would outweigh what he perceives to be high social costs. He argues that such a plan would result in a change in the relative distribution of schooling alternatives so that present disparities in income and opportunities among social and racial groups would increase. He argues that the free market approach would probably lead to greater social and racial segregation of pupils.

Henry Levin is a Research Associate with the Economic Studies Division of the Brookings Institute.

The American public schools have been severely criticized in recent years. . . . The utter failure of traditional schooling to impart even basic reading skills to substantial numbers of youngsters has stimulated a barrage of proposals, from educators and noneducators alike, to change the educational system.

While some critics suggest that changes within the present structure would cure the impotence of the inner-city schools, others see a necessity for much more radical changes in the structure itself. Among the former group are proponents of new instructional techniques and remedial programs, while some of the latter group would turn over the schools to the community and others would dismantle the present system of public schools altogether, replacing them with private schools that would be—in part—publicly financed. . . .

In the light of their records of failure in educating the disadvantaged, how is it that [the traditional public schools] have survived? . . . In the main, the continued existence of these schools derives from the fact that they do not have to be effective to survive. In most cases they perform for a captive audience. Pupils are assigned to them for better or for worse, and each school can retain most of its students because the majority of pupils have no other alternatives.

The proponents of the market approach believe that by giving students and their families a choice of schools, and by requiring schools to compete for students, massive increases in educational effectiveness and output would result. For, if schools had to compete for students, they would likely be much more responsive to the particular needs of their clientele. That is, the private schools—in order to achieve goals of profit, or in the case of nonprofit ones, capacity enrollments—must provide what appears to be good schooling in order to attract students.

The father of this approach is the Chicago economist, Milton Friedman, and it is Friedman's basic scheme that dominates the proposals of others who would also replace the public schools with a market of choices [see *Current*, May 1966, page 50]. Before outlining the Friedman plan, however, it is important to point out that all of the advocates of the market approach view basic schooling as a public function. They do so because at the very least, ". . . a stable and democratic society is impossible without widespread acceptance of some common set of values and without a minimum degree of literacy and knowledge on the part of most citizens. Education contributes both." Thus, because of the social benefits derived from a citizenry which has received some basic level of schooling, the responsibility of paying for this education is considered to be a social burden rather than an individual one. But Friedman would separate the financing, which would be public, from the management and operation of schools, which would be private: "Government could require a minimum level of education which they could finance by giving parents vouchers redeemable for a specified maximum sum per child per year if spent on 'approved' educational services. Parents would be free to spend their sum and any additional sum on purchasing educational service from an 'approved' institution of their own choice. The educational services could be rendered by private enterprises operated for profit, or by nonprofit institutions of various kinds."

The result would be that: "Parents could express their views about schools directly, by withdrawing their children from one school and sending them to another to a much greater extent than is now possible." Indeed, the scheme is based upon the plausible premise that: "Here, as in other fields, competitive private enterprise is likely to be far more efficient in meeting consumer demands than either nationalized (publicly run) enterprises or enterprises run to serve other purposes." . . .

In summary then, the government would provide families with a voucher for each school-age child, which would guarantee a maximum specified sum of money which could be paid as tuition to any "approved" school. Nonpublic schools would compete among themselves—and perhaps with the public schools—for students by offering a variety of educational choices. Freedom of entry by schools into the market—provided that they met minimum qualifications—would insure efficiency in the production of schooling, and students and their families would be given a market for educational alternatives in place of the present rigid assignment practices. Moreover, such competition would induce innovation and experimentation in that each school would try to obtain competitive advantages over the others. Thus, the operation of the market would provide far more choices and a greater degree of efficiency in the schooling of all students, especially those pupils who are presently confined to slum schools. . . .

There are two types of benefits associated with basic (elementary and secondary) schooling: private benefits and social ones. The private benefits represent those which accrue to the individual (and his family) tangibly in the form of higher earnings, and intangibly in the form of heightened appreciation, awareness and insights, and so on. If all of the returns to basic education were private ones, a strong case could be made for letting the market determine the production and allocation of schooling among the population. . . .

In terms of private benefits, it is likely to be true that any measure of competition among schools would lead to increases in their effectiveness. The motive for success—profit maximization—would require that a school meet the need of its students better than its competitors for any given cost. The fact that existing policies would have to be re-examined in the light of their educational contributions would probably engender thorough changes in the administration of the schools. By increasing the number of decision-making units, the probability of schools innovating to gain competitive advantages would be far greater than under the present system. While many examples of such change can be envisioned, a notable one would be the introduction of those new curricula and instructional aids which showed great promise relative to their costs. Most of the existing public institutions have been loath to adopt any but the most modest changes in their educational strategies.

Another fruit of competition among schools might be more imaginative recruitment policies for teachers. At present, teachers are hired on the basis of a single-salary schedule, one which fixes the teacher's salary on the basis of how much schooling he has had and the amount of his teaching experience. Such factors as the quality of his schooling, his actual teaching ability, his expected performance as reflected in his preservice teaching and personality traits or his field of specialization have no effect on his salary. Under this system, the more imaginative persons—

who are often able to reap greater returns outside of teaching—either do not enter the schools or leave after short periods of time. On the other hand, those who have few alternatives in the labor market remain in the schools, protected from dismissal by life-long tenure contracts after only three years of experience. Thus . . . the single-salary schedule fosters mediocrity in teacher selection and retention.

Furthermore, it leads to shortages of teachers with training in some specialties and surpluses of teachers with other training. That is, while mathematics and science majors receive higher starting pay in the market-at-large, they receive the same salaries as do other specialists in the schools. It comes as no surprise, then, to find that schools show a shortage of teachers properly trained in science and mathematics and a surplus of social studies and male physical education teachers. As a result, of course, the social studies and physical education teachers are then often assigned to teach secondary courses in mathematics, physics, chemistry, and other shortage areas. Competitive schools would have to hire on the basis of the realities of the market place rather than on the basis of rigid salary schedules.

Moreover, competitive schools would be more likely to adopt a policy of flexible class size depending upon subject matter, grade level, and type of student, which is a more sensible goal than maintaining uniform class sizes. There would also be more willingness to differentiate staffing by substituting teacher aides, curriculum specialists, and other specialized personnel for classroom teachers wherever accompanied by increases in efficiency. . . . Most important of all, individual differences among teachers might be utilized as an asset in the educational process by enabling teachers to pursue their own teaching styles and approaches in place of the present attempts of the schools to standardize curricula, syllabi, and pedagogy along narrow guidelines.

These are some of the changes that we might realistically envision among competitive schools, changes that are not now feasible given the institutional rigidities of the typical school system. Since Friedman might leave the public schools as an alternative, only the best of them —those which could compete effectively—would survive over the long run. That is, competition would keep the remaining public schools on their toes.

In short, it is likely that Friedman is correct in asserting that the market approach is a more efficient device for satisfying the educational preferences of consumers than is the traditional, highly-centralized public school system.

Under a competitive market, we could probably expect that greater educational benefits would accrue to students and their families. Yet, increases in private benefits do not necessarily yield similar increases in social benefits.

Our schools shoulder the primary burden for satisfying at least two social goals: Those of imparting minimum levels of literacy, knowledge and the common values necessary for a stable democracy; and of decreasing disparities in incomes and opportunities associated with race and social class.

Friedman considers only the first of these social objectives. Under his plan, schools would be required to meet minimum standards—such as a common content in their programs—much as restaurants are required to ". . . maintain minimum sanitary standards." But Friedman's analogy is a bad one, for requiring a common content in school programs is more like requiring uniform nutritional offerings in restaurants, not just cleanliness. Who would decide what minimum content was, and how would it be assessed? Would the traditional sequence of courses be considered minimal? Would teachers be required to satisfy certain criteria, or could anyone be hired to teach? All of these issues would have to be reconciled, and it is likely that the common content requirements to which Friedman alludes would lead to far more extensive regulation than he suggests. And obviously the greater the requirements which are imposed, the more alike schools would be; and in the extreme, the very animal which we wish to replace might merely be disguised in the new trappings of a highly regulated private industry.

Beyond the social responsibilities of assuring minimal literacy and basic skills, there is also the responsibility of exposing children to fellow students who are drawn from a variety of social, economic, and racial groups. It has also been asserted that slum children become more highly motivated and are likely to develop greater aspirations when they are exposed to children from the middle-class. Our present system of segregating school populations according to the neighborhoods in which they are located does little to achieve the goal of mixed-class schools. Friedman's approach, however, makes no provision for ensuring that students attend schools in racially and socially diverse environments. Indeed, it is likely that social segregation—one of the by-products of the neighborhood school—would increase under the market proposal. For, experience with private schools suggests even greater segregation of student bodies on the basis of religious, ethnic, racial, economic, and other social criteria.

The significance of the probability of increased socio-economic segregation under a free market system is that such a result would work directly against the second social responsibility of the schools—the equalization of opportunity for all racial and social groups. . . .

In particular. . . . , how have the poor fared in the market place?

If the public sector has failed the poor in the efficient production and allocation of social services, the private market can hardly claim a greater degree of success in satisfying their needs. For example, a recent study of the Federal Trade Commission showed that goods purchased for $1 as wholesale sold for an average of $2.65 in stores located in poor neighborhoods, but only for $1.65 in stores located in the 'general market.' Geographic mobility, education, income, access to capital (credit)— the very things which the poor lack and the middle class possess—are the characteristics that enable one to operate most successfully in the private market. The failure of the market to give rich and poor equal access to privately produced goods and services should, in itself, make us skeptical about applying it to education.

First, while the private market would likely provide many educational alternatives to middle-class children, there would probably be far fewer sellers of educational services to the children of the poor. It is important to note that schooling must be consumed at the point of purchase; therefore geographical location of schools becomes a salient feature of the market place. But if the previous experience of the slums can be used for prediction, few if any sellers of high quality educational services at competitive rates will locate in the ghetto. Not only is there no Saks Fifth Avenue in Harlem; there is no Macy's, Gimbels, Korvettes, or Klein's. . . .

In addition, the fact that many families could increase their expenditures on schooling *beyond the maximum provided by the state* would also tend to bid schooling resources away from the ghettos, particularly in the short run. Not only do the poor lack the incomes to add private expenditures to the proposed public vouchers, but on the average they also have more children to educate. Consequently, public funds will be all they will have to spend on the schooling of their children. Given this situation, the schools which now serve the poor could not hope to obtain the better teachers since such personnel would probably prefer to teach for more money in a middle-class school rather than for less money in a ghetto school.

Even if the slum children were accepted at private schools located outside the ghetto—a highly dubious eventuality given the history of private schools—the poor would have to bear the costs of transportation to such institutions. While the monetary costs of transportation represent only part of such a burden, even $5 a week represents $180 over a school year. Thus, the ghetto resident is likely to face a higher cost of educational services whether he sends his child to a school in or out of the inner city.

Christopher Jencks has suggested that private schools would spring up to serve Negro children if only money equal to what was spent in the public schools were provided for tuition. Unfortunately, experience with this very approach has suggested that such optimism is probably unwarranted. In order to defy the desegregation order provided by the 1954 *Brown* decision, Prince Edward County, Va., abolished its public schools in 1959 and provided tuition grants to students so that they could attend privately operated schools. While a system of private schools did emerge to serve the needs of white students, no private alternatives became available to black pupils. As a result, those Negro children who could not be sent to relatives or friends in other districts received no regular education at all.

The fact that education as a good is difficult to define or measure also violates an important premise of the competitive market. There is no clear concept of what should be considered "educational output," and data purporting to measure even partial outputs are not wholly satisfactory. . . . Given the fact that even professional educators have no objective way of rating schools, how are the parents of the poor going to compare them? Friedman has suggested that they will emulate the rich, for "The rich are always the taste-makers, and that is the method by which the standards of society are raised." Those of us who have observed the criteria by which families select colleges for their offspring might find this assumption difficult to accept. But even if we were to accept it, and its normative undertones, one might question whether the youngster in Harlem and his counterpart in Great Neck and Scarsdale have the same schooling needs. Further, the only way that the poor could emulate the rich in purchasing education would be if the poor possessed the resources of the rich, as well as their exalted tastes. Indeed, it is the discrepancy in the initial income distribution which is likely to raise the greatest difficulties in a market approach to education.

Friedman tacitly assumes that the initial distribution of income among households is appropriate, and he . . . considers that a "major merit" of the voucher system is that parents with higher incomes and greater desires for education could add their own monies to the standard tuition grant provided by the government. That is, the middle- and upper-classes—having higher incomes and fewer children—could purchase much better educations for their offspring than could the poor.

This argument ignores completely the crucial role which has been given education in increasing the future opportunities and incomes of youth. True equality of opportunity implies that—on the average—an individual of any race or social class has the same opportunity to achieve a given income or occupation as a member of any other race or class. Of course, it is sham to assert that any such situation exists today; but under the market approach to education, the disparity in income distribution among rich and poor and among Negroes and whites would probably increase. . . .

Thus the free market remedy as Friedman has proposed it would probably have greater private benefits than does the present system. Even the poor might experience some improvement in their schooling from a market which gave them alternatives to their present schools. Yet offsetting these private gains are the social costs imposed by a system which would tend to change the relative distribution of schooling alternatives in such a way that the present disparities in income and opportunities among social and racial groups would increase. Moreover, the free market approach would probably lead to greater racial and social segregation of pupils among schools than presently exists. These are tremendous costs to inflict upon a society which is preaching equality on the one hand and on the other hand is reeling from urban riots that are largely attributable to the frustrations of unequal opportunity.

The Friedman approach might nevertheless be modified to avoid some of its deleterious consequences while taking advantage of the benefits of a competitive system. Since we are particularly concerned with the educational deficiencies of the inner-city schools and their disadvantaged clients, we might inquire into how the market approach might be adapted to the specific needs of ghetto children. The simplest way to implement the market approach without putting the poor at a disadvantage would be to grant tuition payments which are inversely related to family income and wealth. Disadvantaged children might be given vouchers which are worth two or three times the value of the maximum grants given children of the well-to-do. Such a redistributive system of grants would overcome many of the initial market handicaps faced by slum families. Thus, differences in tuition would be based upon relative educational needs, costs, and the family resources for fulfilling those needs.

However, since it is unlikely that this differential voucher plan would ever be adopted by the electorate, we ought to consider other market proposals. One of the most meritorious of these is the plan recommended by Theodore Sizer, dean of Harvard's Graduate School of Education. Sizer would have the state provide tuition payments—and thus schooling alternatives—*only* for children of the poor. These family allowances ". . . would allow that one section of our population that suffers most seriously from segregated schooling—the poor—to move, at their own initiative, and if they want to, into schools of their choice outside their neighborhoods." This specific application of the Friedman proposal appears to be politically feasible and it is likely to spawn both the private and social benefits that we discussed above. . . .

Recent emphasis on improving the public education system has focused on community involvement in the public schools. The premise on which the community approach rests is that a school should serve the particular needs of its clientele rather than some general set of requirements which are defined at a highly centralized level. Several efforts have been made to initiate individual community-run public schools in the large cities; but the boldest over-all move in this direction is that recommended for the New York City schools by the Mayor's Advisory Panel on School Decentralization. The Bundy Report—as the New York study is commonly called—proposes that some 60 or so largely autonomous school districts be set up in New York City, each representing a distinct community or set of communities.

Such community school districts would carry out most of the educational functions for their residents and would—in addition—"promote coordination in the planning and operation of health, recreation, and other human resource programs in the city." Responsiveness to the particular educational needs of local residents would be insured by Community School Boards composed of 11 members: "six selected by a panel elected by the parents of children who attend schools in the district; five selected by the Mayor from lists of qualified persons presented by the central education agency after consultation with parents and community organizations."

Given community schools and the promise that they appear to hold in adapting to the special needs of their students, it is possible to suggest a method by which they, too, can benefit from the competitive market. Communities could plan their educational requirements and solicit bids from private industry, universities, and nonprofit groups for fulfilling these needs. Educational contractors would compete for the particular educational services that the community wished to buy. . . . Thus, the groups selling educational services to the community schools would have an incentive to perform well or else chance losing a customer.

The purchasing of educational services on the private market by community schools holds particular promise at the present time, for many firms which have been developing educational programs and technology over the last decade have not really had a chance to test their products in a "natural" environment. Such firms appear to be very anxious to show that their approaches are worthy of implementation. Indeed, the potential rewards to be reaped by educational contractors who can show successful implementation are likely to be enormous.

There are several ways to create competition within a public school system. . . . The proposal for community schools represents a more general framework in which the competition of the market place might be used to advantage. The time is ripe to experiment with at least one of these plans for the children of the ghetto. Do we have any buyers?

The demand for alternatives—whatever their form—results from numerous perceived weaknesses in our schools. These demands, whether or not they have resulted in alternatives, have had such an impact upon our present system that it will never be the same. Accordingly, projections about the alternative movement per se, although appropriate, may be too narrow in scope. Therefore, some of the selections in this section go beyond the alternative issue as such. In such cases, the reader is invited to ruminate about the place and prospects of the alternative movement within a context of broader projections. Is there a place for alternative schools in these broader projections? Are alternatives taken for granted as institutions which will exist when and if these projections are realized?

David Selden

VOUCHERS—SOLUTION OR SOP?

Numerous teacher organizations have come out loudly against the alternative schemes reflected in voucher proposals. David Selden, President of the American Federation of Teachers, addresses himself to some major weaknesses of voucher proposals as he sees them. Selden is convinced that

From *The Record*, February, 1971, pp. 365–371. Reprinted by permission of the publisher.

the voucher idea "tends to divert attention from the real and basic needs of children and the schools."

One of today's most controversial educational issues is the voucher plan—a scheme designed to give students choice of school rather than requiring them to attend schools to which they are assigned. Parents would be given certificates equal to the cost of educating their children and could then spend these certificates in any public or private school with room to accommodate their children.

Opponents of the voucher plan are divided into two camps: those who believe that it will not work and those who believe it will. Those who oppose the voucher plan on grounds of impracticality have found themselves at a serious disadvantage because, as each new detailed objection has been registered, proponents of the plan have added new qualifications and safeguards designed to eliminate the objection. Those who oppose the plan as a matter of principle are raising more fundamental objections. They hold that the voucher plan is a dangerous and divisive proposal which could even destroy the public school system.

Innocence Abroad. Actually, there is no single voucher plan. One of the first to use the term was conservative economist Milton Friedman who was trying to find a way to turn the schools over to private enterprise. Later, Christopher Jencks and his associates at the Harvard Graduate School of Education saw vouchers as a way to bring about educational changes. They were and still are deeply concerned about the failure of American schools to educate underclass students, particularly those who live in the black slums and ghettos of our big cities. Jencks and others observed that while schools in nearby Boston and in other cities are overcrowded and run-down, many middle-class suburbs of those cities have underutilized school facilities.

Furthermore, the voucher advocates took heed of the central finding of the Coleman Report to the effect that the most influential element in a child's education is his social milieu. If such children could be helped to leapfrog out of the city and into suburban schools, they would thus be receiving intrinsically better educational service on the one hand and a more learning-supporting environment on the other.

Jencks and his associates further observed that throughout the nation there are a number of small, highly innovative private schools which are apparently achieving spectacular results. Yet many of these experimental schools live a hand-to-mouth existence. If a way could be found to give such schools financial security, the probability of developing useful, new educational techniques would be increased.

Hence, vouchers. What has happened to the original pure-hearted voucher concept, however, is a classic example of good intentions gone bad.

Mechanical Problems. One of the early problems encountered in making the voucher scheme viable was the obvious fact that putting an urban educational price tag on a poor kid would still leave him unable to afford a suburban school. Therefore, one of the first elements that was added to the concept was that children from poverty slum families would be given added educational green stamps, so that they could afford a more expensive education than they would get if they stayed in their urban attendance districts. This voucher override caveat introduces a vital cop-out right at the outset.

Although educational arguers concede that suburban education is better and that it costs more, they do not concede that *urban* education could be improved if more money were to be spent in the cities. The more vociferous critics of our public schools proceed from the premise that we could educate children if we, (1) really wanted to do a job, and (2) had the right idea about how to teach. They vigorously dispute assertions by teachers and their organizations that well-qualified and well-paid teachers with small classes, reasonable classroom-hour loads, ample remedial assistance, and good physical surroundings have much to do with the quality of instruction. Yet many of these same critics support the voucher plan, despite its initial concession that good education will cost more than we are now spending in slum schools.

Money alone is not an absolute determinant of educational quality. A study by the NAACP in 1969 showed that a large proportion—although not the majority by any means—of so-called compensatory education programs financed under Title I of the Elementary and Secondary Education Act proved to be educationally worthless. On the other hand, it is impossible to effect any large-scale improvement in education without having more money to hire teachers and other personnel and to invest in new schools and equipment. And if more money can be made available for education, it should be spent to improve the public schools in the areas of greatest need.

The voucher bounty idea would introduce incentives for operators of private schools and, of course, for suburban school boards. Supporters of the plan pooh-pooh the possibility that the profit motive would stimulate added hucksterism in education. However, unless safeguards against profiteering were carefully drawn and enforced, voucher money would most certainly tempt unscrupulous educational entrepreneurs in the same way that the GI Bill stimulated the growth of all those electronics, watchmaking, and key punch "schools." Most of the victims of those enterprises were ex-servicemen from the underclass who were looking for educational shortcuts. The greater educational need of underclass children and their parents makes them more vulnerable to the blandishments of fly-by-night school operators.

Open Enrollment. The term voucher plan is so catchy that one almost takes for granted that this is something new, but it is not. In the early, liberal, integrationist days following the U.S. Supreme Court's 1954 school desegregation decision, many school districts adopted so-called open enrollment plans. Black children who otherwise would have been attending all-black slum schools were permitted to transfer to other schools if those schools had space to receive them. Many of these plans also provided free busing, again on a voluntary basis. While most of the open enrollment plans were theoretically "two way," it was inevitably black children who rode the bus—a segregating activity in itself.

Most open enrollment plans have been abandoned or have dwindled to insignificance. As a matter of fact, they never did enlist masses of students, and for the most part, the children who rode the bus were those with strong parental support and high motivation. These were the very children who were more likely to succeed regardless of the school they attended. They were also the very children whose presence could have provided stimulation for less striving children in their ghetto schools.

Most observers of the open enrollment plans quickly came to the conclusion that the programs were ineffective in combatting racial segregation and that very little, if any, educational gain resulted.

As an aside, the open enrollment plans, confined mostly to Northern cities, simply proved that a *little* busing would accomplish nothing; the much more extensive busing program now being followed in many Southern cities bears educational promise through its significant effect upon the social mix in schools.

Racism and Politics. Another scheme very close to the voucher idea is "freedom-of-choice," now outlawed by many court decisions. The freedom-of-choice plans were designed to *promote* racial segregation. They were based upon outright subsidies, very similar to vouchers, given to parents to trade in at the "school of their choice." Of course, black parents were not permitted to use their vouchers at white schools.

The original proponents of vouchers abhor racial discrimination, and they have again proposed mechanical regulations which would supposedly guard against use of the vouchers to promote freedom-of-choice academies. For instance, they would require that at least 25 percent of the student population be of a minority ethnic group before a school would be eligible to receive voucher students.

The proposed 25 percent safeguard illustrates another basic problem of the voucher idea. Since the plan's success seems to depend, in part at least, on federal aid, one can readily see the shape of the future. The percentage figure would loom as a major proving ground over which pro and con lobbyists would clash, just as they now struggle to influence percentages in taxes, tariffs, and oil depletion allowances.

Even if Congress passed a proper percentage, however, it still would have to be enforced. Ironically, some of those who purport to fear the specter of federal intervention in local affairs are also advocating the use of vouchers, not recognizing, presumably, the massive federal regulatory apparatus which would be necessary to prevent abuse.

European Experience. School finance systems very similar to vouchers have been in use in a number of European countries for many decades. In Belgium, Holland, and Denmark, for instance, children receive equal subsidies, regardless of the sponsorship of the school they attend— public, private, nonsectarian, or religious. Contrary to the objections usually raised, the effects of government subsidies have been far from catastrophic. While the percentage of students at religious-sponsored schools has increased somewhat, the proportion now seems to be stabilized. Furthermore, apparently the religious schools are becoming less and less sectarian and more and more like the public schools. It is predicted that there will be very little difference between the two types of schools in five to ten years.

The European system, however, couples close supervision by the state with certain standard requirements—in staffing and equipment, for instance—which all schools must meet. Of course, all schools must teach a standard curriculum prescribed by the state, and there are single national teacher-salary schedules and pension systems.

It cannot be said that public subsidy of private schools creates illiberal, divided, and strife-torn societies, since the three countries under discussion are among the most liberal and peaceful in the world. But it must be noted that economic and social conditions in those countries differ greatly from those in the United States. First, there is no large economically deprived underclass in Belgium, Holland, or Denmark. Second, there is no large racially isolated group. Third, government is much simpler and more centralized. What seems to have become acceptable in small, middle-class, ethnically homogeneous countries under strong centralized control or supervision would not necessarily be applicable to the United States with its huge problems and deep unresolved racial, sectional, and religious antagonisms.

Incidentally, France does *not* subsidize private schools.

Religious Warfare. The dynamite which lies ready for detonation just below the surface of the voucher controversy is the growing issue of public support for religious-related schools. At several meetings called by the sponsors of the voucher plan in an effort to "clarify" the situation, the line-up of religious teams was as apparent as if they had worn colored jerseys. On the one side were those Jewish and Protestant organizations traditionally zealous in maintaining the principle of separation of church and state. On the other side were the Catholic organizations and a scattering of other denominations trying desperately to save their church-related school systems. Even though Jencks and company say that vouchers would not be used to any great extent to solve the financial plight of the church schools, spokesmen for those institutions quite obviously think otherwise.

Jencks thinks that the church schools would have a hard time meeting his 25 percent minority race qualification. Church spokesmen, however, feel that with federal support tuition for such schools could be reduced and the number of "free" students could be greatly increased, thus helping to improve racial integration in such schools and at the same time preventing their possible collapse. The religious advocates of vouchers point out that church-related schools now enroll hundreds of thousands of children who otherwise would be the responsibility of the public system. Unless these schools receive financial aid, they will be forced to curtail operations and send students flooding into already overcrowded public facilities. Vouchers seem to offer a way out.

The tuition subsidy plan now in use in New York state, which provides state funds for college students to attend institutions of their choice, whether public or private, seems to be in conformity with constitutional requirements. Other scholarship plans using federal funds have also been in existence for many years without arousing successful legal objection. Even so, introduction of the voucher plan is almost certain to result in speedy legal challenge by its opponents on grounds of separation of church and state.

Several cases now in the judicial works will have a bearing on the legal status of vouchers. One of these is *Flask v. Gardner*, which challenges the use of federal funds to pay for educational services conducted in religious-sponsored schools under Title I of ESEA. If the courts should decide that the use of funds in this way is unconstitutional, the legality of the voucher concept so far as the religious-related schools are concerned would be dubious indeed.

The other test case is *Lemon v. Kurtzman*. Pennsylvania now provides state aid directly to private schools—most of them church-connected. A number of organizations have filed amicus briefs in opposition to the use of funds for such a purpose, but U.S. Attorney General John Mitchell announced in September, 1970, that his department would file an amicus brief on the side of the state, thus declaring in favor of such subsidies.

Polarizer. The Nixon Administration has not been slow to realize the political potentialities in the voucher controversy. Donald Rumsfeld, who was appointed by the President to become Director of the Office of Economic Opportunity (presumably on the basis that since he voted against every bill which created OEO he could not be accused of favoritism), started down the Spiro Agnew polarization trail in 1970. Rumsfeld was seeking quite obviously to exploit another of those neat splitters which have become the hallmark of the current administration's political style.

By pushing the voucher plan, Rumsfeld attacked teachers, who are almost universally opposed, and the "liberal elements" who favor strict separation of church and state. At the same time, he declared himself in support of people who, according to cynical political analysis, are thought to be in the hard-hat category. He also gave aid and comfort to people who secretly hope vouchers will lead to a revival of the Southern freedom-of-choice plans.

In promoting the voucher plan, Rumsfeld displayed a flair for half-truths. In a speech given September 23, 1970, before the San Francisco Chamber of Commerce "Urban Roundtable," he first detailed the all too obvious defects and shortcomings of our current system of education. Then he totaled up all the money spent by all levels of government on education. In the same paragraph he threw in an observation— unsupported—that "the pupil-teacher ratio is lower today than ever in the nation's history."

What Rumsfeld left out was that the percentage of gross national product for education remained practically constant for decades and that "pupil-teacher ratio" is an almost meaningless figure. Furthermore, if the ratio has gone down, how much has it decreased? A page later in the same speech, he rejected the idea that the amount of money spent on education has much to do with the quality of education. What we need, he said, are new ideas, and he charged that the American Federation of Teachers and other teacher organizations don't want any new ideas, since they are against the voucher plan and have been against other "experiments" launched under the aegis of the OEO.

Quoting directly from the Rumsfeld remarks, he stated: "They [teacher interest groups] charge that money, not new approaches, is the answer to improving educational skills." He then went on to quote President Nixon, "When we get more education for the dollar, we'll start asking for more dollars for education."

As a matter of fact, the voucher plan does not add a single new educational technique, nor can it guarantee that giving pupils more mobility will result in the development of new techniques.

Lizard or Dragon? One of the chief objections which can be leveled fairly at the voucher idea is that it, like so many catchy educational schemes, tends to divert attention from the real and basic needs of children and the schools. Whether education is carried on by people—teachers and paraprofessionals—or by machines watched over by people, there *is* a relationship between cost and educational effort.

No one would deny that it is possible to waste school money, but all other things being equal—the educability of students, the intelligence of teachers and administrators, the social milieu in which the school must operate—the more money you spend on education, the more education is produced. It is silly, if not malicious, to suggest that money-starved school systems will have "to do better" before the great white fathers in Washington will give them more support.

Like a bright, shiny, quick-moving lizard running over a rotting log, the voucher scheme diverts our attention from the decay underneath. But what will we do if Mr. Jencks' entertaining little lizard grows up to be a fire-breathing dragon?

Harold G. and June Grant Shane

FORECAST FOR THE SEVENTIES

All of the chapters in this book are addressed to issues which are, for the most part, of recent origin. The readings have shown that in a relatively short period of time, certainly less than a decade, dramatic changes

From *Today's Education*, January, 1969, pp. 29–32. Reprinted by permission of the authors and publisher.

have taken place in education and even more dramatic changes have taken place in the way professionals, students, and the general citizenry look upon it. Given such changes it is difficult to speculate about what education will look like, much less what we will need by way of formal schooling, in the next few years. Nevertheless, these are some of the matters to which the following selection is addressed.

Harold and June Shane expect a change in emphasis from upper-level to lower-level education. As a corollary of an increased attention and support for the individual student, they predict a gradual abolition of grade levels. The Shanes also offer us some brief comments on two very interesting notions—biochemical and psychological controls as possibilities in learning. Regarding alternatives, the authors note that the next decade's war on educational problems will involve a rapid expansion of educational facilities and services in economically blighted areas, both in terms of enlarging existing facilities and creating new types of learning environments.

Harold Shane is University Professor of Education and June Grant Shane is Professor of Education, School of Education, Indiana University.

During the last five years, there has been a marked increase in long- and short-range speculation regarding possible educational futures that may lie before us in the remaining years of the twentieth century. For the past three years, we have studied approximately 400 published and unpublished articles and books in which such conjectures and projections occur.

These current writings clearly indicate that education and schools, as they exist today, will change drastically during the 1970's and will be modified almost beyond recognition by the end of the century. The paragraphs that follow summarize some of the more important developments that could occur in the next decade and propose some of the new roles in which the teacher is likely to be cast. In conclusion, we give thought to the question: For what kind of world should children who will live most of their lives in the twenty-first century be prepared? Here, then, as many scholars see it, are some of the possible designs of educational futures in the seventies.

Education will reverse its traditional pattern of expenditure. From the beginning, more money has been spent per student in higher education, with secondary education coming in a strong second and elementary education, a poor third. Preschool and kindergarten programs have not even been in the race for funds. But now, major support for early childhood education seems highly probable because of our belated recognition that we have spent literally billions at the upper-age ranges to compensate for what we did not do at the two- to seven-year age levels.

Now priorities for education of the youngest will bring to public education nonschool preschools, minischools, and a preprimary continuum. As nonschool preschool programs begin to operate, educators will assume a formal responsibility for children when they reach the age of two. We will work with parents of young children both directly and through educational TV programs for young mothers. And we will offer such services as medical-dental examinations and follow-up, early identification of the handicapped and deprived, attacks on nutritional needs, and—of major importance—early referral to cooperating social agencies for treatment of psychobehavioral problems.

New programs for two-year-olds will involve the coordination of community resources, under school auspices, to equalize educational opportunity for these children before cultural deprivation makes inroads on their social and mental health.

The minischool, as envisioned here, is one that provides a program of carefully designed experiences for the three-year-old—experiences deliberately devised to increase the sensory input from which the children derive their intelligence. Each minischool presumably would enroll six or eight children under a qualified paraprofessional. A professionally prepared childhood environmental specialist would directly supervise clusters of approximately six minischools.

We will probably build these small schools into housing projects, make them part of new schoolhouse construction, or open them in improvised space in convenient buildings.

The preprimary continuum is a new creation intended to replace contemporary kindergartens for the four- and five-year-old. This program presupposes that the young learner will spend from one year to four years preparing himself to perform effectively in a subsequent primary continuum, the segment of education now usually labeled grades one through three. The preprimary interval should sharply reduce the problems of widely varied experience and social adjustment encountered by children who are arbitrarily enrolled in grade one at age six regardless of their previous cultural environment.

Major environmental mediation for two- to six-year-olds, as described above, will permit schools to abandon the current transitional concept of nongrading. In the coming decade, a seamless primary, middle-school, and secondary continuum of coordinated learning experiences will begin to replace the nongraded programs of the sixties.

Here, progress and the time spent on a given topic will become completely individual matters, as one emergent design for learning serves all ages. The intellectually advantaged child, for instance, might spend only two years in the primary or intermediate continuum, accomplishing what most children would accomplish in three or four years.

In this personalized educational continuum, the question of how to group children will no longer be relevant. The child will simply work with others in ephemeral groupings during whatever time certain shared learning experiences happen to coincide.

Admission age quibbles, too, will become irrelevant after several years of minischool and preprimary experience. There is no need to group children for first grade at the magic age of six, since they would be phased into their primary school year at any time from age four at one extreme to age eight at the other.

Promotion problems will also vanish, since in a continuum of learning there are no specific points at which a student passes or fails; he merely moves ahead at his own pace. Grade cards are likewise destined to disappear: Evaluation of progress will be continuous, and a progress report can be made in a parent conference whenever pupil performance analysis is in order.

The school will provide more learning experiences that parallel or accompany conventional academic content. The creative and enjoyable will begin to vie strongly with the utilitarian and academic dimensions of education. Such paracurricular ventures as educational travel, school camping, informal dramatics (including sociodrama), enlarged intramural sports programs that stress mass participation, and engaging youth in useful service to the community are due to increase in frequency and extent.

Biochemical and psychological mediation of learning is likely to increase. New drama will play on the educational stage as drugs are introduced experimentally to improve in the learner such qualities as personality, concentration, and memory. The application of biochemical research findings, heretofore centered in infra-human subjects, such as fish, could be a source of conspicuous controversy when children become the objects of experimentation.

Enrichment of the school environment in the seventies—especially in the ghetto—to "create" what we now measure as intelligence by improving experiential input also will become more accepted. Few are likely to make an issue of efforts to improve educational opportunities for the deprived child. However, there could be a tinderbox quality to the introduction of mandatory foster homes and "boarding schools" for children between the ages of two and three whose home environment was felt to have a malignant influence. Decisions of the 1970's in these areas could have far-reaching social consequences. Although it is repugnant to permit a child's surroundings to harm him, there is no clear social precedent for removing a child from his home because it lacks the sensory input needed to build normal intelligence and, therefore, in effect condemns him to a lifetime of unskilled labor.

The next decade will see new approaches to "educational disaster areas." Most of America's large cities, and some suburban and rural sections, contain a central core that can only be described in this way. Damage surrounding this core decreases from severe, to extensive, to moderate, to negligible.

Up to now, perhaps, we may have spent too much energy and money on just the worst schools of these central cores. In such neighborhoods, we cannot create a decent educational opportunity until the *total* social setting is rehabilitated. In the early 1970's, we may find it both more efficient and more educationally sound to direct our attention initially to improving those areas and schools where educational damage is moderate to extensive rather than drastic. For such areas, immediate attention may prevent their deteriorating in the near future into severe disaster areas. Once the deterioration in these outer ring schools is reversed, greater educational resources will become available to help us close in on the ghetto schools where damage is severe or total.

It would be unthinkable to ignore the children who live in our worst educational disaster areas until we can mobilize the greater forces needed to bring these schools up to necessary standards of excellence. Therefore, until inner cities regain their socioeconomic and educational health, we often will transport their children to outlying areas. In the next decade, this will involve a rapid buildup of facilities in these areas both in terms of enlarging existing schools and of creating new types of learning environments. Removing children from inner-city problem areas has the added merit of stimulating them through contacts with children from other social groups.

Later in the seventies, the elementary school changes will cause the junior and senior high schools to modify their programs. Their curriculums will presumably become more challenging and interesting. Wider age ranges, increased pupil interchange within and between schools, and individualized programs built around new instructional media will inevitably influence emerging secondary school organization.

In the late 1970's or early 1980's, it is not unlikely that students will graduate from high school with knowledge and social insight equal or superior to that of the person who earned a bachelor's degree in the 1960's.

On entering college, these students will be ready to begin postbaccalaureate studies and our undergraduate college programs *in their present forms* will be unnecessary.

If this seems farfetched, bear in mind that the young person pictured here will have had the benefit of carefully developed learning opportunities in a skillfully mediated milieu since he was two or three years old.

During the next 10 years, business will participate in education to a greater extent. Although many of their activities are neither widely known nor generally understood, major corporations are already contracting to tackle pollution, teach marketable skills to the deprived, administer police protection, reclaim slums, and manage civic governments.

John Kenneth Galbraith has noted that the modern corporation already has the power to shape society. Frank Keppel commented recently that the revival of U.S. metropolitan schools depends as much on the action of leaders of finance and commerce as it does on educators. And Hazel Henderson commented last summer in the *Harvard Business Review* that industry's expansion into such areas as housing, education, and dropout training is probably the best way to handle our central needs if suitable performance standards and general specifications are properly controlled.

The growth of a cooperative business-and-education relationship will be of great portent in the seventies as corporations both expand the production activities of the education industry and assume more management and control responsibilities.

The roles and responsibilities of teachers will alter throughout the next decade. Future-think suggests that between 1970 and 1980 a number of new assignments and specialties will materialize if present trends continue.

For one thing, the basic role of the teacher will change noticeably. Ten years hence it should be more accurate to term him a "learning clinician." This title is intended to convey the idea that schools are becoming "clinics" whose purpose is to provide individualized psychosocial "treatment" for the student, thus increasing his value both to himself and to society.

In the school of the future, senior learning clinicians will be responsible for coordinating the services needed for approximately 200 to 300 children. In different instructional units (an evolution of the "team" concept) we will find paraprofessionals, teaching interns, and other learning clinicians with complementary backgrounds. Some will be well-informed in counseling, others in media, engineering, languages, evaluation, systems analysis, simulation, game theory, and individual-need analysis.

But on the whole, the learning clinician will probably not be appreciably more specialized in subject matter disciplines than he was in the 1960's except for being more skilled in using educational technology. He will do more *coordinating* and *directing* of individual inquiry and will engage in less 1968-style group instruction. He will be highly concerned with providing and maintaining an effective environment, skilled in interpersonal transactions, and able to work with persons of different ages and learning styles.

Ten years from now, faculties will include:

1. *Culture analysts,* who make use of our growing insights into how a subculture shapes the learning style and behavior of its members.

2. *Media specialists,* who tailor-make local educational aids, who evaluate hardware and software and their use, and who are adept in the information sciences of automated-information storage and retrieval, and computer programing.

3. *Information-input specialists,* who make a career of keeping faculty and administration aware of implications for education in broad social, economic, and political trends.

4. *Curriculum-input specialists,* who from day to day make necessary corrections and additions to memory bank tapes on which individualized instructional materials are stored.

5. *Biochemical therapist/pharmacists,* whose services increase as biochemical therapy and memory improvement chemicals are introduced more widely.

6. *Early childhood specialists,* who work in the nonschool preschool and minischool programs and in the preprimary continuum.

7. *Developmental specialists,* who determine the groups in which children and youth work and who make recommendations regarding ways of improving pupil learning.

8. *Community-contact personnel,* who specialize in maintaining good communication, in reducing misunderstanding or abrasions, and in placing into the life of the community the increased contributions that the schools of the 1970's will be making.

As educators turn a speculative eye on the next decade, they must seek to answer a question that most of them have hesitated to face. For what kind of world should we strive to prepare children and youth who will spend most of their lives in the next century? We say this question is crucial because educational policy decisions in the 1970's will not only anticipate tomorrow, they probably will help to *create* it.

Recent publications in the physical, natural, and social sciences suggest emerging changes in society that seem likely to characterize the world of 2000 A.D. A number of future-think writers agree that unless unforeseen catastrophes intervene, such developments as the following are probable:

The individual's personal freedom and responsibility will be greater.

The IQ of the average child will be 125, perhaps 135.

Cultures throughout the world will be more standardized because of the impact of mass media and increased mobility.

Access to more information will carry us toward an international consensus as to what is desirable in family life, art, recreation, education, diet, economic policies, and government.

Cruelty will be more vigorously rejected and methodically eliminated.

Leaders will be those who are the most able, regardless of their racial origins, religious beliefs, family backgrounds, or lack of great wealth.

The worldwide status and influence of the female will greatly increase.

Differences in wealth and ownership between haves and have-nots will narrow.

Through the mediation of trends, society will begin to design or give direction to the future so that the years ahead will better serve human welfare.

The changes described above will open many more doors for educational leadership. During the coming decade, however, education must do more than just lengthen its stride to keep pace with trends and innovations. We must bring social perception and long-range vision to the task of designing and planning schools that can help bring about the best of many possible tomorrows.

Robert J. Havighurst

REQUIREMENTS FOR A VALID NEW CRITICISM

One thing which schools do not lack in this country is criticism. Indeed, most if not all the issues in this book are functions, in part, of criti-

From *Phi Delta Kappan*, September, 1968, pp. 20–26. Reprinted by permission of the author and publisher.

cism of one kind or another leveled at public education. Robert J. Havighurst, one of the most distinguished social scientists in this country and a
leading scholar in the area of school-society interrelationship studies,
offers some criticism on criticism. The author states his position with respect to the seriousness of education's ills, and identifies two themes
which are recurrent in contemporary criticisms of the schools—that the
schools fail to educate the children of the poor and that they are doing a
poor job in their education of the middle-class child. Havighurst also
speaks his mind on the validity of reform suggestions, including alternatives, made by contemporary critics.

I. How Bad Is Urban Education?

On November 2, 1967, the New York City School Board reported the
results of school achievement tests that had been given the preceding
April to all pupils in the second and fifth grades. *The New York Times*
reported the results in a page of tables and headlined the story on page
one with "City Pupils Losing Ground in Reading and Arithmetic." Let
us examine some of the test results.

The national average reading scores for these grades in April were 2.7
and 5.7 respectively. New York City school children averaged definitely
below these levels, and there was some evidence that the New York City
average was lower than it had been the year before.

The New York Times did not point out the fact that almost 300 of the
650 elementary schools had reading averages for their second grades of
3.0 or higher—that is, three-tenths of a year above the national average.
Nor did *The Times* report that 44 elementary schools had reading scores
for their fifth grades averaging 7.0 or more—1.3 of a year above the national average.

During that same month of November, the New York State Board of
Regents called for "a concerted effort to reform urban education." The
"Bundy Report" of the Mayor's Advisory Panel on Decentralization of
the New York City Schools, which was published November 9, com-
mences with the statement, "The New York City school system, which
once ranked at the summit of American public education, is caught in a
spiral of decline." *The Times* on that date referred in an editorial to
what it called "the deterioration of New York's gigantic school system."

The Saturday Review for November 18 carried the following headlines on its front cover—*Requiem for the Urban School* and *Education
in Washington: National Monument to Failure.*

The unwary middle-income parent, with several school-age children,
is very likely to read these pieces in *responsible* newspapers and journals, and to decide to move to the suburbs, where he is assured by the

same press that the schools are good. This person may live in Queens District 27, where 20 out of 27 schools are well above average in reading achievement, or in Queens District 26, where every one of the 24 elementary schools averaged at least .4 of a year above the national average at the second grade and at least one year above the national average at the fifth grade. But if he follows the *responsible* press, unless he explores the fine print, he is misled to suppose that he cannot find "good" public schools in the city.

Although these examples are taken from New York City, they can be duplicated in every large city. In some areas of the city, where the people of average and above-average income live, school achievement is above the national average, and about the same as it is in the "better" suburbs. In the low-income areas, school achievement is low.

How bad is education in our big cities? Does a dispassionate examination of the facts justify such widely publicized statements and slogans as "our children are dying," "requiem for urban education," "the end of the common school," "death at an early age," all applied to the work of the public schools in large cities?

We spend much more on education now than we did in 1955, much more per child, and a great deal more of our gross national product. Yet we are not making much headway with the education of disadvantaged children.

The children who are doing so poorly in our public schools constitute about 15 percent of the total group of children. They come predominantly from the homes of parents who are in the bottom quarter of the population in income, educational level, and occupational status. An equal number of children in such homes do fairly well in school—hence we cannot simply say that the children of the poor do poorly in school. Many of them do very well. But about 15 percent of children come from poor families *and* do poorly in school. We call these children "socially disadvantaged" because there is ample evidence that their home environments give them a very poor preparation for success in school.

Since World War II the families that produce these children have collected in large numbers in the slums of the big cities. Before World War II the majority of these children were living in rural and relatively isolated areas, and consequently their failure in school did not create an obvious social problem.

The other 85 percent of American children are doing quite well in school, according to the ordinary standards of judgment applied by most Americans to the schools.

I find the situation far from desperate. It is encouraging, but rough in spots, and the rough spots are most clearly seen in the big-city slums. We are learning to do the job for disadvantaged children, but making a good many mistakes in the process.

The Criticisms of Urban Education. What are the criticisms? There are two major themes of criticism of urban education, and they are quite different. The first and most general is that the schools are failing to educate the children of the poor, and it is the fault of the schools rather than the fault of the slum culture and home environment to which the children of the poor are subjected.

The second criticism is that the educational system is doing a poor job for the middle-class child and youth. The argument is that the present middle-class establishment is failing to govern the country effectively and failing to solve the country's international and domestic problems, and at the same time attempting to train the next generation to carry on this pattern of civic failure. One of the leading critics, writing an article entitled "In Praise of Populism," says "Indeed, the essential idea of this resurgent populism, in my opinion, is that the powers-that-be in the world are incompetent, their authority is irrational, they cannot cope with modern conditions, and they are producing ultimate horrors." [1]

Who Are the Critics? There is a group who appear at this time to have easy access to the responsible newspapers and journals. These include Paul Goodman, Edgar Friedenberg, Nat Hentoff, John Holt, Herbert Kohl, and Jonathan Kozol. These are not irresponsible people. On the contrary, they feel a tremendous moral responsibility to report their perceptions of the schools and their hypotheses for the betterment of the schools.

There are certain personal characteristics of these critics which are relevant to their criticisms. I do not propose to psychoanalyze them, and I have shared these qualities at one time or another in my own career. All of these characteristics do not apply equally to all of the critics. For one thing, they tend to be anarchists. That is, they do not like rules and institutions set up by society to regulate the conduct and development of its members. For another, they tend to be hostile to authority and therefore critical of the Establishment. A third characteristic is that some of them are young men agonizing in public over their discovery that the world is a difficult place.

[1] Paul Goodman, "In Praise of Populism," *Commentary*, June, 1968, pp. 25–30.

To this group of critics should be added another group who are especially concerned with one or another disadvantaged minority group, and
claim that the schools are failing to educate properly the children of
these groups either by discriminating against them or by offering them
inappropriate forms of schooling. The principal minority group on
whose behalf these critics speak is the Negro group, though there are
similar arguments on behalf of Puerto Ricans, Spanish-Americans of the
Southwest, rural whites of the Appalachian-Ozark mountain area, and
American Indians.

What Is Wrong with the Schools? The critics tend to attribute the
shortcomings of the schools to the fact that they are operated by "the
Establishment." The Establishment consists of the bureaucrats who administer the schools and who in turn are supported by the political leadership of the big cities, backed by a middle class satisfied with the
school system in its present form. Thus Jason Epstein, writing on the
Bundy Report that recommends decentralization of the public schools of
New York City, says,

. . . the urgent matter is to wrench the school system away from the bureaucrats who are now running it and whose failure now threatens the stability of
the city itself. As a practical matter the children of the ghetto, who now comprise nearly half the total public school enrollment, are largely without a functioning educational system at all, and the present school administration has
shown that it is incapable of supplying them with one.[2]

Related to this criticism is the contention that the size of big-city systems makes them bad. When a single school board and a single superintendent and his staff have to take responsibility for more than about 50
schools or 50,000 pupils, it is argued that the school system becomes
rigid, unable to adapt to the various educational needs of various subgroups and sections of the city.

Third, there is the criticism of the common school, or the system of
public education. Thus Peter Schrag, editorializing in *The Saturday Review* for April 20, 1968, on the subject "The End of the Common
School," says,

Although criticism of schools and teachers has always been a great national
pastime, there is something fundamentally new in the declining faith in the
possibilities of reform, and particularly in the kind of reform that can be accomplished within the existing school structure. The characteristic view, reflected in the pressures for decentralization and for the establishment of com-

[2] Jason Epstein, "The Politics of School Decentralization," *New York Review of
Books*, June 6, 1968, p. 26.

peting institutions, is that school systems tend to be self-serving, bureaucratic monsters that need replacement rather than reform. Although these demands have arisen during a time when the schools can attract more resources and more sophisticated staffs than ever before, they also coincide with the moment when the schools have achieved a near-monopoly position as gatekeepers to social and economic advancement: Where the schools were once considered benign, happy institutions for the young, they are now increasingly regarded as instruments of power.

Schrag says that there will have to be a number of alternative forms of education that may replace the single public school.

A few such competing institutions have already been established. In the large cities there are a few community schools, storefront academies, and programs for dropouts. Most of these operations are considered in some measure remedial and temporary. Most of them are inadequately financed and do not begin to meet the problems of miseducation, even in the communities where they are located. Yet the problems that led to the establishment of such institutions are going to be with us for a long time, and unless the public schools begin to accommodate far more diversity and to offer far more choice than they now do, the desperate need for alternatives will continue.

What Do the Critics Propose? As one would expect from critics who tend to be anarchists and who are hostile to the forms of authority, the positive proposals for educational improvement tend to be few and weak. There are three broad approaches.

1. Abolish the present school system and allow new institutions to emerge. This kind of proposal tends to be supported by critics who believe that there is too much bureaucracy with consequent rigidity in the present school system. They are not much concerned with the nature of the new institutions, since they tend to distrust institutions. With John Holt in *How Children Learn,* they follow Rousseau in their belief that children will learn best if allowed to initiate their own education. Paul Goodman writes, "We can, I believe, educate the young entirely in terms of their free choice, with no processing whatsoever." [3]

2. Experiment widely and freely with new procedures, looking for teachers with enthusiasm, creativity, and iconoclasm. New ways of working successfully with disadvantaged children and youth will emerge from such experiments.

3. Require the schools and their teachers to do a much better job of teaching disadvantaged children. This is the proposal especially of some Negro educators, who believe that the school system at present, both

[3] Paul Goodman, "Freedom and Learning: The Need for Choice." *Saturday Review,* May 18, 1968, p. 73.

North and South, tends to *reject* Negro children, to assume they cannot learn well, and to avoid the effort of teaching them effectively.

There are two principal weaknesses in the positions taken by the critics. First, many of them, and especially those who speak for minority groups, are ignoring the basic research on the importance of the preschool years in the preparation of a child for success in school. They ignore the following basic proposition:

The child's cognitive and social development in the years before age five are extremely important in his readiness for school work and his achievement in school. This proposition has been established by the empirical work of Bernstein in London, Martin Deutsch in New York, Robert Hess and his co-workers at the University of Chicago, and Skeels and Skodak at the University of Iowa. This proposition is widely discussed and amplified in the writings of J. McVicker Hunt, Benjamin Bloom, and Jerome Bruner.

Second, they ignore the post-war work on methods and materials of teaching mathematics, science, social studies, and foreign languages which has effectively reformed the curriculum of the intermediate and high school grades, and vastly improved the education of the majority of children and youth who do average and superior work in school.

Nevertheless, the critics serve a valuable purpose in contemporary education. They are sensitive people, aware of the needs for improvement in our society and in our education. They are especially useful as our social conscience.

II. Ways Out of the Educational Mess

Granting the proposition that major changes must be made in big-city education, how shall we decide what changes to make, and how shall we make them? There are three groups of people with something to say on this topic—the establishment, the anarchists, and the activists. All are prepared to talk about changing, though all are not equally prepared to take actual responsibility for changes.

The Establishment as a Change Agent. It is customary to describe the Establishment as a bureaucratic organization wedded to things as they have been in the past. The national organization of school superintendents and the organization of school principals have been accused of standing athwart the path of progress.

Yet some city school systems have been remarkably ready to exercise leadership in the making of changes. For instance, the New York City system which has been pilloried in *The New York Times* as a deteriorating system has been one of the most flexible, most experimental, and most responsive of all big-city systems to the social situation and the social needs of the big city. A list of outstanding changes in the New York City schools in the past 30 years would include:

The establishment of a system of specialized high schools serving the entire city with outstanding programs for the ablest students.

A long history of special programs for gifted elementary school children, centered at Hunter College.

Programs in certain high schools to meet the local community needs of a particular ethnic group, such as the program at the Benjamin Franklin High School when Leonard Covello was principal there.

Science teaching programs in the intermediate grades and the high schools that led the way to the improved science courses which swept the country after 1960.

The Statement on Integration adopted by the New York City Board of Education in 1954, shortly after the Supreme Court decision on segregation. This was not only the first policy statement on integration to be adopted by a big-city board of education, but one of the strongest; and it was put into effect by a positive open enrollment policy and by a vigorous rezoning program during the first years, when these measures could be fairly effective.

The Demonstration-Guidance Project in Junior High School 43 and the George Washington Senior High School. This was the first of the attempts by the big-city systems to enrich their programs for socially disadvantaged children.

The Higher Horizons Project in a large number of elementary schools, which was carefully and critically evaluated by the Research Bureau, and was the first big-city project for the socially disadvantaged to warn us that the job was not going to be easy. While other cities reported rosy but carelessly compiled results of their projects, New York City forced educators to face the facts.

The More Effective Schools Program, a carefully designed project to improve the education of the socially disadvantaged, which has been evaluated carefully and critically by an independent research agency.

The study of Puerto Rican children in New York City schools made by J. Cayce Morrison in the 1950's, which helped the school system to recognize and go to work on this special problem.

A series of experiments in delegating responsibility for the conduct of schools to local district school boards, stretching over the last 70 years. Notable in this series was the project in the Bronx headed by Joseph Loretan in the late 1950's, when he was district superintendent there.

A set of current experiments in the delegation of responsibility to local community committees for choosing administrators and teaching staff and for adapting the curriculum to local community conditions. This is a radical and controversial experiment which no other big-city school system has been able to try. Whatever becomes of it, it will give us valuable knowledge on the problem of relations between the school system and local communities.

It is a curious thing for the critics to proclaim the proposition that New York City schools are failing, when these schools are leading the country in working at the problem of educating socially disadvantaged youth, defining the problem, and studying it scientifically and experimentally.

During this period of the last 30 years, the great majority of books on the problems of education in the big city have come from New York City. These have been written by a wide range of people with a wide range of motives and experience.

Still, many of the great cities have been slow to innovate, and there certainly is a problem in all big-city systems where a bureaucratic structure stretching from the office of school principal to that of superintendent tends to perpetuate practices to which the organization has already grown accustomed. An example is the use of federal funds under Title I of the Elementary and Secondary Education Act to supplement educational services in schools located in poverty areas. The tendency has been to use these funds to support "more of the same" rather than to innovate. That is, the money has been used to pay teachers for an extra hour of classes after school, for Saturday morning instruction, for summer instruction, and to reduce the size of classes. This has not worked very well, and has given rise to criticism of big city systems for failure to try bold new experiments.

The Anarchists as Change Agents. The anarchists have been strong on criticism and weak on constructive proposals for change. They are, of course, opposed to the creation of a new set of organized and institutional practices, since, as anarchists, they mistrust procedures which tend to become rigid and confining. They proclaim "the end of the common school" and tell us that we are killing off the minds and spirits of children, but they are wary of writing proposals that could be put into an organized educational system. They favor experimentation of many kinds, but do not argue for careful evaluation of such experiments. For instance, Peter Schrag, writing in *The Saturday Review* of June 15, 1968, on "Learning in a Storefront" makes the following approving statement:

The East Harlem Block Schools, which operate nursery and primary classes in four locations, have discovered no new pedagogical secrets, operate according to no rigid theory, and have conducted little validating research. What they are doing, however, is to demonstrate that educational programs directed by parents and often staffed by parents are not only effective—at least in the judgment of those same parents—but that they represent a community focus and center of interest limited only by the financial resources their sponsors can attract.

He notes in passing, as though it were not an important matter, that there is no validating research on these schools. He also notes that the project costs $2,000 per child per year for 135 children, but he gives no indication that such a program would have to be supported by a thorough research validation if it would have any chance of gaining the public support that could spread it to cover one hundred times as many children. It would have to do this to produce a significant impact on the education of disadvantaged children in New York City. Instead, Schrag points out the importance of getting the schools into the hands of parents. "It is the parents who are minding the store," he says. It is this kind of anti-institutional and anti-organizational emphasis which is both the strength and the weakness of the anarchist position.

But the ablest of the anarchists recognize the need for new institutionalized procedures. Thus Paul Goodman, who calls himself an anarchist, also says explicitly that new institutions are necessary. After speaking of the present educational establishment as a hoax on the public and calling for an end to it, he says in the letter which appears in this *Kappan*, "Of course our society would then have to re-open or devise other institutional arrangements for most of the young to grow into the world; and in my books I propose many of these, since this is the problem."

To see the anarchist position most ably stated, and stated in most positive terms, one should read more of Goodman's writing. His article on "Freedom and Learning: The Need for Choice" in *The Saturday Review* for May 18, 1968, expands the ideas expressed in the above-mentioned letter. Here he argues that the educational system which has developed into such a large and expensive set of operations since 1900 is a hoax on American society. It tends to force conformity on the younger generation, and conformity to a set of adult institutions which are bad for everybody. He calls for more free choice in learning and says, "Free choice is not random but responsive to real situations; both youth and adults live in a nature of things, a polity, an ongoing society, and it is these, in fact, that attract interest and channel need. If the young, as they mature, can follow their bent and choose their topics, times, and teachers, and if teachers teach what they themselves consider important —which is all they can skillfully teach anyway—the needs of society will be adequately met; there will be more lively, independent, and inventive people; and in the fairly short run there will be a more sensible and efficient society."

Up to age 12, Goodman, says, there is no point to formal subjects or a prearranged curriculum. Teaching should be informal, and should follow the child's interest. If let alone, a normal child of 12 will, Goodman believes, learn most of what is useful in the eight-year elementary curriculum by himself.

However, Goodman recognizes that some families do not provide an adequate setting for their children to learn the elementary school curriculum, and he has a proposal for a kind of school to serve these disadvantaged children. He says, "Since we have communities where people do not attend to the children as a matter of course, and since children must be rescued from their homes, for most of these children there should be some kind of school. In a proposal for mini-schools in New York City, I suggested an elementary group of 28 children with four grownups: a licensed teacher, a housewife who can cook, a college senior, and a teen-age school dropout. Such a group can meet in any storefront, church basement, settlement house, or housing project; more important, it can often go about the city, as is possible when the student-teacher ratio is 7 to 1. Experience at the First Street School in New York has shown that the cost for such a little school is less than for the public school with a student-teacher ratio of 30 to 1. . . . The school should be located near home so the children can escape from it to home, and from home to it. The school should be supported by public money but administered entirely by its own children, teachers, and parents."

Looking at the positive suggestions of the more constructive anarchists, of whom Goodman is a good example, we see that they want education to be institutionalized to a minimal degree, with a wide variety of small school and college units in which pupils and teachers work as far as possible on their own initiative.

The Activists as Change Agents. A broad group of people are prepared to work within the present educational system but want major changes or additions to it. This group might be called "institutional me-liorists," to distinguish them from the anarchists. This group accepts the notion that the educational system must have a complex institutional structure and therefore differs from the anarchists on this major point. The activists want broad and fundamental changes in the educational system.

There is much disagreement among the activists. Many of them have just one program which they emphasize, such as:

Pre-school programs for disadvantaged children starting as early as age 3.

Decentralization of the public school system to place responsibility and decision making more in the hands of parents and local community leaders.

Educational parks.

Black teachers for black schools.

Alternative educational systems to the public schools, supported with public funds.

The U.S. Office of Education has been promoting activist programs through its very large funds under Title III of the Elementary and Sec-ondary Education Act. Several of the educational foundations have been supporting activist projects.

To this writer, who is an activist, it appears that there are some seri-ous weaknesses in the activist approach, but that these weaknesses are being corrected.

A major weakness is a general lack of systematic reporting and evalu-ation of the results of experimental work. Several major big-city pro-grams of compensatory education for disadvantaged children have been given wide publicity as successful on the basis of preliminary and inade-quate evaluation, only to withdraw their claims after more systematic study of their outcomes.

But there have been some outstanding examples of careful research evaluation of innovative programs. For instance, the Higher Horizons Program in New York City elementary schools was evaluated by the Bu-reau of Research, and its successor program, the More Effective Schools, has been carefully studied by the Center for Urban Education. The fact that these evaluations did not support some of the hopes and expecta-tions of the sponsors of the programs is an unfortunate fact which the big city systems must learn to use constructively.

At present there are some serious and sophisticated evaluations of several types of pre-school programs for disadvantaged children supported by the U.S. Office of Education. This should go a long way toward helping the educational systems to make rational judgments about the practical wisdom of expanding pre-school programs at public expense as a regular part of the public school program.

After a period of uncritical spending on innovations designed to improve the education of disadvantaged children and youth, stretching from Head Start through Title I of ESEA to the Job Corps, the federal agencies are now going in for evaluation, under pressure from congressmen and the Bureau of the Budget. The USOE is engaged in cost-benefit studies of the Title I program, and here there is another kind of danger. The educational benefits of pre-school and other innovative programs may not be fully measurable in terms of gains of children on reading-readiness tests and ordinary standardized tests of school achievement, applied immediately after an experimental program lasting a year or so. Yet cost-benefit studies are limited to assessing the costs of benefits that are measured. If the benefits of certain experimental programs cannot be measured simply after a short trial of the program, we should take the time and make the effort to measure the benefits in more complex ways over longer periods of time.

Working on Motives Rather Than Skills. Recently some of the activists appear to have discovered a principle that may produce much more effective ways of teaching disadvantaged children than the conventional way. The conventional way is to work directly on the mental skills of the child—his vocabulary, reading, writing, arithmetic. *Teach, teach, teach* with all the energy, time, patience, and techniques available. This has not worked very well. Hence some experimental methods have been tried that work on *motives* rather than skills and drills. The aim is to help the pupil *want* to learn, to help him see himself as a learner in school, as he now may see himself as a basketball player, a fighter, an attractive person to the opposite sex, a helper in the home, etc.

The theory underlying this approach might be outlined as follows: When a person *wants* something, he *tries* to get it. For example, when a child wants to read, he tries to read, and will use whatever help he can get from teachers, parents, other pupils, television, street signs, books around the house. He will drill himself, or accept the teacher's drill methods.

The desire to learn may be conscious or unconscious. One may have an explicit desire to be a good basketball player, or a good dancer, or a good reader, or a good singer. In this case, one seeks opportunity to improve oneself. On the other hand, one may have only a generalized and vaguely felt desire to please somebody else, or to be like somebody. In this case one accepts opportunity to move in the desired direction, but does not actively seek it.

Programs aimed directly at improving mental skills have had remarkably little success with children beyond the age of 7 or 8. Only a few people, generally with highly personal methods, appear to have succeeded with classes in slum schools beyond the third grade. For example, Herbert Kohl taught a sixth-grade class in Harlem with a kind of freedom and spontaneity that seems to have motivated many of his pupils to care about their school work. Perhaps it is significant that he did relatively little drilling, and did not bother to correct spelling and grammar. In fact, he drew criticism from his supervisors because he did not emphasize the mental skills in the usual way. And Jonathan Kozol, in Boston, made friends with his pupils, took them on trips with him, visited their homes, but did not seem to stress the conventional training.

A rather common element of motivating situations is the presence of a model—a person who is accepted by the pupil as one he would like to be like. The habit of *modeling* one's behavior after that of others is learned very early in life, and becomes largely unconscious. A person forms the habit of imitating his parents and other persons in authority and persons who are visible to him and attractive to him. Teachers may or may not be effective models, depending on their behavior toward pupils and on the attitudes of pupils toward them.

Examples of Motivating Situations. There are a growing number of experiments with inner-city youth that seem to be successful and yet do not represent what we think of conventionally as good teaching. The methods are erratic; the teachers are not well-trained. These *experiments have in common a motivating element.*

Storefront Academies and Mini-schools. Small, informal schools and classes springing up in the inner city appear to be accomplishing more than the conventional schools with disadvantaged youth. For example, the "street academies" of New York City appear to be working successfully with some dropouts and failing students from the high schools. These are described in an article by Chris Tree in *The Urban Review* for February, 1968, and are now a part of the Urban League's Education and Youth Incentives Program. The mini-school idea has already been presented.

Such projects must have methods, and the methods are being worked out pragmatically. It is too soon to say with any assurance what such a program would accomplish if it were expanded and made a part of the school system. Careful, empirical evaluation will have to be made to find out what kind of children and youth profit from this type of school and what kind do not.

Perhaps the essential factor in whatever success these schools have is that of acceptance by the teachers of the pupils as persons who want to learn, and the acceptance by the pupils of the teachers as people they want to be like.

Tutoring Projects. A few years ago there was a wave of tutoring projects which put college students and middle-class adults in the role of tutors to inner-city pupils of the intermediate and high school grades. These seem to have been largely discontinued, even though the tutors often reported that they got great personal satisfaction from their work and that it helped them to understand better the social structure of their society. Several careful evaluations of the effects of tutoring on mental skills of pupils throw some doubt on the value of the project from this point of view.

More recently there has been a development of tutoring by students only a little bit older and more skilled than the pupils being tutored. Some of these projects have shown surprising success. For example, Robert Cloward of Rhode Island University has evaluated a tutoring program in New York City in which teen-agers somewhat retarded in reading tutored middle-grade pupils in slum schools. Both tutees and tutors gained more in reading achievement tests than their controls did in a carefully designed experiment.

I have been told by several teachers of primary grades that they have occasionally asked an older or more advanced child to help a slow first-grader, with good results.

Whatever success these procedures have must be due more to motivation than to method. Getting *involved* with someone in a helping relationship apparently increases the desire to learn on the part of both the helper and the helped.

Games. Games have an accepted place in schools, as activities for recess and sometimes physical education and even spelling lessons. Generally they have been used as a change from the serious business of the school. But now games are being used as part of the planned curriculum. The reason is that games are motivating to most players, and they try to learn in order to win the game. There are now a good many mathematical games available, as well as games in geography. James S. Coleman and his colleagues have been working out games for high school students. The Mecklenberg Academy in Charlotte, North Carolina, has a number of games available for high school students.

It is not clear to what extent games can be used in slum schools, though there seems to be no reason to suppose that inner-city children cannot be interested in games aimed at teaching geography and arithmetic.

Self-Concept Building. Middleclass white Americans have difficulty understanding the demand for courses in African culture and history, for African languages such as Swahili, and for units on the Negro in American history in the elementary school. It is a waste of time if one is only interested in understanding the present world and in learning "useful" foreign languages.

But the need of a disadvantaged minority group to learn about its own cultural history in a positive way is related to the need for a positive self-concept—a self-concept of a person as a member of a social group that has a dignified and competent past. This need is hardly recognized by the white middle-class American, partly because he does not feel the need consciously and partly because his own competence and success as a person give him a positive self-concept which he can pass on to his children. Yet many children of Negro and other disadvantaged groups are told by their parents that they come from inferior stock, that they have "bad blood," that they suffer from their social past of slavery or of defeat by the white man.

While the best basis for a positive self-concept as a person who can learn in school and can succeed in American social and economic life is achievement—in school, in play, and in work—it may be that Negro children, in particular, would gain something from a study in school of the contributions of the Negro group to American life and culture, and of African history and culture.

When we find the good and effective ways to teach disadvantaged children and youth, we will still have to solve the problem of social integration of ethnic and poverty-plagued minority groups into the economic and political life of our large metropolitan areas. The solutions will go hand in hand. Big city and suburban governments as well as big city and suburban school systems will be remade in this process of social urban renewal.

I see the educational establishment reorganized and revitalized, together with the socio-political establishment. The work will largely be done by activists who learn to innovate creatively and to evaluate their innovations scientifically.

Questions for Discussion

1. Had the opportunity been available, do you think you would have desired to attend an alternative school like one of those described by Stretch? Why?
2. What impact do you see the alternative-school movement having upon the profession of teaching? Are you bothered by the fact that some alternative schools do not see a need for "certified" teachers? Does the teacher-power movement (see Chapter 4) have anything to gain or lose as a result of the drive for alternatives?
3. Do you think you are being adequately educated and professionally trained to operate successfully in an alternative school—whatever its form—or in a school of the future based upon the ideas in the Shane article?

Topics for Further Study

1. If possible, visit a "new," "free," or "grass roots" type of school in your city or town. By talking to administrators, teachers, governing board members, and students, try to construct the underlying philosophy of the school. Does this philosophy, in your opinion, differ significantly from what you might find by visiting the public school in the same area? If so, what are these differences?
2. In this chapter we have deliberately concentrated our discussion on nonparochial alternatives to the public schools. But this alternative is too important and too controversial to leave unexamined. Do you believe that the parochial school is about to be "starved out"? What, if any, has been the recent controversy surrounding state support for church-related schools in your state? Illinois provides an interesting case study of this question. After studying the controversy in your state and in Illinois, through newspaper and journal literature, predict the future of the parochial school as an alternative to the public school.
3. Education, housing, and employment in the ghettos of our big cities are the major domestic concerns of most Americans today. As you study the basic questions associated with poverty, do you feel that the alternatives to public schools discussed in this chapter might help to solve some of the social ills which are concentrated in the ghettos? What do you feel the alternatives should be trying to accomplish in the big-city ghetto?
4. Gaze into your crystal ball and predict what you think will be the status of alternatives to the public schools in the year 2000. Include as a basis for your prediction, your guess as to what might be the agreed-upon school-society goals that you would expect to find at the turn of the century. (See the Goslin article in Chapter 1.)
5. Interview a number of education professors concerning their predictions for nonpublic competitors to the present school system. What are your general findings? Before actually doing this survey, anticipate the type of response that you might expect to receive.

EPILOGUE

TO claim that America today is beset with problems, conflict, and grave discord is to claim the obvious. Never before have we been so aware of the domestic dislocations which confront our society. This awareness both frightens citizens and leads them to question and criticize ideas and institutions whose authority a short time ago was taken for granted. Only a few years ago, for example, we were basking in the glory of our public schools. We gloried in the efficient manner in which a pluralistic school clientele had been "Americanized," and the statisticians gave us "proof" of the schools' success through numbers which showed at a glance how many youngsters were finishing high school and entering colleges and universities on their upward social mobility trip through the terrain of the American Dream. True, the launching of Sputnik moved many of us to look at our schools with a critical eye, but most were confident that the schools, with a few relatively minor curricula adjustments, could produce the technological and scientific know-how we felt we needed.

Today, to put it mildly, the school has not escaped the general questioning and criticism which pervades society. Indeed, in many ways it has become the specific focus of demands for social change. Whether or not the school is a contributor to social ills, directly or otherwise, whether it can do anything about such ills, what constitutes legitimate criticism, what is positive reform—all, of course, are issues in themselves. These, along with the issues in this book—which show that traditional educational philosophies, processes, structures, governance patterns, and curricular offerings are now being seriously and dramatically challenged—testify to the fact that like society at large, our schools are going through a very critical period of transition.

Each of the issues examined in the preceding chapters has arisen out of challenges to time-honored educational ideas and practices. Even the historical role of the school as a mirror of the larger society is being vigorously questioned from all quarters in society. Such a relationship, it is argued, has made the school a supporter of the status quo and a perpetuator of social ills. Clearly, then, the points of view discussed by Pounds and Bryner in Chapter 1 can be seen as more than academic exercises in educational philosophy. They represent a range of options, albeit a limited range, for school-society relationship patterns. During this era of conflict over just about everything in our society, including the school, educators as well as citizens are increasingly looking to new conceptions of formal schooling and new ways in which schools ought to serve and relate to the society in which they operate. Can and should the schools regard social changes as surface phenomena relative to some world of basic and eternal truths? Is the main function of education to be found in time-tested elements perceived as essential to social progress? Should the schools take on the role of reconstructing society? Should compulsory-education laws be eliminated? These are only a few of the questions raised by Pounds and Bryner, the significance of which is made obvious by a study of the issues presented in this book. Study of the issues shows too that questioning of the sort reflected above is not limited to professional educators. It comes from virtually every segment of our society.

Traditional patterns of school governance are being called into question by community groups, teachers, and students. These groups are not fighting for the same changes, however, and the school-control issue is, thus, made much more complex. It has led, indeed, to the unlikely alliance of student radicals and supporters of local self-governance. Their common enemy is the educational bureaucracy and the teacher, who has been intensifying his militant "professionalism" in a drive to throw off a previously weak role in educational governance and policy-making. Adding to these complexities faced by the school has been the broadening role of the courts in the educational enterprise. The courts have called upon the school to serve as an active agent for change concerning perhaps the major social issue of our times—race. Other groups and institutions, meanwhile, are demanding that the school abandon an abrasive and denigrating melting pot ideology, to employ cultural and ethnic diversity as an educational resource. These demands, moreover, are coming at a time when many schools are already bankrupt and many others face this condition as a likely eventuality in the near future. In light of this financial situation, many people are now calling for a denial of strict adherence to the time-honored concept of local support through the property tax.

All of the issues analyzed in this book show promise of having a continued impact on educational decision-making in the United States. Indeed, the alternative school movement is, in part, a response to the cumulative impact of such issues. No one can deny the quick and steady growth of this movement. In 1960 there were but a handful of such schools in the United States, while now they number in the thousands. And the cry for alternatives becomes louder.

Clearly, then, the conflict between the traditional and new responses to the issues of the times, as well as the conflict among the new responses themselves (such as teacher power vs. local community control), reflects the transitional nature of the school. During this period of change, it is important to identify numerous other problem areas which might result in greater intensification of the conflict in the future. Here are just a few:

1. the increasing influence of business and industry on education;

2. the effects of technology and the media on the environment of the child;

3. the conflict over the use of drugs to induce psychological and physiological reactions which are conducive to learning, retention, etc.;

4. the impact of the sexual revolution upon the schools;

5. the influence of the Women's Liberation Movement upon teaching as a profession and the education of women in general;

6. the consequences for education of the changing status of the black American and other "Third World" groups in society;

7. the influence on school control of the changing federal-state-local relationship;

8. the significance of changing value patterns for the training of teachers;

9. the effect on public schools of the financial-support crisis now surrounding nonpublic schools;

10. the consequences of increased interest in promoting internationalism, as opposed to emphasis on the nation-state;

11. the influence on education of the growing antagonism of youth toward the corporate world;

12. the ramifications of inadequate vocational education for an increasingly technological society;

13. the implications for education and society of the failure to effectively educate both the handicapped and the gifted.

Each of these problem areas calls into question many traditional notions. As more and more accepted ideas are challenged, it becomes increasingly apparent that American education is undergoing drastic change. What does all this mean for the prospective teacher? It suggests, among other things, that present and future educators must be sensitive to their times and be willing to question the time-honored while the new is pressing to have an impact. Leadership in education must emerge which has the courage and insight to identify impending areas of conflict before they become social crises. The placing of such a responsibility upon educators requires that they be able to exercise an open mind when their beliefs and practices are called into question.

Implicit throughout this book has been the idea that the professionals who staff our schools must become expert in the use of the tools of analysis so that the examination of issues becomes a logical and natural part of their approach to the study of education. Only by this means will it be possible to gain a better understanding of the issues. If educators are to maintain an atmosphere of openness for study during these changing times, they must combine an analytic approach to problems with an attitude of tolerance toward both change and ambiguity. We hope that this book has provided prospective teachers with the tools to pursue such a direction.